Dictionary of the
BRITISH EMPIRE
AND
COMMONWEALTH

Dictionary of the
BRITISH EMPIRE
AND
COMMONWEALTH

Alan Palmer

JOHN MURRAY
Albemarle Street, London

FOR CATHERINE AND JOANNA
WITH LOVE

First published in 1996
by John Murray (Publishers) Ltd.,
50 Albemarle Street, London W1X 4BD

A catalogue record for this book is available from the British Library

Cased ISBN 0-7195-5650-3
Paperback ISBN 0-7195-5657-0

Typeset in 10 Plantin by Servis Filmsetting Ltd, Manchester
Printed and bound in Great Britain by The University Press, Cambridge

Contents

Preface

'Gentlemen, from that tower the world is ruled!': thus, towards the end of the nineteenth century, the German Emperor, William II, enlightened the officers of his suite on a visit to Windsor. Strictly speaking, as so often in his reign, the Kaiser sacrificed accuracy for hyperbole: the Round Tower was no powerhouse of government; and Queen Victoria did not exercise sovereignty over the whole globe – merely over a fifth of its land-surface and almost a quarter of its population. Yet William's rhetorical flourish echoed the mood around him. In these closing years of the Queen's reign the British people, so long indifferent to overseas colonies, were prodded by the coming of cheap newspapers into a proud – and often arrogant – consciousness of empire. Never in any previous epoch had such a vast accumulation of territories owed allegiance to a single sovereign.

Yet, even so, the British Empire had still not attained its full extent. That apogee was reached some two decades later when, after the first of the world wars, the peace settlement briefly stamped imperial authority on a quarter of the globe, extending across Africa from Cairo to the Cape, and through mandated Palestine, Transjordan and Iraq to much of the Middle East as well. But the empire had always been marked off from other supranational political combinations by a resilient mutability, a capacity to adjust to changing world circumstances, and already the character of sovereignty was responding to critical scrutiny. As early as 1917 the term 'Imperial Commonwealth' was in use; by 1926 – the year in which Queen Elizabeth II was born – the 'autonomous communities within the British Empire' were recognized as 'members of the British Commonwealth of Nations'; and in December 1931 the Statute of Westminster placed on equal footing the sovereignty of parliaments of the United Kingdom and of associated dominions devolved from it overseas. There were, in 1931, six dominions: Australia, Canada, the Irish Free State, Newfoundland, New Zealand, South Africa. When, eighteen years later, the appellation 'British' was dropped from formal usage there were still only six – Australia, Canada, Ceylon, New Zealand, Pakistan, South Africa – but now, as well as the dominions, there was in association with them an independent republic, India. That was the decisive moment of transition, the guarantee of continuity between old Empire and new Commonwealth. Over the following forty years this, largely tentative, relationship between Crown and peoples overseas grew to maturity, especially in the 1960s when twenty former colonies gained independence. Characteristically, a Commonwealth Secretariat was created almost as an afterthought, not until 1965. Thirty years later the Commonwealth had become an association of 51 members. If the remaining dependencies of Australia, New Zealand and Great Britain are added to these 51 members, then no fewer than 77 territories, large or small, are linked by the loose bonds of Commonwealth.

The *Dictionary of the British Empire and Commonwealth* is a reference companion intended, not only for students of history and current affairs, but for all who seek to understand global events which are shaping the future of the English-speaking peoples, as they move towards the twenty-first century. The Dictionary looks back to the imperial past, offers guidance for the transition from Empire to Commonwealth and provides outline histories of today's 76 overseas members and dependencies. Different countries have reacted differently to the impact of events. Occasionally, when faced by an external challenge like world war or economic depression, there have been close similarities in their response. More often, however, they have asserted an independence of judgement, shaped by geography, by sentiment and sometimes by old resentments bitterly held. The emphasis in the selection of entries for this Dictionary is deliberately placed in these overseas territories and outside the British Isles. United Kingdom affairs, which are fully covered in so many other reference books, receive scant treatment. Moreover, when there are entries on British public figures, they are assessed principally in relation to territories overseas, not to their achievements at home or in narrowly European affairs.

Compared to Rome and Byzantium, or the mighty dynasties of Asia, the British Empire was short-lived, and the Commonwealth has yet to prove its durability. Yet among the other great imperial Powers of modern times only France – with the world's second largest colonial empire – has shown a similar desire for continuity in change: in 1958 the constitution of the Fifth Republic envisaged a French 'Community of States', and in 1974 four former colonies (French Guiana, Guadeloupe, Martinique, Réunion) became integrated regions of France. But the Commonwealth, though more nebulous in character, retains a balanced legacy of shared interests and experience. Language, religion, institutions upholding law and order, the stimulus of books and artistic expression, and pastimes carefully codified into competitive sport – all have been exported to the extensions of Britain across the oceans. Of equal importance has been the cultural feed-back: for even in the nineteenth century the enriching experience of empire enabled habits of thought from overseas to fertilize stale minds at home and broaden our everday vocabulary.

To decide on a chronological starting-point for the Dictionary was difficult. Readers will see that the traditional North American colonies of King George III's time receive less attention than the spread of his granddaughter's 'dominion over palm and pine'. The American rebellion proved a salutary lesson in how not to misgovern distant settlements; it gave birth to a great nation, but it did not destroy other bonds of colonial attachment. Even after according recognition to the independent United States, George III still ruled over more of the Americas at the end of the century than at his accession. The Dictionary therefore gives a greater emphasis to the Caribbean possessions and to Canada than to the thirteen lost colonies. Moreover, if there is any moment in the eighteenth century when British expansion overseas decisively changed course, that date falls not in the year of American defiance, nor of American independence, but in January 1788. For in that month, within three weeks of each other, an Association for Promoting the Discovery of the Interior Parts of Africa was founded in London, and the Union Jack was run up in an antipodean cove named after an undistinguished Home Secretary, Lord Sydney. Britain's imperial mission thereafter sought fulfilment, not only in Asia and the Americas, but in all the continents of the world. This phase of overseas expansion forms the core of the Dictionary. There can be no closing date: even today, as I finish reading the proofs of this Dictionary, we learn that on 1 November 1995 the Cameroon Republic will become the 52nd member of the Commonwealth – a response to the invitation mentioned in the entry headed 'Southern Cameroons'. The Commonwealth remains a growing community.

Much that was achieved in the old empire was inspired by a nobility of purpose; at times it was defended by a valour that won Victoria Crosses on far-flung battlefields. And much that was accomplished materially in those years has endured: new cities; seaports; bridges; railways; irrigation projects and dams; schools and universities. But many aspects of imperialism were deplorable: arrogant assumptions of race and caste; the cruel intolerance of religious zeal; the exploitation of slave and semi-slave labour. A list of Villains of Empire (and indeed, more recently, of Villains of Commonwealth) is no harder to compile than a roll of honour for heroes and heroines. This Dictionary includes, dispassionately, both saints and sinners – together with the great majority of distinguished men and women of Empire and Commonwealth who, like so many of us, fall clearly into neither category.

I wish to thank the staffs of Rhodes House, the Bodleian Library and the London Library for their assistance. The Dictionary has benefited from the skill and experience of Douglas Matthews, who undertook the exacting task of compiling the index. I am grateful to him and, once

Preface

again, to Grant McIntyre, Gail Pirkis and Elizabeth Robinson for their editorial guidance and careful scrutiny of typescript and proofs. Many friends lent me books and pamphlets or, from their experience, broadened my knowledge of distant places overseas: I thank, in particular, Margaret Ackrill, Clare Brown, Ray Lawton, Christine Mason and Helen Rogers in Oxford and also my cousin in Brisbane, the ornithologist William Peckover, who sent me interesting material on Papua New Guinea. I alone, of course, remain responsible for all comments and assessments of events within the Dictionary. My wife, Veronica, has saved me from many pitfalls and I am, as ever, grateful to her for constant help and encouragement. The book is dedicated to her nieces, Catherine Clarke and Joanna Connelly, for all the pleasure they bring us.

Woodstock, Oxfordshire   Alan Palmer
October, 1995

AUCKLAND COMMONWEALTH CONFERENCE, NOVEMBER 1995

The 1995 Commonwealth Heads of Government Meeting at Auckland, New Zealand, took place after this book went to press. Two important issues raised at the meeting were the resumption of French underground nuclear tests in the Pacific and the contempt for human rights shown by the Abacha regime in Nigeria. Most members condemned the French action, though with John Major dissenting for the United Kingdom. Nigeria was suspended from the Commonwealth for executing nine civil rights protestors, including the eminent playwright Ken Saro-Wiwa, an environmental activist protecting the interests of his Ogoni people in Nigeria's southern, oil-rich Rivers state. The executions were carried out while the Auckland conference was in session and despite appeals for clemency from many governments. The Commonwealth Heads of Government announced that Nigeria would be expelled from the Commonwealth unless democratic rule was restored within two years. The meeting also warned the Gambia and Sierra Leone of the need to respect the 1991 Harare Declaration on democratic principles and human rights.

There was a further significant development at the Auckland meeting. On 12 November 1995 the Republic of Mozambique joined the Commonwealth, as a 'unique and special case'. President Joaquim Chissano's application for membership had won strong support from the southern African Commonwealth states, all of whom are Mozambique's neighbours (South Africa, Swaziland, Zimbabwe, Zambia, Malawi and Tanzania). Mozambique was under Portuguese colonial administration from 1752 to 1951 and is the first Commonwealth member never to have owed allegiance to the British crown.

Cross-references (shown by the symbol *) are given only when they amplify or help to clarify the topic under discussion.

Current place-names are used for contemporary affairs, but (in general) not for the imperial past. Alternative place-names in frequent use are given in brackets.

Road distances and areas of specific regions are generally not metric in the text. To convert miles to kilometres, multiply by 1.61; to convert square miles to square kilometres, multiply by 2.59.

Entries refer only to events which took place before 16 October 1995.

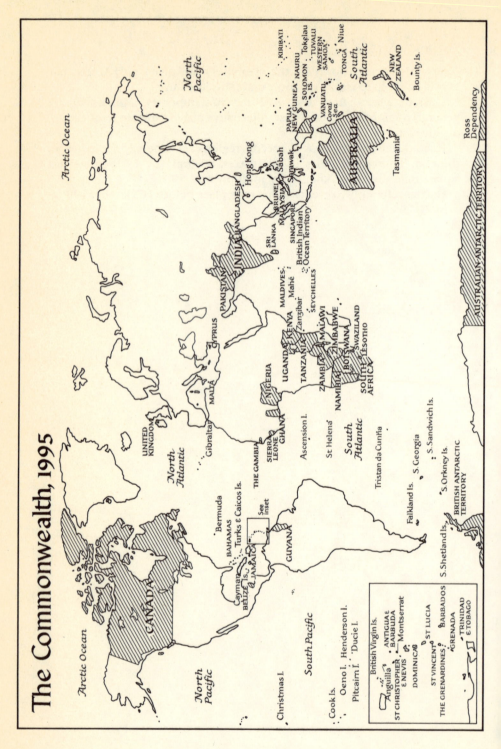

The Commonwealth, 1995

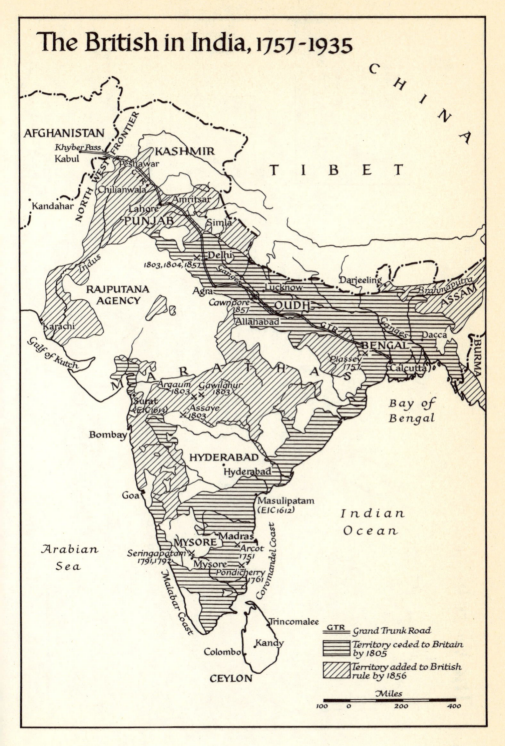

The British in India, 1757-1935

CHINA

TIBET

AFGHANISTAN

Khyber Pass
Kabul

KASHMIR

Peshawar

Kandahar

Chilianwala

Amritsar

Lahore

Simla

PUNJAB

Indus

Delhi
1803, 1804, 1857

RAJPUTANA
AGENCY

Agra

Cawnpore
1857

Lucknow

Darjeeling

Brahmaputra

ASSAM

Karachi

OUDH

Ganges

Gulf of Kutch

Allahabad

Ganges

BENGAL

Dacca

BURMA

M   A   R   A   T   H   A   S

Plassey
1757

Calcutta

Argaum
1803

Gawilghur
1803

Surat
(E.I.C 1613)

Assaye
1803

Bay of
Bengal

Bombay

HYDERABAD

Hyderabad

Goa

Masulipatam
(EIC 1612)

Indian
Ocean

Arabian
Sea

Madras

Arcot
1751

MYSORE

Seringapatam
1791, 1792

Mysore

Pondicherry
1761

Coromandel Coast

Malabar Coast

Trincomalee

Kandy

Colombo

CEYLON

GTR Grand Trunk Road

Territory ceded to Britain
by 1805

Territory added to British
rule by 1856

Miles

100   0   200   400

The West Indies

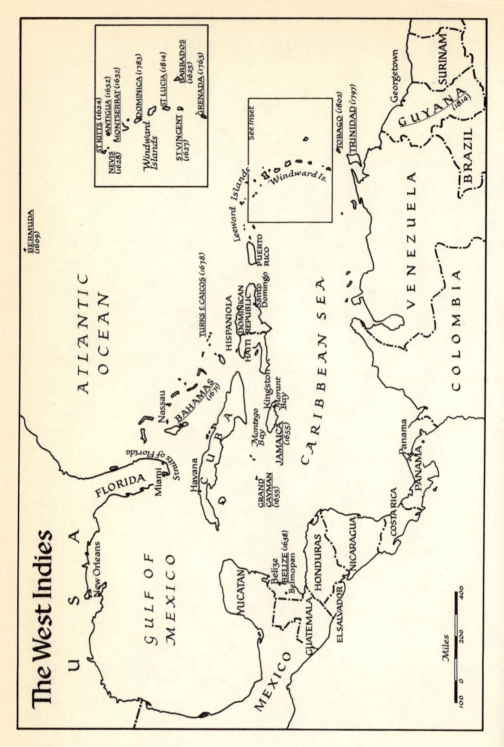

BERMUDA *(1609)*

Inset:
ST KITTS *(1624)*
NEVIS *(1628)*
ANTIGUA *(1632)*
MONTSERRAT *(1632)*
DOMINICA *(1783)*
ST LUCIA *(1814)*
Windward Islands
ST VINCENT *(1627)*
BARBADOS *(1625)*
GRENADA *(1763)*

See Inset
Leeward Islands
Windward Is.
TOBAGO *(1802)*
TRINIDAD *(1797)*

ATLANTIC OCEAN

TURKS & CAICOS *(1678)*

Nassau
BAHAMAS *(1671)*

HISPANIOLA
HAITI
DOMINICAN REPUBLIC
Santo Domingo
PUERTO RICO

CARIBBEAN SEA

Montego Bay
Kingston
Morant Bay
JAMAICA *(1655)*

Straits of Florida
FLORIDA
Miami
Havana
CUBA
GRAND CAYMAN *(1655)*

GEORGETOWN
GUYANA *(1814)*
SURINAM
BRAZIL
VENEZUELA
COLOMBIA

U S A
New Orleans
GULF OF MEXICO

Belize
BELIZE *(1638)*
Belmopan
YUCATAN
HONDURAS
NICARAGUA
COSTA RICA
PANAMA
Panama
EL SALVADOR
GUATEMALA
MEXICO

Miles
100 0 200 400

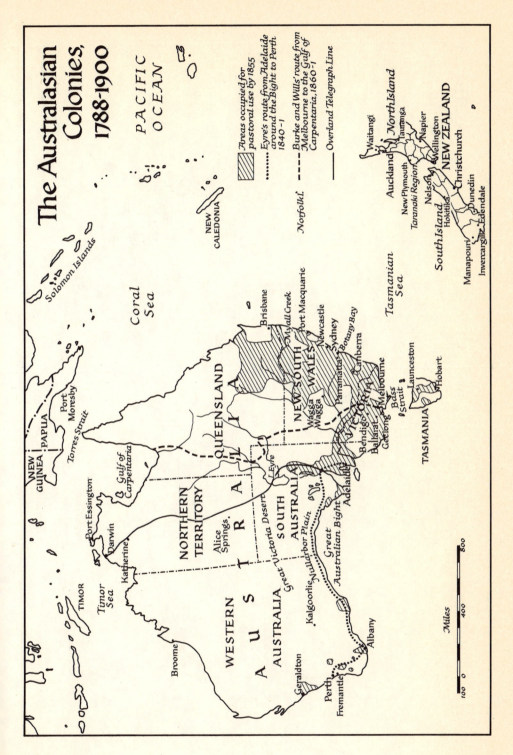

The Australasian Colonies, 1788-1900

PACIFIC OCEAN

Areas occupied for pastoral use by 1855

Eyre's route from Adelaide around the Bight to Perth 1840–1

Burke and Wills' route from Melbourne to the Gulf of Carpentaria, 1860–1

Overland Telegraph Line

Solomon Islands

NEW CALEDONIA

Coral Sea

Norfolk I.

NEW ZEALAND

North Island

Waitangi
Auckland
Tauranga
Napier
New Plymouth
Taranaki Region
Wellington
Nelson
South Island
Hokitika
Christchurch
Dunedin
Manapouri
Invercargill
Edendale

Tasmanian Sea

PAPUA
NEW GUINEA

Port Moresby

Torres Strait

TIMOR

Timor Sea

Darwin
Port Essington
Katherine

Gulf of Carpentaria

NORTHERN TERRITORY

Alice Springs

Great Victoria Desert

Broome

WESTERN AUSTRALIA

SOUTH AUSTRALIA

QUEENSLAND

Brisbane

Myall Creek
Port Macquarie
Newcastle

NEW SOUTH WALES

Parramatta
Sydney
Botany Bay
Canberra

Wagga Wagga

VICTORIA

Bendigo
Ballarat
Geelong
Melbourne

Bass Strait

Launceston

TASMANIA

Hobart

L. Eyre
Adelaide

Great Australian Bight

Kalgoorlie
Nullarbor Plain
Geraldton
Perth
Fremantle
Albany

Miles

100 0   400   800

XV

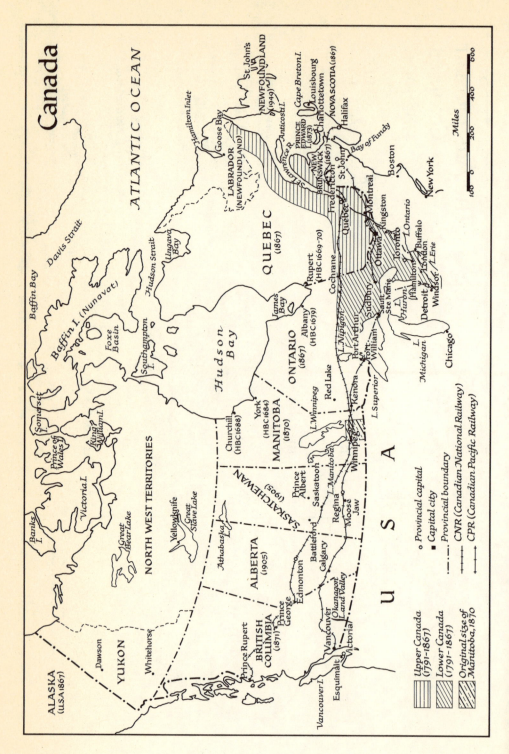

Canada

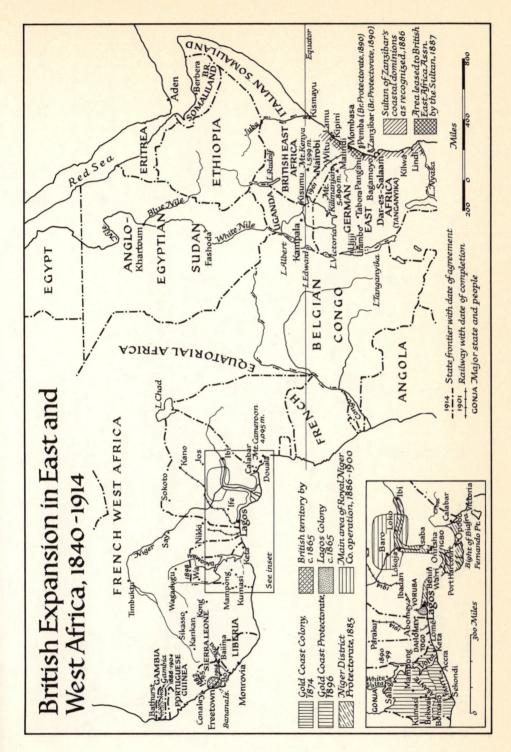

British Expansion in East and West Africa, 1840–1914

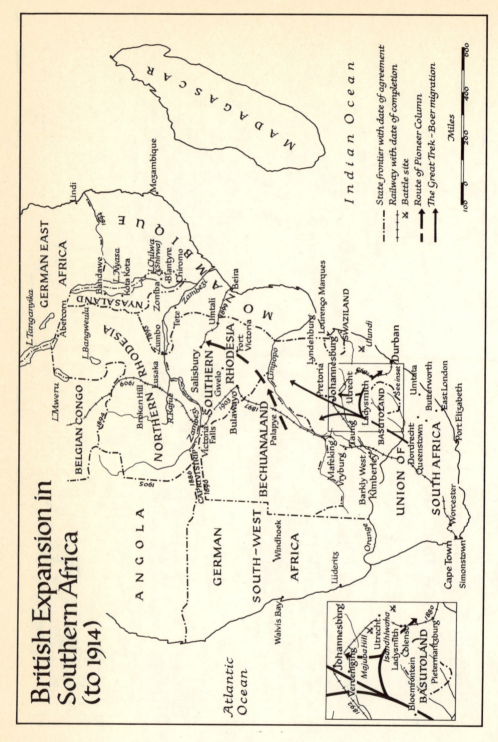

British Expansion in
Southern Africa
(to 1914)

Dictionary of the
BRITISH EMPIRE
AND
COMMONWEALTH

Abdication. In November 1936 the wish of the recently-acceded King Edward VIII (1894–1972) to marry the American divorcée, Wallis Simpson (1896–1986), caused a constitutional crisis of concern to all the Empire. The British government, headed by Stanley Baldwin, thought the proposed marriage threatened the integrity of the Monarchy but agreed to seek the opinion of the dominions. Although Edward VIII was especially popular with the younger generation in Canada – where he had a ranch in Alberta – the Canadian Prime Minister (Mackenzie *King) offered to support Baldwin in whatever course he chose. So, more guardedly, did *Savage in New Zealand. *Lyons in Australia and *Hertzog in South Africa rejected the idea of even a morganatic union. Indian opinion was divided, with the Muslims having no objection to the marriage. Ultimately, on 10 December Edward VIII chose to abdicate rather than give up 'the woman I love', having reigned a mere 42 weeks. He went into voluntary exile in France after being created Duke of Windsor by his successor, George VI. The Duke, who was to serve as governor of the Bahamas 1940–45, married Wallis Simpson in June 1937.

Abdul Rahman Putra, Tunku (Prince) (1903–90), Malaysian statesman: son of the Sultan of Kedah, he was educated at Cambridge, later becoming a barrister (Inner Temple, London). After World War II he established a Malayan nationalist party (UMNO) which, under his leadership, became the Alliance Party in 1954. In 1957 he helped negotiate independence for *Malaya, where he was Prime Minister until 1961. As in effect the founding father of *Malaysia in 1962 it was natural for him to continue as chief minister in the new Federation. He held office until 1970, retiring from active politics after anti-Chinese riots in Kuala Lumpur. The Tunku also served as Secretary-General of the Islamic Conference of Foreign Ministers from 1969 to 1973.

Abeles, Sir Peter (1924–), Australian transport magnate: born in Budapest, emigrated from Hungary to New South Wales in 1949 and set up Alltrans Ltd a year later. A merger with Thomas Nationwide Transport (TNT) in 1967 gave him interests in air courier services and container shipping as well as road transport. Further expansion in 1979

3

brought Abeles and Rupert *Murdoch control of Ansett Transport Industries, with extensive airline services in Australia.

Aborigines: inhabitants of Australia for more than 40,000 years, heirs to a Pleistocene culture which created red ochre rock paintings, extant in isolated sites. When white settlement began in 1788 there were at least 300,000 aborigines, with hunters and food gatherers spread across some 500 tribal territories: by 1888 only 50,000 survived. The chief reasons for this decline were: (i) exclusion from historic hunting lands; (ii) endemic smallpox; (iii) spread of new diseases and alcohol; (iv) open conflict; (v) deliberate slaughter (as at *Myall Creek). Whole tribes speedily perished: around Sydney the Iora were extinct by 1840; the last Tasmanian aborigine died in 1876. Between 1890 and 1930 official policy favoured setting up aboriginal reserves, emphasis thereafter shifting to assimilation. Aborigines only became full citizens in 1967, after a federal referendum. At the 1986 census they numbered 227,645 in a total population of 15,763,000. But they form almost 20 per cent of the population of the *Northern Territory, where there are many self-contained aboriginal communities and a large area was designated aboriginal land in 1984. A protracted *land rights campaign led in December 1993 to federal legislation protecting 'native lands' throughout Australia. In 1972, during a demonstration in Canberra to support this campaign, an aboriginal flag (black above red, with a yellow central circle) was flown for the first time.

Achebe, Chinua (1930–), Nigerian novelist and poet: born Albert Chinualmogo, a mission teacher's son, in Ogid; educated at University College, Ibadan. His first novel, *Things Fall Apart* (1958), portrayed the *Ibo in the late nineteenth century. He gained a wide readership in England with his *Anthills of the Savanna*, which was short-listed for the Booker Prize in 1987. Achebe was awarded the Commonwealth Poetry Prize for 1972. From 1973 to 1981 he was Professor of English at the University of Nigeria.

Aden. The volcanic peninsula of Aden, 100 miles east of the southern entrance to the Red Sea, was annexed by Britain in 1839 and developed as a coaling station on the route to India. To the original territory were added the offshore island of Perim and the large island of Sokotra, formally a British Protectorate from 1876. Kamaran island, 200 miles north of Perim, was seized from the Turks in 1916. Until April 1937 Aden was administered as a dependency of British India; from 1937 to 1963 it was a British Crown Colony. Treaties with the Hadhramaut, Wahidi and Mahri sultanates in 1938–39 made much of southern Arabia a British protectorate. In 1959 mounting Arab nationalism led to the formation of a London-sponsored South Arabian Federation of Emirates, to which the crown colony acceded in January 1963. Aden's prosperity depended, however, on free passage through the Suez Canal, and from 1956 onwards Israeli–Egyptian conflicts weakened the port's commercial viability, despite the construction of an oil refinery. Nationalist unrest (see *Aden Emergency*, below) forced the abandonment in 1968 of plans to give the South Arabian Federation independent sovereignty within the Commonwealth. When British forces withdrew in November 1967 the former colony and protectorate became the People's Republic of South Yemen.

Aden Emergency. Sporadic attacks by Arabs on units from the British garrison in Aden from 1957 onwards developed into a colonial liberation 'emergency' in September 1965 when both the original Arab 'National Liberation Front' (NLF) and the British troops were attacked by FLOSY, the Egyptian-backed 'Front for the Liberation of Occupied South Yemen'. When Nasser withdrew Egyptian support of FLOSY the British agreed with the NLF to evacuate Aden, the last troops pulling out on 29 November 1967. The two-year emergency cost the lives of 129 British servicemen.

Afghan Wars. In 1839 fear of a Russian advance to India's *north-west frontier caused a British invasion of Afghanistan. The allegedly pro-Russian amir, Dost Mohammed, was deposed and the three principal towns – Kandahar, Ghazni and Kabul – occupied; but confused orders from London, inept generalship and a breach of faith by Afghan chiefs led in January 1842 to the annihilation of a British column of 4,000 troops and 12,000 non-combatants in the Jagdallak Pass, pulling back from Kabul to Jallalabad. A punitive force re-entered Kabul, razed Ghazni and released prisoners held by the Afghans before retiring to India. Dost Mohammed resumed his reign, remaining on good terms with the British until his death in 1863. A second Afghan War (1879–80) was caused by his successor's apparent intrigues with the Russian military adventurer, Stoletov. A puppet pro-British ruler could not prevent an Afghan uprising in which the designated British Resident in Kabul, Sir Louis Cavagnari, was murdered. General *Roberts occupied Kabul (August 1880) but at once had to go to Kandahar where a British brigade was encircled, his force of 10,000 men marching 320 miles in 23 days. Dost Mohammed's grandson, Abdurrahman, was installed as amir (reigned 1880–1901), authorizing Britain to supervise Afghanistan's foreign relations while not invervening in internal affairs. Unrest following the Russian Revolution led to border incidents and a third British invasion through the *Khyber Pass (May–August 1919) when the town of Loe Dhaka was occupied. In November 1921 a definitive treaty settled frontier disputes and recognized Afghanistan's independence.

African National Congress: oldest non-white political movement in South Africa; founded at Bloemfontein in January 1912 with the Zulu

Methodist minister, John Lagalilabale Dude, as first president. As early as 1914 the ANC sent a delegation to London to protest at the *Native Lands Act. At Kimberley in 1926 an ANC conference agreed to adopt the tactics of passive resistance brought to the Transvaal by *Gandhi twenty years earlier. Even after the imposition of *apartheid Chief Albert *Luthuli, president of the ANC from 1952 to 1967, accepted the principle of non-violence. So too, at first, did his successor, Oliver Tambo (1917–93), who continued to serve the ANC as president in exile from 1978 to 1991. The ANC leaders were arrested on treason charges in 1956 but the case against them collapsed. By then, however, many young blacks were turning to militancy, with guerrilla operations directed by MK, the *Umkonto we Sizwe* (Spear of the Nation) movement, led by Chris Hani (1942–93), in exile from 1963 to 1990. South Africa's withdrawal from the Commonwealth was followed by stern repression of the ANC. Apart from the exiles, the ANC leaders were imprisoned: Nelson *Mandela was incarcerated for 28 years. The ANC remained illegal until February 1990 when, after five years of violent conflict, President de Klerk sought talks to prepare for multi-racial power sharing. A Convention on a Democratic South Africa opened in Johannesburg in December 1991 but agreement was delayed for two years, partly through clashes between the ANC and *Zulu Inkatha. In the first multi-racial election (April 1994) ANC won 252 of 400 seats and filled 18 of 27 cabinet posts in President Mandela's government. (See also *Zambia* and *Zimbabwe*.)

Afrikaaner National Party: political organization established by the former Boer general and first Minister of Justice in South Africa, James *Hertzog, in 1912. The party opposed South African participation in both world wars and upheld white supremacy. When Hertzog favoured collaboration with *Smuts in a United Party coalition in 1934, Dr Daniel *Malan reformed the National Party, making it anti-British and fundamentally republican and preaching the doctrine of *apartheid as a religious obligation for Afrikaaners of the Dutch Reformed Church. The party came to power after the general election of March 1948 and continued to win substantial majorities in successive elections up to September 1989. The rigours of apartheid led to a widening breach between Malan's successors, *Strijdom and Vorster, and other Commonwealth leaders: the National Party promoted the referendum of October 1960 which led to the withdrawal of South Africa from the Commonwealth and the establishment of an independent Republic in 1961.

Aga Khan III, Aga Sultan Sir Mohammed Shah (1877–1957), Muslim leader and Indian statesman: born in Karachi; succeeded his father as Aga Khan in 1885. As 48th Imam of the Ismaili sect, 1893–1957, he was effective leader of more than 12 million Muslims, in three continents, whom he consistently urged to integrate with other communities in whatever country they lived. He began to play a major role in the political life of British India on the Viceroy's Legislative Council from 1902 to 1904, becoming first president of the All-India Muslim League in 1906. In 1915 he went to Egypt to counter Turkish assertions that the British and their allies were enemies of Islam. He led the British–India delegation to the *Round Table Conferences (1930, 1932) and was chief Indian delegate at the League of Nations Assembly in 1932 and 1935–37. In Britain he was known as a breeder of race-horses and the owner of five Derby winners. But the Aga Khan was also a generous educationist, the effective founder in 1920 of Aligarh Muslim University, now in the Indian state of Uttar Pradesh. From 1934 onwards his influence in All-Indian Muslim affairs declined, *Jinnah receiving wider popular support, but his authority over the Ismaili sect was never challenged. He died in Switzerland and was buried in a magnificent tomb at Aswan, in Upper Egypt. His grandson Karim (b. 1936) succeeded him as Aga Khan IV and leader of the Ismaili Muslims.

Aggrey, James Kwegyir (1875–1927), pioneer African teacher of racial equality: born at Anamabu, now in Ghana, and educated at Cape Coast Methodist School, to the west of Accra. He became a teacher at 15 and headmaster of his old school at 21. In 1897 he was founder-secretary of the Aborigine Rights Protection Society in the Gold Coast and was soon accepted as the chief translator of the Bible into Fante. For much of the following twenty years he was in North Carolina, at Livingstone College, but in 1920 he became the only African appointed to the Phelps–Stokes Commission of Inquiry into educational needs in Africa. He travelled over the central and southern colonial states of the continent, known and respected as the 'Interpreter of Races' because of his work for mutual understanding between black and white. From 1924 onwards he helped establish Achimota College, near Accra, as an institution for higher education, but died in September 1927 from meningitis, only nine months after Achimota opened.

AIDS (Acquired Immune Deficiency Syndrome): worldwide medical problem of the late twentieth century. The spread of an HIV virus which destroys natural immunities and thereby causes the AIDS condition was identified in southern Africa in 1979, although it was not until the summer of 1985 that the widespread prevalence of the AIDS condition aroused major international concern. The worst-affected Common-wealth countries have been Zambia, Kenya, Tanzania, Zimbabwe and, especially, *Uganda. In January 1994 it was estimated that one in ten Ugandans carried the HIV virus, and almost a third of the adult popula-tion of Kampala, the Ugandan capital, were believed to be infected. Commonwealth health ministers discussed ways of combating AIDS at meetings at Melbourne in 1989 and Cyprus in 1993. All Commonwealth countries participated in the London world conference of February 1988, which called for enlightened sex education and 'a spirit of social tolerance' towards sufferers from the condition.

Airlines. The spread of civil aviation had a twofold significance for the Empire and Commonwealth: it drew outlying communities not served by *railways closer together, notably in Australia and northern Canada; and it provided speedier links between London and the imperial capitals. There was a commercial flight from Montreal to Ottawa as early as October 1913, but air transport companies came into being only after World War I. *Qantas, based in Queensland, was founded in 1920, and there were also ferry flights for fur traders in Canada that year. In 1924 the first scheduled Canadian service began flights from the Dominion Skyways aerodrome at Rouyn, Quebec Province: in May to Angliers and in September to Haileybury, across the Ontario border, neither flight exceeding 100 miles. Backing from the great railway companies helped Canadian civil aviation; significantly, Canadian Airways, established by a merging of smaller companies in 1930, was based on Winnipeg, the railway 'gateway to the West'. The government-sponsored Union Airways began flights in South Africa in 1929. There were nine commercial airlines in New Zealand by 1939 but they offered no challenge to older means of transport until after 1945, when they were nationalized. In New South Wales ventures by the pioneer trans-ocean pilot Kingsford *Smith in 1929–30 and, soon afterwards, by the Holyman brothers culminated in the founding of Australian National Airways, the growth of Ansett Air and, in 1946, the setting up of Trans-Australian Airlines. Meanwhile in London five companies merged in 1924 to form *Imperial Airways, which was envisaged as a future Royal Mail service for the empire (see *Airship projects*, below): routes opened to Egypt and the Persian Gulf in 1927, to the Indian Empire (Karachi) in March 1929, to South Africa in April 1932, to Malaya in December 1933 and, in collaboration with Qantas, to Brisbane in April 1935. The main 'hops' were made by flying boats, but the opening service from England to Capetown necessitated six changes and the use of five different types of aircraft; when in March 1936 a weekly link from Penang brought Hong Kong into the Imperial network, there were so many stops between London and the colony that the first flights took 10 days. Air links between England and Canada were first made through US cities by Pan-Am and Imperial flying boat services in the summer of 1939, but Air Canada launched a transatlantic service in July 1943, despite wartime conditions. Air links improved rapidly after the war: by December 1945 BOAC and Qantas jointly ran a three times a week service from London to Australia, flying 12,000 miles in 63 hours. The coming of jet aircraft in 1958 soon made fast, long-haul flights the commonest form of intercontinental passenger transport.

Airship projects. The success of the Germans with long-distance Zeppelins and a pioneer Atlantic round-trip in Britain's R34 in July 1919 aroused government interest in developing airships as successors to steamships 'to link the Empire together'. In 1924 Britain's first Labour Government launched the Imperial Airship Scheme for a passenger/mail service to India and the dominions. Progress with the project was slow, though given a fresh impetus by the transatlantic Zeppelin service introduced by the Germans in 1928. Airship terminals were approved in Ismailia and Karachi (where mooring masts were completed in 1930) and in Montreal (where the mast was never finished), and surveys were made for other sites at Durban and Perth. The Government-built R101, designed to carry 100 passengers in ocean-liner comfort at a top speed of 70 mph, left Cardington in Bedfordshire on the evening of 4 October 1930 to inaugurate the service to Karachi and back. Seven and a half hours later the R101, having covered 300 miles in heavy rain and strong winds, struck a small hill outside Beauvais and was destroyed; only 8 of the 54 passengers and crew survived. The magnitude of the disaster led to the immediate abandonment of all airship projects and a shift of government backing to the flying-boat services of *Imperial Airways.

Alberta, the most western Canadian prairie province, capital Edmonton. Until 1869 much of the future province was controlled by the *Hudson's Bay Company, under the authority of a charter from Charles II (1670). From 1870 to 1905 it formed part of the Northwest Territories of the Dominion, administered virtually as a colony from Ottawa until popular pressure forced the establishment of a territorial legislature in 1888 and a non-elective executive council in 1897. Full provincial status followed in 1905. The rich agricultural land was opened up by the *Canadian Pacific Railway in the 1880s; and the CPR was largely responsible for the founding in 1883 of Calgary, the biggest city on the dominion's high plains. The most rapid growth of Alberta's population came in the first decade of the twentieth century, with 'homesteaders' attracted by a succession of good harvests and high wheat prices: population increased from 73,000 in 1901 to 374,000 in 1911. The province has remained rich in cereals (especially barley) and stockraising of cattle is still a primary industry. But Alberta has always been rich in mineral resources: copper and coal in the late nineteenth century have been supplemented by the exploitation of natural gas reserves and the development of oilfields, with pipelines running from Edmonton eastwards to Montreal and westwards, across the Rockies, to Vancouver.

'All Blacks': popular name given to the Rugby Union *football players of New Zealand, derived from their black jerseys, shorts and socks. The term came into use in 1905/6 when a New Zealand team won 32 of 33 matches played in Britain and France, an achievement followed by victories in all 30 matches during their next tour. The All Blacks have remained formidable; on 20 June 1987 they won the first Rugby World Cup Final at Auckland, defeating France 29–9.

Allenby, Edmund Henry Hynman, Viscount (1861–1936), British soldier: born in Suffolk, educated at *Haileybury and Sandhurst, saw action in Bechuanaland in 1888 and made his reputation as a cavalry commander in the Boer War. After commanding the Third Army at Arras he was appointed to lead the Egyptian expeditionary force against the Turks in June 1917, and in the autumn he advanced through Gaza and Jaffa to capture Jerusalem on 9 December. Between 18 September and 30 October 1918 his imaginative use of cavalry rolled the Turks back, forcing them to sue for peace. Allenby, promoted Field Marshal in 1919, became effectively an imperial pro-consul in the Levant at the end of World War I. After an Egyptian nationalist insurrection in the spring of 1919 he was appointed special High Commissioner in Cairo, with the difficult task of ending the British Protectorate over Egypt while ensuring the safety of the *Suez Canal; he became a substantial presence in the newly independent state and consolidated the Anglo-Egyptian *condominium in the *Sudan. Allenby's forcefulness – including a threat to resign if his advice was ignored – induced the British Government to declare the Protectorate at an end on 28 February 1922; a fortnight later Egypt became an independent kingdom, linked for defence purposes in a special relationship to Great Britain. Allenby remained as High Commissioner in Cairo until his retirement in 1925.

American colonies. *Newfoundland was the earliest English colony in North America, but projects for settling the mainland were advanced by *Ralegh at Roanoake and, more successfully, by the *Virginia Company, with the foundation of Jamestown in 1607 and the first commercial export of tobacco ten years later. Between 1620 and 1640 more than 20,000 immigrants, 'vexed and troubled' by religion, settled in New England: the charter of the Massachusetts Bay Company was confirmed by Charles I in 1629, and Boston was founded a year later. Maryland was formed in 1634, as a proprietary colony for Roman Catholic gentry, many of whom turned to African slave labour to work the tobacco plantations; Protestantism asserted itself there in 1688–89, as it had already in the Carolinas, which were founded by 'Lords Proprietors' early in Charles II's reign. New York – the Dutch colony of the New Netherlands – was seized by an English expedition in 1664. Pennsylvania and much of Delaware were promoted by William Penn, with proprietary grants from Charles II and James II, to provide cheap land and religious toleration to hard-working Dissenters; many were Quakers or German Pietists. Georgia, too, had philanthropic and religious origins, with a Protestant settlement at Savannah in 1733; Georgia only became a royal colony in

1753. *Colonial assemblies, in New England dating from James I's reign, developed a natural independence, jealously protective of the new society they represented. They increasingly resented the Westminster Parliament's control of overseas commerce and its disregard of their desire to penetrate the interior of the continent. From 1764/5 onwards, the taxing of commodities (sugar, tea, etc.) in the colonies to raise revenue for the Crown, and the Declaratory Act of 1766 which asserted Parliament's right to annul colonial legislation, convinced the colonists their civil liberty was in jeopardy. The obtuse policies of government ministers, more interested in trade with the East and West Indies, denied the right of Americans to petition the king directly. Common grievances brought together in a patriotic union of defiance thirteen colonies, whose interests and economic structures varied considerably. The simultaneous enactment in 1774 of Coercive Acts to gag the mounting indignation in Boston and of a *Quebec Act benefiting French Canadian Catholics was the catalyst of rebellion. The first skirmishes at Lexington on 19 April 1775 were followed fourteen months later by the Declaration of Independence. Dogged American resistance, persistent strategic blunders by the British, and aid to the ex-colonists from France (especially the French fleet), ensured that independence became a reality in September 1783, with the signing of the first peace treaty of Versailles.

Amery, Leopold Charles Maurice Stennet (1873–1955), imperialist writer and statesman: born in India, the son of a civil servant attached to the Forestry Department. He was educated at Harrow, where he was a contemporary of *Churchill, and at Oxford, subsequently becoming a barrister and a Conservative MP for a Birmingham constituency (1911–45). Amery was in South Africa during the *Boer War and admired *Milner, whose ideas on imperialism he interpreted in his own writings, particularly in the seven-volume *The Times History of the War in South Africa* (published 1900–1909), to which he was the chief contributor as well as its editor. After two years on the Western Front and in the Balkans, Amery joined the cabinet secretariat in 1916 and drafted the *Balfour Declaration of 1917 on a Jewish 'national home'. He was First Lord of the Admiralty in Bonar Law's cabinet (1922) and Colonial Secretary (1924–29), also becoming Dominions Secretary when the office was created in July 1925. He warmly supported *imperial preference, established the *Empire Marketing Board, and was responsible for organizing the *Imperial Conference of 1926, at which the *Balfour Definition on the form of the Commonwealth was agreed. Amery was too critical of Britain's foreign policy in the 1930s to hold office, but from 1940 to 1945 he was Secretary of State for India and Burma, seeking independence for a united subcontinent within the Commonwealth. Amery firmly believed in imperial expansion, but not in centralization on London; he championed 'a freely co-operative

Commonwealth', a vast family whose unity was symbolized by allegiance to a common Crown.

Amin, Idi (1926–   ), Ugandan soldier and President: a Muslim from northern Uganda who rose to the rank of sergeant in the *King's African Rifles and was Commander-in-Chief of the Ugandan Army in January 1971 when President *Obote was overthrown by a military coup in Kampala. For eight years he was titular Head of State in Uganda, as dictatorial Chairman of the Defence Council. Ugandan Asians were expelled in 1972 and most British nationals followed them soon afterwards. His arbitrary rule, which favoured the narrow interests of the Muslim community of his own tribe, alienated other Commonwealth countries and also Israel. British relations with Uganda were broken off in 1976. Tension increased following the sudden death of the Archbishop of Uganda early in 1977 and armed clashes between Ugandan troops and their Kenyan and Tanzanian neighbours. In April 1979 Tanzanian troops and Ugandan exiles marched on Kampala, forcing Amin to leave the country and seek refuge in Libya.

Amritsar: town in the Punjab (India), barely 30 miles from Pakistan's second largest city, Lahore. The Golden Temple, the holiest of Sikh shrines, lies in Amritsar, which became notorious when on 13 April 1919 the local British commander, Brigadier-General Reginald Dyer, ordered his troops to fire on a prohibited political demonstration in a public courtyard, the Jallienwalla Bagh. At least 379 Indians were killed and 1,200 wounded. A government inquiry subsequently censured Dyer and he resigned his commission, but the massacre left a legacy of bitter resentment against the British among younger Indians. In June 1984 and in May 1988 there was again severe rioting in Amritsar, and heavy loss of life, when the Indian army sought to seize Sikh extremists demanding autonomy. The Sikhs found refuge in the Golden Temple and more than 30 other shrines, which suffered severe damage in the Indian military operations.

Angliss, Sir William (1865–1957), Australian businessman: born in Dudley, Worcestershire, and a butcher's boy in London before emigrating to Victoria in 1884. There he borrowed money to open a butcher's shop, gradually building up a chain of meat suppliers, pioneering wholesale refrigeration and acquiring cattle and sheep stations. In the *Gold Rush of 1892/3 he shipped meat from Victoria to Western Australia and in 1900 he began to supply refrigerated meat in bulk to England. He was soon recognized as the leading Australian meat exporter and was spokesman for the industry at the *Ottawa Conference in 1932. Angliss, knighted in 1939, was a member of the Legislative Council of Victoria (1912–52) and promoted several charitable concerns to encourage child immigration from Britain.

Anguilla: the most northerly of the Leeward Islands in the Caribbean. It covers an area of about 60 square miles and has a population of 7,000. There were English settlers on the island in the mid seventeenth century but it was only recognized as a British possession by the Treaty of Utrecht in 1713, received little formal administration until 1825 when it was linked with *St Kitts and Nevis, and was given colonial status as part of the Leeward Islands Federation in 1871. Resentment at alleged exploitation by St Kitts led in 1967 to Anguilla's unilateral declaration of independence and the despatch to the island of police and British paratroops. In 1969 it became a British dependency, a status regularized in December 1980 by the Anguilla Act. In 1982 a constitution provided for a twelve-seat House of Assembly. Queen Elizabeth II undertook the first royal visit to Anguilla in February 1994.

Antarctic Territories. In 1773/4 the British seaman, Captain James *Cook, made the first recorded voyage across the Antarctic Circle, sighting South Georgia and part of the South Sandwich Island group, but it was another half-century before the Antarctic continent was circumnavigated, by the Russian naval officer Thaddeus von Bellingshausen in 1820/1, and the English sealing captain John Biscoe in 1830. Successive British, American, Russian, French and Norwegian expeditions claimed Antarctic territories during the nineteenth century but Commonwealth claims were not clearly defined until the inter-war years of the twentieth century. The *Ross Dependency was placed under New Zealand's jurisdiction in July 1923 and in July 1933 the Australian Antarctic Territory was established (see *Australian Dependent Territories*), an area almost as large as mainland Australia itself. The twelve-power Antarctic Treaty (signed in December 1959 and operative from June 1961) pledged a status quo over territorial claims in Antarctica and gave pledges of peaceful development and international scientific co-operation. Only after the treaty came into force did London, in March 1962, formally establish the British Antarctic Territory, an area of 660,000 square miles including the South Orkney and South Shetland Islands and the Antarctic Peninsula, but without permanent residents. The territory includes a chain of research stations and is administered by a Commissioner resident in the *Falkland Islands. Formal claims by Chile and Argentina to segments of the British Antarctic Territory lapsed with the conclusion of the 1959 treaty.

Antigua and Barbuda: Caribbean islands in the Lesser Antilles group. Antigua was discovered and named by Columbus in 1493 but colonized by the English from 1632, with a settlement established on neighbouring Barbuda in 1661. The islands were administered as part of the Leeward Islands Federation for 85 years until 1956, when Antigua became a Crown Colony and part of the short-lived *British West Indies

Federation from 1958 to 1962. The islands became an associated state of the United Kingdom in February 1967, gaining full independence within the Commonwealth on 1 November 1981. The estimated population of Antigua is between 81,000 and 85,000 with about 2,000 people living in Barbuda. On Antigua the chief crops are cotton and tropical fruits, although there is also an oil refinery. St John's, the chief town on Antigua, was a naval base in the eighteenth century and in 1805 was used by Nelson, who had previously served there as a junior officer.

Anyaoku, Emeka (Eleazar Chukwuemeka), Ndichie Chief Adazie of Obosi (1933–   ), third Secretary-General of the Commonwealth: educated at Merchants of Light School, Oba, Nigeria and University of Ibadan. He entered the Nigerian diplomatic service in 1962 and was briefly Minister of External Affairs, 1983. Apart from this intermission, he worked for the *Commonwealth Secretariat from 1966, succeeding Shridath *Ramphal of Guyana as Secretary-General in July 1990. He is author of *The Racial Factor in International Politics* (1977) and was chief secretary to the *Eminent Persons Group on their southern African mission in 1986.

ANZAC: acronym for the Australasian expeditionary force of World War I, the Australian and New Zealand Army Corps; in use in Cairo in 1915, it became widely known after the courage of the Corps at Ari Burnu ('Anzac Cove') on the *Gallipoli peninsula (25 April 1915). Of 16,000 Anzacs landed that day, 2,300 were killed and 6,000 wounded. In the Sari Bair battle of August 1915 another 4,000 Anzacs perished. After eight months of intense fighting against the Turks the survivors were withdrawn to Egypt. Anzac divisions later fought at Arras, Messines and Passchendaele, helped check the final German offensive in March 1918, and served under *Allenby in Palestine; Anzacs – Australians of the 3rd Light Horse Brigade – were the first regular troops to enter Damascus (1 October 1918).

Anzac Day: 25 April, the anniversary of the *Anzac landing of 1915, is observed in Australia and New Zealand as *Remembrance Day for the dead of the twentieth century. The earliest commemoration was in 1916.

ANZAM: acronym for the 1948 security pact between Australia, New Zealand and Malaya which set up a Commonwealth Strategic Reserve for action against Communist insurgents during the *Malayan Emergency.

ANZUS Pact: security treaty concluded at San Francisco by Australia, New Zealand and the United States on 1 September 1951. The treaty provided for collaboration should any of the three countries, or 'territories under its jurisdiction in the Pacific', be the victim of 'an armed attack'. The Pact emphasized mounting Australasian independence of the United Kingdom in world affairs. In 1985 the Pact became effectively inoperative when, in New Zealand, the Labour government of *Lange sponsored a South Pacific Nuclear Free Zone.

Apartheid: an Afrikaans word for 'apartness', used by *Malan in the South African election campaign of May 1948. After his electoral victory a series of apartheid laws extended the long-established total racial segregation of the *Transvaal to other provinces of the Union. Among them were: *the Mixed Marriages Act (1949); the *Group Areas Act (1950); the Suppression of Communism Act (1950); and the General Law Amendment Act (1963) which gave the police rights of arbitrary arrest and detention of suspects for 90 days without recourse to the courts. Sexual relations between whites and non-whites were forbidden by strict enforcement of an earlier Immorality Act. Strikes by African workers were forbidden by laws passed in 1953 and 1957, and the meagre voting rights allowed by the *Representation of the Natives Act in 1936 were withdrawn. Movement of non-whites was regulated by *Pass Laws. In 1959 Prime Minister *Verwoerd introduced the Bantu Self-Government Act, which provided for seven native African states within the Union, each with a non-white chief minister. Apartheid was condemned as morally unjustifiable in the United Nations Assembly as early as 1952. There was widespread revulsion in the Commonwealth after the *Sharpeville shootings (1960) in which 67 Africans demonstrating against the Pass Laws were shot. The hostility of Commonwealth prime ministers in March 1961 led Verwoerd to declare that South Africa would leave the Commonwealth rather than modify the apartheid laws, a threat implemented on 31 May 1961. In the new Republic the severity of apartheid was intensified, notably in 1985/6; abroad, calls were made for economic pressure to be imposed on South Africa. At the 1985 *Commonwealth Heads of Government meeting in Nassau, only Margaret *Thatcher stood out against sanctions. By 1990 South Africa's isolation was so marked that President de Klerk began talks with *ANC leaders to end apartheid, a task accomplished by midsummer 1991.

Ascension: a volcanic island in the South Atlantic, administratively a British Dependent Territory annexed to *St Helena, 700 miles to the south-east. The name was given by the Portuguese, who discovered the island on Ascension Day 1501; uninhabited until 1815/16 when it was garrisoned by the British, who feared that it might serve as a base for a bid to rescue Napoleon I from St Helena. The island, a cable station, was under Admiralty control until the Colonial Office assumed responsibility in 1922. A satellite communications centre was set up in 1966 and an airstrip – nicknamed the 'Miracle Mile' – was constructed, the island acquiring considerable strategic importance as a staging-post for the

Ashanti

*Falkland Islands from 1982 onwards. Ascension has long been a breeding ground for sea-turtles and tern.

Ashanti: an Akan-speaking people grouped in a confederacy inland from the Fante tribe of the *Gold Coast, militarily powerful throughout the eighteenth and nineteenth centuries. Their symbol of kingship was a Golden Stool, which was revered as embodying the spirit of the Ashanti nation. The Ashanti, skilled craftsmen in house-building and in fashioning golden and silver objects, long retained slavery and controlled the trade routes from western Africa to the Gold Coast. They were frequently at war with the British settlers. Desultory campaigns in 1824–27 and 1863–64 inflicted defeats on the British which went unavenged until the winter of 1873/4 when Sir Garnet *Wolseley was ordered to stamp out slavery and human sacrifices practised as part of the military caste system of the Ashanti king, Kofi Karikari. This expedition required the construction of a road through fever-ridden swamp and forest, for which it was necessary to build more than 200 bridges, in order to reach and capture the Ashanti capital, Kumasi, after a battle in which the Highlanders of the Black Watch distinguished themselves. Despite Wolseley's victory, the Ashanti reverted to traditional ways under Karikari's successor, King Pempeh. A gold boom along the coast in the early 1890s encouraged the Colonial Secretary, *Chamberlain, to order the opening up of West Africa, an undertaking which revived the highly developed Ashanti sense of nationhood. Another military expedition in 1896 deposed Pempeh, and Ashanti was made a British Protectorate (August 1896). An inept demand by a colonial governor to be enthroned on the Golden Stool precipitated a major revolt in 1900, swiftly suppressed. Ashanti was formally annexed to the Gold Coast colony on 26 September 1901, and a railway from the coast to Kumasi was completed two years later. Since 1957 Ashanti has been a province in *Ghana.

'Ashes', The: a term dating from 29 August 1882 when, following the first series of Test Matches to be lost to a visiting Australian team, the London journalist, R. S. Brooks, inserted in the *Sporting Times* a mock obituary 'in affectionate memory of English *cricket' which ended: 'The body will be cremated and the Ashes taken to Australia.' When, a few months later, the English captain avenged the defeat, an urn containing the ashes of a bail or ball was presented to him. This trophy remains at Lord's, the headquarters of cricket in London, but notionally each of the 57 series of Test Matches between the two countries since 1883 has been 'a contest for the Ashes'. The Tests have been fiercely competitive; on at least one occasion, during the '*bodyline controversy' of 1932/3, they strained Anglo-Australian relations. England 'held the Ashes' 1883–90, 1894/5–96, 1903/4–05, 1911–12, 1926–29, 1932/3, 1953–56,

1970/1–72, 1977–83, 1985–88. During the intervening years, and in the four series from 1989, Australia has 'held' them.

Assiniboines: a native North American 'Indian' people, Siouan-speaking hunters who migrated in the early seventeenth century from modern Dakota into the eastern Canadian prairies, giving their name to the Assiniboine River and to an early *Hudson's Bay Company's settlement on the *Red River, later incorporated in *Manitoba. In alliance with the *Cree, they were often at war with the *Blackfoot confederacy. Their numbers were weakened by smallpox in the eighteenth century and by the virtual extinction of the wild herds of buffalo in the third quarter of the nineteenth century. Many were killed by American whisky-traders in the Cypress Hills region along the US–Canadian border in 1873 after protracted disputes over alleged horse stealing. The last land rights of the Assiniboine were surrendered to the Dominion of Canada by treaty in September 1877: in return for token gifts and the promise of assistance in discovering how to become farmers, the Assiniboines abandoned nomadic life and were settled in tribal reservations.

Athabasca: a long river, lake and region of north *Alberta and north *Saskatchewan, perpetuating the name of a native 'Indian' language spoken over a wide section of western Canada from Hudson Bay to the Pacific. The chief Athabascan-speaking peoples were the Sarcee, Dene and *Chipewyan in the main Athabasca region, the Kutchin in the *Yukon, and the Carrier Chilcochin and Tahltan in *British Columbia. Athabasca was a rich *fur country, opened up by adventurers (so-called 'Pedlars') exploring north-west Canada in the 1770s, ahead of the organized trading communities of the Hudson's Bay Company. Rich mineral deposits around the shores of Lake Athabasca aroused interest in the mid twentieth century, with Uranium City (Saskatchewan) founded in the 1950s in expectation, never entirely fulfilled, of a boom.

Athletics. Modern competitive field and track athletics date only from c.1850, and national representation was haphazard before the formation of the International Amateur Athletic Federation in 1912. Although an Australian, Edwin Flack, won both the 800 metres and the 1,500 metres at the first revived *Olympic Games (Athens, 1896), the chief Commonwealth medal winners before World War I came from Britain, Canada and South Africa. The decision to institute four-yearly *Empire Games (first held in Canada in 1930) stimulated a wider interest in athletics; and in a close finish at the Berlin Olympics of 1936 the New Zealander Jack Lovelock won the Gold Medal for 1,500 metres with a world record of 3 mins 47.8 secs. At the next Olympics (London, 1948) the outstanding Commonwealth athlete was the Jamaican Arthur Wint, who won a gold medal for 400 metres and a silver for 800 metres, thus setting the standard for a tradition of excellence maintained by Jamaican sprinters, men and women, for half a century. Hopes of being the first 'four-minute miler' excited competition between British athletes (Bannister, Chataway and Brasher) and the Australian John Landy. Success came to Roger Bannister at Oxford on 6 May 1954 (3 mins 59.4), a record beaten by Landy in Finland by 1.5 seconds within seven weeks; when on 7 August 1954 the two men faced each other in the mile race at the Empire and *Commonwealth Games in Vancouver, British Columbia, Bannister defeated Landy, though without breaking his record. A young Western Australian, Herb Elliott, began championship athletics in that same year: between 1954 and 1960 Elliott competed in 44 mile or 1,500 metre races and was unbeaten, his best achievements being world records of 3 minutes 54.5 secs for the mile (1958) and 3 35.6 for 1,500 metres (1960). The New Zealanders Peter Snell (1962) and John Walker (1975) ran world mile records and the Australian Ron Clarke a record 5,000 metres (1965), but the most persistent Commonwealth challenge for middle distance running between 1974 and 1988 came from a British quartet – Steve Ovett, Sebastian Coe, Dave Moorcroft and Steve Cram. Among Commonwealth athletes in the last decade of the century Kenyans attained new levels in middle and long distance running and black sprinters and hurdlers dominated British men's track events, while Sally Gunnell from Essex and Elizabeth McColgan and Yvonne Murray from Scotland were the outstanding women athletes.

Attlee, Clement Richard (1883–1967), British Prime Minister: born in Putney (London), educated at *Haileybury and University College, Oxford; became a barrister, but concerned himself with social problems in the poorer parts of London's East End. A major in World War I, he served at Gallipoli and in Mesopotamia as well as in France. He entered Parliament as a Labour MP in 1922 and remained in the Commons until he was created Earl Attlee in 1955. For the last twenty years of his Commons years he led the Labour Party, and was Prime Minister of the first Labour government with parliamentary majorities (1945–51). As a member of the commission which prepared the *Simon Report he visited India twice in 1928–9, and in 1935 he devoted an early broadcast as party leader to India's claim for dominion status. He later selected *Mountbatten as Viceroy and personally piloted the Indian Independence Bill through every stage in the Commons until it became law on 18 July 1947. While serving as Deputy Prime Minister in the Churchill coalition, Attlee was also Dominions Secretary (February 1942 to September 1943), and came to recognize the need for post-war decolonization, beginning with independence for *Burma and dominion status for *Ceylon. He regarded the Empire and Commonwealth as 'the creation of sea power', arguing (in 1945) that in 'the air age' it was strategically indefensible, except through UNO. He waived Foreign Office proposals that Britain assume trusteeship for Italy's former colonies in Cyrenaica and Somaliland and urgently sought to end Britain's *Palestine mandate. In May 1947 Attlee set up a cabinet committee on the future of the Commonwealth, chairing its meetings himself; 'We want no unwilling partners in the British Commonwealth' was his dictum. His views on the looser structure of the Commonwealth links prevailed in the *London Declaration of April 1949.

Australia, the largest island in the world to form a single political entity. *Aborigines from south-east Asia crossed into the continent 60,000 years ago. *Tasman in the 1640s discovered much of the western and northern coasts of 'New Holland'; *Cook charted the eastern coast in 1769–70 and spent a week ashore at *Botany Bay in *New South Wales. The *First Fleet established a penal colony at Sydney in 1788: settlements followed at Newcastle (1801), Hobart and Launceston in Tasmania (1803–4), and Perth in *Western Australia in 1829, the year Britain formally annexed Australia, as 'New Holland' had been known since 1817. By 1802 *Bass and *Flinders had virtually completed the charting of the coasts. The opening up of the interior followed the crossing of the *Blue Mountains (1814) and the journeys of *Sturt, *Mitchell and *Eyre between 1829 and 1841, although the first expedition from south to north (*Burke and Wills) dates only from 1860/1. Further exploration was made by *Warburton, the brothers *Forrest, and *Giles, in the early 1870s. Pastoral settlement encouraged *sheep farming; there was a flourishing *wool trade to England by 1850, the year when the *Australian Colonies Act effectively accorded self-government to New South Wales, Tasmania, *South Australia and *Victoria. *Queensland (part of NSW until 1859) did not have a legislative assembly until 1860, nor Western Australia until 1890; the *Northern Territory only became self-governing in 1978. The *Australian Commonwealth Act brought federation into being on 1 January 1901, although not until 1909 was *Canberra accepted as the site of Australia's capital. Catalysts for social change have included: the *Gold Rushes of 1851–4 and 1892–3; swifter means of transport across the oceans and inland; and the effects of *World War I (in which one in ten of the male population was killed or wounded), the *Great Depression of 1929–34, and *World War II, in which the Timor Sea, Coral Sea and Pacific Ocean were major areas of conflict. Revised *immigration policies admitted more than 2 million 'New Australians' between 1946 and 1966, many from parts of southern Europe with traditionally high birth rates. The coastal cities grew rapidly; by 1986 only 16.4 per cent of the population of 15.8 million lived outside towns, while more than half were concentrated in Sydney, Melbourne and Brisbane. Greater independence from the United Kingdom in world affairs, shown in the *ANZUS Pact and emphasized by differences over *Vietnam and Britain's membership of the *European Community, contributed to a rise of republican sentiment, especially during the premiership of Paul *Keating.

Australia Acts

Australia Acts (1986): these measures (a Statute of the Westminster Parliament and a Statute of the Canberra Parliament) completed Australia's legal independence by removing residual powers of the British government to intervene in federal or state matters. Thus the Privy Council lost the right to hear appeals from Australian courts. Queen Elizabeth II's status as sovereign was not changed; the Queen signed the Act on 2 March 1986 while on a visit to Australia.

Australia Day (26 January): a national holiday to commemorate the raising of the British flag at Sydney Cove on 26 January 1788 in the presence of the first Governor of New South Wales, Arthur *Philip.

Australian Colonies Act (1850). An act 'for the better government of the Australian colonies' passed in London by the Whig government of Lord John Russell, prompted by requests for clarification from *New South Wales, where a legislative council had functioned since 1824. It effectively gave self-government to three of the four existing Australian colonies: New South Wales, *South Australia and Van Diemen's Land (*Tasmania). The Act also provided for the establishment of *Victoria as a colony independent of New South Wales and promised it, like the other three colonies, a two-thirds elective legislature. The Colonial Secretary, the third Earl Grey (1802–94), favoured the creation of a general assembly for all Australia but was persuaded that distances between the colonies were too great and common interests too few, as yet, for confederation to be effective. Grey refused to grant *Western Australia self-government because the colony was still dominated by a penal settlement system. The petitioners from Australia were not given all they sought; an assembly could not appropriate revenue raised in the colony, nor take final decisions over land policy. Elected legislatures came to New South Wales, South Australia and Tasmania in 1855 and Victoria in 1856.

Australian Commonwealth Act (1900): a statute of the United Kingdom Parliament, passed on 9 July 1900, which provided for the formation of a federated Commonwealth of Australia on 1 January 1901: the six colonies – *New South Wales, *South Australia, *Tasmania, *Western Australia, *Victoria and *Queensland – became 'states', with the Northern Territory remaining part of South Australia until it became a federal responsibility in 1911. The Act followed nine years of discussions which reflected growing alarm at the colonial activities of France, Germany and the United States in the Pacific and south-east Asia. A federal convention at Hobart in 1897 prepared a draft constitution but it proved unacceptable to the New South Wales legislature. Further conferences were held by the Australian colonial prime ministers at Sydney and Melbourne in 1898, with reference back to London, where the Colonial Secretary, *Chamberlain, strongly favoured federation on strategic grounds. Edmund *Barton, a barrister from Sydney and the leading figure at the federal convention, became the first Prime Minister of the Australian Commonwealth. Elections for a Senate and House of Representatives were held on 31 March 1901 and on 9 May the Duke of York (later King George V) opened the first Federal Parliament at the *Melbourne Centennial Exhibition building, senators and deputies adjourning to the neighbouring state Parliament House next day. The Federal Parliament did not move to *Canberra until 1927.

Australian Dependent Territories. The Commonwealth of Australia is responsible for seven groups of external Dependent Territories. The largest (2,362,875 square miles) is the Australian *Antarctic Territory, placed under federal sovereignty by Order in Council in February 1933 and formally accepted by proclamation in August 1936; between 1954 and 1959 three scientific research stations were opened in the territory. The oldest dependency is Norfolk Island, 900 miles east of Sydney; it was a penal settlement, 1788–1813 and 1826–55, and has been an Australian dependency since 1913; as the home of descendants of the *Bounty mutineers since 1856, it remains popular with tourists. Christmas Island in the Indian Ocean, 200 miles south of western Java and some 1,500 miles from the Western Australian coast, was annexed by the British in 1888 and administered from Singapore until 1958, when sovereignty was transferred to Australia; until 1987 rock phosphate was mined. The Cocos (Keeling) Islands are a coral archipelago in the Indian Ocean, 1,700 miles off Western Australia: they were discovered by Captain William Keeling of the East India Company in 1609, annexed in 1857, and administered successively by the colonial authorities in Ceylon and Singapore until placed under Australian sovereignty in 1955: in World War I a cable station on the main island was being raided by a landing party from the German cruiser *Emden* (November 1914) when the Australian cruiser *Sydney* caught the *Emden*, forcing her on to a coral reef and wrecking her. The remaining Dependent Territories are uninhabited: Heard and McDonald Islands, in the Indian Ocean 2,500 miles from Fremantle, have been Australian since 1947; Ashmore and Cartier Islands, 200 miles off the Northern Territory and under Australian control since 1933/4, are reefs serving as nature reserves; the Coral Sea Islands are also reefs, technically Australian since 1969 and sheltering a meteorological station.

Australian New Guinea: see *Papua New Guinea*.

Ayub Khan, Mohammed (1907–74), second President of *Pakistan: born, the son of an NCO, near the *north-west frontier, and commissioned into the Indian Army in 1928. He served with distinction in Burma between 1942 and 1945. By 1951 he was commanding general of the Pakistan Army, and became Minister of Defence in October 1954. Mounting disorder led four years later to a proclamation of martial law by the first President, General Mirza, but it was Ayub Khan (newly promoted Field Marshal) who became chief martial law administrator. He succeeded Mirza on 28 October 1958 and won presidential elections in 1960 and, after amending the constitution, in 1965. Ayub Khan favoured a system of 'basic democracies', with powers devolved as privileged concessions down from the presidential office. Despite limited land reform, his militaristic repression alienated the Bengalis of eastern Pakistan (*Bangladesh), and he lost prestige in western Pakistan by a failure to check Indian military incursions in the Rann of Kutch area and in Kashmir. Student riots in 1968 and rivalry in the high command forced him from office on 24 March 1969, his successor being General Yahya Khan: civil war between West and East Pakistan (1,000 miles apart) followed two years later.

Azikiwe, Nnambi (1904–   ), first President of *Nigeria: an *Ibo, born at Zungeru in northern Nigeria; educated at a Methodist school in Lagos and several American universities, where he studied politics and developed interests in West African poetry. In 1934 he became editor of a newspaper in Accra, and over the next eleven years won wide respect as a moderate champion of national independence, emerging as Premier of Eastern Nigeria in 1954, despite a judicial inquiry into his conduct as Chairman of the African Continental Bank (1944–53). British confidence in 'Zik' made it natural for him to be appointed Nigeria's Governor-General in October 1960, becoming at the same time a Privy Councillor, and in 1963 he became Federal President. His chief rival, the *Hausa political spokesman *Balewa, worked with him in uneasy partnership as Prime Minister from 1957 onwards. Mounting tribal divisions weakened the authority of the civilian government and in January 1966 a military coup – led principally by Ibo officers – deposed Azikiwe after assassinating Balewa. Although Azikiwe was accepted as Ndichie Chief Owelle of Onitsha in 1973, he took no further part in federal politics until 1979, when he led the Nigerian People's Party in elections won by the rival National Party. A military coup in December 1983 ended Azikiwe's political activities.

Baden-Powell, Robert Stephenson Smyth (1857–1941), British soldier: the son of an Oxford mathematics professor. He joined the 13th Hussars in India, specializing in reconnaissance and scouting. After serving against the *Zulus and *Ashanti, he attracted attention by his skill in policing the Bulawayo district during the Matabele uprising of 1896. He then returned to India to command 5th Dragoon Guards (1897–99), and published a manual, *Aids to Scouting*. As the situation in South Africa deteriorated in 1899 he was sent to Cape Colony to raise two regiments, but in October took command of the small garrison in the railway junction of *Mafeking, where for 31 weeks he withstood a siege by a *Boer army 10,000 strong. This episode made Baden-Powell a hero of Empire; he was promoted from colonel to major-general, subsequently becoming Inspector-General of Cavalry and commanding the first Territorial division in north-east England. He was knighted in 1909 but in 1910 retired from the army to devote his time to the scouting movement, which he had established in 1907 to encourage boys to use their initiative in leisure-time activities of service to others. In 1912 Baden-Powell married Olave St Clair (1889–1977) who, from 1916, organized the Girl Guide movement which Baden-Powell's sister had established in 1909 to complement her brother's work for boys. The scouting movement attracted members throughout the Empire, especially in the 1920s and 1930s. It became worldwide in scope, particularly strong in the United States and in Hungary. By 1980 it had more than 13 million members in over a hundred countries. 'B-P', as Chief Scout, actively supported the movement until his death (in Kenya). He was created a baron in 1929 and in 1937 received the Order of Merit.

Bahadur Shah Zafar II (1775–1862), titular King of Delhi: the last descendant of the great Moghul warrior sovereigns – Babur, Humayun and Akbar – who between 1526 and 1605 established a Muslim empire across northern and central India from Bengal to Gujarat. By the time of Bahadur's birth Moghul authority had been eclipsed by the *Marathas, basically a Hindu confederacy. Bahadur acceded in 1837, confirming an earlier treaty with the British by which the Moghul heir would remain nominal King of Delhi and receive a pension of £200,000 a year. Bahadur was thus able to maintain for twenty years the ceremonial trappings of monarchy in his fortress-palace above Delhi's walled city, although effective sovereignty was exercised by British Governors-General through an administration based on Calcutta. But in May 1857 Bahadur, an octogenarian contemplative poet without political ambition, was induced by Muslim soldiery who seized Delhi to become the spiritual leader of the *Indian Mutiny, although he played no part in those events. After John Lawrence's Punjab relief force entered his capital in September 1857, he was charged with rebellion and incitement to murder and sentenced to life imprisonment, spending his last years in exile at Rangoon.

Bahamas: Atlantic archipelago of some 700 islands, of which fewer than 20 are inhabited. The north-western island, Grand Bahama, is 50 miles off the Florida coast; the most easterly, Watling Island (San Salvador), was probably Columbus's first landfall in the 'New World', in October 1492. British settlers arrived from *Bermuda in the early seventeenth century, and a company of merchant adventurers established a precarious trading settlement on Eleuthera Island in 1649. Spain sought to annex the islands in 1781 but following the Treaty of Paris (1783) they were organized as a British Crown Colony, a status maintained until January 1964, when internal self-government was granted. On 10 July 1973 the 'Commonwealth of the Bahamas' became fully independent within the greater Commonwealth. A bicameral legislature meets in the capital, Nassau, on New Providence Island; executive power is vested in the Queen's nominee as Governor-General. Tourism is the main industry; salt, rum and crawfish the leading exports.

Bahrain: an archipelago in the Persian Gulf, some 20 miles off the coast of Saudi Arabia and forming an independent Arab emirate. It was never part of the British Empire or Commonwealth, but had special treaty relations from 1820 onwards and became a British Protectorate in 1861, with later treaties strengthening British defence commitments in 1882 and 1892. The ruling Emir affirmed Bahrain's total independence on 15 August 1971, signing at the same time a treaty of friendship with Great Britain. Until World War II the chief industry of Bahrain was pearl fishing; lately an aluminium industry has developed. Oil was discovered in 1931 and, from 1932, welled by the Canadian-registered Bahrain Petroleum Company. The chief export is Saudi petroleum, brought to a refinery by pipeline and processed on Bahrain Island.

Baker, Sir Herbert (1862–1946), architect: born in Kent and educated at Tonbridge School before receiving training from the fashionable domestic architect, Sir Ernest George. Baker went to South Africa at the age of thirty and so impressed *Rhodes with his grandiose concepts that, within a year, he was commissioned to remodel Groote Schurr, Rhodes's home on Devil's Peak outside Cape Town, and later the official residence of South Africa's prime ministers. Baker, an ardent imperialist closely associated with *Milner, made his reputation in Africa. His works included Government House in Pretoria and Government House in Nairobi, parts of the Anglican cathedrals of Cape Town, Pretoria and Harare (formerly Salisbury), the Rhodes Memorial behind Groote Schurr, and the massive Union Buildings on Meintje's Kop, Pretoria. When in 1911 it was decided to create an Anglo-Indian capital city at *New Delhi, the principal planning was entrusted jointly to Baker and *Lutyens, architects too different in vision to form a happy partnership. Baker's liking for courts, pillars and arches opening on to broadening vistas pavilioned New Delhi in splendour; his three-chambered legislature is now India's Parliament House, and the two sandstone blocks of his Secretariat Building remain. Baker brought his form of imperial architecture to London with the building of India House and South Africa House and, more compactly, to Oxford in *Rhodes House. He was knighted in 1926.

Baker, Sir Samuel (1821–93), explorer: born in London. In his mid twenties he twice visited Ceylon, establishing in 1848 the first settlement at Nuwara Eliya, later the centre of *tea cultivation. From 1861 to 1865 he explored the Upper Nile, penetrating to Ethiopia from Khartoum, discovering the Karuma Falls on the White Nile in January 1864 and the lake which he named Albert Nyanza two months later. After accompanying the future King Edward VII on a journey to Egypt and up the Nile in 1869, he entered Ottoman service and was appointed by the Khedive Governor-General of Equatorial Nile, with headquarters at Gondoroko, thus becoming effectively the Governor of the Sudan. For four years he took vigorous action in suppressing the slave trade on the upper Nile, but returned to Europe in 1873. In his remaining years Baker travelled widely, respected as an expert adviser by successive British governments. Repeatedly he warned them of the danger of a hostile Power damming the upper waters of the Nile and thus ruining Egypt by depriving the fertile delta of water (see *Fashoda*).

Balewa, Alhaji, Sir Abu Bakar Tafawa (1912–66), Nigerian Prime Minister: a *Hausa, born at Bauchi, northern Nigeria; became a teacher at the age of twenty and was briefly a headmaster and schools inspector before helping to found the most efficient political party in *Nigeria, the Northern People's Congress. From 1954 to 1957 he held successively the portfolios of Works and Transport as a member of the Council of Ministers in Nigeria's federal government, and he was Federal Prime Minister from 1957 (a year in which he went on pilgrimage to Mecca) until his death. The British colonial authorities admired Tafawa Balewa's skills in creating an independent federation: in the Order of the British Empire he was advanced from Member in 1952 to Commander in 1955 and Knight in 1960, becoming a Privy Councillor a year later. Within the federation he worked in uneasy partnership with *Azikiwe but, as a Hausa, he offended both the *Ibo in eastern Nigeria and the *Yoruba in western Nigeria. Anger at centralization around a narrow power base provoked unrest in the army. In January 1966 Tafawa Balewa was assassinated during a military coup by young officers.

Balfour Declaration (2 November 1917). Arthur Balfour (1848–1930), Conservative Prime Minister from 1902 to 1905, served as Foreign Secretary in the Lloyd George coalition from 1916 to 1919. In this capacity he sent a letter to Lord Rothschild, representing British Zionists, which pledged British support for a Jewish national home in post-war *Palestine, provided safeguards could be reached for the 'rights of non-Jewish communities' there; and provided, also, that the political status of Jews in other lands should not be endangered by the creation of a national home. Allied governments supported the Declaration, which in 1920 was recognized by the League of Nations in assigning to Great Britain the Palestine *mandate.

Balfour Definition (November 1926). At the *Imperial Conference of 1926 the Secretary of Dominion Affairs and Colonies, L. S. *Amery, invited the ex-Premier and elder statesman Earl Balfour (1848–1930) to chair a committee of dominion prime ministers who would examine the constitutional status of the United Kingdom and the overseas dominions. A month later Balfour issued a report in which he defined the imperial relationship: Great Britain and the dominions constituted 'autonomous communities within the British Empire, equal in status, in no way subordinate to one another in any aspect of their domestic or external affairs, though united by a common allegiance to the Crown and freely associated as members of the British Commonwealth of Nations'. This definition, clarifying the nature of *dominion status, paved the way for the Statute of *Westminster of 1931. The Balfour Report insisted that, over foreign affairs and defence issues, 'the major share of responsibility rests, and must for some time continue to rest, with His Majesty's Government in Great Britain'.

Ballet. Although classical ballet was foreshadowed in productions in London during the mid eighteenth century, it was not until the 1830s that the art form became popular, notably through the visits of dancers from Paris and Vienna. Australia was not far behind England: two- and three-act ballets were being performed in Sydney and Melbourne by 1840/1, and the popularity of dance was maintained by visiting European opera companies and by individual artists (such as the notorious Lola Montez, who scandalized Sydney in 1855). In the early years of the twentieth century interest was stimulated by the visits of the Anglo-Danish ballerina, Dame Adeline Genée, to both Australia and New Zealand and, later, by the pioneer visits of Anna Pavlova and her company to South Africa and Canada. Pavlova's tours of Australia in 1926 and 1929 were especially beneficial as they included visits to outlying townships with little experience of the performing arts. Her company included a Czech dancer, Édouard Borovansky (1902–1959), who returned to Australia with Colonel de Basil's Ballets Russes de Monte Carlo and settled in Melbourne, building up an indigenous company. This 'Borovansky Ballet', which had its first professional season in 1944, formed the nucleus of the Australian Ballet, founded in 1962 with Dame Peggy van Praagh (1910–   ) as artistic director. Outstanding among several distinguished smaller companies is the Perth City Ballet, founded by Diana Waldron in 1961, and presenting specifically Australian works as well as the established classics. Although the Borovansky Ballet toured New Zealand and dance companies visited cities on both islands in 1953/4 and 1957, it was not until 1961 that the New Zealand Ballet was set up in

Wellington. The senior Canadian company, the Winnipeg Ballet, gave its opening performance in 1939, and in 1953 became the first ballet company in the Commonwealth to receive a royal charter. The National Ballet of Canada was founded in Toronto in 1951 and the Grands Ballets Canadiens in Montreal in 1952. In South Africa professional companies were slow to emerge: the Johannesburg City Ballet of the 1950s derived from the amateur Johannesburg Festival Ballet set up in 1944; and the prime source in Cape Province was the University of Cape Town Ballet Company. Aspiring dancers from the white dominions long tended to come to London to launch their careers, generally with the Sadler's Wells Ballet (from 1931: Royal Ballet, 1956) or Ballet Rambert: Robert *Helpmann, Elaine Fifield, Kathleen Gorham, Lucette Aldous (Australia); Alexander Grant, Rowena Jackson, Bryan Ashbridge (New Zealand); Nadia Nerina, Margaret Barbieri (South Africa); Dame Merle Park (Rhodesia); Lynn Seymour (Canada). But by the 1980s Canadian and Australian companies also enjoyed a world reputation.

Banana, Revd Canaan Sodindo (1936–), first President of Zimbabwe: born at Esiphezini, Matabeleland, and studied at Wesley Theological Seminary, Washington DC, becoming a Methodist minister in 1962. As a political moderate, he became Publicity Secretary of the People's Movement in Rhodesia in 1976 and joined ZANU (Zimbabwe African National Union). After being held in detention from 1977 to 1979 he was chosen as Zimbabwe's President in April 1980. He held office until December 1987 when, after constitutional changes, he was succeeded by *Mugabe.

Banana trade. Bananas, apparently indigenous to Fiji and some Pacific islands, were introduced to the Caribbean by Spaniards from the Canary Islands in the late sixteenth century and flourished, especially on *Jamaica. But a banana trade developed only in the 1870s, with improved shipping to both New York and London. By 1890 bananas for export were the principal crop of smallholders in Jamaica and, to a lesser extent, in Dominica, British Honduras, St Lucia, St Vincent and Grenada. The Jamaican market continued to expand after World War I, regular 'banana boats', designed for the trade, sailing from the Thames to Kingston. A Banana Producers' Association was established in Jamaica in 1929, partly to counter the political influence of monopolies such as the United Fruit Company, which in most years bought up half the crop. Norman *Manley, as legal spokesman for the banana growers, negotiated an agreement with the UFC by which for each stem exported the company gave one cent to a welfare organization. In 1936 the BPA itself became a private trading company. All exports to Britain were suspended during World War II. In Jamaica, banana production suffered from a fungoid disease originating in Panama, which ruined several crops, and from the hurricane which struck the island on 17 August 1951. The Caribbean banana trade had recovered by 1954 and remained buoyant until 1967, when exports faced fierce competition from the growth of the EEC, many of whose members had links with African banana-producing states. In Jamaica the government appointed a special commissioner with responsibility for marketing of the island's bananas in the United Kingdom. Some safeguards for the trade were provided by the *Lomé Convention of 1975 and several Caribbean countries have increased their exports, notably *Belize. Commonwealth countries outside the Caribbean which export bananas include Nigeria, Uganda, Tonga and Western Samoa.

Banda, Dr Hastings Kamuzu (*c*.1900–   ), President of Malawi: born at Kasungu in Nyasaland; worked as a clerk-interpreter in the Rand gold-fields, where he was greatly influenced by James *Aggrey's teachings. Backing from the African Methodist Episcopal Church enabled Banda to study medicine in Tennessee. He later qualified as a doctor of medicine at Edinburgh. During World War II he was a general practitioner in Liverpool and on Tyneside, moving in 1945 to Kilburn, north London, where he was a doctor for eight years and established close contact with *Nkrumah, *Kenyatta and other African political exiles. From Kilburn and from Kumasi, Kenya (where he practised medicine from 1953 to 1958) he gave advice to the Nyasaland African Congress (later MCP, Malawi Congress Party). Banda returned to his homeland, with the prestige of a promised liberator, on 6 July 1958 and led the MCP in opposition to the *Central African Federation. He was imprisoned from March 1959 to April 1960 but released at the insistence of the Colonial Secretary (Iain *Macleod) and, with *Kaunda and *Nkomo, invited to a conference in London. When Nyasaland received self-government in February 1963 he became Prime Minister, remaining in office when Malawi became independent (July 1964). A one-party election in 1965 ensured that he became President in July 1966. His dictatorship was not challenged until 1992 when Malawi's foreign aid sponsors insisted on improvements in human rights. After electoral defeat in May 1994 he was succeeded by Bakili Muluzi of the United Democratic Front. In January 1995 Dr Banda was held under house arrest, accused of ordering the murder in 1983 of four political rivals, but was considered too ill to plead.

Bandaranaike family: founders (in 1951) and leaders of the Sri Lanka Freedom Party. Solomon Bandaranaike (1889–1959) was born in Colombo, studied law at Oxford, and as leader of the Ceylon National Congress promoted the interests of the Sinhalese at the expense of the Tamils. In 1940 he married Sirimavo Ratwatte (1916–   ), daughter of a wealthy landowner from Ratnapura. Solomon Bandaranaike was an able health minister from 1948 to 1951, effectively combating malaria. Electoral successes in 1956 enabled him to become Prime Minister of a

United Front coalition. He secured the closure of British naval bases in Ceylon but incensed Tamils by insisting that Sinhalese become the sole official language. When he was assassinated by a Buddhist monk in September 1959 his widow was accepted as leader of the Sri Lankan Freedom Party, which won the general election of July 1960, enabling Mrs Bandaranaike to become the world's first woman Prime Minister. Resentment of Sinhalese domination and socialist policies led to electoral defeat in 1956 but she returned to power in May 1970, introducing the reforms which in 1972 created *Sri Lanka. Resistance to further socialism was shown in a turbulent general election of July 1977 which Mrs Bandaranaike lost, amid accusations of unconstitutional practices. These charges led in October 1980 to the withdrawal of her political rights for seven years. She sought election as President of Sri Lanka in 1988 but received little support from the voters.

Bangladesh, a People's Republic covering the north-eastern sector of the Indian sub-continent, with more Muslims than any other member of the Commonwealth. The capital is Dhaka. Until 1947 Bangladesh (together with part of Assam) formed the province of East Bengal in British India. Upon partition the region became the Eastern Province of Pakistan, separated from Pakistan's Western Province by 1,000 miles of the Indian Republic. Complaints that the Bengali Pakistanis were being exploited by the central government in Karachi prompted the formation in 1954 of a movement for autonomy, the Awami League, led by Sheik Mujibur *Rahman. Despite an Awami electoral victory in December 1970, the central government refused to modify the constitutional relationship between the provinces, and on 26 March 1971 the Sheikh formally proclaimed Bangladesh's secession; a government-in-exile was set up in Calcutta three weeks later. This move led to civil war and, in December 1971, to a fortnight's conflict between India and Pakistan, but it was militarily impossible for the central government to retain its hold on the dissident province, and most world powers recognized Bangladesh's independence early in 1972. The new Republic was the most densely populated country in Asia: 71.3 million people (less than 30 per cent of whom were literate) lived in an area smaller than England and Wales and prone to catastrophic cyclones and floods. Under these conditions Mujibur Rahman could not create the socialist parliamentary democracy favoured by the Awami League. In January 1975 he assumed dictatorial powers, but he was murdered in a military coup seven months later, the leader of the rebels himself being assassinated soon afterwards. Major-General Zia Rahman became President in April 1977 and was able to prepare the country for democratic elections in February 1979 which were won by his Bangladesh Nationalist Party. The President was assassinated at Chittagong in May 1981, while seeking to stamp out a secessionist movement among the tribesmen in the hilly south-eastern region of the country. A bloodless military coup led by General Hossain Ershad, on 23 March 1982, effectively imposed military dictatorship until Ershad was deposed in December 1990. Two months later a democratic general election, contested by 70 parties, was won by the nationalists led by Begum Khaleda Zia, widow of the President killed at Chittagong. The Begum became Prime Minister on 19 March 1991 with a pledge that, after 16 years of presidential government, parliamentary rule would be restored. Floods and famine are estimated to have cost the lives of over five million Bangladeshis in the first twenty years of the Republic's independent existence. The principal exports are jute and cotton textiles, with the USA as the chief market, but Bangladesh remains dependent on massive foreign aid.

Banks, Sir Joseph (1743–1820) botanist: born in London, educated at both Harrow and Eton and at Christ Church, Oxford. His enthusiastic study of natural history led to his election as a Fellow of the Royal Society at the age of 23. Soon afterwards he undertook a botanical expedition to Newfoundland and, together with the Swedish botanist Daniel Solander, accompanied Captain *Cook in HMS *Endeavour* for the expedition of 1768–71, using his considerable inherited wealth to fit out the ship with scientific equipment. Banks's initial study of botanical and geological specimens during the first week of May 1770 led him to suggest that the name Botany Bay be given to the inlet which Cook had discovered. As President of the Royal Society from 1778 to 1820, Banks continued to show great interest in New South Wales, advocating systematic colonization. He preferred sponsored plantation, but he was ready with evidence for the Commons committee which in 1779 examined the feasibility of penal settlements in the unknown subcontinent. Banks corresponded with the first five Governors of New South Wales and financed many early expeditions of scientific exploration within the colony. His vision was not limited to Australia, however: he encouraged the introduction of new food plants into the West Indies, notably the breadfruit tree, which he had found in Tahiti; and he took a prominent role in setting up the Africa Association, to promote scientific and humanitarian exploration in regions long exploited by slave-traders.

Banting, Sir Frederick Grant (1891–1941), Canadian physiologist: born in Alliston, Ontario and studied medicine at Toronto. He served with the Canadian Army on the Western Front, in 1918 receiving the Military Cross for bravery at the battle of Cambrai. In 1921 he collaborated with J. J. R. Macleod and C. H. Best in research on pancreatic secretions, discovering the hormone insulin which proved an effective cure for diabetes. Banting and Macleod were joint recipients of the Nobel Prize for Medicine in 1923. Banting's research received generous backing from the Ontario legislature, including the establishment in 1930 of Toronto's

Banting Institute for the advancement of medicine. Banting was knighted in 1934 and, on the outbreak of World War II, was put in charge of medical research throughout the Dominion. He was killed while flying to England in 1941 on a medical mission.

Bantu: originally a wide range of languages in southern Africa, but also the name applied collectively to the African peoples of South Africa under *apartheid. The Bantu Self-Government Act of 1959 was an attempt by the Pretoria government to create black homelands and thus counter Pan-Africanism by reviving the traditional ethnic rivalries of tribal communities – Zulu, Xhosa, Sotho, Tonga, Venda, Tswana, etc.

Baptist War (1831): a Creole slave revolt in Jamaica, caused by despair at the slow progress made by the emancipationists in Britain. Fear that planters were witholding freedom from their labourers led to revolts in several Caribbean islands, notably Barbados. The most serious conflict began on 27 December 1831 at Kensington estate in western Jamaica, where the slave labourers were encouraged by the Jamaican-born Baptist preacher, Sam Sharpe, to take oaths pledging themselves to give up all forced labour after Christmas. Sam Sharpe favoured passive resistance, but the slaves set fire to the sugar canes and used captured weapons to safeguard their rights. In the course of the so-called war, the slaves destroyed more than £1.25 millions-worth of property and killed 12 whites. The vengeance shown towards the rebels was brutal: 207 slaves were shot down in the fields and more than 300 executed. In a colony in which there were ten times as many blacks as whites, the revolt aroused grave fears among the settlers and deep hostility towards the London-based Baptist Missionary Society. Sam Sharpe is remembered as a martyr-hero by the Jamaican people.

Barbados, the most easterly of the West Indian islands, was uninhabited when first occupied by the British in 1627. It became a Crown Colony in 1662, received internal self-government in 1961, and attained independence within the Commonwealth on 30 November 1966. Sugar plantations, using African slave labour, were established as early as 1660 and sugar has remained the principal export, despite several disastrous hurricanes, notably in 1831 and 1898. With 254,000 people living in an island only 166 square miles in area, there is an extreme density of population: some 1,500 people to the square mile, more than three times the figure for Jamaica. But the equable winter climate, together with the islanders' passionate enthusiasm for cricket, brings half a million visitors to Barbados each year.

Baring, Evelyn (1841–1917): see *Cromer, Earl of.*

Barotseland: now forms the western province of *Zambia, with its administrative capital in Mongu. The region was settled in the 1840s by a migration of the Sotho-speaking Lozi tribe (Barotse), forced northwards from the borders of Natal by the incursion of the Boers and other white settlers. Barotseland, regarded by *Rhodes as an important corridor giving access to the southern shore of Lake Tanganyika, was secured for the British South Africa Company by the Anglo-Portuguese Convention of 11 June 1891. When Northern Rhodesia was created in 1911, Paramount Chief Lewanika was allowed considerable autonomy and British officials maintained this system of indirect rule after the Colonial Office assumed responsibility for Northern Rhodesia in 1923. The Lozi form 9 per cent of the population of modern Zambia, although the identity of Barotseland has virtually disappeared in the Lusaka government's quest for integration of ethnic groups.

Barton, Sir Edmund (1849–1920), first Australian Prime Minister: born and educated in Sydney; called to the bar in 1871, becoming a QC in 1879. He sat in the Legislative Assembly of New South Wales, 1879–87 (for the last four years as Speaker), 1891–94 and 1899–1900, as well as being a member of the Legislative Council, 1887–91 and 1897–98. From 1887 onwards he vigorously championed the union of the Australian colonies (at first, including also New Zealand). Barton travelled widely, establishing branches of the Australasian Federation League, and in 1897 he was leader of the Federal Convention at Hobart which prepared a draft constitution, rejected by the legislature of Barton's home state. Barton patiently presided over further meetings of Australian political leaders in Sydney and in Melbourne before going to London as head of a delegation to explain the proposed character of the Commonwealth of Australia. When in January 1901 the Commonwealth came into being, Barton was a natural choice to head the Federal Government. He remained Prime Minister (and Minister for External Affairs) for only two years, concentrating on protective tariffs, defence needs, and on *immigration restraints to safeguard a 'White Australia'. After receiving a knighthood in 1902 Barton retired from politics at the age of 54, but he served as a judge in the Australian High Court from 1903 until 1920, concerning himself particularly with decisions upholding states' rights.

Bass, George (1771–c.1802), naval surgeon, naturalist and explorer: born in Lincolnshire, and sailed for New South Wales as surgeon of HMS *Reliance* in 1795. With the young naval officer Matthew *Flinders, Bass made two small boat expeditions to survey the coast south of Port Jackson (Botany Bay). In December 1797 Bass made a more extensive survey during which he rounded Cape Howe and deduced that there was a strait separating *Tasmania from the mainland. When a further voyage with

Flinders in December 1798 duly circumnavigated Tasmania, the channel was named Bass Strait in his honour. He left naval service in 1799 and undertook several commercial ventures based upon Port Jackson; he seems to have perished on a voyage to South America in which his ship was carrying contraband.

Basutoland: see *Lesotho*.

Batman, John (1800–40), pioneer of white settlement in Melbourne: born in Parramatta, New South Wales, migrating to Van Diemen's Land (*Tasmania). There, in 1835, he joined fourteen other settlers in establishing the Geelong and Dutigalla Association, to open up the Yarru River estuary around Port Philip on the mainland. Batman concluded a 'treaty' with eight aboriginal chiefs in the area, by which he gained possession of some 600,000 acres in return for token gifts. His diary for 8 June 1835 noted an ideal 'place for a village . . . all good water and very deep'. The authorities were slow to back Batman; but Governor Bourke travelled to the region in 1837 from Sydney, named the settlement after the Prime Minister (Melbourne) and authorized land sales. Batman's chosen site became a municipality in 1842.

Batten, Jean (1909–82), pioneer aviator: born at Rotorua, North Island, New Zealand, a dentist's daughter who became fascinated by the challenge of long-distance flying. In 1929 she came to England, began flying lessons in north London and was licensed as a pilot and flight mechanic in 1932. After two unsuccessful attempts to emulate Amy *Johnson, in May 1934 she flew from Lympne to Darwin in 14 days 22 hours and 20 minutes, knocking four days off Johnson's record time for a solo flight. In April 1935 Batten flew back to England, the first solo double journey. These achievements were followed by a pioneer solo flight from England to Brazil (November 1935) and by the first solo from London to New Zealand (October 1936), covering 14,224 miles in 11 days, including a two and a half day stop in Sydney. Her final record was in October 1937, when she flew from Sydney to Croydon in 5 days 21 hours. Briefly she was fêted as a heroine of the Empire, but during World War II no use was made of her skill as a pilot and she soon faded from the public eye, even in her homeland. Most of her later years were spent in obscurity abroad; she was living in Majorca when she died, from a dog bite that turned sceptic.

Baxter, James Keir (1926–72), New Zealand poet and dramatist: born in Dunedin; worked as a labourer, journalist and teacher. *Beyond the Palisade*, the first of 30 volumes of poetry, appeared in 1944. Conversion to Roman Catholicism led him to abandon a casually irresponsible life and set up a religious community beside the Wanganui River. His pre-Catholic poems appeared in 1958 as a single volume, *In Fires of No*

Beaconsfield, Earl of

Return. After he was appointed to a Fellowship at Otago University in 1966 he published several plays, including *The Sore-footed Man* (1967) and *The Temptation of Oedipus* (1969). *Autumn Testament* (1972) reflected the full maturity of his poetry.

Beaconsfield, Earl of (1804–81): see *Disraeli, Benjamin*.

Beaglehole, John Cawte (1901–71), New Zealand historian: born and educated in Wellington; came to London in 1926 to study for a doctorate at University College. He was irritated by the attitude of English academics towards 'colonials' but, on returning home, found himself shunned for his left-wing views. The scholarship of *The Exploration of the Pacific* (1934) and *The Discovery of New Zealand* (1939) won him wide respect. His greatest achievement was to edit *The Journals of Captain Cook* (1955–67) and *The* Endeavour *Journal of Sir Joseph Banks* (1962). His eminence as an Australasian historian was recognized in 1970 with the Order of Merit, never previously awarded to a New Zealand writer. From 1963 to 1966 he was Professor of British Commonwealth History at Victoria University, Wellington.

Beaverbrook, Lord (William Maxwell Aitken, 1879–64), newspaper proprietor: born at Maple, Ontario, the son of a Scottish Presbyterian minister. He entered a law firm but was attracted by business expansion and in 1909 founded the Canadian Cement Company. A year later, already a rich man, he emigrated to England. He was fortunate that the Conservative leader, Bonar Law, was a fellow-Canadian; within three months of reaching England, Aitken was an MP, receiving a knighthood a year later. For much of 1915–16 he was in France, on liaison work with the Canadian Army, but he was back at Westminster in time to help make Lloyd George head of a coalition government in December 1916. A month later Aitken received his peerage. Lord Beaverbrook was Minister of Information in 1918. In 1916 he had purchased the *Daily Express*, intending to publicize his views on the need for strict interdependence of the mother country and the white dominions. He founded the *Sunday Express* (1918), and purchased the London *Evening Standard* (1923). Although he helped Bonar Law become Prime Minister in 1922, Beaverbrook held no public office between the wars, choosing to concentrate on newspaper campaigns advocating 'Empire Free Trade'. He supported Edward VIII in the *abdication crisis and backed Neville Chamberlain's policy of appeasement, the *Daily Express* confidently stating on each day in the first half of 1939 that 'There will be no war this year'. Churchill made use of Beaverbrook's dynamic energy as Minister of Aircraft Production (1940–41), Minister of Supply (1942) and Lord Privy Seal (1943–45), sending him on special missions to Moscow and to Washington. Beaverbrook remained a firm imperialist, turning his newspapers against any public figure who advanced the independence of India and Pakistan, for he felt that the end of the Raj would be followed by the collapse of the Empire and Commonwealth as a whole.

Bechuanaland: see *Botswana*.

Belize (formerly British Honduras), the only member of the Commonwealth on the Central American mainland, lies in the south-east of the Yucatan peninsula, with Mexico to the north, and Guatemala to the south and west. The first settlers (in the mid seventeenth century) were woodcutters from *Jamaica, attracted by the mahogany and logwood of the dense forests which still cover two-thirds of Belize. Despite Spanish incursions the settlements prospered although the region remained a haunt of British buccaneers until 1780, when a government 'Superintendent' was at last sent out from London. A Spanish attempt to eject the British in 1798 was defeated at the battle of St George's Cay, an island off Belize City. Claims of sovereignty by newly independent Guatemala were first made in 1821 and have never been totally abandoned: attempts to settle the dispute by treaty in 1859 were rejected by the Guatemalan government, as also in 1946 was an offer by *Attlee to refer the question to the International Court of Justice. The region became the colony of British Honduras in 1862 but was administered from Jamaica (660 miles to the east) until 1884. From 1953 to 1956 there was strong opposition to membership of the *British West Indies Confederation. Self-government was conceded in January 1964. The colony's name was changed to Belize in 1973: independence followed on 21 September 1981. Relations with Guatemala were so tense that Britain stationed 1,800 soldiers in Belize, with RAF support, but when, in November 1992, Guatemala formally recognized Belize, it was agreed to withdraw them. On 31 October 1961 a hurricane swept a ten-foot tidal wave into Belize City, causing such loss of life that it was resolved to build a new capital, Belmopan, 50 miles inland; the government moved there in August 1970. A further hurricane destroyed banana plantations in 1974. Mestizo peasants in the southern mountains (like their Mayan ancestors) base their subsistence farming on cocoa, but sugar, citrus fruits, bananas and fish are Belize's chief exports.

Bell, Gertrude Margaret Lowthian (1868–1922), traveller, archaeologist and political adviser: born in Durham, the daughter of a wealthy ironmaster, and educated at Lady Margaret Hall, Oxford, becoming in 1888 the first woman to be awarded first class Honours in Modern History at the university. After translating two Persian classics, she settled in Jerusalem in 1899 to learn Arabic, visiting Switzerland in her leisure moments to climb the Matterhorn. Between 1905 and 1914 she made extensive journeys in the Ottoman Empire, undertaking pioneer archaeological surveys of central Anatolia around Isaura and Kerbela. In

1913–14 she penetrated Arabia, from Damascus as far south as Ha'il in northern Nejd and northwards to Baghdad. British Military Intelligence sent her to Cairo in November 1915 as specialist adviser to the Arab Bureau; she was attached to Headquarters in Basra in 1916, and from 1917 to 1920 was Oriental Secretary to the British administration in Baghdad. She attended the Paris Peace Conference in 1919–20 and the Cairo Conference on the Middle East in March 1921, helping consolidate the Hashemite dynasty on the throne of Iraq. She was also honorary Director of Antiquities in Iraq under the British mandate, and founded the National Museum in Baghdad (where she was buried, in the British cemetery). No other woman exercised such influence on British imperial policy in the Middle East.

Bengal: a former Presidency and province of British India, with its geographical core formed by the Ganges–Brahmaputra delta, stretching northwards to Bhutan and Sikkim. The first British settlements were *East India Company factories, dating from 1633. A centre of trade was established on the Hooghly River at Calcutta in 1690, protected by 'old' Fort William from 1696. The EIC's Presidency of Bengal was formed in 1699, but the territory remained under the overlordship of the Moghul emperors until 1740, when the ruling Nawab asserted his independence. Sixteen years later resentment at the EIC's commercial penetration induced Nawab Suraj-ud-Dowlah to launch a surprise attack on Fort William (see *Black Hole*). In June 1757 Robert *Clive recovered Calcutta and defeated Suraj-ud-Dowlah at *Plassey. Thereafter pliant Nawabs accepted the acquisition by EIC soldiers and officials of a vast dominion, which included Oudh and Agra (until 1833) as well as the modern Indian provinces of Bihar and Orissa and present-day *Bangladesh. By the end of the nineteenth century Bengal had a population twice that of the United Kingdom. Almost all the people were Bengali-speaking, but there were some 78 variants of tongue. In 1905 *Curzon, as Viceroy, imposed partition on the huge province: 31 million people formed a new province, East Bengal and Assam, in which Muslims outnumbered Hindus by 3 to 2; while Bengal proper (including Bihar) retained 50 million people, overwhelmingly Hindu. Curzon's partition provoked fierce opposition, stimulating Bengali nationalism but intensifying sectarian divisions, and in 1912 all Bengali-speaking people were reunited in a revived Presidency of Bengal. There was, however, no longer any genuine political unity. The *partition of 1947 detached east *Pakistan (Bangladesh), although West Bengal has remained one of India's twenty-five states, twelfth in area but – with 68 million inhabitants – ranking third in population.

Bennett, Richard Bedford (1870–1947), Canadian Prime Minister: a barrister by profession, born in New Brunswick, but politically associated with the high plains, representing Calgary in the Canadian House of

Commons, 1911–17 and 1925–38. As a masterful Director-General of National Service in 1916–17 Bennett aroused some criticism among his Conservative supporters, but he was accepted as party leader in 1927 and won a clear majority in the election of July 1930, for two years serving as Finance Minister as well as heading the government (until October 1935). His 'Progressive Conservatives' favoured free enterprise at home and strong Commonwealth links. Like *Beaverbrook, he strongly supported 'Empire Free Trade', and in 1932 he convened (and chaired) the *Ottawa Conference to examine ways of promoting imperial preference during the world depression. His political centralism, giving greater authority to the Civil Service within the federation, was resented by the premiers of the provincial assemblies, and when in January 1935 he proposed drastic reforms, reminiscent of the 'New Deal' measures across the American border, the voters turned against him, forcing the Progressive Conservatives into opposition for twenty-two years. Bennett settled in England in 1938; he became a viscount in 1941.

Bhutto family: an aristocratic Rajput dynasty who entered Pakistan politics, establishing the People's Party in 1967 to promote a form of moderate Muslim socialism. Zulfikar Ali Bhutto (1928–79), a lawyer educated at Christ Church, Oxford, served from 1963 to 1966 as Foreign Minister under *Ayub Khan, taking a strongly anti-Indian stance in the *Kashmir dispute. When in December 1971 Pakistan was defeated by India in the short war over Bangladesh's secession, Bhutto became President and took Pakistan out of the Commonwealth (30 January 1972). After amending the constitution to make the Prime Minister chief executive of the Republic, Bhutto resigned the presidency in August 1973 but continued to head the government, as well as holding the portfolios of Defence, Foreign Affairs and Atomic Energy. Victory in elections in March 1977 was followed by accusations of vote-rigging from opponents who were alarmed at Bhutto's policy of nationalizing basic industries. After four months of rioting and virtual anarchy in several cities, the chief of the army staff, General Zia-al-Haq (1924–88), carried through a military coup on 5 July 1977. Bhutto was arrested in September and on 18 March 1978 he was sentenced to death for conspiracy to murder. Despite appeals for clemency from world leaders, he was hanged at Rawalpindi on 4 April 1979, after being held for thirteen months in the death cell. His daughter, Benazir Bhutto (1955–   ), who completed her education at Lady Margaret Hall, Oxford while her father was prime minister, returned from exile in April 1986 and led the People's Party in opposition to Zia, marrying Asif Ali Zardar in 1987. Benazir Bhutto won a slender electoral victory in November 1988 and herself became Prime Minister, Defence Minister and Finance Minister on 2 December. On 1 October 1989, in a reversal of her father's policy, she brought Pakistan back into the Commonwealth. Early in 1990 she became the first head of government to give birth to a child. Her modern, westernized practices lost her support in rural areas and she fell from office in October 1990, after the Islamic Democratic Alliance won elections. A further shift of opinion brought her back to power in 1993.

Biafra. Tribal conflict in federal *Nigeria was so intense in the first years of independence that on 30 May 1967 the predominantly *Ibo eastern region seceded from the federation, asserting independence as the Republic of Biafra, under the leadership of Colonel Odumegwa Ojukwu (1933–   ). Early Biafran successes were countered in July by a full-scale invasion ordered by the Nigerian President, General Yakubu Gowon (1934–   ). Enugu, the Biafran capital, fell in September and the vital harbour, Port Harcourt, in May 1968. Improvised resistance by the Biafrans continued until January 1970, since the Nigerians had difficulty in policing the villages and roads of the region. While London backed the federal government, the Biafrans received limited support from the French. The suffering from battle casualties was intensified by famine, with 300,000 Biafran refugees seeking sustenance from the Red Cross in improvised camps during the closing months of 1969.

Big Brother Movement: an organization which, between 1925 and December 1982, provided funds, accommodation and employment assistance to encourage young men to emigrate to Australia. Some 12,500 boys and men, mostly from the United Kingdom, took advantage of the scheme. Since 1983 its funds have been used to provide awards and scholarships for young people.

Bishop, William Avery (1894–1956), Canadian air ace: born at Owen Sound, Ontario; came to Europe with the Canadian Expeditionary Force in 1914 but transferred to the Royal Flying Corps in 1915. He destroyed 72 aircraft, more verified 'kills' than by any other air ace except the German, Baron von Richthofen. In 1917 Bishop was awarded the Victoria Cross for his valour in a dog-fight in which his Nieuport 17 plane shot down seven enemy aircraft. He also received the Distinguished Service Order and Bar, the Military Cross, the Distinguished Flying Cross and the Legion of Honour. In 1938 he became Canada's first Air Marshal and was titular commander of the Royal Canadian Air Force throughout World War II.

Bjelke-Petersen, Sir Johannes (1911–   ), Australian politician: born in Dannevirke, New Zealand, the son of a Danish pastor who migrated to Queensland in 1913. Before entering politics he farmed on a large scale, accepting traditional prejudices on such issues as law and order. In 1947 he was elected to the state legislature as Country Party member for Nanango, representing Barambah, 1950–87. After serving as Queensland's Minister for Works and Housing for five years, he became Premier of the state government in 1968 and led a Country–Liberal coalition ministry until 1983 when – the Country Party having changed its name to the National Party in 1982 – he headed an exclusively National government for four years. Bjelke-Petersen was the most autocratic state premier of his generation, and a passionate champion of states' rights. Although his right-wing policies alienated progressive reformers, he raised the standing of Queensland (and of Brisbane in particular) within the Australian Commonwealth, and in 1982 he received a knighthood. His party lost its hold on the electorate after he stepped down in 1987, and was forced into opposition in December 1989 after 32 years in power, amid accusations of patronage and manipulation of electoral boundaries. Bjelke-Petersen completed his memoirs, *Don't You Worry About That*, in 1990, but later that year (29 October) he appeared in court formally charged with corruption. In November 1991 his trial on perjury charges was abandoned after the jury failed to reach a verdict.

Black Hole of Calcutta: episode in the Anglo-French struggle for supremacy in India on 20–21 June 1756. When the principal ally of the French, the Nawab of Bengal, Suraj-ud-Dowlah, seized the ill-defended trading station of Calcutta, he ordered a subordinate to hold captive 146 British prisoners. They were forced into an area 18 ft by 14 ft 10 in: only 23 were found alive next morning. Reports of the alleged atrocity incensed British authorities in Madras: Robert *Clive was sent to recapture Calcutta, finally defeating the Nawab at *Plassey.

Blackbirding. Between 1863 and 1904 some 57,000 native inhabitants of *Vanuatu and the Solomon Islands were enticed or kidnapped by Australian seafarers and brought to Queensland and northern New South Wales, where they were employed under conditions close to slavery and for extremely low wages on sugar and cotton plantations, occasionally on sheep stations. The Queensland legislature passed a succession of measures designed to check the abuses of this so-called 'blackbirding'; and in 1872 the Pacific Islanders Protection Act – one of the less remembered reforms of the first Gladstone ministry – required the presence aboard each vessel engaged in recruiting island labourers of an official agent of the colonial government. Half-hearted attempts were made by the Queensland authorities to ban blackbirding in the early 1890s but the practice was only stamped out after 1904, when it was declared illegal by the Federal Parliament in Melbourne.

Blackfoot Indians. The Blackfoot nation was, in origin, a confederacy of three closely associated warlike tribes of the prairie: the Piegan, the Blood and the Blackfoot. Archaeological evidence suggests they are descended from the original settlers on the plains, following the Ice Age. They united in a loose, defensive confederacy, first to resist the intrusion of other migratory peoples, notably the *Assiniboine and the *Cree, but later to safeguard their traditional way of life from the westward movement of Canada's *métis and European settlers. There were frequent battles in the plains as the Blackfoot sought to protect the buffalo herds, on which they depended for their well-being, from the depredation of ruthless hunters. As late as 1870 fierce fighting between the Blackfoot and the Cree over apparent encroachment on hunting grounds caused several hundred deaths in a battle fought where the city of Lethbridge, Alberta now stands. Although the Blackfoot won the encounter, thereafter the diplomatic skill of their paramount chief, Crowfoot, restrained the ferocity of the warriors, most effectively during the first years when the *'Mounties' sought to impose peace in the plains. In 1877 Crowfoot, together with 34 chiefs of the Blackfoot confederacy, signed a treaty with representatives of Manitoba and the Northwest Territories which provided the Blackfoot with land for each family in reservations, annuities promised in perpetuity, provision for technical and academic education, and hunting rights in unsettled tracts in return for the surrender of ancestral territorial claims. When the *Canadian Pacific Railway crossed the borders of a Blackfoot reservation in 1883 an Indian war was only averted through the mediation of the much-respected missionary Fr Albert Lacombe, but in general the Blackfoot nation accepted the need for change and became primarily farmers. In 1958 the Blackfoot chief Akaya-ni-Muka, who anglicized his name as James Gladstone (1887–1971), became the first Canadian Senator of Native American origin.

Blamey, Sir Thomas Albert (1884–1951), Australia's first Field Marshal: born near Wagga Wagga, New South Wales; commissioned in the Australian Army in 1906, attended the Indian Army Staff College at Quetta, 1911–13, and fought with the *Anzacs at Gallipoli in the rank of Major. He served later on the Western Front, winning the Distinguished Service Order. In 1918 he was Chief-of-Staff of the Australian Corps in France, but retired from the army in 1925 and was for nine years Chief Police Commissioner in Victoria, receiving a knighthood in 1935 for his services. When World War II began Sir Thomas Blamey was head of the Australian Manpower Bureau, but he returned to active service with the rank of Lieutenant-General. He commanded the Australian Imperial Force in Egypt and Libya, 1940–41, and the Australians and New Zealanders in the Greek campaign of April 1941. He arrived back in Australia in March 1942 and became Commander-in-Chief of the Australian Army, responsible for home defence. From September 1942 to January 1943 he was in New Guinea, personally supervising the repulse of the Japanese as a prime step to removing their threat to the Australian mainland. He recaptured Papua and remained in command of Allied

Land Forces in the south-west Pacific until 1945. He was appointed Field Marshal a year before his death.

Bligh, William (1754–1817), naval officer and colonial governor: born in Plymouth and went to sea when he was fifteen. He was sailing master of HMS *Resolution* on Cook's voyage of 1776–80. Bligh, a harsh disciplinarian, survived the famous mutiny aboard his vessel, HMS *Bounty*, in 1789 and was at sea again in the Pacific two years later, subsequently commanding warships at the battles of Camperdown (1797) and Copenhagen (1801). Bligh was appointed Governor and Captain-General of New South Wales in 1805. Once again his severity aroused discontent; his attempts to curb the activities of rum traders led to the so-called *Rum Rebellion of 1808, when the New South Wales Corps arrested and imprisoned him, on doubtful charges. Bligh returned to England in 1810–11, and was exonerated and promoted to Rear-Admiral.

Blue Mountains. There are two ranges of Blue Mountains in the Commonwealth: in eastern Jamaica, the thickly-wooded Blue Mountains are popular with tourists; the (better-known) Blue Mountains of Australia are part of the Great Dividing Range and come to within thirty miles of central Sydney. The discovery of a route across the Blue Mountains in 1813 made possible the penetration of the Australian interior. Governor Macquarie authorized the building of a road across the Blue Mountains in 1814–15, thus enabling the colonists in New South Wales to find good, new pastoral lands. The town of Bathurst, the earliest settlement west of the range, dates from the completion of the road.

Bodyline controversy. In an attempt to regain the *Ashes during the 1932/3 cricket season in Australia, the English tourists (led by Douglas Jardine, 1900–58) resorted to new tactics, designed to restrict the prolific scoring of *Bradman. By bowling fast, short-pitched deliveries the bowlers forced the batsmen to either expose their bodies to injury or risk being caught in a trap of seven fielders on the leg side. Both the Australian captain (Bill Woodfull, 1897–1965) and the wicket-keeper (Bert Oldfield, 1894–1976) were injured, although Bradman found he could play the ball well away from the body. The response of spectators, together with Press comments on the English tactics, endangered relations between Australia and the 'mother country'. In London the MCC (then cricket's governing body) was so incensed by the Australian attitude that threats were made to cancel the rest of the series; the Secretary of State for the Dominions (a close confidant of the King) put pressure on the MCC not to exacerbate matters. England won the series of Test Matches 4–1. The most successful of the English fast bowlers, Harold Larwood (1904–95), became a scapegoat for tactics he had been told to employ: he was never selected to play for England again, and he emigrated to Sydney after World War II. Belatedly, in the Queen's Birthday Honours for 1993, Larwood was made a Member of the Order of the British Empire.

Boer: a word applied in the nineteenth century to non-British white South African Calvinists. The Boers were mainly of Dutch descent, but they also included Flemings, Germans and French Huguenots; all Boer families were farmers in origin. The first Calvinist settlements were established near the Cape of Good Hope with the backing of the Dutch East India Company, soon after 1652, but the region came under British rule in 1795 during the wars with revolutionary France. Disapproval of British social customs, and resentment at inadequate compensation for the abolition of slavery, led some 10,000 Boers to migrate from the eastern Cape into the highlands of the interior in the *Great Trek of 1836/7. The Boer trekkers established virtually independent republican communities across the *Orange River and in the *Transvaal, but were frustrated by British colonialists in *Natal. By the Sand River Convention (January 1852) the British conceded autonomous rights to the Boers of the Transvaal; the Bloemfontein Convention (1854) gave a similar status to the Orange Free State. Relations between the British and the Boer states were uneasy, partly because their boundaries were ill-defined, but more particularly because of the settlers' need for British aid in meeting recurrent threats from the militant *Zulus. In 1877, as a protective measure, the Transvaal was annexed by the British, but regained autonomy after the First Boer War (*see below*) by the Convention of Pretoria of 1881. Worsening relations under *Kruger culminated in the Second Boer War (1899–1902). The Boers of the Transvaal and the Orange Free State acknowledged British sovereignty at *Vereeniging in May 1902. Subsequently the former Boer generals – *Botha, *Smuts, *Hertzog – shaped the changing fortunes of *South Africa. Politically, as the importance of farming declined in the economic structure of southern Africa, the use of the term 'Boer' was replaced by the linguistic and ethnic concept of 'Afrikaaner'.

Boer Wars. The First Boer War (1881) was an attempt by the *Transvaal to recover the independence lost in 1877. The British, taken by surprise, were defeated at *Majuba Hill. Boer autonomy was restored by the subsequent Convention of Pretoria. The Second Boer War – 'The South African War' – lasted from October 1899 until May 1902. Its principal cause was the conflict between the colonial ambitions of Joseph *Chamberlain and Cecil *Rhodes and the defiant independence of the Transvaal's Boer President, *Kruger, in alliance with the Boers of the *Orange Free State. There were three main phases to the war: (1) October 1899–January 1900, Boer victories at Colenso and Spion Kop, with British garrisons besieged in Kimberley, Ladysmith and *Mafeking; (2) February–August 1900, offensive by British Imperial troops under Lord Roberts, capturing Johannesburg (31 May) and Pretoria (5 June), with formal annexation of the Orange Free State (May) and Transvaal (1 September); (3) September 1900–May 1902, guerrilla resistance by Boer commandos. This long third phase was countered by *Kitchener, with a system of intense fortification: 8,000 blockhouses, linked by 3,700 miles of barbed wire, covered the Boer lands; civilian sympathizers with the Boers were concentrated in internment camps, where some 20,000 died from disease. Peace was restored in May 1902 by the treaty of *Vereeniging: the Boers acknowledged direct British rule of their territories. The Second Boer War was the first occasion upon which volunteers from the overseas empire fought beside troops from the United Kingdom. Some 16,500 men came from the Australian colonies (588 were killed or died); Canada sent 8,500 volunteers, and 8,000 came from New Zealand. A quarter of a million soldiers of the regular army were shipped from England to South Africa, where there were fewer than 15,000 troops at the start of the war. British battle casualties were under 6,500, but 16,000 men died from enteric fever.

Boldrewood, Ralph: pen-name of Thomas Alexander Browne (1826–95), Australian novelist. He was born in London, but went to Sydney as a child and for 25 years was a squatter in Victoria around Swan Hill and in New South Wales west of Wagga Wagga, with sheep grazing rights. His best-known work, *Robbery Under Arms*, describing life in the bush and goldfields and written in the early 1880s, appeared in book form in 1888; it was the first Australian adventure story to become popular in Britain as well as 'down under'.

Borden, Sir Robert Laird (1854–1937), Canadian statesman: born at Grand Pré, Nova Scotia; called to the bar in 1878 and entered the Canadian Parliament as a Conservative in 1896. He became head of his party in 1901 and led the opposition to *Laurier for ten years. From October 1911 to October 1917 he presided over a Conservative government. He then formed a two-party coalition, primarily in order to secure the passage of a *conscription bill, and remained Prime Minister until July 1920. Borden, who received a knighthood in 1914, was a determined war leader with a strong vision of Empire who insisted that the dominions were to have equal status in world affairs with the United Kingdom. On 14 July 1915 he became the first dominion prime minister to attend a British cabinet meeting. He represented Canada in the Imperial War Conference of 1917 and, at the Paris Peace Conference in 1919, secured acceptance of the principle that representatives from the self-governing dominions could sign the peace treaties on behalf of their governments. When in August 1930 *Bennett formed his Conservative administration,

Sir Robert Borden became Canada's chief delegate to the League of Nations in Geneva.

Botha, Louis (1862–1919), soldier and first Prime Minister of the Union of South Africa: born in Natal, spent his boyhood on a farm near Vrede, Orange Free State. He served in a campaign against the *Zulus in 1884, later farming in the Transvaal. Although Botha's political views were more liberal than those of *Kruger, he raised a volunteer force to counter the *Jameson Raid (1895) and early in the *Boer War became Assistant General in the Transvaal army (October 1899). He gained victories at Colenso and Spion Kop, and in March 1900 was made Commandant-General of the Transvaal. Botha failed to save Johannesburg and Pretoria, but reorganized his commandos for two years of guerrilla warfare. After securing generous peace terms at *Vereeniging, he became a leading champion of reconciliation with the British, in collaboration with General *Smuts. In 1907, with the introduction of responsible colonial government in Pretoria, he accepted office as Prime Minister of Transvaal. It was he who proposed in the Legislative Assembly that the Cullinan diamond, the largest ever mined, be presented to Edward VII to affirm 'the loyalty and attachment of the people of the Transvaal to his person and throne'. After leading the Transvaal delegation to the Union Convention of 1908/9 it was natural for Botha to become South Africa's first Prime Minister (1910), a post he held until his death. He curbed unrest in the Rand and threw his support behind the United Kingdom on the outbreak of World War I, but was faced with armed rebellion by 5,000 pro-German Boers in November and December 1914. When the revolt had been crushed, Botha personally took command of Union forces invading German South-West Africa (*Namibia), capturing the colonial capital, Windhoek, on 17 May 1915 and receiving the surrender of the last German troops at Tsumeb on 9 July. Together with Smuts, General Botha attended the Paris Peace Conference in 1919 and signed the Treaty of Versailles on 28 June, but he died soon after returning to Pretoria.

Botswana, an independent southern African republic within the Commonwealth, formerly the Bechuanaland Protectorate: capital, Gaborone. Botswana is larger in area than France but has a population of only 1.3 million; almost a sixth of the land surface is set aside for wild life preservation, while the Kalahari desert covers much of the south and west. The region was claimed by the British in 1885, when the lands south of the river Molopo were organized as the Crown Colony of *British Bechuanaland. In 1889 the lands north of the Molopo were assigned to the *British South Africa Company, but were administered by a Resident Commissioner appointed from London. When the Crown Colony was absorbed by Cape Colony in 1895 the chiefs of the three principal tribes in modern Botswana – the Bakwena, Bamnagwato and Bangwaketse – travelled to England; the Colonial Office assured the three chiefs that, provided they accepted the construction of a railway across their lands linking Mafeking and Bulawayo, the region north of the Molopo would remain the Buchuanaland Protectorate. This status remained virtually unchanged for 70 years. A constitution providing for an elected legislature and an executive council was introduced in 1961. The first election, held in 1965, brought a landslide victory for Sir Seretse *Khama's multiracial Democratic Party. Under his leadership the Protectorate won independence as Botswana on 30 September 1966 and Sir Seretse served as President until his death in 1980, when he was succeeded by Dr Quett Masire (re-elected in 1989). Cattle-rearing is Botswana's chief industry, although there are valuable diamond mines at Jwaneng and Orapa; many thousands of Botswanan workers migrated to South Africa in the 1970s and 1980s.

Bounty **Mutiny**. On 28 April 1789 the crew of HMS *Bounty*, an armed transport carrying breadfruit seedlings from Tahiti to the West Indies to augment basic food yield on the sugar plantations, mutinied while at sea off Tonga. William *Bligh, the allegedly brutal captain of the *Bounty*, was cast adrift in an open boat, together with 18 members of the 45-man crew who refused to support the mutiny. Fletcher Christian (1764–93) sailed HMS *Bounty* back to Tahiti, where he landed 18 mutineers, before proceeding with the remainder of the crew and some Tahitian women to *Pitcairn Island, where the *Bounty* was set on fire. Bligh and his companions survived a 3,600-mile voyage of six weeks before reaching Timor, where they were rescued. The Admiralty sent the frigate HMS *Pandora* to Tahiti, where 14 mutineers were arrested; four were drowned when the frigate was wrecked in the Torres Strait; ten were eventually court-martialled in England, three of them being hanged. The Pitcairn settlers were unmolested; their descendants moved in 1856 to Norfolk Island (*Australian Dependent Territories).

Boyd, Arthur Merric (1861–1940), patriarch of a remarkable family of Australian artists and writers: born in Opoho, New Zealand but settled in Victoria in 1886, where he won respect as a water-colour painter. Three sons achieved distinction: Merric Boyd (1888–1959) was a ceramic artist who perfected new techniques for his pottery, at Murrumbeena; Penleigh Boyd (1890–1923) became a landscape artist and etcher; Martin à Beckett Boyd (1893–1973) was a novelist and poet who spent much of his life in Britain and is best known for his Langton tetrology of novels, published 1952–62. Of Merric Boyd's sons, Arthur Merric Bloomfield Boyd (1920–) became a painter, potter, sculptor and theatrical designer, and Guy Martin à Beckett Boyd (1923–) a sculptor; he produced the mural reliefs for Melbourne and Sydney airports. Robin Gerard Penleigh Boyd (1919–71) was an influential architect and writer, best known for his book, *The Great Australian Dream* (1972).

Bradfield, John Job Crew

Bradfield, John Job Crew (1867–1943), Australian civil engineer: born at Sandgate, Queensland, and studied engineering at Sydney University. He was responsible for the underground railway system of Sydney, for work on irrigation dams, and (mainly) for the principal design of Sydney Harbour Bridge. Bradfield presented his original plans as early as 1913, but work on the bridge did not begin until 1923, the construction contract going to the Yorkshire firm of Dorman Long. Bradfield's design called for the longest single-span bridge in the world, capable of carrying six lanes of roadway, four railway tracks and two footpaths across a 550-yard expanse of water. Bradfield was present at the opening ceremony in March 1932.

Bradman, Sir Donald George (1908–), the peerless Australian cricketer: born on a farm at Cootamundra, New South Wales, the family moving to Bowral, 80 miles south of Sydney, when he was two. His first-class cricket career covered the years 1927 to 1949; he played for New South Wales in seven seasons and for South Australia in ten, captaining Australia in 24 of the 52 Test matches in which he played. Bradman's great concentration and tenacious courage dominated the Australian tours of England in the summers of 1930, 1934, 1938 and 1948 but his highest score – a record 452 not out, for New South Wales against Queensland at Sydney – was made in the first week of January 1930, when he was only twenty-one. Statistically, no batsman in the world has matched Bradman's figures at the end of his career: in all first-class cricket, an average of 95 runs an innings; in Test cricket, an average of 99.9 runs; in Sheffield Shield contests between the Australian states, an average of 110 runs. For the thirty Test matches in which he played against England in England, his batting average was 102.8; even in the notorious *bodyline series in Australia (1932/3) he averaged 56.6. On 1 January 1949, after returning home from his fourth tour of England, Bradman received a knighthood, the first conferred on a playing cricketer. After his retirement he was chairman of the Australian Cricket Board, 1960–3 and 1969–73.

Brady, Matthew (1799–1826), earliest of the notorious Australian *bushrangers: born in Manchester, transported to New South Wales in 1820 for stealing groceries. For further crimes he was sent to the penal settlement in what is now *Tasmania, but in 1825 he escaped and, with a gang of other ex-convicts, terrorized the island, even taking over a whole township on one occasion. Informers betrayed him; he was hanged in Hobart at the age of twenty-seven.

Braithwaite, Errol Kaumu (1930–), Caribbean historian and poet: born in Bridgetown, Barbados. He won widespread academic respect with his *The Development of Creole Society in Jamaica, 1770–1820*, published in Britain in 1971. Two years later great interest was aroused by the publication of *The Arrivants; a New World Trilogy*, which comprised three volumes of his poetry: *Rights of Passage* (1967); *Masks* (1968); and *Islands* (1969).

Britain: see *United Kingdom*.

British Bechuanaland, south of the Molopo River, was a Crown Colony from 1885 to 1895 when it was absorbed into Cape Colony, subsequently forming a district in Cape Province, South Africa. The (much larger) Bechuanaland Protectorate, north of the Molopo, was never governed from Cape Town or Pretoria and now constitutes *Botswana.

British Borneo: see *Sabah*.

British Broadcasting Company/Corporation (BBC): see *Broadcasting*.

British Columbia, Canada's westernmost province, on the Pacific coast: capital Victoria, on Vancouver Island. British Columbia is predominantly mountainous, with four almost parallel north–south ranges separating the Pacific littoral from the prairies of Alberta; these ranges are heavily forested and rich in fir, spruce and red cedar, making lumbering the chief industry. The coast was charted by George *Vancouver in 1795 and claimed by the Hudson's Bay Company, as 'New Caledonia', in 1821. Vancouver Island was constituted a Crown Colony in 1849, by royal charter recognizing that land rights were retained by the Company. Rumours of gold on the Thompson and Fraser Rivers led to a gold rush, with 10,000 prospectors in the second fortnight of May 1858 alone setting out to seek their fortunes on the Fraser. The probability of further gold discoveries led, in 1859, to the proclamation of a new colony of British Columbia, comprising the mainland from the Pacific as far east as the watershed of the Rocky Mountains. The first governor of the mainland colony, *James Douglas, was already effective governor of Vancouver Island, and exercised dictatorial powers both in levying taxes to pay for the roads to open up the interior and in controlling the second gold rush in the region, to Lake Cariboo in 1862. In 1866 the mainland and island were united as the colony of British Columbia, with the Company losing its land rights over the following three years. From 1859 to 1871 there was a protracted dispute with the USA over possession of the *San Juan Islands, facing Victoria. The united colony of British Columbia became the sixth Canadian province on 20 July 1871, after agreement that a transcontinental railway would be built. The *Canadian Pacific Railway finally reached the coast at the newly established city of Vancouver in 1885, completing expansion 'from sea to sea'; the Canadian

Northern line did not reach the city until thirty years later. The Trans-Canada Highway, linking British Columbia with the east, was officially opened in September 1962. Extensive hydro-electric power enabled the growth of manufacturing industries, mostly associated with forestry or mining. Vancouver city, with its fine natural harbour, has become the third largest metropolitan area in Canada, with a pipeline to the *Alberta oilfields since 1953. Esquimalt, a suburb of Victoria, was the Pacific base for the Royal Navy until 1906, when dockyards and Admiralty buildings were handed over to the new Royal Canadian Navy.

British Council, the principal agent for the United Kingdom's cultural relations overseas. It was established in London in 1935, receiving a royal charter in 1940. Although the Council has offices in more than 90 countries, its chief educational work is concentrated within the Commonwealth where, as well as maintaining libraries, it manages several large-scale programmes on behalf of the *Overseas Development Administration, particularly in India. In recent years the British Council has helped with the establishment of the Allana Iqbal Open University in Pakistan, with forestry research projects in Kenya, and with English-language teaching to provide a wider range of higher educational studies in Pakistan, Zambia and Nigeria. The British Council also provides specialist study courses in the United Kingdom for Commonwealth visitors and, with the *Commonwealth Science Council, helps to promote technological training.

British East Africa: see *Kenya*.

British Empire Exhibition (1924), held at Wembley, was the first major celebration of Empire held in London since an Imperial Exhibition in Kensington in 1886. It was intended to stimulate interest in the overseas empire and its achievements, and to counter post-war disillusionment by appealing to patriotic pride. The main stadium, England's principal sporting arena, was completed a year ahead of the exhibition. Around the stadium were 'Palaces' of Industry, Engineering and Art, special pavilions publicizing Australia, Canada, South Africa, New Zealand, and, in a small pavilion of its own, the 'Queen's Dolls' House', designed by *Lutyens. In all, the Wembley exhibition covered fifteen miles of street frontage, packed into 220 acres. It was opened by King George V on 23 April 1924 and was the occasion of the first royal broadcast. The exhibition remained open for 150 days and attracted 27 million visitors. Wembley Stadium survives (though modernized), and some of the other buildings became industrial warehouses; Queen Mary's Dolls' House is now at Windsor.

British Guiana: see *Guyana*.

British Honduras: see *Belize*.

British Indian Ocean Territory comprises five coral atolls, the largest being Diego Garcia. The Territory, originally including three islands administered since 1976 by the *Seychelles, was established for defence purposes by Order in Council in November 1965. The Territory has no permanent population.

British Kaffraria. The region between the Great Kei River and Natal was the Crown Colony of British Kaffraria from 1847 to 1866, when it was annexed to Cape Colony. Most of the region was included in the Transkei 'homeland' of the Xhosa nation, established by the South African Republic in 1976.

British Nationality Acts. The concept of British citizenship was first defined by the British Nationality Act of 1948, passed by the first (Labour) ministry of *Attlee. The Act confirmed the principle of joint citizenship among members of the Commonwealth, so that a person from a dominion or colony resident in the United Kingdom was entitled to the same civic rights as a native-born resident, while a reciprocal status would be given to a person born in the United Kingdom who settled in a Commonwealth country. This concept was overturned by the Conservatives nearly a quarter of a century later. A bill introduced in the House of Commons by the first Thatcher government on 14 January 1981 restricted the right to live in the United Kingdom to British citizens, while denying that right to citizens of British dependent territories and British overseas citizens. These restraints were denounced by Opposition parties in both Houses of Parliament as being both divisive and discriminatory and, on 20 October, their morality was questioned in the House of Lords by the Archbishop of Canterbury, Dr Robert Runcie. But the bill was enacted on 30 October 1981 and became effective from 1 January 1983.

British North America Act (1867). After conferences between delegates from the Canadian Maritime Provinces, and Upper and Lower Canada, at Charlottetown (Prince Edward Island) early in September 1864 and at Quebec five weeks later, representatives from *Canada, Nova Scotia and New Brunswick came to London in 1866 and agreed with the Colonial Office on setting up a confederation. These proposals were embodied in the British North America Act by which Quebec, Ontario, Nova Scotia and New Brunswick constituted the 'Dominion of Canada', formally proclaimed on 1 July 1867. 'Dominion' was chosen in preference to 'Kingdom' out of deference to republican sentiment across the border in the USA. The Act foreshadowed later imperial devolution in strengthening overseas territories by promoting colonial confederation.

British Somaliland, a protectorate on the Red Sea established in 1885 on land evacuated by the Egyptians. It was across the Gulf from *Aden, which it long supplied with food. Until 1898 it was (like Aden) adminis-tered from India, then by the Foreign Office, with the Colonial Office in charge from 1905 until 1960, except during World War II. The people remained nomadic, though Berbera was developed as a port and capital. In 1899 much of the interior fell under the capricious rule of the fanatical Mohammed bin Abdulla Hassan (c.1870–1920) and his dervishes. Six hard-fought campaigns over 21 years failed to break the power of the 'mad Mullah', who succumbed to influenza in November 1920 after being bombed by RAF biplanes and hounded by the Somaliland Camel Corps for nine months. The Italians occupied the Protectorate for eight months in 1940–41. British control was finally relinquished on 1 July 1960 when the Protectorate joined the larger and more populous Trusteeship territory of Italian Somaliland, to form the independent Somali Republic.

British South Africa Company was founded by Cecil *Rhodes in 1887 and received a royal charter in 1889. The original purpose of the Company, which had its headquarters in Kimberley, was to develop the area north of Bechuanaland, and in 1890 and 1891 Rhodes sent pioneer columns to claim sovereignty over land as far north as Nyasaland (*Malawi). The Company's activities were principally concentrated in the territories named 'Rhodesia', after the BSAC's director-general, where the city of Salisbury (Harare) was founded in 1890. The *Jameson Raid – in which more than 400 troopers from the Company's police force participated – led to criticism of the BSAC in the British Parliament, and in 1896 Rhodes resigned as the chartered company's director. But he took up his responsibilities again in 1898, and the BSAC's semi-feudal administration of the Rhodesias survived his death. It was not until 1924 that the chartered company surrendered its sovereign rights to the British government.

British Virgin Islands: a group of 36 islands (eleven uninhabited) off the Greater Antilles in the Caribbean. They are part of an archipelago of more than 100 islands, all within a hundred-mile radius of Puerto Rico: the remaining islands have been a dependency of the United States since 1917 (when they were purchased, for strategic reasons, from Denmark). The British Virgin Islands were discovered by Columbus, settled by the Dutch in 1648, and seized by the British in 1766. From 1871 to 1958 they were administratively part of the federated Crown Colony of the Leeward Islands, but representative government was introduced in 1950, and the islands declined to join the abortive British West Indies federa-tion (*see below*) eight years later. In 1967 the status of the islands as a colo-nial dependency of the British Crown was confirmed in a constitution, amended ten years later. Executive authority remains vested in a governor appointed from London, although he is assisted by a five-man council, four of whom come from an elected legislature. Road Town on Tortola, the largest island, serves as a political and business capital. American influence is considerable: the US dollar is the unit of currency; tourism is the main industry, either directly in the form of visitors to the islands, or indirectly in so far as their influx to the American dependency provides the peasant farmers of the British islands with a steady export market.

British West Indies Federation. Proposals were put forward at a conference in Montego Bay in 1947 for a federation of the ten British colonies in the Caribbean, with membership extended to British Guiana and British Honduras on the South American mainland. Further conferences were held in London in 1953 and 1956, but lack of common interests and purpose delayed implementation of the proposals until January 1958 when a Federation (limited to the islands) was established, with its capital at Port of Spain, *Trinidad – 1,200 miles away from the largest of the British Caribbean islands, *Jamaica. Sir Grantley Adams (1898–1971), the leader of the Barbados Labour Party and a long-term believer in federalism, became Prime Minister. Complaints that the richer islands (especially Jamaica and Trinidad) were being forced to accept responsibility for the poorer islands soon made federal government virtually impossible. Sir Alexander *Bustamente, in Jamaica, attacked the idea of Federation and, after a Jamaican referendum in 1961 favoured secession, the Federation was dissolved on 31 May 1962, pending the granting of independence to the 'Big Two' – Jamaica, and Trinidad and Tobago. Talks continued intermittently in London for three years over the possibility of setting up a small federation, but without success. In 1968, however, the Commonwealth Caribbean countries agreed on forming a free trade area (*Carifta) which, in 1973, expanded into the *Caribbean Community (Caricom).

Broadcasting. The possibilities of developing wireless telegraphy for the spread of news and information was considered by the first *Imperial Conference of prime ministers in 1911, when a system of relay stations across the Empire was proposed, but not implemented until long after World War I. In 1920–21 pioneer public broadcasting was developed almost simultaneously by the Marconi Company at Writtle in Essex and at Montreal from 'Station XWA'. Government policy in Britain favoured centralization under Post Office licence and gave monopoly rights to the BBC (British Broadcasting Company), which began a news and entertainment service from 'Station 2LO' in the capital on 18 October 1922; the 'company' became a 'corporation', under royal charter, on 1 January 1927.

There was a similar acceptance of government responsibility in most of the overseas dominions and territories: thus, in 1932, the ABC (Australian Broadcasting Commission, re-structured as a corporation in 1983) took over the development of radio from an Australian Broadcasting Company and began co-ordinated transmission from twelve radio stations across the continent, with television channels opening in Sydney and Melbourne in 1956. Similarly, in New Zealand the opening of a small wireless service in Otago during the summer of 1920/1 was followed by a more extensive Broadcasting Company, expanding between 1925 and 1931; a period of public control under a Broadcasting Board (1932–35); and the development of the New Zealand Broadcasting Service as a government department between 1936 and 1962. With the opening of the first television stations in 1960/1, administrative power was transferred to a New Zealand Broadcasting Corporation (1962). In Canada the first 'nation-wide' network was set up in 1926 by the Canadian National Railway, with a chain of stations broadcasting to earphone receivers aboard CNR express trains. In 1932–33 this network, and 47 smaller private radio stations, came under the control of the federal Canadian Radio Broadcasting Commission (Canadian Broadcasting Corporation from 1936, with television stations in Montreal and Toronto from October 1952). Ceylon had a broadcasting service as early as 1925, and All-India radio grew rapidly, but development was slow in central Africa and the West Indies. Even in the Union of South Africa there were fewer than 25,000 licensed wireless sets in 1930; the SA Broadcasting Corporation was not founded until 1936. Rhodesia (Zimbabwe) gained a broadcasting service in 1941, when a studio opened in Salisbury (Harare); Namibia had to wait for the coming of High Frequency Modulation in 1961.

Empire-wide development became the responsibility of the BBC, largely through the vision of Sir John Reith (1889–1971; manager of the company 1922–27, director-general of the corporation 1928–38). On 21 May 1927 an experimental short-wave transmission, using the Dutch station at Hilversum, relayed news reports to Australasia, South Africa and India, a success which encouraged the BBC to plan an 'Empire Service', first transmitted from Daventry on 19 December 1932. On Christmas Day in that year King George V (as he wrote in his diary) 'broadcasted a short message of 251 words to the whole Empire' from Sandringham, thus beginning an annual tradition associating the sovereign and his or her 'people in far-off places'. Reith's legacy to the BBC – high standards of factual accuracy and a dignified sense of moral mission – ensured that radio formed a valuable bond of Commonwealth unity throughout World War II and on state occasions until the funeral of King George VI in 1952; thereafter the visual image of television made a greater public impact than descriptive reporting.

Even before World War II, commercial broadcasting was challenging the public service presentation of light entertainment, and the spread of television intensified this rivalry, especially in Canada and in Australia, where the Sydney newspaper magnate Sir Frank Packer (1906–74) built up a media empire of television and radio stations. The distinction between public and private broadcasting had become blurred by the middle of the 1960s; thus in Canada, a quarter of the income of the 'public' CBC came from advertising. The corporations accepted an obligation to meet specialist needs: in maintaining contacts with isolated communities in the Canadian North and the Australian outback, for example; and by broadcasting in minority languages while also persisting with English-language lessons, notably in Africa and the Indian subcontinent. The Commonwealth Broadcasting Association dates from February 1945.

Brooke, Sir James (1808–68), Rajah of Sarawak: born at Benares, the son of an East India Company official. He was sent home to Norwich for his schooling but ran away and enlisted in the Bengal Infantry at the age of sixteen, and was subsequently wounded while fighting in Burma. In 1838 he travelled to Borneo and visited *Sarawak, returning there in 1840 to help the ruler put down a rebellion. On 24 September 1841 Brooke was invited by the Sultan of *Brunei, as nominal sovereign of all Borneo, to take over the government of Sarawak. Rajah Brooke modernized the administration, imposing a simpler system of taxation and suppressing piracy. A Commission of Inquiry set up in Singapore to examine complaints of cruelty against him found no evidence to support the charge, and Brooke was confirmed in his position as British Commissioner and Consul-General in Borneo. Apart from a short visit to England in 1847, Brooke remained in Sarawak until 1863. Upon his death, five years later, he was succeeded as Rajah by his nephew, Sir Charles Brooke (1829–1917).

Bruce, Stanley Melbourne (1883–1967), Australian Prime Minister: was born and received his schooling in the city from which his middle name was taken. He read law at Trinity Hall, Cambridge and rowed in the University crew for the 1904 Boat Race before being called to the bar of the Middle Temple. He returned to Melbourne in 1911, but enlisted in the Royal Fusiliers in 1914, serving with them beside the Anzacs at Gallipoli and winning both the Military Cross and the French Croix de Guerre. He was elected to the Federal Parliament as a Nationalist Party member in 1918, representing Australia at the League of Nations in 1921, and was head of a coalition government and Minister for External Affairs from 1923 to 1929, developing an 'English' style of conservatism, relaxing federal controls but tightening immigration laws. He lost his seat in the election of October 1929, but was back in parliament as a United Australia Party member from 1931 to 1933. He was chief Australian delegate to the Ottawa Conference (1932) and thereafter spent most of his life in Europe. From 1933 to 1945 he was Australian High Commissioner in London, attending League of Nations meetings in Geneva and assisting Churchill's war cabinet over questions of Australian policy. He received a peerage in 1947 (taking the title Viscount Bruce of Melbourne), and was the director of several British companies as well as serving as founder Chancellor of the Australian National University in Canberra.

Brunei: an independent sovereign sultanate within the Commonwealth, on the north-west coast of Borneo: capital Bandar Seri Bagawan. The Sultanate was a British Protectorate from 1888 until 31 December 1983; supreme political power is vested in the ruler, Hassanal Bolkiah Mu'izzadin Waddaulah (1946–   ; acceded 1967). Oil was discovered in 1929 and, with liquefied natural gas, remains the chief industry and source of revenue, although offshore production is greater than onshore. The interior is rich in timber.

Brunner, Thomas (1821–74), explorer and surveyor of New Zealand: born in London; joined the New Zealand Company in 1841 and was sent as a pioneer settler to the base at Nelson on South Island. In 1846 he set out on a journey into the interior, to look for good grazing land. Brunner established friendly relations with the Maori people and, with the aid of the Maori guide Kehu, traced the routes of the main rivers of north-western South Island and conducted geological surveys which revealed the first coal deposits in the island. He reached Titari Point before turning back for Nelson to complete a 19-month journey. On further expeditions into Westland he discovered the lake which bears his name. In later years he served as Commissioner of Public Works in South Island.

Buchan, John (Lord Tweedsmuir, 1875–1940), author, imperial publicist and Governor-General of Canada: born in Perth, the son of a Calvinist minister; educated at Glasgow University and Brasenose College, Oxford before becoming a barrister. Throughout his life he was an enthusiastic supporter of the imperial ideal, stressing in numerous books the importance of the links of the United Kingdom with South Africa and, later, with Canada. His experience of the Empire began when he served as assistant private secretary to *Milner, 1901–03. From 1910 onwards he wrote adventure stories, historical novels in the tradition of Scott and Stephenson, and biographies. His most famous counter-espionage trilogy – *The Thirty-nine Steps*, *Greenmantle*, and *Mr Standfast* – was published between 1915 and 1918; the three books are marked by an original ingenuity of circumstance, a poet's feeling for landscape, and a sense of heroic imperial patriotism. He was Conservative MP for the Scottish Universities (1927–35) and, as Baron Tweedsmuir, served as Governor-General of Canada, 1935–40.

Buckley, William (1780–1856), 'wild white man' of Australia: born near Macclesfield; a large and physically strong bricklayer, he was sentenced to transportation in 1802, probably for receiving stolen goods. In December 1803, two months after reaching Australia, he escaped from a penal settlement in Port Philip Bay and for 32 years lived with aboriginal tribes, eventually surrendering, in May 1835, to the pioneer settlers of Melbourne. Buckley was pardoned, and used his knowledge of the aborigines to serve as an interpreter before migrating to Tasmania in 1837.

Buddhism: came from Nepal with the spiritual quest of Siddharta Gautama (*c.*567–487 BC); spread to India, Ceylon, Burma, Tibet, China, Japan and Indonesia. Within the modern Commonwealth Buddhism is strongest in Sri Lanka, where it is the faith of 70 per cent of the population, mainly Sinhalese. It still has nearly 5 million adherents in India.

Buganda, originally a kingdom in East Africa; passed under British imperial 'protection' in 1894 at a time when the Foreign Office in London was concerned about French ambitions to control the Upper Nile (see *Fashoda*). Although the ruler of Buganda, Kabaka Mwanga, led a rebellion in 1897 which hampered British military movements, his people – the Baganda – were subsequently given a special status within British *Uganda. An agreement concluded in 1900 effectively gave the Baganda freehold land tenure, and the colonial authorities developed the chief towns of the Baganda, Kampala and Entebbe, as the administrative and commercial centres for all four provinces of the Uganda Protectorate. The Lukiko (the traditional council of Buganda), regarding the emergence of a Ugandan nationalist movement under Milton *Obote with deep suspicion, sought a federal structure for the proposed independent state. Tension with the British authorities led in November 1953 to the deportation to Britain of the last Kabaka, Mutesa II (Sir Edward Mutesa, 1924–69), who in exile became a popular hero of his people. He was allowed to return to his kingdom in October 1955 and was elected President of Uganda in 1963, but in February 1966 he was overthrown by Obote, who then sought to impose a unitary constitution. When in May 1967 the Bugandan Lukiko rejected this constitution, Obote ordered a military assault on the Kabaka's palace, forcing Mutesa to flee to England, and in September the hereditary kingdom of Buganda was abolished. North Buganda and South Buganda survive as two of the ten provinces in the Republic of Uganda.

Burke and Wills Expedition (1860–61). In 1860 the Royal Society of Victoria, encouraged by the government of the colony, raised funds for a Great Northern Exploration Expedition, designed to find a permanent route from Melbourne across the interior of the continent to the northern coast, a project intended to forestall the South Australian government, who were backing the explorer J. M. *Stuart. The Victoria expedition was led by Robert O'Hara Burke (1820–61), an Irish-born Inspector of Police and former officer in the Austrian Army. His chief scientific adviser was a Londoner, William John Wills (1834–61), a meteorologist with medical training and Surveyor of Crown Lands for Ballarat. The expedition left Melbourne in August 1860 and Burke established bases at Menindee and Cooper's Creek, before setting out in November with Wills, John *King and Charles Gray to cross the Great Artesian Basin. Mistakenly, the party took only three months' provisions with them. They reached the Gulf of Carpentaria in February 1861, thus completing the south–north crossing. Gray died as they sought to return to Cooper's Creek, which they reached on 21 April 1861, only to find that the base party had returned to Menindee. Burke made the ill-judged decision to set out for Adelaide: both he and Wills perished from starvation in June. John King, a 23 year old Irish settler, was succoured by aborigines and was rescued, in poor health, in September. He lived for another ten years before succumbing to tuberculosis.

Burma. As early as 1612 the *East India Company had established three factories (trading stations) and agencies in the Empire of Burma, the most important one being at Syriam, near modern Rangoon. The Burmese empire, formidable in the twelfth century, recovered some of its lost central authority towards the end of the eighteenth century and in 1824 was considered to pose a military threat to British trading interests in Assam and Bengal. The First (Anglo-)Burmese War of 1824–26 led to annexation by the British of Assam, Arakan and Tenasserim. Lord *Dalhousie annexed Pegu, including the Irrawaddy delta, in 1852 after a Second Burmese War. Ten years later Arakan, Pegu and Tenasserim were linked together as British Lower Burma, while Assam remained part of Bengal. In 1885 King Thebaw (1858–1916), encouraged by the French, confiscated the property of the Bombay–Burma Company. A powerful Anglo-Indian army swiftly overran his kingdom and deposed Thebaw, who was interned at Ratnagiri in western India. For half a century Burma was treated as an Indian province, but in April 1937 received separate, non-colonial status, enjoying limited self-government under a crown-nominated governor who was responsible to the 'Secretary of State for India and Burma'. A nationalist revolutionary movement, the Thakin Party, was organized by the student leader Aung Sang, but had gained little following before the outbreak of World War II. The Japanese invaded Burma on 20 January 1942 and had absorbed all the country by late May, setting up a puppet government in Rangoon, at first supported by the Thakin. An abortive Allied offensive in the Arakan jungle (October 1942 to March 1943) failed to loosen the Japanese hold, but the Fourteenth Army under General *Slim inflicted a decisive defeat on the Japanese at Imphal (March to June 1944) and recovered the Irrawaddy basin and Rangoon in a gruelling campaign (February to May 1945), fought through the monsoon season. The Thakin became the central group of an Anti-Fascist People's Freedom League (AFPFL) which, having helped defeat the Japanese, wanted an assurance of independence from the British. This was conceded personally by *Attlee in talks with Aung Sang in London in December 1946; and Aung Sang became acting Prime Minister on 27 January 1947. He was, however, assassinated at a cabinet meeting in Rangoon on 19 July 1947 and it was left to his successor, U Nu (1907–   ), to secure the formal grant of independence to Burma, on 17 October 1947. The Socialist Republic of the Union of Burma came into being on 4 January 1948, outside the Commonwealth. In September 1988 the military regime of Saw Maung changed Burma's name to Myanmar.

Burnet, Sir (Frank) Macfarlane (1899–1985), Australian virologist: born at Traralgon, Victoria; educated at Geelong, Melbourne University and Melbourne Hospital, early specializing in virus research. In collaboration with Dame Jean Macnamara (1899–1968) he identified the existence of two viruses, rather than one, in poliomyelitis. As Director of the Walter and Eliza Hall Institute of Medical Research in Melbourne (1944–65) he concentrated on immunology. In 1960 he shared the Nobel Prize for Medicine with the British zoologist, Sir Peter Medawar, for work on immunological tolerance in relation to skin and organ grafting. Burnet was knighted in 1951 and in 1958 received the Order of Merit. He served as inaugural chairman of the Commonwealth Fund from 1966 to 1969, the year in which his principal scientific study, *Cellular Immunology*, was published.

Burnham (Linden) Forbes (Sampson) (1923–85), first President of *Guyana: born, a school-teacher's son, in British Guiana; studied law at London University and became a barrister in 1948. He returned home the following year and helped establish the People's Progressive Party, serving as Minister of Education in 1953. Subsequently he broke with the more militant (and predominantly East Indian) members of the party, led by Cheddi *Jagan, and in 1957 set up the People's National Congress, a more moderate socialist movement, supported by the non-Indian population. Burnham became Prime Minister in 1964, secured independence in May 1966 and remained in office until his death. In October 1980 he became President of the Co-operative Republic of Guyana, under a constitution of his own devising.

Bushrangers: lawless men, akin to English highwaymen, and generally escaped criminals, who in the nineteenth century took to the southeastern Australian bush and lived by robbery. The earliest leader of a bushranger gang was Matthew *Brady, in Tasmania. Although some bushrangers of the 1820s and 1830s were romanticized in legend – notably Jack Donahoe, the 'wild colonial boy' of New South Wales – this form of banditry was at its height in the period 1850–80, with Ned *Kelly as the most notorious folk hero of all.

Bustamente, Sir (William) Alexander (1884–1977), first Prime Minister of *Jamaica: born W. A. Clarke, the son of an Irish planter, near Kingston, Jamaica. He called himself 'Bustamente' while spending an adventurous youth in Panama and New York, and later legalized the surname by deed poll. In 1934 he returned to Jamaica and became a militant trade unionist. His demagogic gifts led the authorities to intern him as a potential trouble-maker in 1940. On his release he formed the Jamaica Labour Party and from 1945 to 1953 was leader of business in the colonial legislature. Despite long political rivalry with Norman *Manley's National Party, Bustamente shaped his island's political future until ill-health in 1965 forced his retirement two years later. He strongly opposed the *British West Indies Federation, firmly believing in Jamaican independence. When this was achieved in August 1962 he served as the island's first Prime Minister. He was knighted in 1955, and in 1969 was proclaimed 'National Hero' of Jamaica.

CAB International. In 1929 the second Labour Government set up a Commonwealth Agricultural Bureau to disseminate information on research in agricultural science to member bodies within the Commonwealth and Empire. From 1985 other countries were allowed to affiliate to the organization, which was renamed CAB International although it remained predominantly a Commonwealth institution. CAB has always specialized in entomology, helminthology, biological control, animal genetics and health, dairy technology, forestry, plantation crops, field crops, plant breeding, soils and fertilizers. CAB International now comprises four institutes and five editorial divisions, all in Britain, and provides information for specialized study from the world's largest agricultural and horticultural database at its headquarters in Wallingford, Oxfordshire.

Cables: see *Telegraph and Telegraphic Cables*.

Calcutta Riots (August 1946). In late March 1946 *Attlee sent three cabinet colleagues – *Cripps, Lord Pethick-Lawrence, A. V. Alexander – to India to discuss preparations for self-government in the subcontinent. The ministers remained in India for seven weeks and put forward several proposals for Indian independence, but the predominantly Hindu *Indian National Congress was suspicious of the plans and the Muslim League followers of *Jinnah hostile, favouring an independent *Pakistan. After the failure of the mission, the League called on Muslims to resort to 'direct action' in support of the Pakistan cause. The government of Bengal (including Calcutta) was predominantly Muslim League; accordingly, when Jinnah called a Direct Action Day on 16 August 1946, there was chaos in Calcutta, with the Muslim and Hindu communities provoking each other to riot and arson. Over three days more than 20,000 people were killed or seriously injured during communal violence in Calcutta alone; at least a quarter of the casualties were fatal. Order was restored by the Viceroy (Field Marshal Lord Wavell, 1883–1950; Viceroy 1943–47) only with great difficulty, and through the mediation of *Gandhi. The anarchy in Calcutta intensified the speed with which London sought an end to the Raj and the withdrawal of British troops and administrators from the subcontinent. Independence followed a year later (15 August 1947).

Calwell, Arthur Augustus (1896–1973), Australian politician: born in West Melbourne; received a strict Roman Catholic education before entering the Civil Service. He was a prominent member of the Australian Labor Party from 1940 to 1972, serving as Minister of Information for the last two years of World War II. As Minister of *Immigration in the *Chifley Government (1945–49) Calwell enforced a 'white Australia' policy but, controversially, admitted considerably more southern and eastern European workers than had earlier administrations. He led the Labor Opposition from 1960 to 1967 and was deeply critical of Australian involvement in the *Vietnam War.

Cambridge, Ada (1844–1926), Australian novelist: born in England; a Norfolk farmer's daughter who married a clergyman, George Cross, in 1870 and emigrated to Victoria soon afterwards. She lived at first on the Murray River but settled at Melbourne and wrote some twenty novels championing women's social rights in a predominantly masculine society; her best-known are *The Three Miss Kings* (1891) and *Materfamilias* (1898). Her early memoirs, *Thirty Years in Australia* (1903), form a valuable document of social history.

CAMHADD (Commonwealth Association for Mental Health and Development Disabilities) was established in Sheffield in 1983, with support from the Commonwealth Foundation, to co-ordinate research into mental disabilities and associated projects in Commonwealth countries faced with similar problems. The first CAMHADD centres overseas were established in Bombay, Nairobi and Lusaka (1985–87).

Canada. The name 'Canada' is probably an adaptation of an *Iroquoian term, *kanata* (meaning 'community'), which appears in a narrative by the Breton navigator Jacques Cartier, who discovered the St Lawrence River in 1535. The French continued to open up North America over the next century and a half: *Quebec was founded in 1608; Montreal (Ville-Marie) in 1642; and in 1662 the Royal Province of New France was established, making it possible within twenty years to travel overland from Quebec to New Orleans through French territory. The *Hudson's Bay Company, incorporated in London in 1670, planted the first fur trading posts at Fort Rupert (1669–70) and Fort Albany (1679), but there was already an English presence in *Newfoundland (where Humphrey *Gilbert established the settlement of St John in August 1583) and, after 1621, a predominantly Scottish presence in *Nova Scotia, even though the French only formally ceded the peninsula by the Treaty of Utrecht (1713). The British foothold in Canada remained precarious until, after the capture of Quebec by *Wolfe, the French surrendered their Canadian territories to Britain by the Treaty of Paris (1763). *Prince Edward Island, in the Gulf of St Lawrence, thereupon became part of Nova Scotia, but was recognized as a separate colonial province in 1769. The subsequent loss of the American colonies in 1783 and the northward migration of more than 40,000 United Empire Loyalists changed the character of Canada, tightening the specifically British connection: *New Brunswick became a province in 1784, with its development closely linked with the other two 'Maritime Provinces', Nova Scotia and Prince Edward Island. In 1791 Pitt's *Canada Constitutional Act gave the settlers of Upper and Lower Canada their first representative institutions. However, failure to understand local needs led in 1837 to the rebellions of *Mackenzie and *Papineau. Two years later the *Durham Report recommended 'responsible government', conceded in 1848. Conferences were held at Charlottetown (PEI) and Quebec City in 1864, on westward expansion and the strengthening of links between the colonies, and in 1867 the *British North America Act formally constituted the Dominion of Canada. The founding provinces – Quebec, *Ontario, New Brunswick, Nova Scotia – were joined by *Manitoba (1870), *British Columbia (1871), Prince Edward Island (1873), *Alberta (1905), *Saskatchewan (1905), and Newfoundland (1949). The completion of the *Canadian Pacific Railway in 1885, treaties with the *'Indian' tribes, the establishment of a stable frontier along the *49th Parallel, and the opening up of the prairies had led, by the coming of the twentieth century, to the development of an integrated wheat economy, which supplemented earlier industries based upon the *fur trade, *forestry, fisheries and mineral deposits.

The population, officially 2,383,500 in 1851/2, doubled in the next 33 years. Completion of the CPR increased the flow of immigrants: Scandinavians, Poles, Slovaks and Ukrainians joined older settlers (French, British, Irish, Dutch, German) during the last two decades of the nineteenth century. Jewish refugees from the Russian Empire, Romania and central Europe settled mainly in Montreal and Toronto. In 1899 some 7,000 Dukhobors, a primitive religious sect from Russia, settled in Saskatchewan, with many families moving on to British Columbia in 1908. Canada accepted 1,640,000 immigrants in the four years preceding World War I, three-quarters of them coming from the United Kingdom and the United States. In 1913 a record 440,000 immigrants settled in the Dominion, bringing the population to about eight million in 1914 and (officially) 8,787,949 in 1921.

Under the leadership successively of Sir Wilfrid *Laurier (Liberal, 1896 to 1911) and Sir Robert *Borden (Conservative, 1911 to 1917) Canada emerged as a World Power. More than 400,000 Canadian soldiers crossed to the Western Front in *World War I, fighting tenaciously at Ypres and with courageous self-sacrifice at *Vimy Ridge in April 1917. Opposition to *conscription in 1917–18 led to rioting in Quebec but did not prevent the growth of a Canadian Army of 630,000 men. Some 22,000 Canadians served in the Royal Flying Corps or the Royal Air Force, the most famous air ace being William *Bishop. Canada's war dead numbered 56,700, with 150,000 Canadians severely wounded. During the inter-war period Canadians participated in the work of the League of Nations, although they refused to accept commitments in Europe, such as the Geneva Protocols of 1922–23. Canada declined to back British policy over *Chanak, and in 1923 a Canadian signed the first treaty independent of the United Kingdom, a fisheries agreement with the USA. Diplomatic representation in capitals outside the Empire began in 1927, with the appointment of a minister in Washington.

Although the Statute of *Westminster (1931) removed the British Parliament's limitations on Canada's legislative autonomy, the federal structure was, at that time, under strain: French-speaking Canadians in Quebec became increasingly separatist; rural communities complained of exploitation by the big cities; and the western provinces maintained that the eastern provinces ignored their interests. From 1930 to 1935 the Conservatives under Richard *Bennett sought to use tariffs to strengthen Canadian trade, achieving some success by promoting imperial preference at the Ottawa Conference of 1932 but losing the confidence of electors during the following three years by increasing centralization. Between 1935 and 1957 the Liberal Governments of *King and *St Laurent harnessed the Dominion's natural resources, thereby increasing Canada's industrial output, while also collaborating closely with the US in defence of North America.

On 10 September 1939 Canada declared war on Germany without a dissentient voice in either House of Parliament, but isolationist sentiment was stronger than in 1914 and in Quebec there remained deep opposition to any compulsory military service. Out of a population of 11.5 million in 1941, some 1.1 million men and women served in the armed forces, the Canadian Army suffering especially heavy casualties in defence of *Hong Kong, in the Dieppe Raid of August 1942 (when, of 5,000 Canadian participants, 3,379 were killed or taken prisoner), in the break-out from

Normandy in August 1944, and along the Dutch–German border in February 1945. Large-scale immigration resumed after World War II, with refugees from Eastern Europe and, in the 1960s, immigrants from the Caribbean and some 500,000 Americans, mostly opponents of the Vietnam War. In addition to half a million Newfoundlanders absorbed by the Dominion in 1949, the existing population increased by 20 per cent between 1941 and 1951, and by another 30 per cent by 1961. Immigrants tended increasingly to come from the Caribbean: 11,628 out of 212,166 arrivals in 1990. By 1994 Toronto was reputedly the most ethnically mixed city in the world, and the estimated population of the Dominion had risen to 28.8 million. Canada was a founder member of NATO, and sent troops to support more than twenty United Nations peace-keeping missions, many undertaken between 1963 and 1968, when Lester *Pearson headed a Liberal government. During his administration, support grew rapidly in Quebec for the separatist Parti Québecois. The separatists won the provincial election of 1976, even though by then the Federal Prime Minister was a French-Canadian, Pierre *Trudeau. In his third ministry (1980–84) Trudeau completed a reform of the system of government, which was embodied in the *Canada Act (1982), proclaimed by Queen Elizabeth II in Ottawa on 15 April 1982. The new Constitution formally asserted Canada's complete and independent sovereignty, but Quebec's persistent opposition has delayed its final acceptance. This constitutional uncertainty led to the downfall of *Mulroney in 1993 and the subsequent electoral defeat of his successor, Kim Campbell.

Canada Act (1982). Proposals for a reformed constitutional structure were agreed by the *Trudeau government in November 1981, accepted by Parliament in Ottawa and, at the Canadian Parliament's request, approved by the United Kingdom Parliament. The Queen, visiting the Dominion specifically for the occasion, proclaimed the Act as in force on 15 April 1982. The Act 'patriated' the constitution by declaring that future political or administrative changes could be decided only by Canada's own assemblies. It confirmed that executive power was vested in a Governor-General appointed by the sovereign on the advice of the Canadian Government, and preserved the existing form of a bicameral legislature, with a nominated Senate and a House of Commons chosen by election at least every five years. The Act sought to safeguard Canada's multi-national cultural heritage and included a Charter of Rights. Nevertheless it failed to satisfy separatist opinion in *Quebec. An amendment – the Meech Lake Accord of 3 June 1987 – devolved certain federal powers, while recognizing Quebec as 'a distinct society'. The legislatures of Newfoundland and Manitoba rejected the Accord. A compromise Charlottetown Accord (September 1992) effectively provided a new Federal structure, with 25 per cent of the seats in the Commons reserved for Quebec. It was, however, rejected in a national referendum on 26 October 1992 by a clear majority, and by six of the ten provinces (with Quebec remaining hostile). Constitutional confusion continues to prevail in Canada.

Canada Constitutional Act (May, 1791): a statute of the Westminster Parliament, introduced by William Pitt 'the Younger' and providing for the first representative assemblies for Upper Canada (capital, Ontario) and Lower Canada (capital, Quebec City). The assemblies contained both nominated and elected members and possessed principal control of taxation. Despite its name the Act did not apply to all Canada: the Maritime Provinces already had representative assemblies. Conflict between Upper and Lower Canada over trade and taxation, and the differing traditions of French Catholics and British Protestants, made the constitutional arrangements unworkable within forty years. The *Durham Report of 1839 recommended a transition to responsible government but Lord John Russell's Canada Act of 1840 (effective from February 1841) fell short of Durham's proposals. It did, however, replace the cumbersome arrangements of 1791 by a united Canadian legislature, thus paving the way for the responsible federal government introduced by the *British North America Act of 1867.

Canadian Pacific Railway. When *British Columbia joined the Dominion in 1871 the Federal Government agreed to start work on a transcontinental railway within two years, and to complete the east-to-west link by 1881. Exploratory surveys of BC's forests began on the agreed day of Union but progress was slow, partly because of technical problems but also because of the world-wide economic depression which began in 1873, the start of the slump coinciding with a major financial scandal over railway funding in Canada. Not until 1876 were Ontario, Quebec and the Atlantic seaboard linked by a 700-mile route, and the transcontinental project – four times as long – was in such serious trouble and so little had been achieved by 1881 that British Columbia threatened to secede from the Dominion. Only then did the Ottawa government authorize the 'Canadian Pacific Railway Company' syndicate to complete the route in return for a 25-million-dollar subsidy, extensive land grants, and a monopoly guarantee north of the US border (to prevent the encroachment of American railroad companies). The subsequent engineering achievements were spectacular: 1,200 miles ran across prairie, but 500 miles cut through mountains. The last spike linking lines from east and west was driven into the track at Craigellachie, in the Eagle Pass over the Rocky Mountains, on 7 November 1885; but the first scheduled transcontinental train did not reach British Columbia until 4 July 1886, while the official opening came in May 1887. The CPR opened up the prairies and facilitated migration from east to west. As early as 1888, in the face of stiff opposition from the provincial government of Manitoba, the CPR agreed to give up its monopoly and accept competition from a Canadian Northern Railway, operational from 1897 but not reaching Vancouver until 1915, a year after a third railway – the Grand Trunk Pacific – had completed a line to Prince Rupert. Canada could not sustain the competition of three continental routes. While the CPR survived as a private venture, the other lines passed in 1923 under federal control as the Canadian National Railway (CNR). After 55 years of competition, falling passenger numbers led to the setting up in 1978 of a government-funded organization ('Via Rail') to safeguard passenger services on both the CPR and the CNR.

Canberra: capital of the Commonwealth of Australia. The site, 150 miles south-west of Sydney, on grazing uplands beside the Molongo River, was chosen in 1908 for the future federal capital. Canberra was named and inaugurated in 1913, with urban planning entrusted to W. Burley Griffin (1876–1937), a landscape architect from Chicago, who served as Federal Capital Director of Design and Construction until 1920, when so many changes were proposed to his original 'cobweb' plan that he retired into private practice: the landscaped central lake of Canberra preserves his name. The Commonwealth Parliament moved from Melbourne to Canberra in 1927. The establishment of government departments and of the Australian National University (founded as a post-graduate institution in 1946 but expanding rapidly from 1960 onwards) led to the growth of new suburbs, notably Queanbeyan on the federal capital's border with New South Wales. Residential areas to house, ultimately, half a million people are planned. Between 1961 and 1990 the population rose from 56,449 to slightly less than 300,000.

Canning, Charles John (1812–62), first Viceroy of India: the third son of the statesman George Canning (1770–1827); succeeded as Viscount Canning in 1837. After receiving his education at Eton and Christ Church, Oxford, Canning became a Peelite politician, serving for five years as Under-Secretary for Foreign Affairs. In February 1856 he succeeded *Dalhousie as Governor-General of India, with the initial tasks of settling the future of newly-annexed Oudh and supporting the ruler of Afghanistan in a conflict with Persia over the possession of Herat. Soon, however, he was confronted with problems of service within the Bengal Army and, in particular, suspicion of enforced conversion to Christianity. Insensitivity to native traditions sparked off the great *Indian Mutiny a year after Canning took up his duties. He was slow to realize the extent of the Mutiny. He gave a free hand to the military commanders to suppress the insurrection, but subsequently protested at vindictive punishments and insisted on merciful treatment of the rank-and-file of mutineers, becoming widely known as 'Clemency Canning'. But he was criticized by officials with long experience of India for ordering the landowners of Oudh who had supported the rebels to forfeit their land. He supported proposals to end the authority of the *East India Company as a governing agency and, at Allahabad on 1 November 1858, proclaimed Queen Victoria as the Sovereign of all India. He served as Viceroy until retiring in 1862, shortly before his death. His viceroyalty saw the introduction of educational reforms and public works programmes which his successors were to develop. In 1858 he was created an earl.

Cape Colony. The Dutch East India Company founded a settlement at Cape of Good Hope in 1662. The embryonic colony was seized by the British in 1795, restored to the Dutch in 1802, recaptured by Admiral Popham in 1806, and finally ceded to Britain by the Convention of London (31 August 1814) the Dutch receiving an indemnity of £6 million. Administration was autocratic, with an executive council set up in 1823 and a legislative council in 1827, but representative government followed in 1853. In the early years five military campaigns were fought against *Bantu 'Kaffirs' and *Zulus. Attempts to stamp out slavery led to conflict between British emigrants and Dutch settlers (*Boers), which culminated in the *Great Trek of 1835. Cape Colony assumed responsibility for *Natal in 1843 but was in long dispute with the Dutch over the *Orange River colony, which in 1854 became a 'Free State', two years after the *Sand River Convention had recognized Boer government in the *Transvaal. The discovery of precious stones in Griqualand in 1867 led to the first South African *diamond rush and to the annexation of the region to Cape Colony in 1870. Bechuanaland (*Botswana) was annexed in 1894 during the period when Cecil *Rhodes (colonial Prime Minister, 1890–96) was following the forward policy towards the Transvaal which contributed to the Second *Boer War. In May 1910, Cape Colony was merged in the new Union of *South Africa as the province of Cape of Good Hope.

Cape-to-Cairo Railway Project. The imperial idea of British colonial possessions stretching from 'Cape-to-Cairo' seems first to have been advocated in 1876 by Edwin Arnold (1832–1904), chief editor of the *Daily Telegraph* and an authority on the recent history of British India. Sir Harry *Johnston, with support from Lord *Salisbury, restated the case for 'a continuous band of British dominions' across Africa from south to north in an article in *The Times* on 22 August 1888. But it was the railway engineer and close friend of Cecil *Rhodes, Sir Charles Metcalfe (1853–1928) who, in the London periodical *Fortnightly Review* for April 1889, first wrote confidently of 'the iron track that must ultimately join the Cape with Cairo and carry civilization through the heart of the Dark Continent'. Rhodes enthusiastically supported the idea, which was however checked by German penetration of East Africa after their

Caribbean Community (CARICOM)

occupation of Dar-es-Salaam in 1888, and by French ambitions which culminated in the *Fashoda Crisis of 1898. No British-controlled 'iron track' ever linked the Cape to Cairo, and only in the years 1919–22 did British rule, directly or indirectly, extend from north to south across the African continent.

Caribbean Community (CARICOM). A Commonwealth regional body which was established, as the Caribbean Common Market, by the Treaty of Chaguaramas in Trinidad on 4 July 1973. The founder-members were Barbados, Guyana, Jamaica, and Trinidad and Tobago; but Belize, Dominica, Grenada, St Lucia, St Vincent and Montserrat became members in May 1974, while Antigua and St Kitts and Nevis were admitted two months later. The Bahamas would not join the Caribbean Common Market, but in July 1983 became a member of the Caribbean Community for political, educational and social purposes. Caricom was originally seen both as an extension of *Carifta, the Free Trade area established in 1968, and as a means of dealing with EEC representatives in the talks which culminated in the *Lomé Convention of 1975. The principal administrative institutions of Caricom are a Council of Ministers and a Secretariat with headquarters in Georgetown, Guyana, but there are also regular meetings of Heads of Government to determine general policy and, in particular, the relationship between Community members and other international organizations. Special institutions – notably the Caribbean Development Bank – provide for the needs of less developed countries in Caricom. Six non-Commonwealth countries possess observer status at Caricom meetings: Dominican Republic, Haiti, Mexico, Puerto Rico, Surinam and Venezuela.

CARIFTA: acronym for the Caribbean Free Trade Area, established by Commonwealth countries in the Caribbean in 1968 to remove customs duties between member states. Since less than 6 per cent of the total trade of Carifta members was with each other, the effect of abolishing these customs duties made little difference to the members' general economy. But it proved an important step towards greater regional consultation, facilitating the formation of Caricom (see *above*).

Carnarvon, Lord, Colonial Secretary: see *Herbert, Henry*.

Carroll, Sir James (1858–1926), champion of Maori rights in New Zealand: born at Waroa, the son of a blacksmith of Irish descent and Tapuke, a Maori chieftainess. In 1879 he became an interpreter in the House of Representatives, gaining experience of government practice. He was elected as Member for the Eastern Maori seat in 1887 and represented Waiapu (Gisborne) from 1894 to 1919; he received a knighthood in 1911 and, for the last five years of his life, was a member of the

Legislative Council. *Seddon brought him into the government as Minister of Native Affairs in 1899, with responsibility for introducing and implementing the Maori Councils Act of 1900. He remained Minister until 1912, gradually extending native government.

Cartier, Sir Georges Étienne (1814–73), Canadian federalist: born at Antoine, Quebec, and educated in Montreal; became a barrister in 1835 and sat in the Canadian legislature from 1848 until the creation of the Federal Parliament. Cartier, who wrote several French-Canadian songs, was proud of his Québecois cultural heritage but worked vigorously to ease friction between the two cultures. As Attorney-General in 1857 he took a prominent role in drafting the early proposals for federation sent to the home government in London, and over the following four years he shared the premiership with Sir John *Macdonald. With the achievement of Federation in 1867 Cartier became first Minister of Militia in the Dominion Parliament, strongly supporting westward expansion during the last six years of his life. He became a baronet in 1868 and died while visiting London to enlighten the first Gladstone government about Canadian affairs.

Cartier, Jacques (1491–1557), French pioneer in Canada: born in St Malo. On his first voyage to North America in 1534 he formally took possession of Canada in the name of King Francis I. A year later he became the first European to sail up the St Lawrence River. He made a third visit to Canada in 1541. His name has been given in Quebec Province to the highest peak, a river and a lake, and in Montreal city to a district and a bridge (1930) across the St Lawrence.

Casey, Richard Gardiner (1890–1976), Australian and imperial statesman: born at Brisbane; educated at Melbourne and Cambridge; served in the Australian Army from 1914 to 1918, seeing action at Gallipoli, in Egypt and in France; awarded MC in 1917 and DSO in 1918. In 1924 he became the first Australian liaison officer with the Cabinet Secretariat in London, but abandoned diplomacy for politics in 1931 and sat as a United Australia Party member of the Canberra Parliament for nine years and, on the outbreak of World War II, was Minister for Supply and Development. He returned to diplomatic life in 1940 as Australian envoy in Washington, but in March 1942 was brought into the War Cabinet by *Churchill as Minister of State in the Middle East and was in Cairo until October 1943, including the critical months when Rommel threatened to overrun Egypt. From 1944 to 1946 Casey was Governor of Bengal, a time of great tension, culminating in the *Calcutta Riots. Casey returned to Australian political life in 1949 as a Liberal representative in Parliament, and from 1951 to 1960 served as Minister for External Affairs under *Menzies. On retiring from parliamentary life in 1960 he became a life peer, Baron

Casey. He was Governor-General of Australia from 1965 to 1969 and was created a Knight of the Garter at the end of his term of office.

Catchpole, Margaret (1773–1841), Australian transportee: born in Suffolk, near Ipswich, where she became a domestic servant in the household of the Cobbold family of brewers. She was imprisoned for stealing a horse to follow a seaman lover to London, and narrowly escaped hanging. Subsequently she escaped from Ipswich gaol but was recaptured and, in 1801, transported to New South Wales. After completing her sentence of detention she remained in Australia as a nurse and midwife, briefly managing a farm outside Sydney. She was a literate woman and corresponded with her family in Suffolk and with the Cobbolds. In 1845 Richard Cobbold (1797–1877), the novelist rector of Wortham, on the Suffolk–Norfolk border, used her letters as source material for his *Margaret Catchpole*, the first widely-read book in England to describe conditions of life in colonial Australia.

Cavendish-Bentinck, Lord William (1774–1839), first Governor-General of India: born in London, the second son of the third Duke of Portland. From 1792 to 1814 he served in the army, seeing action in the Netherlands, with Britain's French and Russian allies in central Europe, on the retreat to Corunna, and in Sicily, Spain and Genoa. In 1803 he was appointed Governor of Madras but was criticized, and in 1807 recalled, for having imposed a ban on sepoy beards and turbans, thereby provoking in 1806 a grave mutiny at Velore. In 1827, however, he became Governor-General of Bengal and carried through such beneficial reforms in the financial system, the judiciary and the social system that it was natural for him to be appointed Governor-General of India in 1833. He campaigned vigorously against the Thug fanatics and banned *suttee, the burning to death of widows at their husband's funeral ceremony. Cavendish-Bentinck encouraged the employment of native Indians in government posts but, working closely with his friend Macaulay, imposed English as the standard unifying language of the subcontinent. He returned to England in 1835 and for the last two years of his life was Liberal MP for Glasgow.

Cayman Islands: three coral islands in the Caribbean, 150 miles northwest of Jamaica and 400 miles south of Miami. The islands were discovered by Columbus in 1503, formally acknowledged as British by Spain in the Treaty of Madrid of 1670, but not systematically settled until after 1734, when George Town was founded on the largest island, Grand Cayman. The islands long remained a dependency of Jamaica; they were constituted a Crown Colony in July 1859, receiving a constitution as a British Dependent Territory in August 1972. The most profitable industry is tourism, but the islands were famous for turtles, and both sharkskin and turtle products long headed their list of exports.

Central African Federation (1953–63): an attempt to unite Southern Rhodesia (*Zimbabwe), Northern Rhodesia (*Zambia) and Nyasaland (*Malawi) in a common dominion, governed from Salisbury (Harare). The federation was the brain-child of the white leaders in Southern and Northern Rhodesia, Sir Godfrey *Huggins and Sir Roy *Welensky.

Cetewayo (Cetshwayo, *c.*1840–84), Zulu King: succeeded in 1873 to the *Zulu kingdom established half a century earlier by his uncle Shaka (d.1829). Cetewayo was faced by the implacable hostility of the British colonial authorities who wished to advance from Cape Colony into central Africa and therefore needed to eliminate the Zulu state. A full-scale invasion of his territories in January 1879 was met by assegai-armed warriors who virtually wiped out a 1,200-strong column of British troops and auxiliaries at *Isandhlwana. But the Zulus over-stretched their resources in a ferocious attack on the mission station at *Rorke's Drift a few days later and were finally defeated at Ulundi in July 1879. Cetewayo was taken prisoner and held in captivity at Cape of Good Hope and, briefly, in England before being restored as a British puppet ruler in 1883. His former subjects, however, refused to acknowledge his authority and drove him into exile. He died a few weeks later, a broken man, at Ekowa.

Ceylon: island in the Indian Ocean, separated at its most northern tip from the Indian peninsula by the 33-mile-wide Palk Strait. Portuguese traders established settlements on the west and south of the island in 1505 but in 1658 lost them to the Dutch East India Company. The British annexed the island to the Madras Presidency in 1796 and began to penetrate the central highlands, where the Portuguese and the Dutch had left a Sinhalese Kandyan kingdom, dating from the sixth century BC, to flourish undisturbed. Ceylon was declared a British colony in 1802, although it was not until 1815 that the power of the Kandyan Kingdom was finally destroyed. An executive council and a legislative council were introduced in 1831–32. The economy was mainly dependent on the production of *tea and *rubber. The main seaport was Galle until the late 1870s, when the building of a breakwater gave Colombo a vastly superior artificial harbour. British colonial officials were accustomed to consulting the native aristocratic Sinhalese families, but it was not until the period 1918 to 1924 that reforms allowed representatives of all classes of both native peoples (Tamils as well as Sinhalese) to sit in the legislative council. The Japanese occupation of Malaya, Singapore and the Dutch East Indies in 1942 emphasized the strategic importance of Ceylon; Trincomalee became the main base of the Eastern Fleet; and the head-quarters of South East Asia Command were at Kandy from April 1944 until the surrender of Japan. These naval and military developments were matched by mounting political activity among Sinhalese and Tamils. Ceylon was accorded dominion status by the Ceylon Independence Act of 1947 and the island became a self-governing state on 4 February 1948. Until 1956 the United National Party formed the government, but a socialist Sri Lankan Freedom Party, founded by Solomon *Bandaranaike, grew rapidly in strength and was the principal force in the 'People's United Front' which came to power in April 1956 and closed all British military and naval establishments. Although the Front was defeated in the 1965 elections, it recovered the political initiative in 1970 and in 1972 secured the passage of a new constitution which enabled the island to become the 'Democratic Socialist Republic of *Sri Lanka', though retaining membership of the Commonwealth.

Chamberlain, Joseph (1836–1914), British Colonial Secretary: born and educated in London but spent his adult life in Birmingham, where he entered local politics as a social reformer and served as Mayor (1873–75), concentrating on improving housing and sanitation. In 1876 he became a Liberal MP, drastically reorganized the party machine, and entered Gladstone's cabinet as President of the Board of Trade (1880). Since he combined extremely radical views on domestic issues with a strong imperialistic pride, he found himself at variance with his colleagues, apart from his friend, Charles *Dilke. He resigned from Gladstone's government in 1886 in opposition to the Irish Home Rule Bill. After spending four months in the United States negotiating a treaty over fishing rights off the coasts of Canada and Newfoundland he broadened his horizons with a visit to *Egypt, where he was impressed by the effects on the country of British administration. When Lord *Salisbury formed his third (Conservative–Unionist) government in June 1895, Chamberlain became Colonial Secretary, a post he held until September 1903. He favoured closer links between the home government and the self-governing colonies, successfully piloting the *Australian Commonwealth Act through Parliament in 1900 and presiding over the Colonial Conferences of 1897 and 1902 in London as a step towards imperial federation. He promoted trade within the Empire, notably exploiting the resources of the West Indies, and also gave attention to improved health services, personally ensuring the establishment of two Schools of Tropical Medicine. He was, however, mainly concerned with the *'scramble for Africa', tightening British control of the *Gold Coast and backing projects by *Rhodes for expansion northwards along the *Cape–to–Cairo route. Allegations that he connived at preparations for the *Jameson Raid of December 1895 were refuted by a Parliamentary Inquiry, although later evidence suggests that he knew and approved of a revolt in Johannesburg aimed at toppling the Transvaal government. He warmly backed the attempts of *Milner to reach an understanding with *Kruger, but could not check the drift towards armed conflict. At the end of the *Boer War in 1902 he visited South Africa to encourage a speedy reconciliation, the first occasion on which a Secretary of State undertook a specifically political mission to any colony. From 1903 onwards Chamberlain supported tariff reform, urging the abandonment of free trade in favour of *imperial preference, but this campaign split the Unionists and weakened his own health. On 11 July 1906 he was paralysed by a stroke and could take no further part in political life. He was the father, by different wives, of both Sir Austen Chamberlain (1863–1937), who as Foreign Secretary won a Nobel Peace Prize in 1925, and of Neville Chamberlain (1869–1940), Prime Minister from May 1937 until May 1940.

Chanak Crisis, 1922. In September 1922 the Turkish Nationalist army under Mustafa Kemal ejected the Greeks from the town of Smyrna (Izmir), which by the Treaty of Sèvres had been placed under Greek control for five years, pending a plebiscite on the city's future. Kemal's victory challenged other aspects of the peace settlement, notably the demilitarization of the Dardanelles, around which a neutral zone 50 miles deep had been established by the victorious allied Great Powers (Britain, France, Italy). The zone was protected by a small British force with headquarters at Canakkale, then generally called 'Chanak'. When Kemal's troops reached the approaches to Chanak the British Prime Minister, Lloyd George, was prepared to risk war with nationalist Turkey in order to uphold the peace settlement. But an appeal by *Churchill, as Colonial Secretary, for military help from 'the Empire' revealed the determination of the dominion governments that London should no longer settle issues of war and peace for the Commonwealth as a whole. Australia, South Africa and Canada refused to support British policy over Chanak; only New Zealand and Newfoundland, reluctantly, promised troops. The crisis passed without a war, thanks largely to the moderation of Britain's military and civilian representatives at Chanak and in Istanbul; and, after discussions at Mudanya, a revised treaty with Turkey was concluded at Lausanne. The Chanak Crisis (which led to the immediate downfall of Lloyd George) had two interconnected consequences for the Commonwealth as a whole: an emphasis by the dominion prime ministers at the Imperial Conference of 1923 on the right of the overseas governments to conduct independent foreign policies; and the creation in July 1925 of the post of 'Secretary of State for Dominion Affairs', to whom cabinet responsibility for 'the autonomous communities within the Empire' would be transferred from the Colonial Secretary.

Chifley, (Joseph) Ben(edict) (1885–1951), Australian Prime Minister: born at Bathurst in New South Wales; he became an engine driver on NSW Railways and was a militant trade unionist before entering federal politics, sitting as a Labor member of the House of Representatives (1928–31 and 1940–51). After a year in Parliament he became Minister of Defence, and on his return to the House was rapidly advanced by the Labor Prime Minister, John *Curtin. He was Treasurer from 1941 to

Chinese labourers

1949, responsible in 1942 for introducing Australia's first uniform system of income tax. As he had served as Minister of Post-War Construction from 1942 to 1945 it was natural that he should inherit the premiership on Curtin's death in July 1945. The Chifley government increased social services, maintained full employment, encouraged immigration, and nationalized Qantas but failed to nationalize the banks. His humour and warmth of personality made him popular with traditional Labor voters, but his failure to check the mounting Communist influence among dockers and miners alarmed many wavering supporters and he was defeated by *Menzies in the general election of December 1949. He remained Leader of the Opposition until his death.

Chinese labourers. The population of China, which had already doubled in the course of the eighteenth century, jumped from 275 million in 1795 to over 400 million by 1850, a growth unaccompanied by any increase in the amount of land under cultivation. Inevitably, over-population led to emigration, in the first instance to south-east Asia but subsequently across the Pacific and Indian Oceans. The principal British colonies affected by this migration were the *Straits Settlements on the Malay peninsula, and *Singapore in particular. By 1911 more than a third of the population of Malaya was Chinese; when Singapore fell in 1942 there were more Chinese in the city and island than native Malayans. Most Chinese in Malaya were employed in the rubber plantations, but some worked alongside Indian immigrants to develop local commercial enterprises.

Elsewhere, however, the Chinese were almost invariably employed as labourers ('coolies') supporting white adventurers. They came to New South Wales and Victoria in 1852/3, participating in the *gold rush to Bathurst, Bendigo and Ballarat; and in the 1860s they made their way to the new Queensland diggings. The threat of a Chinese 'flood' induced the colonial legislatures to seek to impose a ban on all Asian newcomers, foreshadowing the 'White Australia' policy of the *Immigration Restriction Act of 1901.

Gold also brought Chinese labourers to Canada, the first influx travelling north from San Francisco to British Columbia in 1852. They came in greater numbers ten years later but by 1871 there were still only 1,500 Chinese labourers in the province. Attempts by British Columbia to legislate against the Chinese were disallowed by the Federal Government in Ottawa, despite provincial protests that their numbers were increasing rapidly (to 4,000 in 1881). The need for swift work on the *Canadian Pacific Railway led in 1882 to the recruitment of 10,000 coolies, shipped to Esquimalt from Hong Kong, and a further 7,000 from Kwantung Province followed; the coolies received a mere $1 a day. Some were also exploited as strike-breakers in the coal mines at Nanaimo in 1883, a usage which intensified the anti-Chinese prejudice of the white labourers. As the railway neared completion in 1885, the *Macdonald government in Ottawa gave way to provincial pressure and imposed a 'head tax' of $50 each on Chinese immigrants, payable on arrival. Although this measure cut immigration, racial clashes continued and in 1887 there was a grave anti-Chinese riot in Vancouver. By the turn of the century there were 14,000 Chinese in British Columbia, and the 'head tax' imposed in 1885 was doubled. It was raised to $500 in 1903 in a further attempt to check immigration. But deep feeling remained: in September 1907 the 'Asiatic Exclusion League' ransacked the Chinese districts of Vancouver, causing more than $30,000-worth of damage. Eventually, in 1923, the Immigration Act specifically excluded all Chinese settlers from Canada.

Although the employment of cheap Chinese labour to work the Rand mines in the annexed *Transvaal caused an outcry in Britain, in 1903 Balfour's Conservative government in London authorized the recruitment of up to 100,000 Chinese coolies to be shipped from Hong Kong to Durban. However, since Natal had long kept out unwanted Asian immigrants by imposing a language proficiency test, they were treated as indentured labour, with no immigrant rights of settlement, and were housed in strictly guarded compounds. By December 1904 some 20,000 of these coolies were reported to be working in the Rand mines, under conditions hardly distinguishable from slavery. The scheme was condemned by Australia, New Zealand and Canada and vigorously attacked in Britain by the Liberal Opposition and the embryonic Labour Party. The issue contributed to the Conservative–Unionist electoral defeat of January 1906. The incoming Liberal government stopped all further recruiting of Chinese labourers but could not annul the contracts under which 47,000 coolies were by then working underground. Not until January 1910 were the last Rand labourers shipped home to China.

Despite the indignation aroused by this episode, during World War I Chinese coolies were again recruited to serve in Europe as heavy labourers, and housed under primitive conditions. Some 1,600 Chinese died in France or Flanders, and in February 1917 more than 500 were drowned when the ship carrying them to Marseilles was torpedoed in the Mediterranean. By the autumn of 1918 a Chinese Labour Corps of almost 100,000 men was supporting Haig's armies on the Western Front.

Chipewyans: an *Athabascan speaking tribal group, originally settled between the tundra and the boreal woodland north of the Churchill River in present-day Manitoba. Their menfolk were tough hunters of caribou and were notorious for treating women as lowly animals. Some 5,000 Chipewyans survive.

Chisholm, Caroline (1808–77), pioneer Australian social worker: born Caroline Jones in England, near Northampton. At the age of 22 she married Captain Alexander Chisholm, an officer in the East India

Company's army, and for eight years lived in Madras, where she founded a school for the daughters of European soldiers. In 1838 the Chisholms settled at Windsor, New South Wales, but Captain Chisholm returned to military life in India in 1840. Caroline, however, stayed in New South Wales, working in Sydney for the well-being of impoverished new immigrants, travelling with families into the outback, and – with the backing of the Governor of New South Wales, Sir George Gipps (1791–1847) – finding accommodation for several thousand women and children while their husbands sought employment. She returned to England in 1846, with some 600 statements from immigrants about their life in New South Wales. This material, and her own experiences, she used to increase knowledge in Britain about the colony; she gave evidence before two parliamentary committees. In 1849 she founded the Family Colonization Loan Society, which chartered ships to bring settlers to Australia. By 1854 she was in Victoria, visiting the gold fields, where she arranged improved shelter for the diggers. She remained in Australia until 1866, opening a girls' school in Sydney in 1862. Financial difficulties forced her to return to England, where she received an annual Civil List pension of £100 for the last eleven years of her life.

Christianity in the Commonwealth. Although there are more Muslims and Hindus in the Commonwealth than Christians, the pervading religious influence on the expanding Empire in the last two centuries came from Western Christendom. In India, Sri Lanka and Canada Jesuit missions antedated the coming of the British, as did the Capuchins in Trinidad and Belize (which like Grenada and St Lucia remain mainly Roman Catholic in their religious observance). Early colonial charters usually emphasized the duty of settlers to sustain Anglican teachings, and in 1698 new East India Company Statutes stipulated that chaplains be sent out to the Company's stations prepared to learn Portuguese, the common language of Christian traders in the subcontinent. The Archbishop of Goa, a Portuguese colony, was papal 'Patriarch of the East Indies'; his authority was only diminished after 1884, when a Roman Catholic hierarchy was established in British India. But the Company, and later the army, brought Anglicanism to India: St Mary's Church, Madras (1680) was followed by Company churches in Calcutta (1709) and Bombay (1718). Nineteenth-century *hill stations copied English parish churches, architecturally and liturgically. In 1880 the Anglican 'Brotherhood of the Epiphany' established a *mission house in Calcutta, the nucleus of the Oxford Mission to India (and Bangladesh) which, with an indigenous sisterhood ('Handmaids of Christ'), continues relief work in districts hit by famine and leprosy. Non-Anglican influences were at work, too. The Salvation Army was in India as early as 1882; and in 1908 the Presbyterian, Congregationalist and Dutch Reformed churches south of Bombay formed a 'South India United Church'. In September 1947 this United Church and the South Indian Methodists joined four Anglican dioceses (Madras, Tinnevelly, Travancore, Dornakel) in the 'Church of South India', a Christian union which preserved internal diversity but was, in 1955, accorded 'limited inter-communion' by the English episcopate.

When Thomas Middleton (1769–1822) became the first Bishop of Calcutta in 1814 his diocese also included Ceylon, Malaya and New South Wales; and in that same year it was from New South Wales that *Samuel Marsden took Christianity to New Zealand. The *First Fleet was accompanied by a chaplain, Richard Johnson (1753–1827), who built the earliest Christian church in Australia (1794). William Broughton (1788–1853) – who in 1831–32 founded King's School, Parramatta, as a pioneer English public school overseas – became first Bishop of Australia (1836), while the Cambridge tractarian George Selwyn (1809–78) became Bishop of New Zealand (1841). By the end of the century there were twenty dioceses in Australia and nine in New Zealand. Many Anglican provinces overseas reflected the differences of worship current at the time in England: thus Sydney remained 'low' church Evangelical and Adelaide – like Christchurch in New Zealand's South Island – conventionally 'broad' church, while Brisbane became 'high' church Tractarian in tradition, founding the 'Bush Brotherhood' in 1899 as an Anglo-Catholic mission to serve the Queensland outback. But it was the Methodists of Australia who sent the first missions to the Solomon Islands (1879) and co-operated with Anglicans in despatching the earliest missionaries to New Guinea (1890). In New South Wales suspicion of Irish immigrants, free or convict, had delayed acceptance of a Vicar-General for Roman Catholics in Australia until 1836, when the Yorkshireman William Ullathorne (1806–89), a Benedictine priest descended from Sir Thomas More, made his second pastoral journey to Sydney. In Western Australia, in 1847, the Benedictines set up a mission station for the conversion of aborigines at Moore River, 82 miles north of Perth; it became the Abbey of New Norcia in 1867. In the Australian Census of 1986, while a quarter of the population acknowledged no religious faith at all, the largest denomination was Roman Catholic (26 per cent), with Anglicans some quarter of a million behind (23.9 per cent) and a growing number of Orthodox (2.7 per cent). A Roman Catholic bishopric was established in New Zealand in 1848, but the predominant creed there remains Anglican (22.5 per cent in 1986), ahead of Presbyterians (17.6 per cent) and Roman Catholics (14.8 per cent).

During the late eighteenth century bishoprics were established in the American colonies and in Nova Scotia (1787), but attempts to build up Anglicanism in Canada on the Church of England model were soon abandoned. A 1981 survey of Canadian Christians recorded some 45 per cent Roman Catholic, 15 per cent 'United Church of Canada' (a 1925 union of Methodists, Congregationalists and some Presbyterians), 9 per cent 'Canadian Church' (episcopal Anglican), 3 per cent Presbyterian, 2.2 per cent Lutheran. Here, too, the number of Orthodox is rising (1.2 per cent); but the only staunchly Orthodox Commonwealth country remains *Cyprus.

In Africa, missionaries from London were working among the native inhabitants before the British took over *Cape Colony; there they found the Calvinist Dutch Reformed Church already a source of strength to the Boers. Significantly, the CMS (Church Missionary Society, established in London in 1799) was originally called the 'Society for Missions in Africa and the East'. Evangelical Christians were prominent in the movement against *slavery: West Indian planters remained hostile to the Established Church, though bishoprics were set up in 1824 for Barbados and Jamaica and an Anglican 'Province of the West Indies' followed in 1883. In Africa the Evangelical CMS made the most headway; the first black Anglican bishop was Samuel Adjayi Crowther (c.1805–91), a liberated Yoruba slave educated by the CMS and consecrated in 1857 to serve Sierra Leone and south-western Nigeria. In Zanzibar from 1864 and later in what are now Zambia and Malawi, UMCA (the Universities Mission to Central Africa) was active in sweeping away slavery. In England a 'Colonial Bishoprics' Council', established in London in 1841, was followed in 1867 by the earliest Lambeth Conference, a (normally) decennial gathering of Anglican bishops from throughout the world under the presidency of the Archbishop of Canterbury. In South Africa, the greatest successes among non-whites were achieved by the Methodists, though as early as 1910 bishops in the House of Lords supported protests against the inclusion of a colour bar clause in the constitution of the new *South Africa, thus foreshadowing the opposition of most Christian churches to *apartheid. The Vatican, long accustomed to special status in Portuguese, Belgian and French colonies, did not appoint a 'Vicar Apostolic to Catholic Missions in British Colonial Africa' until 1927, although by that date the 'White Fathers', a basically French society which had opened a mission station south of Lake Nyasa in 1889, had more than 500 village schools in Northern Rhodesia.

In Africa and New Zealand there have also been manifestations of an indigenous Christianity. Some African 'churches' began as breakaway prayer groups from Evangelical missions: Mothoagae in Botswana, 1902; Jemisimihan Jehu-Appiah's 'Army of the Cross of Christ' in the Gold Coast (Ghana), 1919; Josiah Oshitelu's Aladura 'Church of the Lord' in Nigeria, 1925. The Lumpa Church of Alice Lenshina, a prophetess exalted by a spiritual vision in September 1953, spread rapidly through the Chinsali district of Northern Rhodesia until it was bloodily suppressed as an allegedly anarchic force in 1964, on the eve of Zambian independence. Similarly, Alice Lakwena's militant 'Holy Spirit Battalion' aroused deep suspicion in *Uganda in 1986–87, as did the 'Tent of the Living God' sect in Kenya in 1990. By contrast, the New Zealand

Anglican church has treated the two indigenous Maori adaptations of Christianity, Ratana and Ringatu, with tolerance; a Maori churchman, F. A. Bennett, was consecrated as assistant bishop in 1928, to guide and interpret his people's spiritual needs.

Churchill, Winston Leonard Spencer (1874–1965), British Prime Minister: son of Lord Randolph Churchill (1849–94), who as Indian Secretary in 1884–85 annexed Upper *Burma. Winston was educated at Harrow and Sandhurst before serving with the 4th Hussars on the North-West Frontier and the 21st Lancers at *Omdurman. He went out to the *Boer War as a reporter and was taken prisoner but escaped. From 1900 to 1904 he was a Unionist MP for Oldham, but opposed *tariff reform and became a Liberal. As Colonial Under-Secretary he made an extensive journey in Africa in 1907, including a visit to pioneer settlements in Kenya. He gained cabinet experience as a reforming President of the Board of Trade (1908–10), as Home Secretary (1910–11), and as First Lord of the Admiralty (1911–May 1915). In World War I he promoted a strategy for defeating Turkey by forcing the Dardanelles, a plan which led to the disastrous *Gallipoli campaign. After six months as Chancellor of the Duchy of Lancaster Churchill left the Government, and in 1916 commanded a fusilier battalion on the Western Front. He was Minister of Munitions (1917–18) and War and Air Secretary (1919–21), pressing for armed intervention to check the spread of Russian Bolshevism. As Colonial Secretary in 1921–22 he visited Cairo and Jerusalem for protracted discussions over Middle Eastern affairs, especially Britain's role in *Palestine. He was out of Parliament from November 1922 to October 1924, then rejoined the Conservative–Unionists and served as Chancellor of the Exchequer (1924–29). Then for the following ten years he was out of office, criticizing successive governments for contemplating concessions to *Gandhi at the *Round Table Conferences of 1931 and (later) for failing to meet the military challenge of Nazi Germany. When World War II began he returned to the cabinet as First Lord of the Admiralty, and became Prime Minister of the wartime coalition formed on 10 May 1940. His personal prestige, courage and inspiring oratory won him acceptance in the United Kingdom as a great war leader. He remained a firm believer in 'the Empire', but he was criticized in Australia and New Zealand for concentrating on European issues, for using Commonwealth troops in distant theatres of war while their homelands were threatened, and for failing to check the rapid advance of the Japanese in 1941–42 which led to the loss of Hong Kong, Malaya and Singapore and the invasion of New Guinea. After defeat in the General Election of 1945 he was Leader of the Opposition to the two Labour governments of *Attlee (1945–51), and he strongly opposed the *Indian Independence Act of 1947. In his second Ministry (1951–55) he was increasing out of touch with a changed world order, though a strong supporter of Nato and of collective partnership against the menace of Communism in both Europe nd Asia. Although he declined the dukedom offered him in 1945, he was created a Knight of the Garter in 1953, the year in which he also received the Nobel Prize for Literature, for his historical studies. He remained an MP until a few months before his death, in January 1965.

Cinema, as a mass entertainment art form using professional actors, originated in Paris in the late 1890s but soon spread to the USA and Britain. As early as 1903 the British North Borneo Company produced a short documentary about the tobacco and rubber plantations under its jurisdiction. The 'educational' advantage of film as a means of spreading the idea of Empire was raised at the Imperial Conferences of 1926 and 1930, and from 1928 the *Empire Marketing Board in London sponsored a film unit: the distinguished Scottish director John Grierson (1898–1972) made his pioneer documentary on deep sea fishermen, *Drifters*, for this unit in 1929: other Marketing Board documentaries included *Song of Ceylon* (1934) – a beautiful forty-minute film of the island, produced by Grierson but directed by Basil Wright and ostensibly promoting tea – and *Cargo from Jamaica* (1935), promoting Caribbean sugar. Some feature films combining adventure, entertainment and enlightenment received material help from the government in London or the colonial authorities: among these were four famous British films directed by Sir Alexander Korda (1893–1956): *Sanders of the River* (1935); *Elephant Boy* (1937); *The Drum* (1938); and *The Four Feathers* (1939).

Among the overseas dominions, Australia took an early lead in film production and in the building of cinemas – there was 'a picture palace' for every 4,400 people as early as 1927. Raymond Longford (1878–1959), a Melbourne man by birth, directed – and often acted in – silent feature films from 1909 until the coming of 'talkies' in 1929: some were pioneer epics, including *Margaret Catchpole* (1911) and *The Mutiny on the Bounty* (1916), while *The Sentimental Bloke* (1919) and *Ginger Mick* (1920) became vintage classics of Australian life. Hollywood competition led to the virtual collapse of the native film industry in the 1930s; it revived in collaboration with the UK's Ealing Studios immediately after World War II, when the success of *The Overlanders* (1946) made Chips Rafferty (1909–71) Australia's first international star. Rafferty's later films included *Eureka Stockade* (1947), *The Sundowners* (1960), and *Outback* (1970). English directors made several distinguished Australian films, among them Michael Powell's *They're a Weird Mob* (1966) and *Age of Consent* (1969), and Nicolas Roeg's *Walkabout* (1970). In the 1970s two outstanding Australian directors emerged: Peter Weir (1944–   ) with *Picnic at Hanging Rock* (1975), *The Last Wave* (1977) and *Gallipoli* (1981); and Fred Schepisi (1939–   ) with *The Devil's Playground* (1976), *The*

Chant of Jimmie Blacksmith (1978) and *A Cry in the Dark* (1988). Bruce Beresford's *Breaker Morant* (1979) dealt with the court martial of an Australian in the Boer War; Gillian Armstrong's *My Brilliant Career* (1979) evoked the outback at the turn of the century; George Miller's *The Man from Snowy River* (1982) broke box office records in Australia; Peter Faiman's *Crocodile Dundee* (1986) made Paul Hogan a world star. In 1992 Baz Luhrmann's *Strictly Ballroom* found romantic comedy, not in the bush, but in the suburban pursuits of 'new' and 'old' Australians.

The Indians became the Commonwealth's most prolific film-makers: in 1979 the Bombay studios produced 714 feature films, each running for an hour or more. The earliest Indian film to win wide recognition was *Aan* (1949), directed by Mehboob (Ramjankhan Mehboobkhan, 1907–64), which ran for 3 hrs 10 mins but was cut by an hour for the English version (*Savage Princess*, 1952). Mehboob's *Mother India* (1956) and *A Handful of Grain* (1959) were also shown abroad. Satyajit Ray (1921–92) began directing in 1953 and won acclaim at Cannes for his earliest feature film, *Pather Panchali* (1955), the first of a rural trilogy completed by *Aparajito* (1956) and *Apu Sansar* (1959). His *Charulata*, or *The Lonely Wife* (1964) gently satirized the Victorian India of the 1870s. In *Ashani Sanket*, or *Distant Thunder* (1973) Ray analyses the reactions of a Brahmin to the Bengal famine of 1942, and in *Jana-Aranya*, or *The Middleman* (1975) he depicts the corrosive influence of the experience of commerce on the ideals of a young graduate. His *The Chess Players* (1977), set in Mutiny Lucknow, used chessboard symbolism to enhance the power politics of annexation. Ray's *Ganashtru* (1979) moved Ibsen's *Enemy of the People* to modern India. Ismail Merchant (1936–   ) began producing films in 1961, in partnership with the American director James Ivory and the Polish refugee Ruth Prawer Jhabvala: the partnership was responsible for many westernized films including *Shakespeare Wallah* (1965), *Bombay Talkie* (1970) and *Heat and Dust* (1983). Aparna Sen directed *36 Chowringhee Lane* (1981), a study of Anglo-Indian spinsterhood in modern Calcutta.

The Canadian film industry long specialized in making documentaries, under government patronage. A Motion Picture Bureau was set up in 1921 and its sponsorship was developed further by the National Film Board, established in May 1939 and headed until 1946 by John Grierson. By 1952 Norman McLaren was winning international recognition for his presentation of the Canadian scene. The National Film Board experimented with two feature-length films (one English, one French) in 1945, but not until the 1970s did the film industry become commercially viable. Early successes included Gilles Carle's *La Tête de Normande St-Onge* and *La Vraie Nature de Bernadette*, and Silvio Narrizzano's *Why Shoot the Teacher?* (1976), a study of Saskatchewan in the early 1930s. The Canadian-born director Ted Kotcheff (1931–   ) made feature films in England and Australia before *The Apprenticeship of Duddy Kravitz* (1974), about Jewish Montreal in the late 1940s. Denys Arcand's *Jesus of Montreal* (1989) and Michel Brut's *Paper Wedding* (1990), an exposure of the corrupt manipulation of immigration laws, again showed the vitality of the French-Canadian film industry.

In several parts of the Commonwealth the spread of *television stimulated nascent film industries. The New Zealand Film Commission encouraged the production of Geoff Murphy's *Goodbye Pork Pie* (1980) and Sam Pilsbury's *The Scarecrow* (1981) but international recognition came with Jane Campion's *Angel at the Table* (1990) and the Oscar-winning *The Piano* (1993). A Nigerian film industry was established in 1972, and some seventeen feature films were produced there over the following twenty years. A flourishing industry has also proved profitable in Hong Kong, where Sir Run Run Shaw (1907–   ), a veteran film-maker from Singapore, created Shaw Movietown at Sai Kung in the New Territories and by the late 1980s was turning out nearly 200 films a year, mainly for the two television channels he owned.

Civil disobedience: a refusal to obey laws or pay taxes, thus constituting a non-violent means of forcing concessions from a hostile government. The tactic was first used by Mohandas *Gandhi in 1907 in the Transvaal against the racially discriminatory laws of South Africa. On his return to India Gandhi developed passive resistance further, notably in opposition to the *Rowlatt Acts of 1920 and in defiance of the salt tax in 1931.

Clarke, Marcus Andrew Hislop (1846–81), Australian journalist and author: born in London, the son of a barrister. He emigrated to Victoria at the age of 17 and worked in a bank and a sheep station before becoming a free-lance journalist and eventually a librarian. In 1870 he spent a month in Tasmania, collecting oral legends from the convict era. From this experience he wrote *His Natural Life*, the misadventures in a brutal society of a transportee, innocent of any crime. The tale appeared as a serial in the *Australian Journal* (1870–72) and later in novel form as *For the Term of his Natural Life* (1874). Although Clarke wrote four other books concerned with the 'early days' of a 'young country', none could match the enduring fame of his first novel.

Clipper ships. Technically clippers were long, low schooners with three-masted square rigs and a sculpted hull, deeper aft than forward and with a raked stern, capable of attaining a speed of 20 knots in good sailing weather. The first genuine clippers were designed in New York in the mid 1840s; some sailed as passenger vessels on the Atlantic run and (in 1852/3) from England to Australia. But the name is most closely associated with the tea trade from China: in 1866, five clippers raced the 16,000 miles from Foochow to London in 99 days, with the first of the new season's tea crop. The coming of steam and the opening in 1869 of the

Suez Canal heralded the end of tea clippers, but the two most famous ships, *Thermopylae* (launched 1868) and *Cutty Sark* (1869), were converted to wool clippers: between 1883 and 1895 they sailed in competition with seven or eight other clippers from Sydney or Newcastle, NSW to London with cargoes of *wool. In 1885 the *Cutty Sark* made the voyage home from Sydney in a record 73 days. Since 1957 the *Cutty Sark* has been a museum ship at Greenwich, south London.

Clive, Robert (1725–74), Governor of Bengal: born near Market Drayton; entered the *East India Company and reached Madras in 1744 as a penniless clerk. He was taken prisoner when a French force seized Madras in 1746 but escaped and became a junior officer in charge of Indian sepoys, rising rapidly in rank after showing bravery while besieging Pondicherry in 1748. In 1751 he was allowed to put into practice an enterprising initiative by which he marched from Madras to seize Arcot, the capital of the Carnatic. Although commanding no more than 230 men, he held Arcot through seven and a half weeks of siege by ten thousand troops and, with reinforcements, helped defeat French plans for expansion of their interests in India. After two years in England, he returned to Bombay in 1755 as a colonel. After the Nawab of Bengal, Suraj-ud-Dowlah, seized the trading station of Calcutta in June 1756, Clive was sent to avenge the *Black Hole atrocity and defeated the Nawab at *Plassey (23 June 1757). For the following three years Clive was effectively the ruler of Bengal, establishing the supremacy of the East India Company, with Mir Jafir serving as a puppet Nawab. In 1760 Clive returned to England, entered politics and received an Irish peerage, as Baron Clive of Plassey. But by 1764 the Company's administration of India showed such incompetence that Clive was sent back, as Governor of Bengal and Commander-in-Chief (1765). He swiftly reformed the administration, restored military discipline and obtained from Mir Jafir formal recognition of the Company's overlordship in the province. Clive's health gave way and he returned finally to England in 1766. Sustained attacks by political enemies at Westminster led to a parliamentary inquiry into Clive's handling of the East India Company's affairs. The inquiry cleared Clive, but during the long struggle he became dependent on opium, and committed suicide soon after the final vindication of his name.

Cobb & Co.: coach firm. Freeman Cobb (1830–78) was born in Brewster, Massachusetts and in 1849 was employed by American coaching lines during the California Gold Rush. In May 1853 he went to Melbourne and with two other Americans formed a partnership, known as Cobb and Co., which began a regular coach service between central Melbourne and its port in July 1853. The firm began operating an 'American Telegraph Line of Coaches' between Castlemaine, Bendigo and Melbourne. Freeman

Coffee

Cobb sold the business in May 1856 and returned to America, but the name 'Cobb and Co.' was retained as the business spread to New South Wales and Queensland under the management of James Rutherford (1827–1911), also an American. Rutherford ran the company in Australia until his death: the last Cobb and Co. coach ran from Sulat to Yuleba on 14 August 1924. Freeman Cobb himself left Massachusetts for South Africa in 1871 and established a new 'Cobb and Co.', which ran mail coaches between Port Elizabeth and Kimberley for five years at the height of the *diamond rush. Another of his original partners in Melbourne, James Swanton, extended Cobb and Co.'s operations to New Zealand in 1871, with services in the Taranaki area of North Island.

Coffee. The first coffee to be drunk in England (during the 1650s) probably arrived with travellers returning from the Ottoman Balkans, but the earliest regular trade in coffee was organized by the East India Company, with shipments from their Red Sea trading post at Mocha (now the seaport of Al Mukha in Yemen). Within the Empire and Commonwealth, centres of concentrated coffee production have changed, often because of natural disasters, particularly drought and disease. *Jamaica appears to have been the first British colony to export coffee to the London market, a trade recently revived. By 1826 *Ceylon was yielding a good crop and produced fine quality coffee until about 1870, when a fungoid disease ruined cultivation throughout the island. Malaya was exporting coffee by 1895. In the early twentieth century there was a rapid growth of production in tropical Africa (where coffee is now grown in 21 countries). The outstanding development was in *Kenya where, though the experiments of the first white settlers often overcropped fertile land and left it exhausted, the area under coffee plantation increased from 32 hectares in 1905 to some 11,260 hectares in 1920 and to 39,000 hectares by 1930. Until 1947 the *Kikuyu were not allowed to grow coffee, a grievance which contributed to *Mau Mau unrest: the colonial authorities maintained that fragmented holdings were liable to disease (which might spread to white farms) and made the harvesting of a crop for export difficult. In both modern Kenya and *Tanzania this problem has been met by the spread of co-operative settlements. Coffee remains the chief crop export in Tanzania and *Uganda. Other Commonwealth countries successfully exporting coffee include *Ghana and *Sierra Leone. Coffee cultivation is spreading in *Zimbabwe and in three Indian states (Karnataka; Kerala; Tamil Nadu). It is a leading crop in *Papua New Guinea and is also cultivated in *Vanuatu.

Colenso, John William (1814–83), first Anglican Bishop of Natal. Colenso was a Cornishman, from St Austell, who gained great distinction as a mathematician at St John's College, Cambridge and taught mathematics at Harrow School before becoming vicar of Forncett St

Mary, Norfolk in 1846. When the See of Natal was created in 1853 he was appointed bishop, to work among the *Zulus. Colenso rejected conventional *missionary attitudes. Since polygamy was traditional in African society, he refused to insist on monogamy as a prerequisite of acceptance of Christianity. He taught printing to the Zulus and was responsible for a pioneer Zulu grammar, a dictionary, and translations of the New Testament and four books of the Old Testament. As a theologian he advocated applying critical scholarship to the Old Testament, and developed doctrines of universal atonement which his metropolitan bishop, Robert Gray of Cape Town, denounced as heretical, deposing Colenso in 1863. An appeal by Colenso to the Judicial Committee of the Privy Council challenging Gray's jurisdiction in Natal was upheld and, though Gray excommunicated Colenso in 1866, he remained in office and was allowed by a series of court rulings to retain control of the see's funds and endowments until his death. In 1875 he exposed the maltreatment of the native peoples by colonial officials, whom he considered corrupt: he denounced the Zulu War four years later. The Zulus respected Colenso, whom they honoured as '*Sobantu*' (father of the people). His daughter Harriette Colenso (1847–1932) championed South Africa's blacks for another half-century.

Colombo Plan. Commonwealth Foreign Ministers, meeting at Colombo in January 1950, proposed that the richer members of the Commonwealth should provide money, advice and technical training for the poorer members in southern and south-eastern Asia. Details of the plan were settled by a meeting of the Commonwealth Consultative Committee, also in Colombo, in February 1951. The Australian Prime Minister, *Menzies, insisted that the character of the Plan be changed in order to secure American backing, in the hope that this would check the spread of Communism. What had begun as the initiative of seven Commonwealth nations was transformed into a source of technical assistance and economic development between 26 states, 15 of them outside the Commonwealth. Headquarters were established in Sri Lanka, at Colombo itself. The 'Colombo Plan Staff College for Technical Education' functioned in Singapore from 1975 to 1987, when it moved to the Philippines.

Colonial assemblies were established in Virginia (1619), Massachusetts (1632), Connecticut (1639), *Nova Scotia (1758) and *Prince Edward Island (1773), and in the older Caribbean colonies, notably *Barbados and *Jamaica, where the Houses of Assembly had considerable influence in shaping laws to preserve slavery and the slave trade. Composition of the assemblies varied considerably; their powers were limited to matters of local taxation, customary law and defence. In the Caribbean possessions settlers and planters reproduced the English structure of vestry meetings. When *Grenada, *Dominica and *St Vincent were acquired from the French, they too received colonial assemblies (by 1775). The existence of these assemblies proved of such value to the Americans in the War of Independence that colonial policy turned against local legislatures in favour of direct, paternal control from London; this trend delayed the further spread of representative institutions in *Canada and ensured that when *Trinidad (1802) and *St Lucia (1814) came under British sovereignty they were administered as Crown Colonies, with legislative councils nominated by executive officials appointed by the home government. The post-emancipation social conflicts in Jamaica led to the abolition of the Jamaica Assembly in December 1865; a local legislature survived in Barbados, although as late as 1937 only 2.5 per cent of the Barbadian population had the vote. Thereafter progress towards self-governing assemblies in the Caribbean was slow until after 1944, when Jamaica became the first West Indian colony with a House of Representatives elected by full adult suffrage.

In Australia, nominated Legislative Councils were set up for *New South Wales in 1823, Van Diemen's Land (*Tasmania) in 1825, *Western Australia in 1832 and *South Australia in 1842, but there were no elected delegates before 1843, and then only to a few seats in the New South Wales assembly. Bicameral parliamentary assemblies followed in 1856 for *Victoria, New South Wales, South Australia and Tasmania, in 1859 for *Queensland, and in 1890 for Western Australia. In *New Zealand there was no colonial assembly prior to the institution in 1852 of a House of Representatives, elected for five years on a franchise which, though without explicit racial bias, effectively excluded Maoris by requiring a property qualification. *Cape Colony was granted a representative 'House of Assembly' by Letters Patent in 1850, and a partially representative assembly was established in *Natal in 1856; in all the African assemblies, membership was strictly limited to residents of European descent. *Newfoundland, a colonial possession since 1583, remained too sparsely populated to warrant a legislative assembly until 1832: responsible government followed in 1855.

Colonial Development Corporation: established during the first Attlee Labour government by the Overseas Resources Development Act (1948), in order to promote the welfare of colonial peoples and increase their productive capacity and trade. The CDC's structure and activities were based on several earlier projects, notably the Colonial Development Fund of 1929, which had provided grants or loans for underdeveloped territories, particularly in the West Indies. In 1963 the name of the CDC was changed to *Commonwealth Development Corporation.

Colonial Land and Emigration Board: set up as a sub-department of the *Colonial Office in 1840 after a Parliamentary Select Committee in

1836 reported on settlement policy in the new colonies. The Waste Lands Act of 1842 imposed a minimum price for the purchase of land in the colonies, with a stipulation that half the sum should go to the Emigration Board to provide funds for settlers to travel to Australia and New Zealand. The Board functioned until 1878.

Colonial Laws Validity Act (1865): defined and developed the principle, hurriedly established in the Colonial Laws Confirmation Act, that Parliament in Westminster should have the right to declare invalid any laws passed by a legislative assembly in a dominion or colony overseas which ran counter to British statute law. The continued existence of the Act aroused resentment in Australia and Canada. The Statute of *Westminster in 1931 formally declared the Act inoperative.

Colonial Office. The first central administrative body for colonies was the Commission of Trade, established by Charles I at his accession in 1625. Nine years later it was renamed 'Commission for Foreign Plantations', generally known as the 'Laud Commission' after its chairman, Archbishop Laud. In 1643 this body was succeeded by the 'Parliamentary Commission for Plantations', duly replaced in 1660 by privy councillors who formed the 'Lords of Trade and Plantations', and subsequently functioning as the 'Board of Trade and Plantations' from 1696 to 1782. Colonial affairs were the business of the Home Office from 1782 until 1801, when an embryonic Colonial Office was established at 14 Downing Street, although there was no designated *Colonial Secretary until 1854. From 1825 and for most of the nineteenth century the Colonial Office was divided into five departments: General; North America; West Indies; Australia; Africa and Mediterranean. A Dominions Department functioned from 1907 until July 1925, when the new *Dominions Office relieved the CO of responsibility for Australia, Canada, the Irish Free State, New Zealand, Newfoundland, South Africa and Southern Rhodesia. As Crown Colonies moved towards self-government, the CO became increasingly divided administratively: by 1955 there were 30 departments.

In 1812 the Office had a permanent staff of 17 with 7 assistants. This increased to 29 in 1849, but even in 1900 – the peak of the *Chamberlain era – there were only 33 permanent first division civil servants at the CO. Numbers then grew rapidly: an establishment of 125 in 1909; 187 in 1919; and 431 in 1925, on the eve of the creation of the Dominions Office. Continuity in administrative policy was preserved by three influential Permanent Under-Secretaries: Sir James Stephen (1789–1859), who joined the CO in 1825 and was Under-Secretary 1836–47; Sir Frederic Rogers (1811–89, created Baron Blachford 1871), Commissioner of Land and Emigration in the 1840s and 1850s, Under-Secretary 1860–71; Sir Robert Herbert (1831–1905), in office 1871–92.

Colonies, Secretary of State for

The literary dilettante Sir Henry Taylor (1800–86) was a senior civil servant at the CO from 1824 to 1876, specializing in West Indian Affairs and (unpopularly) supporting Governor *Eyre. The CO never handled the affairs of all overseas possessions: the India Office concerned itself with the subcontinent, and also with Malaya until 1866, central Arabia, Mesopotamia (Iraq) and the Gulf until 1921, and Aden until 1937; the Foreign Office administered Cyprus in 1878–80 and was responsible for the Nigerian Protectorates until 1900. The CO remained at 14 Downing Street until 1875, when it moved into a wing of the neo-Italianate building designed by Barry, primarily for the Foreign Office. During World War II some CO departments were housed elsewhere in Victoria (London), and from 1947 until 1966 the Office was in Great Smith Street, mainly in Church House. Plans to build an imposing Colonial Office opposite Westminster Abbey, announced in 1950, never left the drawing-board. The CO merged with the Commonwealth Relations Office to form the *Commonwealth Office in August 1966.

Colonies, Secretary of State for. Ministerial responsibility for colonial affairs was long ill-defined (see *above*). The attempt to impose taxes on the American colonies led in January 1768 to the appointment of a 'Secretary of State for the American Colonies' but the post was abolished by the Establishment Act of 1782, which assigned colonial responsibilities to the Home Secretary; in January 1788 it was in honour of the occupant of this office, Lord Sydney (Thomas Townshend, 1733–1800), that the earliest settlement in Australia was named. But when in July 1794 Henry Dundas became the first Secretary of State for War, the increasing demands of military operations overseas thrust more colonial business onto him than to any other member of Pitt's cabinet: accordingly, in March 1801 Dundas's successor, Lord Hobart, was formally gazetted 'Secretary of State for War *and Colonies*'. Jurisdictional confusion was increased by the existence (from 1665 to 1863) of the 'Secretary-at-War', who was an executive minister responsible for army administration. Several of Hobart's successors considered themselves to be primarily Colonial Secretaries, notably Lord John Russell (1839–41), Lord Stanley (1841–45), and the third Earl (Henry) Grey (1846–52). The departmental union ended in June 1854 when Sir George Grey (1799–1882) was specifically designated Colonial Secretary in Lord Aberdeen's coalition government. Thereafter until 1966 every Colonial Secretary held cabinet rank (except in the small, inner-core War Cabinets of 1916–19 and 1940–45). Among 48 Colonial Secretaries were Henry *Herbert (Lord Carnarvon), Joseph *Chamberlain, Winston *Churchill, Arthur *Creech Jones, Malcolm *Macdonald, Iain *Macleod and Alfred *Milner. The post of Colonial Secretary lapsed in August 1966, the responsibilities passing to a Commonwealth Secretary (see *Commonwealth Office*).

Colony. In constitutional usage, an overseas possession in which the settlements form proprietary domains of the mother country – as opposed to a *dominion, in which a self-governing community freely maintains associations with the United Kingdom (see *Balfour Definition*). Persistent memories of past complaints of exploitation led to the gradual abandonment of the term in the period 1966 to 1982, when the rapid transition of the ex-colonial empire into a loose association of self-governing, independent states was nearing completion. The concept of 'Dependent Territory' replaced 'Crown Colony' in official terminology.

Committee of Imperial Defence. No attempt was made to establish a co-ordinated plan for imperial defence, agreed by the army and navy chiefs, until after the crises in Africa (1896–1902). A Colonial Defence Committee was, however, established during the Eastern Crisis of 1878 when war with Russia seemed likely, and was revived in 1885 for similar reasons. From 1890 onwards individual cabinet ministers occasionally recommended a systematic assessment of the needs and resources of the Empire in case of a major war, but the matter was only taken up urgently in 1902 at the insistence of St John Brodrick, the War Secretary, and Lord Selborne, the First Lord of the Admiralty. Accordingly, in March 1902 the Committee of Imperial Defence was set up by the Balfour government to consider the strategical military and naval needs of the Empire. The Committee consisted of the Prime Minister, the two service ministers, the Lord President of the Council, the Commander-in-Chief of the Army (Chief of the General Staff from 1904), the First Sea Lord, and the heads of naval and military intelligence. The Committee began the process of inter-service collaboration which was to reach a peak during World War II. To stress awareness of commitments to the Empire as a whole, from September 1906 the chief military adviser to the government on land operations and strategy became 'Chief of the Imperial General Staff' (CIGS), a title retained until 1964. Defence questions, especially sea power, dominated the first *Imperial Conference (1911).

Commonwealth. An association of peoples linked by a desire for collective well-being. In the USA the term survives for Virginia, Massachusetts, Pennsylvania and Kentucky. After the execution of Charles I 'England' became 'a Commonwealth or a Free State' on 29 May 1649, reverting to 'Kingdom' at the Restoration of Charles II in 1660. The future Liberal Prime Minister, Lord Rosebery (1847–1929), described the British Empire as 'a Commonwealth of Nations' in a speech at Adelaide on 18 January 1884; his words may have influenced the subsequent preference for the egalitarian 'commonwealth' rather than 'dominion' as the title of the newly federated *Australia. The phrase was also used in 1916 by Lionel *Curtis, for a book advocating a federal union of mother country and dominions. The term 'Imperial Commonwealth' received official sanction at the *Imperial War Conference of 1917, while the *Balfour Definition referred to 'British Commonwealth of Nations' (1926). With the clarification of the concept of *Head of the Commonwealth in 1949 the word 'British' dropped from formal usage. A non-executive *Commonwealth Secretariat was set up in 1965. By January 1995 the Commonwealth formed an association of 51 independent states and their dependencies. Of these states, 17 acknowledged the direct sovereignty of Queen *Elizabeth II; 5 retained their own monarchs; 28 were republics; *Malaysia and *Western Samoa were elective monarchies.

Commonwealth Accord on Southern Africa (1985). In August 1985 the South African Prime Minister, P. W. Botha, reaffirmed the Republic's commitment to *apartheid, rigidly enforced by special 'state of emergency' powers. The suspension of civil rights intensified Commonwealth hostility to apartheid, manifested at the *Commonwealth Heads of Government Conference in Nassau, 16–23 October 1985. The intransigent opposition of Margaret *Thatcher to imposing sanctions against South Africa led to a compromise which accepted only minor restraints on trade pending a visit by an *Eminent Persons Group to the Republic. The Heads of Government did, however, issue a declaration of 'accord' on southern Africa which condemned apartheid, sought the release of *Mandela and other political prisoners, and called for the lifting of the ban on the *African National Congress and for talks on far-reaching constitutional reforms. At the same time, agreement was reached on promoting the education of apartheid's victims, principally through *Nassau Fellowships.

Commonwealth Agricultural Bureaux: see *CAB International*.

Commonwealth Association for Mental Health and Development Disabilities: (see *CAMHADD*)

Commonwealth Broadcasting Association was founded in London as the Commonwealth Broadcasting Conference in February 1945, changing its name in 1974. It was established to give technical assistance and professional advice in both radio *broadcasting and television, taking particular advantage of the co-ordination achieved during World War II. A secretariat was created in London in 1963. Thirty years later, more than 60 organizations were affiliated.

Commonwealth conferences: popular name given to *Commonwealth Prime Ministers' Meetings (1949–61) and (from 1962) *Commonwealth Heads of Government Meetings.

Commonwealth Day. The tradition that member states should corporately honour the Commonwealth on a particular day was inherited from the earlier observance of *Empire Day, on 24 May each year; from 1959 until 1966 Commonwealth Day continued to be celebrated on 24 May. The date was changed in 1967, at first to Queen Elizabeth II's 'official' birthday on the second Saturday in June, and ten years later to the second Monday in March. It is an occasion when the Queen, as *Head of the Commonwealth, customarily broadcasts a short message to the peoples of the Commonwealth.

Commonwealth Development Corporation, the successor, from 1963, in name and character, to the *Colonial Development Corporation, with headquarters off Millbank, London. It continues to promote economic growth by investment in dependent territories and, with British ministerial consent, in any independent Commonwealth member or developing country. Almost three-quarters of the investments remain within the Commonwealth. From 1987 to 1993 the CDC provided more funds to preserve and develop natural resources (agriculture, fisheries, forestry) than for construction work.

Commonwealth education conferences. Commonwealth education ministers first met at Oxford in 1959. They established a scholarship and fellowship plan to assist graduates seeking higher degrees in other Commonwealth countries, and established a permanent committee to encourage Commonwealth co-operation in education; the Committee became a division of the Commonwealth Secretariat in 1965. Since 1959 Education Conferences, generally lasting for a fortnight, have been held every three years, with ministers and specialist advisers in attendance. The 1990 Conference in Barbados gave particular attention to the problems of smaller and poorer member states. Health and drugs, together with ways of improving basic education, were among major issues discussed in 1994 at Islamabad.

Commonwealth Foundation: established in 1966, with funds from member countries, to assist non-governmental organizations and individuals to share professional experience, exchange information and take part in mid-career retraining programmes.

Commonwealth Fund for Technical Co-operation (CFTC). The Heads of Government Conference at Singapore in January 1971 agreed to set up a technical assistance programme for sharing the services of expert advisers and financing the training of personnel among Commonwealth developing countries. Implementation of the programme became a responsibility of the *Commonwealth Secretariat, into which the CFTC was integrated in 1993. The Fund was of great value in

African ex-colonies, where there was need for rapid development of technological skills. Under the CFTC an industrial training and experience programme was introduced in 1986, enabling a relatively advanced industrialized country such as India to assist the smaller developing Commonwealth states. The CFTC also provides practical help in improving health services.

Commonwealth Games. A series of four-yearly competitive meetings, concentrating on *athletics, *swimming and diving. They began as the 'British *Empire Games' at Hamilton, Ontario, in 1930, were called 'British Empire and Commonwealth Games' (1954–66), but became the 'British Commonwealth Games' for the ninth meeting at Edinburgh (1970). This title was retained in 1974 at Christchurch, New Zealand, but the word 'British' was subsequently dropped. The Commonwealth Games have been held at: Edmonton, Alberta, 1978; Brisbane, 1982; Edinburgh, 1986; Auckland, 1990; Victoria, British Columbia, 1994. Thirty-two member states boycotted the 1986 Edinburgh Games in protest at Margaret *Thatcher's opposition to imposing sanctions on South Africa over *apartheid. Malaysia will host the 1998 Games.

Commonwealth Heads of Government Meetings: the name given from September 1962 to the periodic meetings of Commonwealth leaders, popularly called 'Commonwealth Conferences' and previously known officially as *Commonwealth Prime Ministers' Meetings (1949–60). The meetings normally take place every two years, though occasionally more often. They are private and informal; no agenda is issued; no votes are taken; communiqués are issued at the end of the conference, often supplemented by 'declarations' on particular issues – declarations were especially common in the 1970s and 1980s, on the affairs of southern Africa. Meetings were held in London in 1962, 1964, 1965, 1966, 1969 and 1977. The first overseas conference was at Lagos in January 1966, when the British Prime Minister, Harold Wilson, was criticized for not using force against *Rhodesia. At Singapore in January 1971 Edward Heath provoked strong opposition by supporting arms sales to South Africa in order to counter the Soviet threat of destabilization to the African continent. But the meeting took two important decisions: to set up the *Commonwealth Fund for Technical Co-operation; and, in the *Singapore Declaration, to define the fundamental principles to which the leaders believed the Commonwealth to be committed. At Ottawa (1973) and at Kingston, Jamaica in April 1975, the principal topics were Rhodesia and southern Africa in general. The 1977 meeting produced the *Gleneagles Agreement on sporting links. The Lusaka meeting in June 1979, the first attended by Margaret *Thatcher, advanced the prospects of an independent *Zimbabwe and issued the *Lusaka Declaration on racism. Southern African affairs were again discussed at Melbourne (1981), New Delhi (1983) and Nassau (1985), where the *Commonwealth Accord on Southern Africa was drawn up and *Nassau Fellowships established. But, in addition to southern Africa, world trade was a prominent topic at Vancouver (1987), and the environment at Kuala Lumpur (1989), whence the *Langkawi Declaration was issued. From Zimbabwe in October 1991 came the *Harare Declaration on democracy, human rights and the status of women. The Harare meeting also encouraged the abandonment of apartheid and discussed the liberalization of world trade. Later meetings were held at Limassol (1993) and Auckland (1995).

Commonwealth Health Development Programme: a project established in 1986, making use of the CFTC (*Commonwealth Fund for Technical Co-operation) and of the three-yearly meetings of health ministers, to strengthen health service collaboration and contacts between specialized institutions among member states. Since 1989 the programme has given particular attention to *AIDS.

Commonwealth High Level Approval Group: an inner core of ten heads of government, available for rapid summons in an emergency.

Commonwealth Immigration Acts (1962; 1968). The *British Nationality Act of 1948 confirmed the long-established principle of uncontrolled entry into the United Kingdom for all Commonwealth citizens. An influx of immigrants in the late 1950s, especially from the Caribbean and the Indian subcontinent, led the Macmillan government in November 1961 to introduce a Bill which required Commonwealth immigrants to possess a 'special skill' or have a job awaiting them before they could be admitted. The Wilson government's Commonwealth Immigration Act of March 1968 was rushed through Parliament to create a voucher system for *Kenya Asians. Subsequently the Heath government totally changed the British approach to *immigration: the Immigration Act of October 1971 imposed a single system of control on Commonwealth and 'alien' immigrants, while allowing free entry to 'patrials' (those with parents or grandparents born in the United Kingdom).

Commonwealth Institutes. In 1886 an Imperial Exhibition was held in London to make the British public familiar with the pattern of Empire. Many exhibits were retained for inclusion in an Imperial Institute, opened by Queen Victoria in 1893 in South Kensington. Apart from the central tower – which was incorporated in the Imperial College of Science – this building was demolished after World War II. Its educational work was transferred to the Commonwealth Institute, Kensington High Street, which was opened by Queen Elizabeth II in 1962. Gifts from many

Commonwealth Nassau Fellowships

Commonwealth countries were used in the construction of the building, designed originally by Sir Robert Matthew and characterized by a hyperboloid roof of copper from Zambia. Exhibitions display the work and art of every Commonwealth country and, in addition to specific educational courses, there is a comprehensive library and resource centre. In Scotland there is a smaller Commonwealth Institute at Rutland Square, Edinburgh.

Commonwealth Nassau Fellowships: see *Nassau Fellowships*.

Commonwealth Office. The Dominions Office was created as a distinct department of state on 1 July 1925, taking over from the *Colonial Office all responsibility for relations with Australia, Canada, Irish Free State, New Zealand, Newfoundland, South Africa and Southern Rhodesia. On 3 July 1947 the title was changed to Commonwealth Relations Office (CRO) and the range of business was extended to include India and Pakistan. The affairs of Ceylon (1948), Ghana (1957) and Malaya (1957) also became a CRO responsibility. In August 1966 the Colonial Office and the CRO were merged to form the Commonwealth Office. There were only two Commonwealth Secretaries – Herbert Bowden and George Thomson – for on 1 October 1968 a further departmental amalgamation created the *Foreign and Commonwealth Office, headed by a Secretary of State for Foreign and Commonwealth Affairs.

Commonwealth Prime Ministers' Meetings. The *Imperial Conferences of George V's reign were succeeded after World War II by more frequent consultations, generally called by the media 'Commonwealth Conferences'. From 1949 to 1961 these largely informal gatherings were officially designated 'Commonwealth Prime Ministers' Meetings'. All were held in London: in April 1949 (where consideration was first given to defining the title *Head of the Commonwealth), in 1951, 1953, 1956, 1957, 1960, and in March 1961 (a meeting at which *Verwoerd announced that South Africa would leave the Commonwealth because of the widespread condemnation of *apartheid). The presence of executive presidents from Cyprus, Ghana and Pakistan led to the renaming of the conferences in 1962; they became *Commonwealth Heads of Government Meetings and were no longer automatically convened in London.

Commonwealth Principles, Declaration of: see *Singapore Declaration*.

Commonwealth Science Council (CSC) is an autonomous inter-governmental body, attached to the *Commonwealth Secretariat in London. The Council meets every two years to promote scientific collaboration between member states and, since 1982, especially to apply science and technology to the development of natural resources on land and – in the Caribbean – under the seas. The CSC has also convened scientific confer- ences on specific issues, notably on industrial disasters (India, 1990), on chemical problems in developing countries (London, 1991), and on toxic waste (Trinidad, 1991). A Science and Technology Fellowship scheme operates as part of the Secretariat's education programme.

Commonwealth Secretariat was established in June 1965 by a deci- sion of the 1964 Commonwealth Heads of Government meeting in London. Hitherto intra-Commonwealth affairs had been regulated by British civil servants. The limitations of this method were emphasized at the 1964 meeting by President *Nkrumah of Ghana, who was supported by the representatives of Nigeria, Pakistan, Trinidad and Uganda. The Secretariat was designed to assist in internal co-operation between member states and, at the insistence of the veteran Sir Robert *Menzies, was never intended to possess executive powers. The Secretariat's effectiveness was much increased in 1971 by the establishment of the *Commonwealth Fund for Technical Co-operation (CFTC), fully inte- grated in 1993, and by the growth of the *Commonwealth Science Council's activities and of programmes to help women in the Commonwealth and youth work. Respect for the neutrality of the Secretariat's multi-national staff has made it possible to send observers to mediate in troubled regions of the Commonwealth and to observe parlia- mentary elections in three continents. The first Secretary-General was a Canadian, Arnold *Smith. He was succeeded by Sir Shridath *Ramphal of Guyana (1975–90). Chief Emeka *Anyaoku of Nigeria became the third Secretary-General, with a term extended to 2000. His successors will serve four or eight years. A 1993 restructuring cut the Secretariat's staff from 431 to 360. Headquarters remain at Marlborough House, Pall Mall, London. The Secretariat was accorded formal Observer Status by the UN Assembly in 1976.

Commonwealth Sugar Agreement (1951). From the outbreak of World War II until 1952 the Ministry of Food in London not only con- trolled *sugar imports to the United Kingdom but served as agents for supplying sugar to Canada and to certain colonies. Throughout 1950 West Indian sugar producers negotiated with London to safeguard the British Caribbean trade in the face of competition from Brazil, Cuba and African sources when the traditional markets recovered their freedom from Ministerial regulation. Accordingly in December 1951 the second Attlee government accepted a Commonwealth Sugar Agreement which, though less than the producers would have liked, assured the West Indies of an increase of some 25 per cent on current production for the United Kingdom market, the site of the world's largest sugar refinery (Tate and Lyle, at Plaistow Wharf in London). The agreement, guaranteed to last until 1960, checked the spread of unemployment through the plantations for a decade.

Commonwealth Telecommunications Bureau, with headquarters in London, is the specialist secretariat of the Commonwealth Tele-communications Organisation, an informal partnership of repre-sentatives of Commonwealth governments and certain Cable and Wireless establishments who meet in conference every three years. Since the Nicosia Conference of 1982, the Bureau has co-ordinated the activ-ities of the Organisation, dealing in particular with the growth of the global system of satellite transmission.

Commonwealth Yearbook: a (nominally) annual publication by Her Majesty's Stationery Office in London giving detailed information on the background and current problems of the member states and of the struc-ture and function of Commonwealth organizations. It was first published under its present name in 1987.

Condominium: a territory existing under joint sovereignty. *Sudan formed a condominium, administered as the 'Anglo-Egyptian Sudan', from January 1899 until 14 December 1955; and *Vanuatu was known as the New Hebrides, an Anglo-French condominium, from October 1906 until 30 July 1980, when the present Commonwealth Republic was estab-lished.

Confrontation: the name President Sukarno of Indonesia gave to his policy of protracted opposition to *Malaysia, which he condemned as a 'neo-colonialist' federation while himself seeking to add *Brunei, *Sarawak and *Sabah to Kalimantan (the Indonesian part of Borneo).

'Confrontation' began in 1962 as an economic weapon: trade links were cut between Indonesia and Singapore, and British property in Indonesia was expropriated. By 1963 Indonesian troops had infiltrated the jungle frontier across Borneo and guerrilla units were raiding the Malayan peninsula, often dropped by parachute. Some 45,000 Malaysian, British and Australian troops were deployed in Malaysia to check the infiltration. The cost of 'confrontation' and the loss of trade with Commonwealth countries intensified unrest in Indonesia and thereby contributed to Sukarno's political eclipse in October 1965. Confrontation was formally ended in the following summer, with a return to normal relations between Malaysia and her neighbour.

Congress Party: see *Indian National Congress*.

Conscription: see *Military Service*.

Constantine, Learie Nicholas (Baron Constantine; 1901–71), cricketer and West Indian diplomat: born at Diego Martin, Trinidad, the grandson of a slave. Like his father he played cricket for both Trinidad and West Indies, touring England in 1923, 1928, 1933 and 1938 and Australia in 1930/1, and playing Lancashire League cricket for ten years for Nelson, a town where he became extremely popular. He was an all-rounder and a particularly agile fielder. During World War II he remained in England as a Minister of Labour welfare officer, helping Caribbean families, and in 1944 won an historic lawsuit against a London hotel which 'failed to receive and lodge him', on account of the colour of his skin. In 1945 he was invited to captain a Dominions' XI, which defeated England at Lord's. Nine years later he was called to the Bar by the Middle Temple. He was elected to Trinidad's first Parliament, served briefly as Minister of Works, and was High Commissioner for Trinidad and Tobago in London, 1962–64. He was knighted in 1962 and in 1969 received a life peerage, becoming the first coloured West Indian to sit in the House of Lords.

Cook, James (1728–79), circumnavigator and cartographer: born at Marton in North Yorkshire; learned his seamanship at Whitby; served briefly as a seaman; studied navigation and received a master's certificate at the age of 31. From 1759 to 1767 he was in North American waters, where he made a detailed survey of the St Lawrence River. In 1768 he commanded HMS *Endeavour* on a three-year voyage of circumnavigation which enabled him to chart the coasts of New Zealand (1769) and part of the eastern coast of Australia and southern New Guinea. He spent a week (29 April–5 May 1770) at the inlet which his companion *Banks named Botany Bay. Cook confirmed the existence of the Torres Strait, sailing back to England by way of Java and the Cape of Good Hope. In his second voyage (1772–75) he followed the edge of the Antarctic ice cap and explored the South Pacific, discovering Norfolk Island and several Polynesian archipelagos. His third voyage (1776–79) enabled him to discover the Sandwich Islands (1778), and chart the Pacific coast of North America before returning south to Hawaii in January 1779. There, in Karakakoa Bay, he was attacked and killed by natives who had earlier appeared friendly (14 February 1779).

Cook Islands: self-governing territory in free association with New Zealand. A Polynesian archipelago of fifteen islands, many of which were discovered by Captain Cook in 1773, although outlying atolls were discovered in 1823 by the intrepid London missionary John Williams (1796–1839), who translated the New Testament into the local Raratongan language but was eventually killed and eaten in *Vanuatu. The sparsely populated atolls produce copra, pearl shell and tropical fruit. The Cook Islands became a British Protectorate in 1888 but were annexed to New Zealand in June 1901. In August 1965 they were constituted a self-governing territory, with a unicameral parliament and a fifteen-man council of native chiefs. Rarotonga is the administrative capital. The islands, which suffered considerably from a hurricane in January 1987, remain closely associated with *Niue, New Zealand's other overseas self-governing territory, 580 miles from Rarotonga.

Copper. Historically, the greatest copper producing regions of the Commonwealth are *Canada and *Zambia, but there are also valuable copper deposits in India (especially Bihar province), South Africa, Australia, Botswana, peninsular Malaysia and Papua New Guinea (where the industry has grown remarkably since 1972). Canada was exporting copper by 1863, with large deposits in *British Columbia, where there was a copper boom in the 1890s around Rossland. It was also extensively mined around Sudbury, Ontario, where in 1890 Canada's first two smelting furnaces came into operation. By the 1870s Newfoundland was among the fifteen largest copper producing regions in the world, but early deposits were soon exhausted, as also happened at the Eustis Mine of eastern Quebec Province, where production started in 1865 but ended in 1939. The Noranda complex, opened in 1927, marked the coming of widespread production to north-western Quebec, with newer resources tapped 220 miles to the north at Chibougamau in the 1950s. In Zambia, what was formerly called the 'Northern Rhodesian copperbelt' effectively dates from 1906, when the first productive mine was opened at Broken Hill (now Kabwe), but the years 1924–30 saw the most rapid growth, with the native labour force leaping from 1,300 to 30,000 and the mining companies extending their operations to Ndola, Kitwe, Roan, Chingola, Kalulushi, Chambishi, Mufulira and Chililambombwe. The belt was about 90 miles long and 30 miles wide. Much of the capital for later development was Anglo-American in origin. The wealth of the copperbelt has left Zambia almost entirely dependent for foreign exchange on sales of copper.

Cree Indians: one of the most famous of Algonquin-speaking native peoples of Canada, traditionally divided into three groupings: Woods Cree, from the lands around the Churchill River and its mouth in Hudson Bay; Swampy Cree, from around the northern ends of Lake Winnipegosis and Lake Winnipeg; and, later, the Plains Cree, from mass migrations of the older groups into northern Saskatchewan. The Woods Cree made contact with fur traders and the *Hudson's Bay Company outposts as early as 1660 and became the first of the Canadian Indian peoples to acquire firearms. Relations with the traders were generally friendly, however, and many *métis were of Cree descent. Their southward migration encroached on *Blackfoot lands, causing frequent wars, notably in 1879 when the Blackfoot defeated the Cree in battle on the site of modern Lethbridge, Alberta. The *'Mounties' concluded settlement treaties with the Swampy Cree in 1875 and with the Woods and Plains Cree in 1876. Famine, caused by the disappearance of the buffalo, hit the Cree hard and in early 1885 Chief Big Bear and Chief Poundmaker led separate Cree revolts to coincide with the rebellion of *Riel, destroying the town of Battleford and the settlement of Frog Lake along the North Saskatchewan River. When the Canadian Army suppressed the rebellion, both chiefs surrendered; they received the relatively lenient sentence of two years' imprisonment, for 'treasonable felony'. The surviving Cree returned to their designated reservations.

Creech Jones, Arthur (1891–1964), Colonial Secretary: born and educated in Bristol; became a junior clerk in the Civil Service. He was imprisoned from 1916 to 1919 for opposing conscription. On his release he became an active trade unionist with particular interest in the movement within the British colonies. He sat as Labour MP for Shipley (Yorkshire), 1935–50 and for Wakefield, 1954–64. While serving as Parliamentary Secretary to Ernest Bevin he became a co-founder in 1940 of the Fabian Colonial Bureau, a group which clarified Labour Party thinking on colonial issues. He was Colonial Under-Secretary from August 1945 until October 1946, when *Attlee appointed him Colonial Secretary. In cabinet he sympathized with the Zionists over *Palestine. At the *Colonial Office Creech Jones sought, not always successfully, to promote social justice (particularly in the African colonies) while preparing spokesmen whom he had met in England for the responsibilities of independent government. He also backed proposals for the building of a large and grandiose Colonial Office. After his rejection by Shipley's voters in 1950, he gave particular attention to educational projects at Oxford, notably the foundation in 1954 of Queen Elizabeth House, Oxford as a centre for the study of developing countries, inside and outside the Commonwealth.

Cricket. The earliest reference to the playing of cricket in a British colony is to a match in Virginia in 1709; the first two countries to play against each other were Canada and the USA, at New York in 1844; and both these countries were visited by the first overseas touring team from England (1859). But Commonwealth cricket is more closely associated with the eight overseas Test Match countries: Australia, where the original Test Match was played, against England at Melbourne in March 1877; South Africa, from 1888: the West Indies, 1928; New Zealand, 1929; India, 1932; Pakistan, 1954; Sri Lanka, 1982; Zimbabwe (against India, at Harare, in October 1992). The contests between England and Australia have been played 'for the *Ashes' since 1882, while England and the West Indies have competed for the Wisden Trophy since 1963, and Australia and the West Indies for the Frank Worrell Trophy since 1964/5. A quadrennial limited-overs World Cup competition was established in

1975 in which, in addition to the Test countries, East Africa (1975) and Canada (1979) have taken part. Cricket is also played enthusiastically in Hong Kong. An individualistic version survives in Corfu, from the years when the *Ionian Islands were a British Protectorate. Traditionally cricket served as a bond linking Empire and Commonwealth partners in friendly rivalry, but the 'bodyline' dispute of 1933 strained relations between Australia and 'the Mother Country'. Women's cricket matches date from 1745 in England, 1886 in Australia, early in the twentieth century in South Africa and New Zealand, and from the second half of this century in India and the Caribbean. International women's matches began in 1934/5 with an English tour of Australia and New Zealand. A Women's World Cup competition was introduced in 1973: the fifth final, in which England beat New Zealand at Lord's in 1993, attracted enthusiastic support. (See also: *Bradman*; *Constantine*; *Sobers*.)

Cripps Mission. Sir Stafford Cripps (1889–1952), the independent Labour MP who served as ambassador to the Soviet Union from 1940 until February 1942, entered Churchill's Coalition War Cabinet as Lord Privy Seal on his return from Moscow. In March 1942 Churchill sent Cripps on a special mission to India in the vain hope that he would win the support of *Gandhi and his *Indian National Congress Party for the conflict with Japan by promising that India should have an assembly with powers to draft the constitution of an independent state once the war ended. Cripps envisaged a federal India with semi-autonomous states, able to choose freely whether to remain inside or outside the Commonwealth. Gandhi, however, sought immediate independence; the British offer was 'a post-dated cheque on a crashing bank', he said. In March 1946, while Cripps was President of the Board of Trade in Attlee's government, he headed a second cabinet mission to the subcontinent in the hope of establishing a unified federal India, but the Muslim concept of an independent *Pakistan was by then too far advanced for this second mission to succeed. (See *Calcutta Riots*.)

Cromer, Earl of (Evelyn Baring: 1841–1917), British pro-consul in *Egypt: born in Cromer, and commissioned in the artillery (1858). While serving in the Ionian Islands he was appointed aide-de-camp to the High Commissioner, and spent the rest of his life in the imperial administrative service. He gained experience in Malta and Jamaica (1864–67) and was private secretary to the Viceroy of India (1872–76). From 1877 to 1879 he gained experience of Egyptian affairs as British representative on a commission to deal with the mounting debts of the Khedive Ismail. After three more years in Calcutta as financial member of the Viceroy's council Baring received a knighthood, and in 1883 was appointed British 'agent and consul-general' in Egypt. He held this office until 1907, effectively ruling Egypt and enjoying greater autocratic powers than any Viceroy of

India. He rescued the country from near-bankruptcy, restored its agricultural prosperity by irrigation schemes, built up a railway network, westernized education, reformed the administration of justice, completed a land survey and created a Land Bank to encourage systematic husbandry. He warmly backed *Kitchener in the reconquest of the *Sudan, and was largely responsible for setting up the *condominium which governed the Sudan after Kitchener's triumph. From 1892, when he received a barony, Sir Evelyn Baring was known as Lord Cromer, becoming a viscount in 1899 and an earl in 1901. After returning from Egypt in 1907 he became a prominent Free Trade supporter in the House of Lords. Lord Cromer's son, Sir (Charles) Evelyn Baring (1903–73; created Baron Howick in 1960), was Governor of Southern Rhodesia from 1942 to 1944 and Governor of Kenya (1952–59) during the *Mau-Mau emergency.

Crown Agents. From 1875 until 1903 the agents-general for the colonies in London were a sub-department of the *Colonial Office; from 1881 they specialized in the affairs of the Crown Colonies. In 1903 the 'Crown Agents for the Colonies' were assigned their own establishment, in Whitehall Gardens, later moving to Millbank. The agents were appointed by the *Colonial Secretary to act as commercial and financial representatives in the United Kingdom for the governments of all British colonies, protectorates or dependencies. During the inter-war period, and until 1958, the Crown Agents also acted for *Iraq and Jordan. In 1954 the department was renamed 'Crown Agents for Overseas Governments and Administrations'. Their function has changed. Instead of two nominated Crown Agents, the department is a statutory body headed by a chairman and managing director. Crown Agents provide professional services for more than 100 governments and some 300 organizations, mostly within the Commonwealth. They purchase and transport materials and equipment, manage investment policies, supervise agricultural and engineering projects, and offer advice on recruitment and training. The Crown Agents are now in Sutton, Surrey.

CSIRO (Commonwealth Scientific and Industrial Research Organization). A Commonwealth of Australia statutory body founded in 1949 to co-ordinate research, particularly in veterinary science and horticulture. CSIRO succeeded the Council for Scientific and Industrial Research, which dated from 1926 and was itself a successor to an original federal Institute of Science and Industry. For ten years CSIRO was directed by Sir Ian Clunies Ross (1899–1959), a former chairman of the International Wool Secretariat and Professor of Veterinary Science at Sydney University. Clunies Ross ensured that CSIRO gave particular attention to controlling the spread of disease among livestock and fruit trees, and instituted a major soil research programme. CSIRO has been attacked for its controversial decision to reduce rabbit numbers by introducing myxomatosis. The organization has also developed new ways of processing textiles.

Curtin, John Joseph (1885–1945), Australian Prime Minister: born, the son of an Irish Roman Catholic policeman, at Creswick, near Ballarat, Victoria. He became a socialist in 1906 and was secretary of the Timber Workers' Union, 1911–15, but then moved to Western Australia, where between 1917 and 1928 he built up the Labor movement. From 1928 to 1931 and from 1934 to 1945 Curtin sat in the Federal Parliament as Member for Fremantle, and in 1935 became head of the Labor Party. When Fadden's six-week coalition ministry was defeated on the budget in October 1941, Curtin formed the ministry which shaped Australian policy throughout the war against Japan. As Prime Minister, Curtin sought the return of Australian troops from the Middle East; and he built up a close relationship with the United States, which has sometimes been over-emphasized. From the closing months of 1943 he stressed the need for a powerful British fleet in the Pacific to counter the mounting political influence of the American, General Douglas MacArthur, Allied Supreme Commander in the south-west Pacific. Curtin attended a conference of dominion prime ministers in London in May 1944, where he advocated an institutional link which would formulate common policies for the British and Commonwealth governments in the post-war world. On Curtin's sudden death (4 July 1945), he was succeeded as Prime Minister by his Finance Minister, *Chifley, rather than by his External Affairs Minister, *Evatt.

Curtis, Lionel George (1872–1955), servant of Empire and Commonwealth: born in London; educated at *Haileybury and New College, Oxford; a barrister by profession. He spent the years 1899 to 1909 in South Africa, where – like *Amery and *Buchan – he was much influenced by the imperial ideals of *Milner. As town clerk of Johannesburg (1901–03) he promoted the development of the city, and as Assistant Colonial Secretary in the Transvaal (1903–07) he supported policies of agricultural reconstruction and helped advance the idea of a united South Africa. On his return to England he helped draft the *Selborne Memorandum (1907). In 1910 he founded the *Round Table, a quarterly review of imperial problems, and began a series of visits to the overseas dominions to promote the idea of Commonwealth collaboration. In 1916 he published two books – *The Problem of the Commonwealth* and *The Commonwealth of Nations* – in which he advocated a federal union of the empire. In later years he argued that imperial union was a step towards a federal super-state which would include not only the Commonwealth, but also the USA, Europe west of the Rhine, and Scandinavia; Quebec should be capital of the federation, Curtis suggested. His writings concentrated, however, on Commonwealth affairs, from which he evolved a general philosophy of government in his three-volume *Civitatis Dei* (1934–37). Curtis helped draft the Montagu–Chelmsford Report, which was a basis for the *India Act of 1919, and in 1920 he published *Dyarchy*, a study of India's constitutional problems. He was also a founder of Chatham House (London's Royal Institute of International Affairs), and he remained an active trustee of *Rhodes House in Oxford.

Curzon, George Nathaniel (Lord Curzon of Kedleston; 1859–1925), Viceroy of India and Foreign Secretary: educated at Eton and Balliol College, Oxford; served as Conservative MP for Southport from 1886 to 1898. His duties did not prevent him travelling widely in North America, the Far East and India (1887–8 and 1892), Russia and the Caucasus (1888–9), Persia (1889–90), Afghanistan and along the route of the ancient river Oxus (1894). From these journeys he derived the material for three detailed studies which won him respect at Westminster, at the age of 35, as a leading authority on the imperial frontiers in Asia. As Parliamentary Under-Secretary for Foreign Affairs from 1895 to 1898 he asserted a more aggressive national pride than did Lord *Salisbury, who was head of the government and Foreign Secretary. Curzon was created a baron in 1898, and began a seven-year term as Viceroy of India in January 1899. He was the youngest of all Viceroys, and the most active: he gave minute attention to the improvement of education, public services and communications; he encouraged agricultural and irrigation projects; and he strengthened the *North-West Frontier, which he organized as a province. But Curzon made two major mistakes: in 1905 he aroused Indian national resentment by partitioning Bengal arbitrarily into an eastern and a western province; and he quarrelled bitterly with *Kitchener, who became Commander-in-Chief in 1903 and sought to reorganize the Indian Army independent of the Viceroy's wishes. Curzon took little part in public life between 1905 and 1915, but he was a member of the War Cabinet from December 1916 until 1919, and Foreign Secretary from October 1919 until January 1924. At the Foreign Office his greatest achievement was to settle frontiers with Turkey in the Treaty of Lausanne (24 July 1923), following the *Chanak Crisis. Curzon, who was created an earl in 1911 and a marquess in 1921, was disappointed in May 1923 when King George V thought it right to choose a member of the House of Commons (Baldwin), rather than a peer, as Prime Minister. Curzon's haughty arrogance made him many political enemies. At the time of his death he was Lord President of the Council in Baldwin's second Ministry.

Cyclone: a tropical or sub-tropical, intensive, fast-moving storm, in which torrential rain concentrated on a small area is accompanied by strong winds, clockwise in the southern hemisphere and anti-clockwise in the northern. The wind speed is 64 knots or more (over 72 mph).

Cyprus

Technically, 'cyclone' is the name for a tropical storm in the Indian Ocean, the Arabian Sea and off northern Australia; such a storm is a 'hurricane' in the Atlantic, the Caribbean and most of the Pacific; in the Philippine and China Seas and in the north-west Pacific it is a 'typhoon'.

*Bangladesh has suffered grievously from cyclones and flooding as swollen rivers burst their banks: death tolls of more than 100,000 followed cyclones on 11 October 1960, 29 May 1963, 12 May 1965, 28 April 1989, and 29 April 1991. Cyclones also hit Burma, on 28 May 1926, and Sri Lanka and Southern India, on 24 December 1964. At Christmas 1974, Darwin in Australia's *Northern Territory was razed to the ground by 'Cyclone Tracy'. Papua New Guinea was devastated in September 1994. Hurricanes swept Barbados in 1780, 1831 and 1898, Jamaica in 1944 and 1951, Sierra Leone in 1975, Dominica in 1979 and 1980. In Belize more than 700 people were killed on 11 September 1931, and 'Hurricane Hattie' caused devastation on 31 October 1961 when a tidal wave flooded Belize City, while 'Hurricane Fifi' destroyed plantations in September 1974. Several typhoons have hit Hong Kong, notably on 18 September 1906.

Cyprus, an eastern Mediterranean island 40 miles from the Turkish coast in the north and 60 miles from Syria in the east. Cyprus became a British Protectorate in 1878 but remained within the Ottoman Empire until World War I, when it was annexed to Britain (5 November 1914). In May 1925 it became a Crown Colony. With Greeks forming 80 per cent of the population, there were widespread demands for union (*enosis) with Greece. Riots led to the suspension of the Legislative Assembly in November 1931, all power passing to a governor, who from October 1933 accepted advice from an informal council of six Orthodox Christians and two Muslims. A consultative assembly met in 1946 but differences between Greeks and Turks prevented revival of the legislature. Similarly, in 1948 an offer of a constitution from London was declined by the Greek community because it did not provide institutional links with Athens, while counter-proposals from the Greek government in 1951 and 1953 were rejected by Great Britain. From April 1955 until February 1959 the Greek guerrilla organization EOKA, led by George Grivas (1898–1974), fought the British authorities with a series of acts of terrorism and murder. In March 1956 the British exiled Archbishop *Makarios, leader of the Greek Cypriot community, to the Seychelles but he was allowed to travel to Athens in April 1957. When Sir Hugh Foot (Lord Caradon; 1907–90) became Governor in December 1957 he promoted talks with Makarios, Fazil Kuchuk (the Turkish Cypriot leader) and the British, Greek and Turkish governments which enabled Cyprus to become an independent republic within the Commonwealth on 16 August 1960. Makarios became President; Kuchuk, Vice-President. Co-operation between the Turkish and Greek communities was minimal, however, and in 1970 the Turks established their own political assembly in northern Cyprus. An abortive coup by EOKA veterans in July 1974 provoked an invasion by Turkish troops, who occupied almost half the northern part of the island. On 13 February 1975 a Turkish Cypriot Federated State was proclaimed, and in November 1983 a unilateral declaration of independence set up 'The Turkish Republic of Northern Cyprus', accorded recognition only by the Turkish government in Ankara: 15,000 Turkish regular troops remained in the island. 'Northern Cyprus' forms 37 per cent of the island and includes the historic port of Famagusta. Attempts by Makarios's successors, by the UN and by Commonwealth leaders to secure reunification have failed. UN peace-keepers and British air bases remain. Grapes, citrus fruit and textiles form the main exports. Reafforestation has restored much woodland burnt in the inter-communal violence, especially in the Paphos Forest.

Dalhousie, Lord (1812–60), Governor-General of India. As President of the Board of Trade in London (1845–46) Dalhousie promoted railways at the height of the boom and this interest, together with the introduction of a telegraph system, he carried with him to India, where he served as Governor-General from 1848 until 1856. His forward policy led to the annexation of the Punjab (which he entrusted to the administration of the brothers Henry and John *Lawrence) and Pegu, as well as Oudh and the Irrawaddy delta in Burma. His extensive reforms alienated traditionalists and Brahmin priests and therefore contributed to the discontent manifested in the *Indian Mutiny, which broke out a few months after Dalhousie's return to England.

Dampier, William (1652–1715), English navigator: born in Dorset, near Yeovil; became a plantation manager in Jamaica in 1674; but by 1679 was commanding a pirate ship in the Caribbean and the Gulf of Campeche. Eventually, in 1686, Dampier sailed for the East Indies, and for three months in 1688 he used the western coast of 'New Holland' (Australia) as a base. When he returned to England he published a (discreet) account of his voyages (1697). He received a naval commission, as captain of HMS *Roebuck*, and returned to New Holland waters. When he found no suitable harbours along today's northern coast of Western Australia he set sail for the Timor Sea. In 1699 he discovered and named New Britain island (Papua New Guinea). *Roebuck* was wrecked on Ascension Island in 1701 but Dampier was rescued by an East Indiaman. His conduct led to a court martial, at which he was declared unfit to serve as a naval officer. He remained, however, a skilled navigator; in 1709, as a privateer in the South Pacific, he rescued Alexander Selkirk, the prototype Robinson Crusoe, who had been marooned for four years on one of the Juan Fernandez Islands.

Datuk Seri's Report

Datuk Seri's Report (1991): see *Mahatir Report*.

De Beers Consolidated Mines. In July 1871 *diamonds were found on a farm owned by the brothers De Beer at Vooruitzigt, close to the border of Cape Colony with the Orange Free State. The site, known first as 'New Rush', was in 1873 renamed Kimberley after the Colonial Secretary; it rapidly developed as a municipality. In 1871 the De Beers brothers sold their rights for 6,000 guineas (£6,300) to speculators who four years later sold on to the Cape government for £100,000. The site was then divided, the principal purchaser being Cecil *Rhodes. The original name was perpetuated by Rhodes in the De Beers Mining Company, which he formed on 1 April 1880 and which absorbed other companies, among them (in March 1888) a group controlled by Alfred Beit (1853–1906). The rival Barnato Diamond Company was purchased on 18 July 1889 with a cheque made out for £5,338,650, thus allowing De Beers Consolidated Mines Ltd to acquire a monopoly of diamond sales on the London market and thus provide the capital Rhodes used as a springboard for his imperial ventures. Despite the intrusion of the Anglo-American Corporation (founded 1917) and other concerns, De Beers has continued to control the mining and marketing of southern Africa's resources. In 1969 the De Beers Botswana Mining Company was formed to mine diamonds at Orapa, where production began in 1971, and in 1976 De Beer's mineralogists discovered diamonds at Jwaneng, where since 1982 an embryonic Botswanan Kimberley has come into being. So strong has been De Beers's hold on the centralized selling of diamonds that an attempt by Zaire to act independently in 1981 was abandoned two years later.

Deakin, Alfred (1856–1919), Australian Prime Minister: born and educated in Melbourne; became a lawyer and sat in the Victoria legislature (1879–1900); he introduced laws to protect workers in sweated industries and promoted irrigation schemes on the Murray River. He worked for federation for twenty years, sat in the House of Representatives (1901–13) and was the first Attorney-General. Deakin headed three governments: September 1903 to April 1904; July 1905 to November 1908; April 1909 to April 1910. Politically Deakin was a Liberal, and his ministries were prone to attack by Labor for repressive trade union legislation; but 'affable Alfred' was also a reformer, who gave the Australians their first federal old age and sickness benefits. Outside Australia Deakin won respect for his ideal of imperial 'unity through diversity' and his vigorous support for *imperial preference.

Dee, John (1527–1608), Welsh astrologer: a Cambridge mathematician who survived more than thirty years of suspected dabbling in sorcery to present to his Queen in 1577 a study of the art of navigation, in which he described himself as being 'careful for the godly prosperity of this British Empire, under our most peaceable Queen Elizabeth'; this is the first recorded use of the term 'British Empire'. In 1580 Dee prepared for Elizabeth the earliest known description of the newly discovered lands.

Delamere, Lord (Hugh Cholmondeley; 1870–1931), Kenyan pioneer settler: born in Cheshire; succeeded his father as third Baron Delamere in 1887, while still at Eton. From 1888 he travelled abroad each year, seeking adventure in Australia and New Zealand and, from 1890 to 1895, undertaking five shooting expeditions to Somaliland. In December 1896 he left Berbera in a caravan of 200 camels to trek a thousand miles south-westwards, reaching the Aberdare foothills of modern *Kenya in September 1897. In November 1903 Delamere acquired a 99-year lease on 100,000 acres of good sheep country around Njoro. He encouraged systematic farming by settlers from Britain and South Africa, showing particular interest in maize production, but he lost heavily on risky experiments, such as ostrich farms. In October 1907 he became president of the Colonists' Association, supporting white settler interests against the official administration, which was more sympathetic to the welfare of the native peoples. He remained the white settlers' chief spokesman until his death: from 1907, as unofficial adviser before Kenya became a Crown Colony; and as Council member for the Rift Valley (1920–31). He sought the creation of an East African dominion as racially discriminatory as was (pre-apartheid) South Africa; he was particularly hostile to the political aspirations of the Indian traders (see *Kenya Asians*). As well as developing three huge ranches he founded Nyama Ltd, a large-scale meat trading concern which sought to export refrigerated lamb on the New Zealand model. Despite criticism of his intemperate political gestures by successive colonial administrators, in 1929 Delamere received a high government decoration (KCMG). The fall in wheat prices that year (see *Great Depression*) meant that he died close to bankruptcy.

Delhi Durbar (1877: 1903: 1911). In the Indian subcontinent and the Malay Peninsula, a durbar is traditionally a court levee in the presence of a ruler. A tented durbar was held on the outskirts of Delhi in January 1877 for the proclamation of Queen Victoria as Empress of India. Edward VII's spectacular Coronation Durbar of January 1903 lasted for two weeks, with *Curzon as Viceroy taking precedence over the sovereign's brother, the Duke of Connaught. In December 1911 George V and his consort came in person to Delhi, where ten square miles of tents were to house 25,000 people for his Coronation Durbar. The King–Emperor announced two important administrative changes for India at the Durbar: the restoration of Bengal as a single unit, in place of the unpopular partitioned Bengal imposed by Curzon; and the transfer of the seat of government from Calcutta to *New Delhi, thus associating the *Raj with the historic walled capital of the Mogul emperors.

Dependent Territory: used since 1968 in preference to *colony to describe a possession of the Crown acquired by settlement, conquest or annexation and for which the United Kingdom or a dominion retains responsibility for foreign relations, defence and internal security. In January 1995 Britain had fourteen dependent territories: *Anguilla; *Bermuda; British *Antarctic; *British Indian Ocean Territory; *British Virgin Islands; *Cayman Islands; *Falkland Islands; *Gibraltar; *Hong Kong; *Montserrat; *Pitcairn Islands; *St Helena with *Ascension and *Tristan da Cunha; *South Georgia and South Sandwich Islands; and the *Turks and Caicos Islands. Seven areas constitute the *Australian Dependent Territories. *Tokelau and the *Ross Dependency are dependent territories of *New Zealand.

Depression, economic, of 1930s: see *Great Depression*.

Dewali: see *Diwali*.

Diamond rush. The discovery of *diamonds on Du Toit's farm, 540 miles north of Cape Town, in March 1869 prompted a rush of prospectors from Cape Colony and Natal. Attention was concentrated on Griqualand West and the area close to the Orange River, where in 1873 the town of Kimberley was founded. The initial rush was given fresh impetus by the *De Beers discoveries and by the initiative of Cecil *Rhodes.

Diamonds. The first country to mine diamonds was India, where the Koh-i-noor (which is believed to have come from Hyderabad in the early fourteenth century) passed into British possession in 1849 with the annexation of the Punjab; there are still diamonds in modern India's Madhya Pradesh province. For half a century after the *diamond rush of the 1870s the South African mines were the chief producers of the gem. The Cullinan diamond, mined in the Transvaal (1905) and the largest in the world, was presented by General *Botha to King Edward VII at Sandringham on 9 November as a gift from the Transvaal people. The Cullinan was cut into four stones and incorporated in the Imperial Crown, worn by King George V, King George VI and Queen Elizabeth II at their coronations. Diamonds are still extensively mined in South Africa. They come, too, from other Commonwealth countries: Botswana, Ghana, Sierra Leone, Namibia, Tanzania, and Western Australia.

Diefenbaker, John George (1895–1979), Canadian Prime Minister: born at Normanby, Ontario; educated at Saskatchewan University, served with the Canadian Army in France (1916–17) but was invalided home, and in 1919 became a barrister. After building up a considerable law practice, he entered the Federal Parliament in 1940. In 1956 he became leader of the Progressive Conservatives and in June 1957 formed a minority government, thus ending Canada's 22 years of Liberal rule. After gaining a majority of 153 seats at the election of March 1958 – the largest margin of victory in Canadian history – Diefenbaker sought closer economic ties with the United Kingdom in the hope of combating rising unemployment. He at once convened a conference at Montreal, which agreed to establish a system of Commonwealth Assistance Loans. But Diefenbaker received scant support in London and could not break the American hold on the Canadian economy. Ironically, it was suspicion that Diefenbaker was subservient to America (primarily over defence issues) that brought about his downfall, in April 1963. He continued to lead the Opposition until 1967, and sat in Parliament until his death.

Dilke, Sir Charles Wentworth (1843–1911): born in Chelsea; succeeded in 1869 to the baronetcy bestowed on his father and namesake, a Liberal MP; he studied law at Trinity Hall, Cambridge before setting out on a world tour. On his return Dilke wrote *Greater Britain* (1868), his own choice of title. He was radical MP for Chelsea (1868–86), at first voicing republican views though he later became a friend of the Prince of Wales (Edward VII). Dilke was President of the Local Government Board (1882–85), with a seat in Gladstone's second cabinet, but his parliamentary career was cut short when he was cited as co-respondent in a divorce suit (1885–86). Dilke shared many of the imperialistic sentiments of Joseph *Chamberlain, though he never joined the Unionists. He continued to study imperial problems, making visits to Greece, the Ottoman Empire and India and completing *Problems of Greater Britain* (two volumes, 1890). Dilke returned to the House of Commons as Liberal MP for the Forest of Dean in 1892 and, until his death, concentrated as a backbencher on colonial issues and imperial defence. He maintained a regular correspondence with Alfred *Deakin; but he also championed native rights in the protectorates of Basutoland, Bechuanaland and East Africa, and sought to amend the South Africa Bill of 1909 to avoid acknowledging a colour bar.

Disraeli, Benjamin (1804–81; from 1876 Earl of Beaconsfield), British Prime Minister: born in London of Jewish parentage but baptized a Christian (Anglican) at the age of twelve; privately educated, and worked as a solicitor's clerk while writing *Vivien Grey* (1826), the first of four political novels. Disraeli toured the Levant and, after several setbacks, won election as MP for Maidstone in 1837. He represented Shrewsbury (1841–47) and Buckingham (1847–76). In his first years in the Commons Disraeli was spokesman for the flamboyant Tory 'Young

England' movement. After 1846 he led the protectionist Tories in the Commons against the Peelite free traders, and served as Chancellor of the Exchequer in 1852, 1858–9 and 1866. After securing the passage of a second parliamentary Reform Bill, enfranchising virtually all male house-holders in the towns (1867), he succeeded Lord Derby as Prime Minister (February 1868), but eight months later suffered electoral defeat. In a letter of 1862 Disraeli described 'these wretched colonies' as 'millstones round our neck', but in his Crystal Palace speech of June 1872 he empha-sized the duty of a government to 'reconstruct as much as possible our colonial empire', and his second Ministry (1874–80) is generally regarded as one of reform at home and empire-building abroad. Yet Disraeli's imperial promotion was limited to purchase of a majority shareholding in the *Suez Canal; a *Royal Titles Act creating Queen Victoria Empress of India; and the establishment of a protectorate over *Cyprus. To offset these gains were defeats at *Isandhlwana and in the Second *Afghan War. He lost the general election of April 1880 and died a year later, mourned by Queen Victoria, whose imperial aspirations he had gratified and flattered.

Diwali, principal festival common to all Hindu communities in India, marking the start of a New Year. It is a festival of light, marked by fire-works and decorative clay lamps and solemnized by prayers to Lakshmi, goddess of wealth and good fortune. Diwali is generally celebrated in late October or early November.

Dobell, Sir William (1899–1970), Australian portrait painter: born at Newcastle, NSW but studied art at the Slade School, London, exhibiting at the Royal Academy. He returned to Sydney in 1939, perfecting his technique while serving with wartime camouflage units. His portraits, which seemed to critical contemporaries like extended caricatures, first aroused great interest in 1943/4. Dobell became the outstanding portrait artist of his generation, probably best remembered for his portrait of *Menzies, commissioned in 1960 by *Time*. He was knighted in 1966 and died at Lake Macquarie, endowing the art foundation which carries his name.

Dominica: independent Republic within the Commonwealth. The mountainous island lies in the *Windward Group of the Lesser Antilles, 95 miles south of *Antigua. Dominica was discovered by Columbus in 1493, a source of dispute between France and Britain in the eighteenth century, and only formally recognized as British in 1815. Despite a good harbour at Roseau (the capital) and fertile soil, volcanic in origin, the island's development was slow. From 1871 to 1939 Dominica was part of the *Leeward Islands Colony but in 1940 passed into the Windward Islands Colony, and belonged to the abortive *British West Indies

Federation (1958–62). Internal self-government in 1967 was followed by independence, as 'The Commonwealth of Dominica', on 3 November 1978. Tourism, bananas and lime products are the main sources of revenue. Hurricanes caused great devastation in September 1979 and 1980. A few hundred Caribs, the original native people of the West Indian islands, survive in a reservation some 40 miles from Roseau.

Dominion: a self-governing territory, formerly with colonial status, and enjoying free association with the United Kingdom. The word was first used as a designation of sovereignty in the *British North America Act (1867): the politicians in Quebec preferred 'Kingdom of Canada' but 'Dominion' was chosen in London, possibly to avoid antagonizing the Americans so soon after their disastrous experience with the 'Empire of Mexico'. Australia in 1900 chose 'Commonwealth' in preference to a word which seemed to imply domination. However, in 1907 the Colonial Conference decided that all self-governing imperial territories were 'British Dominions'; an Order in Council of 9 September 1907 duly elevated the colony of New Zealand to a 'Dominion'. But the unified South African colonies became a 'Union' (1910), and southern Ireland a 'Free State' (1922). The only other Commonwealth countries designated 'dominions' were *Newfoundland (1917 to 1933), *Pakistan (August 1947–March 1956) and *Ceylon (February 1948–May 1972). The relationship between autonomous Commonwealth communities and the United Kingdom was clarified by the *Balfour Definition (1926), and the concept of dominion status was fundamental to the Statute of *Westminster (1931).

Douglas, Sir James (1803–77), colonial governor: born in Demerara, Guyana. At the age of 16 he went to Canada and lived a tempestuous life working for the *Hudson's Bay Company. In 1843 he founded Fort Victoria as a fur-trading outpost for the Company on Vancouver Island, becoming Chief Factor in 1849 and Governor of Vancouver in 1851. When gold was found on the Fraser River in 1858 Douglas enforced arbitrary measures to control the *gold rush, and in 1859 was appointed the first governor of the new mainland colony of *British Columbia. He levied taxes for roads to open up the coastal interior, and in 1859–60 nearly precipitated war with the USA over rival claims to the *San Juan Islands. Douglas remained Governor of Vancouver until 1863 (the year he was knighted), and Governor of British Columbia until 1864. In retirement he campaigned vigorously for a transcontinental railway.

Drysdale, Sir George Russell (1912–81), Australian landscape painter: born in Sussex but emigrated to Victoria at the age of eleven and received his schooling at Geelong, becoming a large-scale farmer. The interest aroused by his *The Rabbiter and his Family* at the first Contemporary Art

Society exhibition (1939) induced him to become a full-time artist. He settled in Sydney where his first one-man exhibition was mounted in 1941. The impact of drought and scorching sun on the outback led him to experiment freely with convincing surrealism; his first exhibition in London in 1950 attracted widespread interest, as did his paintings at the Venice Biennale four years later. He also completed two series of paintings, of women of the bush and of aborigines. Drysdale was knighted in 1969. With *Dobell and *Nolan he lifted Australian art to unprecedented heights in the decades following World War II.

Durham Report (1839). 'Radical Jack' Lambton (1792–1840), who became Earl of Durham in 1832, was a leading champion of parliamentary reform in England, and of colonial development. In 1838 the Whig Prime Minister, Lord Melbourne, appointed Durham governor-general of the British provinces in North America with a special commission to 'adjust important questions' in Upper and Lower Canada by examining the causes of the rebellion of *Mackenzie and *Papineau. Durham's high-handed behaviour towards rebels and loyalists was mischievously exploited by his political enemies at Westminster; he resigned on 9 October 1839, only nineteen weeks after reaching Quebec. On his return Durham produced a *Report on the Affairs of British North America*, which was debated in the House of Lords in February 1839. It recommended the unification of the Canadian provinces in order to promote a common citizenship and counter French-Canadian separatism; it also urged the speedy grant of responsible government to the Canadians, since Durham believed that, as a general principle, a colony could only mature into a nation by accepting political responsibility. The Report's recommendations on a united Canadian legislature were embodied in the Canada Act of 1840, but responsible government was conceded only gradually and not fully implemented until the *British North America Act (1867). By advocating devolution of responsibility to colonial assemblies, the Durham Report revolutionized concepts of imperial sovereignty.

Earthquakes in the Commonwealth have most frequently hit the Indian subcontinent, the Caribbean and the south-western Pacific. Jamaica was rocked on 7 July 1792 and Kingston suffered badly on 15 January 1907. In New Zealand there were earthquakes around Wellington in 1848 and 1855, and Napier, on Hawke's Bay, was virtually destroyed on 3 February 1931. So, too, on 14 October 1968 was the town of Meckering, when an earthquake shook south Western Australia. Rabaul, in Papua New Guinea, suffered the double disasters of an earthquake and a volcanic eruption on 2 June 1937. But the most devastating earthquakes have been in India and Pakistan: Assam, 12 June 1897; from Lahore through the lower Himalayas to *Simla, destroying the towns of Kangra, Palampur and Dharmsala, 3 April 1905; around Bihar, January 1934; in Baluchistan, wrecking the hill station of Quetta, 30 May 1935; in northern Pakistan, 29 December 1974; and in Maharashtra state, India, on 30 September 1993. Minor earthquakes have been known in Kenya and southern Cape Province.

East Africa Company: see *Imperial British East Africa Company*.

East Africa Protectorate: the name given to *Kenya from June 1895 to July 1920, when it was constituted a Crown Colony.

East India Company: the principal institution by which British trade and influence were extended through east Asia between February 1601, when the first five ships of the newly chartered 'Honourable Company' sailed for Sumatra, and the *India Act of 1858. The Company enjoyed trade monopolies between British ports and India until 1813, and China until 1833. For two and a half centuries 'East Indiamen', the Company's ships, were the finest vessels afloat: they were fitted out with considerable space for cargo, but carried passengers in relative comfort, and were well-armed. 'Factories' (trading stations) were established at Masulipatam on the Coromandel coast of India in 1612 and a year later at Surat in Gujarat, 14 miles up-river. Good relations with the Moghul emperors allowed a flourishing trade to develop: fortified factories followed at Madras (1639), Bombay (1661) and Calcutta (1691); *St Helena was acquired in 1651 as a port of call on homeward voyages. Complaints of peculation led to the grant of a royal charter to a rival EIC in 1691, with its powers increased in 1698; ten years later the rivals amalgamated and played an increasing part in Indian affairs as Moghul authority declined.

Administratively the Company was divided into three Indian Presidencies – Calcutta, Madras, Bombay – each of which raised a sepoy army, with British officers trained in the EIC's own military academy at Addiscombe, Surrey. At its peak 'John Company's Army' (as the combined forces were widely called) could put into the field more than 100,000 men to supplement the regular British Army in India. *Clive consolidated the Company's hold on Bengal in 1757, which marked the effective beginning of the British *Raj in India. But when in 1772 the Company's solvency was endangered by a financial crisis in Britain, Lord North's 'Regulating Act' (May 1773) reformed the administration: Warren *Hastings became the first Governor-General of *India, while the Company received a (short-lived) monopoly of the tea trade with America. Parliamentary control of the Company was tightened by Pitt's India Act of August 1784, which placed the EIC under a Board of Control of six commissioners with a president who, from 1802 until 1858, was a cabinet minister. Charter Amendment Acts in 1813, 1833 and 1853 further trimmed the EIC's administrative independence at a time when, territorially, the Company's power was at its zenith with the establishment of the *Straits Settlements, the absorption of Mysore and the Carnatic and, in 1823, the final defeat of the Marathas. But the *Indian Mutiny, which began among sepoys of the Company's largest army in Bengal, exposed the weakness of the Board of Control. With the passage through Parliament of the *India Act (1858) all control finally passed from the Company to the Crown. By 1862 the Company's soldiers were absorbed into the *Indian Army, and the Company's training college in Hertfordshire had become *Haileybury College.

Eastern Caribbean Organization (OECS). The possibility of hostile governments giving support to small revolutionary factions in the West Indies led a group of Eastern Caribbean states (*Barbados, *Antigua, *Dominica, *St Christopher and Nevis, *St Lucia and *St Vincent) to establish in 1981 an organization to promote unity and solidarity in defence of their sovereignty, integrity and independence. The Barbadian prime minister, J. M. G. M. (Tom) Adams (1931–85), who in December 1979 sent troops to help St Vincent suppress a Rastafarian rising on Union Island, proposed a security pact between OECS members in September 1982; he was supported by Jamaica and the United States. When *Grenada seemed paralysed by allegedly Cuban-backed unrest in October 1983, the OECS invited US intervention. On 17 November 1983 it was announced in the Barbadian Parliament that a Regional Security Force would be set up, with headquarters in Barbados and units in each island. Implementation of this pact was delayed through mistrust in London of US involvement in Commonwealth affairs, by resentment in other islands of Barbadian OECS leadership, and by Tom Adams's death.

Egypt, a tributary state of the Ottoman Sultans from 1517 until World War I, was never part of the British Empire, although it formed a British Protectorate from 1914 to 1922. British troops under Sir Garnet *Wolseley occupied Egypt in 1882 to suppress a nationalistic revolt which threatened to cut the revenue of the country's European creditors, including the *Suez Canal Company. What was intended as a temporary occupation acquired permanency from the need to suppress the Mahdist rebellion in the *Sudan and to put Egyptian finances in order. Successive constitutions, imposed by the British, confirmed the sovereignty of the Khedive (the hereditary governor of Egypt) and extended elective representation in a legislature. In practice, however, the modernization of the country was supervised by senior British civil servants (often with Indian experience) and the *de facto* rulers of the country were the three British Consuls-General: Lord *Cromer until 1907; Sir Eldon Gorst (1861–1911), from 1907 until his death; and Lord *Kitchener (1911–14). The British maintained a peacetime army of 5,000 men in Egypt and, on the

Indian model, built up an Egyptian army under British officers. Alexandria became the principal base of the Royal Navy in the eastern Mediterranean, and by the turn of the century half of Egypt's foreign trade was with Britain, while over 70 per cent of vessels using the Suez Canal were British.

In 1914 and 1917 serious consideration was given to annexing Egypt, but proposals were rejected, partly to avoid friction with France and partly because of the growing strength of Egyptian nationalism. The British recognized Egypt's sovereign independence in 1922, with a grandson of the first Khedive becoming King Fuad I. Despite Egypt's independent status, the British High Commissioners exercised great influence on the choice of ministers: *Allenby, as High Commissioner 1919–25, was especially forceful; and Sir Miles Lampson (1880–1964), as High Commissioner 1934–36 and ambassador until 1946, handled both King Farouk (1920–65; reigned 1936–52) and Egyptian politicians with chastening severity. An Anglo-Egyptian Treaty in 1936 promised the gradual withdrawal of British troops, except from the Suez Canal Zone, but Mussolini's invasion of Egypt in 1940 and the subsequent Libyan campaigns against the Italians and the German Afrika Korps postponed British departure. In *World War II, as in its predecessor, Cairo was the natural centre for strategic operations in the Middle East, even though the Egyptian kingdom remained technically neutral until 26 February 1945, when Farouk declared war on Germany. The continued presence of British garrisons and the emergence of the state of Israel with the ending of the *Palestine mandate fanned radical Egyptian nationalism. In July 1952 a military coup overthrew Farouk and established a Republic, in which Gamal Abdel Nasser (1918–70) was the dominant political figure. In November 1954 the British accepted a treaty providing for withdrawal of British troops from the Suez Canal bases within 20 months. The last troops left on 13 June 1956, but six weeks later Nasser nationalized the Suez Canal. This action precipitated the *Suez Crisis, the last occasion upon which the Commonwealth – though far from united – sought to exert pressure on Egypt.

Eire. The ancient name 'Eire', as an alternative to 'Ireland', was revived in the preamble to the 1937 Constitution, approved by the Dáil (the Lower House of the Irish Parliament) in Dublin on 14 June 1937 and effective from 29 December; it replaced the provisions of the Irish Free State. Eire remained within the British Commonwealth, though with an elected president from May 1938 and observing neutrality throughout World War II. When John Costello, a constitutional lawyer, became Eire's Taoiseach (Prime Minister) in 1948 he clarified the country's anomalous status: the Republic of Ireland Bill, presented to the Dáil on 17 November 1948, formally severed all links with the British crown and the Commonwealth from Easter 1949 (18 April).

Elder, Sir Thomas (1818–97), Australian businessman and pastoralist: the youngest of four sons of the shipowner, George Elder, from Kirkcaldy, Scotland, all of whom developed business interests in South Australia. Thomas Elder settled in Adelaide in 1854 and put his money into Walaroo and Moonta copper mines, which prospered. In 1863 he joined a fellow Scot, Robert Barr Smith (1824–1915), in establishing Elder, Smith and Co. which accumulated pastoral lands, in South Australia, Western Australia and Queensland, greater in extent than the partners' native Scotland. Elder, Smith and Co. became the world's largest wool brokers and developed interests in mines, banks, shipping and brewing (Elders IXL). On visits to India and the Middle East Thomas Elder realized the potential of 'the ship of the desert' for expeditions into the Australian interior, establishing a stud of 124 camels and bringing Afghans to manage them. Camels (first used by ⋆Burke and Wills) were supplied for the expeditions of ⋆Giles, ⋆Warburton and others which Elder, Smith and Co. financed. In 1887 Thomas Elder received a knighthood (GCMG).

Elizabeth II (1926–), Queen and Head of the Commonwealth: acceded on 6 February 1952 while in Kenya on the first stage of a proposed journey to Australasia. As Princess Elizabeth she had already visited South Africa, Malta and, with her husband Prince Philip (1921–), made an extensive five-week journey across Canada and into the USA in 1951. A Prime Ministers' meeting soon after her accession agreed that Commonwealth members should employ a form of royal title best suited to their needs but should recognize the sovereign as ⋆Head of the Commonwealth. The Queen's first Christmas broadcast in 1952 emphasized her belief in the Commonwealth as 'a most potent force for good, and one of the true unifying bonds in this torn world', and the rapid spread of air travel allowed her to shed the old identification of the sovereign with the exclusive needs of the United Kingdom. In her Coronation Oath on 2 June 1953 the Queen promised 'to govern the peoples of the United Kingdom of Great Britain and Northern Ireland, Canada, Australia, New Zealand, the Union of South Africa, Pakistan and Ceylon and of' her 'Possessions and the other Territories to any of them belonging or pertaining, according to their respective laws and customs'. In landing at Sydney on 3 February 1954 she became the first reigning sovereign to set foot in Australia and, subsequently, New Zealand. The Queen has visited almost all Commonwealth countries, drawing closer to her subjects by the informal 'walkabouts' introduced in 1963 on a later Australian tour. She regularly hosts Commonwealth Heads of Government meetings wherever they may be held. Mounting republican sentiment in Australia during the ⋆Keating premiership, and to a lesser extent in Canada and New Zealand, is no reflection on Elizabeth II's conscientious fulfilment of the pledge which she broadcast (from Cape

Town) on her twenty-first birthday, dedicating her life to 'the service of our great Imperial Commonwealth'.

Eminent Persons Group. The Nassau Commonwealth Heads of Government Meeting (October 1985) agreed to send an Eminent Persons Commonwealth Mission to South Africa for talks on ways of easing apartheid and advancing 'the fulfilment of the objectives of the (*Commonwealth) Accord'. The group comprised Malcolm *Fraser (Australia) and General Olusegun Obasanjo (Nigeria) as co-chairmen; Lord Barber (ex-Chancellor of the Exchequer), Dame Nita Barrow (Barbados), John Macela (Tanzania), Swaran Singh (India), Archbishop Edward Scott (Canada); and a small secretarial staff led by Chief *Anyaoku (Nigeria). The Group spent six months travelling widely in southern Africa; the most publicized phase was an abortive second visit to Pretoria (14–19 May 1986), abruptly cut short when South African defence forces launched raids into Zambia, Zimbabwe and Botswana against alleged ANC guerrilla targets. The Group's subsequent report in June 1986 condemned apartheid as 'awesome in its cruelty . . . creating human misery and deprivation and blighting the lives of millions'. It praised the willingness of *Mandela and other black leaders to seek a non-racist compromise, but doubted the desire of the South African Government to promote reform. The firm tone of the Eminent Persons Group hardened world opinion against South Africa's racial policies.

Empire Day (24 May). In 1902 King Edward VII proposed that the birthday of his mother, Queen Victoria, should be honoured as Empire Day in order to record the assistance given by 'the colonies to the mother country' in the (recently ended) *Boer War. Thereafter 24 May was duly celebrated officially by schoolchildren across the Empire, though with diminishing display after the death of King George V in 1936. From 1949 onwards popular usage favoured *'Commonwealth Day', but it was not until December 1958 that formal sanction was given to the change of name. The association with Queen Victoria ended in 1967, when 'Commonwealth Day' was observed on 19 June. Even thereafter, however, 'Victoria Day' continued to be celebrated in parts of Canada.

Empire Games. Teams from the United Kingdom, Australasia, Canada and South Africa took part in a Festival of Empire (which included *swimming) at the Crystal Palace in London in 1911. But the first meeting to be called the British Empire Games was held at Hamilton, Ontario in 1930, with eleven competing countries. The greatest emphasis was on men's *athletics. At the Second British Empire Games (London, 1934) women had equal status with men. For these Games the Empire Pool at Wembley was constructed, in order to encourage competitive swimming and diving. The Third and Fourth British Empire Games were held in Sydney (1938) and Auckland (1950). In 1954 the Games returned to Canada – Vancouver – but were renamed 'British Empire and Commonwealth Games', as were the subsequent Games in Cardiff (1958), Perth, Western Australia (1962) and Kingston, Jamaica (1966). Thereafter they were called *Commonwealth Games.

Empire Marketing Board was formed in Britain by the second Baldwin government in 1926, at a time when *Churchill was Chancellor of the Exchequer and *Amery Colonial and Dominions Secretary. The Board promoted the marketing of food and goods produced in the Empire, thereby increasing knowledge of the overseas dominions and colonies in British schools. A film unit was established (see *Cinema). The Marketing Board became a casualty of government economies in 1933.

Enosis movement. Support in *Cyprus for union (enosis) with Greece began late in the nineteenth century when the island was still part of the Ottoman Empire, though under British protection. But it was in 1931 that serious riots in support of enosis first rocked the island. A sustained campaign, including guerrilla operations by EOKA ('National Organization of Cypriot Fighters') continued from 1955 until 1959, and was revived in the independent Republic of Cyprus in 1964. The movement only died down when the failure of an EOKA coup against President *Makarios in 1974 precipitated a Turkish invasion of northern Cyprus and the partition of the island.

Eskimos, the name widely given to the native Inuit peoples of northern Canada. Inuit is a language and culture common to a naturally wandering people who under rigorous Arctic conditions have developed hunting and survival skills which enable them to live in Greenland, Alaska and the Russian tundra as well as in the *Northwest Territories. The coastal Inuit live on fish and marine mammals; inland Inuit hunt caribou. By the mid-1960s Canadian eskimo numbers had fallen to little more than 13,000, but greater medical attention and a birth rate of some 3.8 per cent a year have lifted numbers to about 30,000 Inuits, spread thinly from the Alaskan border to the east of Hudson Bay and on the islands of the Arctic Ocean. The first friendly contacts between kabloona (Inuit for 'whites') and Inuits date from 1822–23, but it was not until December 1953 that the Canadian Government established a Department of Northern Affairs and Natural Resources. In Baffin Island an Eskimo Rehabilitation Centre was set up at Frobisher Bay (subsequently renamed Iqaluit), and a West Baffin Eskimo Cooperative at Cape Dorset. Abraham Okpik was the first Eskimo to be appointed to the Council of the Northwest Territories, in October 1965; a massive educational programme has since been introduced.

Eureka Stockade: the culmination of unrest in Ballarat, Victoria, at the height of the *Gold Rush in 1854. Diggers resented the corruption of a system which treated them as third-class citizens, who had to buy licences to work and carry them at all times. Rioting began when magistrates refused to convict the licensee of the Eureka Hotel, Ballarat, of the murder of a digger (witnessed by other workers) on the goldfield. The hotel was burnt down. Troops sent to Ballarat on 28 November found a thousand diggers entrenched behind a stockade thrown across the ruins of the hotel and flying the 'Eureka Flag' of defiance: a white cross on a blue background and showing the five stars of the Southern Cross constellation. On 3 December the troops broke the stockade and, during the fighting, 30 diggers and 5 soldiers were killed. When 13 diggers were charged with high treason, they were acquitted by juries sympathetic to their grievances. A Royal Commission thereupon investigated conditions in the gold fields and secured some basic rights for the miners. The defenders of the stockade were led by an Irish immigrant, Peter Lalor (1827–89), who later entered politics and was Speaker of the Colonial Legislature in Melbourne, 1880–87.

European Community. The 'Common Market' of Belgium, France, West Germany, Italy and Luxembourg came into being on 1 January 1958 as a 'European Economic Community' (EEC); in January 1986 existing institutions were consolidated in a single body, henceforth known as the European Community (EC). Attempts by Britain to join the EEC in 1963 and 1967 were blocked by the French President, Charles de Gaulle, not least because he wished France to be the sole member-country with wide colonial links. The persistent British campaign for membership weakened such 'empire trading' connections as had survived World War II: Canada, for example, doubled exports to the USA in the years 1958–67 while the British were knocking at the gates of the Common Market. By 1967 the only ex-colonies in the Commonwealth offering preferential terms to British importers were Malawi and The Gambia. When, after de Gaulle's retirement, the British resumed talks with the EEC in the summer of 1970, care was taken to safeguard Commonwealth interests; concessions over dairy products from New Zealand and Caribbean sugar were agreed by an EEC ministerial meeting in Luxembourg in June 1971, and the Treaty of Accession (22 January 1972) offered twenty Commonwealth countries a special relationship with the Community which was eventually defined in the first *Lomé Convention (1975). Separate agreements on commercial co-operation have also been signed between the EC and Canada, India, Pakistan, Sri Lanka, Bangladesh, Cyprus, Malta and (as members of the Association of South East Asian Nations) with Malaysia and Singapore. Community agreements have also been reached with New Zealand, over the supply of butter and lamb. Australia accepts reciprocal customs tariff preference with the United Kingdom, but maintains almost exactly the same volume of trade with the USA as with the EC collectively.

Evatt, Herbert Vere (1894–1965), Australian statesman and lawyer: born at East Maitland, New South Wales, and educated at Sydney University; became a barrister in 1918 and a Doctor of Laws in 1924. He specialized in trade union cases, winning great respect as a defender of civil liberties in the 1920s, and served as a judge, 1930–40. Dr Evatt was returned to Parliament in Canberra in the 1940 election as an Australian Labor Party representative and served *Curtin and *Chifley as both Attorney-General and External Minister, 1941–49. At the San Francisco Conference (1945) he won international respect for upholding the interests of smaller nations during the drafting sessions for the UN Charter, successfully piloting 26 amendments clarifying the legal status of the General Assembly and its councils. As Leader of the Opposition to *Menzies from 1951 to 1960 he opposed anti-Communist witch hunts and the attempt in courts to proscribe the Australian Communist Party. After retiring from politics Dr Evatt was Chief Justice of New South Wales, 1960–62. He also published studies on dominion government and the concept of the United Nations.

Eyre, Edward John (1815–1901), explorer and colonial governor: at the age of 17 he emigrated from his native Scotland, worked on sheep farms in New South Wales, and overlanded stock to South Australia. From Adelaide he set out to explore the interior beyond the Flinders Range and, after a 400-mile journey, discovered the shallow salt lake named after him. In February 1841, accompanied by an aborigine, he became the first white man to cross the Nullarbor Plain from the vicinity of Adelaide to reach the Western Australia seaport of Albany in July. From 1841 to 1844 he was a protector of aborigines in South Australia. After returning to Britain in 1845 and publishing an account of his expeditions, he was appointed Lieutenant-Governor of New Zealand, where he served from 1846 to 1853. For six years he was Governor of *St Vincent in the West Indies, with such success that he was made Governor of *Jamaica in 1864. A year later he put down the *Morant Bay rebellion with such harshness that there was widespread indignation in London. He was suspended and tried by a Royal Commission of Inquiry in Kingston, Jamaica, which commended his swift action in stamping out the revolt but blamed him for allowing excesses which caused 600 deaths and imposed severe floggings on both men and women. Eyre was recalled to England, where he faced attempts by eminent intellectuals and liberal campaigners to bring him to court on charges of murder. His legal expenses were paid from public funds. For 27 years he received a colonial governor's pension.

Fairbridge, Kingsley Ogilvie (1885–1924), educationist: born at Grahamstown, Cape Colony, but contracted malaria in Mashonaland as a child. Despite chronic health problems, in 1908 he went to Oxford to study forestry as a Rhodes Scholar, and became interested in social work. After marrying a nurse, Ruby Whitmore (1890–1966), he founded a Child Emigration Society (1913) in the belief that orphaned and under-privileged children might find a purpose in life as pastoralists in a new continent. The Fairbridges then travelled to Western Australia and the same year (1913) founded a farm school for 35 orphaned immigrants at Pinjarra, near Perth, which after World War I accommodated 200 boys and girls. Pinjarra became the model for 'Fairbridge Schools' across Australia, and also for a Canadian experiment. Ruby Fairbridge continued her husband's work after his death, and at one time had 400 pupils. Interest died down with changing attitudes to emigration, and by 1970 only the Pinjarra School survived. Fairbridge's enterprise is commemorated by scholarships bearing his name which enable British students to spend terms at Commonwealth universities.

Falkland Islands (Malvinas in Spanish): British dependent territories in the south Atlantic, some 300 miles east of the Strait of Magellan and 8,000 miles from the United Kingdom; they are linked with *South Georgia, 800 miles to the south-east. East Falkland has the only town, Stanley, which the 1986 census showed as housing 1,200 of the 1,916 Falkland Islanders, their economy being dependent on sheep and fishing. Attempts to found settlements on the islands by Spain, France and Britain in the eighteenth century ended in Britain's favour in 1771, but the islands were considered unprofitable and the British withdrew in 1774. However, when newly-independent Argentina sought possession as residual legatee of the Spanish colonial empire, Britain sent a naval expedition and formally made the Falklands a Crown Colony (1832). The Argentines never abandoned their claims, taking the question to the United Nations in 1946 and assuming so threatening an attitude in 1977 that the Callaghan government despatched warships to the area. Political discussion of Argentine claims in London and Buenos Aires made no progress (1978–81), although the Thatcher government cut down on defence of the islands until in 1981 protection was limited to a single detachment of marines on East Falkland and an ice patrol vessel armed with two 20-mm guns. In March 1982 the Argentine dictator, General Galtieri, ordered the seizure of the Malvinas, an occupation completed on 2 April. The Thatcher government responded by sending from England a task force of 20 warships, with support aircraft and 6,000 fighting troops, a brilliantly-executed logistical operation which recovered the Falklands by 14 June, though at the cost of a thousand British and Argentinian lives and the loss of four naval vessels and a chartered container ship. A strong military garrison was thereafter based in the

Famine

Falklands. A Falkland Islands Development Corporation was established in June 1984, and a new constitution affirming the right of Falkland Islanders to self-determination came into force in October 1985.

Famine has, over the centuries, proved a chronic scourge in Africa and the Indian subcontinent. The aborigine population of Australia has also suffered from food shortages following long droughts, particularly the rainless years 1895 to 1902. The first famines to arouse wide sympathy in Britain were in Bengal in 1860–61, 1874, 1877 and especially in 1896–97 (2.5 million deaths) and 1900 (more than 3 million deaths). The *Ngaa Nere* (great hunger) of southern Africa in 1898–1900 ravaged the Masai and Kikuyu peoples of *Kenya with particular intensity; on this occasion (as also more recently), the drought caused cultivated areas to lapse into bush and even into desert. Occasionally human folly has created famine: the Xhosa ('kaffirs') of the eastern Cape Colony lost one-fifth of their population in 1857 from shortage of food after accepting prophecies that, if cattle were slaughtered, a great wind would arise and sweep the white men into the sea. More often, local food shortages have sprung from enforced cultivation of cash crops to the neglect of staple needs: ground-nuts in The Gambia and cocoa in modern Ghana, for example, pushed out rice. The gravity of natural disasters has been compounded by political upheaval and maladministration. Thus, in British India, where improved transport and *irrigation barrages lessened the impact of famine at the height of the Raj, the threat of Japanese invasion and confusion over the respective responsibilities of imperial and provincial administration aggravated the famine of 1943, in which more than 3 million people died. The worst recorded African famines, intensified by civil wars and neglected roads and railways, began as recently as 1983/4 and continue to afflict the continent, despite unprecedented international relief work. Although the greatest suffering has hit non-Commonwealth lands in north-east Africa, there have also been grave shortages of food in northern Kenya, Uganda and parts of Tanzania. The impact of famine in other lands has occasionally led to mass migration of refugees across Commonwealth frontiers: as early as 1928/9 a drought in Rwanda (Ruanda-Burundi, then the most fertile of Belgium's colonial territories) precipitated a flight into Uganda, a tragedy repeated and intensified by military unrest during 1994.

Farrer, William James (1845–1906), wheat herborist: born in Westmorland, he began studying medicine at Pembroke College, Cambridge but developed tuberculosis and emigrated to New South Wales, where he worked as a surveyor for the Department of Lands, 1875–86. He then settled at Lambrigg, on the Murrumbidgee River (near modern *Canberra) and experimented systematically with cross-breeding strains of wheat to discover one which would resist the rust disease but withstand Australia's climatic variations. In 1901 he perfected 'Federation', the strain principally used by the successful Australian wheat industry for more than a quarter of a century. This rust-resistant strain also benefited other Commonwealth countries, notably Kenya.

Fashoda Crisis (1898). Fears that the French wished to secure political mastery over the upper Nile, thereby threatening control of the waters which irrigated *Egypt, prompted the despatch of British troops under *Kitchener deeper into the *Sudan after his victory at Omdurman (2 September 1898). After travelling 400 miles further up the Nile Kitchener reached the small town of Fashoda on 19 September. There he found a French force under Captain Marchand which had crossed the continent from Brazzaville in an eighteen-month journey. Marchand claimed that Fashoda belonged to France, whereas Kitchener asserted that the whole of the Sudan (including Fashoda) had passed under British sovereignty by right of conquest. Lord *Salisbury, the British Prime Minister, refused all compromise with France unless Marchand withdrew, and the Royal Navy was put on war alert on 27 October. Eight days later the French accepted Salisbury's demands and ordered Marchand back to Paris. By an agreement signed in March 1899 France renounced all claims to the Nile valley. The crisis was the outstanding British diplomatic victory in the *scramble for Africa, but was regarded in France as such a humiliating defeat that when the Anglo-French Entente Cordiale was established in 1904, Lord *Cromer ordered the name of Fashoda to be expunged from the map, to save the French embarrassment: since then, the town has been known as Kodok.

Fiji: a Melanesian group of some 100 inhabited and 200 uninhabited islands in the south-west Pacific, with their capital, Suva, on the largest island, Viti Levu. Tasman discovered the islands in 1643; Cook visited them in 1774; Bligh surveyed them after the mutiny on the *Bounty* in 1789. In October 1874 the British negotiated treaties with the Fijian tribal leaders and constituted the island a Crown Colony. Indians were brought in to work on the sugar plantations, their numbers increasing so rapidly that by 1966 they outnumbered the Fijians. However, the Fijian birthrate increased over the following twenty years, so that the latest census shows the Fijians forming 48.4 per cent of the population and the Indians 46.4 per cent. The islands achieved prosperity from sugar, gold, coconut oil and bananas. In October 1970 Fiji became an independent state in the Commonwealth, under a Fijian Governor-General appointed by Queen Elizabeth II, but successive military coups in May and September 1987 led to the proclamation of a republic and a decision to allow membership of the Commonwealth to lapse.

Film industry: see *Cinema*.

Fires. No cities in the Empire and Commonwealth have experienced such dramatic conflagrations as London in 1666 or Chicago in 1871. The wooden buildings of pioneer or plantation societies were, however, naturally inflammable. Much of Kingston, Jamaica has been burned down on four occasions: 1780, 1843, 1862, and 1882. Central Georgetown, Guyana was gutted in 1945. St John's, Newfoundland's capital, was destroyed by fire and rebuilt three times in the nineteenth century: 1816, 1842, and 1892 – by which date the citizens decided that stone was preferable to wood. However, on 25 April 1900 the largely stone and brick city of Ottawa was swept by a fire which left 12,000 homeless in Ottawa itself and in Hull, across the river; a later fire destroyed the original Parliament Buildings (1916). Lyttleton in New Zealand, the port of Christchurch, was levelled in the 'Great Fire' of 24 October 1870, and many smaller wooden-built townships suffered a similar fate, as did part of the Lambton Harbour district of Wellington in 1912. New Zealand's countryside was exposed to 'bush burns', but fires sweeping rapidly across the countryside have always posed a greater menace in Australia, especially after periods of drought. In Victoria a wave of bush fires in late January 1851 culminated in Black Thursday (6 February) when, with the Melbourne shade temperature reaching 117 °F (47 °C), strong northerly winds swept the flames through the colony. Similar high temperatures and strong winds fanned another bush fire in Victoria on Black Friday (13 January 1939), when the town of Noojee, 70 miles east of Melbourne, was destroyed. Parts of New South Wales and South Australia experienced bush fires at the same time. In January 1967 fires cut the main road between Melbourne and Geelong, and in Tasmania destroyed 650 houses around Hobart. All the south-eastern states suffered from bush fires in February 1983. Arson was suspected, as it was in January 1994 when the fires in New South Wales reached the outskirts of Parramatta and came within 10 miles of central Sydney.

First Fleet: the convoy of nine ships, escorted by HMS *Sirius* and HMS *Supply*, which brought the first British settlers to Australia. The fleet, under the command of Captain Arthur Philip, sailed from Portsmouth on 17 May 1787. Five hundred animals were taken aboard when the fleet put into Cape Town in October. The voyage lasted 252 days and there were 48 deaths at sea. The settlers disembarked at Port Jackson, Sydney Cove, on 26 January 1788, with basic supplies for two years. Of 1,030 people landed from the ships, 548 men and 188 women were convicts transported to the new penal settlement. Another 220 women convicts were transported aboard the *Lady Juliana*, which left English waters in July 1789 and reached Sydney on 3 June 1790, a fortnight ahead of the notorious *Second Fleet.

Fisher, Andrew (1862–1928), Australian Prime Minister: born in Scotland; became a miner in an Ayrshire coalfield at the age of ten, emigrating in 1885 to Queensland, where he worked in the mines and as an engine-driver. He helped build up the trade union movement and the new Labor Party. In 1893 he was elected to the Queensland legislature and in December 1899 was a member of Queensland's short-lived Labor ministry, the first socialist parliamentary government in the world. He became leader of the Australian Labor Party (ALP) in 1907 and was Prime Minister on three occasions: November 1908–April 1909; April 1910–June 1913; September 1914–October 1915. In his second ministry he introduced maternity allowances and extended old age and invalid pensions, but he never had a sufficient majority to promote extensive socialist measures. On the outbreak of World War I Fisher pledged Labor support of the war effort 'to the last man and the last shilling'. From 1916 to 1921 he was Australian High Commissioner in London, where he showed himself a staunch supporter of the unity of Empire.

Flinders, Matthew (1774–1814), navigator: born in Lincolnshire, the son of a surgeon. He became a naval officer and saw action against the French in 1793 before sailing for New South Wales aboard HMS *Reliance* (1795–97). With Bass he explored the hinterland around Port Jackson in 1796, later surveying the coast of Van Diemen's Land (Tasmania), confirming the existence of the Bass Strait and discovering the island in the Furneaux group which is named after him. A brief spell of leave in 1800 was followed by a second voyage of discovery, in which Flinders circumnavigated the continent (1801–03). Among the regions which he surveyed in detail were the sites of present-day Adelaide and Melbourne, much of the Great Barrier Reef, and the Gulf of Carpentaria. His ship, the *Investigator*, was scarcely seaworthy after the voyage northwards and he arrived back at Sydney only after a remarkable show of seamanship. During a voyage home, undertaken in poor health, he was detained by the French on the island of Mauritius, where he was held from December 1803 to 1811. When he eventually reached England he prepared for publication a magnificent survey of the southern continent, *A Voyage to Terra Australis*. It was published in London on 18 July 1814; Flinders died the next day. More than any other writer he brought the name 'Australia' into common usage.

Florey, Howard Walter (1898–1968), Australian pathologist: born and educated in Adelaide. He came to England in 1921 as a Rhodes Scholar at Oxford and served medicine for the rest of his academic life, in both Britain and Australia. Florey was Professor of Pathology at Sheffield (1931–35) and at Oxford (1935–62). At the same time as he was making Oxford a world centre for pathological research and serving as Provost of The Queen's College (1962–68), he was also an adviser on medical research in Canberra (1947–57) and Chancellor of the Australian National University (1966–68). His greatest work was on antibiotics; and in 1945 Florey shared the Nobel Prize for Chemistry with Ernst Chain and Alexander Fleming for their joint development of penicillin. Florey was knighted in 1944, received the Order of Merit and a peerage in 1965 (Baron Florey of Adelaide and Marston), and in 1960 became the first Australian to be honoured with the Presidency of the Royal Society.

Flying Doctors. In 1928 John Flynn, a Presbyterian minister in Queensland and founder of his church's Australian Inland Mission, set up an Aerial Medical Service to bring speedy assistance by radio and plane to outback areas. The service was based at Cloncurry in Queensland: pedal-operated wireless transmitters could summon help for treatment and, if necessary, removal to hospital. The service became a state responsibility in 1933, with the name changed to Flying Doctor Service of Australia in 1942; it was honoured with the courtesy prefix 'Royal' in 1954. The service goes far beyond medical needs: the radio network has been used for important messages and for teaching purposes. A flying doctor service was established in Kenya in 1957 on the initiative of the Nairobi surgeon, Sir Michael Wood (1919–88).

Football: Association ('Soccer'): an ancient pastime but, as an organized competitive sport, a British creation, dating in London from the formation of the Football Association in 1863 and in Scotland from the founding of Queen's Park Club in Glasgow in 1867. Football spread first to continental Europe and then to South America, largely on the initiative of British businessmen and specialist technicians working abroad. The only country in the overseas empire where the game developed rapidly was South Africa, whence it spread to neighbouring Southern Rhodesia. An English touring team played three international matches in South Africa as early as 1910, although a professional league was not formed there until 1959, around Johannesburg. In Australia the earliest matches date from 1880 and, despite the appeal of other codes of football, there was always some interest in New South Wales and Queensland. The following increased rapidly after World War II, with immigrants arriving from southern Europe. In 1966 OFC (Oceania Football Confederation) was set up, to co-ordinate the promotion of the sport in Australia, New Zealand, Papua New Guinea and Fiji. Since gaining independence Nigeria, Ghana, Kenya, Tanzania and Zimbabwe have all been members of the African Football Confederation. Canada has shown little interest in this code of football.

Football: Australian Rules: dates from 1858, when some Irish members of the Melbourne Cricket Club devised a specifically Australian game for its members to play during the winter. The sport owes much to

Gaelic football and was popular with the Irish at the gold diggings. There were few rules, but a code of laws was drafted in 1866, and in 1877 the Victoria Football Association (VFA) was founded, the oldest football body of any code in the southern hemisphere. The 18-man team comprises six trios of full forwards, half-forwards, centres, half-backs, full-backs and 'ruck' (who are, in effect, roving forwards). An oval ball is used, the object being to gain 6 points by kicking goals through central posts 7 yards apart: one point may be scored for 'behinds' (near-miss kicks), or for a kick through the posts touched by a player after leaving the boot. It is a long-kicking game, with no off-side rule and no knock-on rule; a player may run with the ball only if he bounces it at least every 10 yards. Australian Rules Football was played in New Zealand's South Island in the late 1860s, but it developed mainly in Western Australia, Victoria, South Australia and Tasmania. A 'League' variation brought the code to Sydney in 1897, and after World War II it spread through Queensland to Papua New Guinea, and is also played in Darwin. The code has never spread to other lands. It remains especially popular in Victoria.

Football: Canadian Rules. The most popular sport in Canada is ice hockey, and lacrosse – a game adapted from Canadian Indian origins – constitutes a national sport. Canadian Rules Football was a variation of the Rugby code, as modified in 1874 by McGill University in Montreal. Subsequently it owed much to the parallel development of American Football, although in Canada the game is played over a larger area, with 12 rather than 11 players, and is considered more open and fast-moving. The game was long based on the eastern cities of Toronto, Hamilton, Ottawa and Montreal, but it also enjoys a following in Winnipeg, Regina, Calgary and Vancouver. The growth of professionalism since World War II has brought many Americans into the Canadian sides and, by reaction, may more recently have contributed to the revival of Canadian interest in the Rugby Union code.

Football: Rugby. Traditionally the game dates from November 1823 when, at Rugby School in Warwickshire, William Webb Ellis livened up a familiar pastime by picking up a football and running; the incident may be a legendary tale, but the location is correct. The running game developed in London, the Universities, Yorkshire and Lancashire during the early 1860s and was played in Edinburgh as early as 1858; although the Rugby Football Union was only set up in London in January 1871, there are records of Rugby matches in South Island, New Zealand even earlier: May and September 1870. Rugby Union football rapidly became the national sport of New Zealand, attracting the Maori people as well as players of European descent. By 1888 New Zealand could send a touring side to the British Isles, although the famous *All Blacks appellation dates from 1905/6. The earliest representative overseas tour made by any

Rugby XV was a visit by New South Wales to New Zealand in 1882, seven years after the sport was first organized in Australia. The initiative in South Africa was taken by Stellenbosch University, whose students spread interest in the game through the Southern African colonies in the early 1880s. Provincial unions were followed in 1889 by the establishment of a South African Rugby Football Board at Kimberley, where matches are known to have been played during the *diamond rush. *Rhodes himself gave financial backing to the earliest British tour of Cape Colony, in 1891. South Africa began fielding a dominant international side – the Springboks – soon after the federation of the colonies in 1910, maintaining a particularly intensive rivalry with New Zealand until 1981, when the anti-apartheid sporting ban left the Republic isolated; however, non-whites were eligible to win international caps from 1993; and in 1995 South Africa was invited to host the World Cup – and won it. Namibia showed resource in beating Ireland twice in international matches in July 1991. The Union code has achieved great popularity in Fiji and also in Western Samoa, who beat Wales at Cardiff in the 1991 World Cup. In Canada there were Rugby clubs in Ontario in 1882, but the game was most popular in British Columbia, the province contributing 14 players to the first All-Canada International XV, who lost to the British Lions at Toronto in September 1966. Canadian Rugby skills developed rapidly in the 1980s: Scotland were beaten in May 1991, and by 1993 Canada had also won victories over Wales and France. Rugby Union in Australia long suffered from the rival attractions of Australian Rules Football and Rugby League, but it survived in New South Wales and around Brisbane, even though no Union matches were played in Queensland between 1919 and 1929. By 1963 the Union game had vastly improved at both state and Commonwealth level. With an impetus from Italian immigrants, it continued to gain popularity until the skill and determination of the Australians gave them victory in the World Cup Final at Twickenham on 2 November 1991.

Rugby League football began with the secession from the Rugby Union in August 1895 of 21 clubs in the north of England over the right to reimburse players for income lost through taking time off work to play football. Variations were introduced into the laws, reducing the size of a team from fifteen to thirteen and amending the rules to make for an allegedly faster running game. The code became popular in Australia, especially around Sydney, and in New Zealand (where it long remained an amateur game). A mixed team of Australians and New Zealanders came to Britain in 1907/8; separate national sides competed thereafter. By 1963 Australia had consolidated a world ascendancy never effectively challenged.

Foreign and Commonwealth Office. The Foreign Office was established in London in March 1782, with Charles James Fox as Foreign Secretary taking over the conduct of relations with other governments from the 'Secretary of State for the Northern Department'. From 1878 until 1880 the Foreign Office was responsible for *Cyprus, and before World War I handled the affairs of *Egypt, which was then technically a vassal state of the Ottoman Empire. During the *scramble for Africa the Consular Service of the Foreign Office looked after *Zanzibar (1890 to 1913), *Uganda (1893 to 1905), East Africa (*Kenya, 1895–1905), and also the protectorates in *Nigeria until World War I. On 1 October 1968 the Foreign Office merged with the *Commonwealth Office to accept ministerial responsibility for relations with foreign governments, Commonwealth governments and dependent territories alike.

Forestry is the science of productively controlling, tending and managing large tracts of woodland. It provided the practical skills on which were based the two major historic industries of Canada, logging and sawmilling: Canada's timber trade began when the Napoleonic wars cut Britain off from her traditional Baltic suppliers; Quebec City thus became the chief timber port in the world, with the sawmills multiplying rapidly with the coming of steam power in the late 1820s. These forest-based industries were boosted by the completion of the *Canadian Pacific Railway, and the coming of light steam-driven donkey engines enabled the cedars and Douglas firs of *British Columbia to be felled for export. So extensive was the timber industry in Canada that in 1906 *Laurier, as Prime Minister, presided over an inaugural Forestry Convention, to stress the need for orderly felling and long-term planning. This protective initiative foreshadowed the concern shown later this century in other dominions, where much forest is state protected: almost all in New Zealand, and some 75 per cent of woodland in Australia, with particular care given to safeguarding the eucalyptus of New South Wales and Queensland. In some parts of the Commonwealth trade has remained consistent – the *rubber industry of Malaysia, for example. Elsewhere, greed and lack of planning has outstripped resources: thus, the mahogany trade of *Belize (then British Honduras) flourished in the early years of the century and reached a peak in the late 1920s but then declined rapidly, though some 44 per cent of land in Belize remains forested. The *Langkawi declaration of 1989 showed a growing collective Commonwealth concern for protection of the environment and the development of renewable natural resources. Financial aid has been given for the planting of trees in Sri Lanka and Cyprus, and in 1991 the Harare Heads of Government Meeting backed a programme for pilot schemes to sustain and develop tropical forestry, put forward by President Hoyte of Guyana (where more than 80 per cent of the land surface is covered by tropical forest). In Britain the Natural Resources Institute of the *Overseas Development Administration proposed co-operative ventures to safeguard the rainforests of Ghana. In several African Commonwealth countries attempts have been made to check the felling of trees by finding alternative sources of revenue for forest communities: thus in The Gambia, co-operatives have been set up to market organic honey.

Forrest, John (1847–1918), Australian explorer and politician: born at Bunbury, Western Australia, and educated at Perth; entered the Surveyor-General's department in 1864, becoming Surveyor-General himself in 1883. Forrest undertook three major expeditions into the interior: in 1869 he explored eastwards from Perth to the fringe of the Great Victoria Desert; in 1870 he followed the coastal route to South Australia; and in 1874, accompanied by his brother Alexander Forrest (1849–1901), he travelled from Geraldton around the northern fringe of the desert and down to Lake Torrens and Adelaide. Forrest became Western Australia's first Premier (1890–1901). He was largely responsible for maintaining the settlement at Kalgoorlie, after the *gold rush, by ensuring a permanent water supply; he also completed the conversion of Fremantle into a modern port. He entered federal politics in 1901 and held several ministerial posts, including Home Affairs, Defence and Treasury. In 1918 he became Baron Forrest of Bunbury, the first Australian to receive a peerage. He died at sea on the voyage back to Fremantle after taking his seat in the House of Lords.

Forty-ninth Parallel of latitude: forms the boundary between the United States and Canada across more than 3,000 miles of prairie, from Lake of the Woods in Ontario westwards towards Vancouver, British Columbia. This, the longest undefended frontier in the world, was originally proposed by John Quincy Adams (later President of the USA) in 1814. It received formal definition by the Webster–Ashburton Treaty of August 1842 and was clarified in the Treaty of Washington of June 1846, which settled the *Oregon Question. A Canadian–American survey amicably traced the international boundary along the southern limits of Saskatchewan and Alberta in 1872/3.

Fox, Sir William (1812–93), New Zealand Prime Minister: born in London and educated at Wadham College, Oxford; called to the Bar of the Inner Temple in 1842. A year later he became resident agent for the New Zealand Company at Nelson in South Island, becoming principal agent in 1848 and entering colonial politics. In May 1856 he became New Zealand's second Prime Minister, but his government lasted only twelve days. He was again Prime Minister from July 1861 until August 1862, from June 1969 until September 1872, and for five weeks in March–April 1873. Essentially, however, there were no political parties at this time and so influential was Fox that his opponents dubbed the eight governments between 1869 and 1877 'The Continuous Ministry', believing that all power was held by Fox, and the Auckland financiers who backed him. Business boomed in the Fox years; Wellington and Auckland developed as cities; the railway network spread; new roads were built; and there was a jump in immigration, mainly from Scotland. Fox was knighted in 1871.

Franklin, Sir John (1786–1847), explorer and colonial governor: born at Spilsby, Lincolnshire; entered the Royal Navy as a midshipman in 1801, saw action at the Battle of Copenhagen, and was serving aboard HMS *Bellerophon* in the Battle of Trafalgar. He commanded the survey ship *Trent* in Canadian Arctic waters in 1818. A year later he led an expedition from Fort York on Hudson Bay to Coppermine in the Arctic Circle, and back by way of Fort Providence. A second expedition (1825–27) reached the Mackenzie River, crossed to Garry Island in the Arctic Sea, established a winter base (Fort Franklin) on the Great Bear Lake, and returned along new trails to Montreal. He was knighted in 1829 and returned to naval service in the Aegean, before accepting office as Lieutenant-Governor of Van Diemen's Land (Tasmania; 1834–43). His gubernatorial term saw a marked improvement in the conditions for transported convicts. In 1845 he returned to the Canadian Arctic, seeking the elusive North-west Passage. His party sailed from Baffin Bay and up Lancaster Sound, but were never sighted again after 26 July 1845. Later expeditions found evidence that Franklin's expedition had been trapped in the ice for 19 months; that Franklin himself had died in June 1847; and that, though the expedition had gone on to discover a north-west passage, all the survivors had perished after abandoning their ships in April 1848 and attempting to reach the Hudson's Bay Company outpost on Back's River.

Franklin, (Stella Marian Sarah) Miles (1879–1954), Australian novelist and feminist: born, the eldest of seven children, at Talbingo in New South Wales, the great-great-granddaughter of a *First Fleet trans-portee. Most of her childhood was spent on bush farms, but the family later settled on the outskirts of Sydney where she wrote the first of several autobiographical novels, *My Brilliant Career* (1901), which was used as the basis for a film in 1979. Miles Franklin became a feminist, emigrated to Chicago in 1906 and worked as a secretary for a women's trade union movement. With the coming of war she crossed to Britain and served as a nurse on the Macedonian Front (1916–18). She returned to Australia in 1927 and in 1928 published *Up the Country*, the first in a series of novels written under the pen-name of 'Brent of Bin Bin': her true identity was not revealed until twelve years after her death. Under her own name she wrote *All That Swagger* (1936) and *My Career Goes Bung* (1946). Her will established the annual Miles Franklin Award, a prestigious Australian literary prize.

Fraser, (John) Malcolm (1930–   ), Australian Prime Minister: a grazier's son, born and educated at Melbourne; completed his studies at

Magdalen College, Oxford, as a Rhodes Scholar. When he entered the Federal Parliament as Liberal member for Wannon in 1955 he was the youngest MP in the House. He was Army Minister (1966–8), Education Minister (1968–9 and 1971–2), Defence Minister (1969–71), and became Leader of the Opposition in March 1975. Eight months later he succeeded Gough *Whitlam as head of a caretaker government, pending a general election. On 13 December 1975 Fraser's coalition gained a record majority in the federal House (91 seats to 36), and his government was re-elected in 1980, despite clear signs of economic recession. Malcolm Fraser was a convinced anti-racist, and his governments showed genuine concern for the aborigines at home as well as seeking to relieve the burden of apartheid on South Africa's blacks. He lost support electorally, however, over his government's failure to deal with falling overseas prices for Australia's primary products or to counter the recession which by late 1982 had left more than 10 per cent of the work-force unemployed. Fraser lost the election of March 1983 to Labor, under Bob *Hawke. Soon afterwards he resigned from Parliament to concentrate on farming in western Victoria. He remained staunchly opposed to racism, however, and in 1986 was co-chairman of the Commonwealth *Eminent Persons Group when it reported on conditions in southern Africa.

Fraser, Peter (1884–1950), New Zealand Prime Minister: born at Fearn in the Scottish Highlands; emigrated in 1910 and worked on the Wellington waterfront. He was an organizer of the dock and shipping strike of 1913, the first big trade union confrontation in New Zealand. Fraser was a founder of the New Zealand Labour Party in 1916 and represented Wellington Central in parliament from 1918 until his death. He became Minister of Education and Health in 1935 and, when *Savage died in March 1940, succeeded to the premiership. He believed strongly in imperial unity and worked well with Churchill, Roosevelt and *Evatt, although always asserting his government's right to control the disposition of the dominion's fighting units. In 1945 Fraser was chairman of the San Francisco Conference sub-committee which decided the form of UN trusteeship; and in the same year he organized a gift of £10 million from the dominion to the United Kingdom to assist post-war reconstruction in 'the mother country'. Fraser comfortably won the general election of 1946. His peacetime government encouraged state control of industry and gave patronage to the arts but, ironically, Fraser was challenged by militants in the Watersiders Union at Wellington, which he had helped to create. He lost the election of 30 November 1949, by 12 seats in a House of Representatives of 80 members. Eleven months later he suffered a stroke and died shortly before Christmas.

Freeman, Sir Ralph (1880–1950), civil engineer: born and educated in London; in 1901 joined a firm of consulting engineers which became

Freeman, Fox and Partners in 1938 and specialized in the design of steel bridges. His knowledge, together with the plans of *Bradfield, made possible the construction of Sydney Harbour Bridge, which was opened in March 1932. He was also responsible for designs to bridge the Zambezi; and for preliminary work on the major steel road bridges spanning Britain's estuaries (Forth, Humber, Severn), and on the Auckland Harbour Bridge, completed by his partner and successor, Sir Gilbert Roberts (1899–1978).

Frere, Sir (Henry) Bartle (1815–84), imperial civil servant: born in Brecknock, Wales; educated in Bath and at *Haileybury. He entered the Bombay Civil Service in 1834 and spent 33 years immersed in Indian affairs, notably as Chief Commissioner of Sind (1850–59), confidential adviser to Lord *Canning, and Governor of Bombay (1862–67). He was sent to *Zanzibar in 1872 on a successful mission to the Sultan to suppress the *slave trade. After escorting the Prince of Wales (Edward VII) on the first royal visit to India (1875), Frere was created a baronet. Lord *Carnarvon persuaded him to accept the post of Governor of the Cape and first High Commissioner of South Africa in 1877. Frere believed he should promote a confederation of southern Africa, and expected to become Governor-General of a new dominion. He found, however, that he was heavily committed to war against both the Kaffirs and the Zulus (under *Cetewayo); his attempts to satisfy the grievances of the Boers in the *Transvaal were repudiated by Beaconsfield's government in London. Although Frere was personally popular in South Africa, the Cape Parliament refused even to consider his plans for a federation. In London he was made a scapegoat for the first *Boer War, and he was recalled in August 1880 by the second Gladstone government, formed four months earlier.

Freyberg, Bernard Cyril (1889–1963), soldier and Governor-General of New Zealand: born in Richmond, Surrey. When he was two his family emigrated to Wellington, where he became a champion swimmer and was trained as a dentist. He sought adventure in Mexico and returned to England in 1914, enlisting Churchill's support in securing a commission in the Royal Naval Division, with whom he served at *Gallipoli, winning the Distinguished Service Order. Freyberg commanded a battalion on the Somme in 1916 and won the Victoria Cross at the battle of the Ancre (November 1916). In 1917 he became the youngest brigadier in the British Army, and fought at Passchendaele. By the end of World War I he had been wounded six times and received two Bars to his original DSO. In 1923 he came within 500 yards of swimming the English Channel. He retired as a major-general in 1937 but was recalled in 1939, to the Second New Zealand Division. Freyberg commanded the Division in Egypt, Greece, Crete, Libya and Tunisia, and in Italy from Calabria to Trieste, including the attempted breakthrough at Monte Cassino. He was knighted in 1942 and received a third Bar to his DSO. It was natural that, as New Zealand's most distinguished soldier, he should become Governor-General, a post he held from 1945 to 1952, continuing his wartime work of strengthening collaboration between the United Kingdom and dominion governments. He collaborated amicably with the New Zealand Prime Minister, Peter *Fraser. In 1951 he was created Baron Freyberg. For the last eleven years of his life he was Lieutenant-Governor and Deputy Constable of Windsor Castle.

Froude, James Anthony (1818–94), British historian: born in Devon; educated at Westminster School and Oriel College, Oxford. He is best known as the friend and literary executor of Thomas Carlyle, and writer of stirring narrative histories of sixteenth-century England. But Froude was also the first distinguished man of letters to travel widely in the Empire, of which he became a proud propagandist. In 1874/5 he spent several months in South Africa, campaigning both in Orange Free State and Cape Colony in favour of federation. He visited Australia in 1884/5 and the West Indies in 1886/7. Froude's considered views on 'England and her colonies' were published in *Oceana* (1886) and *The English in the West Indies* (1888). For the last two years of his life Froude was Regius Professor of Modern History at Oxford.

Fur trade opened up land routes into Canada, beginning with the first contacts between the French and the Algonquian-speaking peoples of modern *New Brunswick, *Quebec and *Nova Scotia in the early sixteenth century. From 1608 onwards the trade was regulated by Samuel de Champlain (*c.*1567–1635), to the benefit of such French ports as St Malo and Honfleur. After the first brief occupation of Quebec by the British (1629–31), the French allowed greater initiative in the collection and distribution of furs to be taken by the settlers themselves. Two fur traders, Pierre Radisson (*c.*1636–*c.*1710) and Medard Chouart des Groseilliers (1618–*c.*1690), undertook a long journey westwards in 1661, probably penetrating as far as *Manitoba, and returned to Montreal with a rich bounty of pelts obtained from the Wood *Crees. French colonial officials taxed the two traders so heavily that on their return to Europe they offered their services to Charles II and, with his backing, established the first trading posts of Rupert's Land, in 1668, and the chartered *Hudson's Bay Company in 1670. Thereafter the fur trade was conducted by individual agents of the Company in the north-west, and by the more systematic establishment of French forts and settlements along a retreating frontier. The Company's factors – notably James *Douglas – used fur-trading as a means of establishing control over huge tracts of land along the Rocky Mountains and the Pacific coast, making *British Columbia a valuable possession even before its mineral resources were developed. By World War I the fur trade had dropped to twelfth place in the value of Canadian exports. Trapping was gradually replaced by regular fur farming, and the trade continued on a large scale until World War II, with regular auctions in Winnipeg and Montreal. In the year 1938/9, 6.5 million pelts were taken and there were 10,455 recognized fur farms in the dominion: half a century later the number of pelts had fallen to 4.6 million and the number of farms to 1,040. Despite the vagaries of fashion and changing social attitudes to furs, mink continues to be the most valuable animal raised on these farms.

Gallipoli: a peninsula extending for more than 50 miles on the European side of the Dardanelles; heavily fortified during the Ottoman Empire. The Gallipoli Campaign of World War I, the brain-child of Winston *Churchill, has remained an evocative imperial symbol, the high hopes at its inception dashed by muddle and by inexperience of amphibious warfare. Soon after Turkey entered the war as Germany's ally, strategic plans were prepared which aimed to force the Dardanelles by sea, reach Constantinople, and open up communications with Russia across the Black Sea. Failed naval attacks in March 1915 were followed by operations designed to seize the forts on the peninsula and secure a safe passage for the fleet. On 25 April the first landings were made on five beaches by British, Australian and New Zealand (*Anzac), and Indian troops, with a French corps seeking a beachhead on the Asian shore. The Turks, strengthened by a German military mission and German artillery, were not taken by surprise, as had been hoped. Confusion over landing beaches and hesitancy in exploiting opportunities brought the invasion to a halt within a couple of days. Further landings in early August achieved initial success, but the trench warfare became so compressed that, in seeking to advance 400 yards on a one-mile front, 4,000 British Commonwealth soldiers were killed. After a visit to the peninsula by *Kitchener in November 1915 it was accepted that the army must be evacuated, a task successfully accomplished between 10 December and 9 January 1916. Exact casualty figures are disputed: it is probable that some 46,000 British Commonwealth servicemen were killed, or died from wounds. Because the population of both dominions was so much smaller, the frustrated hopes and high casualties of the campaign left greater bitterness in Australia and New Zealand than elsewhere in the Empire: the Australians lost nearly 9,000 killed with 20,000 wounded, the New Zealanders some 2,700 killed with 4,700 wounded.

Gambia. The Gambia, the most northerly Commonwealth state in Africa, forms an enclave in Senegal. It extends inland for 200 miles along both banks of the Gambia River, but covers an area less than half the size of Wales. The Portuguese discovered the river estuary in the fifteenth century; English traders followed, from 1587 onwards, and there was competition from French, Dutch and Latvian trading companies before British rights over the estuary were recognized in 1783. In 1816 a garrison was stationed on Banjul island to help ensure the effective abolition of the slave trade. In 1843 The Gambia became a Crown Colony, with Bathurst (now Banjul) as the capital. Between 1866 and 1888 The Gambia, like other settlements in West Africa, was a *Foreign Office concern. Sporadic discussions with the French were held between 1883 and 1887 over ceding the colony to French Senegal in return for concessions on the Ivory Coast, but The Gambia was re-established as a Crown Colony in 1888; two years later a definitive treaty settled its boundaries with Senegal. The fever-ridden colony became an economic liability rather than an asset, its chief export ground nuts, as it is today. An independence movement, led from 1960 by the veterinary expert Dawda Kairaba Jawara (1924– ; knighted 1966), achieved success in February 1965. The Gambia became a republic within the Commonwealth on 24 April 1970, ten years after Senegal gained independence from France. Trade needs linked the ex-colonial neighbours, and when President Jawara frustrated an attempted coup in July 1981, he called on Senegalese troops to assist him. Seven months later a Senegambia Confederation was set up, but it was unwieldy, and was dissolved in December 1989. The Gambia remained politically unstable for three reasons: increasing Islamic militancy among junior army officers; alleged corruption, especially over the assignment of foreign aid; and latent tribal rivalries separating the Mandingo (*c.* 40 per cent of the population) from the Fulas (*c.* 20 per cent), the Woloffs (*c.* 16 per cent), and the smaller numbers of Sarahulis and Jolas. Protests by officers who had received no pay culminated in a coup, on 23 July 1994, led by Lieutenant Yayah Jammeh who, as chairman of a five-man military council, assumed the Presidency. Jawara and his ministers found refuge in Dakar, Senegal.

Gandhi, Indira Priyadarshani (1917–84), Indian Prime Minister: born in Allahabad, the only child of Jawaharal *Nehru; educated in Visva-Bharati and at Somerville College, Oxford. She supported her father's activities from 1939 onwards and was arrested in 1941 for hindering the war effort. On her release from prison she married Feroze Gandhi, but acted as her father's official hostess until his death in 1964, when she entered the government as Information Minister. On the death of Lal Shastri on 11 January 1966 she consolidated her position in the *Indian National Congress, and became Prime Minister a fortnight later. Her government was marked by attempts to modernize Hindu social practices, notably by encouraging birth control, and by worsening relations with *Pakistan over *Kashmir and the emergence of *Bangladesh. Accusations of electoral corruption were upheld by the Indian High Court in June 1975 and she was barred from public office. This verdict she refused to accept. A fortnight later she invoked the Maintenance of

Internal Security Act to have 700 opponents arrested, and assumed dictatorial powers pending a general election. The dubious political campaigning of her younger son, Sanjay Gandhi (1946–80), further weakened her position: she lost both the election and her seat in Parliament (March 1977). Rivalries among her opponents soon enabled her to recover the political initiative, however, and she gained a landslide electoral victory in January 1980. The death of the unpopular Sanjay in an air crash on 23 July 1980 eased problems within the party, but Mrs Gandhi was faced with increasing unrest among Hindus in Assam, who resented the arrival of Muslim Bangladeshi immigrants, and among Sikh extremists seeking autonomy for the Punjab. Ill-advisedly, she ordered the Indian Army to attack Sikh strongholds among the shrines of *Amritsar (June 1984): some 700 Sikhs were killed. Mutinies in Sikh regiments culminated in the assassination of Mrs Gandhi in Delhi by two of her Sikh guards on 31 October 1984. In the subsequent communal violence across northern India more than 3,000 lives were lost. She was succeeded by her elder son, Rajiv *Gandhi.

Gandhi, Mohandas Karamchand (1869–1948), Mahatma of the Indian people: born at Porbandar; called to the Bar of the Inner Temple in London (1891) and practised law in Bombay for two years. In 1893 he settled in South Africa, where he spent 21 years leading the Indian community in resistance to racial segregation. There he encouraged the practice of civil disobedience, or 'passive resistance', which he was to develop later in India; and in 1914 he reached a compromise settlement with *Smuts on the status of Indian immigrants. After his return to Bombay in 1915 Gandhi's spiritual prestige ensured that he was soon accepted as the leader and prophet of the *Indian National Congress movement. His opposition to the Raj was intensified by the *Rowlatt Acts of 1919 but, in campaigning for Indian independence, he always sought to curb terrorism and promote Hindu–Muslim unity. Even so, he was imprisoned in 1922 as an agitator. He urged his followers to boycott British goods and encourage native village industries, making the Asoka spinning-wheel the symbol of his movement. From 1924 onwards he travelled the country in great simplicity, stressing the need to avoid both communal violence and the rigid caste values which perpetuated 'untouchability'. His protest march to the sea in 1930, aimed at breaking the salt law, led to a further term of imprisonment; he was released for talks with the Viceroy and for participation, in September 1931, in the London *Round Table Conference on India's future. Although his ascetic figure and the simplicity of his life made a deep impression on the English public, Gandhi's political demands were too advanced for the British to accept. On his return to India he was briefly rearrested, but was released when he began a 21-day self-purification fast. In 1942, with the threat of Japanese invasion imminent, he rejected the *Cripps Mission; he was again imprisoned, from August 1942 until May 1944, for obstructing the war effort with his support for a 'Quit India' campaign. British policy changed under the *Attlee government and Gandhi sought to collaborate with the last two Viceroys (Wavell and Mountbatten) but could not reach agreement with the Muslim leader, *Jinnah. Gandhi regarded the partition of India as potentially disastrous, but accepted it with reluctance, and welcomed the grant of Indian independence as 'the noblest act of the British nation'. He threatened (and began) 'fasts unto death' in order to shame the instigators of communal violence into accepting his pleas for mutual tolerance. His moderation alienated radical nationalists. He survived one assassination bid, but ten days later was shot dead in Delhi by a young Hindu journalist (30 January 1948).

Gandhi, Rajiv (1944–91), Indian Prime Minister: elder son of Indira *Gandhi and grandson of *Nehru; born in Delhi; after failing his engineering examinations at Cambridge he became a pilot with Indian Airlines, marrying in 1968 an Italian, Sonia Maino. He took no part in politics until after the death of his brother Sanjay in 1980. He was persuaded to take over the premiership on his mother's assassination (October 1984) and gained a record victory in the ensuing general election. Although he introduced a vigorous policy of technological innovation, he was hampered by the legacy of his mother's anti-Sikh campaign and ordered further military action at *Amritsar in May 1988; he was defeated in the general election of November 1989. During a further election campaign he, too, was assassinated (21 May 1991).

Ghana: an independent west African Commonwealth republic: capital, Accra. The Danes, and to a lesser extent the Swedes and Dutch, competed with the British for trading stations in the Gulf of Guinea from the seventeenth century onwards. As part of the campaign against the *slave trade the British posts along the Gold Coast were linked administratively with *Sierra Leone in 1821. The neighbouring Danish settlements were purchased in 1850, but not until 1874 did the Crown Colony of the Gold Coast break free from Sierra Leone. Although Lagos (in what was to become *Nigeria) was part of the Gold Coast until 1886, the chief colonial thrusts were always inland, mainly against the *Ashanti confederacy. The Ashanti lands were not finally annexed until 1901, when the 'northern territories' also became a Protectorate of the Crown Colony. From 1884 German commercial agents began to conclude treaties of protection with tribal chiefs in neighbouring Togoland – a German colony swiftly overrun by the British and French in August 1914: some of Togoland became a British mandate, administered from Accra, 1919–56. In March 1946 a new constitution gave the Africans a majority in the colony's legislature. A Convention People's Party was established in June 1949 by Kwame *Nkrumah who, in his campaign for independence, associated the Gold Coast peoples by name with historic Ghana, the West African empire which flourished *c.*750–*c.*1240 in lands to the north-west. Nkrumah secured UN backing for the incorporation of the mandated Togo territories in a new Ghana, which on 6 March 1957 became the first black African Dominion. This status was short-lived, for on 1 July 1960 Ghana was declared an independent Republic, though remaining within the Commonwealth. Nkrumah's establishment of a one-party state in 1964, coinciding with a fall in the world price of cocoa and closer ties with the Soviet bloc, led to his overthrow on 24 February 1966 in the first of five military coups which shook Accra's political life over the following fifteen years. Democratic elections in 1969 were followed by three years of civilian rule, with Dr Kofi Busia as executive President. But democracy could only survive until the next economic recession, in 1972, when a military dictatorship was set up by Colonel (later General) Ignatius Acheampong. A rival general, Akuffo, ousted Acheampong on 5 July 1978 but was himself overthrown in June 1979 by junior officers led by Flight-Lieutenant Jerry Rawlings (1947–   ; the son of a Scottish father and a Ewe tribe mother). An attempt was made to stamp out corruption and six senior officers, including Acheampong and Akuffo, were publicly executed outside Accra. For two years Rawlings retired from active politics and allowed a civilian government to function, led by Dr Hilla Limann. Another coup on 31 December 1981, however, allowed Rawlings to make himself President. Support from the International Monetary Fund helped Rawlings to rein in Ghana's galloping inflation; and in 1992 a multi-party constitution was introduced. It provided for a 200-seat Parliament and an executive President who would be elected for a four-year term, renewable only once. Rawlings won the presidential election on 3 November 1992, but more than 70 per cent of voters boycotted the subsequent parliamentary election and in January 1993 President Rawlings nominated a new government, drawn exclusively from his National Democratic Congress party. Cocoa remains Ghana's principal cash crop for export, followed by timber. The completion of the Soviet-sponsored Volta Dam at Akosambo in the year of Nkrumah's downfall provided hydro-electric power for the Accra–Takoradi region and boosted the 'pioneer industries'; but most Ghanaians continue to be dependent upon agriculture for their livelihood.

Gibraltar: settled by the Moorish invaders in 711; held by the Spanish from 1462 until its capture in 1704 by Admiral Sir George Rooke; confirmed in British possession by the treaties of Utrecht (1713), Paris (1763), and Paris (1783). Throughout the nineteenth century and most of the twentieth 'the Rock' served as Britain's principal base covering western Mediterranean and southern Atlantic trade routes. Spanish demands for the return of Gibraltar were taken up by the UN in 1963, but a referendum held on 10 September 1967 showed 12,138 Gibraltarians wished the colony to remain British while only 44 favoured a return to Spanish rule. Self-government was introduced in 1964 and expanded in May 1969, a move that led the Spaniards to close the land frontier with Andalusia. Talks to reduce tension were held between the Spanish and British foreign ministers, in Madrid in 1977 and Lisbon in 1980, but a proposed reopening of the frontier in 1982 was postponed because of Spanish resentment of Britain's use of Gibraltar as a staging-post for the *Falkland Islands in the conflict with Argentina. Free movement across the land frontier was resumed on 5 February 1985, eleven months before Spain joined the European Community (of which Gibraltar was already an associate member). The British decision in March 1991 to make drastic cuts in the military and naval presence on the Rock led to closer contact between the Gibraltar government and Madrid.

Gilbert and Ellice Islands: On 10 November 1915 these two groups of islands in the south-west Pacific were annexed, at the request of local native assemblies, and became a British Crown Colony. The union was severed on 1 October 1975, the two groups of islands subsequently becoming *Kiribati and *Tuvalu.

Gilbert, Sir Humphrey (c. 1539–83), English seaman and colonizer: born in Devon, a half-brother of Sir Walter *Ralegh. After serving in Ireland and the Netherlands, receiving a knighthood in 1570 and representing Plymouth as an MP, he promoted schemes for planting colonies across the Atlantic. His first voyage (1579) was unproductive, but four years later he sailed from Plymouth with five ships and landed at St John's in Newfoundland on 5 August 1583. There he founded the first successful English colony in the New World. After charting much of Newfoundland's southern coast Humphrey Gilbert sailed for Plymouth on 1 September, only to perish in a storm off the Azores.

Giles, (William) Ernest Powell (1835–97), Australian explorer: born in Bristol; emigrated to Adelaide at the age of 15, and worked as a digger on the Victorian gold fields before undertaking surveys north-west of the Darling River, 1861–65. His main expeditions, in 1872 and 1874, took him deep into the Northern Territory, where he discovered Lake Amadeus. In 1875/6 he crossed from Port Augusta to Perth, covering 2,500 miles in five months; he then returned along a more northerly route, slightly south of the Tropic of Capricorn. He published an account of his travels, *Australia Twice Traversed* (1889).

Gleneagles Agreement (1977). The *Commonwealth Heads of Government, meeting in London in 1977, adjourned to Gleneagles (Scotland) to discuss UN calls to put pressure on South Africa by cutting sporting links with the Republic until progress had been made towards racial integration. The Heads of Government agreed on a declaration by which each member of the Commonwealth acknowledged a duty 'to vigorously combat the evil of apartheid . . . by taking every practical step to discourage contact or competition by their nationals with sporting organizations . . . in South Africa'. The degree of implementation of this agreement varied among member states: it was not possible to prevent all 'rebel' cricket tours; and in 1981 Robert *Muldoon of New Zealand aroused strong opposition overseas, and among liberals at home, by tolerating a South African Rugby tour of the dominion. But the ban remained in force until October 1991, when the formation of a non-racial South African Olympic Committee encouraged the Harare Heads of Government meeting to recommend the resumption of international contacts, provided progress continued towards racial integration. The isolation imposed at Gleneagles effectively ended on 10 November 1991 when South Africa's cricketers played (and lost) a one-day international match with India in Calcutta.

Gluckman, (Herman) Max (1911–75), South African anthropologist: born in Johannesburg; graduated from the University of the Witwatersrand before becoming a Rhodes Scholar at Exeter College, Oxford, in 1934. After conducting field research among the Zulus and Barotse, he divided his academic life between Zambia, Oxford and London, specializing in research into the ways in which persistent conflict nurtured and maintained social cohesion in the tribal societies of central Africa. His seminal *Custom and Conflict in Africa* (1955) was followed by *Politics, Law and Ritual in Tribal Society* (1965), and two studies of Barotse concepts of jurisprudence.

Gold Coast: some 330 miles of West African littoral along the Gulf of Guinea, under direct British rule from 1821 to 1957, organized as a Crown Colony in 1874 and subsequently annexing the *Ashanti lands and surrounding territories. On 6 March 1957 the Gold Coast became the Commonwealth's first black Dominion in Africa, taking the name *Ghana.

Gold Rush: Australia. The first clearly identifiable gold deposits in Australia were discovered in the Wellington district near Bathurst, New South Wales early in 1851 by four young Australians who were introduced to the skills of panning and cradling by Edward Hargraves, a veteran of the California Gold Rush. By May 1851 diggers were coming through the *Blue Mountains from Sydney in great numbers. Gold was also discovered at Clunes, 90 miles north of Melbourne, on 10 July 1851; and six weeks later at Ballarat (67 miles from Melbourne) and Bendigo (85 miles): by the end of the year it was clear that the newly constituted colony of *Victoria contained the richest goldfields yet discovered. Throughout the 1850s, 40 per cent of the world's gold came from these new fields. The social effects of the gold rush changed Australian colonization: settlers of every social class and profession hurried to the goldfields; there was also a rush of immigrants from Europe. Between 1850 and 1860 the population of New South Wales rose from 187,000 to 350,000 and of Victoria from less than 80,000 to 540,000. A new problem was imposed by an influx of *Chinese labourers, especially in the late 1850s around the town of Ararat. Resentment at the imposition of state licences led to unrest, notably at Ballarat, and reached a climax in the *Eureka Stockade incident of 1854. Gold was discovered in Queensland some fifteen years later and there was a minor gold rush to the Palmer River fields in the following decade, but without such drastic social changes. The experience of Victoria was, however, repeated in *Western Australia where in June 1892 gold was discovered at Coolgardie and *Kalgoorlie and, soon afterwards, at neighbouring Boulder. The new gold rush quadrupled Western Australia's population by the end of the century but the discoveries created yet another political problem: a suspicion in Perth that the long-established eastern colonies were exploiting Western Australia in order to lessen the impact of world recession on Melbourne, Sydney and Adelaide.

Gold Rush: Canada. Gold was discovered along the Fraser and Thompson rivers of *British Columbia early in 1858 and attracted a rush of miners up from California, where the boom of 1849–51 had long subsided. The first American ship reached Victoria, on Vancouver Island, on 23 April 1858 and immediately put ashore so many miners and prospectors that the town's population doubled. A succession of vessels maintained the rush throughout that summer, with *Chinese labourers following the original fortune seekers. By 1862 a richer deposit had been found deep in submerged stream-beds near the Cariboo River and an even bigger rush took place, with a special 'Cariboo Road' constructed by military engineers. In eastern Canada there was a small gold rush along the Chaudière river in Quebec in 1864, but without any great social upheaval. The greatest of all rushes followed confirmation that gold had been discovered on the Bonanza Creek of the Klondike in the *Yukon Territory in August 1896, though the news did not break until the following summer. A shanty town, Dawson City, came into being before the onset of winter in 1896/7. The greatest influx of prospectors from the east arrived after the snows melted in the spring of 1898. Over the following seven years $111 million-worth of gold was mined from the area around Dawson City, which at the peak of prospecting had a population of over 30,000. The Klondike boom was, however, short-lived; by 1907 the finest veins were exhausted. Klondike, like the Australian rushes, had enduring consequences: it created its own legends of popular adventure; and it made Canadians aware for the first time of the potential significance of their north-western frontier of development.

Gold Rush: Kenya. In 1930 a lone American prospector panned alluvial gold in what is now Western Province. The discovery, at a time when Kenya's economy was hit by falling prices with the onset of the *Great Depression, prompted an optimistic gold rush. The pickings were few and the find was soon exhausted but, as elsewhere, the rush opened up a hitherto neglected fertile district. The mission-centre of Kakamega became a flourishing town and, with Kenya's independence, a provincial capital.

Gold Rush: New Zealand. An itinerant prospector in South Island, Gabriel Reid, discovered the first important strike in New Zealand at Tuapeka, near Dunedin, in 1861. Thousands of optimists – many of them from Australia – flocked to the vicinity of 'Gabriel's Gully'. The gold strike boosted the growth of Dunedin, increased migration to Otago, and established the recently-formed Bank of New Zealand on a sure footing. Deposits were found soon afterwards on the west coast of South Island and, later, a rich vein on the Coromandel peninsula (North Island), between Auckland and Tauranga. The boom years, when fortune smiled on casual prospectors, were however short-lived.

Gold Rush: Transvaal. Gold was discovered on the Witwatersrand near the village of Johannesburg in 1884, but the extent of the deposits and their value were not appreciated for another two years, until in the spring of 1886 it was confirmed that George Walker had struck a fine reef on his farm, Langlaagte. The gold rush to the Rand, over the following year, differed in two respects – economic and political – from the Canadian and Australian rushes: it attracted investment from capitalists already exploiting the diamonds of *Kimberley; and, while it caused Johannesburg to become the biggest and most prosperous city in southern Africa, it also enabled the *Transvaal burghers to ensure the rapid passage of their republic from penury to affluence, without the vote being given to the thousands of non-Boer workers (Uitlanders) who flocked to the Rand. In 1887 *Rhodes founded the company which became the Consolidated Goldfields of South Africa, for the systematic development of the newly-discovered mineral wealth; but President *Kruger, in deploring the influx of Uitlanders, perpetuated Boer exclusiveness. This contrast in attitudes led to the *Jameson Raid of 1895 and the second *Boer War four years later.

Goldie, Sir George Dashwood (1846–1925), entrepreneur and colonial administrator: born George Goldie Taubman, youngest son of a wealthy Manx landowner; held a commission in the Royal Engineers

141

Golf

1865–67, but left the army to follow a wild and dissipated life in Egypt, the Sudan and Prussian-besieged Paris before taking up a post in 1875 with a family firm trading for palm oil on the Niger. Within four years Goldie (as he now called himself) had bought out his trading rivals and founded the United Africa Company – from 1881 the National Africa Company (NAC). From January 1883 onwards he tried to convince the Foreign Office of the need to frustrate French designs in west-central Africa by penetrating up the Niger and through Sokoto and Chad to the Sudan, thus linking the Niger and the Nile. In 1886 he received a charter constituting the NAC as both a trading company and an administrative body, under the name of the Royal Niger Company, Chartered and Limited. Goldie, who was knighted in 1887, was thus responsible for creating *Nigeria, as the West African territories were first called in 1897. He negotiated with German and French representatives over the frontier lines and used the military experience of *Lugard to establish them in the north. In 1896 Goldie was authorized to send a military force against the Muslim states of Nupe and Ilorin to stamp out slavery. In the following January 500 men (mostly *Hausa) backed up by a 12-pounder gun and six Maxim machine-guns gained a rapid victory for Goldie. But Joseph *Chamberlain, as Colonial Secretary, mistrusted Goldie's chartered independence and insisted on buying out the company in 1900. When the charter was revoked, Lugard took over Goldie's responsibilities as High Commissioner of the new colony of Northern Nigeria.

Golf: was played in Scotland in the mid fifteenth century, although its rules were only agreed and codified at St Andrews in 1754; the first club outside Scotland, Blackheath, dates from 1766. Scottish army officers carried the sport overseas: to the American colonies in the late 1770s and to India after the Napoleonic Wars. The Royal Bombay Golf Club was founded in 1829: the Royal Calcutta in 1842. Golf courses were laid out at Melbourne in 1847 and at Dunedin in the 1860s. Clubs were established soon afterwards in Hong Kong, Singapore and, by the early 1880s, in Sydney, though not until 1898 was the Australian Golf Union formed. Elsewhere, too, Scottish settlers frequently established golf courses at the earliest opportunity: thus in Kenya a Scots district commissioner had provided Kisumu, the railway terminus on the Kavirondo Gulf of Lake Victoria, with a golf course within four years of the town's foundation. Outstanding golfers from Commonwealth countries overseas include the Australian Peter Thomson (1929–   ), who between 1950 and 1972 won the British Open five times, the Australian Open three times and the New Zealand Open three times; the New Zealander Bob Charles (1936–   ), who in 1963 became the first left-hander to win the British Open; and, more recently, Greg Norman of Australia, Ernie Els of South Africa (US Open, 1994), and Nick Price of Zimbabwe (British Open, 1994). Women's golf spread rapidly after the turn of the century, though it was not until 1935 that the Ladies' Golf Unions of Great Britain and Australia competed against each other for the first time.

Gordon, Adam Lindsay (1833–70): Australian poet; born at Fayal in the Azores but educated in England. Emigrated to Adelaide in 1853, joined the South Australian Mounted Police, became a respected steeple-chaser and spent much of his life with horses, though he sat for two years in the colonial legislature. His ballad *The Feud* was published in 1864 and a 'dramatic lyric', *Ashtaroth*, in 1867. He won wide popularity with his collected ballads, *Sea Spray and Smoke Drift* (1867). Three volumes of verse, edited by Marcus *Clarke, were published ten years after his death and established his reputation in England, where he remains the only Australian poet honoured with a plaque in Westminster Abbey.

Gordon, Charles George (1833–85), British soldier: born in Woolwich; commissioned into the Royal Engineers in 1852 and fought in the Crimean War. He became well known as 'Chinese Gordon' for his work in China between 1860 and 1865, when he helped quell the Taiping rebellion. From 1873 to 1880 he served the ruler of Egypt as governor and military commander in the Sudan, continuing further the work begun by Sir Samuel *Baker. He stamped out the slave trade and explored the upper waters of the Nile. Despite a long spell of leave in 1876 Gordon could not preserve his health, and he returned home in 1880. His restless energy made him spend nearly a year helping to administer Mauritius, and he lived for more than a year in Cape Colony and Palestine. In 1884 the British government asked him to return to the Sudan to organize the rescue and evacuation of isolated garrisons imperilled by the fanatical uprising of the *Mahdi (Mohammed Ahmed). Gordon, as an evangelical Christian, believed it his duty, on reaching the Sudan, to seek to end the Muslim upheaval: in March 1884 he found himself besieged in Khartoum. It was not until September that a relief force left Cairo to advance up the Nile; it entered the Sudan early in November, but did not reach the outskirts of Khartoum until 28 January 1885: the Mahdi's dervishes had broken into the Governor's Residence and murdered Gordon two days previously. In death, General Gordon became the outstanding popular hero of Victorian imperialism.

Gorton, Sir John Grey (1911–   ), Australian Prime Minister: born in Melbourne; educated at Geelong and Brasenose College, Oxford. He served as a pilot with the RAAF (1940–44) in England, Singapore, and during the defence of Darwin. After 17 years as a senator representing Victoria, and holding six ministerial appointments, he was chosen to head the Liberal government in January 1968 after the death of *Holt and held office until March 1971. He lost much support for backing the war in *Vietnam and allegedly following US policy too closely, and retired from active politics in December 1975 after failing in a bid to return to the Senate. In 1977 he received a knighthood.

Gosse, William Christie (1842–81), Australian explorer: born at Hoddesdon, near Hertford, into a family who emigrated to Adelaide when he was eight. He joined the surveyor-general's department in South Australia and in 1873 led an expedition westwards from Alice Springs. He discovered a giant sandstone monolith, held in awe by the aborigine peoples. Gosse named the monolith Ayers Rock in honour of Sir Henry Ayers (1821–97), the dynamic South Australian Premier. Gosse's surveys and maps of the interior were of great value to the *Forrest brothers a year later.

Governor-General: the appointed representative of the Queen in those Commonwealth countries outside the United Kingdom of which she is Head of State, and to whom the Sovereign's ceremonial and constitutional duties are delegated. In January 1995 sixteen Commonwealth members had Governors-General: Antigua and Barbuda; Australia; the Bahamas; Barbados; Belize; Canada; Grenada; Jamaica; New Zealand; Papua New Guinea; St Christopher and Nevis; St Lucia; St Vincent; Solomon Islands; Tuvalu. All were appointments made by the Sovereign on the recommendation of the member country's government, without reference to the Government of the United Kingdom. The first Governor-General of the old empire was Warren *Hastings in India, from 1774 to 1785, after North's Regulating Act of 1773 imposed stricter political control on the *East India Company. There were titular Governors-General of India from 1774 until the Republic was established in 1950; between 1858 and 1947 each was also *Viceroy. The only native-born Indian Governor-General was the last, Chakravarti Rajagopalachari. Traditionally, the sovereign executive in a colony was vested in a Governor, with Lieutenant-Governors appointed to any dependencies of the colony. Two successive chief administrators in New South Wales between 1855 and 1861 were called Governor-General, but the practice was then dropped. Canada received a Governor-General on becoming a confederation in 1867; Australia from 1901; South Africa from 1910; but New Zealand, though a dominion in 1907, did not see the status of the sovereign's deputy raised to Governor-General until 1917. Dominion status thereafter carried with it a governor-generalship: the *Irish Free State had Governors-General between 1922 and 1937: all three incumbents were southern Irish. Several members of the royal family were governors-general: Queen Victoria's son, the Duke of Connaught, in Canada (1911–16) and his son, Prince Arthur of Connaught, in South Africa (1920–23); the Earl of Athlone, brother of Queen Mary, in South Africa (1924–31) and Canada (1940–46); the Duke of Gloucester in Australia (1945–47); and Earl *Mountbatten in the Dominion of India (1947–48). The first native-born Australian Governor-General was Sir Isaac Isaacs (1855–1948; served 1931–38); the first Canadian, Vincent *Massey (1952–59); the first New Zealander, Sir Arthur Porrit (1967–72; however, Lord *Freyberg, VC, who was Governor-General 1946–52, had come to New Zealand at the age of two). In 1990 women were appointed Governor-General of Barbados (Dame Nita Barrow) and New Zealand (Dame Catherine Tizard).

Grand Trunk Road, the principal military artery of British India. In 1839 an official of the East India Company, James Thomason (1804–53), began work on renovating, and modernizing to a standard pattern, highways which had been used by pre-British rulers to link the cities of northern India. Engineers, mostly trained at a special technical college in Allahabad, spent the next half-century completing a Grand Trunk Road. It covered 1,250 miles, from the outskirts of Calcutta to Allahabad (a key city on the Jumna, close to its confluence with the Ganges) and on to Agra, Delhi and Lahore; eventually, after another 250 miles crossing six mountain ridges, it reached Peshawar and the *North-West Frontier. On this last section alone there were more than 500 bridges, the most striking being the two-tier rail and road bridge across the Indus completed in 1883 at Attock, 40 miles from Peshawar. Like Roman roads, the Grand Trunk had a succession of official lodgings and transit camps along the route, which was shaded where possible by twin avenues of trees. There were slow lanes on each side of a central 16-foot carriageway for fast traffic. The Grand Trunk Road retained great strategic value up to the time of Partition, and beyond.

Great Britain: see *United Kingdom*.

Great Depression (1929–34). Rash investment and over-production of unwanted goods has rocked the stability of capitalism on more than one occasion; thus British colonial investors lost drastically in the 1840s, the mid 1870s, and the early 1890s. The most widespread depression, however, was the twentieth-century 'world slump' which followed an over-speculative boom in the late 1920s. The unexpected reappearance of Russia as a world exporter of timber threatened Canadian exports in 1928, but far more drastic in its effects was the over-production of prairie wheat in 1929, which lowered the price of this basic crop on both sides of the Atlantic, and also in Australia. The cascading price of wheat dragged down with it that of other products. The agricultural crisis weakened North American financial institutions, already vulnerable because of rash loans contracted in east-central Europe. Prices of export staples in Canada, Australia, New Zealand and Kenya dropped to a quarter of their peak in the earlier post-war years, while overhead costs mounted and banks imposed inevitable restraints on capital lending. Exports of grain to

Great Trek

Europe were hampered for several years by the imposition of high import duties and the coincidence of good harvests in Europe with droughts in Canada and Australia. All overseas dominions suffered from the cumulative effects of earlier land speculation and, in particular, from the misfortunes of ex-servicemen who turned to farming after World War I with little experience of growing crops or raising sheep and cattle; additionally, excessive sheep-farming led to a collapse of wool prices in Australia and New Zealand. The Wall Street Crash of 24 October 1929 was followed by tumbling share values in London on 28 October and soon afterwards in financial centres of the Empire overseas. The cessation of overseas loans worsened the impact of the slump, especially on nascent industries, and there was a drastic fall in commodity prices throughout the Empire. The immediate consequence of the Depression was a sharp rise in unemployment: by 1932, 28 per cent of the labour force in Australia was without work, a level only exceeded in (immediately pre-Nazi) Germany. The proportion was little better in New Zealand, where 80,000 men were unemployed in October 1933. In the newer suburbs of spreading cities, tenants were unable to pay their rents and were evicted. There were violent riots in Sydney in June 1931 and, during 1932, in such traditionally placid New Zealand cities as Auckland, Dunedin and Wellington. Every government imposed internal economies, improvised relief schemes and resorted to 'sustenance' public works projects (though these were limited by a shortage of state funds). At the *Imperial Conference of October 1930 in London, the British refused Canadian requests to help wheat sales by a preferential tariff, but the *Ottawa Conference of July 1932 accepted imperial preference as a means of bolstering the economies of the dominions. At the same time, to safeguard the pound, a 'sterling block' was created: all dominion and colonial currency reserves were to be in pounds, pegged to an agreed exchange rate. The swing politically, in urban areas, was as much to the Right as to the Left: the semi-Fascist New Guard movement had 50,000 members in Sydney in 1932; and there were attempts, on a smaller scale, to raise similar para-military organizations in New Zealand and Canada. Popular support in Canada backed the 'protest' economic theories of the former Royal Flying Corps Major, Clifford Douglas (1879–1952), who advocated monetary reforms to provide 'social credit' for consumers and thereby increase purchasing power: the Depression was the midwife to social credit schemes initiated by the state governments in British Columbia and Alberta, and Douglas also had some following in New Zealand. In general, by 1935/6 economic stability had returned in the wake of governmental supervision of trade and careful investment, although the incubus of unemployment was lifted only with the coming of World War II.

Great Trek: the epic migration of 10,000 Boers from Cape Colony to seek new farmland on which to settle, beyond the authority of the British

146

crown. The Boers complained of inadequate compensation when slavery was abolished in 1834 and resented charges of cruelty against them with regard to the southern African native peoples, who (they alleged) raided their settlements without fearing any response from the colonial administration. The first *Voortrekkers* followed several hundred pathfinders who had crossed the Orange River in 1835, about 5,000 from the eastern Cape in 1836/7 under five different leaders, and some 9,000 more over the next eight years. One group settled immediately north of the river, where they established the *Orange Free State; others crossed the Vaal river; and many sought to establish themselves in *Natal, despite increasing hostility from the *Zulu king, Dingale (Dingaan in Afrikaans). Defence of the settlers in Natal was entrusted to Andrius *Pretorius, who on 16 December 1838 decisively defeated Dingale on the banks of the Ncome ('Blood River'). Thereafter some 6,000 *Voortrekkers* settled in Natal, founding the city of Pietermaritzburg. When the British annexed Natal in 1843, most of the *Voortrekkers* moved to the high veld of the *Transvaal. The *Voortrekkers* (who included the eleven year old *Kruger) became the legendary national heroes of the Boers, who regularly celebrated 16 December – 'Dingaan's Day' – as the Afrikaaner patriotic festival. On a hill outside Pretoria a huge mausoleum – the Voortrekker Monument – was opened on 16 December 1950 by Dr *Malan at the beginning of South Africa's *apartheid era.

Grenada, an independent Caribbean Commonwealth state on the most southerly of the *Windward Islands. The island was discovered by Columbus (1498), colonized by the French, and captured by the British (1762) but restored to France (1779). It was finally ceded in 1783 by the first Treaty of Versailles. From 1885 until the British West Indies Federation was set up in 1958 Grenada was the heart of the Windward Islands Crown Colony, with the colonial governor resident in the island's chief town, St George's. Independence was granted on 7 February 1974. A left-wing New Jewel Movement seized power in March 1979, establishing a People's Revolutionary Government led by Maurice Bishop (1944–83). Bishop, who sought closer links with Castro's Cuba and was regarded with strong disfavour by the US government, was assassinated on 19 October 1983 by even more radical Marxists. In alarm, Jamaica and other eastern Caribbean governments appealed for armed intervention by the United States. Six days later an American task force of 6,000 men, backed by 15 warships, and with token support from Jamaica, invaded Grenada. The Marxist government disintegrated: 45 Grenadans, 25 Cubans and 18 Americans were killed. Democratic government was reintroduced with elections in December 1984, and again in March 1990. The army of occupation withdrew in June 1985. Despite the pro-American sympathies of the *Thatcher government, the invasion by the US of an island of which the Queen was Head of State caused some resentment in Britain, not least because American bombing severely damaged the airport at Point Salines, where building work was nearing completion by a British company (who employed many Cuban labourers). Grenada's chief exports have long been cocoa, nutmegs and bananas.

Grey, Sir George (1812–98), colonial governor and New Zealand Prime Minister: born in Lisbon; served as an infantry officer (1829–38). A year later he sailed for Western Australia and conducted expeditions in the north-west of the region, compiling a vocabulary of aboriginal dialects before spending two years as Resident Magistrate in Albany, then Western Australia's main port. Subsequently Grey served as a colonial governor for 27 years, in South Australia (1841–45); New Zealand (1845–53 and 1861–68); and Cape Colony (1854–61). He brought financial prosperity to each of these, but his autocratic ways often provoked conflict with the *Colonial Office and he was recalled from the Cape for (prematurely) advocating a South African federation. After two years in England he returned to New Zealand as a private citizen in 1870, sat as a member of the House of Representatives (1874–94), and headed the government from October 1877 to October 1879. In 1891 he was a delegate to a National Australasian Convention, but he doubted the wisdom of federal links between New Zealand and the Australian colonies. Grey spent his last four years in England. He is not to be confused with the baronet Sir George Grey (1799–1882), who in 1854–55 was the first *Colonial Secretary.

Griffin, Walter Burley (1876–1937), American architect: largely responsible for planning Australia's federal capital, *Canberra.

Group Areas Act: an early segregationist measure of *Malan's government in the *apartheid era in South Africa. On 27 April 1950 a Group Areas Bill was introduced in the South African Parliament which proposed the delineation of specific areas in which different races in South Africa might trade or reside. The proposal, which imposed the migration of coloured and native peoples from favoured areas to specific townships, was instantly attacked abroad. The strongest critic was *Nehru, on behalf of the Indian minority. The United Nations Assembly urged the South African Minister of the Interior, Dr T. E. Donges, to delay implementation of the measure, but the South Africans were not prepared to compromise. The law was not repealed until 1991.

Gurkhas: the principal racial inhabitants of the independent Himalyan kingdom of Nepal; a warrior people of Rajput Hindu origin. The heartland of Nepal, with its capital at Kathmandu, was never part of the British Empire, and the Gurkhas fought fiercely in defence of their outlying provinces in 1814–15, though finally ceding Kumaon and Garwhal to the British by the treaty of Segowlie (2 December 1815). Good relations between the British authorities and the ruling dynasty in Kathmandu enabled Gurkhas to be recruited for the army of the *East India Company, and their loyalty during the Mutiny made them welcome in the *Indian Army from 1857 onwards. On the eve of World War I there were ten regiments of Gurkhas, each of two battalions. They were in action on the Western Front at Neuve Chapelle as early as November 1914, at Gallipoli with particular distinction in May and August 1915, in Mesopotamia, and in Palestine. Between the wars they fought in 1920 on the *North-West Frontier; in World War II they were employed on three continents, notably at Keren in east Africa and on the Mareth Line in Tunisia, at Monte Cassino, and in the capture of Rangoon. When the Indian Empire was partitioned some regiments remained with the new Indian Army, but a Brigade of Gurkhas was incorporated in the British Army: it saw active service in Malaysia, Cyprus and the Falklands, and long maintained two battalions in the *New Territories of Hong Kong. The courage of the Gurkhas has won them a succession of awards of the Victoria Cross, from Rifleman Kulbir Thapur's in 1915 to Lieutenant Rambahadur Limbu's in Sarawak half a century later. Drastic British defence cuts in 1994, and the impending handover of Hong Kong to China, have left the future of the Brigade of Gurkhas in doubt.

Guyana, formerly British Guiana; an independent Co-operative Republic, capital Georgetown; the only member of the Commonwealth on the mainland of South America. The region was first settled in 1616 by the Dutch, who developed the Demerara sugar plantations and built the canals which still irrigate the coastal belt. The British occupied the Dutch possessions in 1796 and 1803 but found the colonists so suspicious of each other that not until 1831 were the settlements brought together to form the colony of British Guiana. With the abolition of slavery, immigrants from the East Indies were settled in the colony to work on the sugar plantations; by 1970 more than half the population was of East Indian descent. The colony refused to join the *British West Indies Federation in 1956. Internal self-government was established in 1961 and independence followed on 26 May 1966; but there was chronic unrest in Guyana, caused in part by the economic uncertainties of the sugar industry and in part by the political clash between the People's Progressive Party of Cheddi *Jagan, predominantly East Indian and long-established, and the West Indian followers of Forbes *Burnham's People's National Congress. From 1964, when he came to power, Burnham built up the PNC until in 1980 a new constitution proclaimed Guyana a 'co-operative republic' with a nominated 'single list' parliament and a strong executive president. After Forbes's death in 1985 President Desmond Hoyle tried to preserve the autocratic character of the government but, faced by mounting discontent, was forced to permit the introduction of proper procedures for the elections of 1992. The veteran Cheddi Jagan won the Presidential election and took office on 9 October 1992; his PPP gained an overall majority of 7 in a 65-member National Assembly.

Haggard, Sir Henry Rider (1856–1925), British novelist: born at Bradenham Hall, Norfolk; went to South Africa in 1871 and was secretary to the Governor of Natal. In 1877 he helped establish a sound administration in the *Transvaal, where he served as Registrar of the High Court before returning to East Anglia in 1879 to farm and plan a literary career. After drawing on his African experiences for *Cetewayo and his White Neighbours* (1882), he turned to fiction and wrote more than thirty adventure novels. The most famous, *King Solomon's Mines* (1886), had astonishingly high sales by the standards of the times – 5,000 copies within two months of publication; it was followed by *She* (1887). Both tales, set in Africa, convey the excitement of tribal societies maintaining mysterious traditions amid settings of limitless wild life. Haggard awakened the heroic thrill of Empire in Africa, as *Kipling was to do for India. In 1912 he received a knighthood.

Haileybury College: a British public school, 5 miles south-east of Hertford. The main residential quadrangle was built for the *East India Company, who in 1809 moved their training college there from Hertford Castle where it had opened in 1806. Most senior officials in India at mid century had been educated at Haileybury, among them Bartle *Frere and John *Lawrence. The Company's change of status forced the closure of the college in 1858, but it reopened as a school four years later and continued to educate men who went on to serve the Empire not only in India but in Australia, New Zealand and notably in Canada (where Charles Farr of the Hudson's Bay Company founded a town in Ontario which he named after his old school). A Haileybury housemaster, Cormell Price, became the first headmaster of the United Services College, which opened at Westward Ho! in Devon in 1874, with *Kipling as an early pupil: USC left Devon in 1904, found a home at Windsor in 1906, was expanded and renamed Imperial Services College in 1912, and amalgamated with Haileybury in 1942. When India gained independence in 1947, the incumbent British Prime Minister (*Attlee) and three junior members of his Labour government were Haileyburians.

Hammond, Dame Joan Hood (1912–   ), operatic soprano: born in Christchurch, New Zealand but studied the violin and singing at Sydney Conservatorium and became well-known in New South Wales as a golfer (who represented her country against Great Britain in 1935), a squash player, a swimming champion and a pioneer woman sports writer. She made her first public appearance as a singer in 1929. An arm injury forced her to give up instrumental work, and in 1936 she began studying singing in Europe. She sang in a performance of *Messiah* in London in 1938 and made her professional operatic début in Vienna a year later. After serving as a volunteer ambulance driver in London during World War II she emerged as the outstanding operatic soprano of two post-war decades. She sang leading roles in more than thirty operas and was a recording artist for the HMV company; her *Turandot* was the first piece of classical music to win a gold disc for sales of more than a million. Joan Hammond, who retired in 1971, was made OBE in 1953, CBE in 1963, and DBE in 1974.

Harare Declaration (1991): a statement issued by the *Commonwealth Heads of Government in October 1991, during their meeting in Zimbabwe. The declaration was the group's response to the *Mahatir Report on the Commonwealth in the 1990s and beyond. The Harare Declaration reaffirmed the political leaders' confidence in the Commonwealth as a voluntary association of sovereign independent states following the principles set out in the *Singapore Declaration of 1971. It emphasized the need to promote democratic government, respect for human rights, equality for women, educational opportunities for all, non-racialist government in South Africa, sound economic management to alleviate poverty, respect for the environment according to the *Langkawi principles, and support for peace and disarmament under United Nations auspices.

Hariot, Thomas (1560–1621), pioneer English writer on colonization: born at Oxford and educated there, at Oriel College; a mathematician and cartographer, he accompanied Sir Richard Grenville (1541–91) to the Americas in 1585/6. His account of early colonization, *A Brief and True Report of the New Found Land of Virginia*, was published in Armada Year (1588) and by 1591 had been translated into Latin, French and German. Hariot prepared charts and maps for some of the earliest English voyages to Guiana and, after brief imprisonment in the post-Gunpowder Plot scare, spent his last years perfecting navigational instruments. He is reputedly the first Englishman to regularly smoke pipe tobacco, and is known to have died from a form of cancer.

Hastings, Warren (1732–1818), first Governor-General of India: born in Churchill, north Oxfordshire; went out to Calcutta as an *East India Company writer (clerk) at the age of eighteen. His ruthless competence ensured him rapid promotion: he was Resident at Murshidabad, 1758–61, before serving as a member of the Calcutta council for three years. From 1764 to 1769 he was in England, where he gained much respect for his presentation of Indian affairs to parliamentary committees. After returning to India as second-in-council at Madras he became Governor of Bengal in 1772. Lord North's Regulating Act of the following year sought to give unity and cohesion to the Company's activities, by assigning a Governor-General to India; the post was held by Hastings until 1785. He fought against corruption in Bengal but resorted to dubious methods to get one official, Nand Kumar, condemned and executed. Hastings consolidated the Company's power, vigorously pursued war against the Marathas, regularized the collection and spending of the opium revenue, and raised the general level of administration. His work made him many enemies, notably, on the Council of Bengal, Sir Philip Francis (1740–1818), whom Hastings wounded in a duel in 1781. After Hastings resigned and returned to England in 1784, charges of corruption and maltreatment were laid against him by the Whig opposition in the House of Commons; he was impeached in February 1788, and his trial in Westminster Hall continued for 145 sittings, until on 23 April 1795 he was cleared of every charge reflecting on his personal honour: his defence cost him the fortune of £70,000 he had brought home from India. The East India Company gave him an adequate pension, however; he was made a Privy Councillor, and spent his last years on his family estate at Daylesford in Worcestershire.

Hauhau, a *Maori pentecostal religious faith, also known as *Pai Marire* ('goodness and peace'), which strengthened resistance to settlement in the west of North Island. It arose in 1862 from Maori concern over defence of their land rights in Taranaki, when Te Ua Haumene Tiwhakararo experienced a series of visions in which the archangels Gabriel and Michael inspired him to become a prophet of apocalyptic deliverance. Atrocities were committed in many parts of North Island, by adherents of the faith and by their enemies, although around the exposed southern settlement of Wanganui friendly Maoris kept the fanatics away from the *paketa*. Te Ua surrendered to government troops in February 1866, but the religious war smouldered on until the following year.

Hausa, the largest ethnic group, and the most widely spoken language, in modern *Nigeria; also a minority group in *Ghana. The Hausa formed a loose confederation in West Africa in the eleventh century, and their centre, Kano, was a trading centre in the sixteenth century. In 1804 the Fulani, cattle-keeping kinsmen of the more settled Hausa, accepted the leadership of a fanatical Muslim, Uthman dan Fodio, and their horsemen swamped the Hausa communities, eventually organizing them into the Sultanate of Sokoto. The warrior qualities of these Fulani/Hausas made them formidable enemies of the colonialists in the 1890s, although some Hausa were content to serve in the West African Frontier Force.

Havelock, Sir Henry (1795–1857), British soldier: born near Sunderland; read for the Bar in the Middle Temple before entering the army in 1815. Eight years later he went out to India, where he spent most of his life, distinguishing himself in campaigns against the Afghans and Sikhs and in Persia. On the outbreak of the *Indian Mutiny he took command of a column, mainly of Highlanders, and marched from Allahabad to relieve Cawnpore on 17 July 1857, covering 120 miles in nine days and gaining four victories in engagements on the way. Despite four more victories against the sepoy forces, he was not able to reach Lucknow until *Outram arrived with reinforcements for his sick and depleted army. Havelock, by now a major-general, resumed the advance on Lucknow in September 1857 and relieved the town, but was himself besieged there until November. By then he had contracted dysentery, from which he died a week after the end of the campaign. Posthumously he became one of the most respected heroes of mid Victorian England.

Hawke, Robert James Lee (1929–   ), Australian Prime Minister: born a Congregationalist minister's son at Bordertown, South Australia; educated at the University of Western Australia, becoming a Rhodes Scholar at Brasenose College, Oxford in 1953. On returning to Australia he worked for the Council of Trade Unions, serving as President of ACTU throughout the 1970s and building up a strong position in the Labor Party even before he became a member of the House of Representatives in 1980. When Labor returned to power in March 1983 after eight years in opposition, Bob Hawke became Prime Minister. His middle-of-the-path democratic socialism was electorally successful in 1984, 1987 and 1990. He commanded greater respect internationally, and especially among his Commonwealth colleagues, than he enjoyed within his party at home, and on 5 December 1990 he was succeeded as head of government by Paul *Keating, his Treasurer for the preceding seven years.

Head of the Commonwealth. The nature of the title to be used by the sovereign of the United Kingdom in presiding over a free association of member states was given careful study by King George VI and his advisers from 1947 onwards. The King, considering 'Head of the Commonwealth' in a note dated 9 April 1949, feared confusion in the Commonwealth of *Australia, unless the qualifying adjective 'British' was used. Nevertheless, after discussion with overseas prime ministers he accepted the title, although it was not used in his lifetime. 'Head of the Commonwealth' first appears on an official document in the Accession Proclamation of Queen *Elizabeth II, in February 1952, although it is nowhere included in the printed order of the Coronation Service of 2 June 1953 at Westminster Abbey – an omission which may reflect a growing awareness of the Commonwealth's multi-faith character.

Helpmann, Sir Robert (1909–86), Australian dancer, actor and choreographer: born in Mount Gambier, in the extreme south-east of South Australia; trained for *ballet at Adelaide before coming to England in

1933 and dancing Satan in *Job* for Sadler's Wells Ballet company in that year. He was resident chief male dancer with the company until 1950, and from 1939 onwards was also a choreographer, notably of *Hamlet* (1942) and *Miracle in the Gorbals* (1944). Helpmann was a versatile entertainer, appearing in a dozen films (including Olivier's *Henry V*), directing musicals and acting in London's West End: in 1944 he had the curious distinction of playing Hamlet on the same stage on which he had danced the role two years previously. He remained a guest dancer and choreographer with the Royal Ballet in London until 1963 when, after thirty years, he returned to his homeland and became co-director of the Australian Ballet in 1965, choreographing three further works for them and, with Nureyev, co-directing and appearing in their film, *Don Quixote* (1973). Helpmann was created CBE in 1964 and knighted in 1968.

Henry, Alice (1857–1943), Australian feminist: born in Melbourne; briefly a teacher, before becoming a pioneer woman journalist in 1884 and campaigning for social reforms and women's suffrage. She visited England in 1905, made contact with suffragette leaders on both sides of the Atlantic, and settled in Chicago for some twenty years, concentrating on women's trade union activity, a cause for which she wrote two studies published in the UK, *The Trade Union Woman* (1915) and *Women and the Labour Movement* (1923). She returned to Melbourne in 1933, compiled a bibliography of Australian woman authors, and in the National Council of Women campaigned vigorously for equal pay and for uniformity in divorce legislation.

Herbert, Henry Howard Molyneux, Lord Carnarvon (1831–90), British Colonial Secretary: succeeded his father as (fourth) Earl of Carnarvon in 1849 while still at Eton. He became Colonial Under-Secretary in the short-lived Tory government of Lord Derby (1858–59), and was then Colonial Secretary in 1866–67, strongly supporting Canadian federation and introducing the British North America Bill. As Disraeli's Colonial Secretary from 1874 to 1878 he insisted on action to stamp out *slavery along the Gold Coast, sent *Wolseley to Natal and *Frere to Cape Colony, finally authorizing annexation of the *Transvaal in 1877. Carnarvon was an early advocate of South African confederation. After resigning office in January 1878 over Disraeli's policy towards Russia he continued to campaign for closer unity between the colonies; he was chairman of the Colonial Defence Commission between 1879 and 1882, maintaining an interest in the problem until his death, and in 1887/8 he visited both South Africa and Australia. Carnarvon also served as Lord-Lieutenant in Dublin (1885/6) and early perceived that Ireland was an imperial problem rather than an issue in domestic politics; he was therefore in favour of limited autonomy.

Herero, a Bantu-speaking people, concentrated in central *Namibia and western *Botswana; a pastoral people, with enormous herds of cattle, when German colonization began in 1884. Resentment over loss of land rights led them to take the lead in a revolt against the Germans which continued from 1904 to 1907. Battle casualties, deaths in concentration camps, and expulsion to the Kalahari Desert reduced Herero numbers from 80,000 in 1900 to 15,000 in 1910. After World War I the Hereros passed under South African *mandate and were assigned reserves in which to dwell and recover their pastoral skills. The 1970 census return gave the Herero population in Namibia as 55,670; an estimate suggests it had risen to 99,000 by 1990.

Hertzog, James Barry Munnik (1866–1942), Boer general and South African Prime Minister: born at Wellington, Cape Colony; farmed and practised law. He served as a judge in the Orange Free State from 1895 to 1899 but then took command of Boer troops on their southern front and twice in 1900 led commando columns which penetrated Cape Colony. After the *Vereeniging Peace, General Hertzog opposed the attempts of *Botha and *Smuts to seek reconciliation, but agreed to serve as Minister of Justice in the first government of South Africa after Union, from 1910 to 1912. He established the (*Afrikaaner) National Party in 1912, intensifying traditions of racial segregation and opposing South African participation in World War I and subsequent membership of the League of Nations. His party won so many seats in the 1924 election that he was able to form a government, and he remained Prime Minister until the outbreak of World War II. As he never had an overall parliamentary majority, however, he could govern only by means of uneasy coalitions, notably with the South African Labour Party (1924–29), and with Smuts's United Party (1933–39). The influence of his coalition partners prevented Hertzog from implementing the full racialist segregation outlined in his party's electoral programmes, although he was able to enforce disfranchisement of the *Bantu in 1936. His position within the party was challenged by his more extreme successor as leader, Dr *Malan, but it was the defeat of Hertzog's attempts to remain neutral which led to his political eclipse by Smuts in September 1939.

Herzberg, Gerhard (1904–   ), Canadian chemical physicist: born in Hamburg; studied and taught in Germany until 1935, when he sought exile from the Nazis by emigrating to Saskatchewan, where he taught at the university for ten years. From 1949 to 1969 Dr Herzberg was director of the pure physics division of the National Research Council in Ottawa. His development of spectroscopy made possible the detailed study and detection of atomic and molecular spectra, and in 1971 he became the first Canadian citizen to be awarded the Nobel Prize for Chemistry.

High Commissioners: diplomatic representatives exchanged by Commonwealth members with one another. They have equal status with ambassadors, but slightly different responsibilities: High Commissioners have greater freedom than ambassadors in dealing directly with government departments not primarily concerned with external affairs. Normally the appointment of a High Commissioner in London followed closely on the grant of dominion status, but the interchange of High Commissioners between other Commonwealth capitals has developed much more slowly: thus, as late as 1918 Canada had a High Commissioner in London, but not in any other capital city of the empire. Occasionally a government has appointed a High Commissioner with special responsibility over areas in dispute, as in 1875 when the Disraeli government appointed a High Commissioner to reside in *Fiji with jurisdiction over British settlers on islands outside the empire, in order to prevent *'blackbirding' and other irregularities in the recruitment of labour in the West Pacific.

Hill Stations: were created by the British in India and Ceylon (Sri Lanka) as retreats from the heat of the plains or jungle. Most of them faithfully reproduced and long perpetuated both the social habits of upper middle class mid Victorian England and, as far as possible, its domestic architecture. The most famous was *Simla, which outgrew its original purpose to become, between 1865 and 1941, the effective administrative capital of British India for eight months of each year. More typical was Darjeeling, a hill station compressed along a semi-circular ridge climbing to 7,000 feet above sea level on the southern slopes of the Himalayas. While Darjeeling served Calcutta, Madras had Ootacamund, where the mean temperature for the year was 15°C (59°F), and Murree was a retreat from Rawalpindi. Among some seventy other Indian hill stations the best known were Naini Tal and Mussooree. Both Darjeeling and Ootacamund were close to tea plantations, as also was the most famous of Ceylon's hill stations, Nuwara Eliya, some 25 miles south-east of Kandy, which was established as a retreat by settlers in the 1820s.

Hindu faith. Hindu beliefs developed in the Indian subcontinent in the thirteenth century BC, although the word 'Hindu' was only applied to them in the eighth century AD, apparently by their Muslim adversaries. The faith has not been a dogmatic religion, for it does not believe in an organized Church, nor in militant proselytism; religious practices and mythologies vary considerably. In its purest form Hinduism is a way of good living, based upon respect for truthfulness, physical labour, honesty and tolerance of other beliefs. It worships a supreme spirit (Brahman), manifested in various forms, and it accepts transmigration of the soul. In India, Hinduism's greatest social impact was associated with its rigidly predestined caste system and a code of taboos whose infringement carried the punishment of ostracism; reforming Hindus, even those as saintly in observance as Mahatma *Gandhi, have been frowned on by the orthodox of the community because of their association with *Untouchability, and proposed civil law changes in modern India come constantly under the scrutiny of the strictly orthodox. Most of the world's estimated 800 million Hindus live in the Commonwealth: Hindus form 82.6 per cent of the population of the Indian Republic, 34 per cent of the people of Guyana, 25 per cent of Trinidad and Tobago, 22 per cent of Sri Lanka, and 5 per cent of Singapore. There are also sizeable Hindu communities in Kenya and Tanzania (especially Zanzibar), and smaller groups in Uganda, Zimbabwe and South Africa. In the United Kingdom there are more than 150 Hindu temples. During British rule in India militant Hindus clashed with Muslims in the years immediately preceding Partition and again, fanatically, in 1947, particularly in the Punjab and *Kashmir. The Hindu fundamentalist BJP movement intensified intercommunal violence in India by destroying a mosque at Ayodhya in December 1992: some 1,200 people were killed in communal clashes over the following six months.

Hobson, William (1793–1842), first Governor of New Zealand. As commanding officer of HMS *Rattlesnake*, Captain Hobson was sent from Sydney early in 1837 to safeguard the lives of the first settlers in New Zealand, caught in conflicts between the Maori peoples. When Hobson returned to England he reported on affairs in New Zealand, also delivering despatches from James Busby, the first official Resident. The anarchic state of land-purchasing and a fear that France intended to establish colonies there induced the British government to send Hobson back to New Zealand with orders to settle the land question and, through missionary intermediaries, to secure Maori acquiescence in the annexation of both islands. Hobson sailed from England in August 1839, stopped briefly at Sydney where he was sworn as Lieutenant-Governor of any land he might acquire, and reached North Island on 29 January 1840. He declared all land titles invalid and invited Maori chiefs to discuss the settlement embodied in the Treaty of Waitangi, which was agreed eight days after his arrival and which transferred sovereignty over New Zealand to Queen Victoria. Hobson's genuine attempt to build a colony based on mutual understanding between the races was hampered by his failing health; on 1 March he suffered a paralytic stroke at Waitemata Harbour and had to entrust further negotiations with the Maoris to deputies, most of whom he had hurriedly recruited in Sydney. In May 1840, largely to check the conflicting ambitions of settlers, Hobson formally declared New Zealand a colony independent of New South Wales, and in September proclaimed Auckland to be the capital. He died, however, before he could organize the colony.

Hobson-Jobson: originally a phrase in Anglo-Indian military argot applied to the excitement at any non-European festival in India. It was an attempt to say '*Hosseen Gosseen*', which was in itself a corrupt form of Hassan and Hussein, prophets commemorated in Muslim days of mourning. 'Hobson-Jobson' is best known as the title given to the *Glossary of Anglo-Indian Colloquial Words and Phrases and Kindred Terms* compiled by Sir Henry Yule and Dr Arthur Burnell and published by John Murray in 1886, a curious 870-page compendium which sought to explain the meaning and origin of hundreds of words which have enriched the English language from the Orient, generally by way of the Indian subcontinent. Some echo the 'Hobson-Jobson' confusion: thus 'Upper Roger' for an apparent heir was a corruption of *yuva-raja* ('young king'); and 'chop-chop' for 'hurry up' is described as pigeon-Chinese from the Cantonese dialect, *kap-kap*. Some words retaining primarily Indian associations include durbar, tiffin ('light meal'), pukka ('thorough'), *memsahib. The Eastern origin of others has been largely forgotten; they include bungalow, dinghy, dungaree, khaki, veranda and dam (as in 'I don't care a twopenny dam', the word being the name of the lowest copper coin of Akbar's Moghul empire).

Holland, Sir Sidney George (1893–1961), New Zealand Prime Minister: born at Greendale, Canterbury; became director of an engineering company in Christchurch before emerging as the driving force behind the conservative National Party opposition during World War II. Electoral success in December 1949 enabled him to form a government in which fourteen of his fifteen colleagues were New Zealanders by birth (he personally served as Minister of Finance). The government, strongly hostile to the trade unions, encouraged shipowners to reject wage demands, thereby causing a bitter 23-week strike, which Holland claimed to have mastered. A snap election after the strike, on 11 July 1951, won his party 50 of the 80 seats in Parliament, and he undertook drastic reforms to the economy, boosting a free market and ending government controls. His health gave way, however, and he retired in September 1957, to be succeeded by Keith *Holyoake.

Holt, Harold (1908–67), Australian Prime Minister: born in Sydney but educated in Melbourne; became a solicitor, and sat in the House of Representatives from 1935 until his death. He belonged to the United Australia Party, which reverted to its old name of Liberal party in February 1945. He became deputy leader of the party in 1956 and succeeded *Menzies as Prime Minister on 20 January 1966. He was an enthusiastic supporter of the *Vietnam War, and six months after taking office assured President Lyndon Johnson that in Australia the Americans had 'a staunch friend that will be all the way with LBJ'. Holt won the federal elections of November 1966, and despite mounting anti-war protests proceeded to raise to 8,000 the number of Australian servicemen in Vietnam. On 17 December 1967 Holt went swimming in strong surf from a beach at Portsea, Victoria and is presumed to have drowned, though his body was never found.

Holyoake, Sir Keith Jacka (1904–83), New Zealand Prime Minister and Governor-General: born on the family farm near Pahiatua, North Island; entered parliament as a conservative National Party member in 1932 and from 1949 to 1957 was both Minister of Agriculture and deputy premier in *Holland's government. Holyoake took over the premiership when Holland's health gave way in September 1957, but mounting economic uncertainties cost him the general election twelve weeks later and for three years he led the Opposition, constantly attacking Labour's budget proposals. The National Party won 46 seats to Labour's 34 in the 1960 election and Holyoake became Premier again, winning further elections in 1963, 1966 and 1969 and remaining in office until February 1972. He was a pragmatic conservative in home affairs, while developing trade links with Australia and persuasively seeking recognition by the *European Community of New Zealand's unique relationship with the United Kingdom as a supplier of dairy produce and frozen meat. In the Commonwealth Holyoake won respect for his firm multiracialism, and his hostility to *apartheid in South Africa and to the *Smith regime in Rhodesia. He received a knighthood in 1972, when he retired from party politics. In 1977 he became the first ex-Premier to take office as New Zealand's Governor-General, serving for three years with his one-time deputy, Robert *Muldoon, as head of government.

Hong Kong (Xianggang): British dependent territory, due to become a Special Administrative Territory of the People's Republic of China in July 1997. The sparsely populated main island of Hong Kong in the Pearl River Estuary, which often served as a pirates' lair, was seized during the *Opium War by a British naval party (26 January 1841), largely on the initiative of Captain Charles Elliott, RN (1801–75), Chief Superintendent of the China Trade Commission. Formal cession followed by the terms of the Treaty of *Nanking (1842). Hong Kong was made a Crown Colony in April 1843: *Kowloon and Stonecutters Island were acquired in 1860, and in 1898 the *New Territories were leased from China. Between 1850 and 1900 the population grew from 33,000 to 263,000, despite an epidemic of bubonic *plague in 1894; it stood at 600,000 by 1920 and had increased by another million in 1940. A railway to the Chinese border was opened on 1 October 1910 and reached Canton (now Guangzhou) in 1912. Hong Kong served as the main base of the Royal Navy's China Squadron, and until 1959 the Admiralty maintained a naval dockyard there. Between the wars Hong Kong could claim to be the Empire's third commercial port, as well as being the financial centre for British investment in the Orient. On 8 December 1941 the land frontier was crossed by Japanese invaders, who overran the peninsula in four days; the main island resisted assault until, on Christmas Day, Hong Kong became the first British Crown Colony ever to surrender to an enemy. Civilians and servicemen received brutal treatment by their captors: 33 Hong Kong citizens (British, Chinese and Indian) were beheaded in 1943 for treasonable acts against the Occupying Power. An interim administration of self-liberated internees welcomed formal liberation by the Royal Navy a fortnight after Japan's capitulation in 1945. Civil war in China led to an influx of refugees: the population rose from 610,000 on liberation to 2 million in 1950, 4 million in 1970 and 5 million when Mao Tse-tung died in 1976. There were riots over poor housing conditions in 1952 and, with Communist backing, in 1967. By then Hong Kong was one of the world's leading financial and commercial centres, with Kai Tak – a flying field in the 1930s – enlarged to an international airport in 1952 by French engineers, and with tunnels built in 1966, 1972, 1983 and 1989 linking peninsula and islands. Uniquely, considering its international status, Hong Kong had no form of representative government until 1985, when some elected members were admitted to the Legislative Council. An awareness that time was running out for the leased territories prompted Anglo-Chinese discussions on Hong Kong's future, beginning in September 1982. A Joint Declaration, signed in Beijing on 19 December 1984, provided for retrocession of the whole territory of Hong Kong on 1 July 1997, although it was agreed that the social and economic systems of this 'Special Administrative Region' would remain unchanged for fifty years thereafter. A Joint Liaison Group, meeting to prepare the transfer of sovereignty, ran into difficulties over plans announced by the Governor of Hong Kong in October 1992 to extend democratic government, and over a proposed new international airport at Chek Lap Kok. Despite Chinese protests, on 18 September 1994 the first fully democratic elections were held in Hong Kong.

Hong Kong and Shanghai Banking Corporation: founded in 1865 by a combination of local firms. Apart from the years of World War II, it has since then maintained headquarters on Hong Kong Island, in a succession of architecturally impressive buildings. Originally the bank's operations were concentrated principally in the colony and ★Treaty Ports, but in the late nineteenth century it was responsible for much of the capital which developed both Japan's overseas trade and imperial China's railway system (in association with ★Jardine, Matheson). The Bank long served as the repository for all Chinese Maritime Customs dues, and as a non-governmental central bank for Hong Kong; it issued the colony's currency notes, which carried pictures of the Bank's offices and facsimiles of the Chief Accountant's signature. The Bank's financial ventures in China flourished during the inter-war period, mainly from grandiose new branch premises opened on the Shanghai Bund in 1923. There were also important branches in Singapore and Brunei. After World War II the Corporation extended its range of business, notably in Papua New Guinea, and from 1971 onwards in the south-west Pacific from the financial centre of Vila in *Vanuatu.

Hong Kong Regiment: was the first military force raised in British India specifically for service overseas. It was set up in November 1891, partly as a military experiment, and was recruited entirely from Muslims, mostly living in the Punjab and north-western India. The regiment reached Hong Kong from Bombay on 7 May 1892 and was in action in 1899, dispersing a thousand armed Chinese from the frontier hills of the recently-acquired *New Territories. The regiment took part in the relief of the Peking legations in 1900 but was disbanded in October 1902, apparently because the regiment's existence was thought to threaten recruiting for the *Indian Army, since pay and conditions overseas were so much better than in India itself. The regimental colours of the short-lived regiment were handed over in 1928 to the colony's territorial force, the Hong Kong Volunteer Defence Corps, who fought valiantly in December 1941.

Hongs: European trading houses operating in China, especially in Hong Kong in the nineteenth century. The best known Hong was *Jardine, Matheson; after 1870 they faced competition from Swire and Butterfield (generally known as 'Swire's'). 'Hong' is derived from a Chinese word for a row of buildings, and probably originated with the waterfront warehouses at Canton (now Guangzhou).

Horse-racing became a popular sport throughout the Empire almost as soon as British settlements were established overseas. The first organized race meeting in New South Wales was held in Hyde Park, Sydney in 1810 shortly after the arrival of Governor *Macquarie, who was present; the Australian Jockey Club's headquarters remains in Sydney, at Randwick racecourse. Race meetings date from 1814 in Tasmania, 1833 in Western Australia, 1838 in South Australia and Victoria and 1843 in Queensland. The most famous Australian race, the Melbourne Cup, was first run on 7 November 1861, fourteen years after Melbourne became a city, and the stake had reached over £10,000 by 1890. It is an annual fixture for the first Tuesday in November, a public holiday in the city. Race meetings near Cape Town may antedate the first Australian ones. The Queen's Plate, the most important race in Canada, was first run at Toronto in 1861, six years before federation; the Canadian Derby meeting is at Edmonton, Alberta. India under the Raj had elaborate racecourses with impressive clubhouses at Bombay and Calcutta, and smaller courses at the *hill stations, including Darjeeling. In Hong Kong race meetings have been held in the Happy Valley since the 1840s. The East Africa Turf Club held a meeting at Nairobi in July 1900, four years after British settlers arrived. In New Zealand horse-racing was for many years second only to Rugby Union as a spectator sport, with a 'Derby' at both Wellington and Auckland and an important meeting at Christchurch every November. Outside the British Isles, Australians remain the greatest enthusiasts for horses and their riders: Phar Lap, a New Zealand-foaled Australian winner in the years 1928–32, has passed into popular legend; and a jockey from Wagga Wagga, Arthur 'Scobie' Breasley (1914–), was champion in Britain in 1957 and 1961–63, after riding winners in Australia for more than twenty years.

Hotels. In Australia and New Zealand local hotels were established in pioneer settlements. They gave accommodation to new arrivals and provided buildings where communal problems could be discussed. Most outback hotels were two-storeyed and had a ladies' lounge and a private parlour as well as the ubiquitous bars and billiard rooms. Although many were socially dubious, *gold rush towns like Dunedin and Ballarat included some which advertised family facilities: of these, the Shamrock at Bendigo carried a certain elegance into the twentieth century. Sydney had a Grand Hotel before federation, and the *Melbourne Centennial Exhibition left two long-term survivors, the Victoria and the Windsor. In Canada the growth of hotels was closely linked to the spread of the *Canadian Pacific Railway. However, in general the most famous hotels of the Empire were products of the steamship age. Many followed the pattern of the New British Hotel opened by Shepheard in Cairo in the early 1840s to accommodate travellers to the East on the *P & O service, who before the opening of the *Suez Canal needed overland transit from Alexandria to join a new ship at Suez. Shepheard's, refitted in 1890, survived on its original site until January 1952, when it was wrecked by an Egyptian nationalist mob. The next in the Shepheard's tradition were the Galle Face on Colombo's esplanade (1864, rebuilt 1891) and the Hong Kong Hotel, on the waterfront facing Kowloon (1866). By 1870 Reynolds' (later the Bristol) in Karachi and the Great Eastern in Calcutta were trying to reach Shepheard's standard. Raffles Hotel in Singapore was opened in December 1887 by the Sarkies brothers, Armenians who had already made the Eastern and Oriental at Penang a flourishing concern. Raffles, too, encouraged emulators, among them the Strand in Rangoon (1900), the Taj Mahal Hotel in Bombay (1903), and the Peninsula in Kowloon, built in 1927 – by which time Raffles itself was the centre of social life for much of Malaya. Kenya's hotels sought to meet pioneer needs with socially superior comfort. They came with a rush in Nairobi: Woods (1901) was followed by others, including the Norfolk Hotel (1907; bombed by terrorists on New Year's Eve in 1980). Jet air travel has led to a proliferation of international hotels, opulently standardized in characterless comfort.

Hudson, Sir William (1896–1978), hydro-electric engineer; born in Nelson, South Island; served with the *Anzac Corps in World War I before joining the Armstrong Whitworth Company. He worked on some of the earliest hydro-electric power projects in his native New Zealand in the 1920s, and was briefly in New South Wales, before spending six years supervising hydro-electric development at Galloway, Scotland. In 1938 he returned to Sydney and was appointed Commissioner of the Snowy Mountains Hydro-Electric Authority on its creation in 1949. This post gave Hudson responsibility for supervising the construction of some 90 miles of tunnels to divert the waters of the Snowy River through sixteen newly-built dams served by seven major power stations. By this means (the greatest engineering feat in the antipodes), electricity was generated for New South Wales, Victoria and Canberra, while a huge area around the Murray and Murrumbidgee rivers was irrigated. Hudson retired in 1967, but his forceful direction ensured that the project was completed in 1972/3, earlier than the federal government had anticipated.

Hudson's Bay Company. 'The Company of Adventurers of England Tradeing into Hudson's Bay' received a charter of foundation from Charles II on 2 May 1670 after a preliminary voyage in 1668 had confirmed the *fur-trading potential of this inland sea on the edge of the Arctic, named after the navigator Henry Hudson (d. 1611), who may have discovered it in 1610. The Company was headed by Charles II's cousin, Prince Rupert of the Rhine (1619–82), the famous royalist cavalry commander who spent the last twelve years of his life as Governor of Windsor: the million and a half square miles of territory over which the Company was accorded sovereign rights was called Prince Rupert's Land in his honour. The Company long expected fur-traders to bring their pelts to Company posts established on the shore of the Bay: Fort Rupert (1669–70), Fort Albany (1679), Fort York (1684), Fort Churchill (1688), etc. For a quarter of a century the Company's posts were regularly attacked by the French, though recognition of the Company's claims to Prince Rupert's Land was acknowledged by France in the Treaty of Utrecht (1713). Only after 1760 did the Company show greater initiative, establishing posts inland and opening up the *Northwest Territories. Rival (unchartered) companies – the North-West (1779, a partnership of Montreal traders) and the XY (1800) – stimulated expansion, since the companies were forced to search for new fur-yielding regions. The North-West absorbed the XY in 1804 but was itself united with the Hudson's Bay Company by a new charter granted in 1821, the year in which the Company made a formal claim to 'New Caledonia' (*British Columbia). The following quarter of a century saw the apogee of the Company's influence on the growth of the Canadian nation; it was, for example, a Company official, James *Douglas, who established Fort Victoria as a fur-trading outpost on Vancouver Island in 1843 and became the first

Governor of the province in the west. In 1869 the Company was bought out by the Canadian government and lost both its monopoly and its territorial rights: much of Prince Rupert's Land became *Manitoba. But the Hudson's Bay Company remains one of the largest retailing institutions in the world, still concerned with the fur market.

Huggins, Godfrey Martin (1883–1971), Southern Rhodesian Prime Minister: born in Kent; educated at Malvern College, studied medicine at St Thomas's Hospital, and practised as a surgeon in London before settling in Salisbury, Southern Rhodesia in 1911. After serving as an army surgeon in World War I he became accepted as Rhodesia's principal medical consultant and was elected to the legislature in 1924, becoming Premier in 1933 and heading a 'United Party' government for the next twenty years. He developed the mining industry and fruit farming while consistently working for closer collaboration with Northern Rhodesia and Nyasaland; he organized the colony's considerable war effort from 1939 onwards, his services being recognized with a knighthood in 1941. Huggins collaborated closely with *Welensky in establishing the *Central African Federation of the two Rhodesias and Nyasaland in 1953, and was Federal Prime Minister until 1956. His most lasting achievement in office was the start of work in 1955 on the Kariba dam, which began supplying *hydro-electric power four years later. Sir Godfrey received a peerage in 1955 and retired to England as Viscount Malvern of Rhodesia and Bexley.

Hughes, William Morris (1864–1952), Australian Prime Minister: born in London but spent his childhood in North Wales; emigrated to Queensland at the age of twenty, moving down to Sydney two years later, where he took up the cause of the wharf labourers and entered the New South Wales Parliament in 1894, studying law in his free moments. He was a member of the Federal Parliament from 1901 until his death. Despite increasing deafness he was a superb radical orator, like his near contemporary Welsh compatriot, Lloyd George. Hughes became Attorney-General in 1910 in the second Labor government of Andrew *Fisher, whom he succeeded as Prime Minister on 27 October 1915. Sixteen months later he formed a coalition, breaking with his Labor colleagues because he favoured changes in *military service, including conscription. He was respected in London during the later stages of the war and at the Peace Conference, but the sharp tone of his speeches emphasized the essentially conservative prejudices of his mind: he disliked League of Nations idealism, though he fought tenaciously to secure Australia's *mandate in the Pacific; and he was in some respects a white racist, for he wished to safeguard the established order of the Empire by a closer federation of the existing dominions. He fell from office in February 1923. After breaking with Labor, Hughes was a Nationalist

Party member, but he helped form the United Australia Party in 1931 and was back in office as Minister for External Affairs (1937–39) and Attorney-General (1939–41). He was one of the first politicians to give warning of the Japanese threat to Australia, and during 1940–41 he took over ministerial responsibility for the navy. When war came to the Pacific he served on Australia's War Advisory Council, remaining a member until 1944 when his health gave way.

Hume and Hovell Expedition (1824/5). The first important expedition into the interior south and west from Sydney was undertaken by Hamilton Hume (1797–1873) and William Hovell (1786–1875) with a small party which included six convicts. Hume, who had been born at Parramatta, had a wool station west of Goulburn, at Gunning; the expedition set out from there in October 1824. They reached a river which they found was called Murrumbidgee by the aborigines and then sighted, to their east, a mountain range which they named the Alps. They discovered good pastoral land behind the billabong-lined banks of an even greater river – the longest in Australia – to which Hume gave his own name, though the aborigines knew it as Millewa and it was later renamed Murray River to honour the Speaker of the New South Wales legislature, Sir Terence Murray (1810–73). Hume and Hovell reached the coast of Port Philip Bay two months after setting out from Gunning, though they wrongly believed they were at Western Port, some 50 miles to the south-east. The expedition then successfully returned to Gunning, arriving there before the end of January 1825.

Hurricanes: see *Cyclone*.

Hydro-electric power projects. The engineering techniques of harnessing a large head of water to drive turbines which generate electricity improved rapidly between the two world wars. Pioneering projects at Montmorency Falls, Quebec and Niagara Falls in Ontario were further developed by the Shipshaw hydro-project on Quebec's Saguenay River (which was begun in 1926 but not completed until 1943 because of the Depression) and the Chippewa plant at Queenstown, Ontario. In Australasia, the earliest attempts to take advantage of Tasmania's Great Lake waters ran into difficulties, forcing the state government to set up a Hydro-Electric Department in 1914 (Hydro-Electric Commission from 1930): this initiative led to the completion of projects in the Derwent, Gordon and Pieman catchment areas, giving Tasmania cheaper and proportionately more extensive hydro-electric power than any other Australian state. In the early 1920s William *Hudson gained experience on New Zealand's longest river, the Waikato in North Island, of which he was to make use in undertaking the greatest of antipodean hydro-electric projects, on the Snowy River of New South Wales, where 16 dams and 7

Hydro-electric power projects

major power stations were constructed between 1949 and 1972. In New Zealand, too, hydro-electric plants were developed mainly in the 1950s and 1960s: Arapuni and Maraetai (1952–54 and 1970–71) on the upper Waikato; Kurow on the Waitaki River in South Island; Whakamaru was open by 1956; Waipapa (South Island) in 1961; Atiamuri in 1964. There was also a major project in North Island at Turangi-Tokaanu (1965–74), but a similar scheme in South Island at Lake Manapouri (1963–1971) was delayed by a nationwide protest in 1968 at the environmental damage threatened by plans to raise water levels higher than was originally proposed. The harnessing of British Columbia's fast-flowing rivers, often by major engineering feats, brought industrial growth to isolated areas, notably along the Nechako River, where electricity from an underground powerhouse at Kemano on the Kenney dam is transmitted 51 miles through the mountains to sustain the industrial complex at Kitimat. Twenty other important hydro-electric projects were completed in Canada during the 1950s and 1960s, including harnessing the Whitehorse Rapids in the Yukon and the headwaters of the Manicouagan and Outardes Rivers to serve Quebec Province, new plants along the *St Lawrence Seaway, and the Mactaquac hydro-electric scheme to the west of Fredericton, the provincial capital of New Brunswick. In India during the last years of the Raj priority was given to dams which would serve as *irrigation barrages, but some were also used for electrical power stations and this development has been carried much further by the Indian Republic. There are six hydro-electric plants in Andhra Pradesh, several in Assam and Madhya Pradesh, and new projects in Bihar and Sikkim, while the Tehri Dam in Uttar Pradesh will be the sixth highest in the world. Pakistan's Tarbela Dam across the Indus has the world's biggest embankment, 485 feet high, and provides more than half the nation's electrical energy. Since World War II there has been extensive hydro-electric development in Commonwealth Africa. This has not always been successful: the Akosombo Dam on the Volta, a visionary project of *Nkrumah, was completed in 1966 and was intended to supply power to all of Ghana and much of West Africa, but the low level of water has led to occasional rationing of electricity in Ghana and even a temporary dependence on supplies from the neighbouring Côte d'Ivoire republic. By contrast, the Owen Falls Hydro-electric Scheme at Jinja (completed in 1954) can supply power to the whole of Uganda and a third of Kenya. The Kariba Dam, which created an artificial lake 175 miles long on the Zambezi, was begun in 1955, was producing electrical power by 1959, and is the chief source of energy for Zimbabwe and the Zambian copperbelt. Vast schemes like Kariba have aroused widespread criticism from environmentalists: the creation of Lake Kariba forced 40,000 African people to leave villages which would be submerged, and wild life habitats were devastated. So long as President Banda could count on foreign aid, he was able to develop hydro-electric power in *Malawi, notably by generators installed at Nkula Falls and Tedzani Falls. In 1987 work began on a South African–Lesotho undertaking to dam the Orange River in Lesotho, diverting its waters through tunnels into the Vaal River to provide both countries with hydro-electric power. Despite environmental concerns, and the intrusion of nuclear energy, hydro-electricity continues to spread: the financing of the Pergau Dam in *Malaysia during the 1980s provoked controversy in Britain during February 1994, while in 1990 the *Commonwealth Development Corporation authorized financial aid for a project in Papua New Guinea, much resisted by defenders of the island's unimpaired environmental riches.

Ibo (Igbo): non-Muslim national group and language in eastern *Nigeria. The Ibo exercised great influence on Nigerian politics immediately after independence, largely thanks to President *Azikiwe's prestige. They later became identified with *Biafra and the secessionist movement which culminated in the civil war of 1967–70.

Immigration. Almost every corporate community or settlement in the Commonwealth is a product of immigration. The movement of peoples may have been caused by: (i) a mass exodus – *aborigines, *Maoris, the *Partition of India, African and North American tribes seeking more fertile areas; (ii) the *slave trade; (iii) indentured labour – *blackbirding; *Chinese labourers, etc.; (iv) convict *transportation; (v) hunger and poverty in the homeland; (vi) political persecution – notably of *Jewish communities; (vii) a spirit of enterprise and adventure, often prompted by hopes of making a rapid fortune (see *gold rush*). Most Australians, Canadians and New Zealanders are descended from European immigrants or were born in Europe themselves, while the attempts by white settlers in southern Africa to perpetuate their political and economic supremacy continue to pose problems in social relationships. But over the last 120 years there have also been significant movements of non-whites within the Commonwealth: of peoples from the Indian subcontinent to east and southern Africa and the Caribbean (primarily *Guyana and *Trinidad); of South Pacific islanders to New Zealand, especially between 1946 and 1986; of Chinese by way of Hong Kong to the Malay peninsula; of peoples from the Caribbean to *Canada; and, since 1955, of Pakistanis, Bangladeshi, Indians and former colonial peoples from the Caribbean and Africa to the United Kingdom. Probably the greatest migration of all time was the movement of 14 million people across the new boundaries of India and Pakistan in 1947/8. Attempts to control the influx of settlers have included 'head tax' measures against Chinese labourers in Canada, *Commonwealth Immigration Acts in Britain, and *Immigration Restriction Acts in Australia. Conversely, there have also been many occasions of assisted settlement: in early projects for Australasian colonies put forward by *Wakefield; in smaller undertakings, such as the *Big Brother movement and the enterprise of individuals like *Chisholm and *Fairbridge in Australia, or the 1919 Soldier Settlement Scheme for farming in *Kenya. A mass assisted-immigration project was developed by *Chifley and *Calwell in Australia after World War II. In 1947 the British and Australian governments agreed to allow free passages for ex-servicemen and their dependants and cheap passages for civilian families wishing to settle in Australia. Agreements were also made with UN agencies for refugees, and with Malta, Italy and the Netherlands for assisted emigration. A similar scheme operated in New Zealand, though smaller in scale. In 1948 28,943 assisted immigrants landed in Australia; in 1949 118,840; in 1950 119,109; and over the following thirty years some 2.5 million. The growth of immigration in Australia may be seen by comparing the last forty years of the nineteenth century, when 750,000 immigrants arrived, and the forty years after World War II, when the figure jumped to 3.5 million. Similarly, in Canada the figure of 453,016 immigrants over the first two decades of the century constituted a record when it was made public in 1922, but between 1945 and 1965 the dominion accepted more than 2.5 million immigrants. The peak year for Canada was 1957, with 282,164 newcomers, many from eastern Europe, but by 1992 the figure was again high: 252,537 admissions, of whom 14,722 came from the Caribbean.

Immigration Restriction Acts (Australian, 1902 and 1925). The July 1902 Act was one of the earliest measures of Australia's Federal Parliament. It sought to maintain a 'White Australia' by imposing a dictation test in a European language on any would-be settler; the ruling was changed in 1905 to a test 'in a prescribed language', and the dictation test remained obligatory until 1958. The second Act (1925) gave the Governor-General the right to forbid entry to any group of aliens whom he might specify as undesirable, for either economic or racial reasons. Little use was made of this measure.

Imperial Airways: the principal *airline operating from Great Britain between the wars. At the Imperial Conference of 1921 the dominion representatives pressed the United Kingdom government to encourage overseas aviation links. In December 1923 five air service companies merged to form the Imperial Air Transport Company, with government sponsorship. In 1924/5 'Imperial Airways', based on the world's first purpose-built passenger airport at Croydon, carried 11,395 travellers over 853,042 air miles. Further mergers included the acquisition of the Cobham–Blackburn Company, which by 1927/8 had completed preparations for a flying boat service between Cairo, Khartoum, Kisumu (Lake Victoria) and, ultimately, Cape Town. Additional subsidies from Britain, South Africa and the colonial governments enabled scheduled Imperial Airways flights along this route to begin on 27 April 1932; they took at least 9 days, with hotel breaks for the hours of darkness and a railway journey linking Paris and Brindisi, since Mussolini denied foreign companies the use of Italian air space. By then Imperial Airways had already opened regular routes to Egypt and Basra (1925), and to India (London–Karachi, 30 March 1929); a route was established between London, Penang and Singapore on 9 December 1933. The first scheduled flights to Brisbane began in April 1935: they required more than 30 stops, either to change planes or to refuel, and took 12 days, sometimes more. Flights to Nigeria by way of Khartoum came in 1936, but took at least 7 days. The advent of Imperial Airways was of particular service to communities off the main shipping routes; thus, from 1932 onwards mail could be sent from the Gulf or from northern India to London in 8 days rather than five weeks. In 1936/7 Imperial Airways carried 64,771 travellers over 5,231,655 air miles. A prestigious Short Brothers 'Empire' flying-boat service to Australia, accommodating 18 passengers in some luxury, was inaugurated in 1938: a flying-boat left Southampton on 26 June, reached Darwin on 3 July and landed at Sydney on 6 July. On the eve of World War II the company had 47 aeroplanes and 31 flying-boats and each week provided seven flights from Britain to Egypt, four to India by way of the Gulf, three to Kenya and South Africa, and two to Malaya, Australia and Hong Kong. On 1 April 1940 BOAC (the new British Overseas Airways Corporation) absorbed both Imperial Airways and British Airways, a subsidised company which since 1936 had been operating rival services to Europe.

Imperial British East Africa Company: founded by the Glaswegian shipping magnate Sir William Mackinnon, to open up for 'legitimate commerce' a British sphere of influence inland from a coastal strip around Mombasa, as far westwards as the kingdom of *Buganda, which he had leased from the Sultan of *Zanzibar. A Royal Charter was granted on 3 September 1888 to the Association which Mackinnon had established in the previous year, and as the IBEA Co. it set up its first base at Machakos in 1889. A year later Captain *Lugard founded a second station at Fort Smith, five miles north-west of modern Nairobi. The Company had insufficient resources to develop the region; it never paid a dividend, and in 1895 handed over its responsibilities to the British government. The East Africa Protectorate was formally proclaimed on 15 June 1895, and became the colony of *Kenya on 23 July 1920.

Imperial Conferences. The colonial prime ministers first met in London during the Golden Jubilee celebrations of 1887, and a second conference was held at Ottawa in 1894. The Diamond Jubilee meeting of 1897 was given greater prominence as an imperial gathering by Joseph *Chamberlain, who also chaired the Coronation Conference of 1902. Overseas visitors to the fifth conference (London, 1907) showed a marked hostility to the use of the word 'colonial', and it was therefore decided that future meetings should be called 'Imperial Conferences'; the first – in 1911 – coincided with King George V's coronation. Except at the separate *Imperial War Conference of 1917, the main subjects discussed by visiting ministers were the precise character of a *'dominion', and the right of overseas territories to control their own external policies. The 1926 conference led to the *Balfour Definition, while in October and November 1930 there were lengthy discussions before agreement could be reached on the Statute of *Westminster. Other matters discussed at the Imperial Conferences of George V's reign included *imperial preference, naval defence, the status of the *Irish Free State, and the encouragement of closer links within the Empire by means of *broadcasting and *airlines. The final communiqué issued after the conference of June 1937 gave support to 'the hopes of international appeasement' voiced by the new British Prime Minister, Neville Chamberlain, in his quest for peace. Later conferences were called *Commonwealth Prime Ministers' Meetings and, since 1961, *Commonwealth Heads of Government Meetings.

Imperial Preference: a doctrine favouring the economic confederation of the Empire, first developed in Canada; taken up with enthusiasm by Joseph *Chamberlain in 1897, and in his Tariff Reform Movement from 1903 onwards. The British tradition of free trade left successive governments in London unenthusiastic until the impact of the *great depression in 1931, when the MacDonald National Coalition government turned away from free trade to protection. At the *Ottawa Imperial Economic Conference of 1932 the dominion governments agreed to accept the principle of imperial preference, admitting each other's goods and raw materials either without tariffs or at preferential rates: the dominion governments would impose tariffs only to safeguard native industries. GATT (General Agreement on Tariffs and Trade, concluded under UN auspices in 1947) forced modifications in the application of imperial preference in October 1947, but the system was only finally abandoned by the United Kingdom upon her entry into the European Community in January 1972.

Imperial War Cabinet and Conference (1917). When Lloyd George formed a coalition government in December 1916 he also sought closer links with the Empire in prosecuting World War I, and invited the dominion prime ministers to London for a series of meetings in March and April 1917. He hoped to discuss general issues at the Imperial War Conference, which met in fifteen sessions, and also to form an Imperial War Cabinet which would be a unified executive for the Empire at war. He found, however, that the various prime ministers regarded themselves as responsible solely to their own governments; they discussed general issues at the Conference, and attended fourteen meetings of an enlarged British War Cabinet to consider strategy and problems of supply at a crucial stage in the war. Only General *Smuts (South Africa's Defence Minister) remained in London, as a member of the British War Cabinet, from June 1917 to December 1918. The Conference was attended by *Borden for Canada and *Massey for New Zealand, supported by Canada's Minister for the Army Overseas and New Zealand's Finance Minister. The Newfoundland Prime Minister, Sir Edgar Morris, was present, but Australia was represented only from the second week in April, as William *Hughes's arrival was delayed. A significant innovation was the attendance of an Indian 'assessor' from the *princely rulers, the Maharaja of Bikanir. The Imperial War Conference was important in demonstrating the likely extent and constraints of Commonwealth participation in collective undertakings.

Imperial Wireless and Cable Conference (1928). After World War I the Eastern Telegraph Company (ETC), formed in 1892 chiefly to maintain *telegraph links with India, seemed outdated. Concern shown by the dominions at the Imperial Conference of 1926 over financing a Pacific *telegraph cable and the desirability of speedy transmission of messages between the Empire's capital cities led to the summoning of a special conference in 1928. There it was agreed to set up (in 1929) Imperial and International Communications Ltd, which would take over ETC's responsibilities and co-ordinate all overseas communications of the Empire. The company's name was changed to Cable and Wireless in 1934; it was nationalized on 1 January 1947.

Imperialism: the extension of a country's sovereignty by the acquisition of new territories, of which the natural resources and inhabitants then become chattels of the conquering power. It differs from 'colonialism' in claiming to bring material and cultural advantages to allegedly backward peoples in lands distant from Europe. Although there were manifestations of imperialism as an idea of universal power in earlier epochs of history, the modern form is a product of late Victorian Britain, first proclaimed as evidence of 'the commanding spirit of these islands' by *Disraeli in 1872, proudly developed further by such writers as *Dilke, *Seeley and *Froude, and given a sense of mission at the end of the century by *Chamberlain, *Rhodes, *Milner and their devotees. The English word 'imperialism' was taken into other languages, notably German and Russian; a theory of economic imperialism as a means of obtaining profitable returns by sending capital overseas was expounded by the English sociologist economist J. A. Hobson (1858–1940) in *Imperialism* (1902), and developed by Lenin in *Imperialism as the Highest Stage of Capitalism* (1915). Many historians have interpreted the Great Power rivalry of the years 1880 to 1923 as a series of contests between competing imperialisms, shown most markedly in the *scramble for Africa and claims for spheres of influence in the Middle East, the Far East and the Pacific.

India. The Moghul Empire in India was established in 1526 by Babur, who had led an army southwards from Afghanistan six years before. His achievement was consolidated by his grandson, Akbar the Great (1542–1605), but the empire only reached its territorial zenith under the strict Muslim Emperor Aurangzeb (1618–1707). Technically his sovereignty – though often weakened by rebellion – was acknowledged from the Himalayas and Assam to southern Madras, except in the new Hindu kingdom of the *Marathas in the western Ghats, including Bombay, with its outposts in Coromandel and Mysore. The eighteenth century saw a rapid collapse of Moghul power, which was challenged at first by the Maratha Confederacy and then by the emergence of British power under *Clive in conflicts with the French and the Nizam of Hyderabad. The capture of the Mysore capital, *Seringapatam, in 1799 ensured that the *East India Company, increasingly under governmental control, was master of Benares, Bihar and Bengal and most of the littoral of the Bay of Bengal as far as Coromandel. Permanent settlement of Bengal began in 1793, although great progress had already been made by Warren *Hastings. Lasting reforms were made under *Wellesley and *Cavendish-Bentinck, although the Maratha wars, which had begun in 1775, were not finally ended until 1818. Conflict with Afghans and Sikhs led to the conquest of Sind in 1843 and the annexation of the Punjab in 1849. Under *Dalhousie progress was made on the *Grand Trunk Road, and other links between the cities, such as *railways and telegraph, were introduced; this rapid pace of change contributed to the *Indian Mutiny, which was both a proto-independence movement and a military revolt. The government in London – and 'Clemency' *Canning, the Governor-General in Calcutta – recognized that India could never become a colonial possession: hence the formation of a separate Secretaryship of State for India in 1858 (see *below*), the development of a special *Indian Civil Service, and the decision to preserve a system of *paramountcy, based on co-operation between the British government in India and the *princely rulers, pledged to loyalty. Universities were founded in Calcutta, Madras and Bombay in 1857, and rapid improvements were made in the medical service; but on three occasions it proved impossible to devise ways of countering the ravages of *famine in Bengal. The unique status of India was again recognized by the *Royal Titles Act (1876) and the proclamation of Queen Victoria as Empress of India on 1 January 1877. This imperial ascendancy, which reached its apogee in the viceroyalty of *Curzon, ran parallel with a revival of Indian national pride, shown by the achievements of the *Tagore family and through the rise of the *Indian National Congress, from 1885 onwards. Successive *India Acts (1919 and 1935) and the wartime *Cripps Mission failed to satisfy *Gandhi and the champions of *swaraj*. Ethnic-religious conflicts, dormant within the Congress Party for half a century, emerged in 1934/5 with the secession of the Muslim leader, Mohammed Ali *Jinnah; from 1940 Jinnah's campaign for a separate and Islamic *Pakistan forced the pace towards *Partition. The Muslim demand for 'direct action' precipitated the *Calcutta Riots of August 1946, in which 4,000 people died. The *Attlee government in London, though already committed to independence for India, did not accept Partition until after the arrival of *Mountbatten as the last Viceroy in March 1947. The *Indian Independence Act, creating the dominions of Pakistan and India, was piloted swiftly through the House of Commons by Attlee himself. India, shorn of the Muslim-dominated regions of Baluchistan, Sind, the western Punjab, the *North-West Frontier and East Bengal, gained independence on 15 August 1947. Terrible killings followed Partition and Independence; at least 300,000 people are believed to have died in the subcontinent, either slaughtered in violent clashes or struck down by the diseases which followed so great a disruption of orderly administration. During August, September and October 1947 it is estimated that 14 million people migrated across the boundaries of the two new dominions. Even so, problems of political allegiance remained unresolved. Paramountcy was at an end, and the princely rulers were advised by the Viceroy to allow their territories to join India or Pakistan, according to religion and geographical position. The Nawab of Junagadh, a Muslim, acceded to Pakistan, even though his territories shared no frontier with the new creation, but he then went into exile ahead of a plebiscite in which his former subjects voted for union with India. Hyderabad was a huge state landlocked within the new India, the Nizam the Muslim ruler of a predominantly Hindu population; he refused to accede to either dominion, and after two years of uncertainty the Indian authorities took over Hyderabad in September 1949. The problems of *Kashmir, where the Maharaja was Hindu and the people divided, led to armed clashes between Pakistan and India until 1949. There was further fighting after the *Indian Republic was established in 1950.

India Act (1858): a post-Mutiny resettlement of government. The powers of the *East India Company were abolished; administrative authority was transferred to the Crown; and the Company's troops became the nucleus of the *Indian Army. On 5 June 1858 Lord Stanley (1826–93; 15th Earl of Derby from 1869) ceased to be President of the Board of Control and became Secretary of State for India, with an advisory council of fifteen members to serve him in London; and Governor-General *Canning became the first *Viceroy.

India Act (1919): sought to implement proposals put forward in the previous year's joint report by the Indian Secretary, Edwin Montagu

(1879–1924), and the Viceroy, Viscount Chelmsford (1868–1933), which recommended the introduction of responsible government. The Act was experimental and subject to review every ten years. An all-India Parliament of two Houses was set up: a Council of State of 60 members, some of whom were elected and not more than 20 of whom were to be officials, and a Legislative Assembly of 100 elected members and 40 nominees. Parliament had no power to remove the executive; and the Viceroy retained the right to issue emergency laws without reference to the chambers. Eight provincial groupings – Assam, Bengal, Bihar, Bombay, the Central Provinces, Punjab, the United Provinces and Madras – were governed by a system of 'dyarchy': 'reserved subjects' were administered by the Governor and his appointed Executive Council on the advice of ministers chosen from a partially elective legislature, which had direct responsibility for 'transferred subjects'. The complexities of this system were criticized in the *Simon Report of 1930 and at the *Round Table Conferences; it was superseded by the India Act of 1935 (see *below*), but the principle of dyarchy was retained.

India Act (1935): was largely a consequence of the *Round Table Conferences of 1931/2 and a subsequent white paper of 1933 on Indian government. The Act proposed a federal all-India structure, including the *princely states, but with an administration based upon dyarchy in which the Viceroy and his council retained 'reserved' topics; those included defence, foreign affairs, and any issue endangering financial stability or threatening civil peace. At the same time the Act extended the authority of regional legislatures, to which provincial ministers were to be responsible. This provision was put into operation within two years, but it still gave the provinces no more than limited democratic rights: the electoral system allowed 43 per cent of the people (about 7 per cent of them women) to vote. Discord between the various communities of the subcontinent prevented agreement on a federal structure before the spread of World War II led to calls for greater independence.

Indian Army. The defensive structure devised by the *East India Company was based upon the three administrative Presidencies of Bengal, Madras and Bombay, each of which was accorded an army; the earliest Indian regiment – the 1st Bengal Native Infantry – was raised soon after the battle of Plassey (1757). The Bengal Army was always the largest of the three, with 74 regiments at the time of the *Indian Mutiny. Although control passed to the British Crown in 1858 and Lord *Roberts as Commander-in-Chief of the Bengal Army in 1885 exercised supervisory power over the other two, it was not until 1895 that the three forces were officially amalgamated into a single Indian Army, given unity and cohesion by *Kitchener as C.-in-C. from 1903 to 1909. Most active service was against the Pathans; training envisaged protection of the

*North-West Frontier from a Russian assault (which never materialized). Some duties were ceremonial, and military service carried high social prestige, especially in northern India. For more than sixty years the Indian Army remained the largest ever raised entirely by voluntary enlistment. A high proportion of officers were British, Sandhurst cadets up to the eve of World War I favouring a posting where possible to the Indian Army; the most famous, both eventually Field Marshals, were Sir Claude Auchinleck (1884–1981) and Viscount Slim (1891–1970). Prior to 1919, even the most experienced Indian NCOs could not expect to receive commissions higher than the special rank of Jemadar; thereafter, ten places a year were reserved for them at Sandhurst. The larger *princely states maintained armies of their own, although in peacetime special training was given to selected units, to enable them to join brigades of the Indian Army on the battle fronts of a major war. The Indian Army was in action at Ypres as early as 21 October 1914, and on the Western Front won particular respect at Cambrai in late November and December 1917. Indian troops fought in Mesopotamia (*Iraq) from November 1914 until October 1918, and took part in the *Gallipoli landings, the 1916 campaign in East Africa, and *Allenby's final offensive in Palestine. During the inter-war period the Indian Army fought in the last Afghan War and again against the Pathans in Waziristan on several occasions, notably 1920 and 1936/7. They also defended foreign compounds and legations in Shanghai and in Addis Ababa in 1936. Although an Indian Military Academy was set up at Dehra Dun in 1931, the intake of junior commissioned Indian officers was still under sixty a year on the eve of World War II, and there were fewer than a thousand in the army as a whole. During World War II the Indian Army never fought in western Europe, but in 1940/1 saw action in East Africa, Libya, Syria and Iraq. The 4th and 8th Indian Divisions joined the long advance up Italy, 1943–45, but the main war effort was against the Japanese in Burma and the defence of Assam. By 1945 there were nearly 16,000 Indian officers, up to the rank of brigadier. The old Indian Army ceased to exist on 13 August 1947. Regiments were split up: about one-third of the personnel and equipment went to Pakistan, the remaining two-thirds to independent India.

Indian Civil Service (ICS): was, from 1861 to 1947, responsible for the general executive administration of British India: public works ventures; policing and justice; financial matters; agricultural and forestry development; state railways and roads; and, with great distinction, the Indian Medical Service. The highest posts in the government secretariat were recruited from the ICS, as were nominees for the legislative councils. When, early in the twentieth century, the *Indian Political Service (IPS) was formed, a third of its members came from the civil service. The ICS originated in the covenanted civil service of the *East India Company, an administrative body specifically mentioned in the Regulating Act of 1771 which sought to modernize the EIC. *Wellesley introduced training for the civil service in India by establishing a college at Calcutta in 1800, while in England the Company developed *Haileybury. Parliament, however, remained uneasy over the quality of administration, and in 1853 it was decided to open the covenanted civil service to Europeans, Indians or Eurasians who passed an examination set by the Board of Control. On this basis the Indian Civil Service was formally established in 1861, with appointments made by the Secretary of State for India, on advice from the Civil Service Commissioners. In 1860 there were 154 candidates for 80 places. Ten years later 39 out of 318 British candidates and 1 out of 7 Indians were successful; 3 Bengalis had been admitted in 1869, one of whom was the future Sir Surendranath Banerjea (1848–1925), a founder of the *Indian National Congress. The incentives of promotion and relative security within the ICS encouraged the spread of education among the more prosperous members of the Indian community, although failure to gain admittance tended to leave lasting resentment. From 1879 onwards 69 statutory civil servants could be appointed by local provincial governments, and from 1893 simultaneous examinations were instituted in London and India. By 1946/7 there were only slightly more than 500 British members of the ICS, with education, medicine, forestry and most technical engineering projects administered by Indians. Many British believed the ICS was one of the finest, most incorruptible, missionizing institutions the world had ever known. Eminent Indians, on the other hand, complained that it introduced a new caste system which was exclusive, arrogant, alien, divisive and systematically hostile to reforms for local social or economic advancement. After Independence, parliamentary legislation removed any surviving privileges claimed by Indian members of the ICS.

Indian Independence Act: the name generally given to 'The Government of India Act', a measure only finally agreed by *Attlee, *Mountbatten, *Nehru and *Jinnah on 3 June 1947, then drafted with such extraordinary speed that the Bill had a first reading in the House of Commons on 3 July, a second reading on 10 July, received the Royal Assent on 18 July, and became effective on 15 August 1947. It confirmed the *Partition of the subcontinent and the dominion status of both India and Pakistan.

Indian Mutiny (1857): was often represented by the British as a sepoy revolt which sought to perpetuate traditional habits on behalf of reactionary potentates long discredited. Indian interpretations, on the other hand, see the Mutiny as the first round in a struggle for independence. The outbreak began on 10 May at *Meerut, from where mutineers in three Bengali regiments marched on Delhi and proclaimed King

*Bahadur Shah as emperor. The mutineers were incensed by the cumulative effect on ancient institutions of *Dalhousie's reforms, by apparent attempts at forcible conversion to Christianity, and by the slowness of the authorities in dealing with specific grievances, such as the issue of cartridges greased with cow fat (sacred to Hindus) or pig fat (offensive to Muslims). From Delhi the insurrection spread during the early summer to the areas of main recruitment for the Bengal Army, to Oudh and to central India. No fewer than 56 of the 74 battalions of the Bengal Army mutinied. British troops and civilians were cut off in Lucknow and Cawnpore, although both towns were recovered by the combined efforts of *Havelock and *Outram in the autumn. Late in June British troops took the ridge facing Delhi, but could not fight their way into the city until September. During the winter months Sir Colin Campbell (1792–1863) stamped out rebellion in Bengal, while in the following spring Sir Hugh Rose (1801–85) took Rathgarh, Sagar, the Matlun Pass, Konch and Gwalior to pacify central India. Peace was proclaimed on 8 July 1858, and the whole government was re-ordered a month later by the *India Act (1858). Atrocities committed by both sides during the Mutiny left legacies of suspicion and mistrust.

Indian National Army: in World War II, an army of defectors and prisoners, recruited by the Japanese in 1942–44, and estimated to have numbered over 20,000 men. Their nominal leader was the renegade Congress spokesman Subhas Chandra Bose (1895–1945). Although they included a group of fanatics who committed atrocities, most members were lukewarm opportunists, many of whom deserted and returned to their old affiliations. Treatment of ex-INA members was lenient.

Indian National Congress ('Congress Party'). The Congress was founded in December 1885, partly to encourage the spread of education, including ways of attaining the standards demanded for entry to the *Indian Civil Service. Among Congress founders were two retired members of the ICS, Sir Surendranath Banerjee and the ornithologist Allan Octavian Hume (1829–1912), son of the radical MP Joseph Hume. Political objectives were stressed in Congress from 1905 onwards. The violent defiance urged by *Tilak was toned down by Mohandas *Gandhi who, from 1915, taught Congress the concepts of moderate civil disobedience characteristic of the movement's ideals. With the spread of representative government after the *India Act (1935), Congress did well in the 1937 elections and took office in six provinces. But Congress refused to support India's involvement in World War II, largely in protest at the viceregal government's failure to consult national spokesmen over participation. Several leaders, including *Nehru, were interned between 1942 and 1945, but were released to discuss the problem of *Partition and the preparations for Independence. Under Nehru and his successor

Indian Political Service (IPS)

*Shastri, Congress was the ruling party in the *Indian Republic, embracing nationalist opinions of Left and Right so comprehensively that it was virtually unchallenged until 1967, when allegations were made against the anti-democratic approach of Nehru's daughter, Mrs Indira *Gandhi. Electoral defeat in 1977 gave Congress an opportunity to reorganize and acquire closer party adhesion. Apart from March 1977 to January 1980 and November 1989 to June 1991, the republic has been governed by Congress administrations.

Indian Political Service (IPS): formed at the start of the twentieth century during the viceroyalty of Lord *Curzon. An External Affairs Department administered the *North-West Frontier province and handled relations with Afghanistan, Tibet, Nepal and the Gulf rulers. A Political Department maintained contacts between the Viceroy and the *princely rulers. A third of the IPS was recruited from top members of the Indian Civil Service; two-thirds were senior army officers.

Indian Republic: population of some 846.5 million, more than any other country except China. The short-lived Dominion of *India became an independent Commonwealth Republic on 26 January 1950. Over the following 45 years the *Indian National Congress held power except for 54 months (1977–1980, 1989–91); the chief political leaders have been *Nehru, Lal *Shastri, Mrs Indira *Gandhi, and her son Rajiv *Gandhi. In 1956 the States Reorganization Act swept away such historic provinces as Madras, Mysore and Hindustan in favour of 25 states and 7 union territories, with boundaries following ethnic and linguistic lines as far as possible. A constitutional amendment in 1970 deprived the *princely rulers of their privileges; the princely order was finally abolished in December 1971. Territory was extended on three occasions: in 1954 by union with the former French colony of Pondicherry; in December 1961 by annexation of the Portuguese colony of Goa, which became an Indian state in May 1987; and in 1975 when the Himalayan kingdom of Sikkim, an Indian Protectorate since 1950, became a state within the Republic and King Palden Thondup Namgyal was deposed. Clashes with *Pakistan over *Kashmir between 1947 and 1949 led to full-scale fighting in 1965–66 and again in 1971, when India gave support to the *Bangladesh independence movement. There was also a border clash with China in October–November 1962. Intermittent fighting with Naga Hills tribesmen on the borders of Burma dragged on from 1963 to 1975, and with the peoples of the Mizo Hills in Assam from 1972 to 1985. But the most serious disputes have been with the *Sikhs, especially around *Amritsar. Despite the strain of these commitments, centralized planning allowed agricultural production to keep slightly ahead of the needs of the increasing population, even though there remained a threat of famine, and problems in transporting and distributing food in overcrowded cities (urban population: above 160 million). 'Flexible' Five-Year Plans between 1951 and 1966 boosted agriculture, *irrigation projects and coal and steel output, but the pace slackened in the 1970s, and by 1991 the need for World Bank backing to develop heavy industries prompted free market reforms. In 1993 the rupee was floated and state subsidies to farmers were cut, leaving the future of a mixed economy in doubt.

'Indian' Peoples of Canada. By a confused misconception, pioneer settlers in North America called the Native Americans 'Red Indians'. Official Canadian usage preserves the noun: a federal Department of Indian Affairs was set up in 1880, and 'Minister for Indian Affairs and Northern Development' has long been a recognized cabinet post. Probably as many as 200,000 Indians were scattered across Canada in the seventeenth century; migration was common, and in the nineteenth century Sioux from Montana found refuge in Canada when resisting the advance of American settlers in the late 1860s and the 1870s. From about 1750 increasing contact with fur traders and settlers brought new diseases – especially smallpox, measles and tuberculosis – as well as the scourge of alcoholism; Indian numbers (excluding *métis) had dropped to about 110,000 by 1931, but with improved medicine and living standards rose steadily over the following sixty years, to some quarter of a million. Among the most influential Indian ethnic groups are the *Assiniboine Siouan-speakers, the *Athabascan speakers including the *Chipewyans, the *Blackfoots, the *Crees and the *Iroquoians. In 1763 a royal proclamation reserved all lands west of a line along the heads of rivers running down to the Atlantic for the Indian peoples; the hunting grounds of resident tribes were to be left undisturbed. Penetration of the prairies vitiated these provisions, but as the line of settlement advanced across southern Ontario formal agreements of purchase were made with Indian chiefs whenever possible. A federal Indian Act in 1876 legislated for policies of paternal protection by safeguarding Indian communities in their reservations, though normal civil liberties were not provided for. Many restrictive provisions were removed by the federal Indian Act of 1951 which extended to the Indian peoples full welfare, education and benefit schemes, and established Indian councils with similar authority and functions to municipal councils.

Inuit: the correct name for those Canadians generally called *Eskimos.

Ionian Islands: lie, for the most part, some 20 miles off the north-west coast of modern Greece. Corfu is the chief island; others include Levkas, Cephalonia, Ithaca, Zacynthus (Zante) and Cythera (Cerigo). Until 1797 the islands were Venetian. They were then occupied by the French for two years, enjoyed shaky independence as the Septinsular Republic (1800–07), but then returned to nominal French allegiance. The British occupied most of the islands in October 1809, but not Corfu until the Napoleonic empire collapsed in April 1814. Fear that the Russians would occupy the islands, and a desire to protect their Christian inhabitants from passing under Ottoman rule, prompted the British to seek a Protectorate. The 'United States of the Ionian Islands', formally constituted on 5 November 1815, enjoyed considerable autonomy, protected by the Royal Navy and administered by British Lord High Commissioners. The Protectorate was voluntarily relinquished in April 1864 when the islands were united to the Greek kingdom. The chief legacies of British rule are the fortifications of Corfu, two homes for the High Commissioner (a three-storeyed palace of Malta stone and the summer villa of Mon Repos), and a traditional form of cricket.

Iraq: an ancient word revived at the end of World War I for lands nominally part of the Ottoman Empire since 1534, though often showing great independence from the ruling Sultan. Iraq included Mesopotamia, the region between the rivers Tigris and Euphrates, and parts of other Ottoman provinces to the north and the south. Even before World War I, British interests in the region were considerable: a succession of treaties between the Viceroy in India and sheikdoms in the Gulf culminated in a Protectorate over *Kuwait in 1899; the Euphrates and Tigris Steam Navigation Company, which had monopoly river trading rights at Baghdad and Basra, was registered in London, as was, in 1911–12, the Turkish Petroleum Company, formed to develop *oil resources in the Ottoman provinces of Mosul and Baghdad. When Turkey became Germany's ally in November 1914, military operations in Mesopotamia were entrusted to GHQ at *Simla: General Townshend's army was repulsed from the approaches to Baghdad in November 1915 and forced to surrender at Kut-al-Amara on 29 April 1916. A successful offensive, militarily directed from Cairo rather than Simla, recovered Kut on 25 February 1917 and took Baghdad a fortnight later. When Turkey sued for peace the British had advanced to Mosul and seized the oil wells (3 November 1918). Military occupation enabled the British to decide Iraq's future at the Peace Conference. The country became a British *mandate with Emir Feisal (1885–1933) proclaimed King on 23 August 1921 after a plebiscite which gave him overwhelming support. The RAF helped Feisal put down Kurdish revolts, and an Anglo–Iraqi military alliance was concluded in December 1927, allowing the British the use of airfields even after the mandate ended and Iraq achieved full independence in October 1932. British forces again occupied the country from May 1941 until October 1947 and retained the Habbaniya air base until a radical revolution in July 1958 aligned a new and republican Iraq with Egypt.

Irish Free State. A treaty signed in London on 6 December 1921 accepted *partition of Ireland. It accorded dominion status within the

Empire to an 'Irish Free State' which excluded six of the nine counties of Ulster, whose largely Protestant peoples chose to remain part of the United Kingdom while enjoying some autonomy as Northern Ireland. The Treaty allowed the Royal Navy use of bases at Berehaven, Cobh and Lough Swilly and provided for discussions between Dublin and Belfast over the line of the border. The Irish Free State was officially established on 6 December 1922, although the final line of the border was only agreed in December 1925. Mounting dislike of the British connection led to a change of nomenclature in December 1937, when the Irish Free State became *Eire. The Admiralty handed over the three naval bases to the Irish Navy in 1938. Eire remained neutral in World War II and left the Commonwealth in April 1949.

Iroquoians: a five-nation confederacy of North American *Indians – Mohawk, Oneida, Onondaga, Cayuga, Seneca – all of whom spoke a similar Iroquoian language and had traditional hunting grounds covering much of New York State and Vermont and into modern Canada up to Lake Ontario and the St Lawrence. Although fierce warriors in defence of their rights, they were basically a sedentary people who had become skilled in agriculture and developed their own social relationships before the coming of European settlers.

Irrigation. Modern techniques for providing water for the growth and conservation of trees and crops in soils denied their natural supply of moisture were first developed in North America. The Canadian brothers George Chaffey (1838–1942) and William Chaffey (1856–1926), who had experience of finding water for the wine-growing regions of California, were encouraged by Alfred *Deakin to come to Australia in 1886 and establish an irrigation area fed by artificial canals from the Murray River at Renmark in South Australia and Mildura in Victoria. The project ran into difficulties and had to be financially rescued by inter-state funds. The realization, in the 1880s, that about a third of the Australian continent covered artesian deposits led to the growth of alter-native means of extracting water. However, further irrigation channels were developed this century along the Murray River in New South Wales and also in Queensland, while Sir William *Hudson, the Commissioner of the Snowy Mountains Hydro-electric Authority, ensured that the great project irrigated areas along both the Murray and the Murrumbidgee. Between 1960 and 1972 a major irrigation scheme was undertaken on the Ord River in the north of Western Australia, but without the success that was hoped. During the first years of the twentieth century the Krian works at Perak facilitated settlement in northern Malaya by irrigating more than 70,000 acres through a main canal 21 miles long and a total of 200 miles of subsidiary channels. In Canada the federal government encouraged irrigation in Alberta from 1901 onwards. The abnormal droughts from 1917 to 1920 and again from 1929 to 1938 led the government to extend its activities to 'prairie farm rehabilitation': some 20 major projects and more than 4,000 smaller ones brought water storage to Saskatachewan and parts of British Columbia as well as Alberta. Even greater projects sought to combat the threat of *famine in India: the Lloyd Barrage across the Indus at Sukkur, Sind (now Pakistan) was built between 1923 and 1932, sending water down seven canals to irrigate an area twice the size of Wales. With the setting up in 1960 of the World Bank's Indus Basin Development Fund it was possible to complete other barrages on the Indus and the Mangla Dam on the Jhelum River in the Punjab (on which work started in 1967), to irrigate both India and Pakistan. The Tungabhadra Dams and reservoirs and lakes around Mettur bring water to India's Karnataka province. Irrigation schemes are not suitable for the drought areas of Commonwealth Africa, as the character of the soil leads to rapid salinization even when and where rainfall gives a basic supply of water.

Isandhlwana: an outcrop of rock, about 200 feet high, where on 22 January 1879 some 20,000 *Zulus under *Cetewayo wiped out a British column of Lord Chelmsford's invading army, killing nearly 800 white 'redcoats' and a slightly larger number of native soldiers. A simultaneous attack at *Rorke's Drift, 12 miles away, was beaten off. The defeat was caused by over-confidence, casual siting of defensive positions, and an underestimate of the Zulus' strength and fighting qualities. The battle was regarded in London as the most humiliating defeat for British arms within living memory.

Islam in the Commonwealth. Islam – 'the inner peace which comes from submission to the will of Allah' – spread through Arabia in the last ten years of the life of Mohammed (c.570–632) and was carried so rapidly eastwards and westwards that by AD 712 Muslim armies had entered Sind, now in Pakistan, and taken Toledo in Spain. While the Sunni majority of Muslims has always accepted the legitimate succession of Mohammed's first four caliphs, an influential Shia minority only acknowledges the authority of Mohammed's son-in-law Ali and his descendants. This sectarian division, the emergence of rival caliphates (Baghdad, Cairo, Cordoba) and a shift of political power through Syria to Iraq broke the early unity of Islam. Though receding in Europe by 800, Islam survived as the main culture of Asia west of China. Between c.1000–1350 conquerors, proselytizers and traders carried Islam into India. Trans-Saharan trade extended the influence of the early Muslim communities in north Africa as far westwards as Nigeria, and there were isolated Muslim trading colonies as far south as the mouth of the Zambezi. The spread of the British Empire brought frequent wars with Islamic dynasties in India, with Shia tribesmen along the *North-West

Frontier, and against local fanatical prophets, such as the *Mahdi or the so-called *Mad Mullah of Somaliland. There were also clashes in *Egypt and in *Palestine, under the mandate. But Muslim recruits were welcomed by the British in India, Muslim *princely rulers like the *Aga Khan often emerged as wise imperial statesmen, and Muslim traders carried their occupations and their faith further into British East Africa and brought Islam to the Caribbean and the United Kingdom. Four of the six most populous Muslim countries in the world are members of the Commonwealth: Bangladesh (an estimated 90 million); Pakistan (over 88 million); Nigeria (81 million, 47 per cent of the population); and India (over 75 million, 11.5 per cent of the population). Malaysia, with about 11 million Muslims, is predominantly an Islamic federation. The Tamils of Sri Lanka and the people of the Maldives are Muslim. So too are about 40 per cent of the population of Sierra Leone, mainly in the centre and the north. The 9 million Muslims of Tanzania are unevenly distributed, few inland but two-thirds of the people along the mainland coast and overwhelmingly in *Zanzibar. Muslims form over 16 per cent of the population in Mauritius and about 6 per cent in Kenya, Uganda and Ghana. Immigration and conversion has increased the extent of the Islamic faith in the United Kingdom: at the end of World War II there were 3 mosques; fifty years later, more than 350 mosques serve a million Muslims. Most Commonwealth Muslims are Sunnis; but there are Shias in Baluchistan, Sind, the Punjab, and the Indian provinces of Uttar Pradesh, Bihar and Kerala.

Jacob, John (1812–58), British soldier: a member of a Guernsey family, who spent almost all his life in India. After commanding the artillery in a campaign in Kutchee between 1834 and 1840, he was entrusted by *Outram with the political administration of eastern Kutchee, subsequently leading the Sind Irregular Horse. For nine years he superintended the pacification of Sind, to such effect that in 1851 *Dalhousie ordered a town to be named after him: Jacobabad survives, in modern Pakistan. Briefly General Jacob served again under Outram in Persia and raised and armed 'Jacob's Horse', which remained a cavalry force in the Indian Army until 1947, winning special distinction against the Turks and Germans in the last Palestine campaign of 1918. General Jacob died suddenly at the town named after him; his life and legacy make him an archetypal military servant of the Raj.

Jagan, Cheddi (1918–   ), President of Guyana: born at Port Mourant, into a family of East Indian descent; educated at Howard University, Washington DC and at Northwestern University, Chicago, where he gained a doctorate in dental surgery. From 1947 to 1953 Dr Jagan was a member of the legislative council of British Guiana, building up a powerful political position as leader of the People's Progressive Party, predominantly East Indian and politically on the far Left. The PPP secured an electoral majority in May 1953 but the British government declared the elections invalid, imposed martial law, and in 1954 jailed Jagan for violating orders restricting him to the vicinity of Georgetown. Imprisonment made Dr Jagan a hero with his East Indian followers, and he gained a larger majority at the elections of August 1957 despite frequent violent clashes with the West Indian supporters of the People's National Congress of his rival, Forbes *Burnham. When British Guiana was given self-government in 1961 Dr Jagan was the first Prime Minister, holding office until 1964. But Burnham built up the independence movement and the transition to a co-operative republic, while Jagan was kept out of office until mounting discontent forced a revision of electoral procedure. The PPP gained a majority in the elections of 1992: Dr Jagan became President on 9 October.

Jamaica: the largest British West Indian island; capital, Kingston. It was discovered by Columbus in 1494 and held by Spain from 1509 to 1655, when it was captured by the Cromwellian navy and confirmed as a British possession by the Treaty of Madrid (1670). Sir Thomas Modyford (*c.* 1620–79), an entrepreneur not unsympathetic to buccaneers and pirates, was sent from Barbados by Charles II in 1661 as Jamaica's first governor, bringing with him a thousand Barbadian settlers. On the lowlands they established *sugar plantations dependent on slavery: there were 57 plantations as early as 1670, and more than a thousand by 1780. Coffee and rum were valuable exports between *c.*1783 and 1838: some 14 per cent of slaves worked coffee plantations. Resentment at slow progress towards *slave emancipation led to the *Baptist War revolt of 1831, but when emancipation came in 1833 it brought economic chaos and a catastrophic slump in sugar production. The Jamaican Planters Bank failed in 1847, at the height of a gradual transition from huge plantations to smallholdings, owned or rented by freed slaves or Indian immigrants. Laws blatantly favouring planters, the exploitation of the ex-slave peasantry, and the effects of a long drought left the island disaffected, prompting the *Morant Bay rising of October 1865 and its brutal aftermath. Crown Colony government was imposed a year later, and it was not until 1884 that the islanders were again allowed a partially elected legislative council. Remarkably, women were enfranchised as early as 1919. The *great depression of the early 1930s saw the emergence of a strong trade union movement, led by Alexander *Bustamente, and demands for self-government. Reform of the constitution in November 1944 increased democratic representation in the colonial assembly. Norman *Manley, champion of the *banana trade, became chief minister in 1955, and strongly supported proposals for a *British West Indies Federation, to which Jamaica acceded in 1958. Suspicion that Jamaican funds were being used to support the poorer islands made the Federation unpopular on the island;

a referendum in 1961 went against continued membership, and Jamaica seceded. The island became independent within the Commonwealth on 6 August 1962. Hurricanes in 1944 and 1951 devastated agricultural land, and in the last thirty years the island's industrial exports of bauxite and, in its processed form, alumina have matched sugar and banana production.

James, Cyril Lionel Robert (1901–89), Trinidadian author and political thinker: born at Tunapuna, near Port-of-Spain. As a scholar at Queen's Royal College he became closely involved in radical Marxist politics, although he was too independently-minded ever to become an orthodox card-bearing Communist. He lived for many years in Lancashire, encouraged to settle there by his friend *Constantine, the great all-round cricketer. James wrote for the *Manchester Guardian*; completed a novel, *Minty Alley* (1936), on the problems raised by education in a Caribbean working-class family; and in 1938 published an impressive study of Toussaint l'Ouverture and the 'black Jacobins'. James lectured in the USA until he was thrown out during the McCarthyite anti-intellectual witch-hunt of the early 1950s. In his native Trinidad James became a strong advocate of a *British West Indian Federation, though he was for a time kept under house arrest. His deep love of cricket permeates *Beyond the Boundary* (1963), arguably the finest book written on the sport. James himself, however, insisted that a delight in cricket must never deaden the perception of great issues of social significance. He died as an expatriate settled in Brixton, south London.

Jameson Raid: the principal action in a conspiracy to overthrow the Boer government of *Kruger in the *Transvaal and establish an administration favourable to the non-Boer European workers ('Uitlanders'). Leander Starr Jameson (1853–1917), a high executive in the British South Africa Company and a close associate of Cecil *Rhodes, led a force of 430 mounted men from Bechuanaland across the border of the Transvaal on 29 December 1894, intending to march 180 miles to Johannesburg to support a rising by the Uitlanders. The Jameson raiders were surrounded and taken prisoner by the Boers four days after entering the Transvaal, and there was no uprising in Johannesburg. Rhodes's participation in the conspiracy forced him to resign as the chief minister of Cape Colony. In London a parliamentary inquiry cleared the Colonial Secretary, Joseph *Chamberlain, of complicity; later evidence suggests he knew of plans for the Uitlander revolt, if not of Jameson's projected raid. German support for the Boers in the *Kruger Telegram increased the tendency of the British public to make Jameson a popular hero. He served a brief prison sentence in England before returning to South Africa, where he was Prime Minister of Cape Colony from 1904 to 1908. In the 1911 Coronation Honours List he was created a baronet.

Jardine, Matheson: the best-known trading house in pre-Communist China; long respected as the 'princely *Hong'. The company was established in 1832 by William Jardine and James Matheson to operate the *opium trade from Canton (Guangzhou). It followed the Royal Navy to *Hong Kong in 1841, building the first granite warehouse on the island and making the new colony the centre of its activities throughout the Far East. By 1849 the five British resident partners employed 20 European assistants. The company expanded into all the Chinese *treaty ports, and from the early 1860s had offices in Japan. By 1888 the principal director, William Keswick (1835–1912), was also a director of the Hong Kong and Shanghai Bank, and his company controlled the colony's civilian dockyard and principal industrial enterprise, a sugar refinery; it also maintained (until 1922) the colony's main fire brigade. Jardine's faced competition from other Hongs (notably Swire's) but profited from Germany's and Russia's lost markets after World War I. After China's Communist revolution Sir John Keswick (1906–82), chairman 1952–56 and grandson of William Keswick, found new ways of maintaining British commercial relations in the traditional market and presided over the Sino-British Trade Council, 1963–73. Nevertheless, by the early 1980s there was intense trade rivalry with China Resources Holdings Ltd, the state-owned institution which handles Communist China's overseas investments. Although Jardine's activities in Hong Kong, Australia and Malaysia remain considerable, in 1984 the headquarters moved from Hong Kong itself to Bermuda.

Jewish Communities in the Commonwealth. In 1995 there were at least 300,000 members of the Jewish faith in Great Britain, about the same number in Canada, some 120,000 in South Africa, more than 90,000 in Australia, and sizeable congregations in New Zealand, India, Zimbabwe and Kenya. The longest-surviving continuous Jewish settlement in the Commonwealth is in Bombay, and antedates the Christian era. Many other communities have their origins in flight from persecution (although there were Jews in the *First Fleet to Australia, and as early as 1838 Joel Samuel Pollack recorded in two volumes his experiences as a Jewish pioneer in New Zealand). The earliest Jewish refugee settlers in the colonial empire were victims of the Portuguese Inquisition who fled to Barbados and Jamaica in 1654 from Brazil and, about the same time, from Goa and other Portuguese settlements in India to Madras. Tsarist persecution in Russia itself and in Poland during the 1880s and 1890s led to major emigration to Canada (especially *Saskatchewan) and to small settlements in Cyprus, which were augmented by refugees from Romania. In 1839 the British first showed sympathy with Jewish aspirations for a National Home in Syria, and in July 1902 Joseph *Chamberlain tentatively suggested to the Zionist leader, Theodor Herzl, that a Jewish autonomous settlement might be founded at El Arish in

Sinai, a proposal strongly opposed in Cairo by Lord *Cromer, who thought its survival possible only if water were diverted from the Nile. Soon afterwards Chamberlain offered the Zionist movement 5,000 square miles of fertile highlands in East Africa. Three Jewish commissioners visited present-day Kenya, but on the Uashin Gishu plateau they met a Masai column in full war-paint, and *Delamere and the settlers seemed scarcely less hostile. The offer was considered by the Zionist Congress of August 1905 and politely declined on the grounds that Uganda (*sic*) was unsuitable for refugees from Russia. Although firm backing for Jewish aspirations for a National Home was given by the *Balfour Declaration of 1917, the pledge proved incapable of realization in mandated *Palestine. The flight of Jewish refugees from Hitler's Germany was so great that quota restrictions on immigration were imposed before 1939, even by such sympathetic Commonwealth members as Canada (which accepted 8,000 refugees) and Australia (9,000). South Africa admitted some 8,000 refugees in the first two years of the Nazi era, but hardly any after 1935, when *Hertzog began showing increased sympathy towards Hitler. In the United Kingdom, although London's first 'great synagogue' was opened in 1722, the Jewish Disabilities Act which enabled members of the Jewish faith to sit in Parliament became law only in 1858; British Jews could not enter the older universities until the removal of religious tests in 1871; and there was no Jewish member of a cabinet until 1909. Elsewhere in the old Empire, Jewish believers fared better: there was a Jewish synagogue in Montreal in 1777 and disabilities preventing Jews sitting in the Lower Canada legislature were removed in June 1832. In Australia Jewish charitable societies flourished early in Sydney (1832), Melbourne (1839) and Adelaide (1852), though not in Perth until 1897, nor Brisbane until 1908. Two Australian Governors-General were Jewish, as also was the great World War I army commander, Sir John *Monash.

Jinnah, Mohammad Ali (1876–1948), founder of Pakistan: born in Karachi; practised as a barrister and in 1910 became a member of the Viceroy's Legislative Council. He joined the *Muslim League in 1913 and for more than fifteen years sought to co-operate with the Hindu leaders, particularly *Gandhi. But Jinnah believed Gandhi was working for narrowly Hindu objectives at the Round Table Conferences of 1931, and in 1934 he began to transform the Muslim League from a largely Islamic cultural movement into a political force. At a Muslim Congress in Lahore during March 1940 Jinnah pledged support for the British war effort, at the same time calling for the eventual establishment of a separate Pakistan in an independent and partitioned India. His compatriots and co-religionists respected him as *Qaid-i-Azam*, the 'great leader', although some of the League's politicians questioned the wisdom of *Partition. Electoral successes in 1945/6 throughout predominantly Islamic regions in India made Jinnah advocate 'direct action' to prevent disputed areas falling under Hindu control. This policy precipitated the *Calcutta Riots in which more than 4,000 people were killed and some 16,000 seriously injured. The British authorities, previously not unsympathetic towards Jinnah, turned against him; both *Attlee and *Mountbatten felt greater confidence in Gandhi and *Nehru. The Pakistan created in 1947 was consequently smaller than Jinnah had anticipated: 'maimed and moth-eaten', he complained, when he took office as the new Dominion's first Governor-General. His health was by then too poor to enable him to handle the delicate questions of internal migration raised by Partition or the *Kashmir dispute, and he died after only thirteen months in office.

Johnson, Amy (1903–41), British pioneer aviator: born at Kingston-upon-Hull; educated locally and at Sheffield University; learned to fly while working at a solicitor's office in London. She qualified as a pilot and in 1929 became the first woman ground engineer. In May 1930 she set out from Croydon in her de Havilland Gipsy Moth and flew solo through sandstorms and monsoons to Darwin and eventually to Brisbane. She made the flight from England to Australia in 20 days and became the heroine idol of the Empire – 'Amy, wonderful Amy', as a popular song declared; she was made CBE at the age of 27. Her 'British courage and endurance' were taxed again by a solo flight from London to Tokyo across Siberia (1931), and by another sensational Empire solo, from London to Capetown in 1932. Marriage, ultimately unsuccessful, to the airman Jim Mollison (1905–59) enabled her to make joint flights to Karachi (1934) and to the Cape and back (1936), but the couple were fortunate to survive three crashes. She joined the Air Transport Auxiliary and was killed in the Thames Estuary on 5 January 1941 when the plane she was ferrying was apparently shot down, more than a hundred miles off course.

Johnston, Sir Harry Hamilton (1858–1927), African explorer and colonial administrator: born in Kennington, South London. He showed precocious linguistic skills as a boy at Stockwell Grammar School, went out to Africa in search of adventure, and was invited by the Earl of Mayo to join an expedition into Angola. Alone he then penetrated the Congo Basin, winning support from *Stanley and the backing of the Royal Society for a scientific expedition to the Kilimanjaro region in 1884. His proposals for setting up a colony in that area were rejected by the *Colonial Office, but he was appointed vice-consul for the Cameroon and the Niger delta in 1885. His somewhat high-handed treatment of local chiefs brought him to the attention of Lord *Salisbury, who thought him a young man of vision; when Johnston was home on leave in 1888, Salisbury discussed with him the spread of British interests across Africa. Johnston worked closely with *Rhodes over *Nyasaland and served as Commissioner for south central Africa from 1891 to 1896, receiving a knighthood. After two years as Consul-General in Tunis he returned to *Uganda in 1899, where he built up the administrative service. Johnston was disliked and mistrusted by other would-be empire builders in East Africa. After Salisbury's retirement he left government service, giving his backing to the Congo Reform Association and writing several semi-autobiographical novels and ethnological and zoological works.

Jubaland: disputed East African region, adjoining Kenya's former *Northern Frontier District (NFD).

Judicial Committee of the Privy Council: survives as a final Court of Appeal, from the years before the introduction of Cabinet government when executive power was held by the sovereign, in council with his or her chosen advisers. The Judicial Committee hears appeals from the Channel Islands, the Isle of Man, professional disciplinary committees in the United Kingdom, but especially from the courts of British dependencies and from such Commonwealth countries as choose to retain the right of appeal to Westminster after gaining independence. In January 1995 there were 17 of these Commonwealth members: Antigua; Bahamas; Barbados; Belize; Brunei; Dominica; Gambia; Jamaica; Kiribati; Mauritius; New Zealand; Singapore; St Christopher and Nevis; St Lucia; St Vincent; Trinidad and Tobago; Tuvalu. The Judicial Committee is under the presidency of the Lord Chancellor and includes judges from the Commonwealth as well as members of the Privy Council with experience of high judicial office. Appeals from Commonwealth countries are usually heard by a board of five judges.

Kalgoorlie, mining town in Western Australia, 340 miles north-east of Perth. The town sprang up on the site of the aboriginal settlement of Kalgurli when in 1893 a 'golden mile' was discovered during the *gold rush. Despite acute shortage of water in the early years, Kalgoorlie had 35,000 inhabitants by 1898 and, with outlying districts, some 200,000 by 1905/6. The working of alluvial deposits soon had to give way to deep mining, but Kalgoorlie was still attracting immigrants during the *Great Depression. Friction developed between native-born Australians and newcomers from southern Europe (mainly Serbs and Montenegrins) who, from failing to understand safety precautions, were blamed for several accidents; they were also alleged to have offered bribes to secure good jobs beyond their skills. Xenophobic resentment reached a climax in the midsummer heat of late January 1934, when drunken brawls developed into riot and arson in both Kalgoorlie and neighbouring Boulder. There were two deaths and the destruction of some 70 buildings before extra police, drafted in from Perth, restored order.

Kamba (Wakamba): an historic East African people, one of the first tribes met by pastor Johann Krapf of the Church Missionary Society on the journey during which he sighted Mount Kenya for the first time, in November 1848. The Kamba had land around Machakos, where in 1889 the earliest *Imperial British East Africa Company station was set up. Famous for their tribal dancing and their wiliness of mind, they were less warlike than their old enemies, the *Masai. Their principal reserves lay to the north-east of Nairobi: there are an estimated 2 million Wakambas in modern Kenya.

Kashmir: a disputed mountainous region in northern India. It became part of the Moghul Empire in 1526, then was seized in 1756 by Afghans who in 1819 lost it to the *Sikhs of the Punjab. When in 1846 the British defeated the Sikhs, they gave Kashmir to the neighbouring Rajput ruler of Jammu, whose descendants remained (Hindu) Maharajas of Kashmir until the end of the *princely states. In 1931 Sheikh Mohammed Abdullah (1905–82) launched the Muslim nationalist movement which was to win him renown as the 'Lion of Kashmir'; he was imprisoned in both 1931 and 1946 for his 'Quit Kashmir' campaign, aimed as much against Hindus who, as he saw it, had infiltrated his homeland from Jammu, as against the British. After *Partition and Independence, the Maharaja announced in October 1947 that he would accede to India, not to Pakistan, as most Kashmiris wished. The Maharaja's action was challenged both by Sheikh Abdullah and by Pakistan, who sent army units into the province. After fighting between the two dominions, India denounced Pakistan as the aggressor and appealed to the United Nations: a UN supervisory commission established a provisional demarcation line in January 1949 which left most of the territory within India but acknowledged small Pakistani enclaves in the west. Sheikh Abdullah accepted incorporation with India in the hope of lowering tension, but in 1953 the Indian authorities charged him with high treason and he was imprisoned until 1968. Pakistan continued to dispute the settlement and, with UN backing, sought a plebiscite, which India refused. In November 1956 Parliament in Delhi formally declared the whole region the state of Jammu and Kashmir within the Indian Republic; Pakistan thereupon set up an interim administration for 'Free Kashmir' in Muzzaffarabad. During a series of frontier disputes with Communist China in 1962 about a fifth of the area of the state was overrun by the Chinese Army (who continue to occupy it). Fighting broke out again between India and Pakistan in April 1965 but a truce was arranged, through Soviet mediation, at Tashkent in January 1966. A third conflict in the region in 1971 coincided with the Indo-Pakistan war over *Bangladesh. The Simla Agreement of July 1972 defined a new demarcation line while agreeing that the problem should be settled by bilateral negotiation. Though insisting that Kashmiris, and only Kashmiris, had a right 'to decide the future of the state', Sheikh Abdullah served as chief minister in the disputed region for the last seven years of his life. Although his son, Dr Farooq Abdullah (1937–), succeeded him in 1982, the Kashmiri people's patience was running out, and a secessionist rebellion began in December 1989, with Kashmiri guerrillas attacking Hindus and challenging the 400,000 Indian troops deployed in Jammu-Kashmir. The problem remains unresolved.

Kaunda, Kenneth David (1924–), first President of Zambia: born in Lubwa, Northern Rhodesia; trained as a teacher, and after serving as a village headmaster became a welfare officer in the copper mines. He established a Zambian African National Congress but it was considered a subversive organization by the *Welensky government and he was imprisoned for two years. On his release he set up the UNIP (United National Independence Party) which vigorously campaigned against the short-lived *Central African Federation on the grounds that it was exploiting the Zambian peoples for the sake of the Southern Rhodesians. Kaunda's success in elections in 1963 confirmed London's hostility to the Federation, and when Northern Rhodesia seceded and gained internal self-government in January 1964 Kaunda became Prime Minister, assuming office as President of an independent Zambia in the following October. His book *A Humanist in Africa* (1966) preached Christian tolerance and deplored militant racialism, black or white. His ideals marked him out as a wise elder statesman of a Commonwealth in transition, and he showed skill in managing the Lusaka Commonwealth Conference of 1979 and helping to promote a settlement of the Rhodesian problem. But his internal policies seemed frequently at variance with his professed ideals: he considered Zambia too exposed to foreign plots for the safe continuance of democratic government: in 1972 he suspended the constitution and a year later made Zambia a one-party state under UNIP government. This dictatorship he preserved until mounting internal and external pressures led him to accept multi-party and genuine presidential elections in October 1991, when he was defeated by the Democratic Party leader, Frederick Chiluba.

Keating, Paul John (1944–), Australian Prime Minister: born at Bankstown, New South Wales into an Irish Catholic family, his father being a boiler-maker. He left De la Salle College before he was fifteen, attended evening classes and worked as a local government clerk and for a Hong Kong trading company before becoming a trade union official at the age of 23. In 1969 he was elected as Labor member for Blaxland, NSW, in the Federal Parliament. Keating was Minister for Northern Australia in the last weeks of the *Whitlam government of 1975 and remained highly critical of Whitlam's dismissal. He was appointed Federal Treasurer of Australia by Bob *Hawke in March 1983 and

Kelly, Edward

succeeded Hawke as head of the government in December 1990. He advocated republicanism and showed himself markedly less sympathetic to British links than Hawke. He travelled to Balmoral in September 1993 to inform Queen Elizabeth II of his plans for Australia to become a Republic by the centenary of federation in 2001.

Kelly, Edward (1855–80), Australian *bushranger: born at Port Philip, the son of an Irish ex-convict transportee sent to *Tasmania in 1840 for stealing two pigs. Ned Kelly and his younger brother Dan fell foul of the law in north-eastern Victoria at a time when resentment over land squatters caused wild outbursts of social anarchy. Ned, a known horse thief, shot three policemen in an effort to escape arrest in 1878 and with his brother and two companions, Joe Byrne and Steve Hart, took to the hills about a hundred miles north-east of Melbourne. For twenty months the Kelly Gang raided small hotels in outlying townships and held up banks along the Victoria–NSW border until they were cornered in the hotel at Glenrowan, Victoria, in June 1880. All except Ned were killed, the police having set fire to the hotel. Ned was hit several times by shots but survived thanks to the improvised protective armour he wore, made from kitchenware or farm implements. He was, however, subsequently tracked down and put on trial. From prison he wrote two letters justifying his crimes as gestures of freedom from tyranny. He was hanged in Melbourne on 11 November 1880. Legend reveres the police murderer as an outstanding Robin Hood hero of the bush, personally brave and totally contemptuous of laws which he believed favoured greedy land speculators.

Kenny, Elizabeth (1880–1952), Australian nurse: born in Warialda, NSW. At the age of 32 'Sister Kenny' abandoned hospital ward nursing in favour of the bush and the outback. Her wide experience of field work was of value to her in the Australian Army Nursing Service (1915–19), helping her develop techniques for strengthening damaged limbs and muscles. During the poliomyelitis epidemic of 1925 Sister Kenny advocated treatment by muscle therapy rather than through rigid splinting, which she believed prolonged static immobilization. Her methods were criticized by much orthodox opinion, but she vigorously upheld her views and won support from (Dame) Jean Macnamara (1899–1968), the Melbourne physicist who worked on perfecting the Salk vaccine. Sister Kenny's theories of treatment were developed in clinics in Australia as early as 1933, in Britain four years later, and at Minneapolis, Minnesota, USA in 1940. She received higher honour in the United States than in her homeland.

Kenya: independent East African Commonwealth republic: capital, Nairobi. Fossil discoveries made by the *Leakey family suggest that East Africa may well be 'the cradle of mankind', but the earliest chroniclers who visited the region were Arabs from Mesopotamia, in the early tenth century. Vasco da Gama anchored off Mombasa in April 1498 and Portuguese traders followed seven years later; Fort Jesus, a Portuguese outpost on the coast, was garrisoned from 1593 to 1729. Trading communities were then developed by Arabs from Oman who had settled in *Zanzibar. Inland, the *Kamba, *Kikuyu, *Luo, *Masai, *Nandi and some thirty smaller African ethnic groups were little disturbed until the coming of missionaries in 1848 and the opening up of fertile farmland by the *Imperial British East Africa Company in 1888/9. Systematic settlement began with the proclamation of an East Africa Protectorate on 15 June 1895 and the construction of the Uganda Railway from Mombasa to Lake Victoria, 1896–1901 (and on to Kampala in 1925); the Protectorate became the Crown Colony of Kenya on 23 July 1920. Nairobi ('cold water place') was founded as a riverside railhead in 1899 and grew rapidly, attracting Asian traders as well as a social élite from Europe. These white settlers looked for leadership to the pioneer rancher, Lord *Delamere. Proposals to establish a Zionist colony on the Uasin Gishu plateau were opposed by the settlers and rejected by the *Jewish community in 1905; Boer families trekked to the plateau by ox-wagon three years later. A Legislative Council, set up in 1907, aroused resentment among the Africans by seeking to perpetuate exclusive white rule and by moving them from their traditional hunting and pasture lands to new reserves. In *World War I German incursions around Gazi and Taveta were checked in 1914–15 and a successful invasion of German East Africa was launched by *Smuts in February 1916. After the war a Soldier Settlement Scheme, offering land cheaply, virtually by means of a lottery, ran into difficulties through the inexperience of many of the ex-service families taking advantage of it. *Tea and *coffee were among crops ravaged by locusts between 1928 and 1934; cattle suffered from rinderpest. Despite the setbacks, white settlement spread: in 1914 there were 3,000 Europeans in an estimated population of 4.2 million; in 1920/1 about 9,000; and in the last census before Independence, 55,759 out of 8.5 million. In 1923 the Duke of Devonshire, as Colonial Secretary, stipulated that 'the interests of the African races must be paramount', prevailing over the interests of 'immigrant races': white settlers, interpreting this 'Devonshire Declaration' as an intended rebuff to the *Kenya Asians, made few concessions to native Africans. To safeguard African land rights a political movement was launched in 1928 by Harry *Thuku and Jomo *Kenyatta, but the failure of the settlers to make any positive response to Kikuyu grievances over a long passage of time provoked greater violence. Secret societies were founded: the most famous, *Mau Mau, was declared illegal in 1950 but its members began a campaign of ritual killing in 1952. While military measures continued against terrorism until 1956, limited reforms were introduced in 1954 in an effort to promote multiracial co-operation. But Iain *Macleod, becoming Colonial

Secretary in 1959, recognized that these reforms had come too late. In January 1960 a conference at *Lancaster House made clear the British government's decision to accept majority rule based on universal suffrage, and to purchase a million acres of the White Highlands for redistribution as small-holdings to African farmers. Full internal self-government (June 1963) was followed by Independence on 12 December 1963: a year later Kenya became a republic. The first President, Jomo Kenyatta, sought to centralize the government and encourage Africanization, especially at the expense of the Asians. He supported the growth of an East African Community, in partnership with Tanzania and Uganda; but it fell apart in 1977. There was concern in Kenya at the rapid move towards one-party rule, which began with the institution of a unicameral National Assembly in 1966. Civil war was narrowly averted in July 1969 when the Luo political leader, Tom *Mboya, was killed by a Kikuyu gunman. On Kenyatta's death in August 1978 Vice-President *Moi succeeded him and gained electoral successes for KANU (Kenya African National Union). Fulfilment of a four-year Development Programme, launched in 1979, was hampered by the world recession. An abortive coup by air force officers on 1 August 1982 was followed by repression which consolidated the KANU dictatorship. Social and economic problems intensified, for Kenya had the highest birth rate in the world. A population of 20 million in December 1983 had topped 26 million by 1992. While Kenya was self-sufficient in grain in 1975, by 1980 basic foods were imported and there was a growing need of financial aid for industrial projects. A threat to cut off funds unless one-party rule ended led to a restoration of multi-party elections in December 1992, although the electoral procedure was criticized by Commonwealth observers and the President retained the right to nominate twelve members of the National Assembly. KANU won 95 elected seats, and the four-party 'Forum of Restored Democracy' 85 seats. As well as uncertainty over the prospects for democratic government in Kenya, since 1991 there have been frequent ethnic clashes in the predominantly Kikuyu areas of the Rift Valley.

Kenya Asians. Indian and, to a much lesser extent, Malay traders flocked into the East Africa Protectorate as soon as the first towns were established. They were joined by Asian labourers working on the railway from Mombasa to Lake Victoria. So marked was the Indian influence on trade that until 1920/1 currency was based on the rupee, rather than on British coins. Although the Devonshire Declaration of 1923 dashed Kenya Asians' hopes of political recognition (see *above*), London's attitude changed over the following thirty years; Kenya Asian spokesmen were recognized politically by reforms in 1954 and 1958, though the higher civil service posts remained closed to them and they could not buy land in the white highlands. By 1962 there were more than 200,000 Asians in the country, compared with some 56,000 Europeans; the

Indian hold on small-scale commerce was so strong that there was a widespread prejudice against them, not unlike the anti-Semitism of pre-Hitler Germany. Kenyatta's Africanization policies stimulated a mass exodus, particularly in 1968, but there was never the systematic persecution experienced by Asians in *Uganda under *Amin. The Sikhs and the Sunni Muslims remain, and Asians have greater economic and administrative influence in Kenya than in any other African state.

Kenyatta, Mzee Jomo (*c.* 1890–1978), founder-President of the Kenyan Republic: born at Ngenda, the son of a *Kikuyu farmer; educated at the Scottish missionary school at Thogota and worked as a local government clerk in Nairobi, becoming editor of a Kikuyu-language monthly review, and general secretary of the Kikuyu Central Association (KCA) in 1928. He spent most of the years 1929 to 1946 in exile, representing the KCA in Britain and visiting the Soviet Union, the Netherlands, France and Germany and attending occasional classes at Selly Oak and at the London School of Economics. His book *Facing Mount Kenya* (1938) aroused interest in Britain as an 'inside' account of Kikuyu life and culture. He worked on a farm in West Sussex during 1940–41, occasionally lecturing on African affairs. In 1945 he presided over the *Pan–African Congress at Chorlton-on-Medlock. When he returned to Nairobi in September 1946 he was accepted as a national leader by his people. He campaigned for African equality in political representation, an end to the colour bar, higher wages, and land redistribution. He was arrested on 21 October 1952 and in April 1953 unjustly convicted of managing *Mau Mau; he was imprisoned until August 1961, and became president of KANU (Kenya African National Union) on his release. He led the KANU delegation to London for the 1962 talks on Kenya's constitutional future, then became minister of state in a transitional coalition government and first Prime Minister of independent Kenya (in December 1963), and finally President of the republic a year later, an office he held until his death. At first he collaborated with the *Luo spokesman, Tom *Mboya, towards establishing a centralized African republic. After Mboya's murder in 1969 he tightened KANU's hold on the country, banning the Communist front organization (Kenya People's Union) in October 1969; but he worked closely with the more regionalist KANU leader, Daniel arap *Moi, who became vice-president. On Kenyatta's sudden death (on 22 August 1978) Moi, as his successor, ensured that Kenyatta received an impressive funeral, worthy of the founder of a state.

Khama, Sir Seretse (1921–80), first President of Botswana: born at Serowe in Bechuanaland, a great-grandson of King Khama III, the Christian ruler who had placed his Bamangwato people under British protection in 1885. Seretse became titular ruler of the Bamangwato in

1923, but a regency was exercised by his uncle, Tshekedi (1905–59), while Seretse received his education at Fort Hare University and Balliol College, Oxford. In 1948, while reading for the Bar in the Inner Temple, he defied convention and tribal traditions by marrying an Englishwoman, Ruth Williams. Despite support from a gathering of the Bamangwato at Serowe, he was barred from Bechuanaland by successive British governments between 1949 and 1956. On his return home he showed great political skills, joined Bechuanaland's legislative council in 1961, and formed the multiracial Democratic Party a year later. A landslide victory in Bechuanaland's first election led to his appointment as Prime Minister in 1965. He negotiated the transition to independence and, in September 1966, became President of the new *Botswana, having received a knighthood in the same year. His fourteen years of office were marked by interracial harmony and tolerance, and by firm opposition to the racism of neighbouring Rhodesia and South Africa.

Khyber Pass: an historic defile some 33 miles long linking Pakistan with Afghanistan. It gives access from the Kabul river to the Indus valley and down to Peshawar. A road and a railway track run between the steep rock faces of the Safed Koh mountains which, at one point, narrow the pass to 5 yards (4.5 metres). The Khyber Pass was the key British defensive position on the *North-West Frontier from 1833 until World War II. During this period of more than a century, the British also ensured that the Khyber remained a protected route for caravans of mules, buffaloes and camels carrying their merchandise three times a week, despite the threat of raids from Afridi brigands in the surrounding hills.

Kikuyu (Gikuyu): the largest ethnic group in Kenya, forming between a fifth and a quarter of the population. At the time of white settlement they were a warrior people with pastoral lands down the Rift Valley, from the equator to the Nairobi region in the south. In the 1880s and 1890s their numbers dropped because of the spread of smallpox, and from the consequences of rinderpest among their cattle, disasters which left some potentially rich agricultural land around Nairobi unoccupied. This traditionally Kikuyu land was parcelled out among the settlers, initiating conflicts over *land rights which outlasted the years of colonization. Many Kikuyu were skilled and intelligent, and became natural leaders, among them Harry *Thuku and Jomo *Kenyatta. Some supported *Mau Mau in the 1950s, although the Kikuyu elders resisted the movement, which they believed undermined their authority and the traditions of their people. When Kenya gained independence, Kikuyu influence at first dominated the republic, but declined after Kenyatta's death. In the late 1980s Kikuyu support shifted towards the political opposition; between 1991 and 1995, Kikuyu clashes with ethnic groups supporting the government caused more than 1,500 deaths.

King, John (1838–72), Irish-born survivor of the ill-fated *Burke and Wills Expedition across the Australian continent in 1860/1.

King, (William Lyon) Mackenzie (1874–1950), Canadian Prime Minister: born, the grandson of W. L. *Mackenzie, at Berlin, Ontario, a town patriotically renamed Kitchener in World War I. King studied law at Toronto and gained a doctorate at Harvard before entering politics. He sat as a Liberal in the Federal Parliament (1908–11 and 1919–48) with an interlude when he was wartime director of industrial research for the Rockefeller Foundation. King was Canada's Prime Minister from December 1919 to August 1930, apart from three months of minority Conservative government in the late summer of 1926 on the occasion when King forced, and won, a general election following a dispute with the Governor-General, Lord Byng (1862–1935). After five years of leading the Opposition against *Bennett's tariff and centralization policies, King was returned to power in October 1935 and headed the government until November 1948, when he handed over to Louis *St Laurent. King was an astute politician, strongly upholding Canada's independence in world affairs and initially critical of any Commonwealth proposals from London. His spiritualist beliefs puzzled, and at times alarmed, other Commonwealth leaders, several of whom also thought King vain and unaccommodating. Yet he maintained Canada's unity in the face of growing separatist sentiment in *Quebec and despite vacillations over compulsory *military service in World War II. King was a useful wartime link between Washington and London, though he resented any exclusion from top-level consultation. He supported the foundation of the United Nations in 1945; characteristically, he sought to save the UN from domination, either by the Great Powers or by smaller Powers who might assert more influence than King believed was warranted by their size and strength. He refused a knighthood, but on his retirement accepted the Order of Merit.

King's African Rifles. A famous British colonial *native regiment, formed on 1 January 1902 by combining local *askari* (East African equivalent of sepoy) regiments raised in Nyasaland, Kenya and Uganda into a single regiment of five battalions to serve anywhere in the Empire, but primarily in East Africa; they did not serve overseas until 1942. Sikhs and Punjabi Muslims were recruited in India to augment the KAR in its first years. On the outbreak of World War I the regiment numbered 73 British officers and 2,325 *askaris*, only 3 battalions; by 1917 the KAR constituted a corps of 7 regiments and 27 battalions and had fought under *Smuts with great distinction against the Germans in Tanganyika in 1916. It was to the 1st battalion of the 4th KAR that General von Lettow-Vorbeck surrendered the last of the Kaiser's fighting forces on 25 November 1918 at Abercorn (Mbala, Zambia). During World War II the KAR formed the spearhead of the attack on the Italians in Somaliland and Ethiopia in 1941, helped to seize Madagascar from the Vichy French in 1942, and fought in the Arakan region of lower Burma, 1942–45. The KAR were such good jungle fighters that three battalions served in *Malaya against the Communist infiltrators in 1952/3. Their final operations were against the *Mau Mau, a campaign in which Sergeant Idi *Amin of the 4th KAR became a platoon commander. The KAR were disbanded in December 1963, the battalions becoming Kenya Rifles, Uganda Rifles, Malawi Rifles, etc.; at this time there were about a hundred African junior officers in the regiment's seven battalions.

Kingsford Smith, Sir Charles Edward (1897–1935), Australian pioneer airman: born at Hamilton in Queensland; educated at Sydney Cathedral School, joined the Australian army on his eighteenth birthday, transferred to the Royal Flying Corps in 1917, and won the Military Cross for bravery. From 1921 onwards he was an air-taxi pioneer in Australia, founding Interstate Services in 1926 and then promoting commercial *airlines and stimulating an interest in air transport by his long-distance ventures. Among his famous flights were a record-breaking ten-day circuit of Australia in 1927 in company with Charles Ulm and, with Ulm and two Americans in 1928, the first trans-Pacific flight, in his plane *Southern Cross*. He flew from Australia to England in 1929 and completed the journey round the world in the following year. In 1932 he received a knighthood for his services to aviation, and in 1933 flew from England to Australia in a record 7 days and 5 hours. He was lost attempting another pioneer flight from England in November 1935. With his co-pilot J. T. Pethybridge, he is thought to have perished off the Burma coast after leaving Calcutta.

Kipling, (Joseph) Rudyard (1865–1936), author: born in Bombay, son of the principal of the art school in Lahore; spent his school-days at the United Services College, Westward Ho!, Devon, immortalizing them much later in *Stalky and Co.* (1899). From 1882 to 1889 he was a journalist at Lahore, where the collected poems *Departmental Ditties* (1886) and more than thirty short stories on imperial themes had been published by the time he left India to settle in England. *Barrack Room Ballads* appeared in 1892 and *The Jungle Books* in 1894 and 1895. So rapid was Kipling's rise to literary eminence that in 1895, just nine years after his first book was published, he was offered – and declined – the Poet Laureateship. For the Diamond Jubilee of 1897 he published what he believed to be his greatest poem, the five-verse *Recessional*, in which he celebrated 'dominion over palm and pine' with a call for contrition and a warning against becoming 'drunk with sight of power'. The Indian theme returned in the novel *Kim* (1901); a year later he made his permanent home at Burwash in Sussex, and his later writings reflected a romantic delight in English history, best shown in *Puck of Pook's Hill* (1906). He accepted the Nobel Prize for Literature (1907), but refused all other honours. Detractors ignore Kipling's allusive gift of satire, his contempt for colonial affectation, and the depth of his feeling for the animal world and for the 'untouchables' of human society.

Kiribati (pronounced 'Kiribass'): an independent Commonwealth republic in the south-west Pacific, formerly known as the Gilbert Islands archipelago: capital, Tarawa. There are 36 islands in the Kiribati group. The core of them are the 17 Gilberts, which became a British Protectorate in 1892 and, at the request of the islands' assemblies, were developed as the Crown Colony of the Gilbert and Ellice Islands from 1916. Most of Kiribati was occupied by the Japanese in 1942; the islands were cleared by American and New Zealand troops in 1943. As the Ellice Islands are nearly 500 miles away, a movement for independence developed in the early 1970s. After a referendum the Ellice Islands broke away on 1 October 1975 and became *Tuvalu. Internal self-government was then granted to the remaining islands in the Crown Colony on 1 November 1976, and on 12 July 1979 they became independent, as the republic of Kiribati. Considerable renaming followed: Christmas Island became Kiritimati, Fanning Island became Tabuaeran, Washington Island became Teraina. Since 1988 some 5,000 people have been resettled on these last two islands, the principal island, Tarawa, being considered over-populated. The main export is copra, but fishing is a thriving local industry. Coconut trees abound.

Kirk, Norman Eric (1923–74), New Zealand Prime Minister: born at Waimate, South Island; left school at the age of 12 and educated himself while working on traction engines. From local politics in Canterbury he moved into the national arena as Labour MP for Lyttelton (1957–69), later sitting for Sydenham. He became leader of the parliamentary Labour party in 1965, gained a sweeping electoral victory seven years later, and was Prime Minister from December 1972 until his death. During this brief period he ended compulsory military service, brought the last troops home from *Vietnam, and approached world affairs with a strongly humanitarian outlook; he was firmly opposed to racism in South Africa, and to nuclear tests in the Pacific. Inflation jumped alarmingly after the increase in world oil prices in 1973, and Kirk resorted to controls and subsidies. Worry over these economic problems overstrained his health, and he died suddenly, in September 1974: fifteen months later the same problems cost his successor, Sir Wallace Rowling, the general election.

Kitchener, Horatio Herbert (1850–1916), British soldier: born near Ballylongford, Ireland; educated at the Royal Military College, Woolwich and saw war for the first time as a volunteer ambulance driver in France (1870/1). He was originally commissioned into the Royal Engineers and undertook survey work in Palestine and, more extensively, in occupied *Cyprus from 1878 until 1882, when he was made second-in-command of the Egyptian cavalry. Kitchener spent the next 17 years in Egypt; he built up *Wolseley's army for the abortive attempt to relieve Gordon in the Sudan and then, from 1886, served as Governor of the Eastern Sudan and commander of cavalry forces against the dervishes. As Sirdar of the Egyptian Army in 1892 he methodically prepared for the reconquest of the Sudan, advancing up the Nile in 1896 and mounting his main assault on Khartoum in 1898, the campaign being decided at the battle of *Omdurman. He then thrust farther up the Nile to confront Captain Marchand's French expedition at *Fashoda, and forced it to withdraw. He remained Governor of the Sudan until required to go to South Africa as Chief-of-Staff to Lord *Roberts in 1899; he took over command of the army in 1900, and was forced to check Boer infiltrations by a system of blockhouses combined with the detention of their civilian sympathizers in closely guarded camps. Although his methods offended liberal opinion in Britain and on the continent, Kitchener was created a viscount and awarded the Order of Merit in 1902. From 1903 to 1909 he served in India as Commander-in-Chief, completely reorganizing the *Indian Army, limiting the military authority of *Curzon as Viceroy, modernizing training and equipment, and giving the Indian Army its own staff college at Quetta. Kitchener was made a Field Marshal in 1909; as British 'Agent' in Cairo from 1911 to 1914 he was the effective ruler, and the military commander, of Egypt. His presence on leave in England at the outbreak of World War I led to his appointment as Secretary of State for War in August 1914, even though he knew little of military affairs in Europe and never understood the workings of cabinet government. Earl Kitchener of Khartoum (as he then became) was an impressive figurehead who encouraged the recruitment of a vast army of volunteers. He made few contributions to general strategy but travelled to France and Flanders, Egypt, Gallipoli and Salonika with advice to field commanders on specific problems. He was on a military mission to Russia in early June 1916 aboard HMS *Hampshire* when the cruiser struck a mine off the Orkneys. Kitchener is assumed to have drowned.

de Klerk, Frederik Willem (1936–   ), South African President: born in the Transvaal; set up a legal practice at Vereeniging and entered the South African Parliament as a National Party member in 1972, becoming party leader in the Transvaal ten years later. When President Piet Botha (1916–90) suffered a stroke on 18 January 1989, de Klerk succeeded him as head of the party and, in September, as State President. He was more moderate than his predecessors and began dismantling *apartheid in order to secure better contacts for South African enterprises abroad. In

February 1990 he ordered the release from detention of Nelson *Mandela, and began political talks with black leaders. On 1 February 1991 he informed Parliament of his intention to scrap the last apartheid regulations. When South Africa's first multiracial elections were held in April 1994 and victory went to the *African National Congress, de Klerk stepped down as head of state (10 May 1994), agreeing to serve as Second Deputy President under President Mandela.

Korean War. Rival claims to sovereignty over the Korean peninsula, by Communist North Korea above the latitude 38° parallel, and Americanized South Korea below the 38° parallel, led to a surprise attack from the North on 25 June 1950. The UN Security Council – boycotted by the Soviet Union – recommended UN members to help the South Korean Republic repel the invaders, and an international force was set up under General MacArthur. Among the nations who sent fighting troops were Australia, Canada, New Zealand, South Africa, and the United Kingdom. The North Koreans were thrown back in September and October 1950, but the UN advance to the Sino-Korean border prompted intervention by Communist Chinese 'volunteers' who recovered much territory before the momentum of their offensive was checked. In May 1951 the UN established a defensive line slightly north of the 38° parallel which was little changed by later clashes. Peace talks begun in July 1951 did not finally bring about an armistice for another two years, but there was little fighting after September 1951. Casualties in the war were high: Commonwealth contingents lost some 7,000 men.

Kowloon: principal town on the Chinese mainland in the British Dependent Territory of *Hong Kong. Kowloon was acquired from China in 1860, eighteen years later than Hong Kong island. In 1912 a railway was completed between Kowloon and Canton (now Guangzhou), linking the colony with the main Chinese trunk routes and, ultimately, the Trans-Siberian Railway. Overcrowding and alleged discrimination against refugees from the Chinese Communist revolution led to serious riots in Kowloon in 1952 and to the hurried institution of a municipal building programme.

Kruger, (Stephen Johannes) Paulus (1825–1904), President of the Transvaal: born into a Boer family near Colesburg in Cape Colony. At the age of thirteen he accompanied his parents in the *Great Trek, settling to farm land north of the Vaal river. After serving as commandant of the 'South African Republic of the Transvaal' he was appointed to the Transvaal executive council in 1872. In 1882 he became President of the Transvaal, visiting England, Holland and Germany in 1883/4 to explain the Boer position. The *gold rush and the development of the Rand mineral resources threatened the predominantly farming character of the

Boer republic while also bringing it sudden wealth. To keep out foreign 'riff-raff' Kruger purchased German arms and sought German support, upon which he believed he could count after the fiasco of the *Jameson Raid. In September 1899 his advisers told Kruger he could expect a British invasion from Cape Colony and Natal and he therefore ordered pre-emptive incursions, thus precipitating the Second *Boer War. In May 1900 he was forced to evacuate his capital, Pretoria, and in June he travelled to Europe, hoping for armed mediation by Germany, perhaps in combination with Russia and France. He found the Great Powers unresponsive and, with the British army occupying the Transvaal, in November 1900 settled at Hilversum in the Netherlands. Despite failing health he wrote his memoirs, published in 1902, at the end of the war. He died in July 1904, while seeking medical treatment in Switzerland.

Kruger Telegram (3 January 1896): an ill-considered message sent by Germany's ruler, Kaiser William II, to congratulate President *Kruger on repelling the *Jameson Raiders and maintaining the independence of the Transvaal 'without appealing to the help of friendly powers'. The tone of the message provoked the first serious anti-German demonstrations in London, intensified the suspicion of Lord Salisbury's government that Germany had imperial designs in southern Africa, and aroused false hopes in the Transvaal that, in any armed conflict with the British in Cape Colony or Natal, the Boers would be able to count on German military aid.

Kuala Lumpur Statement (1989). The *Commonwealth Heads of Government meeting in peninsular Malaysia in October 1989 issued two important, previously agreed pronouncements: the *Langkawi Declaration on the environment, and the Kuala Lumpur Statement on southern Africa. This statement reaffirmed the Commonwealth's resolve to continue to back the struggle against apartheid and seek a non-racial democracy in South Africa, while also examining the possibilities of multilateral Commonwealth aid for human resource development in a post-apartheid society.

Kuwait: an emirate at the north-western head of the Persian Gulf which developed entrepôt trade links with India under Sheikh Sabah al-Owel who, as ruler from 1756 to 1772, established the present dynasty. Kuwait was never part of the Empire or Commonwealth, but in 1899 it passed under British protection by a treaty which strengthened the emirate against possible encroachment by the Turks or from foreign companies to whom the Ottoman Sultan had given concessions. British forces safeguarded Kuwait in 1914 and, though frequent stress was laid on the emirate's independence, Kuwait served as a British centre for discussions over the future of the Gulf and of the Arab kingdoms on several occasions, notably in December 1922. Kuwait's strategic importance increased with the opening up of the Burgan oilfield from 1936 onwards; the British Protectorate remained effective until June 1961, when it was replaced by a ten-year defensive pact. Direct military involvement lapsed in the 1970s and 1980s, when the Emir and his ministers upheld a strict neutralism. Although British troops, aircraft and warships played a prominent part in the liberation of Kuwait from Iraqi rule in 1990, they intervened as members of a 29-nation UN force rather than in accordance with past policies.

Lamming, George Eric (1927–   ), Barbadian-born novelist: taught in Trinidad and Venezuela but came to England and worked in a factory in the early 1950s. His self-consciously textured novels – notably *The Emigrants* (1954), *Season of Adventure* (1960), *Natives of My Person* (1972) – sensitively convey an inner conflict of cultures while giving literary form to an argot largely unknown outside the Caribbean.

Lancaster House, London: historically part of St James's Palace; built as York House in 1825, modified as Stafford House in 1841, and in 1912 purchased by Viscount Leverhulme, who renamed it to honour his native county. He presented the lease to the government in 1913, intending the house to be used as a museum and for state banquets and conferences. Lancaster House Conferences took place over disarmament and over Cyprus in 1955; over constitutional change in Kenya in January 1960; and over the Rhodesian question and the transition to an independent Zimbabwe in September–October 1979.

Land rights. The problem of land rights was common to almost every pioneer colonial settlement, although its nature varied across the world. In Canada and New Zealand, treaties were made between representatives of the government or colonizing associations and the aboriginal *Indian or *Maori peoples respectively. The Royal Proclamation of 1763 insisted that western land should be purchased from the Indians, not seized; greater care was taken by the federal government over Indian lands in the 1870s and 1880s than elsewhere in North America; the *métis suffered more than pure-blood Indians from the settlers who followed the railways westwards. In New Zealand, misunderstandings over native land law and collective holdings were intensified by the Treaty of *Waitangi, rather than clarified, as had been the original British intention; infringement of land rights provoked the so-called *Maori Wars of 1843–47, 1863–64 and 1869–70 which were followed by confiscations of land; the Native Land Court, established in 1865, put the burden of proof of ownership of title on the Maoris themselves and became, in practice, a legalistic device for denying land rights. Compensation for lost land rights did not begin until the late 1920s, and then largely on the initiative of Sir Apirana Ngata. His

Native Land Settlement Act (1929) provided state-financed land but did not redress specific past injustices, and a renewed protest movement gathered strength in 1974/5. In the Australian outback and in East Africa the white settlers acted on the principle which John Locke had sought to justify in 1690: a man has a natural right to hold property with which he has 'mixed' the labour of his body, for example by enclosing and cultivating unoccupied and unused land. Since the Australian *aborigines were a nomadic people, it was denied that they possessed any rights to hold land or to be compensated for its acquisition, a ruling upheld in a court of law as late as 1971, in respect of the native peoples of the *Northern Territory. A subsequent Federal Commission, headed by Mr Justice Woodward, led to enactment in 1976 of the Aboriginal Land Right (Northern Territory) Act, recognizing native rights. In 1981 the state government of South Australia granted the Pitjantjatjana people some 40,000 square miles of freehold land; other states followed this change of policy; and on 22 December 1993 the Federal Parliament in Canberra enacted the Native Title Bill which, after two centuries, recognized the rights of aborigines to hold land. In East Africa, and especially in *Kenya, the legal claim of the native peoples to their land was presented much earlier and grudgingly acknowledged, notably by the million-acre redistribution scheme to create small-holdings in the so-called 'white highlands' preserve, implemented in 1961. Further south, the pattern for both the Rhodesias and the Union was set by the South African *Natives Land Act of 1913, which imposed segregation and set aside good farm land for white ownership. The denial of land rights continued until decolonization in Zambia, Malawi, Botswana and Zimbabwe, and until the repeal of the key segregation laws in South Africa during May and June 1991.

Lange, David Russell (1932–), New Zealand Prime Minister: studied law at the University of Auckland and was called to the Bar. In 1977 he was elected Labour MP for Mangere, and in 1983 became Leader of the Opposition to the *Muldoon Government. Labour won the 1984 election, with a 17-seat majority, and Lange formed a government on 26 July, also becoming Minister of Education. His government, caught in severe financial difficulties, resorted to a right-wing monetarism which encouraged an optimistic stock market boom in 1986 and helped Lange increase his majority in a fresh election. In world affairs, Lange opposed the presence of nuclear-powered or nuclear-armed ships in New Zealand waters, a decision so resented by the United States that the dominion was effectively forced into isolation, out of the *ANZUS Pact. In his second government Lange faced internal divisions and personally opposed the sale of public assets which some colleagues advocated. In August 1989 he felt compelled to resign, but remained Attorney-General in the government of his successor, Geoffrey Palmer, until Labour's defeat in the general election of October 1990.

Langkawi Declaration on the Environment (1989). Langkawi is the most northerly island off Pensinsular Malaysia in the Strait of Malacca, close to the Thai border. The *Commonwealth Heads of Government, adjourning there from the Kuala Lumpur Conference in October 1989, agreed, for the first time, on a collective declaration recognizing the need for joint action by member-governments to protect the global environment and achieve sustainable development of natural resources, particularly of forests (see *Forestry*).

Lapstone Conference (1938). An informal gathering of some ninety Commonwealth academics, trade unionists and specialists in world affairs met in early September 1938 at the Lapstone Hotel, on the eastern edge of New South Wales's Blue Mountains, to discuss international problems objectively. The conference, which lasted for a fortnight, was arranged by the Australian Institute of International Affairs and the *'Round Table' group of Commonwealth visionaries from London, including Lionel *Curtis. Visitors came from Canada, Newfoundland, New Zealand, the United Kingdom, Eire and India and included the future Labour Foreign Secretary, Ernest Bevin (1881–1951). Lapstone had a double significance: at a time of mounting crisis in Europe and the Far East, it broadened Commonwealth understanding among influential public figures who were not themselves in government; and it emphasized the growing initiative of the overseas dominions in jointly anticipating new trends in world affairs.

Laurier, Sir Wilfrid (1841–1919), Canadian Prime Minister: born at St Lin, Quebec; studied law at Montreal, and became a respected barrister, entering the Quebec legislature at the age of 30 and sitting as Liberal member of the Federal Parliament from 1874 until his death. After brief cabinet experience in 1877 Laurier was in opposition for eighteen years, from 1888 onwards as leader of the Liberals. When he formed a government in July 1896, he became the first French-Canadian Premier, and the first Roman Catholic Prime Minister in the British Empire. He was knighted a year later, amid the Diamond Jubilee celebrations. His long premiership was marked by an emphasis on transcontinental unity, a rapid rise in immigration, and by Laurier's personal encouragement of imperial consultation, combined with insistence on the dominion's right to act independently in foreign affairs: the establishment of a Canadian Department of External Affairs (1909) was the fruit of Laurier's long experience. He insisted, against the wishes of many French-Canadians, on sending volunteers to fight the Boers in South Africa (1899–1902). Agreements with Britain improved prairie exports, but Laurier's desire for a commercial treaty with the United States aroused hostility from business interests anxious to protect Canada from the highly developed predatory capitalism of its neighbour. His attempt to build up a Royal

Canadian Navy was not popular with the electorate, who feared the mounting costs of warship construction. When the Liberals lost the 1911 election, Laurier again became Leader of the Opposition. During World War I he rejected invitations to enter a coalition, largely because he remained hostile to compulsory *military service.

Lavalée, Calixa (1842–91), Canadian composer: born at Verchères, Quebec; received musical training as a pianist at the Paris Conservatoire and in his later years toured North America extensively, giving recitals and organizing concerts, notably at Cleveland, Ohio, where in 1883 he presented the first programme of native North American composers. Lavalée completed several symphonies and string quartets as well as an opera, *The Widow*, but he is best remembered as composer of *O Canada!*, which in 1966 received parliamentary recognition as Canada's *national anthem, although the tune was originally composed as a hymn to St John the Baptist. *O Canada!* was first sung, to words written by Sir Adolphe Routhier, in 1880 for a ceremonial visit by the Governor-General to Quebec City.

Lawrence, Sir George St Patrick (1804–84), British general: born at Trincomalee, a brother of Sir Henry and Baron John (see *below*); trained for service with the *East India Company at Addiscombe and spent all his public life in India (1822–64). He was commissioned into the Bengal Light Cavalry, fought in Afghanistan (1838/9) and organized the evacuation of civilians from Kabul in 1842. After surviving capture by the Sikhs (1848/9), he became the Company's political agent in Mewar (1850–57); and was official Resident and Commander-in-Chief for the Rajputana states (1857–64), retiring with the rank of major-general and a knighthood in 1866.

Lawrence, Sir Henry Montgomery (1806–57), British soldier; born in Matara, Sri Lanka, a brother of Sir George (*above*) and Baron John (*below*). Like Sir George he completed his education at Addiscombe, joining the Bengal Artillery in 1823. He saw active service in Burma (1828), Afghanistan (1838), and against the Sikhs (1845). He was knighted in 1848, in recognition of his administrative work in the Punjab. As a colonel he was in 1856 appointed Chief Commissioner to the Governor of Oudh, where he sensed mounting grievances among the sepoys and warned London of the danger of cutting the number of British troops in India. On the outbreak of the Indian Mutiny, he was promoted brigadier-general and given command of all troops in Oudh. His skill enabled 1,000 Europeans and 800 loyal Indians to hold the Lucknow Residency against 7,000 mutineers; but in supervising the defence he was mortally wounded by a shell splinter.

Lawrence, John Laird Mair (1811–79; Baron Lawrence from 1869), Viceroy of India: born in Richmond, Yorkshire, a younger brother of Sir George and Sir Henry (see *above*). He was educated at *Haileybury and in 1830 entered the East India Company's civil service at Delhi as an assistant magistrate. His skill in handling Indian affairs, and particularly the Sikhs, led to his appointment as Chief Commissioner for the Punjab in 1853, and he received a knighthood shortly before the Mutiny. His local knowledge, advice and prompt action in 1857 secured the capture of Delhi from the mutineers after a three months' siege. From 1859 to 1862 he was in London, enlightening the officials of the newly-established India Office. He returned to India, as the third of the Viceroys, in 1864. His five-year term saw improvements in health and communications (especially railways), new irrigation projects, and a firm refusal to countenance policies likely to antagonize the Russians in central Asia. On his retirement to England he received a peerage, and spent his last years fulminating against the policies which led to the Second *Afghan War.

Lawrence, Thomas Edward (1888–1935), 'of Arabia': born at Tremadoc, North Wales; educated at Oxford School and Jesus College, Oxford, undertaking archaeological work at Carchemish in Syria and learning Arabic (1910–13). He joined the Intelligence Service in Cairo in December 1914, and served in Mesopotamia, April to May 1916. From December 1916 he encouraged the Arabs of the Hejaz to revolt, nominally under Emir Hussein (*c.* 1854–1931) but effectively under the Emir's third son, Emir Feisal (1885–1933). Colonel Lawrence master-minded raids on the Medina–Damascus railway and led the Arabs north-wards on the fringe of the main Palestinian battle front against the Turks and Germans, finally entering Damascus in October 1918. Lawrence continued to support the Arabs at the post-war Peace Conference, and for twenty months in 1921/2 he served as special Arab adviser in the *Colonial Office, when Churchill was Colonial Secretary. He accompa-nied Churchill to Egypt for the Cairo Conference of 1921, securing the throne of *Iraq for Emir Feisal and the Emirate of *Transjordan for Feisal's brother, Abdullah. Lawrence's obsessive desire for individualis-tic anonymity induced him to decline all further offers of public posts. He briefly enlisted in the Tank Corps and then, changing his name by deed poll to Shaw, served for twelve years as an aircraftsman with the RAF (including a posting to India). In 1919/20 Lawrence produced his finely-written account of the Arab Revolt, *The Seven Pillars of Wisdom*, printed privately in 1926 but not published on the open market until after his death in a motorbike accident near his home in Dorset in May 1935.

Leakey, Louis Seymour Bassett (1903–72), Kenyan anthropologist and archaeologist: born at Kabete, Kenya, into a missionary family of great courage, one member – Nigel Leakey – winning a posthumous VC with the *King's African Rifles in Ethiopia in 1941. Louis Leakey spent his childhood among the *Kikuyu people, of whom he later wrote an anthropological study. He graduated from St John's College, Cambridge and in 1936 married Mary Douglas Nicol (1913–   ), who was herself interested in the pre-history of the Dordogne. The Leakeys settled in Nairobi, where Louis was Curator of the Coryndon Memorial Museum from 1945 to 1961: at the same time both Leakeys began a quest for the early hominid fossils which they believed remained in the Rift Valley. In 1948, at Rusinga Island in Lake Victoria, Mary Leakey discovered *Proconsul africanus*, a primitive ape believed to be 1.7 million years old. The Leakeys became famous after their discovery in the Olduvai Gorge (Tanzania) of the skull of *Zinjanthropus* (1959), and of *Homo habilis* (a species some 2 million years old) in 1964. After Louis Leakey's death Mary Leakey made further discoveries, of which the most remarkable were the fossilized hominid footprints found in 1976 at Leatoli, 30 miles south of Olduvai. Their second son, Richard Leakey (1944–   ), became an eminent Kenyan palaeoanthropologist, discovering on the eastern shores of Lake Turkana crania of *Australopithecus boisei* (1969), *Homo habilis* (1972) and *Homo erectus* (1975). Richard Leakey became Director of the National Museum of Kenya in 1968. President Moi made him Director of Wildlife Services in 1989 with authority to check the ivory poaching which threatened to make Africa's elephants extinct. Much was achieved in the first year, but the hostility of officialdom forced Richard Leakey to resign in 1994 and return to his studies of mankind's origins.

Lee Kuan Yew (1923–   ), Singapore Prime Minister: born into a Straits Chinese family in Singapore; educated locally at Raffles College, and at Fitzwilliam College, Cambridge where he gained special distinctions in his final examinations for law; called to the Bar of the Middle Temple, and became an advocate in Singapore in 1951. Three years later he founded the moderate left-wing and anti-Communist People's Action Party (PAP) which in 1959 was successful in the first elections after the establishment of internal self-government. Lee led Singapore into *Malaysia when it was formed in September 1963, but subsequently negotiated Singapore's withdrawal and emergence as an independent republic (in August 1965) when he found Singapore's interests at variance with the needs of the Malaysian federation. Lee remained Prime Minister of Singapore for more than thirty years, building up the prosperity of the city and port while gaining wide respect in the Commonwealth for his moderation and probity. He stepped down from the premiership in November 1990, but remained in the cabinet of his successor, Goh Chok Tong, as Senior Minister; his son, Brigadier Lee Hsien Loong (1952–   ), became Deputy Prime Minister and held ministerial responsibility for foreign trade and defence.

Leeward Islands. The islands form a chain in the Lesser Antilles group in the Caribbean. They comprise *Antigua and *St Christopher and Nevis, the British dependencies of *Montserrat and the *British Virgin Islands, and non-Commonwealth islands such as French Guadeloupe, the US Virgin Islands, and Franco-Dutch St Martin. The Leewards were visited by Columbus in 1493 and their possession was long disputed by the British, French, Spanish and Dutch. In 1871 the present Commonwealth members, together with *Dominica, were loosely federated as the Crown Colony of the Leeward Islands, with an economy based on the export of sugar and molasses. By 1933 the Colony was hardly viable, and proposals were made for union with the *Windward Islands, but, although Dominica was detached and transferred to the Windwards in 1940, the Crown Colony as a whole survived until 1958, when the islands joined the *British West Indies Federation.

Lesotho (**formerly Basutoland**): a constitutional monarchy within the Commonwealth; capital, Maseru. Geographically Lesotho is a mountainous enclave surrounded by South Africa, almost identical in area with Belgium. The Basuto nation is basically a congeries of scattered tribes who fled both the Zulus, and then the *Boers who sought to seize Basuto territory by force in 1856. Paramount Chief Moshoeshoe I was granted British protection in 1868, but the new Protectorate was absorbed into Cape Colony in 1871. The threat of further conflict with the Boers led to a restoration of direct control from London in 1883, with executive power vested in a High Commissioner, originally resident in Pretoria. Apart from the institution of an annual council of a hundred elders in 1903, this improvised political system remained for more than seventy years. The Basuto Council refused to join the Union of South Africa in 1910 but accepted a customs union, and about half the work-force found employment in South Africa. The economy of Basutoland/Lesotho was – and is – based on simple farming, with all land owned communally by the nation, though held in trust by hereditary chiefs. No European settlement has ever been permitted. Independence, as the Kingdom of Lesotho, was attained on 4 October 1966, when the Paramount Chief became King Moshoeshoe II. Political power from 1965 until the last weeks of 1985 was exercised by Chief Leabua Jonathan; political refugees from South Africa often found sanctuary in Lesotho (where Desmond *Tutu was bishop, 1976–78). A border blockade imposed by the South African Republic early in January 1986 was followed by a military coup which overthrew the Chief Jonathan administration in favour of the first of several military councils. King Moshoeshoe II was deposed in November 1990, in favour of his son, King Letsie III. When an election was held on 27 March 1993, all 65 seats in the assembly were won by the BCP (Basotho Congress Party); their leader, Dr Ntsu Mokhele, formed a government on 2 April 1993, pledged to uphold democracy. He was, however, faced by strong opposition from the army (who twice, early in 1994, sought to seize power), and from King Letsie, who until late September 1994 refused to collaborate with the BCP. Unresolved issues echo political uncertainties across Lesotho's border.

Livingstone, David (1813–73), Scottish missionary and explorer: born at Low Blantyre, Lanarkshire; educated himself while working in a cotton mill and in 1837 enrolled as a medical student at Glasgow, later offering his services to the London Missionary Society, for whom he worked in Bechuanaland (Botswana), 1841–49. He married Mary Moffat, daughter of Robert Moffat (1795–1883), the pioneer missionary who ran the flourishing mission at Kuraman (western Botswana) from 1826 to 1870. Mary and their three young children accompanied Livingstone on his earliest journeys into the interior in 1841–43. His first major discovery was Lake Ngami, in 1849. From 1852 to 1856 he travelled from the upper Zambezi to Luanda, crossing the continent and becoming in 1855 the first white man to see (and name) the Victoria Falls. Livingstone was in Britain in 1856/7, undertaking lectures which fired widespread interest in 'opening up the dark continent'. From 1858 to 1864 he led a government-sponsored expedition into central Africa. He discovered Lake Nyasa in 1859, but during the journey (in 1862) his wife Mary died from fever at Shupanga on the banks of the Zambezi. In his final expedition (begun in 1865) he believed he was tracing the source of the Nile, although in reality he had discovered the river Lualaba which feeds the upper waters of the Congo. He suffered great privations and, though deeply shocked at the prevalence of slave caravans, needed the traders' food and medicines to get back to the base he had established at Ujiji on Lake Tanganyika, where he was 'found' by *Stanley on 10 November 1871 and given fresh supplies. However, his health gave way while he was seeking a route back southwards, and he died at Chitambo (Zambia) in May 1873. Faithful native servants carried Livingstone's embalmed body to the coast, and eleven months after his death he was buried at Westminster Abbey, proudly mourned as an epic hero of Empire.

Lomé Conventions. When Britain completed negotiations to join the EEC in 1972, the accession treaty included an offer to 20 ACP (African, Caribbean and Pacific) members of the Commonwealth to conclude special agreements with the European Community over trade and aid. A convention was subsequently signed at Lomé (Togo) on 28 February 1975 between the EEC and 46 ACP countries (almost half in the Commonwealth) for duty-free entry of agricultural products and most manufactured goods to the Common Market, and including special protocols dealing with bananas, beef and sugar. Special funds were created for low-interest loans to develop mineral extraction. 'Lomé II' (October 1979) revised and extended the scope of 'Lomé I' and provided

£3,650 millions of aid over five years to the ACP countries. Further aid was promised by 'Lomé III' (December 1984) and 'Lomé IV' (December 1989; valid for ten years).

London Declaration (27 April 1949): a statement agreed by Commonwealth prime ministers which redefined the nature of the relationship between the Crown and the 'members of the British Commonwealth of Nations'. King George VI was recognized as '*Head of the Commonwealth' (the word 'British' being dropped), and provision was made for the continued Commonwealth membership of any country choosing to become a sovereign independent republic: India, in the first instance.

Lugard, Frederick John Dealtry (1858–1945; Baron Lugard from 1928), British soldier and colonial administrator; born in Madras; educated at Rossall School and Sandhurst; commissioned into the Norfolk Regiment, for service in India, at the age of twenty and soon won awed admiration as a big-game hunter. After secondment to the military transport service he saw action in the Sudan and Burma, his courage and initiative gaining him a DSO (Distinguished Service Order) before he was thirty. From 1888 to 1892 he was in Africa, originally in command of a force sent to check slave traders from expanding their activities to Karonga (now in Malawi). In 1890 the *Imperial British East Africa Company sent him inland from Mombasa with a military column to Kampala in Uganda, where he concluded a beneficial treaty with the Kabaka of *Buganda, and also established for the IBEA a defended trading station at Dagoretti (north-west of Nairobi). He was on leave in England in 1893/4, arousing wide interest with his two-volume – and somewhat proleptic – study, *The Rise of Our East African Empire*, and influencing the government to take over the responsibilities of the IBEA and proclaim a protectorate over the future *Kenya. Between 1894 and 1906 Lugard built up British influence in West Africa, thwarting French ambitions on the Oil Rivers Protectorate (see *Nigeria*), serving as Special Commissioner for inner Nigeria and remaining from 1900 onwards as High Commissioner for Northern Nigeria, where he developed a close paternalistic relationship with local dependent rulers or tribal chiefs; in his reports to London he sounds like the model for the fictional 'Sanders of the River'. In 1897 he raised and commanded one of the finest of the *native regiments, the West Africa Frontier Force. For five years he was Governor of Hong Kong, where on his personal initiative the university was founded in 1911. He then returned to West Africa and governed Nigeria from 1912 to 1919, perfecting his system of indirect rule in which imperial responsibility was based on traditional native institutions. His long colonial experience kept him retained on the Permanent Mandates Commission of the League of Nations for fourteen years after his return from Lagos.

Luo (Jaluo)

Luo (Jaluo): the second largest ethnic group in *Kenya, often called the Kavirondo, and long reckoned physically strong. Most Luo farmed around Kisumu and north-eastern Lake Victoria Nyanza. Traditionally they have resented the dominance of their more numerous neighbours, the *Kikuyu. Luo political leaders have included the murdered progressive *Mboya and the veteran left-wing campaigner, Oginga Odinga (1911–), who set up a National Democratic Party in 1991 to challenge President *Moi.

Lusaka Declaration (1979). At the end of the *Commonwealth Heads of Government meeting in Lusaka on 8 August 1979 a formal statement was issued condemning racism, racial prejudice and discrimination within the Commonwealth. The meeting had in particular discussed peace prospects and constitutional development in the future *Zimbabwe.

Luthuli, Albert John (*c.*1898–1967), southern African political leader: born in southern Rhodesia (Zimbabwe), the son of a Zulu Christian missionary; educated at the Methodist Institution, Edenvale, Johannesburg; became a teacher and lay preacher and was elected tribal chief of the Abasemakholweni in Natal (1936). He visited India and the United States on missionary lecture tours and in 1945 joined the executive of the *African National Congress. His vigorous campaign against *apartheid from its inception caused the *Malan government to depose him from his chieftainship. He was elected president-general of ANC in 1952 but put on trial for high treason at Johannesburg in December 1956; the charges were subsequently dropped, but he was banished to a remote farm where he was kept under house arrest. Luthuli's struggle for African rights won him worldwide recognition, and his advocacy of non-violence led the Nobel Committee to award him (March 1961) the 1960 Peace Prize. The students of Glasgow University elected him Rector, even though he could not leave Natal. In *Let My People Go* (1962) he made a plea for racial moderation, rejecting both white intimidation and black militancy. In September 1967 the South African government announced that Luthuli had been killed by a freight train; the next year his memory was honoured by the bestowal of a United Nations Human Rights Prize.

Lutyens, Sir Edwin Landseer (1869–1944), English architect: born in London; studied architecture in South Kensington, going into practice in 1888 and specializing in country-house architecture, although he was also chief consultant for Hampstead Garden Suburb. In 1913 he became joint architect, with Sir Herbert *Baker, for *New Delhi. The partnership was not a happy one: Baker knew India well and had great experience of monumental building in southern Africa; Lutyens' experience was European, apart from the Rand War Memorial and Johannesburg Art Gallery (1909–11). From 1913 until its completion in 1931 Lutyens devoted his skills to the inventive magnificence of the Viceroy's House, New Delhi, the most imposing palace of the Empire. He was also the principal designer of many cemeteries and memorials for World War I, including the Cenotaph in Whitehall, the Arch of India in New Delhi, and the Somme Memorial at Thiepval.

Lyons, Joseph Aloysius (1879–1939), Australian Prime Minister: born of Irish Roman Catholic parents at Stanley in Tasmania; trained as a teacher in Hobart. From 1909 to 1929 he was a Labor member of Tasmania's House of Assembly, and state Premier from 1923 to 1928. He then moved into federal politics as Postmaster-General under *Scullin, but he was by temperament too conservative and in 1931 left Labor and helped found the United Australia Party, which won most seats in the general election at the end of the year. Lyons completed the formation of his government early in January 1932 and remained Prime Minister until he died from a heart attack on Good Friday, 1939. He steered the country carefully through the *Great Depression, helped as much by rising wool and gold prices as by the cautious deflationary measures he introduced. By July 1934 he had sensed the mounting danger from Japan, and launched a three-year defence programme to bring the army and air force up to strength. In 1915 he married Enid Burnell (1897–1981), who became the mother of eleven children; she was created DBE (Dame of the British Empire) in 1937. As a widow Dame Enid Lyons entered politics and in 1943 was the first woman elected to the federal House of Representatives, where she sat for eight years. In 1949 Dame Enid attained cabinet rank under *Menzies.

Maasai (Masai): a Nilotic people who moved southwards down the Nile from the upper Sudan in the fourteenth or fifteenth century and settled on the highlands above the Rift Valley to the east of Lake Victoria. When the first European contacts were made with them in 1883 they were notorious for their raids on caravans and for maintaining chronic warfare with their Bantu-speaking neighbours, the *Kikuyu. Their young men, the *moran*, formed a powerful warrior force. A 'treaty' between British agents and a prominent medicine man, Lenana, assuring the Maasai of their traditional grazing land, allowed the completion of the Uganda Railway, and the Maasai assisted the British in expeditions against the *Nandi; but in 1911 a second Maasai treaty made them trek southwards from the Lasikipia plateau to Narok. They fought with the British against the Germans in East Africa in World War I, and against the Italians in Ethiopia and the Japanese in Burma in World War II. The Maasai did not play so great a part in the politics of independence as the Kikuyu or the *Luo; since about 1980 they have supported President *Moi against his Kikuyu opponents. Ethnic clashes between Maasai and Kikuyu broke out once more along the Rift Valley in 1991. Kenya's

Macaulay's Education Minute

Maasai Mara National Park is a game reserve on land traditional to the Maasai peoples.

Macaulay's Education Minute. The great Whig historian Thomas Babington Macaulay (1800–59) was in India from 1834 to 1838 as one of the three members of the Governor-General's council; *Cavendish-Bentinck gave him responsibility for deciding the form of education for the peoples under British rule. In his famous 'Minute on Education' of 1835 Macaulay, who was certain that the Indians should ultimately enjoy self-government, advised that English language, literature and methods of study must serve as the basis of schooling and instruction throughout India. The aim, he insisted, should be a class of 'Indians in blood and colour, but English in taste, opinions, morals and intellect', for 'no nation can be perfectly well governed till it is competent to govern itself' – an approach which remained basic to education policies under the Raj.

Macdonald, Sir John Alexander (1815–91), first Canadian Prime Minister: born in Glasgow; taken to Canada by his parents at the age of five and settled at Kingston on Lake Ontario; became a barrister and took a vigorous part in the political life of Upper Canada from 1844 onwards. He was a firm believer in confederation, claiming it was essential in order to expand westwards and to keep in check US dominance over North America. Politically he was a Conservative, but he encouraged change, fighting hard to secure the acceptance of Ottawa as the capital in 1859. Seven years later he led the Canadian delegation which discussed confederation in London. His proposals shaped the *British North America Act of 1867. He was knighted and entrusted with forming the first government of the Dominion, remaining Prime Minister until November 1873 and returning for a second ministry from October 1878 until his death in the summer of 1891. He sought to consolidate the formal Act of Federation by drawing the elements of the Dominion closer together. Among his chief concerns were the growth of transcontinental railways, the pacification of Canada's Native Indian peoples, the containment of *Riel's insurrections, and the ending of the *Hudson Bay Company's territorial sovereignty.

MacDonald, Malcolm John (1901–81), British Colonial and Dominions Secretary and administrator: the only son of J. Ramsay MacDonald (1866–1937; Prime Minister 1924, 1929–35). After completing his education at Bedales and Oxford he was MP for Bassetlaw (1929–35) and for Ross and Cromarty (1936–45). His governmental experience was almost entirely concerned with the Commonwealth: he was Secretary of State for the Colonies in the summer of 1935 and for the Dominions from November 1935 until May 1938, when he returned to the Colonial Office until May 1940, combining the two offices for three months in the winter of 1938/9. From 1941 to 1946 he was High Commissioner in Canada. During the post-war emergencies he served as Governor-General of Singapore and Malaya (1946–48), and then as Commissioner-General for South East Asia (1948–55). After five years as High Commissioner in Delhi and two at Geneva seeking a settlement of Indo-China's problems, he served as last Governor and first High Commissioner in Kenya (1963–1965). His patience and tact induced Wilson's Labour government to retain him as Britain's roving Special Representative in east and central Africa until 1969, when he retired with the Order of Merit.

Mackenzie, Sir Alexander (?1764–1820), Scottish explorer of western Canada: born at Stornoway; joined the North-West Company as a *fur trader and founded the trading post of Fort Chippewayan on Lake Athabasca. From there he set out westwards, discovered the river which carries his name and, following it down to the sea, became in 1792/3 the first European to cross the Rockies and reach Canada's Pacific coast. He was knighted in 1802, returning to his native Scotland for the last years of his life.

Mackenzie, William Lyon (1795–1861), Canadian politician and rebel: born in Dundee; emigrated at the age of 25 and was a radically independent member of the Upper Canada legislature from 1828 to 1830 and 1834 to 1836 while also attacking privilege and social injustice in a newspaper he established, the *Colonial Advocate*. In December 1837, while the Canadian authorities were dealing with the rebellion of *Papineau around Montreal, Mackenzie attempted to seize Toronto, the city of which he had been Mayor in 1834. With a group of some 900 supporters, he was forced to take refuge on an island in the Niagara River. When Canadian militia attacked an American steamer bringing supplies to the rebels, there was a risk of extended fighting along the border. On seeking asylum in New York State, Mackenzie was arrested and imprisoned for a year. In 1848 he was pardoned in Canada, returned to Toronto and even subsequently sat in the provincial legislature for eight years. His rebellion, like Papineau's, helped to arouse interest in London in colonial conditions and thus contributed indirectly to the *Durham Report. Mackenzie was the grandfather of W. L. Mackenzie *King.

McKillop, Mary Helen (1842–1909), Australian religious: born at Fitzroy, Melbourne, of Irish descent, her father having at one time trained for the priesthood. In 1866 she became the founder-Mother of the Sisters of St Joseph of the Sacred Heart, a teaching order devoted to the poor and underprivileged in remote areas, established at Penola in South Australia. The Order spread rapidly and undertook other forms of social work. Attempts by the local priesthood to curb the Sisters' independence and social initiative met determined opposition from Mother Mary. She was accused of alcoholism and insubordination; in September 1871 Bishop Sheil of Adelaide excommunicated her and attempted to disperse the Order. Mother Mary travelled to Rome in 1873 and was reinstated by Pope Pius IX, who in 1875 confirmed her status as Superior-General of the Sisters. Despite such authoritative support, her detractors in Adelaide renewed their campaign and she removed the mother-house of the Order to Sydney. For twenty-five years she supervised the work of the Sisters of St Joseph, popularly known as the 'Little Joeys'. They concentrated on the care of orphans and support for unmarried mothers. Mother Mary suffered a stroke in May 1901 and was an invalid for the last eight years of her life. In 1926 the formal process began of seeking to establish Mother Mary as Australia's first canonized saint. She was declared Venerable in Rome in 1991, and on 19 January 1995 was beatified by Pope John Paul II at an open-air mass at Randwick racecourse during his visit to Sydney.

Macleod, Iain Norman (1913–70), British Colonial Secretary: born in Scotland; educated at Fettes College and Cambridge; after active service in France during World War II joined the Conservative Party secretariat. He was elected MP for Enfield West in 1950 and between 1952 and 1959 was successively Minister of Health and Minister of Labour. On 14 October 1959 Harold Macmillan appointed Macleod Colonial Secretary – 'the worst job of all', in the Prime Minister's words. Macleod held the post for less than two years but showed such patience and determination as to set the pattern of dignified retreat without further bloodshed during the transfer of power in former colonies, particularly in Africa. He immediately ended the State of Emergency in *Kenya, convening a constitutional conference in London and persuading African delegates to attend and, finally, ordering the release of *Kenyatta. In April 1960 he re-established constitutional government in Nyasaland (*Malawi) and ordered the release of *Banda. By October 1960 he had completed the last stages for Nigeria's independence, and went on to prepare for *Tanganyikan, *Ugandan and Kenyan independence, and for the dissolution of the Central African Federation in favour of an independent Malawi and *Zambia. His African policies provoked protests from 70 Conservative MPs and peers, and in the House of Lords on 7 March 1961 the Marquess of Salisbury attacked him as 'too clever by half'. Although outwardly Macmillan gave Macleod his support, later evidence shows that he thought the pace of change was too rapid; on 9 October he 'kicked Macleod upstairs' by making him Chairman of the Party and Leader of the House (of Commons). Macleod declined office under Macmillan's successor, Douglas-Home. He became Heath's Chancellor of the Exchequer on 19 June 1970, but died of a heart attack on 20 July.

Macquarie, Lachlan (1762–1824), colonial governor: born on Ulva in the Outer Hebrides; entered the army at fifteen and saw service in India,

America, Jamaica and Egypt. He was in command of the 73rd Regiment of Foot when he was appointed Governor of New South Wales in 1809; he took his regiment with him to Sydney, where he arrived in January 1810. Macquarie, a man of artistic taste, transformed New South Wales from a penal settlement into a colony, even though the number of convicts transported leapt dramatically during his eleven years of office. He used many of the transportees on public works projects, giving Sydney its first fine buildings and founding new townships such as Windsor and Liverpool and the more distant Bathurst. He encouraged both the exploration of the interior, especially the crossing of the *Blue Mountains, and the importation of merino sheep. His encouragement of emancipationists and his generous treatment of convicts aroused criticism, and led to his recall to England at the end of 1821. He sought to improve contacts with the aborigines, trying to train several families to become farmers and instituting an annual corroboree at Paramatta, where he went into residence in an elegant Government House.

'Mad Mullah': the name generally applied to the fanatical Muslim leader, Mohammed bin Abdulla Hassan (*c.*1870–1920), against whose capriciously tyrannical usurped authority six campaigns were launched in *British Somaliland between 1899 and 1920.

Mafeking: town in the extreme north of Cape Province, South Africa, close to the frontier with Botswana and long serving as the administrative headquarters of *Bechuanaland. At the start of the *Boer War it was a small railway town, swiftly enveloped by a Boer army led by General Cronje. From October 1899 until May 1900 the town sustained a siege of 216 days, largely through the enterprise and ingenious improvisation of Colonel *Baden-Powell, who commanded a garrison of 700 men. Although other besieged towns suffered as severely (notably Ladysmith), Mafeking captured the public imagination. Imperial pride, bruised by the 'black week' of Boer victories in December 1899, was lifted by reports of Mafeking's defiance of Cronje's troops. When confirmation of Mafeking's relief reached London on the evening of Friday, 18 May 1900, the news prompted a saturnalia of wild celebration which continued over a fine spring weekend. The rejoicing was not limited to 'the home country': in Manitoba a new town on the Canadian Northern Railway, pushing north from Winnipeg, was named Mafeking to honour the occasion.

Mahatir Report (1991): at the end of the Kuala Lumpur *Commonwealth Heads of Government meeting in 1989 the Prime Minister of Malaysia, Datuk Seri Dr Mahatir Mohammad, was invited to preside over a committee which would consider the future of the Commonwealth in the 1990s and beyond. He presented the committee's findings in a report to the Harare Commonwealth Heads of Government meeting of October 1991. The report reaffirmed the principles of the *Singapore Declaration, and emphasized the need to promote democratic government throughout the Commonwealth while preserving its character as a multiracial community. The Datuk Seri's report formed a basis for the *Harare Declaration, and its emphasis on multi-party democracy was again stressed at the Cyprus meeting two years later.

Mahdi. The title Mahdi – or Islamic Messiah – was accorded by his followers to Mohammed Ahmed bin Abdullah (1848–85), a one-time minor Egyptian government official from Dongola who turned slave trader and, in 1881, roused the people of *Sudan in a religious war against their Egyptian overlords. He drove the Egyptians out of Kordofan (eastern Sudan) and established a capital at El Obeid, where on 5 November 1883 he annihilated an army sent against him under General William Hicks (1830–83). Subsequently his Dervishes cut off Khartoum, which they seized in January 1885, killing General *Gordon in the assault on the city. The Mahdi died from typhus five months later and was succeeded as head of the 'Mahdia' by his chief lieutenant, Khalifa Abdallahi ibn Mohammed (c.1850–99). On *Kitchener's orders, the Mahdi's tomb at *Omdurman was destroyed in 1898.

Majuba Hill (Amajuba): battle lost by the British on 27 February 1881. Majuba – 'the hill of doves', in Zulu – stands in the Drakensberg Range of north-west Natal, near the *Transvaal border and overlooking the approach to Laing's Nek Pass. During the First *Boer War General Sir George Colley, advancing with 1,500 men into the Transvaal, was beaten off by the Boers at Laing's Nek in late January 1881; sending a force of fewer than 400 men over the hill in an attempt to turn the Boer defences, he was defeated by Piet Joubert. There were heavy casualties and Colley himself was killed. Like *Isandhlwana, Majuba was regarded by patriotic Victorians as a national humiliation. But Prime Minister Gladstone, who had been opposed to a war he blamed on the policies of his predecessor (*Disraeli), decided to make peace with the Boers and recognize the independence of the Transvaal. His critics argued that he thereby neglected his duty to 'avenge Majuba'.

Makarios III, Archbishop (Mikhail Christodoulos Mouskos, 1913–77), first President of Cyprus. The Mouskos family were peasant farmers from Ano Panayia, near Paphos. Their son became a monastic novice at the age of thirteen but was not ordained priest until 1946. Within two years he was elected Bishop of Kitium and in 1950 was accepted as primate (or ethnarch) of the self-governing Orthodox Church in *Cyprus, taking the name borne by his predecessor, Makarios ('Blessed'). As ethnarch he was his people's national spokesman as well as their spiritual leader. He favoured union with Greece, giving support to the *enosis* movement. The British authorities wrongly believed that he controlled the EOKA terrorists, and in March 1956 he was deported to the Seychelles for a year, then permitted in April 1957 to settle in Athens. When in December 1957 a change in British policy opened up the possibility of independence for Cyprus, Makarios modified his stance to work towards this end, becoming the new Republic's President in August 1960. He survived several attempts at assassination by EOKA extremists but was forced into a five-month exile in July 1974 by the abortive EOKA coup which, in its turn, brought Turkish troops to defend the non-Greek minority in the island. Makarios resumed the presidency in December 1974 but never recovered his primacy over the island as a whole. He died of a heart attack on 3 August 1977, shortly after returning from the Queen's Silver Jubilee *Commonwealth Heads of Government meeting in London.

Malan, Daniel François (1874–1959), South African Prime Minister: born at Riebeck West, Cape Colony; received theological training at Utrecht and gained a doctorate before returning to South Africa as a pastor of the Dutch Reformed Church, from 1905 to 1915. During World War I his intensive Afrikaaner nationalism found expression in the columns of his newspaper, *Die Burger*, and he entered Parliament in 1918, accepting office under *Hertzog from 1924 to 1933 and introducing measures to make Afrikaans an official language and seek the repatriation of Indians from South Africa. But Dr Malan thought Hertzog's policies too liberal and in 1933 set up a 'purified Nationalist Party' which opposed Hertzog and, even more intensely, the *Smuts government during World War II. In May 1948 the mistrust felt by many white voters towards Smuts's internationalism gave Malan an electoral victory, and he served as Prime Minister until his retirement from politics on 2 December 1954. In those six years he introduced the policy of 'separation' (*Apartheid) of whites and non-whites which he had advocated in his election campaign. Criticism of successive measures to intensify segregation in education, work, leisure and places of residence was met by the Suppression of Communism Act (1950), which placed on anyone charged with advocating Communism the onus of proving the accusation false. When in March 1952 the South African Supreme Court ruled that these repressive policies were unconstitutional, Malan secured the passage of further legislation to make Parliament the highest Court of South Africa. On his retirement Dr Malan was succeeded by Johannes *Strijdom.

Malaria: a killer disease caused not, as was once thought, by 'bad air', but by the prevalence of the parasite-bearing mosquito, especially in tropical or sub-tropical climates. A cure developed in Peru from cinchona tree bark, brought to Europe by Jesuits in the seventeenth century but only identified as quinine in 1820, served as a palliative for many explorers and settlers in the course of the century. It was only in the mid 1890s that the combined research of the Hong Kong parasitologists Sir Patrick Manson (1844–1922) and Sir Ronald *Ross of the Indian Health Service effectively pioneered the study of the disease. After dangerous field research in East Africa Ross confirmed that malaria was transmitted to humans from bites of the female *Anopheles* mosquito. The use of insecticides and the development of prophylactic regimes had reduced the incidence of malaria by the third quarter of the twentieth century, but more recently Commonwealth health authorities have indicated that they believe malaria to be on the increase, particularly in tropical forest and coastal zones.

Malawi, independent central African republic within the Commonwealth, formerly known as Nyasaland: capital (since 1975) Lilongwe, the previous seat of government having been Zomba. Although *Livingstone reached Lake Malawi (Nyasa) in 1859, the shores of the lake were settled only in the 1890s when the slave trade was stamped out. The Church of Scotland founded a mission centre in the Shire highlands in 1876 and named it Blantyre, after Livingstone's birthplace. The *British South Africa Company's agents developed Nyasaland's agricultural yield of cotton, groundnuts and tobacco but also brought with them a strict colour bar which aroused resentment among the Ngoni peoples, who had themselves migrated northwards to escape Boer penetration of their traditional lands. Many Malawis worked in the Rand goldfields or coal mines. In 1945 the Nyasaland African Congress was formed to campaign for self-rule, later changing its name to Malawi Congress Party. It received advice from Dr Hastings *Banda, who practised medicine in Kenya from 1953 until he returned to his homeland in July 1958. Fierce opposition to inclusion in the Rhodesian-dominated *Central African Federation exploded in riots, and on 18 February 1959 a State of Emergency was declared by the Governor, Sir Robert Armitage. In London, parliamentary criticism of Armitage's actions led to the appointment of the Devlin Commission, which reported that Nyasaland had become a 'police state'. Iain *Macleod, as Colonial Secretary, lifted the State of Emergency and restored normal colonial administration in April 1960. Self-government followed in February 1963, with Banda as Premier; independence was proclaimed on 6 July 1964 and Banda was elected President in July 1966, establishing a single-party state of which he was declared President for Life in 1971. He ruthlessly crushed all opposition groups and silenced dissenters within his own Congress Party. Malawi, unlike other newly independent states, maintained good relations with the Portuguese colonialists and with the Republic of South Africa, where Banda paid a state visit in 1971. Outside pressure, making foreign loans dependent on improved civil rights, led to a referendum in favour of parliamentary democracy in June 1993, and to democratic elections in May 1994 which rejected Banda and forced his Congress Party into parliamentary opposition to the United Democratic Front of President Bakili Muluzi. Personal freedom was restored and efforts were made to stamp out political corruption.

Malaya, Federation of. The political status of the Malay peninsula has changed confusingly during the twentieth century. The British imperial foothold was established by the East India Company and given a political form as the *Straits Settlements (*Singapore, Malacca, Penang). In 1896 a British Protectorate – the Federated Malay States – was established over Perak, Selangor, Negri Sembilan and Pahang. By treaty with Thailand (then Siam) in March 1909 a British Protectorate was also established over Kelantan, Trengganu and Kedah, while from 1915 Britain accepted responsibility for defence and external affairs for Johore, under a treaty with the ruling Sultan. Johore and the 1909 protected area formed the Unfederated Malay States. This cumbersome arrangement hampered the development of the *tin and *rubber trades and proved disastrous during the Japanese invasion of 1941–42. In January 1946 plans were announced for a Malayan Union (excluding Singapore) which was set up three months later, too rapidly to survive among peoples mistrustful of centralized administration. In January 1948 the Union was reconstituted as the Federation of Malaya, but it was immediately confronted with Communist subversion and was considered Malay-dominated by the half-million Chinese in the peninsula. The conflict with Communist guerrillas – the *Malayan Emergency – was still in progress when a ministerial system of government was introduced by the constitution of 1955. Subsequent elections were won by the Alliance Party of Tunku *Abdul Rahman Putra. Independence within the Commonwealth followed on 31 August 1957. Six years later the constitution was amended to permit union with *Sabah, *Sarawak and (briefly) Singapore, in the new Federation of *Malaysia.

Malayan Emergency. A Communist uprising began in Malaya in June 1948 when guerrilla units of the 'Malayan Races Liberation Army' launched attacks on rubber plantations, killing three European planters at Sungei Siput in central Perak. A state of emergency was proclaimed by the federal government on 18 June 1948. The rising was co-ordinated by Chin Peng (general secretary of the Malayan Communist Party since 1947) and gained considerable success in its first three years, with civilian casualties at more than 1,500 in 1950, compared with about 950 terrorists killed, wounded or captured. On 6 October 1951 the British High Commissioner, Sir Henry Gurney (1898–1951), was murdered on his way to Fraser's Hill in southern Perak. General Sir Gerald Templer

Malaysia

(1898–1979) became High Commissioner and C.-in-C. Malaya in February 1952. In two years he effectively broke Communist resistance by using helicopters and specially trained jungle warfare platoons, by moving civilians to new settlement areas which were carefully defended and policed, by supervising the sale and movement of foodstuffs in rural areas to prevent the Communists establishing a regular supply route, and by speeding up the transition to independence. The Malays themselves were not attracted by Communist propaganda after 1949, when it became clear that the movement was dominated by Chinese. By 1954, when Templer returned to London, the number of civilian killed and wounded for the year had dropped to 180. Chin Peng met the Malayan politician Tunku *Abdul Rahman in China in December 1955 to discuss peace, but made an unacceptable demand for political recognition of the Malayan Communist Party. The Emergency did not officially end until 31 July 1960, though there were few casualties in the later years. Australia, New Zealand and Fiji sent contingents to support the British and local units: *askaris* from the *King's African Rifles in 1952–53 and later from the Northern Rhodesia Regiment showed skill in jungle fighting; and several Australian Air Force squadrons were in Malaya, 1950–58.

Malaysia: an elective monarchical federation within the Commonwealth: federal capital, Kuala Lumpur. It comprises the eleven states of the Federation of *Malaya (Johore: Kedah: Kelantan: Malacca: Negri Sembilan: Pahang: Penang: Perak: Perlis: Selangor: Trengganu), *Sabah and *Sarawak. There is a strong central government but each of the thirteen states has its own ruler (by either election or succession) and much autonomy, with a constitution of its own. Religious freedom is guaranteed, although the official faith is Islam, and the rulers of peninsular Malaya are also heads of religion in their state. The federal sovereign is chosen every five years by the rulers from among themselves. The Federation was established on 16 September 1963 and until August 1965 included *Singapore: *Brunei declined an invitation to join. *'Confrontation' with Indonesia (1963–66) and strained relations with the Philippines over Filipino claims to Sabah long forced Malaysia onto the defensive, and Australia still maintains a small force of infantry and aircraft in the Federation. Chronic tension between Chinese and Malays has led to occasional race riots, most notably in May 1969. Malaysia remains the world's largest exporter of natural rubber and tin, but under a federal National Development Policy agreed in 1990 it is planned to become a highly developed industrial state by the year 2020, specializing in electronics, cars and chemicals as well as the traditional clothing and textile industries.

Maldives: an independent Commonwealth republic in the southern Indian Ocean: capital Male. The archipelago of some 2,000 palm-covered coral islands – only 200 of them inhabited – was taken under British protection in 1887 and administered from Ceylon, 400 miles to the northeast, until 1948 when it was accorded self-government. Independence followed in July 1965. The republic was given special status in the Commonwealth in 1982, and admitted as a full member in 1985. The population is Muslim and depends for a livelihood on fishing, on the export of coconut products, and on tourism. The southernmost island, Addu Atoll – more than 250 miles from Male – was developed as a little-known naval base by the British Eastern Fleet in 1942/3, when Japanese attacks on Ceylon threatened the anchorage at Trincomalee; not until 1976 was the air base of Gan on Addu Atoll handed over to the republic.

Malta: independent republic within the Commonwealth; an island 58 miles south of Sicily and 180 miles north of Libya: capital, Valletta. Malta was successively Phoenician, Carthaginian, Roman and, from 870 to 1090, Arab. It was then ruled for 440 years by Norman-Sicilian dynasties, but became the home of the Knights of St John of Jerusalem in 1530, defying capture until treacherously surrendered to Bonaparte in 1798. The Maltese people sought British protection in 1802 in return for a guarantee of their civil and religious (Roman Catholic) rights. The island was formally annexed in 1814, the size and depth of the Grand Harbour making it the natural home of the Mediterranean Fleet from 1814 until 1979. The island was granted a legislature in 1921 but the administration was often in conflict with the Church authorities: on three occasions the assembly's rights were suspended. The Italians and Germans bombed Malta repeatedly between 1940 and 1943 and the population faced severe food shortages; nearly 40,000 houses, churches and public buildings were destroyed, and more than 1,500 civilians were killed (a figure which represents twice as high a proportion of the population as in the London 'blitz'). In admiration of his Maltese people's loyalty and courage King George VI awarded the George Cross to Malta on 16 April 1942. Internal self-government came in 1947. Mounting unemployment following defence cuts led to a referendum in February 1956 in which three-quarters of the Maltese people voted for integration within the United Kingdom, though with Malta retaining an assembly as well as sending MPs to Westminster. The British government proposed a five-year experiment on these lines but the offer was rejected by the Maltese, piqued by London's hesitancy. Mounting unemployment, exacerbated by privatization of the naval dockyard, provoked riots in the spring of 1958, which were followed by twelve months' direct rule by the island's Governor. An interim constitution in 1961 enabled talks to begin on independence, which was granted on 21 September 1964. Dom Mintoff (1916–   ), the former Rhodes scholar who led Malta's Labour governments from 1971 to 1994, favoured increasing neutrality, away from NATO commitments. Malta's request to join the European Community in 1990 was finally rejected in June 1993, principally because of the island republic's small size. Grapes form the island's chief export but the economy is increasingly dependent on tourism; the Maltese government is also developing Valletta's dry-dock facilities and new container ports.

Managing Agency Houses. When the *East India Company's trade monopoly was curtailed in 1813 some employees in India went into private partnership, forming their own mercantile houses to handle imports and exports. As early as 1820 there were twenty of these agencies in the main Indian ports. Though many ran into difficulties within a few years, at least one – Gillanders Arbuthnot, set up in Calcutta in 1819 – continued to attract British investors until 1988. The Managing Agency Houses multiplied after 1833/4, particularly in Calcutta, Bombay and Canton (see *Hongs*), when the EIC finally stopped its commercial dealings. In India the agencies specialized in indigo (1830s–50s), jute and, from about 1851, acted as brokers for the growing *tea industry. Over the period 1860 to 1930 the Managing Agency companies of Calcutta alone gave backing to more than 4,000 tea plantations. Several agencies had shipping interests, too: Mackinnon Mackenzie, founded as a general agency in Calcutta in 1847, began chartering ships in 1851, and five years later set up the company which was to become British India Steam Navigation, a great shipping line which merged with *P & O in 1914. Some had links with other trading concerns in the East: thus Jardine Skinner, founded in Calcutta in 1844, had close ties with *Jardine Matheson of Hong Kong. Later the agencies supported railway construction, especially in the 1880s. The Managing Agencies shaped India's economy under the Raj, enabling the companies they supported to develop local manufacturing industries earlier than elsewhere in Asia. But the hold of the Managing Agencies on the economy began to alarm the government in India during the *Great Depression, and in 1936 a Companies Act placed restrictions on agency interventions in the managed companies. After 1956 the influence of Nehru's preference for a state-controlled economy caused curbs to be imposed on merchant agency capitalism, despite a rapid 'Indianization' of management. In 1970 the system was finally abolished.

Mandates. After World War I, defeated Germany's former colonies and many of the non-Turkish areas of the Ottoman Empire were ceded to the victorious allies under a system of mandated responsibility, monitored by the League of Nations. These mandates fell into three categories. In Class A were lands whose independence was provisionally recognized but which were to be protected by specified Great Powers until the League was convinced they could stand alone: Britain's Class A mandates were *Iraq, *Palestine, *Transjordan. In Class B were territories for which the mandatory Power undertook to promote the welfare of the people and administer them with the prospect of eventual self-government: Britain's Class B mandates were *Tanganyika, British Cameroons (see *Southern Cameroons*), *Togoland. Class C mandates were 'to be administered by the mandatory as integral parts of its territories, subject to safeguards in the interests of the indigenous population': among Commonwealth Class C mandates were several Pacific islands which passed to *Australia and *New Zealand (including *Nauru and *Western Samoa), German New Guinea (Australian mandate, developed as *Papua New Guinea) and, most contentiously, German South West Africa, which passed under South African control, and from 1971 onwards had to fight for its independence as *Namibia. The League mandates still operative in 1946 became the responsibility of the Trusteeship Council of the United Nations. South Africa's refusal to acknowledge this change of management was in 1971 condemned as illegal by the International Court of Justice at The Hague.

Mandela, Nelson Rolihlahla (1918–   ), State President of South Africa: born in the Transkei; studied and practised law in Johannesburg, joining the *African National Congress in 1944 and its executive in 1952. During the early years of *apartheid he campaigned on behalf of a free, multiracial democracy, calling a three-day general strike in 1961 to concentrate world attention on the evil of Afrikaaner nationalist government. He evaded arrest for a year but was jailed in November 1962. While in prison he was charged under the Suppression of Communism Act. His trial lasted from October 1963 to June 1964, and in the course of it he delivered a four-hour defence speech of dignity and vision. Sentenced to life imprisonment, he remained incarcerated in a maximum security island prison for 27 years, until August 1988. Worldwide protests at Mandela's continued detention, and the realization that he alone could moderate the violence of extremism, induced President de *Klerk to order his release on 11 February 1990. After the suspension of the apartheid laws Mandela began a series of talks with de Klerk, and in January 1991 met Chief Buthelezi – leader of the predominantly *Zulu Inkatha Freedom Party – in an abortive attempt to end the violence between rival African factions, exploited by their enemies. Mandela continued his attempts to keep the peace throughout the year. In December 1993 Mandela and de Klerk shared the award of a Nobel Peace Prize. After the ANC's victory in the multiracial elections of April 1994, parliament elected Mandela as State President. He took office on 10 May 1994.

Manitoba: easternmost of Canada's prairie provinces, with its capital at Winnipeg. The Treaty of Paris of 1763 confirmed British rights to the territory, which was administered by the Hudson's Bay Company until a small area around Winnipeg itself was transferred to the new Dominion in July 1870, a 'postage stamp'-sized province created in part as a response to the pleas of *métis communities after the *Red River rebellion. The boundaries of the province were considerably extended west and north in 1881, but did not finally reach Hudson Bay until 1912. Winnipeg grew rapidly as a railway town and attracted many immigrants; Ukrainian and Polish settlements were established in the Manitoba prairie lands. The province remains an important wheat producer, although less than 15 per cent of the land area is farmed; more than half of Manitoba is wooded.

Manley family, Jamaican politicians, from Kingston. Norman Washington Manley (1893–1989) was a much-respected barrister who in 1938 successfully defended his cousin and political opponent, *Bustamente, against charges of sedition. Manley founded the People's National Party in 1938, became Prime Minister in 1955, and strongly supported the *British West Indies Federation. Its collapse in 1962 threw him into political opposition. In 1969 he handed over leadership of the People's National Party to his son, Michael Norman Manley (1923–   ), an active trade unionist from 1952 onwards. As Prime Minister from 1972 to 1980, Michael Manley followed a more radically socialist policy than had his father, showing greater independence of American influence. Rising unemployment cost him the election of 1980 and he failed again in the 1983 election. He remained leader of the parliamentary opposition, during which time he wrote and published a *History of West Indies Cricket* (1988). On returning to power in 1989 he followed more moderate policies, but in March 1993 the electorate again rejected him.

Maori people. The ancestors of the Maori of today were Polynesians who seem to have settled in what is now New Zealand as early as the ninth century AD and had established a flourishing culture by the thirteenth century. When *Cook visited the islands in 1769 the Maori population was probably in excess of 150,000. Cook had occasional armed clashes with Maoris but found many of their chiefs warily friendly; he reported favourably on the quality of flax and timber purchased from them, although it was through whalers and sealers that the Maoris became best known to Europeans. By 1806 regular contacts had been established between traders from New South Wales and the peoples of North Island. *Marsden thought the character and skills of the Maoris whom he met in Sydney far superior to those of Australia's aborigines; hence his missionary desire to convert them to Christianity. The Treaty of *Waitangi (1840) offered its Maori signatories some protection from fraudulent land purchasers, but its interpretation of *land rights was too imprecise to preserve the original economic collaboration between Maoris and *pakeha. The land hunger of the settlers provoked the first of the so-called *Maori Wars (1845/6), which continued intermittently in North

Island for a quarter of a century. War, land-alienation, the transmission of European diseases and the migration of Maoris from high land to the plains, where the customary hygienic safeguards of Maori society proved inoperative, were all causes of a rapid decline in Maori numbers. This was shown by a shorter expectancy of life and a falling birth-rate: by 1896 there were fewer than 45,000 Maoris. Four separate Maori parliamentary constituencies were created in 1867 in an effort to end the armed conflicts between the peoples, and the emergence of Sir James *Carroll to champion Maori rights from 1887 onwards marked the spread of greater multi racial tolerance. (Sir) Maui Pomare (1876–1930), a chief's son, became Minister of Health in 1923, the first Maori to hold an important government office. At the same time the land reformer (Sir) Apirana Ngata (1874–1950) was leading his Young Maori Party in a demand for state subsidies to enable Maori farmers to purchase land. Ngata was Minister for Maori Affairs from 1928 to 1934, steering through a Native Land Settlement Act in 1929 and personally working out the details of land development schemes. Maori standing in the community was enhanced by service abroad, as volunteers, in the two world wars: of 2,227 Maoris who fought in Gallipoli or on the Western Front between 1915 and 1918, almost half became casualties – 336 dead, 734 severely wounded; and in World War II Lieutenant Moana-nui-a-Kiwa Ngarimu was awarded a posthumous Victoria Cross, while the 28th (Maori) Battalion won distinction in Crete, at Alamein and at Cassino. Improved hygiene, food and housing conditions in both islands led Maori numbers to rise again: 82,326 (1936 census); 137,326 (1956 census); 227,000 in the 1971 estimate; and 450,000 (or slightly more than one in eight of the total population) in the 1993 estimate. By then the assignment of only 4 Maori seats out of 103 in the House of Representatives seemed outdated; the mixed-member proportional representation system favoured by New Zealand's 1992 referendum should increase the Maori voice in political affairs.

Maori Wars ('Land Wars'). Resentment by the *Maori people of settler infringement of their land rights and apparent breaches of the *Waitangi Treaty led to Anglo-Maori conflict in five campaigns between 1845 and 1872. The first serious fighting was at Kororareka (Russell) in North Island in 1845, spreading down to Wellington province in 1846 and, more extensively in 1847, across Taranaki province. Tension mounted again, over land acquisition, throughout the late 1850s and there were clashes in Taranaki and Waitara in 1860/1. The unrest was intensified by the impact of *hauhau religious fervour. The authorities were so alarmed that they sent for reinforcements from Britain and raised four regiments in Australia to put down resistance in the Waikaoto region. There were no pitched battles, for the Maori were too shrewd to be drawn into a confrontation in which they would suffer from inferior weaponry and shortage of numbers. The wars were therefore indecisive; in London both the *Colonial Office and the War Office deplored the cost of sustaining a long campaign; in Wellington and Auckland the colonists complained that, while the economy of peaceful South Island flourished, the sterile conflict in North Island was hampering the development of sheep farming. Wiser policies prevailed in Parliament at Wellington, particularly over the activities of the land courts, and a scheme to encourage military colonization by Australians was abandoned.

Marathas, a Hindu people of western India. They live now mainly in the republic's Maharashtra state, inland from Bombay as far as Nagpur – which in 1743 became the Maratha capital. The Marathas emerged as a powerful fighting force under Sivaji (1627–80); by 1700 they had dented Moghul imperial power, gradually building up a confederacy which stretched across the peninsula to Bengal. Though defeated by the Afghans at Panipat in January 1761, they remained a formidable force in opposing the British and their allies. Three designated 'Maratha Wars' were fought: from 1775 to 1782; in 1803; and in 1818. Yet in reality the wars continued intermittently while Maratha power was gradually eroded, mainly by the skill of Governors-General *Wellesley and the Marquess of Hastings (in India, 1813–22) in detaching individual rulers from the confederacy. Their power was finally broken in 1818 when Poona fell. Sagpur was not annexed until 1848, Nagpur itself not until 1853.

Maritime Provinces: collectively, the Canadian provinces of *New Brunswick, *Nova Scotia and *Prince Edward Island along the Atlantic seaboard, first sighted by the Bristol seafarer, John Cabot, in 1497. The region formed the French colony of Acadia, ceded to Britain by the Treaty of Utrecht (1713), although France retained the fortress of Louisbourg on Cape Breton Island (Île Royale) until 1758. The French settlers were deported during the 1750s but returned after the Seven Years' War. There was an influx of New Englanders and, later, of Loyalist refugees from the lost American colonies. By 1784 the 'Maritimes' had developed provincial characteristics of their own, but on 1 September 1864 five delegates from each met at Charlottetown (Prince Edward Island) to discuss federal union between the three provinces. They were joined by a visiting delegation of eight politicians from Upper and Lower Canada who persuaded them, early in October, to adjourn to Quebec City for the first truly confederal conference, which in turn led to the creation of the new Dominion of Canada.

Marsden, Samuel (1764–1838), chaplain and pioneer pastoralist: a controversial figure in antipodean history. He was born the son of the blacksmith at Farsley in Yorkshire and received financial aid from an evangelical society to go to Magdalene College, Cambridge. A sense of vocation prompted Marsden in 1793 to travel out to Australia, where he was both a chaplain to convicts and a very severe magistrate. From 1797 onwards Marsden encouraged large-scale sheep-farming. After fourteen years in New South Wales he returned to England as senior chaplain in the colony, taking with him the first bale of Australian wool; he was received in audience by King George III. On returning to Sydney, Marsden met Maoris brought over from New Zealand: he thought them 'far advanced in civilization' and 'prepared to receive the knowledge of Christianity'. In November 1814, with three missionaries, he accompanied two Maoris back to North Island and at Ramgihoua on Christmas Day preached the first sermon in New Zealand, leaving missionary settlements which he visited on six other occasions. A stained-glass window in St Andrew's Cathedral, Sydney, designed in 1936, shows Marsden as a saintly apostle to Maori warriors, who kneel at his feet. But popular legend also remembers him as 'flogging Sam', a disciplinarian whose harsh treatment of Irish Catholic convicts aroused protests and condemnation from Governor *Macquarie.

Masai: ethnic group in Kenya: see *Maasai*

Mashonaland: the plateau which forms the north-eastern region of *Zimbabwe, including Harare. The Mashona were a Bantu-speaking people. From 1889 to 1923 Mashonaland was administered by the British South Africa Company; it then became the most highly-developed region of *Southern Rhodesia. It is now divided to form three of Zimbabwe's nine provinces: Mashonaland Central, East, and West.

Masire, Quett Ketumile Joni (1925–   ), President of Botswana: a member of the Bangwaketse people; became a journalist and entered politics through his tribal council in the first instance, then joined the Bechuanaland Legislative Council when it was set up in 1961. A year later he helped Sir Seretse *Khama found the multiracial Botswana Democratic Party, becoming Deputy Prime Minister in 1965 and Vice-President during the first fourteen years of independence. When President Seretse Khana died in July 1980, Masire was elected as his successor; he was re-elected in 1984, 1989 and 1994. Masire's moderate statesmanship and careful continuance of his predecessor's policies of cautious non-alignment have given Botswana stability.

Massey, (Charles) Vincent (1887–1967), Canadian Governor-General: born in Toronto; his grandfather, Daniel, pioneered the making of reapers and binders for the prairies (and later members of the family have won distinction on stage and screen). Vincent Massey completed his education at Balliol College, Oxford. He enlisted in World War I, rising to lieutenant-colonel by 1918. After some years in the family business (Massey-Harris Corporation), he set up the Massey Foundation for encouraging the arts in Canada. From 1926 to 1930 he was Canada's first diplomatic representative in Washington, DC at minister level. He returned to diplomacy in 1935, when he went to London as High Commissioner. His eleven years in England were of great value to the Commonwealth, not least because of his skill in maintaining good relations between such disparate characters as *Churchill and Mackenzie *King. On his return to Canada he chaired a Royal Commission on the arts in the dominion; and on 28 February 1952 he took office as Canada's first native Governor-General, retiring in September 1959.

Massey, William Ferguson (1856–1925), New Zealand Prime Minister: an Ulsterman by birth, who emigrated to North Island at the age of fourteen and became a dairy farmer; he retained some narrowly Protestant prejudices from his boyhood. Massey sat in the New Zealand Parliament from 1894 until his death, virtually founding the Reform Party, a conservative body which represented the interests of the agrarian community. After leading the parliamentary opposition for seven years Massey took office as Prime Minister in July 1912. Although he never had a comfortable majority in the House of Representatives until after the election of December 1919, Massey headed the government for 12 years and 10 months, a longer span than any other New Zealander. He was a man of limited vision, converting Crown leaseholds into freehold land, rigorously checking the growth of trade unionism, pleasing his small-farmer supporters by bulk selling of meat during the war years, and always staunchly upholding free enterprise. The first months of the Massey government brought New Zealand to the edge of a protracted class war, with special units – 'Massey's Cossacks' – recruited from the farming community to smash strikes in the Waihi goldfields and on the Wellington waterfront. Although he backed New Zealand's participation in World War I and welcomed Lloyd George's *Imperial War Conference, he was at heart an isolationist, disliking the League of Nations and mistrusting the system of *mandates. He died in office.

Matabeleland: now forms two provinces in Zimbabwe, with the provincial centre at Bulawayo. During the *scramble for Africa Matabeleland was the home of the *Ndebele people, whose king, Lobengula (c.1833–94), conceded to *Rhodes's agents in 1888 a right to develop the country's mineral resources, then unsuccessfully rose against the British South Africa Company's exploitation in 1893. Matabeleland was incorporated in *Southern Rhodesia in 1923.

Mau Mau: developed from 1948 onwards in *Kenya as an underground movement among the *Kikuyu, seeking the recovery of land they considered theirs by right, and the expulsion of the non-African peoples. The movement started in the reserves but spread to Kikuyu squatters on planters' farms. Although Mau Mau was banned in August 1950 it continued to attract support, especially from the young. By 1952 Kikuyu initiates to Mau Mau were reverting to witch-doctor rituals, with oath-taking commitments to kill or be killed; loyal Christian Kikuyu, rejecting such pagan barbarities, became martyrs for their faith. In the third quarter of 1952 more than sixty Kikuyu were murdered for refusing to join Mau Mau. The killing of European farmers and coffee planters began in the first week of October 1952: a State of Emergency was declared on 20 October, and Kikuyu political leaders, including Jomo *Kenyatta, were arrested. A massacre of 97 Africans in the Rift Valley village of Lari on 26 March 1953 turned many Kikuyu against the movement, but Mau Mau gangs found shelter in heavily forested regions. By the end of 1955 methodical combing by army patrols plus local forces and police, supported by helicopters, together with government measures to hasten land reform, had cut numbers down to a hard core of some 1,500 Mau Mau. Their leader, Dedan Kimathi, was captured by Kikuyu police on 21 October 1956; military operations ended a month later, but the State of Emergency was not lifted until February 1960. During the rebellion more than 1,800 Africans and 68 Europeans were murdered, and 166 members of the security forces and some 11,000 Mau Mau were killed.

Mauritius: a volcanic island in the Indian Ocean, forming an independent republic within the Commonwealth: capital, Port Louis. Although discovered by the Portuguese in 1511 it was settled in the seventeenth century by the Dutch, who named it in honour of Prince Maurice of Nassau. The French acquired the island in 1715, holding it until Martinique was seized by the Royal Navy in July 1810; it passed under British sovereignty in 1814 by the terms of Treaty of Paris. It became a Crown Colony and a naval base during the nineteenth century, with dependencies as far distant as Diego Garcia, an atoll 1,200 miles to the north east. The economy of Mauritius was based on sugar production, under French rule with slaves brought from Madagascar or East Africa and under British rule using indentured Indian labour. The island acquired, and retains, a population of mixed descent: in 1992, 52.6 per cent of Mauritians were Hindus from the Indian subcontinent in origin; 28.3 per cent were of African origin; 16.55 per cent were Muslims from Asia; 2.6 per cent were of European descent, mainly French. The even tenor of colonial administration was disturbed in November 1965 by Britain's decision to cut the link with Diego Garcia, which became part of the *British Indian Ocean Territory. Resentment intensified in Mauritius when the Creole population of the atoll was deported, and Diego Garcia itself was leased to the United States as an Indian Ocean naval anchorage.

Mauritius was given independence on 12 March 1968 and for fourteen years was controlled by the moderate Mauritian Labour Party, under Sir Seewoosagur Ramgoolam (1900–85). In the 1982 election, on a wave of anti-American sentiment, all elective seats in the National Assembly were won by a left-wing militant front, led by (Sir) Anerood Jugnauth, QC (1930–   ), who successfully campaigned to make Mauritius a republic in March 1992. He remains Prime Minister. Tourism has increased rapidly: most visitors come from France.

Mboya, Tom (1930–69), Kenyan politician: born, a *Luo, on a sisal estate; educated at Roman Catholic schools in Kenya and at Ruskin College, Oxford. On returning home he became a trade union organizer and was invited to join *Kenyatta in the delegation which went to London in 1960 for the *Lancaster House constitutional conference. He was much respected for his moderation and far-sightedness. After independence, he served successively as Minister of Labour, Minister of Justice, and Minister of Economic Planning. It was expected that he would succeed Kenyatta as President, but on 5 July 1969 he was shot dead in central Nairobi; a member of the Kikuyu was tried for the murder and hanged. Mboya's death nearly plunged Kenya into civil war and there were angry anti-Kenyatta demonstrations by Luos, especially at Kisumu.

Meerut: town about 35 miles north-east of Delhi; established as a military cantonment by the East India Company's Bengal Army in 1806. Early in May 1857, sepoys of the Bengal Army were issued with new cartridges which, as part of the loading drill, the soldiers were required to bite: the bullets were greased with pig fat and cow fat – the pig abhorrent to Muslims, the cow sacred to Hindus. When the sepoys refused to bite the bullets they were punished and humiliated. Resentment at their treatment exploded on 10 May 1857 when four regiments (one cavalry, three infantry) rebelled, wrecking the cantonment and killing several British officers. The *Indian Mutiny spread throughout the region of Bengal from which the army had recruited most of its sepoys. Meerut is now a manufacturing town – oilseed mills, cotton goods, soap – in Uttar Pradesh.

Melba, Dame Nellie (Helen Porter; 1861–1931), operatic soprano: born, educated and trained as a singer at Melbourne. In 1886, four years after contracting an unhappy marriage to a Queensland sugar plantation manager, she left Australia for Europe. The clarity of her voice attracted attention in France and she made her operatic début in *Rigoletto* at Brussels in 1887, having adopted a stage name to honour her birthplace. She first appeared at Covent Garden in 1888, causing a sensation by the even level kept by her voice through two and a half octaves. She continued to make world tours until 1926. In 1902 she returned to Australia for the

first time, to be idolized in Melbourne and criticized in a Sydney newspaper for 'vicious vulgarity' and 'bourgeois bumptiousness'. Melba,
created Dame of the British Empire in 1918, gave her final concert in
Australia ten years later, at the age of 67. Her international fame in the
years before World War I testified to Australia's attainment of cultural
maturity.

Melbourne Centennial Exhibition (1888). To mark the centenary of
the first settlement in Australia and assert Melbourne's claim to pre-
eminence as the first city, the colonial government of Victoria set aside
£25,000 for a centennial exhibition to be held in a 'crystal palace' (which
had already housed an international exhibition in 1880). The event
attracted support from 93 different countries, with far more emphasis on
music and painting than in any previous Australian exhibition. Ultimately
the cost to the colonial government was ten times as much as the original
meagre budget had foreseen, but more than two million people visited the
Centennial Exhibition, emphasizing Melbourne's cultural affinity with
the metropolitan centres of Europe and America's eastern seaboard.

Memsahib: the wife of a sahib, a master or senior person, military or
civilian, in India. From 1840 onwards a memsahib would be expected to
follow a socially-binding code of conduct, requiring the approval of the
Burra Memsahib, the most eminent lady in the society or community of
which the memsahib was a member.

Menzies, Sir Robert Gordon (1894–1978), Australian Prime Minister:
born, a storekeeper's son, at Jepparit, Victoria; educated at Melbourne
University. While practising as a barrister in Victoria he was elected to the
state legislature (1928), entering Parliament in Canberra in 1934 as
United Australia Party member for Kooyong. *Lyons brought him into
the government as Attorney-General in 1935. He aroused lasting hostility
among trade unionists for a heavy-handed resort to law to break strikes,
even those by dockers refusing to load pig-iron for Japan. Menzies
resigned on 20 March 1939, angered by Lyons' failure to back a national
insurance scheme which he favoured. Less than three weeks later Lyons
suffered a fatal heart attack and, though many leading UAP members
resented Menzies' behaviour, he won a bitter contest for party leadership
and became Prime Minister on 26 April. The impact of World War II
absorbed his energies: he reintroduced conscription in Australia and
backed the sending of two Australian divisions to the Middle East, early
in 1940. On 28 October 1940 he established an Advisory War Council,
which included the veteran *Hughes. Soon afterwards he set out for
England and was present at several of Churchill's cabinet meetings in the
spring of 1941. Menzies favoured the setting up of an Imperial War
Cabinet, but could not get support from Churchill himself, *Smuts,

Métis

Mackenzie *King, or most of his Canberra colleagues. When he tried to form a national coalition in August 1941 *Curtin, as Labor leader, refused to serve under him; Menzies resigned on 28 August. After a few weeks as co-ordinating defence minister he moved into Opposition, founding a new Australian Liberal Party which built up its strength on anti-Communism and anti-unionism, prejudices which enabled the Liberals to win the 1949 election. Menzies was again Prime Minister from 19 December 1949 until January 1966, a record sixteen years of continuous office. He supported US policy in the Korean War, backed *ANZUS and *SEATO and anti-Communist measures in *Malaysia, and in April 1965 sent the first Australian battalion into *Vietnam. As an elder statesman, respected throughout the Commonwealth, he was invited to preside over the Five Nations Committee of 1956 which vainly sought agreement with Nasser over the *Suez Canal. At home, Menzies' obsession with 'red subversion' made him seek, unsuccessfully, to outlaw the Australian Communist Party, thus perpetuating class bitterness in political life. Yet, in general, the 'Menzies Years' were prosperous: he encouraged the rapid spread of university education, and general improvements in secondary education. He took pride in shaping *Canberra as the federal capital and in welcoming Queen Elizabeth II on her first visit to Australia. Though never doubting that traditional cricket was the finest of sports, he was glad to bring the Olympic Games to Melbourne in 1956. He was created a Knight of the Thistle in 1963, emphasizing his Scottish family connections, and two years later succeeded Churchill as Lord Warden of the Cinque Ports, an honour never before held by a non-resident of the British Isles.

Métis: a Canadian of mixed descent, part-French and part-Indian; the term originated among early French colonists. With the collapse of the French fur trading companies, many métis took service with the *Hudson's Bay Company, though many more – probably the majority – remained 'freemen', especially skilled as bison hunters. While the Company recognized the existence of a métis way of life in its toleration of the founding of the Red River settlement in 1812, half a century later the newly created Dominion government was less understanding. The province of *Manitoba, which was founded after the *Red River rebellion, fell short of the métis' hopes for political recognition, and the Dominion's purchase of Rupert's Land from the Company in 1869 threatened the incursion into métis lands of new-style Canadian settlers, following the route of the transcontinental railway. These fears made the métis back Louis *Riel and precipitated bitter conflicts in 1869–70 and again in 1885. The transformation of Manitoba after the coming of the railways swamped most traces of métis life in the province, except in remote areas of the north. Probably as many as 100,000 métis survive in Canada, mainly in the *Northwest Territories, but they have not received the attention accorded to the *Eskimos (Inuit) or to the North American Indian communities.

Military Service. The concept of compulsory military service dates from French practice during the Revolutionary era. But, though most continental countries accepted conscription during the nineteenth century, it was long regarded with abhorrence in the United Kingdom and the Empire. Voluntary enlistment brought contingents from Australia, Canada and New Zealand to fight against the Boers in 1899–1900, but as early as 1903 the Federal Parliament in Melbourne passed a Defence Act which provided for conscription for service within Australia, should the nation be at war. A second Defence Act (1909) introduced the practice of peacetime conscription: part-time compulsory military training for boys and men between the ages of 12 and 25 began in 1911 throughout Australia and survived until 1929, although after the end of World War I the training programme was much reduced. In the United Kingdom the first National Service Act became law in February 1916, with conscription retained until April 1920 (although Ireland was always exempted). Attempts by *Hughes to introduce a similar measure in Australia failed, despite a referendum in October 1916 (with a small majority against) and a second referendum in December 1917 (when the 'No' vote was much larger). The New Zealand Parliament introduced conscription in August 1916, although there was fierce opposition to the measure, including two well-publicized Anti-Conscription Conferences. Canada passed a Compulsory Military Service Act in September 1917, but its enforcement in the following spring led to five days of riot in Quebec, in which four people died. The experience of World War I made governments reluctant to impose compulsory service again in the mounting crises of the late 1930s. Eventually, in Great Britain, the National Service Act of April 1939 allowed conscription of men aged 20 to 21; the age limit was extended on the outbreak of war, and included single women from December 1941; male conscription was retained in Britain until 1960. *Menzies restored National Service within Australia in 1939; in 1943 *Curtin committed Australians to compulsory service overseas for the first time, though only in the 'South-Western Pacific Zone'. New Zealand returned to conscription in June 1940. In Canada Mackenzie *King, who depended politically on support from Quebec Province, delayed compulsion until April 1942: even so, there were again protests and evasion from Quebec, and Canada swiftly reverted to voluntary enlistment with the return of peace. So, too, did Australia and New Zealand; but not for long. Full time compulsory military training returned in New Zealand in 1949 and Australia in 1951, where it was modified in 1957 and scrapped in 1959. Most controversially, Menzies yet again introduced a National Service measure in 1965: a proportion of 20 year old Australians were to be chosen by ballot for two years' service in the army, anywhere in the world. This ballot drafting system lasted until 1972, calling up 64,000 men for army enlistment, almost a quarter of whom went to *Vietnam. Military service in the Union of South Africa was based upon the South Africa Defence Act of June 1912 (amended in 1922), which imposed an obligation on all males 'of European origin' to be trained to use a rifle, either in the army or navy reserves or in rifle associations. Any white male between 17 and 60 might be called up for service in time of war; this system was extended into full white conscription during the apartheid era. With the advent of multiracial democracy in South Africa, white conscription began to be phased out in favour of voluntary, professional enlistment, irrespective of colour. Elsewhere in the historic Empire, military service was voluntary. Since gaining independence, several Commonwealth countries have resorted to conscription, generally for brief emergencies, though Singapore has maintained compulsory military service since 1967. Some other Commonwealth countries – Ghana and Tanzania among them – rely on a people's militia to augment the regular army.

Milner, Viscount (Alfred; 1854–1925), British imperial statesman: born in Giessen, Hesse-Darmstadt; spent his boyhood in Germany before completing his education (with brilliant academic achievements) at Balliol College, Oxford. He was a Classics don, a barrister and a political journalist, as well as undertaking voluntary philanthropic work in London's East End. From 1884 to 1889 he was principal political adviser and secretary to G. J. Goschen (1831–1907; Chancellor of the Exchequer, 1886–92). Milner then spent three years in Egypt, helping *Cromer put the country's finances on a sound footing. After five years as Chairman of the Board of Inland Revenue in London, he was sent out to Cape Town by *Chamberlain in 1897 as High Commissioner in South Africa, a post he held for eight years. Milner sought to work with both the mercurial *Rhodes and the highly suspicious *Kruger. By the close of 1898 he had decided that Kruger would either have to reform the Transvaal government or be overthrown by war. His lack of patience with Kruger tempted the Boers to strike first militarily, before reinforcements could reach Cape Colony. By 1900 Milner was immersed in problems of post-war reconstruction and was appointed Governor of the Transvaal and the Orange Free State in addition to his existing responsibilities. He received a peerage in 1901 and, with *Kitchener, signed the peace treaty of *Vereeniging. He worked for reconciliation, yet he never won the confidence of the Boers and he alienated Liberal sympathies at home by encouraging the migration of *Chinese labourers to the Rand. Although only in his early fifties on his return to England, he was regarded as an elder statesman, to be consulted on imperial matters. He joined Lloyd George's inner War Cabinet in December 1916, took part in some of the most vital military conferences of World War I, and went to Russia in

February 1917 to encourage the Provisional Government to prosecute the war vigorously. Briefly he was War Secretary in 1918, finishing his public career as Colonial Secretary (1919–21), travelling to Egypt to help settle the new political relationship between Cairo and London. He disliked the reshaping of Europe at the Peace Conference. His conviction of the need for an effective imperial council in London and his certainty that the colonies should be prepared for self-government by education on the classical English model influenced the approach of 'Milner's kindergarten', men who had served him with respect and admiration – for the most part in South Africa – and who themselves became influential servants of Empire. Among them were L. S. *Amery, John *Buchan and Lionel *Curtis.

Missionaries (see also *Christianity in the Commonwealth*). The earliest Anglican missions abroad were sent by the Society for the Promotion of Christian Knowledge (SPCK, founded 1698/9) to southern India or the Society for the Propagation of the Gospel (SPG, founded 1701), primarily to the American colonies. The West Indies and America also attracted missions from Baptists and Congregationalists in the eighteenth century. The London Missionary Society (LMS), founded in 1795 and including Congregationalists, Anglicans, Presbyterians and Methodists, announced that it would send agents of the Word to 'Tahiti, Africa, Tartary, Astrachan, Surat, Calabar, Bengal, Coromandel and Sumatra': within 30 years the LMS had missions in all these regions except Tartary and Astrakhan; and there were LMS missionaries on no fewer than twenty Pacific islands, as well as Tahiti. Ultimately the most productive mission field for the LMS was in southern Africa, where the Scotsman John Philip (1775–1851) was superintendent in Cape Colony from 1820 until his death, and his compatriot, Robert Moffat (1795–1883), arriving in Cape Town in January 1817, then evangelized in Bechuanaland for most of the period from 1829 to 1870, crossing into Matabeleland and also providing the first mission station for his son-in-law, Livingstone. They offered religious faith, medicine, and schooling. The Church Missionary Society, an Anglican evangelical organization set up in 1799, sent out only five missionaries in the first year of its existence but gradually became a force in India and Australia and, slightly later, in the heart of Africa. All missionary bodies were prominent in the movements against *slavery and the *slave trade and strongly supported the emancipationist movements in *Sierra Leone and *Jamaica, where they fell foul of settler colonial administrators. The second great phase of missionary activity in the 1830s and 1840s brought Methodists, Anglicans and Presbyterians to West Africa, particularly to present-day Ghana and coastal Nigeria; the Universities Mission to Central Africa, though not founded until 1857, was powerfully effective from 1861 onwards. Most criticism has been levelled at the third phase of activity – between 1880 and 1910 – when the missionaries are said to have been agents of imperial penetration in Africa. There is no doubt that Charles Helm, a member of the LMS, assisted Rhodes's agents to secure concessions from King Lobengula of the *Ndebele; this was largely because Helm preferred treaty concessions with a responsible body to the prospect of individual bargains between tribal chiefs and 'riff-raff' adventurers, as had happened in the Congo. There had, moreover, been serious conflicts involving missionizing rivals and local communities, notably between 1878 and 1892 in Buganda where such divisions weakened resistance to paganism and where, in 1886, both Anglicans and Roman Catholics were martyred. British missionaries helped 'carry the flag' to Uganda, Zimbabwe and Nyasaland in particular. The 1910 World Missionary Conference in Edinburgh helped reduce rivalry and conflict, especially in New Guinea and Africa. Since World War II, church missionary activity has often gone in partnership with famine relief; the most notable development is the spread of *Mother Teresa's sisterhood, the Missionaries of Charity, founded in the poorer regions of Calcutta soon after India gained independence.

Mitchell, Sir Thomas Livingston (1792–1855), pioneer explorer of eastern Australia: born at Craigend, in Scotland; served under Wellington in Portugal and Spain and, as a retired major, was appointed deputy to the Surveyor-General in New South Wales, arriving in Sydney in 1827. He became Surveyor-General himself a year later and led four expeditions between 1831 and 1846 in the course of which he was able to explore large stretches of the Boga, Darling, Lachlan, Glenelg, Barcoo, Murrumbidgee and Murray rivers. His most important discovery was what is now the fertile western district of Victoria, which Mitchell named Australia Felix because of its beauty. On his return to Sydney he left a clear track to serve as a pioneer route for squatters entering Australia Felix in search of good pastures. The track was known for many decades as The Major's Line. His later expeditions turned northwards up the Bulloo river to its confluence with the Barcoo, at a point he named Isisford, now 400 miles into the Queensland interior. Mitchell returned to London on several occasions during his quarter of a century as Surveyor. He was knighted in 1839, and acknowledged as the first geographer of the interior: he published *The Australian Geography* (1850) for school use. Shortly before his death, at Darling Point and still in office, Mitchell completed a valuable report on roads in New South Wales, which was published posthumously and set a pattern for further public works projects in the colony.

Mixed Marriages Act, Prohibition of (1949): one of the earliest 'morality' laws of *apartheid in South Africa, passed by the *Malan government, by which race was made an impediment to marriage. There was already a prohibition of legal unions between whites and Africans, and this Act extended the ban to outlaw marriages between whites and all other races. It was followed by the Population Registration Act of 1950, which enforced the legal classification of all individuals by race; and, also in 1950, by the Immorality Amendment Act, which strengthened earlier attempts to check inter-racial adultery by imposing heavy penalties on offenders. These laws, the cause of many tragic suicides, were repealed in 1991.

Moi, Daniel arap (1924–   ), President of Kenya: born at a village in the Rift Valley Province, where his family farmed lands traditionally shared by the Tugen and Kalenjin ethnic groups; educated at the African Inland Mission school at Kabartonjo and the Government African school at Kapsabet; from 1946 to 1956 he was himself a teacher, before becoming Kenya's first African Minister of Education in 1961. He was not originally a supporter of *Kenyatta's KANU movement, becoming (in 1960) chairman of KADU (Kenya African Democratic Union), a more federalist party which enjoyed some liberal white planter support. On independence KADU merged with KANU, and by 1966 Moi presided over KANU in his native province. He served successively as Local Government Minister (1962–64), Home Affairs Minister (1964–67), and Vice-President for the last eleven years of Kenyatta's life. Moi took office as Kenya's second President on 14 October 1978, launched a comprehensive development programme, purged the army, and thwarted a Kenya Air Force coup on 1 August 1982. Thereafter his administration became increasingly dictatorial: KANU was the only legally permitted party until December 1991, and presidential executive powers were strengthened by constitutional changes in January 1988. External financial pressure, together with criticism from Commonwealth leaders and from Anglican churchmen inside Kenya, led to an apparent relaxation of the presidential hold on political life during 1992. At the end of the year a general election returned President Moi for a fourth five-year term.

Monash, Sir John (1865–1931), Australian soldier: born into a German–Jewish merchant's family at Melbourne, educated at Scotch College and Melbourne University, and became a civil engineer, specializing in reinforced concrete construction, including the building of bridges. While at Melbourne University he joined the citizens' forces (militia), was commissioned into the artillery, and by 1913 held the rank of colonel, with nineteen years of part-time service to his credit. He went to Egypt with the first *Anzac troops and commanded the 4th Australian Infantry Brigade at *Gallipoli. From 1916 until May 1918 he led the 3rd Australian Division, with particular distinction at Ypres and Messines. For the last six months of the war he commanded the Australian Corps on the Western Front, inducing Marshal Foch to limit the costly frontal assaults of August 1918 at Amiens and perfecting plans which enabled three Australian battalions to take the key position of Mont-Saint-Quentin on the upper Somme, on 31 August 1918. He received a knighthood in 1918 and on his return home supervised Australian demobilization, while also presiding over the Electricity Commission in the state of Victoria. Sir John retired in 1930 with the rank of full general: Monash University, founded in 1958 to the east of Melbourne, honours his memory.

Montserrat: British dependent territory in the Caribbean, 27 miles south-west of *Antigua: chief town, Plymouth. The volcanic island of Montserrat was visited and named by Columbus in 1493 but not colonized until the English brought in Irish indentured labourers from *St Kitts in 1632. The French captured the island on three occasions (1664, 1667, 1782) but were swiftly ejected, and Montserrat was confirmed by treaty as a British possession in 1783. From 1871 to 1956 Montserrat was linked with its neighbours as part of the *Leeward Islands Colony. The constitution received in January 1960 gave the island partially elective executive and legislative councils. Montserrat, an island prone to earth tremors, is the last of the Leewards to remain a dependency, although occasional talks have been held since the early 1980s to find ways of giving the 11,000 residents their political independence. They flourish on tourism.

Morant Bay Rebellion (1865). Morant Bay, *Jamaica's second largest town and port, was the centre of a riot in October 1865 which the brutality of the colonial governor, *Eyre, turned into a rebellion, swiftly and cruelly suppressed. Prolonged drought, high prices, grievances over land transfers and the maladministration of justice, together with reports of social changes in the USA following the end of the Civil War, all contributed to disaffection on the sugar plantations. Troops fired on a demonstration in Morant Bay town on 11 October: 7 black demonstrators and 21 whites or non-participating blacks were killed, and there was also looting and destruction of property. Eyre imposed martial law, had the principal 'people's spokesman', the Baptist preacher George William Gordon, court-martialled and hanged, and proceeded to punish the whole area: 580 men and women were killed in the repression, 600 were flogged, sometimes with sadistic satisfaction, and about a thousand homes were destroyed. The repercussions of the rebellion – in reality a protracted riot – were considerable: representative government in Jamaica was suspended until 1884; and parliamentary attacks in London censured Eyre and the colonial administration's approach to the problems of a former slave community.

'Mother Teresa' (Agnes Gonxha Bojaxhiu, 1910–) of Calcutta, nun: born in Skopje, of Albanian Catholic parentage; became a nun of the

Dublin Sisterhood of Loreto in 1928, but settled in Calcutta before the end of that year. For eighteen years she taught Bengali destitutes. The suffering of the famine years stirred in her a vocation to acquire medical training and live among the desperately poor. In 1948 she was allowed to train as a nurse, and in 1950 she founded a new religious humanitarian order, the Missionaries of Charity, which in the first instance cared for the people of Calcutta. Within ten years houses of the Order had spread to every densely populated town in the Indian Republic; and by 1965 Mother Teresa had extended the range of the Order's activities to Latin America, eventually to every continent. The Missionaries of Charity care for famine victims, drug addicts, orphans, abandoned children, the destitute, and lepers. Mother Teresa was awarded the Nobel Peace Prize in 1979 and received an honorary Order of Merit, presented to her by Queen Elizabeth II personally in India in 1983. Her Mission remains Calcutta-based. Denigrators complain that, as a Catholic sisterhood, Mother Teresa's creation is too exclusively concerned with Christian salvation and too obedient to ethical teachings which are hostile to family planning; but such criticisms fail to acknowledge the personal inspiration which has won the devotion of hundreds of young Indians who have joined her mission to lift life for society's destitute outcasts.

Mountbatten, Earl, of Burma (Albert Victor Louis Nicholas Francis; 1900–79), Admiral of the Fleet and Viceroy of India: born Prince Louis of Battenberg at Frogmore, Windsor, a great-grandson of Queen Victoria. The family name was anglicized in June 1917 while Prince Louis was serving with battle cruisers in the North Sea in World War I. By the outbreak of World War II he was in command of the Fifth Destroyer Flotilla, his ship HMS *Kelly* being sunk in the battle for Crete (1941). He was Chief of Combined Operations in 1942 but arrived in New Delhi as Supreme Allied Commander, South-East Asia, in October 1943, later moving his headquarters to Peradeniya, outside Kandy, from where he directed the recovery of Burma. By fighting through five months of monsoon and by closer co-ordination of land and air forces, the Burma army under General Sir William Slim (1891–1970; Viscount Slim, 1960) recovered Rangoon: Mountbatten received the surrender of Japanese forces in south-east Asia at Singapore on 12 September 1945. His experience in the Indian Ocean and his ability to work with Asian peoples contributed to the decision to appoint him Viceroy of India (on 27 February 1947) with responsibility for speedily achieving independence. Good personal relations with *Nehru were not matched in his contacts with *Jinnah and the *Muslim League and, in retrospect, he appears to have dangerously hastened the transfer of power. At Nehru's request Mountbatten remained as Governor-General of the Dominion of India from August 1947 until June 1948. His links with the royal family were strengthened by the marriage of his nephew, Prince Philip (1921–   ), to

241

Princess *Elizabeth in November 1947. Mountbatten resumed his sea-going naval career before becoming First Sea Lord (1955–59) and Chief of the Defence Staff (1959–65) at a time when military responsibilities were receding 'east of Suez'. On 27 August 1979 Earl Mountbatten was assassinated by Irish terrorists while aboard a small boat during a holiday in County Sligo.

'Mounties': popular name given to the Royal Canadian Mounted Police. The force was raised in 1873, on the initiative of John *Macdonald, as a constabulary maintained by the Dominion government, and was originally known as the North-West Mounted Police because its duties were to keep order in what was essentially Canada's Indian territory, ravaged by American 'wolfers' (raiding buffalo) and illicit whisky traders. The new 'police cavalry' were issued with scarlet tunics, like the British army. The first recruits successfully undertook a 'great march' west of Winnipeg to round up an American gang who had killed Indians in the Cypress Hills. This led at first to improved relations between the Blackfoot Confederacy and the Mounties, who became the government's chief agents in negotiating Indian treaties, but by the mid 1880s the Indian peoples had come to distrust them. More than any other force the Mounties prevented Canada from sinking into the lawlessness of the 'Wild West'. The prefix Royal was accorded by Edward VII in 1904. The force's responsibilities were extended to *Saskatchewan and *Alberta in 1905, and to Canada as a whole in 1920, when the present name was adopted and the headquarters were moved from Regina in Saskatchewan to Ottawa in Ontario.

Mugabe, Robert Gabriel (1924–   ), President of Zimbabwe: born at Kutame; educated at mission schools and Fort Hare University, supplementing his education by correspondence courses with London University. From 1942 to 1958 he was a teacher at mission schools in South Africa and Zambia as well as in his homeland. When *Nkomo founded the ZAPU (Zimbabwe African Peoples Union) in 1961 Mugabe became deputy secretary-general. He was briefly detained by the Rhodesian authorities but escaped to Tanzania and in August 1963 founded ZANU (Zimbabwe African National Union), which was more socialist than ZAPU. On returning to Rhodesia he was held in detention from 1964 to 1974. From 1975 to 1979 he lived in Mozambique, as director of the guerrilla ZANLA (Zimbabwe African National Liberation Army); and in October 1976 he accepted joint leadership with Nkomo of the Patriotic Front. From September to December 1979 Mugabe was in London for the *Lancaster House Conference on the future of his country. After returning home in late January 1980 to prepare ZANU for the election campaign, he survived two assassination attempts in three weeks. ZANU emerged from the election as the largest single political group, and Mugabe took office as Zimbabwe's first Prime Minister on 4

March 1980. Independence in April 1980 was followed by a cautious policy which avoided confrontation between black and white and narrowly averted a protracted civil war with ZAPU followers. Constitutional changes in 1987 made the presidency an executive post, to which Mugabe was duly elected on 30 December 1987. He was re-elected in March 1990, and ZANU and ZAPU merged and the legislature became unicameral.

Mujibur Rahman (Sheikh Mujib, 1925–75), national leader of the Bangladeshi: born into a family of landowners at Tongipara, East Bengal; studied law at the universities of Calcutta and Dacca. He was a founder member of the Awami League in 1949, campaigning in favour of autonomy for East *Pakistan, and from 1954 until his death he was accepted as leader of the League. Under *Ayub Khan he was arrested on several occasions. Despite the electoral victory of the Awami League in 1970 the Pakistan government refused to make concessions, and in August 1971 he was charged with treason; however, military intervention by India in *Bangladesh in December 1971 secured his release. He declined to accept the post of President of the new Bangladesh, but agreed to become Prime Minister in January 1972; he made a genuine attempt to establish in Dacca a parliamentary democratic socialist administration, in the face of corruption and the hostility of powerful landowners. His assumption of dictatorial powers in January 1975 precipitated military conspiracies, and in the following August he and his wife were murdered in an army coup.

Muldoon, Robert David (1921–), New Zealand Prime Minister: born in Auckland; served with the infantry in World War II; became an accountant and was elected to Parliament as National Party member for Tamaki in 1960. He was Minister of Finance from 1967 to 1972 and became leader of his party, in opposition, in 1974. His electoral promise to promote a generous pensions scheme for over-sixties contributed to Labour's defeat in the 1975 election, and Muldoon became Prime Minister on 12 December 1975. Although he honoured his pledge, Muldoon found that he had to force his free-enterprise party to accept a 'managed economy' in order to check mounting inflation and unemployment. New Zealanders, he urged, should 'think big'. He embarked on ambitious petrochemical projects to boost heavy industry, but lost public support by appearing 'uncaring' in the face of criticism from a powerful anti-nuclear lobby. After seeing his majority dwindle, he called a snap election in July 1984 and lost, to Labour under *Lange. Muldoon gave up his party's leadership but remained in Parliament.

Mulroney, (Martin) Brian (1939–), Canadian Prime Minister: born at Baie Comeau, the son of Irish immigrants; educated at St Francis

Xavier University, became a partner in a Montreal law firm, and in 1976 President of the Iron Ore Company of Canada, a post he held until his election as Progressive Conservative MP for Central Nova Scotia in 1983. He swiftly became party leader, and won a landslide victory over a tired Liberal administration in September 1984. As Prime Minister he reached agreement on free trade with the Reagan administration in Washington and cautiously began a series of constitutional reforms in *Canada, aimed at settling disputes between Ottawa and the provincial governments. His Charlottetown Accord of September 1992 – giving *Quebec special status as a 'distinct society', while also changing the character of the Senate – was put to a national referendum on 26 October 1992 but decisively rejected. Mulroney failed to heal the constitutional rifts, and on 25 June 1993 he was replaced as party leader and Prime Minister by Kim Campbell, who was herself defeated by the Liberals under Jean Chrétien (1934–) in a federal general election four months later.

Murdoch, (Keith) Rupert (1931–), Australian-born newspaper magnate: born in Melbourne, the son of Sir Keith Murdoch (1886–1952), a famous war correspondent in World War I and later head of the *Melbourne Herald* newspaper group. Rupert Murdoch was educated at Geelong and Worcester College, Oxford. He worked for a time as a journalist with the *Beaverbrook group in London, applying his experience to the family newspaper chain in Australia on his father's death. By 1960 he was the second largest publisher in the antipodes, becoming Group Chief Executive of The News Corporation, Australia. He bought the London *News of the World* and the *Sun* in 1969, founded News International, and in 1982 became Chairman of Times Newspaper Holdings Ltd, while still retaining his other interests and branching out into television in his homeland. By 1976 he had moved into the American market, purchasing the *New York Post* and the New York Magazine Company; he became an American citizen in 1985. His interests in Britain continued to grow, with the purchase of the Collins publishing house in 1989 and the formation of the satellite network Sky Television.

Murray, Sir (John) Hubert Plunkett (1861–1940), Australian administrator of Papua: born at Manly, NSW into a Roman Catholic family of Irish descent; his younger brother became the classical scholar and Liberal internationalist, Gilbert Murray, OM (1866–1957). Hubert Murray was educated at Sydney and Magdalen College, Oxford, became a barrister and eventually a circuit judge in his native state; also commanded the NSW Irish Rifles in South Africa during the Boer War. In 1904 he began his long association with Papua as a judicial officer. His humanitarian sympathy with native problems led to his appointment by the Australian government as Lieutenant-Governor of Papua in 1908, a post he held for 22 years, a longer span than any other administrator of a colony in the British Empire. He insisted on modifying the indentured labour service, which he regarded as close to slavery, and to give a primitive native population the best opportunities of development, he excluded Asian immigration. He assigned precise areas to rival missionary activity, scrupulously protected native land rights in supervising sales to Australian settlers, and boosted education with government subsidies, despite the financial stringency caused by the *Great Depression. He was knighted in 1925. Murray's wisdom and tolerance protected the Papuans from the exploitation which had so humiliated and sadly depleted the Australian aborigines.

Muslim League: founded in 1906, primarily as a religious organization to safeguard Islamic worship in British India. The League became a political movement in 1935 under the leadership of *Jinnah as Muslims left the *Indian National Congress Party because it had become predominantly Hindu in policy and aspirations. The breach widened with Congress state electoral successes in 1937. The Muslim League supported India's full participation in World War II but intensified its demand for Muslim autonomy and, from 1942 onwards, advocated a separate Muslim 'Pakistan'. The League's uncompromising attitude imposed *Partition, and in 1946/7 there was no doubt that Jinnah and the League had overwhelming support from India's Muslim population. After Jinnah's death in 1948 the League never again found a charismatic leader: new parties emerged in Pakistan, and in the general election of 1955 the League lost the absolute majority it had possessed since the creation of the state. Thereafter it split into three factions. The neo-fundamentalism of the 1980s led to a revival: the Muslim League won 17 of 73 seats for the National Assembly in 1984 and supported the ruling Islamic Democratic Alliance coalition, 1990–93. In India, too, a Muslim League survives, and sent two members to Parliament in Delhi after the 1989 general election.

Myall Creek Massacre (June 1838). Several whites were murdered in the summer of 1837/8 by *aborigines who resented their intrusion into traditional hunting grounds some 350 miles north-west of Sydney. In June the convict station-hands of a successful squatter, Henry Dangar, took vengeance on aborigines living in Myall Creek – outside the modern town of Inverell, NSW – murdering some thirty men, women and children: eleven whites were summarily tried for the murders, and acquitted. The colonial Attorney-General, John Plunkett, ordered the men to be brought to Sydney for a more conventional trial and seven of the eleven were duly hanged. While the massacre highlighted the tensions between squatters and aborigines, Plunkett's insistence on keeping to the letter of the law emphasized the colonial government's intention to follow, as far as possible, policies of aboriginal protection.

245

Namibia: an independent democratic republic within the Common-wealth: capital, Windhoek. Namibia was from 1880 to 1915 the German Protectorate of *South West Africa; it was then occupied by South African forces, and between the wars was administered from Pretoria under a League of Nations *mandate. Subsequently, South Africa refused to acknowledge United Nations rights of trusteeship in the terri-tory and during the apartheid era sought integration of South-West Africa with the rest of the Union. SWAPO (South-West Africa People's Organization) was established in 1960 and began guerrilla operations against the South Africans in the Damaraland bush country in 1966. The United Nations gave political support to SWAPO and, in response to its leaders' pleas, a resolution formally renaming the region 'Namibia' was carried in the UN General Assembly on 12 June 1968: SWAPO was re-cognized by the UN as 'the sole authentic voice of the people of Namibia' three years later. Despite the despatch of peace missions and frequent dis-cussions with representatives of the South African Republic, Pretoria long refused to accept any compromise with SWAPO, seeking to establish its own puppet administration at Turnhalle. Guerrilla attacks on South African units and institutions by SWAPO from bases in Angola became so severe that in June 1980 and November 1981 the South African army invaded Angola in the hope of crushing SWAPO. With the gradual with-drawal of Cuban support for SWAPO, the Reagan administration was able to cajole the South Africans into a series of talks with UN repre-sentatives and ultimately with SWAPO. In December 1988 South Africa agreed to recognize Namibia's independence. Elections under UN super-vision on 7–11 November 1989 gave the largest number of parliamentary seats to SWAPO, whose veteran leader, Dr Sam Nujoma, was elected Namibia's first President on 16 February 1990. Independence and membership of the Commonwealth followed on 21 March 1990. With the formal transfer of the disputed enclave of *Walvis Bay to Namibia on 28 February 1994 the last vestige of colonial rule in Africa was removed.

Nandi. A warlike, nominally pastoral, people living in north-western Kenya, their traditional lands in hilly country between Kisumu and the Uganda border. Constant raids on the Uganda Railway around Kisumu led, between 1895 and 1905, to five expeditions by British colonial troops against the Nandi. They were only subdued when, after they had lost 500 men and 10,000 cattle, their principal *Orkoiyot* (medicine man) was killed. The Nandi were then confined to a fertile reserve, which they were encouraged to farm, while their old grazing land was opened up to set-tlers.

Nanking, Treaty of (1842): ended the first Anglo-Chinese *Opium War. China ceded *Hong Kong island to Britain, relaxed discriminatory taxes on foreign merchants and opened five *Treaty Ports to foreign trade. At the same time British consular officials were accorded 'extra-territoriality' (the right to try British subjects in China). A further commercial treaty, signed in the following year, strengthened Britain's predominance in the China Trade. The 1842 treaty also recorded China's pledge no longer to call the British 'barbarians' in official documents.

Napier, Sir Charles James (1782–1853), British soldier: was bought an army commission at the age of twelve by his father, though he did not see active service until he was sixteen. He fought in the Napoleonic Wars in Spain and Portugal, lived on Cephalonia during the Greek War of Independence, commanded troops in northern England as a major-general during the Chartist disturbances of 1839–40, and was in India from 1841 to 1847 and 1849/50, subjugating Upper and Lower Sind, where he subsequently established an orderly civil government and in 1844–45 conducted a campaign against the Sikhs in the northern hills. On returning to England he wrote a series of books highly critical of India's government and the administration of the colonies. He has been long remembered for the Latin pun by which, according to *Punch* in February 1843, he laconically reported his successful conquest of Sind: '*Peccavi*!' ('I have sinned.')

Nassau Fellowships. It was agreed at the *Commonwealth Heads of Government Meeting in Nassau (1975) that, with support from UN agencies, the Commonwealth governments would finance awards to be given to victims of *apartheid to allow them to study at universities or other educational institutions in the developing Commonwealth countries. For administrative purposes this scheme for multilateral 'Nassau Fellowships' was assigned to the *Commonwealth Secretariat, whose educational service members decide who should receive the fellowships, and supplemented by an additional programme of Nassau Fellowships awarded by individual Commonwealth governments, according to their own criteria. Applicants were, almost inevitably, refugees living on voluntary support while in exile from South Africa. By 1991, when the social burden of apartheid eased, 250 fellowships had been awarded by the Commonwealth Secretariat and another 600 by individual governments.

Natal. Vasco da Gama sighted the African coast, close to where Durban now stands, on Christmas Day 1497, and called it 'Terra Natalis'. The British established a coastal settlement in 1824, largely for elephant hunters, and in 1835 they founded a city which was named after General Sir Benjamin D'Urban (1777–1849), Governor of the Cape, 1834–38. The Boers, on their *Great Trek, reached the hinterland in 1839/40 and founded the city of Pietermaritzburg, named after the leading Voortrekkers, Pieter Retie and Gert Maritz. Pietermaritzburg, 40 miles inland from Durban and surrounded on three sides by rivers, seemed easily defensible from attack by the *Zulus. The Boers therefore made Pieter-maritzburg the capital of what they called the Republic of Natalia. In 1843/4 the British formally annexed Natalia to Cape Colony, but installed a separate administration a year later and in July 1856 established Natal as a crown colony. The port of Durban grew rapidly in the 1860s with the arrival of Indian labourers who, though brought originally to work on the sugar plantations, soon secured a firm hold on the colony's commercial life. A railway from Durban reached Pietermaritzburg in 1880. Boer troops entered Natal in 1881 and won the battle of *Majuba before an uneasy peace could be established with *Kruger's *Transvaal. But as soon as Natal gained responsible government in 1893 talks were held with the Transvaal to complete the railway link to Johannesburg, opened in 1895. The colony was enlarged by absorbing *Zululand in December 1897. Boer columns again marched into Natal in late October 1899, cutting off a British garrison at Ladysmith and defeating a relief force at Colenso on 15 December, although Natal was cleared of the invaders by February 1900. Three outlying districts of the Transvaal (Vryheid, Utrecht and East Wakkerstroom) were absorbed by Natal in January 1903, after the *Vereeniging peace settlement. Three years later the growing prosperity of the colony was disturbed by an insurrection of the Bambata, who feared they were losing their identity under the combined impact of British settlers, Boers and Indian immigrants. Natal became a province of the Union of South Africa on 31 May 1910. There was serious rioting in Durban in 1949 between Indians (who formed a majority of small traders and labourers) and Africans. Under the South African Republic the old Zulu problem resurfaced in Natal, and the Zulu Inkatha movement has threatened to disturb the precarious racial balance in what is now 'Kwazulu/Natal' since the transition to democratic government in 1994. Durban remains South Africa's principal seaport, with half its population of Asian origin.

National Anthems of the Commonwealth. *God Save the Queen* is generally recognized by the Commonwealth collectively as a Royal anthem, as well as being the anthem of the United Kingdom and Britain's dependent territories. Over the last half-century a growing consciousness of national identity – and the increasing use of anthems at international sporting events – has led to the choice of individual national anthems by 50 Commonwealth states. Almost all titles commend the country by name: *Fair Antigua and Barbuda; March on, Bahamaland; Hail the Name of Ghana; Jamaica, Land we Love; Kenya, Land of the Lion; God Bless our Land of Malawi; God Defend New Zealand; Tuvalu for the Almighty; Oh Uganda; Stand and Sing of Zambia, Proud and Free;* etc., etc. Other national anthems include Barbados's *In Plenty and in Time of Need*, Belize's *Land of Freedom*; Nigeria's *Arise O Compatriots* and Sri Lanka's *We All Stand Together*. When South Africa rejoined the Commonwealth in 1994, *Nkosi*

Sikel'i Afrika ('God Bless Africa') appeared to have ousted the Afrikaaner *Die Stem Van Suid-Afrika* ('The Call of South Africa'). The choice of national anthem has frequently provoked controversy. The Scottish-born schoolmaster Alexander Muir (1830–1906) wrote and composed *The Maple Leaf for Ever* as a Canadian anthem in 1867, the year in which the *British North America Act created the Dominion, and from 1887 it was sung officially as a national song in Ontario's schools. Quebec, however, preferred *Lavalee's *O Canada!* from 1880 onwards. On 31 January 1966 (as the Dominion's centenary celebrations approached) Lester *Pearson, as Prime Minister, formally proposed in Parliament the adoption of *O Canada!* as the anthem. *Advance Australia Fair* was composed by P. D. McCormick for the NSW Highland Society's concert in Sydney on St Andrew's Day 1878; only in 1984 was it recognized as Australia's national anthem, in the face of strong popular sentimental support for the more stirring tune of *Waltzing Matilda*, the bush ballad written in 1895 by 'Banjo' *Paterson.

National Colonization Society: founded in London in 1830 to promote the systematic colonization, particularly of Australasia, advocated by Gibbon *Wakefield.

National(ist) Party in South Africa: see *Afrikaaner National Party*.

Native Regiments. The establishment of locally raised forces goes back at least to 1757 in Bengal (see *Indian Army*), far earlier in the case of the militia of the American colonies. Moreover, trading posts in Africa had long been accustomed to strengthen their defence with locally recruited and hastily trained natives. In 1779 a West Indies Regiment was recruited, primarily in Jamaica; it became regularly established after the Napoleonic Wars, with two battalions, one of which served in Sierra Leone while the other remained based in Kingston. Sierra Leone had its own 'frontier police' from 1829 onwards. Men from the West Indies Regiment, together with levies from *Sierra Leone, Lagos and The *Gambia, also served under *Wolseley against the Ashanti in 1873/4. *Kitchener included an embryonic Sudan Defence Force, as well as Egyptian 'regulars', in the army which defeated the dervishes at *Omdurman in 1898. By then the idea of raising regular, disciplined local armies, originating with the *Gurkhas, had spread across Asia, and they included a *Hong Kong Regiment (recruited in India) and, during the Boxer rising at the turn of the century, a short-lived Chinese Regiment based on *Weihaiwei. The most famous of all native infantry regiments was the *King's African Rifles, raised in East Africa. The Royal West Africa Frontier Force combined units from Nigeria, Sierra Leone and the Gold Coast and, though primarily infantry, also provided its own artillery. A camel corps was raised in Somaliland, and fought as such in

World War I. In 1912 the Northern Rhodesia Police was reorganized along military lines and – still using the name 'police' – took a leading part in the campaign against Lettow-Vorbeck's German colonial army between Lake Tanganyika and Lake Nyasa in June–September 1918; the force was eventually renamed the Northern Rhodesia Regiment in April 1933, and in World War II fought in Italian Somaliland, Eritrea, Madagascar and, with great determination, in Burma, as well as serving later in the *Malayan Emergency. In 1964 the NRR became the Zambia Rifles. Native forces were also raised in the Middle East during the period in which *Iraq and *Transjordan were mandated territories. The best-known force, the Arab Legion, with its headquarters in Amman, was never part of the British Army, though it was led by British officers.

Natives Land Act (1913). The earliest piece of legislation to apply a measure of racial segregation to the Union of South Africa as a whole. The law set aside rural reserves, covering 7.5 per cent of the country, in which Africans might buy, lease and farm land of their own: they were forbidden from doing so in the remaining 92.5 per cent of the country. At that time native Africans formed slightly more than two-thirds of the population of the Union.

Nauru: a South Pacific island republic in the Commonwealth, a raised coral reef only 8 square miles in area, with a population of some 8,500. It was annexed by Germany in 1888, occupied by Australian troops in 1914 and held by Australia under a League *mandate from 1920, and was under UN trusteeship from 1947 to 1968. Independence was conceded on 31 January 1968. It has been rich in phosphate deposits, run since 1970 by the Nauru Phosphate Corporation but now showing signs of exhaustion. Since 1993 generous compensation has been offered by the Australians to Nauruan workers whose health was ruined during the years of mandate and trusteeship.

Naval Bases. To keep open the sea lanes serving the Empire, the Royal Navy required bases around the world. Sailing vessels needed harbours with good dockyards and skilled craftsmen; the coming of steam made ships dependent on coaling stations, such as *Aden or Port Louis (*Mauritius). Some colonies were, in the first instance, strategically placed naval bases: *Gibraltar, for the Atlantic fleet; *Malta, for the Mediterranean. Halifax, in Nova Scotia, founded for the Royal Navy as early as 1749, became Canada's leading ice-free Atlantic port as well as an invaluable base in both world wars. Other harbours were useful only for short periods of time: Nelson's dockyard on *Antigua; *Weihaiwei from 1898 to 1914; Addu Atoll in the *Maldives during and after World War II. Some bases were developed at smaller towns in prosperous colonies: thus Simonstown, 20 miles south of Capetown, first used by the Royal

Navy in 1815, remained directly under Admiralty control from 1898 to 1957, as also did Trincomalee, in eastern Ceylon (Sri Lanka), until 1958. Esquimalt, on the south of Vancouver Island in British Columbia, was a Pacific naval base from about 1860 until 1906, when it was handed over to the Royal Canadian Navy. The naval yards at Wooloomooloo Cove and Sirius Bay, Sydney were maintained by the Admiralty until 1911, when the Royal Australian Navy was formed: the British Pacific Fleet returned to Sydney and expanded them in 1944–46. The China Squadron's headquarters were at *Hong Kong, the navy's only major dockyard east of Malta until the new naval base on the Johore Straits of *Singapore, planned in 1922, was completed in 1937. The always powerful Mediterranean Fleet supplemented Malta with Alexandria in Egypt between 1883 and 1956. As soon as there was a threat of war with Russia during the eastern crises of 1853/4 and 1877/8 the fleet moved up to Besika Bay in Turkish Asia Minor, 40 miles south-east of the Dardanelles; proposals to lease the anchorage from the Sultan were dropped when *Cyprus was occupied, although the navy made little use of the island. Bermuda served the North American and West Indies Squadron, which also used Port Royal in Jamaica. The Admiralty controlled *Ascension Island from 1815 to 1922, and long maintained facilities on *St Helena. The chief bases in the Indian Ocean during the nineteenth century were at Bombay and Calcutta, together with Port Louis, Trincomalee and Colombo. Stanley in the *Falkland Islands was an important coaling station for the South Atlantic Squadron in both world wars. The main naval base in West Africa was Freetown in *Sierra Leone. Naval bases closed rapidly from the mid 1950s onwards: the naval dockyard in Hong Kong went in 1959, and the Royal Navy finally left Malta on 31 March 1979.

Ndebele: a cattle-rearing people who lived south of the Orange River at the start of the nineteenth century but in the 1820s and 1830s were forced by pressure from both the *Zulus and the *Boers to migrate northwards across the Limpopo. Under their king, Mzilikazi, they settled in the fertile region which became *Matabeleland (*Zimbabwe) and conquered *Mashonaland. In 1870 Mzilikazi was succeeded as king by his son Lobengula, who raised an army of 15,000 warriors and established his kraal on the site of modern Bulawayo. Lobengula, an impressive six foot tall and weighing about twenty stone, was a politically astute ruler, more afraid of incursions by Boers than by the British. On 30 October 1888 he concluded an agreement with representatives of *Rhodes by which, in return for a small subsidy, the *British South Africa Company obtained exclusive rights over all metals and minerals in his kingdom. Tensions mounted, however, in 1890, when Rhodes's pioneers occupied Mashonaland, a Ndebele dependency. Lobengula successfully held his men back, until they were provoked by Dr Jameson (see *Jameson Raid*) in

October 1893; the Ndebele were crushed, the Bulawayo kraal was seized (4 November), and Lobengula died in hiding in January 1894. The failure of the Jameson Raid left Matabeleland virtually without police and two years later the Ndebele rose in revolt (24 March 1896), killing the white families who had settled on their lands. A rising in Mashonaland followed in June and it was only with great difficulty that, in October, the Ndebele were forced to accept 'Rhodesian' rule, as a conquered people.

Nehru, Jawaharlal (1889–1964), Indian Prime Minister: born at Allahabad, the son of Pandit Motilal Nehru (1861–1931), an eminent lawyer and an early advocate of Indian home rule; educated at Harrow and at Trinity College, Cambridge, and read for the Bar of the Inner Temple before returning to India and supporting Mohandas *Gandhi from 1920 onwards. He spent nine of the following twenty-five years in prison for advocating civil disobedience and, from 1942, a 'Quit India' campaign. He became vice-president of the Viceroy's Council in 1946, seeking a smooth transition to Independence and finding it easier to work with *Mountbatten than with the intractable *Jinnah. He became both Prime Minister and Foreign Minister on Independence and continued to head the government until his death at the end of May 1964. His encouragement of movements towards republican democracy and of a mixed economy was influenced by socialist experiments elsewhere. He introduced three Five-Year Plans, patiently overcoming the suspicion of individualistic, conservatively-minded rural communities, steeped in respect for traditional Hindu laws. Nehru was also an international states-man, anti-colonialist and firmly non-aligned, ready to mediate in Korea and Vietnam or to support UN peace-keeping missions by despatching Indian troops overseas. Nevertheless, he authorized India's invasion of Portuguese Goa in 1961. At home Nehru's critics seized on three alleged weaknesses: his excessive restraint over the *Kashmir issue and over Chinese Communist incursions into *Tibet; his insensitivity to Hindu religious feelings when seeking to rationalize law; and his preference for concerning himself with world issues rather than with narrowly Indian problems. Within twenty months of Nehru's death his daughter, Mrs Indira *Gandhi, became Prime Minister.

New Brunswick: Canadian maritime province, bounded by the Gulf of St Lawrence, the Bay of Fundy and the US state of Maine. Cartier explored much of the Atlantic coast in 1534 and a French settlement was established seventy years later, becoming (with *Nova Scotia) the colony of Acadia, ceded to Britain in 1713 by the Treaty of Utrecht. It remained sparsely populated until 1763/4 when 6,000 New Englanders were enticed to make the journey northwards and settle, mainly around the Bay of Fundy. Twenty years later a further migration, of United Empire Loyalists, peopled the southern part of New Brunswick, including the lower St John River, at the highest navigable point of which the newcomers founded Fredericton, which became the provincial capital, and the college which became the University of New Brunswick. The United Loyalist influx led to the final separation of New Brunswick from Nova Scotia and its establishment as a province in June 1784. Economic growth of the province suffered from the severity of its winters and from difficulties of communication, for it is cut into regions by river valleys. Responsible government, with executive and legislative councils and a provincial assembly, came in 1848. New Brunswick's Liberal Party was prominent in the original movement for confederation. Although electorally defeated in 1865, its leader Samuel Tilley (1818–96) recovered the voters' confidence in 1867 and carried the province into the Dominion a year later, serving as Canada's first Minister of Customs. The province's economy was originally based upon wood and fishing, and so it has remained. Despite the growth of mining and of processing industries around the port of St John, 85 per cent of the land surface is still productive forest.

New Delhi: capital of British India, 1912–47, and of India since Independence. A series of at least eight cities has stood in the vicinity of modern Delhi, on the right bank of the Jumna river, strategically central to the Indus–Ganges plain. Early seventeenth-century Old Delhi, built by the Moghul emperor Shahjahan and containing his Great Mosque and the Red Fort, was looted and extensively destroyed by the British after the Indian *Mutiny. But the city retained importance as a symbol of past imperial sovereignty and was the site of two accession *Delhi Durbars. The Viceroy's capital was moved from Calcutta to Delhi in 1912 and work began a year later on building a spacious, landscaped New Delhi, with its centre 3 miles south of the Red Fort. The city was planned by Sir Herbert *Baker and Sir Edwin *Lutyens, in often inharmonious partnership. Ceremonies to mark the official completion of the original plan were held in 1931. Significantly, Australia's new planned capital, *Canberra, was being built at exactly the same time as New Delhi.

New Hebrides: see *Vanuatu*.

New South Wales: the most populous state in Australia. It was named by *Cook in 1770 and became, in the first instance, a penal colony 'settled' by the *First Fleet (1788). The original colony of New South Wales included Van Diemen's Land (*Tasmania) until 1825, Port Philip district (*Victoria) until 1851, and Moreton Bay district (*Queensland) until 1859: *New Zealand was very briefly a dependency of the colony (1840–41). The introduction of merino sheep in 1797 shaped the colony's early economy, which also benefited from an increasing flow of free settlers after the turn of the century; they numbered about a thou-

sand in 1810. Sydney was sufficiently developed to have a Chamber of
Commerce in 1823; by 1829 the official area of settlement had been
divided into *nineteen counties, extending beyond the *Blue Mountains
to Bathurst, 100 miles inland. Single women were offered free passage
from England to New South Wales in the 1830s and some 3,000 made
the journey between 1832 and 1836. Penal *Transportation to the
Sydney area continued until 1840, by which time some 80,000 inhabitants of the nineteen counties had come as convicts, as against some
70,000 free settlers. Coal-mining was developed about 75 miles north of
Sydney, where the port of Newcastle on the Hunter River grew from a
penal settlement (1804–24). A nominated legislative council set up in
1823 was followed by a partially elective assembly in Sydney in 1843 and
a bicameral, elected parliament in 1856. Pastoralists in search of grazing
land crossed the nineteen counties boundary about 1835 and became the
first 'squatters'. The *gold rush of 1851, though less dramatic than in
Victoria, led to a rapid rise in population and the creation of new inland
centres, but *railways linking them were slow to come: Redfern (Sydney)
to Granville (for Parramatta) in 1855; Sydney to Wagga Wagga in 1879,
Albury in 1881 (with a change of train for Melbourne from 1883) and
north-westwards to Bourke (460 miles inland) in 1885; unlike its neighbours, New South Wales had standard-gauge railways. Intense rivalry
between free trade Sydney and largely protectionist Melbourne helped
postpone federation until 1901. Within the state, the growth of the urban
complexes around Sydney and Newcastle has led to occasional proposals
for subdivision. However, during the twentieth century New South Wales
has only lost *Canberra, for a federal capital, and the inlet of Jervis Bay, as
a proposed federal port. In 1925 a Royal Commission appointed by the
NSW Government advised against subdivision, though a second Royal
Commission in 1935 recommended a triple subdivision, to be decided by
a referendum in each region. After forty years of campaigning, a constitu-
ent assembly for the New England plateau met at Armidale, 200 miles
north of Sydney, in 1955, though with little response from the state
government. A referendum on the question of the New England plateau
seceding from NSW and forming a new state was held in April 1967; it
was rejected by 198,812 votes to 168,103. The official 1993 assessment
estimates that, of NSW's 6,008,600 residents, some 3,719,000 live
around Sydney and nearly half a million in the Newcastle conurbation.

New Territories: a region opposite to *Hong Kong island and forming
the hinterland of *Kowloon. A treaty signed at Peking (Beijing) on 9 June
1898 provided for the lease to Great Britain for 99 years of some 376
square miles of China's mainland, together with the island of Lan-tao and
the waters of Mirs Bay and Deep Bay; no other lease of land to the British
was controlled by a terminal date. The addition of the New Territories
gave the colony good agricultural land and better military protection; it

also provided a springboard for economic penetration of southern China, bandit-free country through which a railway could be constructed to Canton. Villages in the New Territories became towns during the great influx of population after China's Communist revolution.

New Zealand: a Dominion within the Commonwealth, comprising a more densely populated North Island and a larger South Island, together with offshore Stewart and Chatham islands, the South Pacific dependencies of *Cook Island, *Niue and *Tokelau, and the *Ross Dependency in the Antarctic: the capital, Wellington, is on the North Island. The *Maori communities were well-established in the islands they knew as 'Aoteara' when the first Europeans came there: *Tasman, who sighted and named the coast in 1642 but did not land; *Cook, who landed on North Island in 1769; and French explorers, including Jean de Surville (1769) and Marion du Fresne (1772). From the early 1790s whalers and timber seekers visited the coasts; contact was made with the Maoris by traders from Sydney, and in 1814 *Marsden brought the first Christian mission to the northern 'Bay of Plenty'. Large-scale systematic emigration was planned by Gibbon *Wakefield and the *New Zealand Company in the late 1830s. This activity, together with reports that the French were seeking to colonize South Island, prompted the government in London to entrust William *Hobson with establishing British sovereignty over both islands in 1840: the South – somewhat tenuously – by virtue of discovery; the North by the Treaty of *Waitangi, negotiated with the Maoris. Briefly New Zealand was treated as part of New South Wales, but was created a separate colony in May 1841, with the capital at Auckland. Towns were established, largely on the initiative of the New Zealand Company or its subsidiaries, at Wellington and, in the South Island, at Nelson (1840/1), Dunedin (1848) and Christchurch (1850). In 1846 a doctrinaire constitution, drafted largely by Wakefield's devotees in London, was rejected by the Governor, Sir George *Grey, on the grounds that it failed to comprehend the colony's needs and would have left the Maori at the mercy of settlers. A revised constitution in 1852 was basically federal in character, dividing New Zealand into six regions, though providing for a general assembly to gather at Auckland. Local self-government was conceded in 1856. The *Maori Wars delayed the development of the North Island, and an extension of the federal principle until there were ten regions hampered the growth of any sense of nationhood as the provincial administrations haggled over the allocation of federal funds and the provision of links between the regions of settlement. Some progress towards unity was made in 1865 when the capital was moved southwards from Auckland to Wellington, across Cook Strait from the South Island. So intense was the competition over railway promotion in the early 1870s that the provincial councils were swept aside in 1876, in favour of a unitary state. Nevertheless, while Christchurch in the South Island was linked with Bluff, at the far south, by rail in 1879, the relatively short distance between Wellington and New Plymouth could not be covered by rail until 1886 because of lingering Maori armed resistance in Taranaki, and the Wellington to Napier line was only opened in 1891. Remarkably, the line northwards from Christchurch to Cook Strait was not completed until 1935, nor were the islands linked by rail ferry until 1962. Despite such delays, in the last quarter of the nineteenth century the economy of the South Island boomed, partly because of the *gold rush but also through the spread of *sheep and cattle farming. *Refrigeration came in the early 1880s: the first cargo of frozen New Zealand lamb and mutton sailed for England from Port Chalmers on 15 February 1882, and a factory to export frozen dairy produce was opened at Edendale in the same year. Delegates from New Zealand attended the National Australasian Convention at Sydney in 1891 but preferred to retain their recently found national identity. New Zealand made rapid strides towards genuinely democratic government and comprehensive social legislation: manhood suffrage without a property qualification was introduced in 1879; New Zealand women were enfranchised in 1893, earlier than in any other country; a non-contributory old age pension scheme was effective by 1898, and a national health service began in 1941, seven years earlier than in the United Kingdom. Dominion status was officially accorded to New Zealand on 26 September 1907. Links with the United Kingdom, and especially with Scotland, remained close. In World War I, New Zealand was the first Dominion to base *military service on conscription; casualties were high, both with *Anzac at *Gallipoli (where 2,700 New Zealanders died), and with the First New Zealand Division in France and Flanders. The 1920s saw the spread of *hydro-electric projects and greater cattle rearing in the North Island, as well as in the traditional pastures of the South. But the *Great Depression hit New Zealand hard, with the collapse of wool prices because of excessive sheep farming and the withdrawal of overseas funding for major public works projects: 80,000 New Zealanders were unemployed in October 1933. In World War II the light cruiser HMNZS *Achilles* was in action in the first naval battle, helping to cripple the pocket battleship *Graf Spee* off the River Plate in December 1939; and the New Zealand 2 Division, under General *Freyberg, VC, fought throughout the war in the Middle East and Italy. New Zealanders were also acutely conscious of the Japanese menace in the Pacific, their troops serving in the Solomon Islands in 1943/4. There has never been any inclination in New Zealand towards isolationism in world affairs: the fear of 'Red China' prompted the despatch of troops both to *Korea and to south *Vietnam, though no more than 550 New Zealand volunteers were serving in Vietnam at any one moment, and the war commitment became increasingly unpopular. Mounting distrust of nuclear ships and *nuclear tests led to a realignment of policy, giving full support to the *South Pacific Forum and promoting the Nuclear Free

Zone Treaty, agreed by the Forum at Rarotonga in 1985. Domestic issues have been particularly concerned with renewed problems over Maori *land rights, and with the consequences of a referendum in 1992 in which the electorate supported proposals for constitutional reform to introduce a mixed-member system of proportional representation for the parliamentary Lower House. (See also the entries on: T. Brunner; J. Carroll; P. Fraser; S. Holland; K. Holyoake; N. Kirk; D. Lange; W. Massey; R. Muldoon; M. Savage; R. Seddon.)

New Zealand Company: originally known as the New Zealand Association; founded in London in 1837, largely on the initiative of Gibbon *Wakefield, though supported by Lord Durham, the banker Francis Baring and a number of reformers in the House of Commons. The Association wanted New Zealand systematically colonized rather than, as Wakefield said, settled 'in a most slovenly and disgraceful manner' by ex-convicts, land speculators and other undesirables. Lord Melbourne's government vacillated, hesitantly prepared to support the Association provided that it was transformed into a joint stock company, a move formally made in August 1838. Wakefield's exasperation with this dilatoriness caused him to charter a ship for the Company and send out colonists ahead of government approval, a move which checked French plans to colonize the South Island. From the start, Wakefield won support from Scottish Presbyterians; and in 1848 one of his closest associates in the Company, John Robert Godley (1814–61), interested leading Anglicans in setting up the Canterbury Association. This subsidiary of the Company was to establish a 'respectable' Church of England settlement in eastern South Island which would, from its inception, have churches, schools and all the institutions associated with prosperous early Victorian English society. Only carefully-selected migrants were allowed to join the venture, travelling out to the new province of Canterbury, accompanied by Godley, in 1850 and founding there a city named Christchurch, after Godley's Oxford college. The Canterbury Association was the Company's last and most successful venture. The *Colonial Office had always looked askance at the Company's independence of official policy; in 1850 the government bought out the bondholders, and the Company was dissolved.

Newfoundland: the tenth province of Canada, comprising both the island of Newfoundland and the mainland peninsula of Labrador. The provincial capital, St John's, was founded as a settlement by fishermen from Devonshire in the sixteenth century and is the oldest town in North America. Archaeological evidence shows there was a Viking settlement in northern Newfoundland by AD 1000, and the Norsemen may have arrived in Labrador even earlier. John Cabot sighted and named the island on 24 June 1497. Claims of English sovereignty were asserted in

257

Nigeria

Henry VIII's reign (1537) and reaffirmed by Humphrey *Gilbert when he landed at St John's in 1583. Long disputes with the French over fishing rights were only partially settled by the Treaty of Utrecht of 1713, and not finally resolved until the conclusion of the Anglo-French Entente in 1904. A royal governor was appointed to Newfoundland for the first time in 1729, and permanent settlements developed during the following eighty years; Labrador was attached administratively to Newfoundland from 1809 onwards. The colony received self-government in 1855, at a time when fishing the Great Banks and fish-processing were still major industries, though attention was already turning to the timber potential of the interior. Since Newfoundland looked out towards the Atlantic and Europe rather than the west, colonial spokesmen rejected proposals to join the new Dominion of Canada in 1867; there was a widespread fear of being swamped by Quebec and Toronto. Newfoundland received Dominion status in 1917, but was made virtually bankrupt by the *Great Depression in 1929/31. So grave was the economic situation that in February 1933 a Royal Commission recommended the suspension of Dominion status and the administration of the island and Labrador by seven nominated commissioners, a solution adopted in February 1934. A combination of British loans and money generated by US bases during World War II led to improved conditions. In June 1946 a convention was elected to discuss the former Dominion's future, and a referendum on 3 June 1948 put three choices before Newfoundlanders: results showed that 64,900 wanted the return of responsible Dominion government; 64,100 wanted union with Canada; and 23,300 were happy with the nominated commissioners and a prospect of continued British loans. This third possibility was not offered in a second referendum, held seven weeks later, when 78,323 voters favoured joining Canada but 71,334 still wanted a return to responsible government. Negotiations continued in Ottawa for six months, and at midnight on 31 March 1949 Newfoundland and Labrador were integrated with Canada. The union has led to improved communications by rail and road with the rest of continental North America and to a greater diversity in the economy, especially the development of *hydro-electric projects, newsprint shipments and off-shore oil-wells.

Nigeria: a federal republic within the Commonwealth: capital, Abuja (which replaced the former capital, Lagos, in December 1991). Modern Nigeria has a population of 112.2 million, more than twice as many people as in any other African state, and the ninth largest in the world. Yet the republic has little natural racial, cultural and historic unity. The largest single ethnic group are the Muslim *Hausa, closely linked to the fierce warrior Fulani and associated with the trading centre of Kano from the eleventh to the sixteenth century, and with the Sultanate of Sokoto in the nineteenth century. The non-Muslim *Ibo in the east and the

*Yoruba also have historic associations: there were Yoruba city-states in the mid twelfth century, a Benin imperial confederacy in the early fourteenth century, and an Oyo empire around Lagos at the start of the seventeenth century. A hundred years later, the successors of all these communities were involved in the *slave trade; the earliest British commitments in West Africa were concerned with the suppression of that trade. Lagos was taken in 1851, as a base of operations: it was not annexed until April 1861, and even then was administered from *Sierra Leone and later as part of the *Gold Coast, only becoming a separate colony in January 1886. Parliament showed great reluctance to become entangled in West Africa, though there was some interest in the growing palm-oil trade of the Niger delta, particularly when the French and German governments began to back commercial ventures in the region. After the *West Africa Conference at Berlin in 1884/5, a Niger Districts Protectorate was set up by the British; it was renamed *Oil Rivers Protectorate in 1891, and Niger Coast Protectorate in 1893. At the same time, from 1886 onwards several trading partnerships, unified under charter as the Royal Niger Company, made their own terms with the emirates of the middle Niger. A steady forward policy, taking over Yorubaland in 1893 and Benin in 1897, received purpose and direction from Frederick *Lugard: the Royal Niger Company's lands passed to the Crown in 1900 and were organized as the Protectorate of Southern Nigeria (which from February 1906 included Lagos) and the Protectorate of Northern Nigeria. The whole region became a single Colony and Protectorate on 1 January 1914. The mandated, formerly German, Cameroons (see *Southern Cameroons*) were administered as part of Nigeria between the wars, making the Protectorate Britain's largest colony in Africa. The chief exports were palm-oil, cocoa and tin. Some Ibos became wealthy on river trade and improved their education abroad: among them was Dr *Azikiwe, an advocate of self-government from 1937 onwards. An experimental unitary state of Eastern, Western and Northern regions was formed in October 1954, with internal self-government accorded to the Eastern and Western regions in 1956, but not to the allegedly backward Northern Region until 1959: full independence within the Commonwealth followed on 1 October 1960, and a republic was proclaimed exactly three years later, with Azikiwe as first President. *Oil had been discovered in the already richer south-eastern region in 1958, encouraging a secessionist movement. There was widespread resentment of the narrow power base of government under *Balewa, Azikiwe's Hausa Prime Minister, and rumours of widespread corruption. On 14 January 1966 the civilian government was overthrown in the first of at least six military coups which have heightened Nigeria's political instability. When the army commander General Ironshi was ambushed and killed seven months later, power passed to Colonel (later General) Yakubu Gowon (1934–   ). Inter-racial violence became so intense that the Eastern region finally seceded, as *Biafra, and a civil war weakened the country from 1967 to 1970. General Gowon imposed reforms, including a change of structure by which Nigeria became a federation of twelve 'equal and autonomous' states, but while he was visiting Kampala in August 1975 his government was overthrown in a coup led by Brigadier Murtala Mohammed, who had time to increase the federated states from twelve to nineteen before being murdered by mutinous troops in February 1976. Four years of a cautious transition to civilian rule coincided with peak earnings from oil refineries at Kduna, Port Harcourt and Warri. However, Muslim fanatics seeking to impose Islamic purity brought such anarchy to the Kano region in December 1980 that the federal army moved in; a thousand civilians were killed. Oil revenue began to fall drastically in 1981 and austerity measures were imposed, amid widespread accusations of corruption. A bloodless military coup on 31 December 1983 was followed by nine years of harsh military rule: an Armed Forces Council increased the number of federated states to thirty, while pursuing a strongly centralized policy which emphasized Nigeria's links with the Islamic world. Throughout 1993 and 1994 there was a power struggle between General Sanni Abacha's ruling military council and a civilian political movement which supported Chief Moshood Abiola; the latter claimed victory in presidential elections held on 11 June 1993, but these were declared invalid by Abacha's ruling council. Strikes in support of Abiola virtually closed down the oil industry, Nigeria's main source of export revenue.

Nineteen Counties: a border of settlement officially recognized in *New South Wales in 1829, extending from Taree, at the mouth of the river Manning in the north, inland to Dubbo, Parkes, and as far south as the upper Murray River and the coast at Moruya. Pastoralists who crossed this line of settlement were at the time regarded as 'squatters', though they are accepted now as pioneers opening up Australia.

Niue: a coral island in the South Pacific, closely linked in cultural tradition and language with Rarotonga in the *Cook Islands, 580 miles to the east. Niue, which has a population of less than 2,300, is a self-governing territory in free association with New Zealand; the administrative centre is the port of Alofi. Although only two-thirds the size of the Isle of Wight, it is the largest inhabited coral island in the world. Captain Cook, discovering Niue in 1774, was met by rock-throwing native warriors, their teeth artificially coloured red; he named his discovery Savage Island, and sailed away. Missionaries bravely settled on Niue in 1846, but it remained neglected by the Great Powers until the growth of Anglo-German rivalry led to the establishment of a British Protectorate in 1900; annexation by New Zealand (1,300 miles away) followed a year later. Self-government in internal affairs was granted on 19 October 1974, although defence and external relations remain New Zealand's responsibility. There is a steady migration of the young to New Zealand, since Niue has little employment to offer apart from the production and export of coconuts and honey.

Nkomo, Joshua (1917–), Vice-President of Zimbabwe: born at Matopos, Matabeleland; educated in Natal and the Transvaal and worked as a welfare officer and trade-union organizer on Rhodesia's railways in the Bulawayo region. He presided over the Rhodesian section of the African National Congress from 1957 until 1959, when it was banned in Salisbury (Harare). In 1961 he founded ZAPU (Zimbabwe African People's Union) but it was declared illegal and he was kept in detention by the Rhodesian authorities from November 1964 to December 1974. His leadership of the Zimbabwe movement seemed confirmed when British emissaries visited him in detention while seeking a Rhodesian settlement in 1968 and 1971. In October 1976 he led the ANC delegation to Geneva in a further search for a settlement, subsequently working with Robert Mugabe, the leader of ZANU (Zimbabwe African National Union), in the Patriotic Front's guerrilla campaign against the illegal white government in Rhodesia. Nkomo established ZAPU's headquarters in The Gambia, at Lusaka, and was fortunate to escape death when Rhodesian commandos raided the base in April 1979. Nkomo was in London five months later for the *Lancaster House Conference on Zimbabwe. In Zimbabwe's first elections ZANU received a wider backing than ZAPU and its leader Mugabe became Prime Minister, while the better-known Nkomo became Home Affairs Minister. Relations between the two men were often strained; Nkomo left office in January 1981 and was for a time suspected of planning a coup against Mugabe. In December 1987, however, ZANU merged with ZAPU and there was a reconciliation between President Mugabe and Nkomo, who became one of the republic's two vice-presidents.

Nkrumah, Kwame (1909–72), President of Ghana: born and baptized Francis Nwia Koffi at Nkroful, near Axim, the son of a goldsmith; educated at Roman Catholic mission schools and taught in them for five years before going in 1935 to Lincoln College in Pennsylvania, USA. He studied law in London at the end of World War II, and helped organize the fifth *Pan-African Congress in 1945. Two years later he published *Towards Colonial Freedom*, a reasoned appeal for self-government in Britain's African territories. On returning to Accra in 1949 he advocated 'positive action' to advance decolonization by civil disobedience, strikes and intensive propaganda. He founded the Convention People's Party (CPP), the earliest mass-appeal movement in West Africa. Despite briefly imprisoning him as a dangerous 'subversive', the colonial authorities recognized his national leadership when the CPP began to win a succession of electoral victories. In 1952 Nkrumah became Premier of the Gold

Coast, presiding over its transition into the Dominion of *Ghana in March 1957 and becoming President of the new republic on 1 July 1960. Although he was at first hailed by other Pan-Africans as 'the Redeemer' and 'the Gandhi of Africa', his encouragement of a personality cult aroused suspicion, as did his growing admiration for Mao and Ceaușescu. His dictatorial tendencies led him to interfere with the judiciary and to impose extravagant public works projects which, with a slump in cocoa prices in 1965, led to economic chaos. His ill-advised visit to China in February 1966 gave the army the opportunity to overthrow his government. He found sanctuary in Guinea but his health gave way and he travelled to Romania, where he died in a sanatorium in April 1971. Although the Ghanaian people had toppled a massive statue of Nkrumah in 1966, they honoured him as Founding Father of the nation in July 1972 at a state funeral in Axim.

Nolan, Sir Sidney Robert (1917–92), Australian artist: born in Melbourne, the son of a tram-driver. He became a virtually self-taught painter in the late 1930s, holding an exhibition in 1940 and a year later experimenting with theatrical design for the De Basil Ballet's *Icarus* in Sydney. During army service in World War II he was stationed in the outback of Victoria, an experience which heightened his perception of spacious landscape. He attracted attention in 1945–47 with the first of two series of paintings centred on the Ned *Kelly legend, his grandfather having been one of the policemen who hunted the gang. Later themes to inspire him included the *Burke and Wills Expedition, *Gallipoli, and, in the 1960s, Leda and the Swan. Though Nolan exhibited in Paris in 1948 and his work won great respect in Italy and the United States during the 1950s, he was strangely neglected by British galleries for another twenty years. In many respects his artistry seemed inspired by a similar vision of an untamed continent as the literary work of his friend Patrick *White, for whose famous novel *Voss* he designed the dust-jacket. Nolan returned to theatrical design most effectively in May 1962 for the revival by the Royal Ballet of *The Rite of Spring*, his costumes suggesting an aboriginal colouring of the skin, while as a backcloth he had a merciless sun scorching an arid landscape. Nolan, who was knighted in 1981 and given the OM in 1983, also published *Paradise Garden* (1972), a personally illustrated collection of his poems. For the last nine years of his life his home was in England, along the Welsh marches border.

North-West Frontier Province. During the 1840s the threat of disintegration in the Punjab, which would leave a power vacuum that might be filled with Russian nominees, led successive Governors-General in India to undertake forward policies, thrusting the frontier of British rule northwards into the mountain offshoots of the Hindu Kush. This advance, carried through in two wars against the *Sikhs, was completed in 1849 but left uncertain the north-western frontier line with Afghanistan. The region became a military buffer zone, strategically important because of the *Khyber Pass and the less used caravan routes through the Gomal, Kuram and Tochi Passes. Defence of these routes committed the British Army to a series of eighteen campaigns against Pathan hill tribesmen between 1863 and 1901, when a region covering some 30,000 square miles around Peshawar was formed as the North-West Frontier Province. Resistance continued during the inter-war period, when aircraft were frequently used against militant tribesmen, even as late as December 1938. The Province became an administrative region within *Pakistan in 1947, its military importance again emphasized between 1979 and 1990 when the province sheltered some 3 million refugees forced out of Afghanistan by Soviet invaders. Many of those refugees were insurgent Mujaheddin ('holy warriors'), whose Islamic militancy influenced the people among whom they settled.

Northern Frontier District (NFD): a long disputed region, mostly scrub-desert, stretching for some 400 miles along Kenya's border with the former Italian Somaliland and Ethiopia. From 1893 onwards the fierce Somali peoples of Jubaland and eastern Borana resisted British attempts to settle a frontier on the Juba River. By 1900 the Somalis were seeking to migrate southwards, away from the desert, encouraged by the successes of their kinsfolk under the so-called *'Mad Mullah' in *British Somaliland. Several campaigns had to be waged by the locally-raised East African Rifles and their successors in the *King's African Rifles to check Somali infiltration. By a treaty with Mussolini in July 1924 the British ceded to Italian Somaliland the line of the Juba River and a strip of more than 50 miles south-west of it. Mussolini's invasion of Ethiopia in 1935 made the NFD once again a sensitive area, and the definitive frontier in the north was not settled until 1947. Most of the old NFD now forms Kenya's sparsely populated North-Eastern Province; capital, Garissa.

Northern Territory (Australia). A Dutch sailing vessel from the East Indies, the *Arnhem*, visited the northern coast of Australia in 1623; *Tasman came in 1644; and a French navigator, Nicholas Baudin (1754–1803), made two visits, in 1801 and 1803. But it was *Flinders who made the first detailed survey of the coast. Fear of French activity prompted the despatch of a party from New South Wales to establish a base at Port Essington in 1824, but they found that the tropical conditions and the shortage of fresh water ruled out permanent settlement. Further attempts to establish townships on Melville Island and in Raffles Bay were also abandoned, although New South Wales accepted administrative responsibility for the whole region from 1825 onwards. In 1862 *Stuart, with funds from the colonial government of South Australia, reached the northern coast from Adelaide. A year later the territory was transferred from NSW to South Australia, of which it remained a corporate part until January 1911, when it became the responsibility of the Commonwealth of Australia collectively. The South Australian authorities had more success than their predecessors; they developed the town and port of Darwin on the site of a settlement made in 1862, giving it permanence as the northern terminal of the Overland *Telegraph Line in 1872. Construction of the telegraph route also led to the founding of the inland towns of Alice Springs and Katherine. Although there was good pasturage on the northern tableland, the Territory was slow to develop. One-fifth of the land formed aboriginal reserves. An administrative division in 1926, separating Central Australia around Alice Springs from the far north, was abandoned in 1931, largely as a result of financial constraints. Darwin was heavily bombed by the Japanese on 19 February 1942 and there were a further 63 air raids on the town and port, as well as a raid as far inland as Katherine in March 1942; but in general World War II had a beneficial effect on the Territory, opening up an arterial land route from Alice Springs to Tennant Creek, Katherine and Darwin which later became the Stuart Highway. Improved communications helped tap the Territory's latent mineral resources, especially its extensive uranium reserves. Self-government was introduced for the Northern Territory on 1 July 1978. Much progress has been made in protecting *aborigines and their lands since the Aboriginal Land Rights Act of 1976 provided new criteria for assessing claims: a 1993 survey showed that aborigines form about a quarter of the population of the Northern Territory and that courts of law have confirmed aboriginal ownership of slightly more than a third of the land, while many further claims are under investigation.

Northwest Territories of Canada cover an area of 1,323,000 square miles (larger than India), and in the 1991 census returned 57,649 residents. The whole area, once the great hunting ground of fur trappers, was the responsibility of the *Hudson's Bay Company until 1869 when it was absorbed into the new Dominion of Canada. The *Yukon became a separate territory in 1898. Mining – for lead, zinc and gold – replaced furs as the greatest source of profit after World War II and exploratory projects for oil and gas production multiplied rapidly in the 1980s, especially in the second half of the decade, when crude oil from Norman Wells was piped to a refinery in Alberta. A legislative assembly was set up at Yellowknife in 1979. In November 1992 a referendum in the Territories proposed a division which would allow the creation of Nunavat, an autonomous Inuit (*Eskimo) region, covering 850,000 square miles, with its capital at Iqaluit on Baffin Island. An agreement to establish Nunavat by 1999 was signed by the Dominion Prime Minister, Brian *Mulroney, on 1 June 1993.

Nova Scotia: eastern Canadian province, consisting of the original Nova Scotia peninsula and Cape Breton Island. The whole area formed part of the ill-defined French colony of Acadia, but the peninsula was granted by James I to Sir William Alexander in 1621 as New Scotland (called, in the charter, 'Nova Scotia'). A settlement was established and baronetcies were sold, but the region was ceded to France by Charles I in the treaty of St Germain in 1632; Cromwell ordered re-establishment of the settlement in 1654; and Charles II restored it to France in 1667 – but some Scottish settlers remained, despite the shifts of sovereignty. Nova Scotia was finally ceded to Britain by the Treaty of Utrecht (1713) and became a springboard of assault on French Canada in the mid eighteenth century, with the provincial capital of Halifax founded as a naval base in 1749. From 1759 to 1764 Nova Scotia included *New Brunswick and, from 1763 to 1769, *Prince Edward Island. Cape Breton Island, where the population has remained almost entirely of French or Scottish origin, was not surrendered by France until 1758; it was detached from Nova Scotia in 1784 but failed to develop as a separate province and in 1820 was incorporated again. Highland Scots, Ulstermen and Germans in the later eighteenth century, plus Lowland Scots after the Napoleonic Wars, have shaped Nove Scotia's cultural development. Shipbuilding flourished until the coming of iron, and ship-owning proliferated until one Halifax merchant, Samuel Cunard (1787–1865), began a service of steamships in 1840 to revolutionize transatlantic crossings. Sir Charles Tupper (1821–1915), the medical practitioner who became Premier of Nova Scotia in 1864, secured the backing of the provincial assembly for confederation, despite forceful opposition from Joseph Howe (1804–73), the most respected political spokesman in Nova Scotia for the preceding quarter of a century. Nova Scotia, having first considered a federal union of the three *maritime provinces, entered the new Dominion in 1867. The decisive influence was a pledge to begin work within six months on a railway from Halifax to Montreal, thus giving the historic port access to the west. During the years of agricultural depression in the 1880s and again in the late 1920s, some Nova Scotians complained that they were subsidizing the prairie lands. But the province kept its distinctive character. Although iron and steel mills and coal mines brought heavy industry, especially to Cape Breton Island, and the apple orchards on the west of the peninsula are famous, 75 per cent of Nova Scotia remains forest land, a quarter of it owned by the province; and fishing remains a primary industry. In June 1992 an offshore oilfield went into production, the first in Canada.

Nuclear Tests. The first nuclear weapons tests within the Commonwealth were the explosions of three British atomic bombs on the Monte Bello Islands, off the north-west coast of Western Australia, beginning on 3 October 1952. Further tests took place on the *Woomera range in South Australia, at Emu in 1953 and at Maralinga in 1956/7. A test hydrogen bomb was detonated over Christmas Island in the south-western Pacific on 15 May 1957, a year after America's first thermo-nuclear test at Bikini

Atoll in the Marshall islands. Alarm at the consequences of a proliferation of nuclear explosions led to voluntary abstention from testing by the Great Powers from 1958, and to a partial Test Ban Treaty in 1963. Neither France nor China accepted the ban: both New Zealand and Australia frequently protested at the French continuance of nuclear tests at the mid-Pacific atoll of Muroroa. On 10 July 1985 *Rainbow Warrior*, a Greenpeace vessel about to sail to the French prohibited area to frustrate further testing, was mined in New Zealand's Waitemata harbour by French saboteurs, killing a Greenpeace photographer, straining relations between Wellington and Paris, and encouraging New Zealanders to take the lead in sponsoring the Nuclear Free Zone Treaty of the *South Pacific Forum, agreed at Raratonga that year. The announcement by President Chirac in July 1995 that France would resume nuclear tests led to fresh confrontations with Greenpeace protestors at sea and to strained relations between France and members of the *South Pacific Forum.

Nyasaland: the name given to present-day *Malawi when it became a British Protectorate in 1891. From 1893 until 1907 it was officially called the British Central African Protectorate, and from 1953 until 1963 it was linked with the Rhodesias in the *Central African Federation. On independence, in July 1964, the name of the ancient kingdom of Malawi was adopted.

Nyerere, Julius Kambarage (1922–   ), President of Tanzania: born at Butiama on Lake Victoria; educated at Makerere College and Edinburgh University. He abandoned a teaching career to organize the politically moderate Tanganyika African National Union (TANU) in 1954. In 1958 and again in 1960 TANU won electoral successes throughout the country, and Nyerere became Prime Minister of Tanganyika in May 1961; he was elected President of the Republic in November 1962. When *Tanzania was formed in 1964 he became acting head of the united republic, his status as executive President confirmed by elections in 1965, 1970, 1975 and 1980. Although advocating a specifically Christian socialism and treating cautiously all contacts with China and the Soviet Union, Nyerere accepted the need to impose one-party government on the republic; he accordingly merged TANU with Zanzibar's Afro-Shirazi Party in 1977 to form Chama cha Mapinduzi ('Revolutionary Party'), of which he was chairman until 1985. President Nyerere, a man of scholarship, has also translated Shakespeare's *Julius Caesar* and *The Merchant of Venice* into Swahili for use in Tanzania's colleges and schools. He retired in October 1985 and was succeeded by President Ali Hasan Mwinyi.

Obote, (Apollo) Milton (1924–   ), President of Uganda: born in the Lango region of Uganda; educated at Jinja and at Makerere College, where he gained a doctorate. He migrated to Kenya and from 1950 worked there as a labourer, clerk and salesman, joining the Kenya Africa Union as an early member. He returned to Uganda in 1955 and was admitted to the colony's legislative council in 1957. Three years later he founded the Uganda People's Congress (UPC), and became Prime Minister when Uganda gained independence in October 1962. Dr Obote's desire for a unitary state was in conflict with the influential federal traditions of *Buganda. His revised republican constitution, replacing the office of Prime Minister with an executive President, became effective in May 1967, despite fierce resistance from Buganda to his accumulation of power. While President Obote was attending the Singapore Commonwealth Conference in January 1971, his allegedly corrupt government was overthrown in a military coup led by Idi *Amin. Obote went into exile in Tanzania, but returned to Kampala in 1980, after Amin's downfall, and claimed victory for the UPC in the ensuing general election. He was sworn in once more as President on 15 December 1980. Intercommunal violence, aggravated by food shortages and corruption, culminated in another military coup in July 1986, when Dr Obote found refuge in Zambia.

Oil (Petroleum). The earliest petroleum-producing region in the British Empire was south-western Ontario, where the first well in North America was dug in 1858 at Oil Springs, midway between Lake Erie and Lake Huron; it was followed by several drilled flowing wells at Black Creek Valley in 1862; a small refinery town, Petrolia, developed there and was exporting oil to Europe by 1870. By 1914 oil was also being produced from wells in southern Trinidad (opened in 1909), north Borneo, Assam and Burma. Already, however, British investors were more interested in the potentially rich fields of the Middle East: the first significant flow of oil in the Gulf was at Masjid-i-Suleiman (Persia) on 20 May 1908, within the recognized British sphere of commercial interest; the Anglo-Persian Oil Company opened a refinery at Abadan in 1912; and the Turkish Petroleum Company, committed to developing the resources of the Mosul and Baghdad provinces, was registered in London in 1911/12. After World War I these provinces formed part of British-mandated *Iraq – where a new oilfield was opened up in 1927, with a pipeline to Haifa, in British-mandated *Palestine. A Canadian-registered company developed the oil wells of *Bahrain from 1932 onwards, completing the main refinery in 1937; oil wells were sunk in British-protected Kuwait in 1936 but the output was small until after World War II, when the Burgan oilfield reached its full potential after the Mina al-Ahmadi refinery was opened in 1949. Britain was also responsible until 1971 for the defence and external policies of the *Trucial States emirates in the Gulf: these included Abu Dhabi, Dubai and Sharja, where oil revenue flowed freely in the 1960s. Among Commonwealth members, Canada has experienced a succession of oil booms; Turner Valley in Alberta was opened up in 1936, followed by a second Alberta 'find' at Leduc in 1947, and by Redwater (1948), Pembina (1953), and Swan Hills (1967). There was a big leap in production in the 1960s, especially in Alberta, with the opening up of the Athabasca Valley oilfields, first discovered nearly eighty years before; by the late 1980s more than 80 per cent of Canada's crude petroleum came from Alberta. On the outbreak of World War II the largest producer of petroleum in the Empire was Trinidad, with sixteen companies managing the wells and two large refineries; though Trinidad's share of the market fell considerably with the rise of the Middle Eastern fields, oil production is still the island's chief source of revenue. Nigeria shot to prominence as an oil producer in the early 1960s, with crude oil exports tripling between 1963 and 1966 and rising again in the 1970s; however, though Nigeria became the one Commonwealth member of OPEC, the country's oil revenue has suffered from political instability. The late 1970s saw a rapid rise of production in Australia, especially the Gippsland field (Victoria) and the Carnarvon field (Western Australia). Offshore drilling has brought an oil industry to Scotland and the prospect of oil revenue to, among other areas, Newfoundland and Bangladesh; the Iagafu oilfield in the Southern Highlands of Papua New Guinea also has great recoverable reserves.

Oil Rivers Protectorate: name used between 1891 and 1893 for the British Protectorate on the Niger delta, the embryonic *Nigeria. The 'oil' was palm oil, the main export of the region at that time.

Olympic Games. Four Commonwealth cities have been awarded the right to host the modern Olympic Games: London (1908; 1948); Melbourne (1956); Montreal (1976); Sydney (2000); the winter Olympics of 1988 were held in Canada, at Calgary. The XXIst Olympiad at Montreal suffered from the withdrawal of 19 African and Asian nations in protest at the participation of New Zealand, because the New Zealanders had agreed to send a Rugby Union team to South Africa, already ostracized by many governments because of *apartheid. Three Commonwealth countries – Canada, New Zealand, Kenya – also boycotted the XXIInd Olympiad in Moscow in 1980 in protest at the Soviet occupation of Afghanistan. The earliest threat to boycott any Olympiad was made in February 1938, when the Empire Games Federation, meeting in Sydney, announced that none of its members would participate in the proposed 1940 Games at Tokyo so long as Japanese troops continued to invade China. The venue was then switched to Helsinki, but the Games were then abandoned on the outbreak of World War II. (See also *Athletics*.)

Omdurman: town in the *Sudan, facing Khartoum, 5 miles to the south-east, across the River Nile. The *Mahdi's successor, Khalifa

Abdallahi (*c.*1850–99), made Omdurman his capital from 1885. On 1 September 1898 *Kitchener's troops shelled Omdurman, destroying the Mahdi's tomb. Next day they defeated the Khalifa's Dervishes, who had made a frontal attack on the British camp beside the Nile. The 21st Lancers, in which *Churchill was serving, launched a famous cavalry charge against the right flank of the Khalifa's army. Omdurman was entered before nightfall, and two days later Khartoum was taken.

Ontario: Canada's second largest province, with its capital at Toronto, Canada's second largest city. The province includes the Dominion capital, Ottawa, a city which developed very rapidly from the late 1820s, when it was a military timber base beside a river which gave the township its name. Ontario was first explored by the French in the period 1615 to 1627, when it became a royal province; even so, it was still primarily the home of fur traders and missionaries when ceded to Britain in 1763. Under the *Canada Constitutional Act of 1791 the province became 'Upper Canada', largely the home of settlers of English or Scottish descent, many of whom had emigrated northwards after the American colonies asserted their independence. In 1867 the province entered the confederation as Ontario. By then the peninsula between the three Great Lakes Huron, Erie and Ontario was becoming industrialized, a trend accelerated by the exploitation of its *oil resources, first tapped in 1858. The provincial boundary was extended to Hudson Bay in 1912. Although Ontario is Canada's most highly industrialized province, almost two-thirds of the land surface remains forested.

Opium Trade. The expansion of British commercial control over India ensured that from 1773 onwards the *East India Company enjoyed a monopoly of the drug's growth and production, primarily in the Bengal Presidency. There had long been a small trade in opium between India and China, and opium addiction intensified in southern China with the decline of Manchu administration and government towards the end of the eighteenth century. From the mid 1770s a regular trade developed, by which East India Company ships would carry Bihar opium principally from Calcutta to Canton (Guangzhou), returning with *tea for the London market. By the end of the century opium from the Makwa region (now in Madhya Pradesh) was similarly being shipped from Bombay. Opium exports were worth about a quarter of a million pounds a year to the Company by 1803, and thereafter rose steadily: in the first decade of the nineteenth century, the number of opium chests conveyed aboard the Company's ships multiplied ten times over, to reach 224,968 in 1810/11 and then, during the next decade, to 424,244 chests by 1820/1. Although officially the Manchu emperor had closed all his ports to foreign commerce, the Chinese authorities at first connived at this blatantly illegal trade; but in 1839 the imperial Chinese authorities ordered their commissioner in Canton to put a halt to the opium trade and he impounded 20,291 chests. This intervention was resented by British merchants, and the resultant 'Opium War' (see *below*) of 1839–42 and the Treaty of *Nanking opened a series of ports to British trade, as well as handing over the sovereignty of *Hong Kong. Compensation was paid to indemnify merchants for the confiscated opium but the British did not specifically mention the trade, which they regarded as a normal commercial transaction. The opium trade continued to bring profit to *Jardine, Matheson and other commercial houses in the colony, where the smoking of opium remained legal until 1940. After the so-called Second Opium War (1856–60) the opium trade was 'regulated', and thus tacitly legalized. As late as 1910 imperial China was still importing £7.5 million a year worth of opium from British India, but the collapse of the Manchu empire in 1911 forced the opium trade underground once more.

Opium Wars. The name given to two Anglo-Chinese conflicts. The first began in 1839, after the Chinese government confiscated *opium amassed at Canton. The Royal Navy took *Hong Kong, carrying the war to the Yangtze River in the summer of 1842 when Shanghai, Woosung and Chinliang were shelled and taken, by landing forces who suffered higher casualties from disease and the heat than from battle. The war ended, humiliatingly for China, with the *Nanking Treaty. Chinese seizure of a suspect Hong Kong-registered small vessel, the *Arrow*, led to the second conflict (1856–60). This was a protracted war, in which a truce in 1858 was followed, on China's refusal to ratify the peace terms, by a second campaign in 1860 in which Peking (Beijing) was entered and the Imperial Summer Palace was looted and burnt to the ground. The effect of these wars was to open China's *Treaty Ports to foreign trade, overwhelmingly British.

Orange Free State (OFS). *Boer farmers crossed the Orange River in the late eighteenth century and a few homesteads were made north of the upper river between 1809 and 1820. Full settlement came with the *Great Trek, and in the face of fierce hostility from the Sotho peoples. The Governor of Cape Colony, Sir Harry Smith (1787–1860), annexed the region in 1848, but a change of policy in London left the Boers to develop their own 'Free State', a measure confirmed by the Bloemfontein Convention (1854). Disputes continued, both with the Sothos and with Cape Colony, particularly over OFS claims to Griqualand West after the *diamond rush to Kimberley. President Steyn of the OFS honoured alliance treaty obligations to join the Transvaal in the Second *Boer War, but the OFS was overrun by *Roberts's army in February and March 1900. On 28 May 1900, while the war was still in progress, the territory was annexed as the Orange River Colony. Responsible government was conceded in 1907 and in May 1910 it became a province of the Union of

South Africa, resuming its traditional name. The OFS's capital, Bloem-fontein, became South Africa's legal and judicial centre. Although coal is mined in the north of the province, a goldfield was opened at Odendaalsrus soon after World War II and diamonds are mined at Jagers-fontein, the OFS remains primarily pastoral and agricultural country.

Oregon Dispute. During the settlement of *British Columbia frequent tensions arose between British and Americans over the western bound-ary between Canada and the USA, an area unexplored when the main line of the frontier up to the Rockies was settled in 1818. By the mid 1840s American farmers had moved into the valleys, while the British were established on Vancouver Island. A compromise settlement in 1846 extended the *Forty-ninth Parallel line westwards to Puget Sound, leaving Oregon as part of the USA and enabling Vancouver Island to develop as part of Canada. With the exception of a lingering dispute over the *San Juan islands (between 1859 and 1871), the 1846 settlement has never been challenged.

Ottawa Imperial Economic Conference (21 July to 20 August 1932): summoned by the Canadian Prime Minister, Richard *Bennett, to discuss ways of meeting collectively the challenge of the *Great Depres-sion. Bennett's hopes of securing guarantees of wheat prices were not realized, but he was able to promote the ideal of *imperial preference, which he had long championed. The Ottawa Agreements were a series of documents which ensured that the United Kingdom would allow the import of goods, food and raw materials from the Empire either without tariffs or at preferential rates, in return for guarantees that the dominions would give preference to exports from each other or from Britain, pro-vided always that they did not harm native industries. The Ottawa Agreements were extended in 1933 to cover the colonies as well as the dominions.

Outram, Sir James (1803–63), soldier: born in Derbyshire; educated at Aberdeen; commissioned into the Bombay Infantry in 1819, he became equally respected for subduing rebellious Dangs and Bhils and for hunting wild animals. After serving for three years as Political Agent at Gujarat, he made his name during the First *Afghan War when he rode 355 miles from Kelat through the Bolan Pass with vital despatches. His courage and chivalry led him to be respected, even in his early forties, as the 'Bayard of India'. He added to his legend by bravely defending the Residency at Hyderabad in 1843 against 8,000 Sikhs. As Resident at Baroda from 1847 to 1851 he caused consternation with his report on corruption among senior officials; he was removed from his post but later vindicated, and subsequently received a knighthood. In 1857 he managed a brisk, victorious campaign against Persia. During the *Indian Mutiny he defended Lucknow during its second siege and held the city again until final relief came. After leave in London he returned to India to serve as military member of *Canning's council, but his health was broken. He died at Pau while recuperating, in the winter of 1863. He is buried in Westminster Abbey, as one of the outstanding military heroes of British India.

Overseas Development Administration (ODA): department of state in the British government responsible for development assistance to overseas countries and for co-ordinating Britain's response to disasters (earthquakes, famines, etc.). The ODA forms part of the Foreign and Commonwealth Office and, while not restricted to meeting Commonwealth needs, must necessarily work closely with the *Commonwealth Development Corporation, providing funds to help support voluntary aid agencies working in developing countries.

P & O: the Peninsular and Oriental Steam Navigation Company traces its origins to the initiative of Brodie Wilcox and Arthur Anderson, London shipping agents for the City of Dublin Steam Packet Company, who in 1826 began a regular service to Portugal. In 1837 the government gave them the first overseas mail contract ever accorded to a steamship line, for all communications with the Iberian peninsula. So successful was the company that in 1840 it received a contract for a mail and passenger service to Alexandria, and on to India: 'and Oriental' was thereafter added to the company's name. The direct Suez to Calcutta line opened in 1842, and by the end of the decade had been extended to Singapore and Hong Kong. The Suez to Bombay route began in 1852; in the same year P & O secured the mail contract to Australia. With the opening of the *Suez Canal in 1869 it was possible to run a direct service from the United Kingdom to India and beyond. P & O, Kipling's 'exiles' line', became a projection of Anglo-Oriental life: the stewards were mostly from Goa, the seamen were mainly lascars, many of the engine-room crew came from Bombay. Until World War I P & O was challenged by Holt's Ocean Steamship Company (from 1865 onwards) in the Far East and, more persistently, from 1856 by BI (British India Steam Navigation Co.) Although BI was the first line to send a 'homeward bound' passenger ship northwards through the Suez Canal, its regular line from London to Calcutta, through the canal, did not come into service until 1876. P & O and BI merged in 1914; during the war P & O also took over the New Zealand Shipping Company. By 1939 the P & O group had at sea over 2 million tons of shipping: more than half this tonnage was sunk during World War II. These losses, together with competition from *airlines and the long closure of the Suez Canal after 1956, changed the group's character; P & O now concentrated on fast cruise liners and, from 1965, on cargo container ships. The regular Hong Kong, Singapore and India passenger service ended in 1969, the line from Sydney in the early 1970s. The group's services were thereafter concentrated in home waters rather than on providing a link between the nations of the Commonwealth.

Page, Sir Earle Christmas Grafton (1880–1961), Australian Prime Minister: born at Grafton, NSW; graduated from Sydney University to become a surgeon serving with the medical corps in Egypt and France in World War I; entered Parliament in 1919 and from 1921 to 1939 led the Country Party of rural conservatives. This numerically small group protected farming interests and kept up the price of wool and wheat by striking political bargains with larger parties, enabling them to enter the government in coalitions. From 7 April to 25 April 1939 Page headed the United Australia coalition government, but he was best known as Treasurer (federal finance minister) from 1924 to 1929, successfully concluding a financial agreement for loans from the federal government to help state governments in difficulties. Early in his career Page showed some sympathy with the movement to partition *New South Wales and establish a New England State in the predominantly agricultural north.

Pakeha (or *Paketa*): Maori word for settlers in New Zealand or for native-born New Zealanders not of Maori origin.

Pakistan: independent Islamic Republic within the Commonwealth; capital, Islamabad. The idea of a separate Islamic state in the sub-continent was first put forward by *Jinnah and the *Muslim League in 1942. The Indian Independence Act provided for the establishment, on 14 August 1947, of a dominion comprising Baluchistan, *Sind, the West Punjab, the *North-West Frontier and, 1,100 miles across India, East Bengal and some districts in Assam. *Kashmir was claimed by both Pakistan and India and has remained an area of dispute, causing three short wars between the two states. Pakistan remained a dominion until 1956, when a republic was proclaimed. The parliamentary constitution was suspended in October 1958 by General *Ayub Khan. Student riots, widespread strikes and mounting discontent in Pakistan's more distant provinces forced him to hand power over to General Yahya Khan (1917–80) in the last week of March 1969. The country remained under martial law, although in December 1970 Yahya Khan permitted 'one man, one vote' elections which gave victory to the People's Party, led by Zulfikar Ali *Bhutto. As the election also gave a boost to the secessionist movement in East Pakistan (*Bangladesh), Yahya Khan maintained martial law, thereby provoking a civil war which ended, in December 1971, with independence for Bangladesh and the elevation of Bhutto to the presidency of the republic. Britain's recognition of Bangladesh led President Bhutto to take Pakistan out of the Commonwealth on 30 January 1972. A new constitution in April 1973 provided for a federal parliamentary system which gave the republic a civilian government, until 5 July 1977 when General Mohammad Zia-ul-Haq (1924–88) carried through a bloodless military coup. People's Party leaders were arrested and on 4 April 1979 Zulfikar Bhutto was hanged, having been found guilty of 'conspiracy to murder'. President Zia imposed harsh Islamic punishments for crime under a new legislative code, but relaxed martial law for the first time in eight years in December 1985. Zia – together with the US ambassador and 21 senior army officers – was killed on 17 August 1988 when his aircraft blew up in flight, shortly after taking off from Bahawalpur. Elections in November were won by Benazir *Bhutto's People's Party, and Pakistan rejoined the Commonwealth on 1 October 1989. Criticism of her social policies led to the government's fall in August 1990 and an interlude of Islamic Democratic Alliance rule, until another general election in October 1993 enabled Benazir Bhutto to win a second victory and form a new government. Mounting fundamentalist unrest among Shia Muslims in the north and around Karachi threatened further internal upheaval during the early months of 1995.

Palestine: under Turkish rule from 1517 until overrun in *Allenby's offensives of 1917–18. Three days after Allenby launched his first offensive the *Balfour Declaration promised the Jewish people a national home in Palestine, an undertaking incorporated in the League of Nations *mandate which assigned Palestine to the British. A civilian administration was set up on 1 July 1920, control passing from the Foreign Office to the *Colonial Office in 1921. The region east of the river Jordan, which many observers regarded as an integral part of Palestine, became mandated *Transjordan, an area in which the promises implicit in the Balfour Declaration were held not to apply. Preservation of order in Palestine was entrusted to the RAF and to a specially-recruited Palestinian gendarmerie: regular British ground forces did not return until 1936. Administrative policy was determined by seven successive High Commissioners: Sir Herbert Samuel (1920–25); Field Marshal Lord Plumer (1925–28); Sir John Chancellor (1928–31); General Sir Arthur Wauchope (1931–37); Sir Harold Macmichael (1937–44); Field Marshal Lord Gort, VC (1944–45); and General Sir Alan Cunningham (1945–48). Great difficulties were experienced in holding a balance between the Arab and Jewish communities. After disturbances in 1921 there was a calm until 1928, when the Arabs became alarmed at the rapid growth of the Jewish population, which had doubled in ten years. There were attacks on Jewish settlements and grave rioting in the fourth week of August 1929, especially in Hebron and around Jerusalem, where 229 people died. A British report drawn up by Lord Passfield and published on 20 October 1930 emphasized the plight of the Palestinian Arabs: their shortage of land and work; their fear that within 20 years the Jewish population would outnumber the Arab. But the government rejected the report's recommendation of strict curbs on Jewish immigration. Growing anti-Semitism in Europe increased the rate of Jewish immigration from 4,075 in 1931 to 61,854 in 1935. A series of Arab attacks on Jewish settlements and on British troops in 1936 led to the commissioning of a further report, from Earl Peel, which (on 7 July 1937) recommended *partition into Arab and Jewish states, with the British retaining control of a corridor inland from Haifa and including Jerusalem, Nazareth and Bethlehem. This plan was unpopular with the Jewish community (who published their own partition proposals) and was rejected by the Arabs. To satisfy Arab grievances, the British sought to curb Jewish land purchases and imposed a strict limit to Jewish immigration, so that in 1941, for example, entry permits were issued to only 4,592 Jews; but many 'illegal' immigrants landed from small ships along the coast. Jewish anger at the British restraints led to attacks on British forces, although these were suspended during World War II. Terrorism became more widespread in 1946, notably by the Stern Gang and the Irgun Zvai Leumi, who on 22 July 1946 blew up the southwest wing of Jerusalem's King David Hotel, which housed the British administration: 91 lives were lost. New British partition proposals were rejected by the Jewish community and the Arabs, and on 26 September 1947 the Colonial Secretary told the UN General Assembly that Britain wished speedily to renounce the mandate; the UN then put forward its own partition plan, which was accepted by the Jews as a basis for Israeli statehood. The British mandate ended on 14 May 1948, most towns being evacuated by British troops in April. The Palestinian problem thereafter became primarily the concern of Israel and her Arab neighbours, an international question outside the range of direct Commonwealth influence.

Pan-African Congress, Manchester, 1945: Although four earlier congresses had been held to discuss the diaspora of the African peoples and their problems, the Fifth Congress, convened at Chorlton-on-Medlock, Manchester in October 1945 was the first to have a majority of delegates from Africa (rather than from the Caribbean) and the first to place the emancipation of the African peoples from colonialism at the head of the agenda for discussion. Two hundred delegates attended; the chairman was from British Guiana, one joint secretary was from Trinidad, and the treasurer was also from the West Indies: but the other joint secretary was *Nkrumah, and the assistant secretary was *Kenyatta. Resolutions were passed calling for government discussions to end colonial rule, for universal suffrage for men and women throughout the colonial possessions, for freedom of speech and of the printed word, and condemning all racial discrimination (specifically including anti-Semitism). The presence at Manchester of so many African students and their known political spokesmen in voluntary exile emphasizes the importance of the Congress in the early days of the decolonization movement.

Papineau, Louis Joseph (1789–1871), French-Canadian political leader: born in Montreal; became a member of the legislative assembly of Lower Canada in 1809 and was Speaker from 1815 to 1837. Papineau strongly opposed proposals to unify Upper and Lower Canada, voicing the suspicions of many French-Canadians that the government in London was encouraging land sales to incoming settlers from Britain or America, to the exclusion of the French tradition of seigneurial land-holding. In 1834 he presided over meetings of the assembly in Quebec at which 92 resolutions were passed, listing grievances – including many concerned with land tenure – and seeking control of finance by an assembly which would be totally elective and would also have a share in nominating the executive council. All these requests were rejected in London. The mood in Quebec hardened when further protest resolutions were ignored in August 1837. Papineau encouraged his followers to prepare for rebellion – a mood also prevalent in Ontario, under the leadership of W. L. *Mackenzie. When attempts to arrest the French-Canadian leaders were made in November 1837 shots were fired on both sides; Papineau escaped to the USA and then went into exile in Paris until he was able to return to Quebec under an amnesty in 1847. He sat briefly in the legislature, but no longer commanded a wide popular following; in 1854 he retired into private life.

Papua New Guinea (PNG): independent member of the Commonwealth in the south-west Pacific, the largest nation in Melanesia: capital, Port Moresby. PNG comprises the eastern portion of the island of New Guinea and some ten other islands, including Bougainville, the largest of the Solomon Islands. Culturally PNG is extremely diverse; it is a nation with more than 750 languages. The islands were visited by Portuguese seamen in 1527 and later claimed by the Spaniards, the Dutch and, in the Solomons, by the French. Eastern New Guinea – since 1963 the Indonesian province of Irian Jaya – became a Dutch colony in 1828 but no attempts were made to establish permanent white settlements elsewhere for half a century. German colonial activity in the early 1880s, together with signs of French interest, prompted the colonial government of Queensland to annex the southern coast of New Guinea (Papua) in 1883, to prevent it falling onto the hands of a potential enemy. The British government repudiated Queensland's action but made Papua a British Protectorate in 1884 and, with the backing of the eastern Australian colonies, formally annexed the region in 1888. It was assigned to the newly united Australia in 1902, though not handed over until 1906; the perceptive administrative guidance of Sir Hubert *Murray saved the people of Papua from exploitation by unscrupulous adventurers. Australian troops conquered the German north-western part of New Guinea in 1914 and it was administered by Australia, under League of Nations *mandate, from 1921 onwards. Japanese units landed in northern New Guinea in March 1942, and the Australians poured troops into Port Moresby; there was heavy fighting on the Kokoda Trail, high in the central mountains of the island, in late July and August before the Japanese were gradually forced back to their northern bases. Papua itself was effectively cleared of the invaders by the end of January 1943, but the Japanese sent reinforcements to northern New Guinea, engaging the Australians and Americans there until August 1944. Papua and New Guinea, together with other mandated islands, were administratively united as PNG by the Australians, with UN sanction, in 1949. Australia granted PNG self-government on 1 December 1973, its sprawling territories organized into 19 provinces. Full independence followed on 16 September 1975. Leading exports were copra, coffee, cocoa and palm oil, together with some rubber from Papua, but mineral resources were developed in the 1970s and 1980s; Bougainville in particular yielded copper and, to a lesser extent, silver and gold. Resentment at alleged exploitation of these deposits by other regions prompted the growth of a secessionist movement in the North Solomons province, unrest forcing the copper mines to close in May 1989. A 'Bougainville Revolutionary Army' claimed to have set up an independent government on the island in May 1990, with its capital at Arawa. By December 1993 PNG forces had captured Arawa, but occasional guerrilla clashes continued. Elsewhere in PNG attempts have been made to attract tourists by emphasizing the spectacular flora and fauna and, in particular, the rich natural heritage of bird life, which includes 26 species of kingfisher, 33 species of birds of paradise and no fewer than 55 species of parrot.

Paramountcy: a special relationship, established in 1857 and lasting until 1947, based upon a series of treaties by which the *princely rulers in India were allowed by the British sovereign to retain their autocratic rule in return for pledges of loyalty to the Queen (later to her as Empress, and to her descendants as Emperors). The imperial authorities had a right to intervene if a ruler behaved tyrannically or acted in collusion with the sovereign's enemies.

Park, Mungo (1771–1806), explorer of West Africa: born at Foulshiels, in the Scottish Borders, studied medicine at Edinburgh, and was ship's surgeon on a voyage to Sumatra in 1792, where he made botanical studies which greatly interested Sir Joseph *Banks, who encouraged him to go to Africa. In December 1795 he penetrated inland from the river Gambia, was held captive by Arab traders but escaped, reached the Niger at Seko and explored its banks as far as Bammaku; his health gave way and he was close to death when rescued by slave traders, who brought him back to The Gambia in June 1797. He returned to Scotland, and in his detailed book *Travels in the Interior of Africa* (1799) established the eastward direction of flow of the Upper Niger. Park married, settled in Peebles with a medical practice, and was befriended by Sir Walter Scott and other Scottish men of letters; becoming restless, he accepted an invitation to lead a second, government-sponsored expedition to the Niger in 1805, to trace its course to the coast. He set out from Pisania on the Gambia with a party of 45 men, which had diminished to 7 survivors by the time he reached the Niger at Bambakoo. From Sannsanding he sent back journals outlining his route, together with a preliminary geographical survey, but he then disappeared. It was discovered in 1812 that Mungo's party had reached Boussa, where they were attacked and killed by native tribesmen.

Partition: a principle tacitly accepted in nineteenth-century India under the system of *paramountcy, with the division of the country into directly-ruled provinces and *princely states which retained some autonomy. As a practical solution of imperial problems, however, partition was first proposed by *Churchill and Lloyd George on 4 February 1912 in cabinet discussions concerning Ulster opposition to Irish Home Rule. On that occasion it was rejected by their colleagues, and an amending bill to accept Irish partition, passed in the House of Lords in July 1914, was shelved by the government. However, partition became a reality in December 1920 with the passage of the Government of Ireland Act, which set up a six-county Parliament in Belfast, one year ahead of the grant of dominion status to the *Irish Free State. Partition between Arabs and Jews was proposed in *Palestine by the Peel Report of July 1937 but was rejected by most Arabs and Jews and by the House of Lords; subsequent partition plans in October 1938 and August 1946 were turned down by the Arabs, who also rejected the UN partition plans under which the state of Israel was created. Partition of India into two independent dominions was first seriously advocated by *Jinnah in 1942. It was only accepted by *Mountbatten in 1947 when an alternative proposal for a unitary state with provincial autonomy was rejected. The new boundaries were hurriedly determined by the Radcliffe Commission, without allowing for minority interests, including those of the *Sikhs. Practical application of Partition in the summer of 1947 created immense problems, partly because of uncertainties in the *princely states, but also because two great provinces (Bengal and the Punjab) were divided in the process; there were disputes over division of the *Indian Army, over responsibility for canal waters and large-scale irrigation projects, over the sharing of the government debt and Reserve Bank balance, and over compensation for property lost by refugees seeking safety across the new borders – for Partition necessitated the migration of 14 million people, often under conditions of great hardship, danger and personal tragedy. When the *Cyprus problem became acute in 1956–7 attempts were made to avoid partition because of the suffering and disruption it would bring to the Greek and Turkish communities, but in 1970 Turkish Cypriots established an assembly of their own in the north of the island. When the attempted EOKA coup against *Makarios brought near anarchy to the island in July 1974, the Turkish government in Ankara landed an army to protect its minority population, and eventually established a Turkish Republic of Northern Cyprus: partition was thus imposed on the island.

Pass Laws: legislation introduced by the *Malan government as part of *apartheid, strictly limiting the movements of non-whites. One of the many protests against the Pass Laws led to the *Sharpeville shootings of May 1960. The Pass Laws were repealed in 1991.

Paterson, Andrew Barton (1864–1941), Australian bush balladist and journalist: born, the son of a grazier, near Orange in New South Wales; studied law in Sydney and became a solicitor before taking up journalism. He was a war correspondent for the *Sydney Morning Herald* in South Africa and China at the turn of the century and edited two Sydney news-papers between 1904 and 1908, as well as serving in France and Egypt during World War I. He is best known as 'Banjo' Paterson, the writer of *The Man from Snowy River and other Verses*(1895). In April 1895 he wrote a ballad about the adventures of an itinerant labourer ('swagman') which was first sung – to a variation on a long-forgotten Scottish air – at a concert in Winton, Queensland: as *Waltzing Matilda*, the ballad became widely accepted as Australia's (strictly unofficial) *national anthem.

Pearson, Lester Bowles (1897–1972), Canadian Prime Minister: born, a Methodist minister's son, at Newtonbrook in Ontario; his education at Toronto University was interrupted by service in the army during World War I; he later went to St John's College, Oxford, as a Rhodes scholar. He joined the Canadian diplomatic service in 1928, gaining experience as deputy to the High Commissioner in London during the years of appeasement, and held ambassadorial rank in Washington in 1945/6, helping to establish the United Nations Organization. He entered the Canadian Parliament as a Liberal and was Minister for External Affairs from 1949 to 1957, swiftly becoming accepted as Canada's first world statesman. He helped create NATO, presided over the UN General Assembly in 1952, and in 1956 secured a ceasefire during the *Suez crisis, as well as easing the plight of refugees from Hungary. In 1957 he received the Nobel Peace Prize. A year later he succeeded *St Laurent as Liberal party leader and became Prime Minister in April 1963, remaining in office for five years even though the Liberals did not have a clear major-ity after the 1965 elections. He was not so successful in home affairs, partly because of a distaste for political in-fighting and partly because the electorate disliked his strong support for military participation in UN peace-keeping missions. He improved relations between Canadians of British and of French descent, but was disconcerted by de Gaulle's speech in July 1967 supporting *'*Québec libre*'. After retiring in favour of

Pierre *Trudeau, he chaired a World Bank commission on the problems of developing countries. Pearson received the Order of Merit in 1971.

Petroleum: see *Oil*.

Pindarees (Pindaris): free-ranging robber bands in central India, especially active between October 1814 and midsummer 1817; sometimes employed as bandit mercenaries by the *Maratha princes. The Pindarees ravaged the kingdom of Hyderabad in 1815 and in the following summer crossed the river Kistna into the frontier areas of Madras, which were nominally under British protection; they plundered several districts for twelve days, virtually unchecked. In the summer of 1817 the Marquess of Hastings (Lord Moira, Francis Rawdon-Hastings; 1754–1856), who was Governor of Bengal from 1813 to 1822, resolved to prevent further raids by striking at the Pindarees, even at the cost of renewed fighting with the Maratha princes. He mobilized an army of some 100,000 men, one section of which encircled the Pindaree strongholds in central India while the main force prevented their powerful allies among the Marathas from bringing them assistance. Hastings was thus able to destroy the threat of the Pindarees for all time, while also gaining decisive victories against four of the Maratha princes and advancing the frontier of British authority to the line of the river Sutlej.

Pitcairn Island. With the slightly larger uninhabited islands of Henderson, Ducie and Oeno, Pitcairn forms a British *Dependent Territory in the Pacific, equidistant from New Zealand and the isthmus of Panama. Discovered in 1767, it was uninhabited when in 1790, 9 mutineers from HMS *Bounty* landed there, together with 12 Tahitians, male and female. Nothing was known of the settlement until 1806, and their descendants remained on Pitcairn until 1856 when, as their numbers had increased to 194, they complained that since the island covered an area of less than 2 square miles, it was over-populated; they were removed to Norfolk Island (now an *Australian Dependent Territory). Within eight years, however, a quarter of the families evacuated had returned to Pitcairn, and in 1898 were given legal protection under the British High Commissioner in *Fiji. Since 1970 the High Commissioner in New Zealand has acted as Governor, with a ten-member advisory council on Pitcairn itself. The island exists on subsistence crop cultivation and fishing, selling wooden carvings to its few tourists. The population in January 1994 was 53. For more than a hundred years the families on the island have worshipped as Seventh Day Adventists.

Plague. Bubonic plague, a disease carried by infected rat fleas, has spread across the Eurasian land mass in several waves, most notoriously as the Black Death, in 1347–49, which killed about a quarter of Europe's population. A further famous epidemic struck western Europe in 1664/5. The last pandemic in the British Empire was in 1894, centred particularly in the Far East: one in eighty of the population of Hong Kong died of the plague that year, including Lady Robinson, wife of the colony's governor. It spread to India and was still virulent in parts of Bengal and the Punjab five years later. Although an effective vaccine was developed by the turn of the century, there have been occasional localized epidemics, most recently in late September 1994 at Surat, in the north-western Indian state of Gujarat, in the less virulent form known as pneumonic plague.

Plassey (Palasi): village in western Bengal on the river Bhagirathi. On 23 June 1757 *Clive defeated there the army of the Nawab of Bengal, Suraj-ud-Dowlah, thereby avenging the incident of the *black hole of Calcutta and consolidating the British hold over Bengal.

Polo: a game played in ancient Persia about 600 BC and surviving in northern India when the territory passed under British sovereignty. Polo was first organized as a modern sport by British army officers in Assam in the 1850s; the earliest polo club was established in Calcutta in 1862, nine years before the first match in England. Before World War I it was limited almost exclusively to India, England and USA, played mainly by army officers and by several Indian princes and their entourages. Between the wars polo spread widely in Europe, especially to Spain (before 1936) and to Argentina, but also to other parts of the British Empire, notably Australia, New Zealand, South Africa and Kenya. Quarantine regulations to guard against the spread of African horse sickness hit the sport internationally in the 1950s and contributed to the decline in the number of polo clubs in the Indian subcontinent; the expense and the legendary social exclusiveness of the sport has left it particularly exposed to the vagaries of political change.

Pretorius, Andries Wilhelminus Jacobus (1799–1853), *Boer leader: born near the Cape to a farming family of Dutch origin. He prospered as a farmer but supported the move of his compatriots northwards and was accepted as leader of the *Great Trek of 1837/8 into *Natal. On 16 December 1838 he led the Voortrekker troops who decisively defeated the *Zulu king Dingale at the Blood River battle. As commandant-general of the Boers he secured the *Transvaal from British attack in 1852. When a capital city was founded two years after his death it was named Pretoria in his honour. His son Martinus Pretorius (1819–1901), President of the Transvaal from 1857 to 1871, sought unsuccessfully to unite the Transvaal and the Orange Free State in 1862/3 and, after his resignation as President, took up arms against the British once more in 1877.

Prince Edward Island

Prince Edward Island, in the Gulf of St Lawrence, the smallest Canadian province, with an area of 2,185 square miles, barely a quarter the size of Wales. It was settled by the French, as Île St-Jean, taken by the British in 1758, and annexed to *Nova Scotia in 1763. Six years later a curious and disastrous experiment was made by which the island became a separate colony of Crown territory in which all land was parcelled out in London to veteran officers of the wars: large estates were thus held for the most part by absentee landowners. Despite the fertile soil of the island and the hardy qualities of Scottish immigrants, the colony lagged behind its larger neighbours. Not until 1798 did it receive its present name, in honour of the future Queen Victoria's father, who was at that time in command of British troops in Nova Scotia. The island was given responsible government in 1851 and, at Charlottetown in September 1864, hosted the first conference to discuss confederation. Yet, like *Newfoundland and unlike the two larger *Maritime Provinces, Prince Edward Island at first rejected membership of the new Dominion, looking as it did outwards to the Atlantic rather than up the St Lawrence, to the rest of Canada, from which it was cut off by ice for three months each year. The promise of dominion aid in buying out absentee landlords and of 'continuous communication' with the mainland eventually induced Prince Edward Island to enter the confederation, on 1 July 1873. But, though ice-breaker ferries provided links with neighbouring provinces, no tunnel or other form of communication was ever completed. Almost half the island remains farmland; the sea fishing trade also survives, particularly for lobsters.

Princely States (India). The system of *paramountcy in British India provided for the survival of several hundred princely territories whose traditional rulers continued to enjoy varying degrees of autonomy, provided they did not impose 'gross misrule' on their peoples. From 1921 to 1947 a Chamber of Princes served as a permanent consultative body to advise the Viceroy and his Council on matters of common concern to the states. At the time of Partition and Independence two-fifths of the population of India lived within the 562 princely native states. The British authorities divided the states into three classes: the first division comprised 118 'salute states', of considerable size and with rulers of such prestige that they were entitled to ceremonial gun salutes on formal occasions – a 21-gun salute for five rulers (the Nizam of Hyderabad and the Maharajas of Baroda, Gwalior, Jammu and Kashmir, and Mysore), the remaining Rajas receiving 11- or 9-gun salutes; the second division, of 117 'non-salute states', had rulers with more limited powers; the third division comprised 327 hereditary landowners with the conventional authority of peers of the realm, but no civil or criminal jurisdiction. From 1931 onwards the independence parties in India regarded princely rule as a parasitic anachronism devoted to upholding British interests. On 25

July 1947 the Viceroy, *Mountbatten, told the Chamber of Princes that the rulers should sign Instruments of Accession to one or other of the emergent dominions, India or Pakistan, who would provide for the retention of their sovereignty and state government; decisions over accession were to be taken according to where they lived and to the religion of their subjects. By 14 August all the rulers had signed except the (Muslim) Nizam of (predominantly Hindu) Hyderabad, the (Hindu) Maharaja of Jammu and Kashmir (mostly Muslims), and the (Muslim) Nawab of (predominantly Hindu) Junagadh. Hyderabad was absorbed by India in a 'police action' in September 1949; Junagadh joined India after its ruler had decided on flight; and the fate of *Kashmir long remained unresolved. The sovereignty of the rulers, both in India and Pakistan, was gradually eroded by successive constitutional acts and by restraints on their privy purse, and the princely order in the Indian Republic was finally abolished in December 1971.

Protectorate: the name given by a state to the form of authority it asserts over territory which it seeks to administer without formal annexation and without according to its inhabitants any form of citizenship. In practice, protectorates were established in regions where there was already some form of kingship or disciplined communal life. Frequently the status of protectorate was changed to 'colony', as in *Kenya, but in the Middle East protectorates were loosely maintained, without imposing bonds of government from London.

Qantas. In 1920 two returned pilots from World War I, P. J. McGuinness and W. Hudson Fysh, received backing from the sheep farmer Fergus McMaster to set up the Queensland And Northern Territory Air Service. It was based on Winton, Queensland and used two Avro biplanes, carrying two passengers, mail and light freight, for a service over western Queensland and into Northern Territory. The company expanded until in 1934 it gained support from *Imperial Airways and, as QANTAS Empire Airways Ltd, provided the route from Malaya for the air service from London. Headquarters were established at Sydney in 1938; it was nationalized in 1947; and the name 'Empire' was omitted from 1967 onwards. Among international airlines, only KLM is older than Qantas.

Quebec (Fr. Québec) is the largest of Canada's ten provinces, but less than half the land area of the *Northwest Territories. It was visited by Jacques *Cartier in 1535 and was known as New France from then until 1763. Quebec City, founded at the confluence of the St Lawrence and St Charles rivers, became a fortified capital in 1608; it was on the neighbouring Plains of Abraham that, on 18 September 1759, General *Wolfe defeated the French under Montcalm in the decisive battle for British mastery of eastern Canada. Under British rule the province was known as Quebec (1763–90), as Lower Canada (1791–1846), as Canada East (1846–67), and reverted to the original name of Quebec in 1867 with the creation of the Dominion of Canada. While the growing of cereals and stock-rearing made southern Quebec wealthy agricultural country, the wide-ranging forests farther north ensured that the manufacture of paper and wood pulp became the chief industry, until the exploitation of the iron ore and other mineral deposits in the Ungava region and the spread of industrialization with the coming of *hydro-electric power. The *Quebec Act of 1774 perpetuated French customs and influence. French-speakers formed three-quarters of the population in 1867 and well over 80 per cent a century later. French cultural and religious traditions survive: the province's 1981 census return showed that there were 5,609,685 Roman Catholics in a total population of 6,438,403. The political life of the province has also been influenced by French traditions, notably over *military service. Sir Wilfrid *Laurier became the first Québecois to form a government in Ottawa: later national leaders have included Louis *St Laurent and Pierre *Trudeau. A separatist movement emerged in the 1960s under the leadership of René Levesque and was given publicity by President de Gaulle's support for * '*Québec Libre*' on his 1967 visit to the province. Levesque's Parti Québecois won only 6 out of 110 seats in the provincial legislature in 1971, but on 15 November 1976 became the strongest party in the province with 70 seats. Levesque organized a referendum in the province on 20 May 1980 to decide when Quebec should seek a separatist 'sovereignty association' with the Dominion government in Ottawa, but 59.5 per cent voted against the proposal. Levesque's authority thereafter went into decline: in 1985 his Parti Québecois could win only 23 seats in a legislature increased to 122 members. Nevertheless the Meech Lake Accord of June 1987 recognized Quebec as a 'distinct society' (see *Canada*) within the Dominion, while *Mulroney's proposed federal constitution of September 1992 also promised Quebec at least a quarter of the seats in the Canadian House of Commons. The return of the Progressive Conservatives to power in Ottawa after the October 1993 general election led to a rapid revival of separatist sentiment in Quebec; and in the elections for the provincial legislature on 12 September 1994 the Parti Québecois was again returned to power.

Quebec Act, 1774: a basic charter of British rule in Canada, passed by Parliament at Westminster in April 1774. It gave Canada a legislative council appointed by the Crown to advise a powerful executive, and it extended the territorial limits of Canada southwards to the Ohio and Upper Mississippi rivers. Of most lasting importance was the Act's guarantee that the peoples of the newly conquered former French territories should enjoy continuance of their language, customs, systems of land tenure, civil laws, and freedom to worship as Roman Catholics.

'Québec Libre'. The separatism of the French-speaking community in *Quebec was given a considerable boost when on 24 July 1967 President de Gaulle, in Montreal during a State Visit, made a speech from the balcony of the town hall which included the exclamation, '*Vive le Québec libre!*' ('Long Live Free Quebec'). The speech embarrassed Lester *Pearson's government, and the President's visit was abruptly ended.

Queensland: Australian state, with its capital at Brisbane. *Cook visited the coast in 1770, landing at a point which he called Moreton Bay. A penal colony was established there in 1824, later moving to the site of modern Brisbane. Free settlers moved into the region in 1840, although not officially allowed there until 1841. The Moreton Bay District was removed from the jurisdiction of New South Wales and in June 1859 was set up as the Colony of Queensland, with responsible government. The colony grew into a huge state, more than three times the size of France. Queensland covers the whole of north-eastern Australia, with sugar cane a major crop around Cairns and Mackay, supplemented by tropical fruit, including pineapples and bananas, and with eucalypt forests along the coastal hills. Despite a *gold rush in 1868, wool remained the chief export up to the coming of Federation in 1901 and beyond, for the southern lowlands provide good sheep and cattle country. Railways came to the Brisbane area in 1865 but the gauge adopted was unusually small (3 ft 6 in) and when in 1888 connections were made to Sydney, and ultimately Melbourne, it was impossible to run through carriages or wagons. Mining developed extensively during the 1950s and 1960s. *Oil was discovered at Moonie in 1961. The legislature has at times clung tenaciously to states rights, especially during the *Bjelke-Petersen era (1968–87) when policies were more blatantly right-wing than elsewhere in Australia. Almost half the population of Queensland live in or around Brisbane.

Raffles, Sir (Thomas) Stamford (1781–1826), colonial administrator: born off Morant Bay, Jamaica, the son of a sea-cook. At the age of fourteen he was given a clerkship in the East India Company, and showed such skill that in 1805 he was sent to Penang as secretary to the company's agency there. At the age of 30 he took part in an expedition to seize Java from the Dutch, and on its capture was appointed Lieutenant-Governor. In the four years before Java was restored to the Dutch, Raffles changed the system of land tenure and totally reformed the internal administration. He also acquired a deep understanding of the East Indies, some of which he employed in writing a *History of Java*, published in 1817, the year he received his knighthood. From 1818 to 1823 he took charge of the Company's settlement at Bengkulu, in western Sumatra. On his initiative a trading post was founded on the island of Singapore in 1819, although it was some years before he could convince the Company of Singapore's potential importance. He failed to achieve the scholarly work he had intended, partly because of poor health but also because all his papers were lost in a fire during his return to Europe in 1824. In the last years of his life he helped set up London's first Zoological Society, of which he became president.

Rahman, Tunku Abdul (1903–90), Malaysian statesman: see *Abdul Rahman Putra*.

Rahman, Sheikh Mujibur (1925–75), of Bangladesh: see *Mujibur Rahman*.

Railways were the principal means by which a coastbound colonial and imperial trading power commercially developed the interior of four continents. The earliest colonial railway was a small goods-carrying line, some 16 miles long, linking the Richelieu and St Lawrence rivers east of Montreal: it went into service in 1836, the year steam trains came to London. Canada continued to take the lead in railway development, with the Great Western line from Niagara Falls to Windsor, Ontario, on the St Clair river, completed in the early 1850s; it was soon followed by a Grand Trunk line from Montreal to Toronto and on to the southern end of Lake Huron. These lines set a pattern followed, on a far larger scale, after confederation in 1867: fertile country was opened up, by the carrying of goods and the establishment of railside towns. Ultimately the *Canadian Pacific Railway and its rivals welded the nation together: *British Columbia would never have entered the Dominion without an assurance of a transcontinental line; and it could be argued that had there been no CPR to link Canada's prairie provinces with its seaports, they would more naturally have merged into the American economy and joined the USA.

Railways had less influence in Australia because of the deserts and arid plateaux of the long-unexplored interior: local lines were opened to the public around Melbourne in 1854, Sydney in 1855, Adelaide in 1856, south of Brisbane in 1863, around Launceston in Tasmania in 1871, and – rather curiously – along the coast of Western Australia from Geraldton to Northampton in 1879. Development was hampered by wide variations of rail-track gauge between the colonies; in South Australia there were three gauges for major lines and another three for smaller ones. By 1883 passengers could go from Melbourne to Sydney, with one change of train because of different gauges, and by 1888 from Melbourne to Brisbane with two changes. Gauge variations hampered the movement of goods – especially live cattle – even more than passenger traffic, but the lines gave fruit farming and wine growing districts speedier routes to the cities and ports. Plans to link Adelaide and Darwin, when the *Northern Territory was part of South Australia, were slow to develop: by 1900 there was still a gap of over 1,100 miles between Pine Creek, the end of Darwin's line southwards, and Oodnadatta, which was the terminus of Adelaide's line northwards until 1926, when it was extended to Alice Springs. Like British Columbia in Canada, Western Australia made entry into federation conditional on the building of a transcontinental line: the link between *Kalgoorlie (WA) and Port Augusta (South Australia), across the Nullarbor Plain, was completed in 1917; but it was not until 1970 that, with conversion to standard-gauge track, a through 'Indian–Pacific Service' was introduced between Perth and Sydney. The profitable farming communities of South Island in *New Zealand benefited considerably from the Christchurch to Bluff railway of 1879; but North Island's terrain imposed a need for many narrow tunnels and long climbs so that, even with the coming of diesel locomotives in 1956, the Auckland–Wellington express took 14 hours to cover the 350 miles.

The most extensive railway network of the old Empire was in India. A twenty-mile line from Bombay to Thana opened in 1853, encouraging *Dalhousie to outline plans which would link all the major cities and ports of the subcontinent. In 1859 some 300 miles of track were in service; there were more than 4,000 by 1870; 24,752 in 1900; and by 1910 more than 31,000 miles of track (including narrow gauge mountain railways). The first major trunk line from Calcutta and through Delhi reached Lahore in 1864, Peshawar in 1883 and the Afghan frontier in 1891. Bombay was linked with central India in 1864, though it was not until 1887 that Bombay's magnificent Victoria Terminus was opened, for the Great Indian Peninsula Railway. The railways required extraordinary skills in bridge-building and tunnelling; they were so costly that they never brought good dividends to the shareholders. Strategically, however, and as a form of commercial transport, they were of great value; they even helped reduce the sufferings of the terrible *famine years. British financiers backed proposals to link the Indian lines with the Russian system through Persia, but the government in India opposed the plans on strategic grounds. The line from *Kowloon to Canton (Guangzhou), completed in 1912, gave Hong Kong access to China's railways, many of which were built by British investors. In Malaya the 500-mile-long railway between Penang and the Johore Strait (for Singapore) was opened on 1 July 1909; a through railway link with Bangkok – 1,200 miles from Singapore – began on 1 July 1918.

Apart from local lines around the Cape, railways came later to southern Africa, their spread coinciding with the *Rhodes era, following the *diamond rush and the Transvaal *gold rush. The first train from Cape Town reached Johannesburg in September 1892, with an extension to Pretoria completed by the end of the year. Another line – seen by Rhodes as the first stage of his *Cape-to-Cairo project – ran northwards from Kimberley to Bulawayo by 1897, crossing Matabeleland to the Victoria Falls by 1903, to Lusaka and Broken Hill by 1909, and eventually to mineral-rich Katanga in the (Belgian) Congo. In North Africa Kitchener constructed a military railway from Wadi Halfa, on the Sudanese border with Egypt, up the Nile to reach Khartoum in 1899. The Uganda Railway in East Africa, inland from Mombasa, was begun on the coast in 1896; it was built by Indian labour, and reached Nairobi in 1899, after delays imposed by tribal raids and roving man-eating lions. The 582-mile-post, set up beside Lake Victoria as a first objective, was reached on 20 December 1901. The railway became *Kenya's main artery but was not extended to Kampala in Uganda until the late 1920s. The principal lines in *Tanganyika were built by the Germans, inland from Dar-es-Salaam, to reach Tabora by 1907 and a terminus at Kigoma, 779 miles inland, by 1913. After World War I a link was established between the Mombasa and Dar-es-Salaam lines and the railway services of Kenya, Tanganyika and Uganda were amalgamated in 1948 to give East Africa a network of over 3,600 miles; the joint administration was broken up in 1977. Lines came even later to West Africa, largely because of internal unrest: in Nigeria, the railway from Lagos to Kano opened in 1910; and in what is now Ghana, a line from Seccondee on the coast inland to Coomassie (168 miles), which also became fully operational in 1910, helped to quadruple the colony's exports of cocoa within a single year. Most African lines were opened during the colonial era, but in 1970 work began on the Tanzam railway, to link Dar-es-Salaam with the Zambian copper belt; the line – over 1,100 miles long and constructed mainly by the Chinese – was completed in less than six years.

Raj: a Hindi word for sovereignty. 'The Raj' signifies the period of British rule in India, which ended with Partition in 1947. The term was rarely used until after the British withdrawal.

Ralegh, Sir Walter (1552–1618), English navigator and colonizer: born at Hayes Barton, inland from Budleigh Salterton, south Devon. He was a half-brother of Humphrey *Gilbert, with whom he took part in piratical raids on the Spanish in 1578. After serving Elizabeth I in Ireland, he became one of her favourite courtiers (though often incurring her displeasure). In 1584 he obtained a royal patent to finance an expedition which would take possession in the Queen's name of lands discovered in America: the expedition – led by his cousin, Sir Richard Grenville (1541–91) – reconnoitred America's eastern seaboard and sought to colonize Virginia, apparently bringing back to England the first potatoes and tobacco. Ralegh, a successful naval commander and soldier against the Spanish, never visited Virginia himself, but he undertook two important voyages of discovery: in 1595 he explored the coasts of Trinidad and the lower reaches of the Orinoco, publishing his adventures in *The Discovery of the Empyre of Guyana* (1596). He was a writer of fine prose, and also of poetry. Court intrigues led to his arrest on the King's orders soon after

James I's accession. Condemned to death, Ralegh was reprieved but detained for 13 years in the Tower of London, where he was housed in some comfort with his family and began writing his *History of the World*. He was then allowed to lead a second expedition to the Orinoco, in 1616, primarily in search of gold; but having endangered the fragile peace of Europe by raiding Spanish settlements, on his return he was again arrested, largely to appease the Spaniards. Ralegh was beheaded at Westminster on 29 October 1618.

Ramphal, Sir Shridath Surendranath ('Sonny') (1928–), Commonwealth Secretary-General: born in Guyana; studied law at King's College, London and was called to the Bar of Gray's Inn in 1951. He entered the Guyanese National Assembly in 1965 and was Attorney-General in Guyana until 1973 when he became both Foreign Minister and Minister of Justice. He was knighted in 1970. In 1975 he came to London to succeed the Canadian Arnold *Smith as the second Secretary-General of the Commonwealth, an office he held for fourteen formative years. Despite his intense loathing of *apartheid, he was able to uphold the strict neutrality of the *Commonwealth Secretariat, thus making it possible for the Secretariat to send observers to monitor election procedures and to accept a broadening of responsibilities within southern Africa.

RCMP (Royal Canadian Mounted Police): see *'Mounties'*.

Red River Rebellion (1869–70). Lord *Selkirk's attempts between 1811 and 1818 to establish an agricultural settlement along the Red River valley in Canada's midwest met with limited success, partly because of the harsh winters and recurrent plagues of grasshoppers. On its repurchase of the territory from Selkirk's heirs in 1836 the Hudson's Bay Company established 'Assiniboia', a predominantly *métis community of fur-traders governed by its own council, nominated by the Company. When the newly-formed Dominion purchased the Company's territorial rights in 1869, the community feared that the federal government would treat the region as annexed land and impose government from Ottawa. Such fears and resentments – and suspicions of proposed railway plans and land reallocation – led the Red River settlements to follow Louis *Riel in a separatist movement between November 1869 and February 1870, generally overdramatized as a 'rebellion'. There was little bloodshed, apart from the execution of a belligerent Orangeman, Thomas Scott, largely on Riel's insistence. A military expedition, commanded by Colonel Garnet *Wolseley, occupied Fort Garry (Winnipeg), forcing Riel to go into hiding. Although the 'riverites' could not stand out against the Ottawa authorities the 'rebellion' effectively made their case; henceforth their views would receive a fair hearing. A compromise settlement led to the recognition of responsible government in the new province of *Manitoba; an amnesty followed in 1875.

Refrigeration by vapour compression was perfected in France, but it was an Australian, Thomas Mort (1816–78), who designed the first machine-cooled store, in Sydney (1861). These inventions were of immense practical value to a world-empire, enabling frozen meat, dairy produce and fruit to be carried by ship and by rail. Refrigerated meat from Sydney was landed from SS *Strathleven* in England on 2 February 1880; and the first refrigerated cargo vessel, the *Dunedin*, left Port Chalmers (in South Island, New Zealand) on 15 February 1882, carrying 4,460 mutton and 449 lamb carcasses, which went on sale in London 97 days later. The bulk transport of refrigerated meat was developed about 1900 by Sir William *Angliss of Melbourne. By 1911 refrigerated cargoes to Britain were earning Australia and New Zealand £7 million each a year. India and Canada benefited particularly from refrigerated railway wagons, and the West Indies from cold storage for *bananas.

Representation of Natives Act (1936): a statute of the South African Parliament enacted in April 1936 modified the *South Africa Act (1909) to provide for the election of four additional senators (of European descent) to represent the interests of the 'Natives' (Africans) in the upper House of the legislature. At the same time 'the persons whose names appear on the Cape Native Voters roll' were allowed to elect three members to the House of Assembly and two members to the Provincial Council. The Act also set up a Natives Representation Council of six ex-officio members, four members nominated by the Governor-General, and twelve elected 'native members'. The Council was to consider and report on proposed legislation or general matters affecting the native African population, and on any question referred to it by the cabinet minister responsible for native affairs. Even under the *Smuts administration the Natives Representative Council could function only with extreme difficulty, and in 1947 resigned as a body in protest at proposed laws which would have increased segregation. After *Malan's electoral victory in 1948, these extremely limited civic rights were whittled away; native representation in the assembly was finally abolished in June 1960.

Rhodes, Cecil John (1853–1902), imperial statesman: born, a vicar's fifth son, at Bishop's Stortford in Hertfordshire; received his schooling locally. A tendency to tuberculosis induced him to join an elder brother in Natal, landing at Durban on 1 September 1870. His presence in South Africa so soon after the *diamond rush encouraged him to seek his fortune around Kimberley, and a natural business acumen enabled him to become wealthy by the age of twenty, when he sought admission to Oxford to complete his education. He was rejected by University College but admitted by Oriel College, in October 1873. His university life was interrupted by long periods of business activity in Africa; by his final term, in 1881, he had founded the *De Beers Mining Company (1880) and was a member of the Cape Colony legislature. His most active years began with the Transvaal *gold rush, 1886. He founded the *British South Africa Company a year later, enthusiastically accepting the *'Cape-to-Cairo' expansionist ideal outlined in *The Times* on 22 August 1888. In that year Rhodes began to expand the De Beers Company, and by July 1889 it had a monopoly of diamond sales on the London market. In October 1888 his BSAC received a Royal Charter and he obtained exclusive mining rights in Mashonaland and Matabeleland from Lobengula of the *Ndebele. Rhodes became Prime Minister of Cape Colony on 17 July 1890, at a time when his chartered company's pioneer column was establishing settlements in Mashonaland, including in September the town of Salisbury (now Harare). Government support enabled him to expand BSAC activities to Barotseland (*Zambia) in 1891. Rhodes's hostility to *Kruger's protective system of government in the Transvaal led him to become implicated in the *Jameson Raid, a fiasco which forced his resignation as Cape premier on 6 January 1896. He helped restore peace in Matabeleland after the Ndebele and Shona revolts later that year but, though he remained politically active, he was in poor health. During the Second *Boer War he was besieged in Kimberley, from October 1899 to February 1900. He died at Muizenburg of 'heart disease' on 26 March 1902 and was buried in the Metapo hills, above Bulawayo. His fortune was left mostly in trust to Oxford University (see *below*), but his splendid house of Groote Schurr overlooking Cape Town was left to serve 'the prime ministers of a united South Africa'.

Rhodes House, Oxford: built in South Parks Road (1926–29), as a memorial to *Rhodes; the architect was Sir Herbert *Baker. It serves as a home for the administration, by the Rhodes Trustees, of *Rhodes Scholarships, but is also a university centre and library for the study of the Commonwealth (outside the Indian subcontinent) and the USA.

Rhodes Scholarships. Most of *Rhodes's considerable fortune was left to establish a trust for scholarships to be awarded (from 1903 onwards) to men from the overseas Empire and the USA, enabling them to study for up to three years at Oxford; in a codicil to his will Rhodes extended the scholarship scheme to Germany, in the belief that educational ties 'between the three strongest Powers will render war impossible'. German scholarships were awarded between 1903 and 1913, 1929 and 1938, and since 1956. Rhodes insisted that his scholars must be chosen with care, their selection depending on character as well as academic skills and sporting attainments. Among Rhodes Scholars have been one Governor-General of Australia (Sir Zelman Cowen), one US President (Clinton), a Commonwealth secretary-general (Arnold *Smith) and at least three prime ministers – Norman *Manley (Jamaica), Bob *Hawke (Australia), and Dom Mintoff (*Malta). With the spread of women's education the scholarship scheme ceased to be single-sex in 1976.

Rhodesia. Between 1889 and 1923/4 Rhodes's chartered *British South Africa Company controlled a region northwards from the Transvaal to the Congo Free State, divided administratively in 1911 into Northern Rhodesia (*Zambia) and Southern Rhodesia (*Zimbabwe), with the Zambezi river as a border. The white population of Southern Rhodesia was given an opportunity in October 1922 to join South Africa, but voted in favour of responsible government under the Crown. In October 1923 Southern Rhodesia was given limited powers of colonial government with a legislature in Salisbury (Harare) but, to the white settlers' dismay, with London retaining a veto over laws concerning the native African population. Northern Rhodesia became a Crown Colony in April 1924, though with more limited powers of self-government. Sir Godfrey *Huggins headed a paternalistic administration in Southern Rhodesia from 1933 to 1953, developing the mining industry and fruit-growing resources as well as directing the country's war effort, especially in training flying crews for the RAF. Huggins, with Sir Roy *Welensky – leader of the whites in Northern Rhodesia – brought the two Rhodesias and Nyasaland (*Malawi) together in a *Central African Federation in 1953. The federation, dominated by Southern Rhodesian interests, was dissolved in December 1963, largely because the active African political parties of the north and Nyasaland were determined to assert a right of secession and avoid exploitation by the Salisbury business community and by the ascendant right-wing Rhodesian Front movement. Southern Rhodesia reverted to colonial status on the dissolution of the federation, the leader of the Front, Ian *Smith, becoming premier in April 1964 and holding talks on independence with successive Conservative and Labour governments in Britain. His opposition to majority-rule elections and racial integration was ill received in London, and on 11 November 1965 Smith issued a unilateral declaration of independence (*UDI) which was repudiated by the British government and by the United Nations: the trade embargo subsequently imposed was ignored by South Africa and Portugal. Despite two series of discussions between Smith and a British prime ministerial delegation, aboard HMS *Tiger* (December 1966) and HMS *Fearless* (October 1968), agreement proved impossible. On 2 March 1970 Smith declared Rhodesia a republic and sought to establish a regime similar in character to that of South Africa. Mounting black African resistance, led by *Nkomo and *Mugabe, spread guerrilla warfare across the country and provoked Rhodesian 'hot pursuit raids' against Patriotic Front bases in Mozambique and, later, Zambia. Economic pressure from abroad forced the Smith regime in 1978 to seek a compromise with three 'moderate' black political spokesmen: Bishop Abel Muzorewa, the Revd Ndabaningi Sithole, and Chief Jeremiah Chirau. A draft 'constitution' was approved by the white community in a referendum, and in April 1979 elections were held for 72 black seats in the 100-member legislature. On 1 June 1979 Bishop Muzorewa became Prime Minister of 'Rhodesia-Zimbabwe'. But the new compromise state was considered by the Patriotic Front and its supporters abroad to perpetuate white dominance; the armed struggle in Rhodesia continued until agreement was reached at the Lusaka meeting of Commonwealth leaders in August 1979 that a conference should be held at *Lancaster House to consider the restoration of legitimate government in Salisbury (Harare) and the completion of the transition to an independent Zimbabwe.

Riel, Louis (1844–85), Canadian rebel leader: born into a Roman Catholic *métis family at St Boniface, now in Manitoba. He followed his father's lead in urging the métis community to oppose implementation of the Hudson's Bay Company's decision to surrender their land rights to the new Dominion. In November 1869 Riel led the *Red River rebellion, seeking to set up a republic at Fort Garry (Winnipeg), of which he was executive president. The arrival of troops under Colonel *Wolseley forced Riel to go into hiding. His rejection of approaches from Irish Fenians in America to stir up another revolt induced the Dominion government to offer an amnesty to the former rebels; elected to the federal Parliament in October 1873 Riel took the oath but never sat in the House, and in April 1874 he was denied his seat by a group of staunch Protestant members from Ontario, who expelled him before he even entered the House. He was elected again in September 1874 but outlawed in February 1875 and went into exile in the USA. Although he suffered a mental breakdown four years later, he remained a popular hero to the métis and to many Indians, alarmed by the new wave of settlers into Winnipeg and beyond. Foolishly, in 1885 Riel allowed himself to be persuaded into leading another armed uprising on behalf of those who believed their land rights to be in danger. This 'north-west rebellion' coincided with *Cree attacks on settlements along the North Saskatchewan river. Canadian army units, including artillery, speedily crushed the risings; Riel was taken under arrest to Regina, where he was sentenced to death for high treason. Despite pleas for clemency from Roman Catholics in the east, Riel was hanged on 16 November 1885.

Roberts, Frederick Sleigh, Lord (1832–1914), British Field Marshal: born in Cawnpore, the son of a general who served for more than fifty years with the Indian Army; educated at Clifton College, Eton and Sandhurst; served with the Bengal Army throughout the Mutiny and won the Victoria Cross for his courage at the siege of Lucknow. Although he distinguished himself in a campaign in Ethiopia in 1868, he concerned himself mainly with the defence of India, convinced of Russia's intention to sweep down through Afghanistan and secure mastery of the passes through the Himalayas. In 1879 he defeated the Afghans and occupied Kabul, whence in August 1880 he led a force of 10,000 men in a three-week march through the mountains to Kandahar, where he inflicted another defeat on the Afghans and relieved the beleaguered garrison. This march made 'Bobs' a legendary figure during the years when Victorian imperialism was at its zenith. He was Commander-in-Chief in India from 1885 to 1893, created a baron in 1892; he became Field Marshal in 1895, at the start of four years as C.-in-C. in Ireland. After the disastrous opening months of the Second *Boer War he was sent to take command of the army in South Africa in January 1900 and, with *Kitchener as his Chief-of-Staff, swept victoriously through the Transvaal, capturing Bloemfontein (March), Johannesburg (May) and Pretoria (June), before returning to London. In January 1901 he was appointed Commander-in-Chief of the British Army, a post abolished in February 1904 when he retired. Earl Roberts of Kandahar, Pretoria and Waterford, as he became on returning from the Cape, campaigned vigorously in favour of compulsory *military service. He died in November 1914 at St-Omer, on his way to inspect the first Indian troops to arrive on the Western Front.

Rorke's Drift: a ford and mission station on the Buffalo River, along the borders of *Natal and *Zululand. It was used by Lord Chelmsford as a base camp during his war against *Cetewayo. On 22 January 1879 an improvised defensive wall of biscuit tins and stones enabled a company of the 2nd Battalion of the 24th Regiment to beat off a *Zulu attack which began a few hours after the Zulu victory at *Isandhlwana, 12 miles away. The stubborn defence put up by this force of barely a hundred men excited such admiration in Britain that no fewer than twelve Victoria Crosses were awarded for courage shown in this particular action.

Ross Dependency: a section of the Antarctic, including King Edward VII Land and Victoria Land, formally constituted as a New Zealand Dependency in 1923. It includes McMurdo Sound, where bases were established for the Commonwealth Trans-Antarctic Expedition of 1957/8, a period when extensive surveying was done of the area around the huge inlet.

Ross, Sir John (1777–1856), explorer of the Canadian Arctic: born in a manse in Wigtownshire; joined the Royal Navy as a boy and reached the rank of commander in 1812, when he served in the Baltic and was ordered to survey routes to northern Russia through the White Sea. Two voyages in search of a north-west passage enabled him to survey huge areas of the Canadian Arctic, including Boothia Bay and the Boothia

Peninsula. His nephew (Sir) James Ross (1800–62) accompanied him on some early expeditions, and in 1831 was responsible for discovering the magnetic north pole. Sir James Ross also led the expedition to the Antarctic in 1839–43 in which the volcano Mount Erebus was discovered; many geographical names in the Antarctic record his travels.

Ross, Sir Ronald (1857–1932), physician: born in Alamara, India; studied at St Bartholomew's Hospital in London but from 1881 to 1899 served in the Indian Medical Service. His great achievement was his discovery of the *malaria parasite and his tracing of its life history. For the last six years of his life he was founder-director of the Ross Institute for Tropical Diseases. He received the Nobel Prize for medicine in 1902.

'Round Table'. In 1910 two of *Milner's close associates, Lionel *Curtis and Philip Kerr (later Lord Lothian; 1882–1940), founded *Round Table*, a quarterly review of Empire problems published in London. Kerr remained editor until 1916 and Curtis travelled widely in the Empire during the four years preceding World War I, making speeches on the need for Empire unity and setting up 'Round Table' discussion groups, especially among students. The periodical remained influential throughout the inter-war years, and its supporters were prominent in convening the *Lapstone Conference in New South Wales (1938). *Round Table* remains the principal Commonwealth journal on international affairs, a responsibility of the Institute of Commonwealth Studies of the University of London.

Round Table Conferences: two series of meetings held at St James's Palace, London to discuss the future of India, following the *Simon Commission Report. The first session lasted from 12 November 1930 to 20 January 1931: although the Indian National Congress refused to come, spokesmen for the *princely rulers were present, and agreed to enter an Indian federation. This sign of progress induced *Gandhi to accept talks with the Viceroy; against the advice of *Nehru and the radical wing of Congress, Gandhi agreed to attend the second session, which met from 7 September to 1 December 1931. Although the Conference tacitly recognized that India must receive Dominion status sooner or later, the British delegates could not accept Gandhi's arguments that the change should be made immediately. The chief consequence of the Conference was to make Gandhi a familiar figure to the British public. A third brief session in 1932 achieved nothing, for by then all the Congress leaders (including Gandhi) were under detention for sedition. In March 1939 another Round Table Conference was convened to discuss *Palestine; its members examined proposals for *partition into Jewish and Arab regions, but could not agree.

Rowell–Sirois Report, 1940. A Canadian Royal Commission was appointed in 1935 to examine the relations between the provincial governments and the federal authorities in Ottawa. The Commission was chaired originally by N. W. Rowell, later by J. Sirois. Their Report, presented to Mackenzie *King in 1940, recommended greater attention by the Dominion government to ensuring an even distribution of federal resources. The report was discussed at a two-day conference in January 1941 but was opposed by Ontario, Quebec, British Columbia and Alberta, though backed by the maritime and other prairie provinces. No action was taken, partly because of wartime conditions; but the report emphasized the need for constitutional revision, a task eventually tackled – with great difficulty – by *Trudeau and *Mulroney.

Rowlatt Acts. Sir Sidney Rowlatt (1862–1945), a judge of the King's Bench division in the United Kingdom from 1912 onwards, was appointed chairman of the Indian Sedition Committee in 1917/18. He was to decide the nature of the special powers sought by the Indian government to fight subversion, in the wake of the Russian Revolution. Rowlatt's recommendations were enacted in 1919 and gave the government arbitrary rights of arrest and detention. Their publication was used by *Gandhi as a rallying point for his call to his *Indian National Congress for non-co-operation, but a nationwide strike (*hartal*), called by Congress for 6 April 1919, lacked the self-discipline on which Gandhi relied. Attacks on Europeans were followed by arson. The violence provoked reaction, most tragically at *Amritsar. Yet the Rowlatt Acts remained rather a symbol of persecution than a genuine threat, for they were never in themselves put into practice.

Royal Africa Company: founded under a royal charter of 1660 as the 'Company of Royal Adventurers', with monopoly rights in licences to British slave traders who would use the West African coast. The name was changed to Royal Africa Company in 1672; fortified trading stations reached (in modern terms) from The Gambia, through Senegal and Ghana, to Nigeria. But there were enough gaps in this line of ports for traders to ignore the monopoly and look for their slaves elsewhere, trading in the Indian Ocean with Madagascar and Zanzibar. The Royal African Company was abolished in 1698, its disappearance welcomed as deregulating the *slave trade.

Royal Titles Act (April 1876): provided for Queen Victoria to augment her titles by becoming Empress of India, although it was not until 1 January 1877 that she was proclaimed Empress, by the Viceroy at the tented *Delhi Durbar. The change of style, proposed in the first instance by *Disraeli, pleased the rulers of the *princely states and heightened the sovereign's interest in her Indian possessions, but it was regarded as 'un-English' in the United Kingdom. By the provisions of the Act her heirs became Emperors of India, until the imperial concept was ended when King-Emperor George VI formally relinquished the title on 22 June 1948.

Rubber. British settlers brought the first rubber trees to south-east Asia from Brazil in 1873/4, establishing plantations in central Malaya with such effectiveness that by 1910 they covered nearly 250,000 acres. Their extent had multiplied three times over by 1940, when Malaya produced more than 40 per cent of the world's rubber. Despite the Japanese invasion and the *Malayan Emergency, the area under plantation increased until by 1970 two-thirds of the cultivated land in the Malay peninsula was producing rubber, and Malaysia was the chief rubber supplier to the world, a level maintained over the following quarter of a century. Considerable numbers of Tamils from southern India and Sri Lanka worked on these Malay plantations; but rubber was also cultivated in the Kerala and Tamil Nadu provinces of India, and in Sri Lanka itself. Other rubber-producing areas of the Commonwealth – although on a small scale – include Brunei and south-western Ghana.

Rum Rebellion (1808): a misnomer for what was in effect a military coup, in early colonial New South Wales. Soon after William *Bligh, late of the *Bounty*, took office as governor in August 1806 he made strenuous efforts to check an illicit rum trade involving officers of the New South Wales Corps, an army unit recruited in England to police the penal colony. Early in January 1808 a vessel arrived at Sydney from the Cape with some 8,000 gallons of spirits aboard. Bligh, whose sense of discipline offended many free settlers, was so unpopular that George Johnston, the Corps' commanding officer, had no difficulty in preventing an inquiry into the unloading of the vessel's rum: on 26 January 1808 he had Governor Bligh arrested for having 'exceeded his powers'. In an act of both rebellion and mutiny, Johnston deposed Bligh from office, taking control of the colony as 'Lieutenant-Governor' until an appointed successor arrived from England early in 1810. Johnston was then sent back to England, court-martialled and cashiered – a remarkably lenient fate. The New South Wales Corps was disbanded, and replaced by a regular infantry regiment. Bligh, for the second time in his life, was exonerated.

Rutherford, Ernest (Baron Rutherford of Nelson; 1871–1937), New Zealand-born physicist: born in what is now Brightwater town, near Tasman Bay, Nelson, South Island; educated locally and at Christchurch College before going to Trinity College, Cambridge at the age of twenty-four. In 1898 he became a professor at McGill University, Montreal, beginning the research into radio-activity which he was to carry further as professor at Manchester in the seven years before World War I. As early as

Sabah

1908 Rutherford received the Nobel Prize – for Chemistry, although in reality he was creating the science of nuclear physics. In collaboration with the Danish scientist Niels Bohr, he revolutionized concepts of the atom. During the war years he perfected submarine detection methods for the Admiralty. From 1919 until his death in October 1937 he created a centre of nuclear physics at the Cavendish Laboratory in Cambridge, where in May 1932 his colleagues John Cockcroft and Ernest Walton first split the atom; Rutherford was knighted in 1914, and in 1925 received both the Order of Merit and a peerage. It could be argued that he was the greatest scientist of the English-speaking world since Isaac Newton.

Sabah: known as North Borneo until September 1963, when it became a member-state of *Malaysia. The territory – about the size of Scotland – was in 1877/8 ceded by the Sultan of Brunei and other local rulers to a syndicate which sought to develop its rubber, timber and tobacco resources. In 1881 the syndicate received a royal charter, and as the British North Borneo Company administered the territory, in consultation with the *Colonial Office, until 15 July 1946, when the company's rights passed to the Crown. It then became the Colony of North Borneo and incorporated the rubber-producing island of Labuan, off the south-west coast, which in 1846 had been acquired by the British from the Sultan of Brunei. In January 1942 North Borneo was overrun by the Japanese, who were ejected by Australian forces in June 1945. Indonesian designs on Sabah during the period of *confrontation (1963–65) led to jungle operations by British, Malayan and Australian troops against infiltrating guerrillas.

St Christopher (St Kitts) and Nevis: independent member of the Commonwealth in the *Leeward Islands group, combined area 101 square miles: the capital, Basseterre, is 11 miles north of Nevis's main centre, Charlestown. St Kitts was discovered by Columbus in 1493 and in 1624 was chosen by Sir Thomas *Warner as the island of first English settlement in the Caribbean; Warner also colonized neighbouring Nevis, in 1628. Possession of the islands was disputed by both France and Spain until 1783, although they had been formally ceded to Britain by the Treaty of Utrecht (1713). The colony was dependent on sugar plantations, worked by slaves brought from Africa. Unlike in *Jamaica, *slave emancipation did not bring economic chaos, for the plantations were always smaller and the population large enough to provide a cheap labour force. St Kitts and Nevis were part of the Leeward Islands from 1871 to 1956, and of the British West Indies Federation from 1958 to 1962. *Anguilla was then associated with the two islands administratively until 1980. Independence on 19 September 1983 recognized St Christopher–Nevis as a 'sovereign democratic federal state', giving Nevis an eight-member assembly, with a right of secession. Sugar, rum and tourism are the chief sources of revenue.

St Helena: an isolated British Dependency in the South Atlantic, 1,140 miles from the African coast and 1,800 from South America. It is a volcanic island, discovered by the Portuguese navigator Juan de Nova Castella on 18 August 1502, St Helen's Day. The island was neglected until the opening of regular sailing routes to India, when it became frequented by Dutch, British and French vessels. The Dutch annexed the island in 1633 but never occupied it. From 1659 until 1834 St Helena was controlled by the East India Company, as a useful replenishment station on their ships' long voyages. Some travellers broke their journeys for a rest on the island: thus the future Duke of Wellington spent a month there in 1805, enjoying (as he wrote) 'the most healthy climate'. In 1815 the island was leased by the Company to the British government as a place of internment for 'General Bonaparte' after his defeat at Waterloo. Napoleon landed on 15 October 1815, died on 5 May 1821, and was buried there until his body was exhumed on 15 October 1840 and taken to France aboard a French warship. St Helena became a Crown Colony in 1834. Although rarely visited by ships after the opening of the Suez Canal, St Helena was an important cable station. Administratively annexed to St Helena are *Ascension Island, *Tristan da Cunha and some smaller islands.

St Kitts: see *St Christopher and Nevis*.

St Laurent, Louis Stephen (1882–1973), Canadian Prime Minister: born at Compton, in Quebec Province; studied law at Laval University before being called to the Bar in 1905. He was for many years a professor of law at Laval, but entered Parliament as a Liberal for Quebec East in 1942 and served as Mackenzie *King's justice minister. He gained wider experience as Minister for External Affairs in 1946–48, but was accepted as Liberal heir-apparent and duly succeeded King on 15 November 1948. St Laurent's social reforms included the Old Age Security Act in 1951, but he concentrated particularly on asserting Canada's national independence, notably by assisting Lester *Pearson in his mediations during the *Suez Canal Crisis of 1956, and by securing the appointment of the first native-born Canadian (*Massey) as Governor-General. It was on his initiative that federal and provincial governments promoted the *St Lawrence Seaway, in partnership with the United States. Although he won the general election of 1953 the Liberal hold on the Canadian electorate gradually weakened, partly because of tight checks on credit facilities, especially for farmers in the prairie states, and partly because of a mood of isolationism which mistrusted commitments to the UN and NATO. In June 1957 the Liberals lost a general election for the first time in 22 years. St Laurent resigned from office but continued to lead the Liberals in opposition for a year, before handing over to Lester Pearson.

St Lawrence Seaway. The use of canals to move the products of Canada's central provinces down to the Atlantic dates from 1824–33 when the first Welland Canal was built; it was widened and given new locks (1913–32) to become a ship canal, a decisive step towards completing a deep-water channel between the Great Lakes and the ocean. In 1954 agreement was reached with the United States for canalizing the lower St Lawrence River. Work was completed with remarkable speed: the Seaway was opened by Queen Elizabeth II and President Eisenhower in a ceremony at St Lambert, Quebec, on 26 June 1959. Vessels up to 730 feet long may sail directly from the westernmost Great Lakes to the Atlantic, a distance of some 2,300 miles. At the same time, the Seaway provides *hydro-electric power for the industries of Canada and the USA.

St Lucia: an independent Commonwealth member in the Lesser Antilles group, an island of richly colourful mountain scenery, some 240 square miles in area: the capital, Castries, was rebuilt after a fire in 1948. An English attempt to take the island in 1605 was defeated by the fierce Carib inhabitants, and a second attempt by a party from Bermuda in 1638 ended with their massacre in 1641. French settlers fared better, and left their mark on St Lucia's architecture. After more than a dozen changes of sovereignty, France finally ceded St Lucia by the Treaty of Paris (1814). The island long formed part of the colonial federation of the *Windward Islands, although granted representative government in 1924. Internal self-government in March 1967 was followed by independence on 22 February 1979. Bananas and coconut products are exported; tourists arrive in swelling numbers.

St Vincent and the Grenadines: an independent Commonwealth member: the capital, Kingstown, is about 40 miles south of *St Lucia and 110 miles west of *Barbados. St Vincent Island was discovered by Columbus in 1498 on the feast day of St Vincent of Saragossa (22 January). Attempts by British and French settlers to occupy the island from 1627 onwards were resisted by the Carib inhabitants, but in 1773 they accepted a treaty with Britain which, in return for surrender of sovereignty, guaranteed their land rights. In 1795–96 the Caribs, supported by the French, rebelled but were overcome and deported. Development of agriculture was hampered by volcanic eruptions in 1812, 1902 and (to a lesser extent) in 1970 and 1979. St Vincent became part of the *Windward Islands colony in 1855, received full internal self-government in October 1969 and gained independence on 27 October 1979. Bananas and tourism are the chief sources of revenue. The Grenadines are a string of small islands stretching for some 40 miles south of St Vincent; the best-known are Bequia and Mustique.

Salisbury, Lord (Robert Arthur Talbot Gascoyne-Cecil; 1830–1903), British Prime Minister: born at Hatfeld House, Hertfordshire; educated at Eton and Christ Church, Oxford. He visited Cape Colony, Australia and New Zealand (1851–53), and was then a Tory MP from 1853 until succeeding as 3rd Marquess in 1868; strongly mistrustful of democracy, he wrote prolifically in Tory periodicals with European power politics, High Church Anglicanism and the future of India his greatest interests. He was Secretary of State for India (1866–67 and 1874–78); Foreign Secretary (1878–1880); Prime Minister (1885); both Prime Minister and Foreign Secretary (1886–92 and 1895–1900); and remained Prime Minister until July 1902, when he retired in favour of his nephew, Arthur Balfour. During the years in which Europe became divided into rival alliances Salisbury avoided commitment, seeking practical agreements with other Great Powers to assist British imperial expansion in China, Egypt and the *Sudan, west Africa and, above all, southern Africa. In the first instance it was Salisbury, rather than *Rhodes, who encouraged the *Cape-to-Cairo ideal. Personal travel in the Empire, unknown to previous prime ministers, led him to become a willing participant in the *scramble for Africa, favouring expansion through chartered companies; it was fitting that the chief town of *Rhodesia was named after him. Clashes of rival imperial interests in Africa and the Far East brought him close to war with France and Russia in 1898, particularly during the *Fashoda crisis. The last three years of Salisbury's premiership were overshadowed by the Second *Boer War, a conflict he had not anticipated – perhaps because, from 1895 onwards, he had allowed greater freedom of initiative to *Chamberlain, as Colonial Secretary, than he himself realized.

Samoa Agreement (1899). Samoa is a group of tropical volcanic islands in the Pacific, 450 miles north-east of Fiji, discovered by the Dutch in 1722. Rival attempts at settlement by the British, Germans and Americans led to an uneasy compromise agreed at Berlin in 1889. Continued friction was ended by a unique treaty in November 1899 by which Britain received a free hand in *Tonga and the *Solomon Islands in return for accepting division of the Samoan group between Germany and the USA. The two principal islands and two smaller ones became (until 1914) the German protectorate of *Western Samoa. After the US Congress ratified the agreement in February 1900 the island of Tutuila and its immediate dependencies became American Samoa, which in 1960 was given limited self-government.

San Juan Islands Dispute. From 1859 to 1871 there was tension between *British Columbia and the United States over Canadian claims to the San Juan Islands, in the Juan de Fuca strait, north of the Pacific inlet of Puget Sound. A Hudson's Bay Company outpost, long established on the main island, was retained even after the settlement of the boundary in the west in 1846 clearly left Puget Sound and its approaches in American possession. The island was occupied by US troops in 1859 after the Company's agents manhandled an American squatter who had shot one of their pigs. The indignation of the colonial Governor, James *Douglas, almost caused a war. Rival claims to the islands were finally settled, in America's favour, in 1871 when the dispute was referred to Berlin for impartial German arbitration.

Sand River Convention (1852): gave British recognition to the South African Republic established by the *Boers in the *Transvaal after the *Great Trek. Two years later the Bloemfontein Convention similarly recognized the *Orange Free State.

Sarawak: a region in north-western Borneo, now within the federation of *Malaysia: state capital, Kuching. The right to rule Sarawak was bestowed on Sir James *Brooke by the Sultan of Brunei on 24 September 1841: he and his heirs ruled as the 'white Rajahs' for more than a hundred years. Small accessions of territory were made in the later nineteenth century and in 1905, after Sarawak became a British Protectorate in 1888. The Rajah established executive and legislative councils in September 1941 but within eleven weeks Sarawak had been occupied by the Japanese. Civilian government was not restored until 15 April 1946. A month later the council voted narrowly in favour of becoming a British Crown Colony (effective from 1 July 1946). Sarawak joined Malaysia in September 1963. The traditional exports of rubber, pepper, sawn timber and cocoa beans have been surpassed in value over the last ten years by liquified natural gas and petroleum products, from the spread of northern Borneo's oilfields.

Saskatchewan: the central of Canada's three prairie provinces, forested in the north: capital, Regina. The name comes from a *Cree Indian word for 'swift flowing', applied to the Churchill and Saskatchewan rivers. Fur traders explored the lands in the seventeenth century but there was little settlement before the coming of the *Canadian Pacific Railway. When the Dominion was established in 1867 Saskatchewan was part of the *Northwest Territories. Like *Alberta, it became an administrative district in 1882, and a province in its own right in 1905. For more than a century two-thirds of Canada's wheat has come from Saskatchewan, but it has also become a major source of Canada's oil since World War II. Notable among many immigrants were a community of Hungarians who settled in the Esterhazy district of south-eastern Saskatchewan between 1886 and 1888, and the first Russian Dokhobors, who reached Yorkton in 1899 – although the more spiritually anarchistic soon moved on to *British Columbia.

Savage, Michael John (1872–1940), New Zealand Prime Minister: born in Australia at Benalla, Victoria and did not emigrate to South Island until he was 35; became a trade union official, active in Labour politics in Auckland, and sat for Auckland West in Parliament from 1919 until his death. He became leader of the Labour Party in 1933, and after the *Great Depression attracted support from the traditionally conservative farming community to win the general election of 27 November 1935. On 6 December he formed the country's first Labour government, also taking charge of foreign relations, native affairs and, from 1936, broadcasting. His personality exuded a cheery confidence and he became widely popular. Social reforms, including a marketing act to benefit the farmers, ensured that he won the general election of October 1938, but the additional strain of the war effort overtaxed his health: he died suddenly on 27 March 1940, Peter *Fraser succeeding him.

Scottish Colonial Company. In 1695 the 'Company of Scotland Trading to Africa and the Indies' was formed in Edinburgh to establish Scottish colonies under the sovereignty of the ruler of the United Kingdom in any part of Asia, Africa or America not already colonized. The principal founder was William Paterson (1658–1719), a Bank of England director with experience of the West Indies sugar trade. Friction with *East India Company interests in London deprived the new company of much promised capital, and the attitude of King William (with his Dutch trading interests) was, at best, ambiguous. Paterson was aboard one of the three vessels which sought to colonize Darien (Panama) in July 1698, an expedition which achieved nothing, partly because of the ravages of the climate but also because of Spanish hostility. Further expeditions in 1699 were no more successful. The 'Darien Scheme' was a financial disaster, and only one trading voyage to West Africa was profitable. By 1701 the company was bankrupt, leaving the Scots mistrustful of English (and Dutch) commercial enterprise overseas.

'Scramble for Africa': the rapid partition of the continent by rival European governments, 1880–1911. The main beneficiary was France, with sovereignty over a third of Africa's land-surface. The four main causes of the scramble were: competitive industrialization in Europe, which needed new sources of raw materials and new markets: bankers seeking investment for surplus capital; individual patriots, whose sense of national mission could not be fulfilled within a heavily armed Europe; and a reaction to defensive native confederacies which threatened to check commercial ventures originally undertaken independent of government backing. The scramble was possible only through speedier communication and the superiority of European weaponry. The impact of the scramble was deep, but brief: the 'scurry from Africa' – effectively from 1956 to 1968 – proved even speedier.

Scullin, James Henry (1876–1953), Australian Prime Minister: born in up-country Victoria, near Ballarat; left school early and completed his education at evening classes. After working as a gold-miner and a shop-keeper he became a trade union organizer and sat as a Labor MP (1910–13 and 1922–49). By 1928 he was Leader of the Opposition; forming a government on 12 October 1929, he had the misfortune to be faced immediately with the *Great Depression. To check rising unemployment he put up tariffs, but without any real success, and economies which cut the basic wage by 10 per cent split his party. His most remarkable achievement was to secure the appointment of the first Australian-born Governor-General (Sir Isaac Isaacs, 1855–1948). Scullin's premiership ended in December 1931, after an electoral defeat. He never again held office.

Seato (South East Asia Treaty Organization): established by the Treaty of Manila of 8 September 1954 to link Australia, France, New Zealand, Pakistan, the Philippines, Thailand, the United Kingdom and the United States. The eight signatories pledged themselves to take collective action if any one or more of them should be attacked, or weakened by internal subversion. It was never as cohesive as Nato, nor was it ever extended. Both France and Great Britain argued that its provisions did not apply to Vietnam, Laos or Cambodia; Pakistan ceased to be a member in November 1973; France withdrew in June 1974, after long disputes with Australia and New Zealand over *nuclear tests; and in September 1975 the remaining members decided that Seato no longer served a useful purpose and should accordingly be phased out.

Second Fleet. Three convict transports – *Neptune, Scarborough* and *Surprise* – left English waters on 19 January 1790, together with a store ship, *Justinian*. Aboard the ships were 1,000 convicts and 100 men of the specially-recruited 'New South Wales Corps', intended to relieve the Royal Marines who had accompanied the *First Fleet. Living conditions were grim, with the convicts kept often in chains; discipline was harsh; the voyage was frequently stormy; contagious diseases were prevalent and medicine in short supply. Not surprisingly, when the Second Fleet reached Sydney in late June 1790 it was found that a quarter of the convicts had perished during the voyage, and another 150 were so ill that they died within days of disembarkation. No later convoy sailed under such terrible conditions.

Seddon, Richard John (1845–1906), New Zealand Prime Minister: born at St Helen's, Lancashire; left work in an iron-foundry to emigrate to Victoria, Australia at the age of eighteen. Although he joined the *gold rush to New Zealand's South Island in 1866, Seddon failed to make his fortune then, or later in 1874 at Kumara (Westland), where he entered local politics and showed such a flair for publicity that he was returned to Parliament in 1879; he remained an MP until his death. At heart Seddon was a pragmatic Liberal, ready to support state ownership and the promotion of railways to open up rural communities. His demagogic skills made 'King Dick' – as he was early nicknamed – respected as a political figure, while his energy led him to acquire and retain several government posts at the same time. When he became Prime Minister in May 1893, he was also the minister responsible for mines, public works, defence, and marine. Soon he also became minister for native affairs and labour, and colonial treasurer. As early as September 1893 Seddon completed the legislation giving women the vote. He steered through an Old Age Pensions Bill in 1898 and gave New Zealand universal penny postage in 1901. He was a forceful personality among the colonial premiers who came to Britain for the Diamond Jubilee celebrations of 1897 and for Edward VII's coronation in 1902, sharing many of *Chamberlain's tariff beliefs and securing passage of a Preferential Trade Act in 1902, which favoured British imports. He sent three contingents of New Zealand volunteers to fight against the Boers in South Africa. Early in 1906 Seddon won his fifth successive electoral victory, but the strain was too great even for his iron constitution; he died in June while returning from a visit to Australia.

Seeley, Sir John Robert (1834–95), British historian: born in London; educated at City of London School and Christ's College, Cambridge, where he was Regius Professor of History from 1869 until his death. He believed that 'history is past politics, and politics present history', and from the early 1880s his lectures concentrated on the inevitable progress of Britain's imperial mission. His two main published collections were *The Expansion of England in the Eighteenth Century* (1883) – which included the famous aphorism, 'We seem to have conquered and peopled half the world in a fit of absence of mind' – and *The Growth of British Policy* (1895), published the year *Chamberlain became Colonial Secretary, which supported the fashionable idea of imperial federation.

Selborne Memorandum (1907): William Waldegrave Palmer (1859–1942), who became second Earl of Selborne in 1895, was a son-in-law of *Lord Salisbury, in whose government he served as Colonial Under-Secretary and, after 1900, First Lord of the Admiralty. His close links with South African affairs during the Chamberlain era led to his appointment as High Commissioner in South Africa as *Milner's successor (1905). Selborne saw an urgent need for reconciliation between British and Boers, and for union, fearing that old conflicts between the Transvaal and Cape Colony would otherwise be renewed through economic competition. He put forward his plea for a central government unifying South Africa's peoples as a nation in his *Review of the Mutual Relations of* *the British South African Colonies* (1907). This 'Selborne Memorandum' was used as a basis for discussion among parliamentarians from the four South African colonies when they met at Durban and Cape Town in 1908 and 1909. Selborne remained in Pretoria until 1910, presiding over the creation of the *Union of South Africa which he had advocated.

Selkirk, Thomas Douglas, fifth Earl of Selkirk (1771–1820), colonizer in Canada: educated at Edinburgh University; sat as a Scottish representative peer in the House of Lords (1806/7). He encouraged emigrants, especially from Ireland and the Scottish Highlands, to settle in British colonies rather than the USA. Under his direction 800 Highlanders settled on *Prince Edward Island in 1803. Eight years later he purchased land along the Red River valley – five times the area of Scotland – from the Hudson's Bay Company, for a pioneer settlement on what he called 'the immense open plains . . . of British America'. Highland emigrants again followed his lead, but his enterprise met fierce opposition from the North-West Fur Company who encouraged the *métis to attack Fort Douglas on 19 June 1816, killing the Governor of the Hudson's Bay Company and 20 of his 27-man escort. Lord Selkirk, who remained in Canada until 1818, hurriedly recruited mercenary veterans and led a retaliatory attack on the Company's post at Fort William. He also concluded a treaty with the *Assiniboine Indians giving him land rights in return for an annual tobacco payment. Much of Selkirk's land was reckoned by boundary commissioners in 1818 to lie within the USA but a core of pioneers, enduring great hardship, remained around Fort Douglas to join other immigrants and a large métis community in what became, after the *Red River Rebellion, the province of *Manitoba. Fourteen years after Selkirk's death his heirs re-conveyed the lands to the Hudson's Bay Company who pledged maintenance of the settlement on the Red River.

Seretse Khama (1921–80) of *Botswana: see *Khama, Seretse*.

Seringapatam (Sringapatnam): an island town in the Cauvery river, now in Karnataka state, India. From 1610 until 1799 it was the capital of Mysore and the fortress home of the two powerful usurper sultans, Haidar Ali (1728–82) and his son Tippoo (1749–99), an ally of the French against the British. Tippoo was besieged in the fortress for a month by an army commanded by General George Harris (1746–1829). On 4 May 1799 Harris's troops stormed Seringapatam, killed Tippoo and, by their victory, made possible the annexation of Mysore.

Seychelles: a group of more than 180 islands in the Indian Ocean, forming an independent republic within the Commonwealth: capital, Victoria, on Mahé island. They were colonized as spice islands by the

French from 1756 onwards but were captured by the British in 1794 and administered as a dependency of *Mauritius until November 1904, when they became a Crown Colony. The islands were given internal self-government in October 1975 and independence on 29 June 1976. A political coup on 5 June 1977 brought into office President France Albert René, who introduced a one-party system of government in 1979, giving the Seychelles Popular Front a monopoly of power. The President won popular approval for constitutional amendments in June 1993 which allowed a multi-party election and the return of five Democratic Party members to challenge the SPF. The economy depends largely on fishing and tourism.

Sharpeville Shootings. On 21 March 1960 South African police used automatic weapons to break up a demonstration against the *pass laws which was held at Sharpeville, a township south-west of Johannesburg, in the Transvaal: 67 Africans were killed by the shooting and almost 200 were wounded. There was widespread condemnation of the shootings by South African liberals and by world opinion. In June an attempt was made on the life of the South African Prime Minister, *Verwoerd. Resentment by nationalists of the reaction abroad to Sharpeville led to the final decision to take South Africa out of the Commonwealth and found a republic.

Shastri, Lal Bahadur (1904–66), Indian Prime Minister: born at Benares, where his father was a law clerk in *Nehru's father's practice. Lal Shastri joined the *Indian National Congress at the age of sixteen and was imprisoned on several occasions. He had a clear and orderly mind and entered the Indian cabinet in 1952 as Nehru's minister for railways and transport, later taking charge of commerce and home affairs. In 1963 he left office to help reorganize Congress, but returned to the government early in 1964 when Nehru's health began to fail. Shastri succeeded Nehru on 2 June 1964, becoming India's second Prime Minister. A short war with Pakistan began in September 1965 over the *Kashmir problem. Shastri agreed to go to Tashkent to meet Pakistan's military leader, Ayub Khan, at the invitation of the Soviet Prime Minister, Kosygin. A compromise settlement was reached at the meeting, but the strain of the talks was too great for Shastri. On his return to New Delhi he suffered a fatal heart attack (11 January 1966). Mrs Indira *Gandhi succeeded him.

Sheep. The discovery of extensive pastures in New South Wales, and later in New Zealand, led to a rapid growth of sheep farming and a profitable wool trade. The earliest Australian sheep probably came from Bengal, but the origins of the wool industry may be traced back to the landing of 33 merino ewes from Cape Colony on 16 May 1797. These ewes, and other prime sheep brought from England in 1805, allowed settlers like *Marsden and John Macarthur (1767–1834) to begin large-scale pastoral farming, in both instances near Parramatta, NSW. In 1821 175,000 pounds (weight) of wool was exported to England; within five years it jumped to a million pounds; by 1830 to two million. 'Luxuriant pastures' found in the Darling Downs, inland from Brisbane, began the spread of sheep farming inland. There was a slump in 1840/1, caused partly by prolonged drought, but the wool trade had revived by 1845. The scab parasite devastated flocks in the 1880s; fleece quality fell, wool prices dropped from 1891 onwards, and sheep numbers declined during the long drought from 1895 to 1902. Even so, by 1910 there were 92 million sheep on Australia's farms, which allowed the export of 700 million pounds of wool in the course of that one year; and improved *refrigeration also brought in considerable earnings from frozen mutton exports. Although there had been over-production in the 1920s, wool farmers fared less badly in the *Great Depression than dairy farmers, and on the eve of World War II sheep numbers stood at 110 million, with annual wool exports up to 1,023 million pounds weight. An international survey in 1952 showed Australia as having 18 million sheep, a sixth of the world total. Wool receipts began to drop in the 1960s, even though as late as 1972 there were more than 162 million sheep. By 1992 the figure had fallen to 148 million and the relative value of sheep to the changing economy was in sharp decline. In New Zealand sheep farming followed a similar pattern, spreading rapidly across South Island in the 1850s and 1960s; wool remained the dominion's chief export until World War I, overtaken by frozen lamb (and dairy produce) between the wars and fluctuating uncertainly in the 1930s. By 1952 New Zealand had 35 million sheep, some 13 million more than the United Kingdom. Sheep never made such an impact on the economy of other Commonwealth countries: the extensive sheep farming in Ontario at the time of confederation has survived, though equalled by the farms of Alberta; and sheep remain, too, in traditional pastures in Cape Province. Hopes entertained by *Delamere and other early settlers in Kenya were never fulfilled, although in the 1920s wool was exported to the London market and by World War II there were more than a quarter of a million wool-bearing sheep in the colony. The total number of sheep in Kenya rose to more than 3 million by Independence and to 7 million by 1988, but they were for domestic consumption, and there was no recognized wool trade. The same is true of Pakistan, where there are many million sheep in the fertile, irrigated plain. In the small communities of the Falkland Islands, however, sheep farming, and the accompanying wool trade, remain essential to the economy.

Sierra Leone: independent Commonwealth republic: capital, Freetown. The windward west coast of Africa provided a source of captives for the *slave trade as early as 1562 and was later exploited by the *Royal

Africa Company. The spread of emancipationist beliefs led to the foundation in London of a Sierra Leone Company in 1790 which, having already purchased land from a tribal leader identified as 'King Tom', founded Freetown as a settlement for 60 Europeans and 400 freed Africans, mainly waifs from London, Bristol and other ports. Wesleyan pioneer *missionaries were followed in 1804 by the Church Missionary Society; in 1807 the government took over the Company, and Sierra Leone became a Crown Colony in 1808. Over the following seven years patrolling warships of the Royal Navy landed 6,000 freed men. Sierra Leone became a centre for expansion in West Africa, with The *Gambia and the Gold Coast (*Ghana) originally as dependencies. So unhealthy were the mangrove swamps along the coast that 'Sally Own' (as it was nicknamed) was long regarded as 'the white man's grave'. Although Freetown was an important *naval base the colony remained small, protected by the locally recruited Sierra Leone Police, formed in 1829. Trade with the interior was left mainly to Creole settlers, who began exporting ground-nuts (from 1837) and palm oil. The growth of neighbouring French colonies led the British to extend their jurisdiction inland after 1855 to the upper waters of the Great and Little Scarcies rivers and the river Moa, a region of tropical rain-forests and rising plateaux. In August 1896 a Protectorate was proclaimed over the hinterland and work began on a light railway from Freetown to Baiima, 200 miles inland. Resentment over methods of raising local revenue caused the so-called Hut Tax Rebellion of 1897/8, which was put down by the recently formed West African Regiment in a protracted campaign. A colonial legislative council, set up in 1924, mainly comprised nominees (including three paramount chiefs from the inner Protectorate) but was dominated by Creole settlers. Infantry from Sierra Leone showed great skill fighting in Burma in World War II. Not until 1951 was a constitution introduced representative of all races and unifying Freetown and the hinterland Protectorate; the first Africans joined the government in 1953. Independence was granted in April 1961, the first Prime Minister being Sir Milton Margai (1896–1964). A republic was proclaimed in 1971, with Dr Siaka Stevens (1905–   ), of the All Peoples' Congress, as executive President. He set up a one-party state in 1978 and remained in office until 1985, when he was succeeded by General Joseph Momoh, who appointed a civilian cabinet. A promise in 1991 of multi-party elections in the near future was frustrated by an army coup on 29 April 1992, led by Captain Valentine Strasser who set up a Supreme Military Council for the republic. The SMC faced increasing opposition from insurgents of the Revolutionary United Forces, with their power base in the eastern and southern provinces, around the towns of Kenema and Bo. The insurgency checked the development of government-sponsored palm oil mills and the Forest Industries Corporation, and stopped Sierra Leone's growing tourist industry.

Sikhs: originally a dissentient Hindu sect in the Punjab, their religion dating from the teachings of Guru Nanak (1469–1539), who was born near Lahore and set up a spiritual centre at Kartarpur. Sikhism is a compound of the beliefs and books of Nanak and nine later Gurus, and of Hindu and Muslim holy writings. The Sikhs' spiritual centre is the Golden Temple of *Amritsar, built by the fifth great teacher, Guru Arjan, early in the seventeenth century. The Moghul emperor Akbar (1542–1606) tolerated Sikhism, welcoming its spiritual nobility, but eighty years later the Moghuls and the Sikhs were in bitter conflict, and the last of the great teachers, Guru Govind Singh (1666–1708), called on his followers to accept militancy in defence of their faith. They organized themselves into twelve confederacies against the Moghuls, although the powerful Sikh kingdom in the Punjab emerged only under Ranjit Singh (1780–1839), who became ruler of Lahore at the age of twelve. Ranjit Singh maintained good relations with the British, keeping a frontier along the river Sutlej while extending his lands to the north and west. After his death the Sikh military leaders became alarmed by British expansion in *Sind and advanced across the Sutlej in December 1845, launching a surprise attack on the British post at Mudki. This first Anglo-Sikh War caused heavy casualties on both sides: the Sikhs were defeated at Sobrahan on 10 February 1846 and Lahore was occupied a month later. A second war led to Sikh defeats at Chillianwalla (12 January 1849) and Gujarat (21 February 1849); the Punjab was annexed to British India in March. The Sikhs were among the most loyal communities under the *Raj, and their fighting traditions were nurtured on the North-West Frontier and in both world wars. But they never formed more than 1.5 per cent of India's population and, as a minority people, were poorly treated at *Partition in 1947: Lahore became a city in Pakistan, while Amritsar and the eastern Punjab remained in India.

The 1950s and 1960s were decades of widespread emigration, bringing Sikhism to Britain, where by 1995 the religion could count some 400,000 followers. In India, increasing dismay at the republic's social policies led to the emergence by 1980 of a Sikh secessionist movement, and to communal violence which culminated in the Indian army assaults on Amritsar in 1984 and 1988 and in the assassination of Mrs Indira *Gandhi by a Sikh member of her bodyguard. Demands for Sikh autonomy continue, although with lesser violence since 1990.

Simla (Shimla): the most famous of Indian hill-stations, now the state capital of Himachal Pradesh. It is 140 miles north of Delhi, on a series of ridges, 7,000 feet above sea level. The first Governor-General to retreat from the heat of Calcutta to Simla was Lord Amherst (1773–1857), in 1827. By 1865 it was accepted that the Viceroy and his entourage should leave Calcutta in late March and remain in Simla until October or November, an annual migration which continued until World War II.

Before 1903, when the railway reached Simla, the journey was hazardous and exhausting, the distance equal to that between Warsaw and London. The change of capital to *New Delhi in 1912 lessened the disruption of government. Most homes at Simla were white bungalows, although a Viceregal Lodge was built in 1888 and there were official residences for the Governor of the Punjab and the C.-in-C. of the army.

Simon Commission (1927–30). In November 1927 the British government appointed a special commission to examine developments in India. It was chaired by the Liberal elder statesman, Sir John Simon (1873–1954): among the other six commissioners was Clement *Attlee. They made two visits to India and Burma, in February to April 1928 and October 1928 to April 1929. The commissioners travelled to every provincial capital and sought interviews with all political and religious groups, but found that the *Indian National Congress would not co-operate; nevertheless the commissioners' visits represented the most detailed survey attempted by British parliamentarians. The Simon Report, published in June 1930, recommended an immediate grant of responsible government in the provinces, and negotiations with the *princely rulers over the structure of central government. These proposals fell short of 'dominion status' because the commissioners felt this should not be accorded until Muslim–Hindu communal relations had improved and Indian officers had been trained for senior posts in the armed forces. A *round table conference to give India dominion status was announced nine months before the Simon Report was completed, thereby rendering much of the commissioners' careful study superfluous. It is a sad instance of the vacillations of policy which confused attempts to solve the Indian Question during the inter-war years.

Sind: province in *Pakistan. Sind was a tributary state of the Moghul empire from 1592, maintaining some independence until it was conquered by Sir Charles *Napier's army in 1843. It became a province of British India, and included the towns of Hyderabad, Shikrapur and Sukkur. *Irrigation, notably the Lloyd Barrage, enabled the arid plains to produce wheat, rice and cotton. Karachi was developed rapidly as a port from 1880 onwards.

Singapore: an independent island republic within the Commonwealth. The commercial possibilities of the island were ignored by the Portuguese and Dutch traders who contested the region with the Javanese in the sixteenth and seventeenth centuries. Sir Stamford *Raffles established a trading settlement there in 1819 and the island was purchased by the East India Company from the Sultan of Johore in August 1824, being incorporated in the *Straits Settlements from 1826 to 1946. The island's strategic position and good harbour facilities, together with

311

its value for exporting *tin and *rubber from Malaya, had made it a great port by 1900, even though the Johore Causeway carrying a road and railway to the peninsula was not opened until 1932. The population rose from 200 in 1819 to 350,000 in 1919, nearly three-quarters of them Chinese immigrants. When the Japanese attacked Malaya in 1941 the city's population had risen to 750,000, of whom 584,000 were Chinese. A *naval base was completed in the Johore Straits in 1938, but the defences of the island were incapable of preventing Japanese troops from crossing the Straits on 8–9 February 1942. The island was forced to surrender within a week, and 70,000 Commonwealth troops passed into captivity. Singapore was liberated on 5 September 1945 and became a Crown Colony, joining Malaysia in 1963; complaints of discrimination by Malays at the expense of Chinese induced Singapore to secede two years later. The island became an independent sovereign state on 9 August 1965. Under the leadership of *Lee Kuan Yew, Singapore has enjoyed great commercial prosperity: strict policing and severe penalties impose uniformity of discipline on the community.

Singapore Declaration (1971). At the end of the *Commonwealth Heads of Government meeting at Singapore in January 1971 an agreed Declaration of Commonwealth Principles was published. The Declaration emphasized that the Commonwealth was a voluntary association of sovereign independent states, co-operating in the interests of their peoples to promote understanding between nations at peace. It was outspoken in condemning 'racial prejudice as a dangerous sickness threatening the healthy development of the human race and racial discrimination as an unmitigated evil of society'. The Declaration was re-examined in the *Mahatir Report of 1991 and its principles reaffirmed, with greater precision, in the subsequent *Harare Declaration, while the Cyprus Commonwealth Conference (1993) stressed democratic values.

Slave Emancipation. After more than forty years of campaigning by the opponents of *slavery a Bill to abolish the institution was carried through Parliament in late August 1833. Slavery in the British Empire was accordingly outlawed from 1 August 1834 –, at a cost of twenty million pounds of taxpayers' money, in compensation to the deprived slave-owners.

Slave Trade. The trade in African slaves to the Americas and the Caribbean islands was begun by the Spanish, under crown licence, in 1510. Dutch, Portuguese, French and British seamen participated from the mid sixteenth century onwards. Sir John Hawkins (1532–95) undertook the first English slaving voyage, from Senegal and Sierra Leone to the Caribbean in 1562, and made two further voyages before deciding in 1568 that they were unprofitable. British participation revived in 1610 but did not become intensive until mid-century. The failure of the chartered

*Royal Africa Company was followed by the growth of slave-trading partnerships using ships from London, Bristol and, from about 1750 onwards, Liverpool. The 'slave coast' extended (using current place-names) from Senegal southwards through Sierra Leone, Ghana and Nigeria to Angola, with more than half shipped from the stretch between Lagos and the Niger estuary. Permanent trading posts in The Gambia and Ghana received slaves brought from the hinterland by African merchants or agents of African rulers. The slaves were then shipped under appalling conditions to the southern American colonies or, more frequently, to Jamaica, Barbados and the Leeward Islands. Relatively small ships would carry up to 600 slaves, chained to shelves below-deck throughout the crossing: at least one in ten perished on a voyage, sometimes more than one in eight. It was calculated, however, that a cargo of 600 slaves would earn a profit of £1,500; having unloaded the slaves, the traders would then bring back *sugar and rum to their home ports. The peak period of the British slave trade was between 1765 and 1775, when about 34,000 slaves were brought across from Africa each year (though some estimates suggest a higher figure). The trade declined during the wars with revolutionary France, which coincided with Wilberforce's campaign against *slavery and the slave trade. A bill to abolish the British slave trade was passed in the House of Commons in 1804 but twice rejected in the House of Lords, though a third attempt was successful in March 1807 and the trade was outlawed from May 1808 onwards. At the Congress of Vienna the Foreign Secretary, Lord Castlereagh (1769–1822), secured a general condemnation of the slave trade (February 1815) and it had been abandoned by all the Great Powers by 1820. Royal Navy patrols from Freetown and in the Indian Ocean sought to enforce the ban on slave-trading throughout the nineteenth century, successive rulers of *Zanzibar being among the worst offenders.

Slavery. In the late fifteenth and early sixteenth centuries, when capitalism emerged in western Christendom, the institution of slavery – its origins in ancient times, and long practised in much of Europe, Asia and Africa – was accepted as an economic necessity. Slavery was imposed on the North American indigenous population by early settlers before being developed in a new form by the *slave trade companies for the Caribbean and mainland colonies of the European Powers. Lord Chief Justice Mansfield, in a famous judgment on 22 June 1772 concerning the ex-slave Somersett, held that the right of property in slaves could not be upheld in an English court of law, and that any enslaved person landing on English soil became free. This judgment encouraged the work of philanthropists like the evangelical MP, William Wilberforce (1759–1833), and the Quaker, Thomas Clarkson (1760–1846). Wilberforce denounced slavery and the slave trade in the House of Commons from 1787 until his retirement in 1825. With other evangelicals he set up (in 1787) the Anti-Slavery

Committee, which sought to end the slave trade as a first step towards general emancipation; this task took Wilberforce nineteen years of parliamentary campaigning, largely because of hostility on the part of City interests in both Houses, especially in the Lords. The Act abolishing the slave trade in British possessions came into effect in January 1808. It was followed by British naval support for the 'free town' established by emancipationists in *Sierra Leone. Opposition from the Lords also delayed the final abolition of slavery. Growing resentment at conditions led to slave rebellions in Barbados (1816), Jamaica (1823, 1824 and 1830) and Guyana (1823); and there were still some 750,000 African slaves on British Caribbean coffee and sugar plantations in 1830. The Bill abolishing slavery was carried in 1833 and became effective on 1 August 1834. Campaigns continued against the crypto-slavery of *blackbirding and 'coolie' *Chinese labourers. Moreover, though slavery was illegal in the British Empire, it could not be banned in territories under British protection but not under direct British rule. Thus slavery was not abolished in *Kuwait until 1949, nor in the Emirate of Qatar, a *Trucial State, until 1952. In other parts of the Arabian peninsula, including the outlying regions of the Aden Protectorate, slavery survived even longer.

Smith, Arnold Cantwell (1915–94), first Secretary-General of the Commonwealth: born in Toronto, where he received his basic education; became a Rhodes Scholar at Christ Church, Oxford in 1935; served in the British diplomatic service in Estonia and Egypt before transferring to the Canadian foreign service in 1943 and eventually becoming Canada's ambassador in Moscow during the Khrushchev era. After two years as Assistant Under-Secretary for External Affairs in Ottawa, Smith was invited to head the newly created *Commonwealth Secretariat in 1965; he held office for ten years. He emphasized the strict neutrality of members of the Secretariat, while also seeking to give the Commonwealth strength of purpose. He increased the effectiveness of the Secretariat by securing the establishment of a *Commonwealth Fund for Technical Co-operation, and he encouraged the search for shared principles, finally set down in the *Singapore Declaration. On his retirement in 1975 he was made a Companion of Honour. He later lectured on international relations, and in 1981 published *Stitches in Time – the Commonwealth in World Politics*.

Smith, Ian Douglas (1919–   ). Rhodesian Prime Minister: born at Selukwe; farmed in central *Rhodesia, serving also in the Royal Air Force (1941 to 1946). He sat in the Southern Rhodesian legislature from 1948 to 1953 and then in the legislature of the *Central African Federation until it was dissolved in 1962, when he helped found the Rhodesian Front Party to preserve white supremacy. He became Prime Minister in April 1964, found it impossible to collaborate with Harold Wilson's Labour government (which came to power in London six months later), and on 11 November made what he called 'a unilateral declaration of independence' (*UDI). In talks with Wilson aboard HMS *Tiger* (1966) and HMS *Fearless* (1968), Smith refused to make concessions which would have led to majority black rule. He remained Prime Minister after declaring Rhodesia a republic, in March 1970. External economic pressure and ostracism (except from South Africa and Portugal) eventually forced him to compromise, and he came to London for the *Lancaster House Conference of September 1979 which led to the establishment of *Zimbabwe. Smith was elected a member of the first Parliament in Harare after independence.

Smuts, Jan Christiaan (1870–1950), South African Field Marshal and Prime Minister: born on a farm at Boplass, Riebeeck West, Cape Colony. Although he knew no English until he was twelve and had studied science and literature at Stellenbosch, he travelled to England in 1892 to read law at Christ's College, Cambridge; he gained a Double First and was called to the Bar of the Middle Temple before becoming State Attorney to *Kruger in the *Transvaal. He fought in the Second *Boer War, and in 1901/2 commanded Boer commandos who penetrated deeply into Cape Colony. He later held high office in the Transvaal colonial administration, took a prominent part in drafting the constitution of the Union of *South Africa, and was elected to the first Parliament. From 1910 to 1924 Smuts was Minister of Defence and created the South African Army, with which he conquered German *South-West Africa (*Namibia) in 1915. He commanded the allied armies in East Africa in 1916/17 before coming to Britain for the *Imperial War Conference and serving in the War Cabinet in London (June 1917 to December 1918). He went on a special mission to Switzerland in December 1917, unsuccessfully seeking a separate peace with Austria–Hungary. After playing a leading role in the post-war peace conference and in setting up the League of Nations, he returned home as successor to *Botha. General Smuts was South Africa's Prime Minister from August 1919 until his defeat in the elections of June 1924; he returned as *Hertzog's deputy premier from 1933 to 1939, and headed the government again from September 1939 until May 1948. Smuts was the most internationally-minded South African statesman; he was made Field Marshal in 1941, commanded South Africa's and Rhodesia's armed forces throughout World War II, and made four visits to Britain to discuss general strategy with *Churchill and other Allied leaders. Although he retained traditional Boer concepts of white supremacy, he helped draft the charter of the UN, and in 1948 became Chancellor of Cambridge University. These outside concerns – and the breadth of a mind which could develop and expound the comprehensive philosophy of 'holism' – increasingly isolated him from Afrikaaner voters. In 1947 King George VI invested him with the Order of Merit during the

South African royal visit, but a year later Smuts suffered a more person-ally humiliating electoral defeat than had Churchill in 1945. Smuts's decision to give recognition to the new state of Israel two days before polling in May 1948 may have cost him his own parliamentary seat, and over the Union as a whole the white voters rejected his internationalism, bringing *Malan to power with a mandate to impose *apartheid.

Soames, (Arthur) Christopher (1920–87; Baron Soames from 1978), last Governor of Southern Rhodesia: educated at Eton and Sandhurst; served with the Coldstream Guards in World War II; married Sir Winston Churchill's youngest daughter, Mary, in 1947 and represented Bedford as a Conservative MP from 1950 to 1966. He entered Macmillan's cabinet as War Secretary in 1968, later becoming Minister of Agriculture. From 1968 to 1972 he was ambassador in Paris, and a European Commissioner from 1973 to 1977. After his creation as a life peer in 1978, he was appointed Leader of the House of Lords by Margaret *Thatcher, but his skills as a negotiator were then employed in settling the Rhodesian dispute. He flew to Salisbury as Governor on 12 December 1979 and supervised the restoration of peace so effectively that elections on a multi-racial franchise were held within twelve weeks. At midnight on 17–18 April 1980 he handed over his powers to the new republic of *Zimbabwe.

Sobers, Sir Garfield (1936–   ), West Indian cricketer: born in Bridgetown, Barbados; first played for the West Indies in March 1954, when he was seventeen, as a slow left-arm bowler. He developed into the finest all-round cricketer in the history of the game, perfecting three types of bowling, achieving world records as a batsman and showing great versatility as a fielder, occasionally at cover point but more often at slip or short leg. By April 1974, when he retired from Test cricket, he had repre-sented the West Indies 93 times, 39 of them as captain; he scored 8,032 runs, took 235 wickets, and held 110 catches. At Kingston, Jamaica in 1958 he made 365 not out against Pakistan, a world record for a Test innings which stood until April 1994, when Brian Lara made 375 against England at Antigua. Sobers played for Barbados for twenty seasons, and for South Australia for three; he also captained Nottinghamshire from 1968 to 1974, the first West Indian player to lead an English county side. He received a knighthood in the 1975 New Year Honours List.

Solomon Islands: an independent Commonwealth monarchy in the south-west Pacific: capital, Honiara, on Guadalcanal. The islands were discovered by the Spaniard Mendana in 1568 but left unexploited for three hundred years. Geographically they include Bougainville and Buka which, with several atolls, at present form the North Solomons Province of *Papua New Guinea. In the 1860s the practice of *blackbirding by raiders from Queensland aroused protests overseas but stimulated an interest in the islands which was intensified by German projects of colonization twenty years later. The northern Solomons were acquired by Germany in 1886 and held until 1914. A British Protectorate over the southern islands was proclaimed in 1893 and was extended to the east and further south when Germany abandoned claims to this area under the *Samoa Agreement of 1899. Copra was, and remains, the chief export. Administration was entrusted to a Resident Commissioner, responsible to the Governor of *Fiji as High Commissioner and assisted by a nominated Advisory Council: internal self-government was authorized in January 1976, pending full independence on 7 July 1978. The constitution acknowledges the Head of the Commonwealth as Queen of the Solomon Islands. During World War II there was protracted fighting in the Solomons, which were seized by the Japanese in May 1942. The US 1st Marine Division sailed from New Zealand in late July 1942 to recover the islands and began an invasion of Guadalcanal on 7 August. Japanese resistance was formidable and prolonged until 8 February 1943. The Americans met similar stubborn resistance on New Georgia, another island of the group, June–August 1942. The New Zealanders made costly invasions of Vella Lavella and Green Island in September and October 1943; not until March 1944 were the Solomons finally liberated. Since 1992 there has been tension between *Papua New Guinea and the Solomon Islands over secessionism in Bougainville: Papuan troops landed on outlying islands in the Solomons to destroy alleged secessionist supply bases and in April 1993 there were clashes between Papuan and Solomon naval patrols.

Somaliland: see *British Somaliland; Jubaland; Mad Mullah; Northern Frontier District.*

South Africa. Early proposals by *Milner and others for unifying the South African colonies were revived in the *Selborne Memorandum of 1907, considered in detail at intercolonial conventions in Durban and Cape Town, and enacted in September 1909 (see *above*). Federation became a reality on 31 May 1910, the Union of South Africa enjoying Dominion status until it left the Commonwealth on 31 May 1961. South African participation in World War I brought a *mandate over *South-West Africa. The development of the Union's mineral resources brought prosperity to white South Africans who increased their discriminatory authority over blacks and Indian settlers with the rising power of the *Afrikaaner Nationalist Party. During an uneasy coalition partnership from 1933 to 1939 between *Hertzog's wing of the nationalist movement and *Smuts's United Party, racial segregation was intensified by a series of 'status' bills (including the *Status of the Union Act, June 1934) and a *Representation of Natives Act (April 1936). Hertzog's failure to keep South Africa neutral in 1939 and the subsequent wartime leadership of Smuts pushed the 'native problem' into the background. South Africans fought, mainly on the African continent, throughout the war; and the Union, like Southern Rhodesia, became a vital training area for newly recruited RAF aircrew. The electorate reacted against Smuts's internationalism in the elections of May 1948, which brought *Malan's National Party to power with a sufficient majority to impose *apartheid. The new laws enforced classification of men, women and children by race, giving each separate group a different status which decided where they might live, what work they might undertake and with whom they might not have sex. At the same time the Suppression of Communism Act (1950) marked the beginning, for white radicals as well as for blacks, of an attack on civil liberties and of the conversion of the Union into a police state where great brutality was condoned. Humanitarian sentiment abroad was expressed by condemnation of apartheid at the United Nations and at Commonwealth conferences, and by the award of the Nobel Peace Prize to such champions of individual liberties as *Luthuli in 1960 and Archbishop *Tutu in 1984. Protests after the *Sharpeville shootings of 1960 induced Prime Minister *Verwoerd to hold a referendum on 5 October 1960 among whites of the Union: 52 per cent of voters favoured secession from the Commonwealth and the establishment of a South African Republic; 9 per cent of the white electorate abstained. The Republic came into being on 31 May 1961. The *African National Congress thereafter resorted to an armed struggle against apartheid. In 1962 a Sabotage Act further restricted civil liberties, and saw the beginning of Nelson *Mandela's 28 years of imprisonment. A Terrorism Act in 1967 imposed indefinite imprisonment without trial. On 16 June 1976 there was an uprising in the black township of Soweto, outside Johannesburg, initially as a protest against plans to make Afrikaans the language of teaching for all children. After a week of riots in Soweto and other townships the government admitted that 236 non-whites had been killed and more than a thousand injured, though unofficial estimates place the figure of dead at nearer six hundred. Attempts were made by the government to divide the opposition: the revival of the *Zulu cultural organization, Inkatha, was encouraged from 1975 onwards and a succession of Bantu 'homelands' – Transkei (1976), Bophuthatswana (1977), Venda (1979), Ciskei (1981) – were given a token independence, within the Union's boundaries. The death in police custody of the moderate black activist Steve Biko (1946–77) intensified the struggle inside South Africa and also the call for sanctions against the apartheid government by the international community. When foreign banks refused to extend loans in 1985 the white prosperity of South Africa was jeopardized, and from June 1986 the government imposed an even harsher 'State of Emergency' which curbed white democratic organizations and harassed church leaders. After F. W. de *Klerk became

President in October 1989 a gradual relaxation of tension led to the release of Mandela, followed by meetings between ANC leaders and government spokesmen. The transition to democracy was hampered by the rise of a violent right-wing neo-Nazi Afrikaaner Resistance Movement (AWB) and by increasing militancy within Zulu Inkatha. Even while talks on the transition to multiracial democracy were in progress during 1992, there were mass political killings south of Johannesburg at Boipathong (17 June) and in Ciskei at Bisho (7 September); and the left-wing ANC leader Chris Hani (1942–93) was assassinated on 10 April 1993. During July 1993, after the elections were announced, more than 300 people died in black townships; and on 25 July an evening service in St James's Church, Kenilworth – a 'white' area of Cape Town – was broken up by terrorists who threw hand grenades and used automatic rifles to kill eleven of the congregation. The victory of ANC in the multiracial elections of April 1994 and the succession of Nelson Mandela to the presidency was followed by South Africa's re-admission to the Commonwealth, and by a state visit to the republic of Queen Elizabeth II in March 1995. The transitional programme for South Africa envisages agreement on a constitution by 27 April 1996 but provides for the issue to be left for decision either by a national referendum or, in 1999, by a general election.

South Africa Act (1909): carried through the British Parliament on 20 September 1909 by Asquith's Liberal government, it gave approval to a constitution devised by delegates to conventions held in Durban (October 1908) and Cape Town (February 1909) providing for the federation of Cape Colony, Natal, the Transvaal and the Orange Free State in a single Dominion, the Union of *South Africa, established on 31 May 1910. The Act tacitly accepted racial segregation by providing that, as no general solution of 'the native problem' had been found at the two conventions, the existing franchise arrangements of the four colonies should be preserved in the Union: black Africans living in Cape Province could vote in parliamentary elections, while those living in other provinces could not. All black Africans were ineligible for membership of the Parliament, and their 'needs' and 'wishes' were to be presented in Parliament by nominated senators, appointed because of their alleged special knowledge of the Union's coloured peoples; their rights were limited still further by the South African Parliament's *Representation of Natives Act (1936).

South Australia: sighted by *Tasman and charted in 1802 by Flinders but not settled until 1836, when an attempt was made at systematic colonization for free immigrants, according to *Wakefield's principles. The city of Adelaide was founded that year and named in honour of King William IV's queen-consort; there were never any convict settlements in

South Australia. Within five years the Wakefield settlement had failed and the embryonic colony was bankrupt. The British authorities settled its debts in London and set up a conventionally administered colony in 1842, which was allowed a partially elective legislative council in 1851. It soon became the chief wheat producer among the Australian colonies, so flourishing that it encouraged the expeditions into the interior of James *Stuart, welcomed the grant of extended jurisdiction over the *Northern Territory in July 1863, and sought to complete and control a south-to-north artery. In the talks that led to the formation of the federal Commonwealth of Australia in 1901 the colony's leaders played a mediatory role, helping to curb the rivalry between Melbourne and Sydney. The state remains rich in wool production and wheat, but has developed the *wine trade and the valuable iron ore deposits of the Middleback Range, as well as encouraging light industries around Adelaide.

South Georgia and the South Sandwich Islands: British dependencies in the South Atlantic, 470 miles apart and linked to the *Falkland Islands, 800 miles north-west of South Georgia. Captain Cook took possession of both dependencies in 1775. Sealers used South Georgia as a base intermittently from 1788 until the growth of a whaling industry which sustained the island's few inhabitants in the summer months, from 1904 to 1966. Both dependencies were thereafter used for scientific purposes and left virtually uninhabited until the Argentinians seized South Georgia on 3 April 1982. A British task force recovered the island three weeks later.

South Pacific Commission: a never specifically Commonwealth body, set up in February 1947 by Australia, New Zealand, the United Kingdom, France, the Netherlands and the United States, and since joined by both independent and dependent territories in the South Pacific. The original object was to co-ordinate aid and recovery programmes in those parts of the region which had suffered in World War II, but the Commission has subsequently sought to promote social stability in the islands by providing technical assistance. The Dutch left the Commission in 1962, but it now has 27 members, 15 of whom are in the Commonwealth. Headquarters are at Noumea in the French overseas territory of New Caledonia.

South Pacific Forum: arose from the Pacific Islands Producers' Association set up by *Fiji and *Western Samoa in 1965 to co-ordinate trade with New Zealand. Other Commonwealth islands joined PIPA: *Tonga, *Niue, the *Cook Islands, *Kiribati and *Tuvalu. They invited New Zealand to host a meeting of heads of government at Wellington in August 1971, attended also by Australia's Minister for External Territories. The joint gathering was called a South Pacific Forum; it was agreed to hold annual meetings, like small-scale Heads of Government conferences. *Papua New Guinea, the *Solomon Islands, *Vanuatu and *Nauru have since joined the Forum. Early meetings were concerned primarily with trade matters, but increasingly in the 1980s political questions came to the forefront, particularly criticism of *nuclear tests in the Pacific. New Zealand took the lead in promoting the South Pacific Nuclear Free Zone Treaty, agreed by the Forum at Rarotonga in 1985.

South-West Africa: a German protectorate from 1880 until April–May 1915 when it was overrun by South African troops led by *Botha and *Smuts in a three-week campaign. For the remainder of World War I the region, known to earlier settlers as Damaraland in the north and Namaland in the south, was administered by South Africa, to whom it was assigned as a class C *mandate by the Treaty of Versailles (1919); for administrative purposes the Union government included *Walvis Bay with the mandated territory. The black peoples of South West Africa – Ovambo and Herero – suffered from the restraints and humiliations imposed in the Union itself, especially after World War II when South Africa refused to place the territory under United Nations trusteeship. Repeated instances of expropriation of Herero reserves by white settlers, together with the extension to South-West Africa of the *apartheid laws, were condemned by a resolution of the UN Assembly in June 1968, which also renamed the territory *Namibia. Three years later the International Court of Justice ruled that South Africa's presence in South-West Africa was illegal. South African troops finally withdrew in April 1989.

Southern Cameroons. The West African German Protectorate of Kamerun, lying between French Equatorial Africa and Nigeria, was established in July 1884, originally over the estuary of the Wouri river, though the Germans later penetrated inland to reach Lake Chad. Most of the protectorate was overrun by British and French colonial forces between August 1914 and July 1915, although an isolated garrison held out at Mora until February 1916. The Kamerun was divided between France and Britain, in anticipation of post-war *mandates, accorded by the League of Nations. The British administered the smaller, western parts of Kamerun, subdividing it into the Southern Cameroons and the Northern Cameroons, a backward area always closely associated with *Nigeria, which it chose to join in 1961. The British Southern Cameroons resisted Nigerian political and economic encroachment and responded at an early stage to the African nationalist movement in the neighbouring French trust territory, which became an independent republic on 1 January 1960. The Southern Cameroons themselves voted for union with the republic in February 1961, and the British link finally ended seven months later. The Commonwealth Heads of Government Meeting at Nicosia in 1993 invited the Cameroon Republic to join the

Commonwealth at an unspecified date if its government felt able to observe the principles of the *Harare Declaration.

Southern Rhodesia: see *Rhodesia* and *Zimbabwe*.

Speke, John Hanning (1827–64), explorer of central Africa: born near Ilminster, Somerset. After serving with the Indian army in the Punjab he joined the orientalist (Sir) Richard Burton (1821–90) in exploring Somaliland in 1854. Three years later the Royal Geographical Society sent the two men to equatorial Africa to go inland from the coast facing Zanzibar and explore the lakes. After Burton had left him Speke trekked northwards from Tabora and discovered Ukerewe, the largest lake in Africa, which he renamed Lake Victoria Nyanza. Speke was convinced that Lake Victoria (as it is generally called) fed the waters of the Nile, a belief Burton refused to share. In 1860 Speke set out on a further expedition to Lake Victoria, with Colonel James Grant (1827–92); they explored the lake, where on 28 July 1862 Speke rightly identified the Ripon Falls as the Nile's headwaters. Speke and Grant returned to England in 1863 with botanical specimens. While preparing a report to present to a meeting of the British Association (which Burton was to attend), Speke was killed in an accident when out partridge shooting.

Sri Lanka: an independent 'democratic socialist republic' within the Commonwealth; capital, Colombo. The name Sri Lanka ('resplendent island') was chosen to replace *Ceylon when it became a republic in 1972, during Mrs *Bandaranaike's second premiership. In 1978 a new constitution – not unlike the basic structure of Gaullist France – established a directly-elected executive presidency and a single-chamber assembly. Fear that the central government would be dominated by the Sinhalese nominee for the presidency led to tension between the Sinhalese and Tamil communities, and in May 1983 Tamil Tiger guerrillas began fighting government forces for control of the regions where Tamils formed a majority, in the north and east of the island. Severe fighting took place on the Jaffna Peninsula in 1987, and recurred in November 1993 when the Tigers sought to break out of the peninsula, where security forces had confined them after the withdrawal in 1989 of Indian troops sent two years earlier to police the north. Tamil Tigers have occasionally struck at the heart of the island, notably on 1 May 1993 when a suicide bomber assassinated President Premadasa. At the same time, the *tea economy of the island suffered from a Marxist rising in the south of the island by the JVP (People's Liberation Front). Between 1983 and 1994 Sri Lanka's civil wars killed more than 30,000 people. A general election held on 16 August 1994 brought victory to the People's Alliance, which sought to negotiate a settlement with the Tamils, promising them a high degree of autonomy in the Jaffna area.

Stanley, Sir Henry Morton (1841–1904), journalist and explorer: born John Rowlands in Denbigh; went to New Orleans as a cabin boy, was adopted by a family named Stanley, and took American citizenship. After fighting with the Confederates he became a special correspondent with the *New York Herald* at the age of 26, reporting from East Africa and Spain until ordered to 'find *Livingstone', who was thought to be lost in central Africa. He 'found' Livingstone at Ujiji on 10 November 1871 and the two men jointly explored the northern shores of Lake Tanganyika. Stanley led an expedition of his own to Victoria Nyanza, and again to Lake Tanganyika in August 1874, tracing the Congo river down to the sea. He returned to the Congo on behalf of King Leopold II of the Belgians in 1879, attended the *West African Conference in Berlin, and from 1886 to 1889 led another expedition to Africa to 'find' the German explorer and acting governor of Equatorial Sudan, Emin Pasha (1840–92), who was allegedly menaced by the *Mahdi's troops. Stanley advanced into the interior from the mouth of the Congo, 'found' Emin in April 1888 on the shores of Lake Albert after two years of further exploration, and escorted him to Zanzibar, thus tracing a new route across central Africa from west to east. Stanley published four books, vividly describing his travels in Africa, all of which aroused wide interest in 'the dark continent'. He was a popular lecturer in Britain, Australia, New Zealand and America. After becoming renaturalized in 1892, Stanley sat as Unionist–Conservative MP for Lambeth North from 1895 to 1900, the peak years of *Chamberlain's imperialism. In 1899 he received a knighthood.

Status of the Union Act (South Africa, 1934). Under the influence of the extreme Nationalist, Dr *Malan, the South African coalition government headed by General *Hertzog accepted the so-called 'status bills' of 1934; they sought to clarify the *South Africa Act of 1909 and the Union's interpretation of the Statute of *Westminster. The principal Status of the Union Act of June 1934 emphasized that South Africa was 'a sovereign independent state', with a right of secession from the Commonwealth. At the same time it stipulated that, over South African matters, the monarch should act only on the advice of his or her government in Pretoria, and that all legislation should be enacted through the attachment of a South African Great Seal held by the Prime Minister, not the Governor-General.

Straits Settlements. The East India Company, long in competition with the Dutch in the Malay peninsula, formally acquired Penang in 1786, *Singapore in 1819–24 and Malacca in 1824. These isolated regions, together with Province Wellesley (a mainland coastal strip facing Penang island), were unified as the Straits Settlements in 1826 and administered as an Indian 'presidency', with headquarters moved from Penang to

Singapore in 1836. The *Colonial Office took over responsibility for the settlements from the India Office in April 1867, and they remained a Crown Colony until after World War II, when a hurriedly improvised Malayan Union (excluding Singapore) was followed in January 1948 by the Federation of *Malaya. The cumbersome system of administration in the Malay peninsula had hampered effective defence against invasion in 1941–42, and delayed the economic integration of a region rich in natural resources.

Strijdom, Johannes Gerhardus (1893–1958), South African Prime Minister: born at Willowmore, Cape Province; educated at Stellenbosch. Both a Boer farmer and a lawyer, he entered Parliament as an extreme Afrikaaner nationalist in 1934 and in December 1954 succeeded *Malan as head of a government deeply committed to *apartheid; he remained in office until shortly before his death (September 1958). Strijdom intensified racialist laws, attacking freedom within *universities, depriving Cape coloured voters of their franchise, and politically harassing Albert *Luthuli and the moderate 'white' Opposition. His fanaticism led Strijdom to have 156 supporters of a Freedom Charter charged with treason, but the prosecution case collapsed after their trial had dragged on from December 1956 to January 1958. Strijdom remained contemptuous of criticism of apartheid, whether from the United Nations or from other Commonwealth members.

Stuart, John McDoual (1815–66), explorer: born in Dysart, Fife; left Scotland for South Australia in 1839, having trained as a surveyor. He was draughtsman for *Sturt's central Australian expedition of 1844–46, and in 1858 led the first of six expeditions into the interior to explore the area around Lake Torrens and Lake Gairdner. Further journeys allowed him to explore the Lake Eyre region and, in 1860, to reach the geographical centre of Australia, where Mount Stuart commemorates his achievement. His hopes of crossing from south to north were twice dashed, in 1860 and 1861, but a third expedition in 1861/2 was successful. The route he surveyed then was followed ten years later by the overland telegraph line, and much of it is today covered by the Stuart Highway, along which 'road trains' of heavy trucks travel from Alice Springs to Darwin. Stuart, whose eyesight suffered from the sun and intense heat on his travels, returned to his native Scotland two years before his death.

Sturt, Charles (1795–1869), explorer: born in India, where his father was a judge in Bengal; returned to England for schooling (at Harrow); joined the army, where he served under Wellington in the Peninsula and marched northwards with his regiment to enter Paris on Napoleon's fall. In 1827, as an army captain, he arrived in Sydney on the governor's military staff, and made two expeditions into southern New South

Wales (1828/9 and 1830/1), exploring much of the Macquarie, Darling, Murrumbidgee and Murray rivers. So harsh were conditions that he went temporarily blind and had to return to England on extended sick-leave. Sturt travelled back to Australia in 1835 and in 1838 supervised the overland movement of cattle down to Adelaide. There he spent much of the remainder of his active life, although he led a further expedition into central Australia in 1844–46, publishing a scientific narrative of his discoveries in 1849. Sixteen years of retirement in England gave him the opportunity to pass on detailed knowledge of the inner continent to the Royal Geographical Society, who in 1847 honoured him with their Gold Medal.

Sudan: the northern Sudan was occupied by Egyptian troops sent up the Nile by Muhammed Ali, the founder of the modern Egyptian dynasty, in 1820; the city of Khartoum was established in 1822 at the confluence of the White and Blue Nile, and an Egyptian governor of the Sudan was appointed in 1830. Effective control lapsed later in the country, and in 1881 the Dongola slave-trader Mohammed Ahmed bin Abdullah (1848–85) led an Islamic uprising of which he was the Messiah, or *Mahdi. His Dervish rebellion was so successful that he wiped out an Anglo-Egyptian army sent against him in November 1883, and in January 1885 he besieged and captured Khartoum, killing General *Gordon who had sought to restore order in the province. Fears of French occupation of the Sudan led the British to prepare a full-scale invasion in 1896 which reached a climax with *Kitchener's victory at *Omdurman in 1898. An Anglo-Egyptian *condominium was established in January 1899, reaffirmed by treaty in 1936. The resources of the Nile were developed for *Egypt's benefit, but the whole region was effectively treated as a British Protectorate; there was a British Governor in Khartoum, and the Sudan was divided into eight provinces, each administered by a British District Commissioner. With the contraction of British authority in Egypt it was logical to accept Sudanese demands for independence, and the condominium ended in December 1955. No attempt was made to keep the Sudan in the Commonwealth. Since independence, the competing interests of rival warlords have left the Sudan in a state of almost constant rebellion.

Suez Canal. A 103-mile long lock-free canal linking the Red Sea port of Suez, through the Bitter Lakes and Lake Timsah, with the Mediterranean at Port Said, constructed largely by French engineers and opened by the Empress Eugénie in November 1869. Little interest was taken in the canal project by the British, until it was seen that passage of the canal by British steamships considerably shortened travel between the United Kingdom and India, and beyond. The distance from the English Channel (Eddystone lighthouse) to Bombay was 10,450 miles around the Cape, and only 6,000 through the canal; to Singapore it was 11,350 miles (Cape) and 8,050 (canal); and to Sydney 12,340 miles (Cape) and 11,200 (canal). In November 1875, on the personal initiative of *Disraeli, the British government became the largest shareholder in the Suez Canal Company, by the purchase of the 40 per cent allocation held originally by the ruler of *Egypt (who was chronically insolvent). From 1882, and for the next 74 years, British troops were stationed in the canal zone to keep the waterway open, as the Suez Canal Convention – signed at Constantinople in 1888 by ambassadors of all the Great Powers – confirmed the canal company's rights until 1968, provided that free navigation was maintained for all vessels 'in time of war as in time of peace'. This right was, understandably, denied by the British to their enemies in both world wars, although no attempt was made to close the canal to Italian warships and troopships during Mussolini's war with Ethiopia (1935–36). Agreement was reached with President Nasser of Egypt in October 1954 for British forces to withdraw by midsummer 1956; the last units left on 13 June. Six weeks later Nasser nationalized the Suez Canal Company, thereby causing the prolonged Suez Crisis (see *below*). British troops, supported by French, again held the canal from 5 November to 23 December 1956: Egyptian blockships then prevented passage of the canal until April 1957, and it was again closed on the outbreak of the Six Day Israeli–Egyptian War in June 1967. It was not completely cleared, repaired and reopened until 5 June 1975. The loss of sea-passage through the Suez Canal led to the building of bigger tankers, and to the rapid decline of old sea routes in favour of air transport.

Suez Crisis (1956). The nationalization of the Suez Canal (see *above*) by Nasser on 25 July 1956 provoked a sharp reaction from Britain and France, the main foreign shareholders. Attempts to find a compromise solution, not least by *Menzies as chairman of a Canal Users' Association, were frustrated, both by the intransigence of Nasser and by policies in London and Paris. The British Prime Minister Sir Anthony Eden (1897–1977) was convinced that a failure 'to stand up to Nasser' would lead to him becoming as great a menace as Hitler and Mussolini, twenty years previously. Israel began a campaign against Egypt on 29 October 1956; the British and French governments called for a ceasefire, which was rejected by Nasser. Accordingly, on 31 October Anglo-French forces attacked Port Said and sought to establish themselves as a buffer between the belligerents along the canal - a unilateral action which was condemned by almost every Commonwealth government, by the United States, and in the UN Assembly. Economic pressure led to a drop in the value of the pound sterling and effectively stopped the Anglo-French invasion on 7 November. Among many 'lessons of Suez' for British policy-makers was confirmation of what should have been accepted since the *Chanak crisis in 1922: Commonwealth countries would never give automatic support to rash gestures of belligerence by the United Kingdom government.

Sugar. Sugar was a rare and expensive luxury in Britain at the start of the seventeenth century, when a limited supply came from Mediterranean trading republics such as Venice and Genoa. Good quality refined sugar only became more widely available in the early eighteenth century, brought from the islands of the West Indies, especially *Jamaica. Sugar cane was introduced to the Caribbean by the Spanish and a cargo appears to have been brought back from Hispaniola to Seville as early as 1515. The English trade originated in *Barbados in 1643 and grew rapidly until by the end of the century sugar plantations covered 80 per cent of the island's arable land. By then plantations had spread to *Antigua, *St Kitts, *Montserrat and, most of all, to Jamaica. By 1730 Jamaica was the chief exporter of sugar, with more than 400 plantations on the island, reaching a peak of over a thousand in the 1780s. Convict labour from English prisons worked on the St Kitts plantations for small payment, and there was also cheap Irish labour on several islands. The wealth to be made from the 'sugar and rum' islands influenced maritime strategy during the long wars with the French and their allies (1794–1814). But though recent Caribbean gains were consolidated by the peace treaties of 1814–15, sentiment had hardened against *slavery and the *slave trade, the basic source of effective labour. Significantly, the peak exports from Jamaica came two years before the abolition of the slave trade, and there was a sharp decline of Caribbean exports during the free trade decades of the nineteenth century, from 1847 onwards. *Guyana, too, suffered in the same period. Increasingly the West Indian trade faced competition from the raw sugar of *India and of *Queensland, where the Colonial Sugar Refining Company had eight mills near Brisbane by 1870 and soon spread to the north of the colony. The CSR became notorious for dubious labour practices, including *blackbirding, and later exploited the limited resources of *Fiji, importing many thousands of Indian labourers to work its plantations. Unrefined sugar became a major export of *Mauritius before World War I. By then, too, South African unrefined sugar was worth in export earnings as much as fruit and tobacco put together. Caribbean production was worst hit between the wars, mainly by competition from outside the Commonwealth, especially Brazil and Cuba. It was given some protection after the war and until 1960 by the *Commonwealth Sugar Agreement. As late as 1968 the Commonwealth Caribbean countries were producing a million and a quarter tons a year, with Jamaica accounting for 445,000 tons; the industry then fell into a rapid decline from which it has been only partially rescued by regional agreements (*Carifta; *Caricom) and the *Lomé agreements. Among Commonwealth members India, Australia and South Africa all produce more sugar than do the West Indies, the source of such wealth to British merchants in the eighteenth century.

Suttee (*sati*): the Indian custom by which a widow would burn herself to death on her husband's funeral pyre. The practice, allegedly based on Hindu scriptural texts, was said to have been encouraged by male heirs to a father's property. Vigorous efforts to stamp out suttee were made in the early 1830s by *Cavendish-Bentinck as India's first Governor-General.

Swaraj: an Indian word meaning home rule or self-government. First used in 1905 in protest at the decision of *Curzon as Viceroy to partition Bengal administratively, it was taken up by *Gandhi in 1920–22 at the start of his civil disobedience campaign. Younger Indian nationalists, including Nehru, thought *swaraj* by itself inadequate, and by 1929 had persuaded the Indian National Congress movement to seek *puru swaraj* (complete independence), finally attained in August 1947.

Swaziland: independent southern African kingdom within the Commonwealth: capital, Mbabane. To the north, west and south the kingdom is bounded by the Transvaal, and to the east by Mozambique. In area Swaziland is slightly larger than Northern Ireland but smaller than Wales. The Swazi people settled in the region late in the eighteenth century, and under a succession of powerful chiefs became a political entity, their independence guaranteed in conventions between Britain and the Transvaal in 1881 and 1884. In 1890 a provisional administration was set up in Mbabane, representing the interests of British, Boers and Swazis. Four years later, in a gesture to appease *Kruger, the British agreed that Swaziland should be a protectorate of the Transvaal. After the Second *Boer War, the British entrusted administration to a Special Commissioner with authority over *Bechuanaland and *Basutoland as well. In practice, Swaziland was treated administratively as the south-eastern Transvaal, before and after South African federation. The Swazi chief Sobhuza II (1905–82) was recognized as king of the Swazi nation in 1921. He declined to accept withdrawal from the Commonwealth when, in May 1961, South Africa became a republic. The British accorded Swaziland internal self-government in April 1967, and in September 1968 Sobhuza II was recognized as king of an independent Swaziland. The country's iron ore and coal deposits have been developed with a railway across the Mozambique border to Maputo, rather than accept dependence on South Africa, despite a Swaziland–SA customs union. During the apartheid era relations with Pretoria were strained, and the South African Army raided alleged ANC guerrilla bases in Swaziland in August 1986. By 1993/4 sugar cane production, begun experimentally in 1958, was the chief source of foreign revenue.

Tagore, Rabindranath (1861–1941), Indian poet and philosopher: born into a wealthy family in Calcutta, the son of the Hindu social and religious reformer, Debendranath Tagore (1817–1905). As early as 1878 he published a volume of poems, but then went to England to study law, returning in 1880 to manage the family estates at Shileida for the next seventeen years, collecting legends which he used in short stories, novels and plays while also writing lyric poetry evoking the Bengali landscape. His *Binondini* (1902) was the first novel to present Indian traditions in conventional western form. By then Tagore had become an interpretative philosopher, seeking to make Indian thought comprehensible to western minds. This cultural synthesis he sought to perpetuate by founding in 1901 an international school at Santiniketan, Bolpur, which developed into the Visva-Bharati University. In 1913 he received the Nobel Prize for Literature, the first award to an Asian; at that time he was second only to *Kipling among writers in the Empire. Tagore's finest play, *Chitra*, appeared a year later. He was knighted in 1915, but resigned the honour in 1919 in protest at *Amritsar and the *Rowlatt proposals. He criticized both *Gandhi, for his non-co-operation, and successive Viceroys, for their arbitrary insensitivity to India's ways. On his death Rabindranath Tagore was mourned as India's greatest poet; to western peoples, however, his prose and plays offer fuller enlightenment.

Tahiti: largest island in French Polynesia. It has never been part of the Empire, or of the Commonwealth. *Cook visited Tahiti in 1773, and it became a centre for much British missionary activity at the start of the nineteenth century. A request to establish a Protectorate over the islands was rejected by the British government in 1826, and ten years later a French admiral, Abel Dupetit-Thouars (1793–1864), gave protection to French missionaries and began to build up French influence in the island, arousing protests from the British consul, George Pritchard (1796–1883), himself a missionary there since 1824. Local friction between the English and French was played down in both London and Paris; in 1838 the British again turned down a Tahitian appeal for formal protection. But in 1843 Dupetit-Thouars seized the initiative and proclaimed a French Protectorate, imprisoning Consul Pritchard early in the following year and bringing the two countries close to war. Eventually Pritchard was released and received £1,000 in compensation. British interests in the Pacific were thereafter concentrated on New Zealand, the *Cook Islands and *Fiji. In 1888 Tahiti was formally annexed to France.

Tanganyika: a region of East Africa, with more than 100 tribal communities at the time of colonization. Portuguese merchants first developed coastal settlements which later served Arab traders in slaves and ivory. The interior was virtually unknown to Europeans before the spread of the Church Missionary Society in the late 1840s: in May 1848 the missionary

Tanzania

Johann Rebmann became the first European to see the summit of Mount Kilimanjaro, at 19,340 feet the highest peak in Africa. The whole region, from Kilimanjaro south to Lake Nyasa, was colonized as German East Africa (1885–1914), together with a coastal strip purchased by Germany from the Sultan of Zanzibar in 1890. The Germans undertook the opening up of the interior, and a *railway reached Dodoma and Tabora by 1907 and the shore of Lake Tanganyika in 1913, at Kigoma. The strategic ingenuity of the German commander, General von Lettow-Vorbeck, ensured that military operations continued throughout World War I, causing great devastation of crops, and far more deaths through disease than battle casualties. The peace treaties transferred a small triangle of 'German East' to Portugal and gave Belgium a *mandate for Ruanda and Burundi in the north-west, but most of the region became the British-mandated Tanganyika Territory. Coffee production increased considerably during the inter-war years. A moderate, progressive party - the Tanganyika African National Union – began to campaign for democracy and independence in 1954/5, led by *Nyerere. Responsible government, under UN trusteeship, came in September 1960, and full self-government in May 1961, with Nyerere as chief minister. Independence within the Commonwealth followed on 9 December 1961, and a republican form of government precisely a year later. Tanganyika and *Zanzibar formed a united republic on 26 April 1964, adopting the name *Tanzania six months later.

Tanzania: independent republic within the Commonwealth: capital, Dodoma. The state was formed by the union of *Tanganyika and *Zanzibar in 1964, with the hybrid name accepted on 29 October 1964: Zanzibar retains a separate assembly, headed by Tanzania's first vice-president serving as titular President of Zanzibar. Policy was determined for the united republic by President *Nyerere, as chairman of the Revolutionary Party until his retirement in 1985. He was succeeded by President Ali Hasan Mwinyi, who was re-elected in October 1990 and who, in June 1992, authorized multi-party politics, provided that no organization should be formed representative of a particular region or a particular tribe. Early assumptions of collaboration with neighbouring *Kenya and *Uganda were abandoned, largely through the chronic instability of Ugandan politics. Closer links were established with *Zambia through the construction of the Tanzam *Railway (1970–75), linking the Zambian copper belt with Tanzania's principal port, Dar-es-Salaam. Coffee, cotton, diamonds and tea remain the main exports, and the attractions of the Serengeti National Park have helped to develop a tourist industry.

Tasman, Abel Janszoon (1603–c.1659), Dutch navigator: born near Groningen; joined the Dutch East India Company in 1632 and, after gaining considerable trading and maritime experience, was commissioned in 1642 to undertake a voyage of exploration in the southern and eastern seas. He discovered an island off a great continent, and named the land mass New Holland and the island in honour of Governor Van Diemen of Batavia (Dutch East Indies). Travelling further south, he sighted New Zealand, Tonga and possibly Fiji. He sailed back to Batavia in 1644, along the northern shore of New Guinea, and charted much of the coast of the Gulf of Carpentaria. His later years were spent as a merchant in Batavia, where he died. Although individual Dutch navigators continued to visit the coast of 'New Holland', they did not exploit his discoveries, as the British were to do after *Cook's voyages.

Tasmania: the smallest Australian state: capital, Hobart. The island was discovered by *Tasman in November 1642 and named Van Diemen's Land in honour of the then Governor of the Dutch East Indies. Penal settlements were introduced, with convicts from New South Wales, and free men were encouraged to come there from 1803. A lasting settlement was established by David Collins (1756–1810) at Hobart in 1804. The *aborigine population suffered more there than in the vicinity of any other settlement, partly because of their isolation from the main continent but mainly from drink and disease; although there were some 5,000 aborigines in 1804, the last native of the island died in May 1876. Van Diemen's Land was separated from New South Wales in 1825 and declared a colony, but convicts were transported until 1853 and responsible government came in 1856 when the colony was renamed in honour of Tasman. The discovery in 1871 of rich mineral resources at Mount Bischoff ended the islanders' dependence on sheep farming, and the spread of *hydro-electric power between the two world wars gave Tasmania the cheapest electricity in Australia and boosted light industries; but from 1933 to 1974 the state needed financial help from the Federal Grants Commission in Melbourne.

Tea. The first tea reached London from China by way of Holland in 1658. The popularity of the drink increased rapidly when the East India Company ships varied their cargoes to include tea from southern China as well as spices (and the other novelty drink, *coffee, from Arabia). Within forty years tea-drinking was widespread among the wealthier classes: the Company imported 54,600 lbs of tea from China in 1706, for which customers paid £1 a pound. By 1750 tea-drinking had spread through the English counties and the Scottish Lowlands, imports had risen to 2.3 million lbs annually, and the cost had fallen to five shillings a pound; however, actual consumption of tea may have been twice what these figures suggest, as high excise duties and lax port controls encouraged extensive smuggling. The younger Pitt cut tea duties drastically in 1784 and there was a rapid rise in the Company's tea activities: 16.7

million lbs were imported from Canton to London in 1790 and 26 million lbs in 1820, a year in which 20 ships made the voyage from the Pearl River to the Thames. In 1838, as an experiment, 280 lbs of the first tea grown in Assam was sold in England. A favourable verdict on the taste led, in 1839, to the formation in London of the Assam Company, which enjoyed a ten-year monopoly of tea production in India. Public tea auctions began in Calcutta in 1861, with *Managing Agency Houses soon becoming the main tea brokers. The spread of tea estates in Assam and Bengal – and later in southern India and in the hills between Kandy and Nuwara Eliya in *Ceylon – stimulated competition with the China tea trade, which benefited from the opening of *treaty ports, especially Foochow and Amoy. The introduction of *clipper ships on the China run maintained competition until after the opening of the *Suez Canal. The most rapid growth of Indian tea plantations came in the 1880s and 1890s. By 1910 India was exporting 265 million lbs of tea and Ceylon 182 million, while China exported 17 million lbs directly to the United Kingdom and another 15 million to Hong Kong, some of which was then shipped to Australia and the United States. The third-largest tea producing region in the Empire was Natal (2 million lbs in 1910), while there was also a small tea trade in Mauritius, Fiji and Nyasaland. Despite a slump in 1931/2 the tea industry remained buoyant during the inter-war years. Large-scale tea farming spread to East Africa, with the growth of plantations around Kericho in Kenya, where experimental tea-growing by planters with experience of India had begun as early as 1902. After decolonization the cultivation of tea for export received government backing in Papua New Guinea, Tanganyika and Uganda. There are also tea estates in the Chipinge and Inyanga districts of Zimbabwe. *Sri Lanka has suffered from insurgency in some of the finest tea-growing country. The main tea-producing areas of the Commonwealth remain Assam, Kerala, Maharashtra, Tripura and West Bengal in India, and tea is a secondary crop in Kenya, Mauritius, Malawi and Bangladesh.

Te Kanawa, Dame Kiri (1944–), New Zealand operatic soprano: born in Gisborne, North Island; educated at Auckland; won numerous prizes in her homeland and in Australia before coming to England to complete her training at the London Opera Centre and make her début at Covent Garden in 1970, where she attracted great attention by the clarity of her voice and her stage personality as the Countess in *The Marriage of Figaro,* and subsequently as Elvira in *Don Giovanni.* She went on to sing the major soprano roles in most of the great opera houses. In 1981 she sang at the wedding of the Prince of Wales in St Paul's Cathedral, and was created a Dame of the British Empire a year later.

Telegraph and Telegraphic Cables. The first public electric telegraph was installed in west London in the spring of 1843. The system spread rapidly, with an underwater cable joining Dover and Calais in 1851. The telegraph extended as far eastwards as Berlin and Vienna by 1854; extensions were hurriedly constructed to field headquarters in the Crimea by April 1855, a development of great strategic importance. An electric telegraph 800 miles across India, from Calcutta to Agra, was completed in 1854, while Lahore and Peshawar were linked in 1857, Mutiny year. By 1858 a transatlantic cable linked Britain and North America, although there was no cable to Jamaica and the Caribbean colonies until 1870 – and then, to the *Colonial Office's dismay, only by way of New York and Florida, where it might be tapped. Direct contact between London and India was established in 1865 by a land line from Constantinople to El Faw on the Persian Gulf, which was connected with Karachi. Since this line might be tapped, the *Great Eastern* in 1870 laid cables which avoided foreign soil, except at Lisbon; it joined Gibraltar, Malta, Alexandria, Suez, Aden and Bombay. An amalgamation of the four operating companies on the India route created the Eastern Telegraph Company in 1872 which, with government backing, extended its lines to Singapore and Hong Kong; by 1876 the ETC linked Australia and New Zealand to the main system. In Australia itself, the Overland Telegraph Line between Port Augusta in South Australia and Darwin in Northern Territories had been completed in 1872. The ETC, with Aden as a main base, laid submarine cables from 1879 onwards south to Zanzibar and Durban, where a land-line to Cape Town was already in use. This network, giving London control over two-thirds of the world's cables, had a fourfold importance: it made possible the speedy implementation of an imperial grand strategy, military and naval; it placed public administrators more directly under Colonial Office, India Office or *Foreign Office surveillance; it enabled British newspapers to give detailed reports speedily to a well-informed electorate; and it drastically changed commercial practice by providing up-to-date information on world prices and market trends. In 1902 Britain, Canada, Australia and New Zealand combined to lay a trans-Pacific cable; disputes over the maintenance, renewal, upkeep and strategic value of this line were raised at the *Imperial Wireless and Cable Conference in 1928. Defence strategists long continued to value telegraph communications highly, despite the spread of a chain of wireless transmitters – with which, so it was argued, an enemy might easily interfere.

Tennis. The covered court game of real tennis ('royal tennis' in Australia) started in the monastic cloisters of early medieval France as a handball pastime (*jeu de paume*), but a racket was in use by Geoffrey Chaucer's time (*c.* 1370). It was popular at court in France, Castile, Scotland and England and was played by Henry VIII, notably at Hampton Court Palace, where a court survives. Before 1650 the game crossed to the American colonies. It was taken to Tasmania from Oxford University by

Samuel Travers, who opened a court at Hobart in 1875 and published an explanatory *Treatise on Tennis*; Royal Melbourne Tennis Club was founded in 1882, and the game is still played in both cities. By 1870 outdoor tennis on grass had become popular in Britain; and in 1875 the MCC, magisterially presiding over England's summer pastimes, issued a code of rules for the new 'lawn tennis'; the world's first lawn tennis tournament followed at the All-England Croquet Club in Wimbledon in 1877, attracting 24 contestants. The sport spread overseas rapidly, notably to Victoria, South Australia and New South Wales in the early 1880s, and by 1890 to Cape Colony and British India.

The Lawn Tennis Association of Australasia was founded in Melbourne in 1904, with enthusiastic support from (Sir) Norman Brookes (1877–1968); in 1907 Brookes became the first overseas player to take the Wimbledon title; and in partnership with the New Zealander Anthony Wilding (1883–1915) he secured the Davis Cup for Australasia from 1907 to 1912 and again in 1914. The tennis associations of Australia and New Zealand separated in 1923. Although Canada became a Davis Cup competitor as early as 1912, Australia remained the leading tennis-playing nation in the Commonwealth; and the Australian Championships, begun in 1905, are one of the four competitions in the 'Grand Slam' circuit. Other Australian Wimbledon champions include: G. L. Paterson, 1919; J. H. Crawford, 1933; F. A. Sedgman, 1952; L. A. Hoad, 1956, 1957; N. A. Fraser, 1960; R. Laver, 1961, 1962, 1968, 1969; R. Emerson, 1964, 1965; J. D. Newcombe, 1967, 1970, 1971; and P. Cash, 1981. The outstanding Australian woman player was Margaret Court (née Smith; 1942–   ), champion at home, 1960–66 and 1970 (when she won the 'Grand Slam'), and at Wimbledon, 1963, 1965 and 1970, as well as five times in Paris, five times at Forest Hills, New York and four times in Rome. Evonne Cawley (née Goolagong; 1951–   ) was Wimbledon singles champion in 1971 and 1980. Since World War II the only other Commonwealth country to have Wimbledon singles champions is Great Britain, with Angela Mortimer in 1961; Ann Jones, 1969; and Virginia Wade, 1977. Although South Africa has produced many fine players and admitted non-whites to the national championships in 1972, tennis there suffered from the ostracism imposed by the *Gleneagles Agreement at the height of the apartheid era. India has produced no Wimbledon singles champions, but several outstanding doubles competitors in all tournaments.

Thatcher, Margaret Hilda (1925–   ), British Prime Minister: born Margaret Roberts at Grantham; educated locally and at Somerville College, Oxford, becoming an industrial research chemist. She was elected Conservative MP for Finchley in 1959 and in 1970 became Minister of Education and Science under (Sir) Edward Heath, whom she succeeded as party leader and Leader of the Opposition in 1975. Victory in the General Election of May 1979 made her Britain's first woman Prime Minister, a responsibility held until 28 November 1990 – the longest span of prime ministerial office since Lord Liverpool's administration (1812–27). In home affairs Mrs Thatcher encouraged home ownership, the privatization of publicly-owned enterprises, and the strict application to the economy of monetarist principles. In world affairs she worked in partnership with the US to topple Communism in eastern Europe while also distancing herself from Britain's European partners over moves towards federalization or monetary union. The first achievement of her government in Commonwealth affairs was the transition from Rhodesia to Zimbabwe, a task in which she benefited from the experience of her Foreign and Commonwealth Secretary, Lord Carrington, and from the skill of Lord *Soames. Argentina's invasion of the *Falkland Islands in April 1982 caught the government off-guard but Mrs Thatcher rejected any compromise over sovereignty and won high regard in the United Kingdom for the resolution with which she responded to the challenge. Surprise was felt in October 1983 at her acceptance of US intervention against alleged Communists in *Grenada, a Commonwealth member. Mrs Thatcher recognized the need for agreement with China over *Hong Kong, travelling to Beijing in September 1984 to sign the Joint Declaration ending British sovereignty in 1997. Commonwealth countries remained highly critical of Mrs Thatcher's attitude towards South Africa, especially her vigorous opposition to sanctions at the Heads of Government Conferences in Melbourne (1981), New Delhi (1983) and Nassau (1985), and at the EEC summit in June 1986. She believed she could better lessen the harshness of apartheid by mediation rather than confrontation, and she therefore received the head of the South African government at Chequers in June 1984 and met his foreign minister in Namibia in April 1989. Anger at Mrs Thatcher's opposition to sanctions led 32 countries to boycott the 1986 Edinburgh *Commonwealth Games. Dwindling support from cabinet colleagues over monetary matters led to a party leadership election on 20 November 1990; she announced her resignation two days later as she regarded the result as indecisive. After a further leadership election she handed over the premiership to John Major (1944–   ). On her resignation Mrs Thatcher was admitted to the Order of Merit; in 1992 she received a life peerage; and in 1995 she was invested with the Order of the Garter.

Theatre. India had a tradition of folk theatre, based upon the Rama and Krishna play-cycles, long before the coming of the British; and alone among non-European peoples of the Commonwealth the Indians have nourished a native culture in the theatre, one which has been influenced by Shakespeare, Ibsen and Chekhov without abandoning its indigenous conventions. French settlers brought the theatre to Canada before the British conquest – Corneille's *Le Cid* was presented in Quebec in 1646, ten years after its first performance in Paris. English actors staged Shakespeare in Williamsburg, Virginia in 1752, and when an English touring company first came to Quebec and Montreal in 1795, it instituted a practice regularly observed during the nineteenth century of travelling north after 'playing' America's eastern seaboard. Canada has produced many fine actors and actresses who have made their names in Europe and the United States, but there have no eminent Canadian dramatists; the Dominion's most interesting theatrical venture, the three-month-long Shakespeare Festival at Stratford, Ontario did not begin until 1953, with a specially-designed auditorium opening four years later. South Africa's theatres long struggled against Dutch Puritanism: the earliest playhouse, the African Theatre in Cape Town, opened in 1801 and welcomed English professional tourists in the early 1830s, only to be closed by the municipal authorities in 1839. The opening of a (discreetly named) Drawing Room Theatre at Cape Town in July 1855 was tolerated; but it was not until the *diamond rush and the later *gold rush that popular theatres began to flood southern Africa, attracting famous actors and actresses out from Europe. An Afrikaans professional theatre emerged soon after World War I; but the black community had to wait until the late 1950s before use was made of their native talents, notably in the musical *King Kong*, which was brought to London from Johannesburg in 1961. The first record of a play presented in Australia is of Farquhar's *The Recruiting Officer*, with a convict cast, performed at Sydney on 4 June 1789. Sydney's Theatre Royal opened at Christmas 1832 (with the melodrama *Black-Eyed Susan*) and was followed by a Theatre Royal in Hobart in 1837, now Australia's oldest playhouse. Theatres opened at Adelaide in 1838 and three years later in Melbourne. Music-hall remained widely popular, but from 1882 onwards shrewd managers attracted 'stars' from Europe, bringing to Australia Sarah Bernhardt, the Irvings, the D'Oyly Carte Gilbert and Sullivan productions, and opera and *ballet. Native Australian plays, delighting in the bushranger traditions, were also popular. A rich vein of Australian dramatic writing was tapped either side of World War II; the most famous of these plays, Ray Lawler's *The Summer of the Seventeenth Doll*, came to London in 1957 with an all-Australian cast, after opening in November 1955 in Melbourne. The foundation of the Elizabethan Theatre Trust in 1954/5 encouraged the spread of good production and acting across the continent. Professional theatre and indigenous playwriting was slow to emerge in New Zealand; the New Zealand Players, established in 1952 to bring productions to the cities of both islands, abandoned their uphill task eight years later. The most famous actor of West African origin – from the Fula people of The Gambia – was Ira Frederick Aldridge (1804–67), who made his London début as Othello in 1826 and became respected as a Shakespearean actor on both sides of the Atlantic for forty years.

Thuggee: the practice and beliefs of a fanatical religious fraternity of 'thugs' in India, professional assassins who had taken vows to the goddess Kali and who murdered nominated victims stealthily, either by strangling or by poisoning with datura, a narcotic genus of the family *Solanaceae*, of which the potato is also a member. The thuggee flourished in the early nineteenth century but were gradually extirpated between 1829 and 1840, largely through the initiative of Lord William *Cavendish-Bentinck as Governor-General, and of General Sir William Sleeman (1788–1856), who smashed both the thuggee and the brigands known as dacoits.

Thuku, Harry (1895–1970), early champion of African rights in Kenya: a *Kikuyu, educated at mission schools. In 1921 he began to campaign for the right of the Kikuyu to grow *coffee on their small-holdings, his agitation provoking a riot a year later. In 1928 he founded a movement which campaigned in the first place for African land rights, but which was to become the embryonic Kenya African National Union. In later years Harry Thuku retired from the forefront of politics in favour of *Kenyatta and others with a wider experience. His single-mindedness was vindicated shortly before independence when he became a director of the Kenya Planters' Coffee Union. In 1970 he published *An Autobiography*, an attractive account of the 'Young Kikuyu' and their political and economic struggles.

Tibet Expedition (1904): a reconnaissance in force to 'open up the hidden land', undertaken from India by (Sir) Francis *Younghusband.

Tilak, Bal Gangadhar (1856–1920), Indian nationalist: a Brahmin teacher of mathematics who was goaded into nationalist fury by *Curzon's attitude towards the Congress movement. He became the first leading Hindu to incite violence against the British, and was sentenced to six years' imprisonment in 1908. On his release he founded the Indian Home Rule League, inventing the concept of *swaraj* (self-government), which he claimed to be his birthright. During his imprisonment he wrote *The Secret of the Bhagavad-gita*, giving Indian nationalism a spiritual basis. Despite deeply-held Hindu beliefs he concluded a pact in Lucknow with Muslim leaders in 1916, providing for joint action against the Raj. Tilak's influence steadily diminished with the ascendancy of Mohandas *Gandhi's teachings of non-violence from 1915 onwards, but his radical national beliefs survived as an alternative style of defiance for the Congress. In his last years he disapproved of Gandhi's general policy of civil disobedience, preferring outright confrontation with the British over particular issues.

Tin Trade. Tin was mined in the Malay peninsula long before British settlement, mainly by immigrant Chinese. From the early 1870s British investors developed the tin industry, improving communications and making tin the principal export before the end of the century, even at the cost of destroying the small but traditional tin industry of Cornwall. Malaysia continued to supply nearly half the world's tin. Among other Commonwealth countries, Nigeria produces about one-tenth of Malaysia's output, there is a small Australian tin industry, and also some production in Madhya Pradesh, India.

Togoland: a region in West Africa annexed by Germany in 1884, though its northern boundary remained ill-defined until 1899. German occupation met strong resistance from the native Kabre and Konkona peoples and the colony was only pacified in 1912. Togoland was overrun by the British and French within three weeks of the outbreak of war in August 1914, after a naval assault on the capital, Lomé. The colony had only 35 miles of sea-coast, sandwiched between the British Gold Coast (*Ghana) and French Dahomey. In 1920 Togoland was partitioned: the larger section, including Lomé and all the coast, became a French-mandated Protectorate and gained independence, as Togo, in 1960; Britain received a *mandate for the smaller, eastern region. The line of demarcation, agreed in Paris, separated the Ewe peoples. British Togoland was administered from the Gold Coast. After World War II some Ewe leaders called for reunification of their nation, and a referendum was held in British Togoland, under UN auspices, on 9 May 1956 in which the majority voted for continued association with the Gold Coast. Subsequently it became – and remains – a region in independent Ghana. Some Ewe would still welcome union with their kinsfolk in the Togo republic.

Tokelau (Union Islands): a group of three atoll islands in the Pacific, some 300 miles north of *Western Samoa. They were at one time included in the *Gilbert and Ellice Islands, but have been treated as part of New Zealand since 1 January 1949. So limited were Tokelau's economic prospects that from 1965 to 1975 the government in Wellington encouraged their inhabitants to take advantage of a resettlement scheme in New Zealand. About a quarter of the population migrated, leaving about 1,700 people in the islands, dependent mainly on fishing, revenues from fishery rights and some £2 million a year in aid from New Zealand. In January 1994 a council of elders and a council of elected representatives assumed joint administrative responsibility for Tokelau.

Tonga: an independent monarchy within the Commonwealth since 1970; capital, Nuku'alofa on Tongatapu. The Friendly Islands, as Tonga was long called, lie in the South Pacific, some 470 miles south-east of Fiji. The largest, Tongatapu, was discovered by Tasman in 1643. Unity was achieved between 1820 and 1845, under King Taufa'ahau Tupou I, originally the ruler of Ha'apai island, who was baptized George by Wesleyan

Methodist missionaries in 1831 and who in 1860 insisted on the acceptance of Christianity by all his subjects. In 1862 royal decrees granted Tongans freedom from the arbitrary rule of tribal chiefs, guaranteed their land rights, and set up a council of chiefs as a step towards the benevolent consultative royal democracy which has made Tonga's political evolution unique. The colonial empires respected Tonga's strict neutrality and never attempted to limit royal authority, but Tonga accepted a British Protectorate in 1900 and foreign relations were handled by the British until June 1970. Queen Salote Tupou III ruled from 1918 until her death in July 1967 and gained much popularity in Britain during her visit for Queen *Elizabeth II's coronation in 1953. A party favouring curbs on the power of King Taufa'ahau Tupou IV won the elections of February 1993.

Transjordan: an emirate created in 1921 which remained under British *mandate until 1946 when it became a kingdom, changing its name to Jordan in June 1949 when it absorbed the western bank of the river Jordan which had formed part of *Palestine (1918–48). Under Ottoman rule Transjordan had formed part of southern Syria. The emirate was bestowed on Abdullah ibn Hussein (1882–1951), a prominent participant in the Arab revolt associated with T. E. *Lawrence. Abdullah was a brother of King Feisal I of *Iraq and grandfather to King Hussein (1935–   ), ruler of Jordan since 1952. After some friction in the first two years of the emirate Abdullah remained on good terms with the mandatory power, although regarded with some suspicion by the Colonial Office. Between 1924 and 1930 the British official Resident in Amman, Sir Henry Cox (1882–1937), exercised a pro-consular authority reminiscent of *Baring in Egypt. Emir Abdullah permitted the levying of an Arab Legion commanded by British officers. Under Sir John Glubb (1897–1986) the Legion proved an effective force against pro-Axis agents in Syria and Iraq during World War II.

Transportation. During the Cromwellian interregnum the practice began of sending political prisoners to Barbados: they included royalists captured in the Second Civil War, and Irish rebels spared massacre in 1649/50. Some supporters of Monmouth's rebellion similarly escaped death in 1685, but the system did not become legally recognized until 1717, when it was extended to common felons. Although criminals were also sent to the plantations in Virginia, the verb 'barbadoed' was applied in the eighteenth century to what the nineteenth century would have called 'transported'. The convicts were not slaves, for if they survived they returned to Britain when they had completed their term of sentence. Plantation-owners disliked the system, fearing that the convicts would become trouble-makers among the slaves; and the revolt of the American colonies effectively stopped transportation in 1783. A modified system was proposed four years later, by which the convicts were sent, not as labourers in established settlements, but to new penal colonies in Australia. The *'First Fleet' of convicts reached New South Wales on 18 January 1788. Regular transportation to New South Wales continued until 1840, and was revived in the Port Philip area (soon to become Victoria) from 1844 to 1849. It was used in Van Diemen's Land (Tasmania) between 1803 and 1853, and in Western Australia from 1850 until the system was finally abandoned in 1868. Almost 137,000 men and 25,000 women were transported to Australia during these years; most had been sentenced for theft, but among them were about a thousand political prisoners, including five Scotsmen convicted of sedition in 1793/4, the six Tolpuddle Martyrs of 1834 sentenced for 'administering unlawful oaths' in forming a farm labourers' trade union, 153 Canadians implicated in the rebellions of *Mackenzie and *Papineau, and 100 Chartists, mostly seized in 1842 after a wave of riots. Nearly all political prisoners returned home after relatively short sentences, although some Chartists settled and are said to have influenced the Ballarat diggers who manned the *Eureka stockade. Political prisoners were normally spared hard labour. The first convicts were employed in public works, but from about 1820 onwards some were 'assigned' as unpaid servants to free settlers. Conditions were especially terrible for women transported to Tasmania or Parramatta, NSW. Some, however, prospered: Mary Haydock (1777–1855), a Lancashire lass who began seven years' transportation for horse-stealing in 1790, married a free Irish settler, Thomas Reibey, and inherited his business interests when she was thirty-five. Within ten years she was a millionaire, owning ships and eight farms. When she died Mary Reibey was mourned by Sydney society as a generously charitable matriarch.

Transvaal. The area beyond the Vaal River was settled by *Boers migrating northwards during the *Great Trek in 1836/7 and established as an independent South African Republic, recognized by the British in the *Sand River Convention of 1852. Imminent bankruptcy and a mounting threat from the *Zulus led the British to annex the Transvaal in April 1877. Despite the Zulu victory at *Isandhlwana their threat had been removed by September 1879 and the Boers began again to seek independence, under the leadership of *Kruger. The British failure to respond to this change of mood led to the First *Boer War and the Boer victory at *Majuba Hill: the Transvaal recovered self-government by the Convention of Pretoria (5 April 1881), and most remaining British restraints were lifted in 1884. The *gold rush of 1886/7 led to mounting friction between the newcomers ('uitlanders') and President *Kruger's government, which denied them political and civic rights. After the failure of the *Jameson Raid in December 1895, the Transvaal Boers believed they could count on sympathy from continental Europe in a preventive war against the British of Cape Colony and Natal. Initial victories in the

Second Boer War in 1899 were followed by *Roberts' conquest of the Transvaal and by loss of independence in the Treaty of *Vereeniging. After five years' administration as a Crown Colony, the Transvaal recovered responsible government on 12 January 1907 and became a province of the Union of South Africa on 31 May 1910. The administrative capital of the Union was established at Pretoria, and the Transvaal retained the racially discriminatory laws which ensured continued white Boer dominance of the province.

Treaty Ports. By the Treaty of *Nanking (1842) China confirmed to the British their acceptance of the need to allow freer trading by European merchants inside China. The ports of Canton (Guangzhou), Amoy (Xiamen), Foochow (Fuzhou), Nangpo (Ningbo) and Shanghai were opened for foreign trade, the British being given a privileged position, especially in Shanghai, where the commercial centre along the waterfront 'Bund' was a British extra-colonial creation. Within two years some seventy companies of British or Anglo-Indian origin were operating in the five ports which remained subject to the influence of the *hongs and, from the late 1860s, of the *Hong Kong and Shanghai Bank: commercially, China became predominantly a British imperial market. Even as late as 1895, 65 per cent of China's commerce was handled by the British, while British ships carried 85 per cent of China's imports and exports. By 1914 there were more than thirty treaty ports in China, some far inland up the rivers and not all giving priority to the British. In 1927 the British and other nations began to give up their privileged rights: most had been surrendered to China by 31 December 1929. However, the British held on to concessions in Shanghai until World War II, only formally abrogating their rights in a joint Anglo-American–Chinese treaty signed in Washington in January 1943.

Trinidad and Tobago: independent Commonwealth republic: capital, Port of Spain. The island of Trinidad lies 7 miles off northern Venezuela on the South American mainland; Tobago, with Scarborough as the chief port and town, is 19 miles north-east of Trinidad. Columbus sighted Trinidad in 1498 and it was colonized from 1532 by the Spanish, from whom the British seized the island in 1797, with formal cession confirmed in 1802 by the Treaty of Amiens. At emancipation in 1833 more than half the population were slaves, working on sugar plantations on the west coast between Port of Spain and the town of San Fernando. The free population cultivated and exported cocoa from the northern uplands, and some coffee. All agricultural production fell during the 1840s but picked up again from 1850 onwards with the arrival of Indian labourers, who by 1883 formed a third of the population. In 1888 Trinidad became a Crown Colony linked with Tobago, a poorer, cocoa-producing island, first colonized by the Dutch in 1632 but frequently changing hands until 1814, when it was confirmed as British by the Treaty of Paris. The economy of the Crown Colony changed considerably with *oil exploitation, from 1909 onwards; thirty years later two large refineries were in operation and the island was producing more petroleum than anywhere else in the Empire. The colony – the most prosperous in the Caribbean – merged in the *British West Indies Federation in 1958, with Port of Spain becoming the federal capital. But the federation rapidly became unpopular in the colony as it came to be felt that Trinidad's resources were being exploited for the more distant islands. Soon after the federation broke up Trinidad and Tobago gained independence (31 August 1962), adopting a republican constitution on 24 September 1976, and giving Tobago a measure of self-government by a law passed in September 1980 which set up an island assembly in Scarborough. The rapid growth of the population, together with oil competition from the Middle East, led to mounting unemployment in the late 1960s, and to serious rioting in the spring of 1970 which was exploited by the militant Black Power movement: some army units mutinied and there was widespread arson before order was restored. The construction of a new industrial complex at San Fernando and the harnessing of natural gas reserves led to improved conditions. Oil is still the main source of revenue, and sugar still the main agricultural export.

Tristan da Cunha: a volcanic island in the South Atlantic which, like *Ascension, is administratively a dependency of *St Helena, 1,320 miles to the north-east. There is a settlement called Edinburgh (with a population of about 300) on Tristan, which is otherwise uninhabited, as also are its neighbours, the three Nightingale Islands and Inaccessible Island. South Africa maintains a meteorological station on Gough Island, a haven for penguins. Tristan is named after the Portuguese admiral who discovered it in 1506. It was used by sealers in the eighteenth century, surveyed by Captain Nightingale, RN, in 1760, and formally annexed by the British in 1816. A marine corporal, William Glass, and his family settled on Tristan in 1817. They were later joined by a few settlers from Cape Colony and St Helena, and by 1875 the population had reached 100. From 1942 to 1945 Tristan da Cunha was under Admiralty supervision and constituted HMS *Atlantic Isle*. Attempts to develop a crayfishing industry were frustrated by the sudden eruption of the volcano in October 1961, when the islanders were evacuated to England for two years. Crayfishing is now well developed, but the island receives only six or seven visits from ships each year and there is no airstrip. Despite its isolation, the growth of satellite telecommunications means that since 1992 Tristan da Cunha has had a direct-dialling telephone link with other parts of the Commonwealth.

Trucial States: the name given to a series of Arabian emirates in the Persian Gulf which were in practice, though never officially by name,

British Protectorates from the later years of the nineteenth century until 1971. The collective name was derived from the practice of successive British resident agents at Sharja: from 1823 onwards they entered into treaty relations with the emirs who, in return for British support, gave an annual pledge that they would observe a 'truce', by abstaining from piracy. In 1892 the relationship with London was strengthened when Britain assumed responsibility for the emirates of Abu Dhabi, Ajman, Dubai, Fujaira, Ras al-Khaima, Sharja and Umm al-Qaiwain, as well as for the Sultanate of Muscat and Oman. After Britain's withdrawal from 'east of Suez', the seven emirates combined in 1972 to form the United Arab Emirates, the Sultanate remaining independent (though dropping the name Muscat). Great Britain also had a special relationship in the Gulf with *Bahrain and with *Kuwait.

Trudeau, Pierre Elliott (1919–   ), Canadian Prime Minister: born in Montreal; educated at Jesuit schools, the universities of Montreal and Harvard, and the London School of Economics. He was a barrister in Quebec until his election as Liberal MP for Mount Royal in 1965. He was Minister of Justice under Lester *Pearson, whom he succeeded as Prime Minister in April 1968. His 'contemporary' style appealed to young voters, and he won a good majority at elections held ten weeks after taking office. Much of his premiership was concerned with the need to curb separatism in *Quebec; his policies tempered firm handling of terrorist kidnappings with the encouragement of civic equality between English- and French-speaking communities. He promoted the 1976 *Olympic Games, a costly undertaking which lost him much support in the elections of May 1979, when he went into Opposition for nine months. However, his skill in deflecting separatist threats from Quebec enabled him to bounce back to victory in the general election of February 1980, and to head the government for another four and a half years. Trudeau's 1977 decision to make Canada the first major country in the world to extend its jurisdiction over offshore fishing from 12 miles to 200 miles caused consternation abroad, and left problems – notably with Spain – which continued to reverberate long after his retirement in June 1984.

Turks and Caicos Islands: British dependent territories, 50 miles south-east of the Bahamas, to which they form a geographical appendage. Of the thirty islands only six are inhabited: Grand Turk is the administrative capital, though Grand Caicos is the largest island. The group was discovered in 1512 but remained unoccupied until the arrival of Bermudan fishermen in 1678. From 1799 to 1873 the islands were administered from the Bahamas, but were then incorporated with Jamaica until 1962, when they were constituted a Crown Colony. Fishing and tourism are the chief industries.

Tutu, Desmond Mpilo (1931–), Archbishop of Cape Town: born at Klerksdorf, Transvaal, the son of a teacher; educated at the Bantu High School in Johannesburg, and was himself a teacher for six years before beginning training for the Anglican priesthood in 1958, having been much influenced by the English anti-apartheid campaigner, (Archbishop) Trevor Huddleston (1913–). He was ordained priest in 1961, served a curacy in Johannesburg, studied in London, lectured in theology in Lesotho, and from 1972 held an administrative post in London with the World Council of Churches. He became the first black Dean of Johannesburg in 1975, when he insisted on living in the black township of Soweto rather than the city deanery. He was consecrated Bishop of Lesotho a year later, but returned to South Africa in March 1978 as General Secretary of the South African Council of Churches and led a movement of civil disobedience against President P. W. Botha's government. In October 1984 he was awarded the Nobel Peace Prize, an honour that brought greater publicity to his struggle for multiracial democracy. A few weeks later he was enthroned as Bishop of Johannesburg, and in October 1985 spoke at the UN General Assembly on the South African problem. On 7 September 1986 he was enthroned as Archbishop of Cape Town, the first black head of the Anglican communion in southern Africa. As elected primate of the country, Archbishop Tutu helped promote the reconciliation of President de Klerk and Nelson Mandela, and in 1993 encouraged contact between Mandela and the *Zulu Inkatha leaders, in an effort to reduce communal violence.

Tuvalu: an independent Commonwealth state in the south-west Pacific, previously known as the Ellice Islands and comprising 9 coral atolls, rarely more than 12 feet above sea level. The total resident population is about 8,500, a third living in Funafuti, around the capital, Fongafale. The atolls, close to the intersection of the equator and the International Date Line, became a British Protectorate in 1892 and were part of the *Gilbert and Ellice Islands Crown Colony (1915–75), even though the Gilberts were nearly 500 miles away. During World War II the Japanese occupied the Gilberts (1942/3), but though they bombed Funafuti in April 1943 they did not land in the Ellice Islands. The two groups of islands finally separated after a referendum in Tuvalu in 1974, the Gilberts becoming *Kiribati. Tuvalu's independence was proclaimed on 1 October 1978. Tourist potential is limited: a grass airfield handles five flights a week, and there is a single deep-water wharf, on Funafuti. The economy depends on fisheries, copra, philatelic enterprise and overseas aid. Fears that global warming will cause the islands to sink have led to requests for help in resettlement. Resentment at a lack of response to these pleas led in December 1994 to proposals for dropping the Union Jack from the canton of the flag and proclaiming a republic.

UDI (Unilateral Declaration of Independence), 11 November 1963: an unconstitutional proclamation by which *Rhodesia was declared an independent state on the initiative of the Rhodesian Front Government of Ian *Smith. Both in London and in the UN Assembly UDI was interpreted as a gesture of rebellion on the part of a regime determined to preserve white minority rule. Constitutional legality returned to Southern Rhodesia (*Zimbabwe) in December 1979, with the arrival of Lord *Soames as the last Governor-General.

Uganda: independent Commonwealth republic in east Africa: capital, Kampala. From the early sixteenth century the Uganda region of east Africa was ruled by native kings, of *Luo origin from present-day Kenya. Until the beginning of the *'scramble for Africa' successive British governments were disinclined to intervene in central east Africa, preferring to leave control of the region to the most highly organized of these kingdoms, *Buganda. The accession of a weak ruler (Kabaka) in December 1884 brought anarchy to Buganda and exposed missionaries to danger and death at a time when German traders were showing an increasing interest in the region. To forestall their German rivals, the *Imperial British East Africa Company sent *Lugard to Uganda in December 1890, and over the following fourteen months he imposed order. When in 1893 the IBEA was unable to continue its activities, an appeal was made to the government and on 18 June 1894 a British Protectorate was established, with the administration based in Entebbe. Two years later work began on the 'Uganda Railway' from Mombasa, which brought rapid settlement to inland *Kenya but took thirty years to reach the chief trading town of Uganda, Kampala. Attempts were made to co-ordinate development with Kenya and Tanganyika, and the production of cotton – and, later, coffee – was encouraged; but the Protectorate remained poor. In 1961 Uganda was given internal self-government, with Buganda remaining a kingdom enjoying special federal status. Uganda received independence on 9 October 1962, and the Kabaka of Buganda became President a year later. Mistrust of the Bugandans was exploited by the founder of the Uganda People's Congress, Milton *Obote, who came to power in a coup in 1966, only to be overthrown by a military revolt in January 1971 led by Idi *Amin. Amin's reign of terror fell especially heavily on practising Christians and on the Ugandan Asian business community, who were expelled from the country in 1972 without compensation. Threats to annex border country in 1978/9 prompted a Tanzanian invasion, supported by exiled Ugandans who established a provisional government in Kampala on 14 April 1979. Obote returned as President after elections eighteen months later, but could not check the lawlessness in many districts and was again forced to flee the country by a military coup in July 1985 led by Yoweri Museveni (1945–   ), who became titular President on 29 January 1986. With help from the International Monetary Fund living conditions began to improve in 1988; some property was returned to Ugandan Asians and others dispossessed by the Amin regime. Aspects of Museveni's one-party government have, however, been criticized by Christian church leaders. Until the year 2000 there is a ban on political party activity.

United Kingdom. Although a personal union of the crowns of England and Scotland came about in 1603 with the accession of James VI of Scotland and I of England, and there were Cromwellian experiments with joint administration between 1651 and 1659, Great Britain as a single political unit did not exist until the proclamation of the Act of Union on 1 May 1707: the first Parliament of the United Kingdom was opened by Queen Anne on 23 October. 'The United Kingdom of Great Britain and Ireland' was established in January 1801, after an Act of Union had been passed by Parliament in Dublin on 28 March 1800 and by Parliament in Westminster on 2 July 1800. From 1714 to 1837 the sovereign of the United Kingdom also ruled Hanover, for a hundred years as Elector and then, from October 1814 to June 1837, as King of Great Britain, Ireland and Hanover. However, the accession of Queen *Victoria was not constitutionally possible in Hanover as the Electorate, retaining the Salic Law, denied the crown to a woman. Until the passage of the *British North America Act (1867) all overseas possessions were colonies or dependencies of the United Kingdom. Thereafter the concept of *dominion status evolved gradually, increasingly limiting the direct authority of the United Kingdom to the British Isles. After the Republic of Ireland Act in 1949, constitutional usage changed to 'United Kingdom of Great Britain and Northern Ireland'.

Universities. The first university founded in a British colony overseas was Harvard in Massachusetts (1638), and there were eight other universities in the American colonies at the time of their rebellion. Canadian university education came later: the University of New Brunswick was founded by Loyalists from the rebel colonies as a college in 1785 and given university status in 1823. The oldest Protestant university in Quebec is McGill (Montreal), founded 1821, while the Roman Catholic university of Laval in Quebec City dates from 1852. There was similar sectarian rivalry in other provinces: in Nova Scotia, for example, King's College was founded in 1790, and a Protestant university (Dalhousie) at Halifax in 1838, to be challenged by the Jesuits of St Francis Xavier University from 1853. Toronto had a university in 1827, while a Presbyterian university was established at Kingston, Ontario in 1839. Winnipeg had to wait until 1877; Saskatoon and Edmonton, Alberta until 1907; and Vancouver until 1908. The great and rapid spread of Canadian universities did not come until after World War II. Sydney University (1850) was the first in Australia, followed by Melbourne (1853), Adelaide

(1874) and by state universities in Tasmania (1890), Queensland (1909), and Western Australia (1911). An Australian National University for post-graduate research was set up at Canberra in 1946. Over the following forty years the number of Australian students seeking university places jumped from 15,000 to more than 200,000 and there was a corresponding increase in the number of universities to accommodate them. Christ's College in Christchurch, New Zealand was established soon after the foundation of the city in 1850. The University of Cape Town, founded in 1873, received a charter in 1877 but Stellenbosch, the most prestigious of South Africa's white universities, was not founded until 1918. Black campuses flourished at Fort Hare and Turfloop; from 1959 university segregation was rigidly enforced under the apartheid laws. In British India attempts were made to introduce a university system which taught early nineteenth-century English values: Calcutta, Madras and Bombay universities were founded in 1857; the Punjab University came in 1882, Allahabad in 1887, but Delhi not until 1922; the specifically Hindu University at Benares dates from 1916, the Muslim University at Aligarh from 1920. A university college opened in Colombo in 1921. Hong Kong University was founded in 1912. Most African Commonwealth members did not acquire universities of their own until after independence: but Makerere College, outside Kampala, was a centre of higher education for East Africa as a whole, not merely for Uganda, far earlier than 1961, when it received full university status. In the British West Indies a university college was established in Jamaica in 1948 and later linked with campuses in Trinidad (1960) and Barbados (1963). At first the University of the West Indies was loosely dependent upon University College, London, but it become fully independent in 1962; a year later a separate university was established in Guyana. In London the Association of Commonwealth Universities (with headquarters in Gordon Square) can trace its origins back to 1913; it now represents more than 400 overseas university institutions and publishes the *Commonwealth Universities Yearbook*.

Untouchability. A fundamental problem of Indian social life during the years of attaining independence. The Untouchables were the lowest caste in the recognized *Hindu structure, and they themselves had an involved and extensive concept of sub-castes. Traditional teaching held that it was the duty of Untouchables to accept their predestined fate as a punishment for past sins in a previous life, in the hope that if they observed the taboos they might in their next incarnation become brahmins, while if they broke the taboos they might return as the lowliest of animals or insects. Gandhi campaigned strongly to remove the social discrimination of the Untouchables, with whom he personally associated, calling them 'children of God' (*harijans*). By 1947 there were 60 million Untouchables in India – 17 per cent of the population: most were poor peasant labourers. The

1950 Constitution of India banned Untouchability, making discrimination a criminal offence. The onus, however, was passed to the Untouchables themselves, who had to accept that, whatever traditional teaching might say, they were now socially emancipated.

Vancouver, George (1757–98), British navigator: as a fifteen-year old midshipman accompanied *Cook on his second voyage, and was also on his third voyage into the Pacific. After serving for twenty years as a naval officer, Vancouver undertook exploratory voyages in Australian and New Zealand waters in 1791, before heading north-westwards across the Pacific and discovering the island and sound off the Canadian coast which carry his name. He returned to England by way of Cape Horn in 1795 and wrote a detailed account of his Pacific voyage which was published shortly after his death.

Vanuatu: an independent Commonwealth republic in the Pacific, 500 miles west of *Fiji, comprising 80 islands and formerly known as the New Hebrides group: capital, Vila, on Efate island. The islands, discovered by the Portuguese in 1606, were a source of chronic friction between Britain and France in the mid nineteenth century until an experimental Anglo-French *condominium of the New Hebrides was established in 1887, largely through *Salisbury's patient diplomacy. Renewed tension between the governments led to further discussions in Paris during the negotiation of the Anglo-French Entente of 1904. A comprehensive agreement on conditions of land-holding and the employment of native labour was concluded in February 1906 and reviewed in 1914 and 1922. The condominium was exercised by resident British and French commissioners, with an executive staff from both countries. The New Hebrides served as a launching-pad for the assault to liberate the Japanese-held Gilbert Islands (*Kiribati) in November 1943. The cumbersome condominium ended on 30 July 1980, when the republic of Vanuatu was proclaimed and at once joined the Commonwealth. The absence of direct taxation in Vanuatu ensured that even before independence Efate island was becoming a financial centre for the south-west Pacific, with the *Hong Kong and Shanghai Banking Corporation, three other international banks and six trust companies established in Vila. Cattle exports, cocoa and tourism also boost a sound economy.

Vereeniging: coal-mining town in the Transvaal, some 30 miles south of Johannesburg. On 31 May 1902 the peace treaty ending the Second *Boer War was signed there after a fortnight of discussions between *Milner, *Kitchener and other British military leaders, and a delegation of thirty Boers including *Smuts, *Botha and *Hertzog. By the treaty the Transvaal and Orange Free State accepted British sovereignty in return for a grant of £3 million for repairing and restocking devastated farms and a promise of eventual self-government, honoured in 1907.

Verwoerd, Hendrik Frensch (1901–66), South African Prime Minister: born in Amsterdam, the family emigrating to South Africa when he was a child; educated at Stellenbosch University and at three German universities before being appointed professor of sociology at Stellenbosch in 1927. When Jewish refugees from Nazi Germany were admitted to South Africa, Verwoerd resigned his professorship to edit a nationalist newspaper, *Die Transvaaler*, strongly hostile to South African participation in the war. He was elected a senator in 1948, two years later becoming Minister for Native Affairs, with responsibility for enforcing *apartheid. He succeeded *Strijdom as Prime Minister on 2 September 1968. The *Sharpeville Shootings of March 1960 turned world opinion against his government, and Verwoerd narrowly escaped assassination at Johannesburg by a European farmer three weeks later. In a referendum on 5 October 1960 he sought a mandate from the white voters to take South Africa out of the Commonwealth and gained a small majority; under his leadership, South Africa became a republic in 1961. He was assassinated in the parliament buildings in September 1966 by a Portuguese East African.

Victoria (1819–1901), Queen from 1837, Empress of India from 1877: born in Kensington Palace, the only daughter of King George III's fourth son, Edward, Duke of Kent (1767–1820). She married in February 1840 her first cousin, Prince Albert of Saxe-Coburg-Gotha (1819–61), and was the mother of Edward VII (1841–1910; King-Emperor 1901–10), three other sons and four daughters. The second half of her reign saw the rapid widening of her Empire coincide with the contraction of the world through speedy transport and communications; these were matters in which she took great personal pride. She never set foot in any colony, although in her 69th year she said she had 'a great longing sometime to go to India', and she took lessons in Hindustani. Her romantic concept of Empire was stimulated by the presentation to her in 1850 of the Koh-i-noor diamond, by the ruler of the Punjab, as a pledge of loyalty after his lands were incorporated in the British Empire on 29 March 1849. Yet the Great Exhibition of 1851 celebrated British achievements at home rather than abroad, and foreign countries were allocated four times as much ground space as 'colonies'. The Queen's Proclamation of November 1858 informing her Indian subjects that Crown rule had replaced Company rule marked the start of personal links with local Indian rulers which intensified after the *Royal Titles Act and *Disraeli's evocation to her of Oriental splendour. From June 1887 she had Indian servants at court; the best-known, Abdul Karim from Agra, became a trusted companion. She had some interest in Canada after her eldest son's successful visit there in 1860, and despite her dislike of public duties in London she agreed to open the Indian and Colonial Exhibition of May 1886. Her imperial pride intensified with the Golden Jubilee celebrations of 1887 and reached a climax in the Diamond Jubilee procession of 1897, which included troops from every part of her Empire. She rejected all concepts of a colour-bar and genuinely believed that her governments had a duty 'to protect the poor natives and advance civilization', by which she meant primarily improved education and medical services.

Victoria: name given, in repetitious honour of the sovereign, to numerous places in her Empire. The largest is Victoria Island, in the Canadian Arctic, discovered in the year of the Queen's coronation. The most populous, however, is the Australian State of Victoria, originally known as Port Philip in New South Wales. Convict settlements (1803–4 and 1826–8) were followed by rapid colonization from 1834 onwards, with Melbourne founded in 1837. The region was detached from New South Wales and named Victoria in 1851, shortly before the Ballarat *gold rush, which raised the population of the new colony from 77,000 to 540,000 by 1860. Victoria received responsible self-government in 1855 and was the political centre of Australian life from the establishment of the federal Commonwealth in 1900/1 to 1927, when Parliament moved from Melbourne to *Canberra. By 1993 the population had grown to 4.4 million, more than 3 million of whom were residents of Melbourne; traditional exports of wheat, wool and dairy produce survive, despite the growth of the textile industry, mining and offshore natural gas and oilfields.

Other places named Victoria include the capitals of *British Columbia, *Hong Kong and the *Seychelles, towns on the islands of Grenada, Labuan (Sabah) and Gozo (Malta), a coastal section in the Antarctic *Ross Dependency, mountains in New Zealand and Papua New Guinea, and the famous Victoria Falls on the borders of Zimbabwe and Zambia, discovered by *Livingstone in 1855. Lake Victoria, named by *Speke in 1858, was originally Lake Ukerewe. The vast Victoria railway station in Bombay – the Great Peninsula Terminus – pays tribute to the Golden Jubilee year in which it was completed.

Vietnam War (1965–73): the name generally given to the period of military involvement by the United States and its allies in the civil war between Communist North Vietnam and non-Communist South Vietnam which had begun with guerrilla infiltration from the North in 1970 and was to end with the Communist unification of the country after North Vietnam troops entered Saigon on 30 April 1975, twenty-six months after the last American withdrawal. Great Britain maintained that what happened in Vietnam was outside the range of her concerns as a member of *Seato: but the Australian government under *Menzies and

*Holt enthusiastically backed United States intervention. Combat troops landed in 1965 and reached a peak of more than 8,000 in 1968, but the intervention caused widespread protests in Australia, especially as Menzies introduced a system of conscripted *military service by ballot. By the time Australian forces were withdrawn in 1972, some 47,000 soldiers, airmen and seamen had served in Vietnam, more than a third of them as conscripts; the Australians suffered 2,900 casualties, more than 480 of them fatal. New Zealand, too, sent troops to Vietnam, despite widespread anti-war protests, but there were never more than 500 New Zealand servicemen in Vietnam. Most Commonwealth troops were deployed in Phouc Tey province, but in 1970 some Australians accompanied their allies in raids on alleged supply lines in neutral Cambodia.

Vimy Ridge. A German World War I defensive position, north-east of Arras, stormed by the Canadians in April 1918, an epic assault in which they lost 3,598 men killed and more than 7,000 wounded in taking some 2 miles of the German line. After the war France gave the Canadian people 250 acres of land on Vimy Ridge, where in July 1936 King Edward VIII unveiled an impressive memorial bearing the names of 11,500 Canadians with no known grave killed in the battles around Arras.

Virginia Company: received a Royal Charter in April 1606 to undertake England's first systematic colonization overseas. The Plymouth branch of the Company sought to establish a settlement in what became New England, but met little success; three vessels owned by the London section sailed from the Thames in December 1606, reached Chesapeake Bay on 13 May 1607, and founded Jamestown. The Company was dissolved by James I in 1621, but the colony flourished.

Viticulture: see *Wine Trade*.

Waitangi, Treaty of (5 February 1840): a contentious agreement concluded by William *Hobson with Maori chiefs on North Island eight days after his arrival as the Queen's representative in New Zealand. The 'treaty', which has no standing in international law, was intended to safeguard Maori *land rights from predatory settlers, and to uphold Maori fishery and forestry rights, in return for formal cession of sovereignty to the British Crown. New Zealand was proclaimed a British colony fifteen months later but the administration's failure to fulfil the pledges of the Waitangi treaty exploded in the first of the *Maori Wars in 1845 and continued to provoke protests over the following hundred years.

Wakefield, Edward Gibbon (1796–1862), colonial theorist: born in London; educated at Westminster School and entered the diplomatic service. After two years' experience in Turin (1814–16) he incurred

351

displeasure by eloping with a ward of court. He was allowed to join the embassy staff in Paris in 1820, and served there for six years before abducting an heiress. During three years of imprisonment in Newgate he wrote *A Letter from Sydney* (which he had never visited) advocating systematic colonization: land would be sold to free settlers at reasonable prices in approved areas. On his release from Newgate he became a founder-member of the National Colonization Society and promoted settlement in New South Wales. His South Australian Association (1834) had more success. He accompanied Durham (see *Durham Report*) to Canada, and on his return became the London agent for the New Zealand Land Company (1839–46). The Treaty of *Waitangi was, he thought, too generous to the Maoris; but he appears to have changed his opinion after 1853, when he emigrated to Wellington. For the last nine years of his life, Wakefield helped to establish self-government in the colony.

Walvis Bay: settled by the British in 1878 and attached administratively to Cape Colony; incorporated in the Union of South Africa in 1910. Although Walvis Bay covered an area of less than 400 square miles it was tenaciously retained, even though it formed an enclave in *South-West Africa, a German protectorate, from 1880 to 1915. Between the wars South Africa used Walvis Bay as a port for its mandated territory, and only renounced its claim to sovereignty on 28 February 1994, when Walvis Bay was incorporated in *Namibia.

Warburton, Peter Egerton (1813–89), Australian explorer: born in Cheshire; served with the Bombay Army from 1831 to 1853 when, as a retired major, he became Commissioner of Police in South Australia for fourteen years. In September 1872 he led a party of six into central Australia, and in the following April set out from Alice Springs in search of a route from there to Perth. This he failed to find, and lost the sight of an eye as the party almost perished from thirst and shortage of food. In January 1874 he reached Roebourne, on the Indian Ocean coast of north-west Australia; he published an account of his journey across the 'western interior' a year later, and died in retirement at Adelaide.

Warner, Sir Thomas, (*c*. 1575–1649), 'father' of colonization in the West Indies: born in Woodbridge, Suffolk; took part in an exploratory voyage to Guiana in 1619/20, visiting the Dutch settlement of Surinam and, on the return voyage, landing on the island of *St Christopher, where the climate and fertile soil impressed him. With his wife and some forty companions he sailed from Woodbridge in 1623 and established a settlement on St Christopher. He returned to London in 1625, received financial backing from the Earl of Carlisle, and was knighted by Charles I and granted Royal Letters Patent to be Governor of the island for life.

Warner 'planted' settlements in neighbouring Nevis, *Antigua, and *Montserrat; he paid another visit to England in 1636 but returned to St Kitt's, where his status as Governor was confirmed by Parliament in 1643. He died, and is buried, on the island. His family continued to administer and develop the West Indian islands for 300 years: a direct descendant in eight generations was the Trinidad-born English cricketer, Sir Pelham Warner (1873–1963).

Weihaiwei: town in northern China on the southern tip of the Shantung peninsula, commanding entry into the Gulf of Pechili from the Yellow Sea. When, in 1897/8, Germany's lease of Kiaochau was followed by a Russian lease of Port Arthur (Lu-ta), it was assumed in London that the dismemberment of the Chinese Empire was imminent. Lord *Salisbury's cabinet resolved to secure neighbouring Weihaiwei, even though the Admiralty thought little of the anchorage's potential as a naval base. On 1 July 1898 China leased some 285 square miles, including the old walled town itself and a strategic island. The territory was administered by a resident Commissioner in touch with *Hong Kong. Britain's alliance with Japan in 1902 lessened the importance of the anchorage, especially after the Japanese seized Port Arthur from the Russians in 1904/5. Roads and wharfing were developed, and an abortive attempt was made to promote Weihaiwei as a picturesque resort whose 'excellence of climate is unsurpassed in the Far East'. No troops were stationed there in time of peace, nor was the territory fortified, but the China Squadron asserted a British presence by 'showing the flag' in naval exercises each summer. In 1930 the leased territory was restored to China: it is now called Wei Hai.

Welensky, Sir Roy (1907–   ), Northern Rhodesian politician: born in Salisbury (Harare), the son of a Jewish refugee from Lithuania. He won wide respect both as an amateur heavyweight boxer and as a railway trade union official, and in 1938 became a Labour member of the Northern Rhodesian Legislative Council, on which he served until 1953, when he was knighted for his wartime work on manpower problems. With Sir Godfrey *Huggins he was an enthusiastic advocate of the *Central African Federation, succeeding to the federal premiership in November 1956. His insistence in 1959 on a constitutional change which reduced African representation in Parliament provoked such opposition that Nyasaland's wish to secede from the Federation was backed by *Macleod, the Colonial Secretary in London. After the Federation broke up, Welensky found his political leadership challenged by the Rhodesian Front movement of Ian *Smith, and he retired from politics.

Wellesley, Richard Colley, Marquis (1760–1842), Governor-General of India: elder brother of the Duke of Wellington; born in County Meath in Ireland; sat as an MP at Westminster, 1784–97, supporting

Wilberforce's early campaigns against *slavery. He was Governor-General of India from 1797 to 1805, stamping out French influence in Hyderabad, securing the defeat of Tippoo at *Seringapatam and, in collaboration with his brother, crushing *Maratha resistance (1803). So successful were his policies that the revenue of the East India Company more than doubled during the eight years he held office. He was, briefly, ambassador in Madrid and, from December 1809 to March 1812, Foreign Secretary. From 1821 to 1828 and from 1833 to 1835 he was Lord-Lieutenant of Ireland; but his greatest achievement was the consolidation of British rule over central India.

West Africa Conference (Berlin, 1884–5). An early instance of anticipatory diplomacy, the conference sought, on Bismarck's initiative, to regulate the *'scramble for Africa'; fourteen governments sent delegations to the German capital. The conference, which opened on 15 November 1884 to discuss rival colonial claims in central and west Africa, lasted for fifteen weeks. It formally endorsed free access to the African interior for all European Great Powers, guaranteeing freedom of navigation along the Congo and Niger rivers while asserting what Bismarck called 'much careful solicitude' for the welfare of the native peoples and, in particular, the stamping out of *slavery and the slave trade. Ironically, the conference also recognized King Leopold II of the Belgians as sovereign head of a Congo Free State in which slavery and maladministration were soon to fall to a nadir of iniquity. Britain and Germany together frustrated Portuguese claims to the Congo and limited French ambitions. By defining Germany's sphere of influence in the Cameroons and *Togoland, the conference made possible the growth of British interests in what was to become *Nigeria; Britain also recognized German claims to *South-West Africa.

West Indies Federation: see *British West Indies Federation*.

Western Australia (WA): the largest state in the continent covers a greater area than Western Europe; the capital is Perth. A convict settlement, for less hardened criminals moved there from New South Wales, was founded at Fredericktown (now Albany) in 1826. Three years later Captain Charles Fremantle, RN, established a township at the mouth of the Swan River, declaring the whole region a British possession. The naval officer Sir James Stirling (1791–1865) recommended the development of the area, founded the city of Perth (in 1829), and was acting governor in the colony's formative years. Political development was slow, perhaps because *transportation survived longer there than elsewhere, with 9,668 male convicts being sent there between 1850 and 1868. Partially representative government was introduced in 1870 and responsible government came at last in December 1890, less than two years before the 'golden mile' at *Kalgoorlie changed the character of much of the southern part of the huge colony. At the same time, vast acres of pastoral land were opened up in the Kimberley region and a timber industry was created for the hardwood forests of the south-west. Western Australia entered the federal commonwealth in 1901 with some hesitation; the legislature insisted, as a condition of entry, that a transcontinental *railway should be constructed to link the sparsely populated west with the eastern seaboard cities: the first trains made the journey to Perth in 1917. By 1906 there was a secessionist movement in the state, though it was not until 1930 that the Dominion League of Western Australia was formed, to put forward the claims of the western third of the continent. Mistrust of a tariff policy which seemed to favour New South Wales and Queensland, together with despair over the onset of the *Great Depression, won rapid support for the Dominion League. A compulsory referendum in August 1933 gave a two-to-one vote in favour of secession: in 1934 petitions were sent to King George V and the Privy Council seeking a separate grant of dominion status; but in 1935 it was ruled that secession was impossible, unless supported by a majority of all Australians. Improved communications (including airlines) and the impact of World War II – in which the Japanese bombed the north-western towns of Derby, Wyndham and Broome (1942) – silenced the call for secession. Post-war prosperity came from a mineral boom in the 1960s, notably iron ore production in the Hammersley hills and in the Pilabara and Mount Newman regions, and from oil on Barrow Island.

Western Samoa: independent South Pacific constitutional monarchy within the Commonwealth; capital, Apia on Upolu island. Western Samoa was first formed into a political unit as a German Protectorate by the *Samoa Agreement of 1899. As well as fertile Upolu it comprises the large island of Savai'i and six smaller islands. The people are mainly Polynesians, and in recent years have shown remarkable skill at Rugby Union *football. New Zealand troops occupied Western Samoa in 1914 and the islands were administered by New Zealand as a League of Nations *mandate from 1920 until 1946, and thereafter for fifteen years as a United Nations trusteeship. A UN plebiscite in May 1961 voted in favour of independence, which was accorded on 1 January 1962. The constitution established an elective monarchy with the head of state – Ao o le Malo – chosen for life from the two royal lines of the islands. New Zealand continues to exercise considerable influence in the relations of Western Samoa with other governments. Cocoa, coconuts and bananas are the chief exports. The attractive climate induced Robert Louis Stevenson (1850–94) to spend the last five years of his life at Valima on Upolu, where he is buried.

Westminster, Statute of (11 December 1931): a measure formally passed through the British Parliament which gave legal form to the

Wheat

*Balfour definition of Dominion status (1926); it thus marks the transition from the old British concept of an imperial mission to an acceptance of joint association in a free Commonwealth of Nations. South Africa and Canada ratified the Statute immediately, though both dominions subsequently clarified their relationship to the 'mother country', by the *Status of the Union Act (1934), and the *Canada Act (1982). Australia did not ratify the Statute until 1942, New Zealand not until 1947, as both dominions regarded the issue as a constitutional matter primarily for the United Kingdom, rather than for themselves.

Wheat. The cultivation of wheat in both Canada and Australia began as subsistence farming for expanding communities. In both countries mass production was made possible only by technological revolution in agricultural practices. Problems with *irrigation long restricted the growth of Australian wheatlands to South Australia, although many thousands of acres of New South Wales were sown with wheat, barley and corn in the first decade of settlement. By 1845 there were some 900 wheat farmers in South Australia, the wealthy among them having purchased one of the reaper-harvesters perfected by John Ridley in 1843; by 1850 South Australia was a granary for all the colonies and wheat farming soon spread to Victoria and, later in the century, to New South Wales. In Ontario, Canada's first modern farm implements came from Daniel Massey's foundry at Newcastle in 1847, a primacy challenged by Alanson Harris's at Brantford ten years later. Their reapers and binders made it possible to gather in the first harvests from the prairies in the 1860s. *Saskatchewan was the wheat bowl of the Dominion even before its recognition as an administrative district in 1882. *Alberta and *Manitoba soon overtook Ontario in crop yield, and the spread of railways enabled Canadian wheat to be brought to the Lake ports and shipped to Europe: by 1910 wheat was Canada's largest single export, accounting for 22 per cent of the Dominion's earnings abroad; this proportion rose to 25 per cent in 1930, although the price of wheat was by then already falling because of the *Great Depression. The experiments of the Australian herborist William *Farrer perfected a rust-resistant wheat strain in 1901 which helped farmers in Kenya and India, as well as encouraging wheat cultivation in eastern Australia. Improved irrigation raised the yield from Victoria higher than that from the other two states by 1910: even so, Saskatchewan alone produced a larger crop than all the Australian states together. British India had considerably more land under wheat but realized a much poorer crop from each acre. Similarly, although Cape Colony and New Zealand had almost identical wheat acreage in 1910, the antipodean soil gave almost four times as high a yield as the South African. In Kenya, Lord *Delamere pioneered wheat farming in 1909, but yellow rust destroyed his first crop; even when Kenya's wheat was well-established, by the end of the 1920s, the crops were in several seasons attacked by locusts. All exporting countries suffered during the Great Depression and needed government aid to survive and recover. Australia enjoyed boom years during the 1960s, with extensive exports to China. Although Canada's farmers had a poor harvest in 1988, the average annual yield remains high; the Dominion continues to export more wheat than any other member of the Commonwealth.

White, Patrick Victor Martindale (1912–90), Australian novelist and Nobel laureate: born in London, the son of an Australian sheep-farmer; received his main education at Cheltenham and at King's College, Cambridge; travelled widely in Europe, America and the Australian outback before serving with the RAF in the Middle East during World War II. His first novel, *Happy Valley*, was published in 1939, but he tapped his richest vein of writing after he began farming in New South Wales in 1946. *The Tree of Man* (1955) is a symbolic novel about a young farmer at the start of the century seeking to rear a family in a bush community. It won international regard, as did *Voss* (1957), a mystic allegory about a crossing of Australia by a German idealist, set in 1845. Other novels were centred on an artist in 'boiling, brash, beautiful, ugly Sydney', and on the shipwreck of a sailing vessel in the 1830s; several depicted pre-war and bombed London. In December 1973 White became the first Australian to be awarded a Nobel Prize for Literature; he aroused criticism by 'ungraciously' asking his friend, Sidney *Nolan, to accept it in Sweden on his behalf.

Whitlam, (Edward) Gough (1916–   ), Australian Prime Minister: born in Kew, a suburb of Melbourne, but educated in Sydney and Canberra. After air force service in World War II he became a barrister, and was elected a Labor member of the House of Representatives between 1952 and 1978; served as party leader, 1967–77. He formed a government on 2 December 1972, ended conscription for *military service, brought troops home from the *Vietnam War, gave diplomatic recognition to Communist China, abolished university fees, and introduced a health service (Medibank). This vigorous programme of socialist initiative was checked by the Senate (where Labor remained in the minority), which publicized attempts by cabinet ministers to raise overseas loans without Government approval and refused to approve the Appropriations Bill (budget) unless Parliament was dissolved and a general election called. When Whitlam refused to ask for a dissolution, the Governor-General (Sir John Kerr) on 11 November 1975 dismissed the Government, called on the Opposition leader (*Fraser) to form a government, and accepted his request to dissolve Parliament; in the general election on 13 December 1975 Labor was defeated. The exercise of a sovereign prerogative in this manner by Sir John Kerr remains controversial, and has increased demands within Australia for republican constitutional reform, and for direct presidential election of the head of state.

Windward Islands

Windward Islands: part of the Lesser Antilles group in the Caribbean, comprising Martinique (French) and the Commonwealth islands of *St Lucia, *St Vincent and the Grenadines, and *Grenada. The British islands constituted the Crown Colony of the Windward Islands from 1855 to 1958, with the administrative capital at St George's in Grenada. Tobago was part of the colony until 1889, when it united with *Trinidad. *Dominica was attached to the colony in 1940. There was no common legislature and each island developed its own institutions: most exported sugar and rum. The Windward Islands joined the *British West Indies Federation when it was established in 1958 and maintained a loose association after it broke up; between 1974 and 1979, they separately achieved independence.

Wine Trade: Three regions in the Commonwealth had wine-producing vines before the coming of British settlers: Cyprus, whose Commandaria dessert wine antedated the Ottoman invasion of the island; French pioneer communities in southern Ontario; and South Africa, where the Dutch planted the first vineyards in the coastal region around the Cape in the late seventeenth century. Cape vines were taken by the *First Fleet to New South Wales in 1788 but the Australian wine trade owed more to John Macarthur (1767–1834) and his family, who after a visit to Europe planted French vines in New South Wales in 1820; cuttings from Macarthur's vineyard were sent in 1838 to the Devonian immigrant, John Reynell, in the Southern Vales, south of Adelaide. Another settler, Walter Duffield, had the commercial initiative to send his wines to Europe: on 10 July 1845 'a case of the first wine which has been made in the colony' reached Buckingham Palace as a gift for Queen *Victoria; and ten years later South Australian wines were commended at the first Paris Exhibition. James Busby (1801–71) planted extensive vineyards along the Hunter Valley, south of Newcastle (NSW), the most productive being at Kirkton in 1830, the year he published the first manual on Australian viticulture. Busby also established a vineyard in the Bay of Plenty region of New Zealand's North Island, where in 1833 he became the earliest official British Resident. Many other settlers in the Hunter Valley planted vines, one of the most profitable being the Mount Pleasant wine estate which, though planted in 1880, was not given its trade name until 1925. Similarly, the much-respected winery of Tahbilk, in the Goulburn valley of Victoria, had vines as early as 1845, although it did not begin to export its table wines until after World War II. Dr Penfold, who went into medical practice north of Adelaide in 1844, established a winery which had many good vineyards along the Barossa valley, spread to New South Wales and, after World War II, to New Zealand; its best labels commemorated the doctor's original home, The Grange. The Chaffey brothers, Canadians responsible for many of south-eastern Australia's *irrigation projects, built up the highly profitable wine trade of the Murray river, especially the Mildara wines from Mildura and, from 1887, the Renmark wines. In north-west Victoria, the Milawa vineyard began wine production in 1889. Wine came to Western Australia with Cape Colony cuttings at Houghton in 1833 and with Captain J. S. Roe's Sandalford vineyard, planted 12 miles outside Perth in 1840. At Federation, in 1900/1, Victoria was the leading wine state, with more than 40,000 acres under vines, but South Australia's output leapt considerably in the following decade, and large-scale production in the 1960s increased New South Wales's output. Speedier bulk transport lifted Australia's exports to the United Kingdom in the 1980s and early 1990s. The New Zealand wine industry, too, has expanded: there are seven main wine-producing districts in North Island – Northland, Auckland, Waikato, Bay of Plenty, Gisbourne, Hawkes Bay (Napier), Maatu (Wellington); and Marlborough in South Island. South African vineyards, north of the Cape and from Paarl and Worcester along the Langeberg slopes of the Little Karroo further east, maintained traditions begun by the Dutch settlers, though the export of sherry and red and white table wines suffered from the extensive voluntary boycott of produce from the Republic during the apartheid years. Cyprus continues to export wine, mainly through Limassol from vineyards in the south of the island; and by 1987 Malta, too, was exporting red and white wines, from vineyards previously considered of strictly local interest.

Wolfe, James (1727–59), British soldier: born, the son of a general, at Westerham in Kent; became a junior officer in 1742 and saw service in Germany before fighting against the Jacobites at Culloden and spending eight years on garrison duty in Scotland. As a brigadier he gained great success fighting the French in eastern Canada, and was largely responsible for the capture of the fortress of Louisburg (1758). This brought him command of the expedition to take Quebec. He landed from the river in June 1759, at the foot of the cliffs on which the citadel stood, but could make no impression on the fortifications until he found a lightly guarded gully, up which he led his men under cover of darkness to the Plains of Abraham (12–13 September 1759). The battle for possession of Quebec was brief but cost the lives of both the French general, Montcalm, and Wolfe himself. By securing Quebec, however, Wolfe tipped the military balance in Britain's favour; the French never recovered their hold on North America.

Wolseley, Garnet Joseph, Lord (1833–1913), Field Marshal: born near Dublin; joined the army in 1852, was wounded in Burma in 1853 and fought in the Crimea, twice leading his company in assaults on the Redan Fort at Sebastopol and losing the sight of an eye. During the Mutiny he served in India and later took part in operations in China (1860). From 1861 to 1870 he was in Canada, suppressing the *Red River rebellion without losing a man. In 1873/4 he commanded the expedition against

King Kofi Karikari of the *Ashanti, a brilliantly executed campaign, meticulously prepared. After serving briefly as Britain's first administrator in *Cyprus (1878), he restored British authority in *Zululand and captured King *Cetewayo (1879). He sought to modernize the army during two years as Quartermaster-General in the War Office, and was then given command of the expeditionary force assigned to restore order after xenophobic riots in *Egypt. This campaign against Arabi Pasha was a logistical masterpiece: 40,000 men transported in 61 steamships from Britain to Egypt, with a feint attack on Alexandria covering the main assault from Port Said and Ismailia. Arabi Pasha was defeated at Tel-el-Kebir (13 September 1882) and Cairo was occupied two days later, thereby establishing a British mastery over the Nile delta which lasted for seventy years. On returning to England Wolseley received a peerage, but was sent back to Cairo in 1884 to lead the expedition which vainly sought to rescue *Gordon from the *Mahdi at Khartoum. After commanding in Ireland for five years, Viscount Wolseley became Commander-in-Chief of the British Army on 1 November 1895. In the absence of a general staff this post carried too heavy a responsibility, and after his retirement in November 1900 Wolseley was criticized by a Royal Commission for failing to prepare, in advance, contingency plans for war in South Africa. Yet, perhaps even more than *Roberts or *Kitchener, Wolseley was the archetypal 'Soldier Who Made The Empire'.

Women's Suffrage: active campaigning to extend to women the right to vote began in Britain and in North America during the late 1860s. In Canada Dr Emily Stowe, the first woman general practitioner of medicine in the Dominion, founded a Toronto Women's Literary Club in 1876 which concentrated on suffragist activity, substituting the words 'Suffrage Association' for 'Literary Club' in 1883; it became the Dominion Women's Enfranchisement Association six years later. But the biggest boost came from the Women's Christian Temperance Union, which was influential in the new prairie provinces; its leaders could see no prospect of a prohibition party gaining votes so long as the electorate remained exclusively male. Alberta, Manitoba and Saskatchewan gave women the vote in provincial elections in 1916, British Columbia and Ontario in 1917. The right to vote in federal elections was given to women throughout the Dominion in 1918 – the year in which women over thirty were enfranchised in the United Kingdom. Although Canada's Maritime Provinces duly enfranchised women for provincial elections before 1922, the women of *Quebec (like those of France) did not have the provincial vote until World War II. Women remained unenfranchised in the Dominion of *Newfoundland until 1925.

Within the Commonwealth as a whole, the most rapid progress had already been made in Australasia: New Zealand in 1893 became the first country in the world to give women the vote, with *Maori women having the same (special) rights as their menfolk. Two Australian colonies enfranchised women before federation: South Australia in 1894, and Western Australia in 1899. In the first election after federation women in those states could vote nationally for the lower house. Universal adult suffrage in federal elections for both houses came in 1902 and was made compulsory in 1924, though *aborigines were denied all voting rights until the late 1960s. There were still variations in state elections: women could vote for the New South Wales Parliament in 1902, for the Tasmanian in 1903, Queensland in 1905, Victoria in 1908. Practice in British India varied: women were promised the vote 'in the Governor's provinces' by the *India Act (1935), effective from April 1937; and in many municipalities they could vote for local government and were eligible for election; but some districts still insisted on leaving such matters to their men. In South Africa women of European extraction were enfranchised in 1930, two years later than in Southern Rhodesia. Jamaican women were enfranchised as early as 1919, but there was no uniform pattern in the West Indies: women over 30 had the vote in Trinidad by 1935; and there was general adult suffrage for the Leeward Islands in 1936. Political activity was denied women in most other parts of the Commonwealth until decolonization. Advancement to cabinet posts, though slow in Australia and Africa, was rapid elsewhere. By 1994 women had headed governments in Sri Lanka, India, the United Kingdom, Bangladesh, Pakistan, and Canada.

Wool Trade: see *Sheep*.

Woomera: town in South Australia, the centre of a huge rocket firing range, including territory in Western Australia. It was developed as a result of the United Kingdom and Australia Long Range Weapons Agreement, 1947. Further agreements allowed *nuclear tests in the vicinity between 1953 and 1963. The McLelland Report of December 1985 criticized the *Menzies government for allowing the tests and recommended compensation payments to anyone who had suffered radiation or found their lands contaminated because of inadequate safety precautions. The British intended to make use of the Woomera range for developing the Blue Streak long-range missile, a project authorized in 1957 but abandoned in May 1960.

World War I (1914–18). The immediate causes of the war lay in Europe and in the failure, because of a system of rival alliances and interlocking war plans, to localize a Balkan dispute. Tension and mistrust between the Great Powers had, however, been heightened by imperial rivalry in the Middle East, Africa and, to a much lesser extent, the Pacific. The principal fighting was for more than three years limited to a series of battlefields along the Western Front from Flanders through northern France to

Verdun, and to a far more extensive area in Europe's eastern plains. There were also battle fronts in the Balkans and, from May 1915, in northern Italy. Indian, Canadian, Australian, New Zealand and Newfoundland divisions were brought to Europe and sustained heavy casualties fighting against the Germans on the Western Front. Many overseas territories sent men to Europe as support units and labour battalions. South African troops and *native regiments occupied Germany's African colonies: the campaign in and around *Tanganyika lasted for more than four years but *German South-West Africa, *Togoland and the *Cameroons were soon overrun. Australian and New Zealand forces occupied German possessions in New Guinea and the Solomon Islands and their navies helped track down German warships in the Pacific and the Indian Ocean. The main imperial theatre of war was against the Turkish Ottoman Empire, allied to Germany from November 1914. The principal war fronts were in Mesopotamia (*Iraq), in *Palestine and *Egypt, and in the costly attempt to force the Dardanelles by a landing at *Gallipoli. Fighting ended in 1918: in Asia with the Turkish acceptance of the Mudros Armistice of 30 September; in Europe with the Compiègne Armistice of 11 November; in East Africa with the German surrender at Abercorn (Mdabal, Zambia) on 25 November. A minimum estimate puts the war dead of the British Empire at 947,000, or one in ten of those who enlisted. Of these casualties 743,000 came from the United Kingdom, 60,000 from Australia and 56,700 from Canada. New Zealand suffered high casualties for a country with a small population. These figures take no account of those who died from disease, including the influenza pandemic of 1919 which accompanied returning soldiers home, and in Australia alone cost another 19,000 lives. The principal territorial changes in the ensuing peace-making came in the form of *mandates under League of Nations supervision.

World War II (1939–45): For the first nine months of conflict, this war was even more confined to Europe than its predecessor. Turkey remained neutral; Japan, though allied with Germany, did not enter the war until December 1941. It was Italy's declaration of war as an ally of Germany on 10 June 1940 that opened new battle fronts in East and North Africa; naval warfare was extended to the Mediterranean, where *Malta was exposed to relentless bombing. Southern African and *native regiments from Kenya and other colonies, together with troops from the United Kingdom and India, captured the Italian empire in Ethiopia and the Horn of Africa by April 1941. German intervention to support an Italian attack on Greece in April 1941 brought Australian and New Zealand troops to Greece and Crete, where they fought desperate rearguard actions under the command of General *Freyberg. German control of Crete, together with assistance from pro-German elements in Syria, Iraq and Madagascar, overstretched Allied resources in new theatres of war. The surprise Japanese attacks on bases in the Pacific, *Hong Kong and

*Malaya gained rapid victories, not least because British intelligence reports had underrated Japanese fighting skills. Both Hong Kong and Singapore were lost, together with the Solomon Islands; Australia was directly threatened in New Guinea and experienced air raids in the Northern Territories and north Western Australia, as well as a concerted (and largely abortive) submarine raid on Sydney Harbour, in May 1942. Japanese troops occupied *Burma as well, and crossed the Assam frontier of India. Once again Commonwealth troops fought in distant theatres of war: untrained Canadians, lacking equipment, were killed or captured in Hong Kong, and Canadian commandos suffered heavily in amphibious operations against Dieppe in August 1942. There was occasional friction between the Commonwealth governments and *Churchill over the employment of Australian and New Zealand troops to clear the enemy from North Africa and, in 1943/4, to invade Italy and advance on Rome, rather than concentrating them on the war in the Pacific. Many African soldiers left their continent for the first time and fought in the jungles of Burma. American commitment to defeat Japan tightened post-war links between Canberra, Wellington and Washington. South Africa, Rhodesia and Canada participated in a Commonwealth scheme for training aircrew for the RAF, as well as supplying their own planes for the war in Europe and the Far East. Fighting in Europe ended with the German surrender in Italy on 29 April 1945, followed by the surrender of all remaining German forces by 8 May, five days after the 14th (Burma) Army entered Rangoon. Japan capitulated on 15 August, after the Americans had dropped atomic bombs on Hiroshima and Nagasaki. The advance of the Soviet Red Army into Germany and through east-central Europe threatened a 'cold war' which long delayed a definitive peace settlement. Battle casualties were fewer than in World War I, but civilian deaths by bombing, and through calculated genocide, were far higher.

Yoruba: a historic West African people who built up a loose confederacy of ivory-trading states. Their descendants are now primarily concentrated in western *Nigeria, in the tobacco-producing and cacao-exporting region around Ibadan. The Yoruba Chief Obafemi Awolowo (1909–84) was prominent in the Nigerian independence movement, but was held under arrest from 1962 to 1966 after protests that the Nigerian federal government neglected Yoruba interests.

Younghusband, Sir Francis Edward (1863–1942), soldier and explorer: born at Murree, then in northern India (now Pakistan); educated at Clifton and Sandhurst, then commissioned into the King's Dragoon Guards in India; subsequently explored the Karakoram and the Pamirs, and opened up routes from Rawalpindi to Chinese Turkestan, and from Kashgar (K'a-shin, in Sinkiang, China) to Kashmir. When serving as Political Resident at Indore he was ordered to lead an expedition into

Tibet to discover if the Russians had encroached on the country's neutrality. Tibet's holy capital of Lhasa was entered on 3 August 1904, but only after a tragic misunderstanding led the British column to kill several hundred Tibetan peasants by machine-gun fire. Despite this disaster, Younghusband established good relations with the Tibetans, and found no Russians there. He later served as Resident in Kashmir, supported three Everest expeditions and, in his retirement, founded the World Congress of Faiths.

Yukon Territory: the extreme northwestern lands of Canada, bordering on Alaska: administrative centre, Whitehorse. This mountainous and richly forested region was under *Hudson's Bay Company surveillance until 1870, when it was absorbed by the Dominion of Canada as part of the *Northwest Territories. The rapid growth of population in the Klondike *gold rush induced the federal authorities to make the Yukon a separate territory, in June 1898. It has benefited from the Alaska Highway and roads serving it, and from hydro-electric power harnessing the Yukon River at Whitehorse Rapids and its tributaries at Mayo and Aishik Lake. Mining (including gold) remains the basis of the Yukon's economy, supported by forest industries and fur-trapping.

Zambia: independent republic within the Commonwealth: capital, Lusaka. Until 1851, when *Livingstone sighted and named the Victoria Falls, Europeans had little contact with Zambia. Waves of migration by warring tribes have left within the present republic some seventy distinct peoples, speaking more than thirty dialects. The leader of the Barotse (or Lozi) people, Paramount Chief Lewanika, accepted protection from the *British South Africa Company in 1891. The Company divided the region into two administrative districts (in 1899/1900) which were amalgamated as Northern *Rhodesia in 1911, the Paramount Chief retaining some autonomy. The *Colonial Office took over Northern Rhodesia in 1923, and the colony became increasingly dependent economically on policies determined in Salisbury, the capital of Southern Rhodesia. These commercial links were regularized when the *Central African Federation was created in 1953. Hostility among the African peoples to white dominance intensified in the late 1950s, under the leadership of Kenneth *Kaunda. After Kaunda's United National Independence Party (UNIP) gained electoral successes in 1963, Northern Rhodesia seceded from the Federation, received full internal self-government in January 1964 and – under the name of Zambia – achieved independence on 24 October 1964. Zambia sought to break free from economic dependence on foreign investment in and exploitation of the republic's mineral resources. Prolonged unrest in neighbouring Rhodesia/Zimbabwe during the *Smith era hampered economic growth and convinced Kaunda of the need to turn eastwards, away from South Africa, and ensure that exports from the copper-belt used Dar-es-Salaam: the Tanzam *Railway was completed between 1970 and 1975. UNIP single-party rule, imposed in 1973, ended with elections in October 1991 which brought the Movement for Multiparty Democracy (MMD) into office, with its leader, Frederick Chiluba, succeeding Kaunda as President on 31 October 1991. A move away from Kaunda's planned economy, by introducing free market reforms in 1992/3, led to unrest and allegations of a planned coup by UNIP stalwarts; the subsequent resignation from Parliament of 15 MMD members and several ministers allowed President Chiluba to calm fears of growing corruption. But the abolition of price subsidies, a freeze on public-sector wages, rising inflation and high interest rates left workers on the farms and in the copper-belt suffering greater material hardship under MMD than in the UNIP era.

Zanzibar: island in the Indian Ocean, separated from the east coast of Africa by a 22-mile-wide channel. In the seventeenth century pioneer Portuguese traders were driven out by Arabs from Oman who used the island, and neighbouring Pemba, for slave-trading and the export of ivory. But it was the decision in 1832 of Sultan Seyyid Said (1806–56), the Omani ruler of Muscat, to move his capital to Zanzibar which consolidated its commercial pre-eminence in east Africa. Treaties between Britain and Seyyid Said in 1839 and 1845 and the appointment of a resident British consul (1841) failed to control the slave trade; a further treaty in 1873 was followed by regular naval patrols of the waters around Zanzibar. Said's immediate successors settled the future of territories he had claimed on the African mainland with Mackinnon's British East Africa Association in 1887. While the mainland coast passed eventually to *Kenya, Zanzibar became a British Protectorate in 1890. Trade, however, declined with the rise of the mainland ports of Mombasa and Dar-es-Salaam. On 24 June 1963 Zanzibar was granted internal self-government, and was recognized as an independent Sultanate on 6 December 1963. Five weeks later, however, the left-wing Afro-Shirazi Party forced the Sultan into exile, proclaiming a People's Republic. At the same time President *Nyerere in neighbouring *Tanganyika was forced to seek British aid to put down a similar left-wing revolt. The Afro-Shirazis found themselves isolated, and on 26 April 1964 Zanzibar and Pemba formed a united republic with Tanganyika which was re-named *Tanzania six months later. Zanzibar continues to be overwhelmingly Muslim, and to concentrate, as its main crop, on the growing and export of cloves.

Zimbabwe: independent republic in the Commonwealth: capital, Harare (formerly the city of Salisbury in Southern Rhodesia). There was a powerful kingdom of Zimbabwe in the fourteenth and fifteenth centuries with its capital at Great Zimbabwe, whose ruins suggest that it was built in the eighth century AD. The Shon-speaking people were overrun by successive waves of warrior tribes, finally becoming vassals of the *Ndebele. The name Zimbabwe was revived by Joshua *Nkomo in 1961 for his African People's Union, founded in opposition to white majority rule in *Rhodesia. The African name was also used by Robert *Mugabe, who shared leadership of the Patriotic Front with Nkomo from 1976, and became first President of an independent Zimbabwe in April 1980. Constitutional amendments in 1987 created an executive presidency, as a step towards a one-party state. Experiments in socialist planning between 1980 and 1990 were impeded by prolonged drought and by uncertainty over events across the border in South Africa. Moves were made towards a free market economy in 1990/1, partly in response to pressure from the World Bank. A government-sponsored redistribution of farmland has been criticized for offering former white owners inadequate compensation, and there have been allegations of corruption. But the mineral resources of the country, especially the goldfields, hold out a prospect of prosperity.

Zululand (Kwazulu): the name given to the north-eastern part of *Natal. It comprises a coastal plain and an inland plateau and was given a high degree of autonomy under the *apartheid regime, with Eshowe as the district capital. Historically Zululand was technically independent until 1887, when it became a British Protectorate; it was annexed to Natal ten years later.

Zulus: a warrior, Bantu-speaking people, who became a powerful nation under King Shaka (c. 1787–1828), their ruler from 1816 until his murder by his half-brothers. Under his successor Dingale (c. 1800–40) they challenged the *Boers in their *Great Trek but were defeated at the Blood River (16 December 1838). Shaka's nephew, *Cetewayo, was crowned king in 1873 and at first successfully resisted British attempts to take over *Zululand in 1879, but was captured by *Wolseley after the British victory of Ulundi. Attempts to impose a poll-tax on the Zulus in February and March 1906 provoked a minor rising, ruthlessly suppressed by the Natal authorities, with some 3,000 Zulus hunted down and shot by colonial troops and armed police. Thereafter Zulu political expression was harshly curtailed. A cultural association, Inkatha, was tolerated briefly in the 1920s but was then forced underground until the early 1970s, when it received some patronage from ministers in the South African Republic, as a divisive alternative to the ANC (*African National Congress). Under the leadership of Cetewayo's descendant, Chief Mangosutu Buthelezi, the association developed into the Inkatha Freedom Party in 1975 – predominantly Zulu, but open to all Africans. There was grave violence between Inkatha and ANC supporters in 1991/2, which marred *South Africa's transition to democratic government. In the multi-racial general election of April 1994, Inkatha gained 10.5 per cent of the vote, mainly in the Zulu regions; Chief Buthelezi took office as Minister of Home Affairs in President *Mandela's first coalition government.

APPENDIX

Members of the Commonwealth, 1995

COUNTRY	CAPITAL	JOINED (from 1931)	Est. POP. (1995)	Est. AREA (sq. miles)
ANTIGUA and BARBUDA	St John's	1982	66,000	178
AUSTRALIA	Canberra	1931	17,747,000	7,682,300
BAHAMAS	Nassau	1973	258,000	5,833
BANGLADESH	Dhaka	1972	108,000,000	55,598
BARBADOS	Bridgetown	1966	257,000	166
BELIZE	Belmopen	1981	205,500	8,867
BOTSWANA	Gaborone	1966	1,350,000	224,607
BRUNEI	Bandar Seri	1984	262,000	2,226
CANADA	Ottawa	1931	28,900,000	3,849,658
CYPRUS	Nicosia	1961	725,000	3,542
DOMINICA	Roseau	1978	72,500	289
GAMBIA	Banjul	1965	888,000	4,361
GHANA	Accra	1957	15,600,000	92,100
GRENADA	St George's	1974	85,000	133
GUYANA	Georgetown	1966	810,000	83,000
INDIA	Delhi	1947	846,500,000	1,269,350
JAMAICA	Kingston	1962	2,500,000	4,244
KENYA	Nairobi	1963	26,300,000	224,961
KIRIBATI	Tarawa	1979	66,200	281
LESOTHO	Maseru	1966	1,830,000	11,720
MALAWI	Lilongwe	1964	8,100,000	45,747
MALAYSIA	Kuala Lumpur	1957	19,500,000	127,320
MALDIVES	Male	1982	238,000	115
MALTA	Valletta	1964	367,000	95
MAURITIUS	Port Louis	1968	1,093,000	790
NAMIBIA	Windhoek	1990	1,837,000	318,261

COUNTRY	CAPITAL	JOINED (from 1931)	Est. POP. (1995)	Est. AREA (sq. miles)
NAURU	Nauru	1968	9,050	8
NEW ZEALAND	Wellington	1931	3,495,000	103,736
NIGERIA	Abuja	1960	113,000,000	356,669
PAKISTAN	Islamabad	1947–72; 1989	116,000,000	307,374
PAPUA NEW GUINEA	Pt Moresby	1975	3,772,000	178,260
St KITTS and NEVIS	Basseterre	1983	44,200	104
St LUCIA	Castries	1979	153,250	238
St VINCENT and THE GRENADINES	Kingstown	1979	117,200	150
SEYCHELLES	Victoria	1976	68,200	176
SIERRA LEONE	Freetown	1961	4,260,330	27,699
SINGAPORE	Singapore	1965	2,818,500	244
SOLOMON ISLANDS	Honiara	1978	330,000	249,000
SOUTH AFRICA	Pretoria/ Capetown	1931–61; 1994	40,150,000	471,445
SRI LANKA	Colombo	1948	17,245,000	25,332
SWAZILAND	Mbabane	1968	817,300	6,704
TANZANIA	Dodoma	1964	28,360,000	364,900
TONGA	Nuku'Alofa	1970	94,250	270
TRINIDAD and TOBAGO	Port of Spain	1962	1,253,300	1,864
TUVALU	Fongafale	1978	9,000	10
UGANDA	Kampala	1962	19,517,500	91,000
UNITED KINGDOM	London	1931	56,671,000	94,544
VANUATU	Port Vila	1980	163,500	4,706
WESTERN SAMOA	Apia	1970	162,500	1,097
ZAMBIA	Lusaka	1964	8,780,500	290,586
ZIMBABWE	Harare	1980	10,019,600	150,804

Further Reading

A bibliography of Empire and Commonwealth affairs, past and present, would be vast. Good guides to more detailed study are appended to the volumes of such multi-volume series as the *Cambridge History of the British Empire* (8 vols, 1929–59), the *Cambridge History of India*, and the *Survey of Commonwealth Affairs* (1937–52). Books listed here have been of particular value in compiling this reference companion. The place of publication is London, unless otherwise shown.

In general, for the old colonial Empire and its origins:

K. R. Andrews, *Trade, Plunder and Settlement: Maritime Enterprise and the Genesis of the British Empire, 1480–1630* (1984)
C. Bridenbaugh, *Vexed and Troubled Englishmen, 1590–1642* (New York, 1967)
D. B. Durant: *Ralegh's Lost Colony* (New York, 1981)
W. Foster: *England's Quest of Eastern Trade* (Reprint, 1966)

Of general interest for later years:

C. A. Bayly, *Imperial Meridian: The British Empire and the World, 1780–1830* (1989)
John Bowle, *The Imperial Achievement: The Rise and Transformation of the British Empire* (1974)
V. Harlow, *The Character of British Imperialism* (1939)
L. James. *The Rise and Fall of the British Empire* (1994)
T. O. Lloyd, *The British Empire 1558–1983* (Oxford, 1985)
J. Morris, *Heaven's Command* (1968)
—— *Pax Britannica* (1973)
—— *Farewell the Trumpets* (1978)
T. Pakenham, *The Scramble for Africa* (1991)
D. C. M. Platt (ed.), *Business Imperialism 1840–1930* (Oxford, 1977)

For particular aspects:

J. Darwin, *Britain and Decolonization* (1988)
J. D. Hargreaves, *Decolonization in Africa* (1988)
W. L. Langer, *The Diplomacy of Imperialism* (New York, 1951)
A. N. Porter, *The Origins of the South African War: Joseph Chamberlain and the Diplomacy of Imperialism* (Manchester, 1980)
R. Robinson, J. Gallagher, A. Denny, *Africa and the Victorians: the Official Mind of Imperialism* (1961)
J. Trollope, *Britannia's Daughters: Women of the Empire* (1983)
M. E. Wilbur: *the East India Company and the British Empire in the Far East* (Stamford, 1945)

The most useful atlases have been:

G. Barraclough (ed.), *The Times Atlas of World History* (rev. edn, 1984)
C. A. Bayly (ed.), *Atlas of the British Empire* (1989)
A. N. Porter (ed.), *Atlas of British Expansion Overseas* (1991)

Biographies of Commonwealth statesmen are listed under their respective regions; for British figures see:

N. Fisher, *Iain Macleod* (1973)
M. Gilbert, *Churchill, A Life* (1991) – which supplements the eight volumes and 'companions' of the official biography
D. Gilmour, *Curzon* (1994)
V. Halperin, *Lord Milner and the Empire* (n.d., ? 1954)
K. Harris, *Attlee* (1982)
L. James, *Imperial Warrior: Life and Times of F. M. Allenby* (1993)
J. G. Lockhart and C. M. Woodhouse, *Rhodes* (1963)
N. Nicolson, *Mary Curzon* (1977)
M. Perham, *Lugard* (2 vols, 1956–58)
J. Simmons, *Livingstone of Africa* (1955)
P. Spear, *Master of Bengal: Clive and his India* (1975)
J. W. Wheeler-Bennett, *King George VI, His Life and Reign* (1965)
J. Wilson, *Lawrence of Arabia* (1989)
R. Wurtzburg, *Raffles of the Eastern Isles* (1954)
P. Ziegler, *Mountbatten* (1985)

Works on Australia:

G. Blainey, *The Rush that never Ended: A History of Australian Mining* (Melbourne, 1978)
C. M. H. Clark, *A History of Australia* (6 vols, 1962–88)
H. Cox, *The Wines of Australia* (1967)
L. F. Crisp, *Ben Chifley* (1963)

Further Reading

C. Edwards, *Bruce of Melbourne, Man of Two Worlds* (1965)

M. Flynn, *The Second Fleet* (Sydney, 1993)

M. Gillen, *The Founders of Australia* (Sydney, 1989)

R. Hughes, *The Fatal Shore* (1986)

J. Morris, *Sydney* (1992)

B. Murphy, *Dictionary of Australian History* (Sydney, 1982) is preferable to the attractively produced J. Bassett, *The Oxford Illustrated Dictionary of Australian History* (1993)

J. Ritchie, *Punishment and Profit* (Melbourne, 1970)

Canada:

St John Chadwick, *Newfoundland: Island into Province* (1967)

G. Friesen, *The Canadian Prairies, A History* (1984)

H. A. Innis, *The Fur Trade in Canada* (2nd edn, Toronto, 1956)

C. C. Lingard (ed.), *Canada One Hundred, 1867–1967* (Ottawa, 1967)

W. L. Morton, *The Critical Year: The Union of British North America, 1857–73* (Toronto, 1964)

M. Ormsby, *British Columbia, A History* (Toronto, 1958)

E. E. Rich, *The Fur Trade and the Northwest* (Toronto, 1967)

G. F. G. Stanley, *Louis Riel* (Toronto, 1963)

G. Woodcock, *A Social History of Canada* (1988)

M. Zaslow, *The Opening of the Canadian North* (Toronto, 1973)

East Africa:

Of particular value are the three volumes of the *Oxford History of East Africa* (1963–76); see also:

K. Blixen, *Out of Africa* (1937)

E. Huxley, *White Man's Country* (2 vols, 1935)

—— *Nine Faces of Kenya* (1990)

R. Meinertzhagen, *Kenya Diary, 1902–1906* (1983)

G. H. Mungeam, *British Rule in Kenya 1895–1912* (Oxford, 1966)

C. Chenevix-Trench, *Men Who Ruled Kenya: The Kenya Administration, 1892–1963* (1993)

E. Trzebinski, *Kenya Pioneers* (1985)

Hong Kong and China:

M. Greenberg, *British Trade and the Opening of China, 1800–42* (1951)

J. Morris, *Hong Kong, Epilogue to an Empire* (1988; with Bibliography)

H.-C. and L.-H. Mui, *Management and Monopoly: East India Company's Tea Trade* (Vancouver, 1984)

N. Pelcovits, *Old China Hands and the Foreign Office* (New York, 1948)

372

Indian subcontinent:

Basic are the multi-volume studies of the *History of India* produced by the university presses of both Oxford and Cambridge; B. R. Nanda's biography *Gandhi* (1958) is a more succinct account than the 8-volume life by D. G. Tendulkar (Bombay, 1951–4); see also:

C. Allen and S. Dwivedi: *Lives of the Indian Princes* (1984)
N. Chaudhuri, *The Trading World of Asia and the English East India Company, 1660–1760* (1978)
C. C. Davies, *The Problem of the North-West Frontier* (1932)
R. G. Irving, *Indian Summer: Lutyens, Baker and Imperial Delhi* (1981)
A. Jalal, *The Sole Spokesman: Jinnah, the Muslim League and the Demand for Pakistan* (1985)
S. Jones, *Merchants of the Raj* (1992)
E. W. R. Lumby, *The Transfer of Power in India* (1954)
L. S. Malley, *The Indian Civil Service* (1937)
R. J. Moore, *Escape from Empire: The Attlee Government and the Indian Problem* (Oxford 1983)
J. Morris, *Stones of Empire: The Buildings of British India* (Oxford, 1983)
M. Satow and R. Desmond, *Railways of the Raj* (1980)
S. R. Sen, *1857* (New Delhi, 1957)
P. Woodruff, *The Men Who Ruled India: The Founders* (1953)
—— *The Men Who Ruled India: The Guardians* (1954)

Malayasia and Singapore:

J. Cloake, *Templer, Tiger of Malaya* (1985)
P. Elphick, *Singapore, The Pregnable Fortress* (1995)
D. G. E. Hall, *History of South-East Asia* (4th edn, 1981)
W. D. McIntyre, *The Rise and Fall of the Singapore Naval Base* (1979)
S. Runciman, *The White Rajahs: A History of Sarawak from 1841 to 1946* (1960)
C. M. Turnbull, *History of Singapore, 1819–1975* (Kuala Lumpur, 1977)

Middle East and Egypt:

M. W. Daly, *Empire on the Nile: The Anglo-Egyptian Sudan* (1986)
D. Gillard, *The Struggle for Asia, 1828–1914* (1977)
M. Kent, *Oil and Empire: British Policy and Mesopotamian Oil 1900–1920* (1976)
A. Palmer, *The Decline and Fall of the Ottoman Empire* (1993)
R. Rhodes James, *Gallipoli* (1965)
P. J. Vatikiotis, *History of Modern Egypt* (1991)
M. E. Yapp, *The Making of the Modern Near East, 1792–1923* (1987)
—— *The Near East since the First World War* (1991)

Further Reading

New Zealand and the Pacific:

P. Adams, *Fatal Necessity: British Intervention in New Zealand* (Auckland, 1977)

J. C. Beaglehole, *The Exploration of the Pacific* (1934)

—— *The Discovery of New Zealand* (1939)

P. Freyberg, *Bernard Freyberg, VC* (1991)

W. P. Morrell, *Britain in the Pacific Islands* (1960)

W. H. Oliver (ed.), *The Oxford History of New Zealand* (Oxford and Wellington, 1981)

K. Sinclair, *History of New Zealand* (1969)

Southern Africa:

J. Allen (ed.), *Archbishop Desmond Tutu: The Rainbow Children of God* (1994)

D. Caute, *Under the Skin: The Death of White Rhodesia* (1983)

J. S. Galbraith, *Crown and Charter: The Early Years of the British South Africa Company* (1974)

C. L. Leipoldt, *300 Years of Cape Wine* (Cape Town, 1974)

T. Pakenham, *The Boer War* (1979)

L. A. C. Raphael, *The Cape to Cairo Dream* (1937)

J. C. Smuts, *Jan Christian Smuts* (1952)

P. Snelson, *To Independence and Beyond: Memoirs of a Colonial and Commonwealth Civil Servant* (1993)

L. Weinthal (ed.), *The Cape to Cairo Railway and River Route* (1923)

M. Wilson and L. M. Thompson, *The Oxford History of South Africa* (to 1870: Oxford, 1969)

West Africa:

A. N. Cook, *British Enterprise in Nigeria* (Philadelphia, 1943)

C. Fyfe, *History of Sierra Leone* (Oxford 1962, reprint 1993)

E. Isichei, *History of West Africa since 1800* (1986)

D. Wellesley, *Sir George Goldie, Founder of Nigeria* (1934)

West Indies, Slavery and Slave Trade:

R. T. Anstey, *The Atlantic Slave Trade and British Abolition, 1760–1810* (1975)

R. R. Dunn, *Sugar and Slaves* (Chapel Hill, 1973)

W. Green, *British Slave Emancipation: the Sugar Colonies and the Great Experiment* (Oxford 1976)

B. W. Higham, *Slave Population and Economy in Jamaica, 1807–1834* (1976)

C. Lloyd, *The Navy and the Slave Trade* (1948)

J. H. Parry, P. Sherlock, A. Maingot, *A Short History of the West Indies* (4th ed, 1987)

J. A. Rawley, *The Transatlantic Slave Trade* (New York, 1981)

Army and Navy:

P. Blunt, *Imperial Sunset: The Native Regiments of the British Army* (1988)

M. Chappell, *The Gurkhas* (1993)

A. Clayton and D. Killingray, *Khaki and Blue: Military and Police in British Colonial Africa* (Athens, Ohio, 1989)

P. M. Kennedy, *The Rise and Fall of British Naval Mastery* (1976)

A. J. Marder, *The Anatomy of British Sea Power: British Naval Policy 1890–1905* (1940)

C. Chenevix-Trench, *The Indian Army and the King's Enemies* (1988)

Other books:

J. Arlott (ed.), *The Oxford Companion to Sports and Games* (1975)

Robin Higham, *Britain's Imperial Air Routes 1918–1939* (Hamden, Conn., 1960)

J. Hartnoll (ed.), *Oxford Companion to the Theatre* (3rd edn, 1967)

Viscount Templewood, *Empire of the Air: The Advent of the Air Age, 1922–1929* (1957)

P. Vandyke Price: *Dictionary of Wines and Spirits* (1980)

In a category of its own – for which see the entry 'Hobson-Jobson' in the text – stands H. Yule and A. Burnell, *Hobson-Jobson: A Glossary of Anglo-Indian Colloquial Words and Phrases and Kindred Terms* (1886)

I have found the volumes of *The Statesman's Yearbook* (published annually since 1864) invaluable for statistical information, especially the issues since 1892, when maps illustrating 'subjects of great moment' first appeared. Periodicals of particular interest are: *The Round Table; The Journal of Imperial and Commonwealth History; Australian Historical Studies; Canadian Historical Review; New Zealand Journal of History.*

Index

Entries in the Dictionary are shown in SMALL CAPITALS, with the main reference in *italic* page numbers

Index

Index

Index

Index

Index

Griqualand 65, 270
Grivas, George 102
Groote Schurr, near Cape Town 24, 291
GROUP AREAS ACT (South Africa, 1950) 15, *148*
Guadalcanal 316–17
Guatemala 35
Gunnell, Sally 18
GURKHAS *148–9*, 249
Gurney, Sir Henry 221
GUYANA (*formerly* British Guiana) 51, 57, 127, *149–50*, 151, 167, 183–4, 327, 352

Hadhramaut sultanate 4
HAGGARD, SIR HENRY RIDER *150*
Haidar Ali 306
HAILEYBURY COLLEGE, HERTFORDSHIRE 10, 18, 100, 112, 131, *150*, 176, 207
Halifax, Nova Scotia 250, 265
HAMMOND, DAME JOAN HOOD *150–1*
Hampshire, HMS 200
'Handmaids of Christ' 74
Hani, Chris 6, 319
Harare, Zimbabwe 365; *see also* Salisbury
HARARE DECLARATION (1991) 91, *151*, 218, 312, 322
Hargraves, Edward 139
harijans 347
HARIOT, THOMAS *151*
Harris, Alanson 356
Harris, General George 306
Hart, Steve 192
Harvard University, Massachusetts 346
Hassan, Mohammed bin Abdulla *see* 'MAD MULLAH'
Hastings, Francis Rawdon-Hastings, 1st Marquess of 228, 280
HASTINGS, WARREN 111, 144, *151–2*, 172
HAUHAU (or *Pai Marire*) *152*, 227
HAUSA 22, 25, 142, *152*, 258
HAVELOCK, GENERAL SIR HENRY *152–3*, 177
Hawaii 95
HAWKE, ROBERT JAMES LEE 130, *153*, 191–2, 292
Hawkins, Sir John 312
HEAD OF THE COMMONWEALTH 88, 89, 92, 114, *153*, 211
Heard Island 21
Heath, (Sir) Edward 90, 216, 334
Helm, Charles 238
HELPMANN, SIR ROBERT 27, *153–4*
Henry VIII, King 333
HENRY, ALICE *154*
HERBERT, HENRY HOWARD MOLYNEUX, 4th Earl of Carnarvon 86, 131, *154*
Herbert, Sir Robert 85
HERERO *155*, 321
HERTZOG, JAMES BARRY MUNNIK 3, 6, *155*, 187, 219, 315, 318, 323, 348
HERZBERG, GERHARD *155*
Herzl, Theodor 186
Hicks, General William 218
HIGH COMMISSIONERS *156*
HILL STATIONS (India) 74, *156*, 161
HINDU FAITH *156–7*, 252, 347
Hiroshima 363
HIV virus 7
Hoad, L.A. 334
Hobart, Robert, Baron (*later* 4th Earl of Buckinghamshire) 86
Hobart, Tasmania 19, 331
Hobson, John Atkinson 171
HOBSON, WILLIAM *157*, 255, 351
HOBSON-JOBSON *158*
Hogan, Paul 79
HOLLAND, SIR SIDNEY GEORGE *158*, 159
HOLT, HAROLD 143, *159–60*, 351
Holt's Ocean Steamship Company 273

Holyman brothers 8
HOLYOAKE, SIR KEITH JACKA 158, *159*
Home of the Hirsel, Baron *see* Douglas-Home, Sir Alec
Home Office 85
HONG KONG (Xianggang) 72–3, 80, 106, 149, *159–60*, 186, 201, 211, 246, 251, 254, 270, 287, 335, 341, 353, 363
HONG KONG AND SHANGHAI BANKING CORPORATION *160–1*, 186, 341, 348
HONG KONG REGIMENT *161*, 249
Hong Kong Volunteer Defence Corps 161
HONGS *161*, 186, 341
Honiara, Guadalcanal (Solomon Islands) 316
HORSE-RACING *161–2*
HOTELS *162–3*
Hovell, William 165
Howe, Joseph 265
Howick, (Sir Charles) Evelyn Baring, Baron 99
Hoyle, Desmond 149
Hoyte, Hugh Desmond 127
Huddleston, Archbishop Trevor 344
Hudson, Henry 163
HUDSON, SIR WILLIAM *163*, 165, 181
HUDSON'S BAY COMPANY *163–4*; in Alberta 9; and Assiniboines 17, 289; claims British Columbia 47; early trading posts 60, 132; and Cree Indians 96; Douglas in 109; sovereignty ends 214; in Manitoba 225; métis serve in 234; in Northwest Territories 264; and Riel 293; and San Juan islands 301; Selkirk and 306; in Yukon 364
HUGGINS, SIR GODFREY MARTIN (Viscount Malvern) 69, *164*, 292, 353
HUGHES, WILLIAM MORRIS *164–5*, 171, 233, 235
Hume, Allan Octavian 177
HUME AND HOVELL EXPEDITION (Australia, 1824–5) *165*
Hume, Hamilton 165
Hume, Joseph 177
hurricanes 102, 109, 185; *see also* CYCLONE
Hussein, Emir of Mecca 207
Hussein, King of Jordan 339
Hut Tax Rebellion (Sierra Leone, 1897–8) 309
Hyderabad, Sind 271, 331
Hyderabad (state) 173, 282–3
HYDRO-ELECTRIC POWER PROJECTS 163, 164, *165–7*, 256, 258, 284, 300, 331

IBO (or Igbo, Nigeria) 4, 22, 25, 38, *167*, 258, 259
Ilorin (Muslim state) 142
IMMIGRATION 32, 59, 60–2, 72–4, 91, *167–8*, 275
IMMIGRATION RESTRICTION ACTS (Australia, 1902, 1925) 72, 167, *168*
Immorality Amendment Act (South Africa, 1950) 239
IMPERIAL AIRWAYS 8, 9, *168–9*, 283
IMPERIAL BRITISH EAST AFRICA COMPANY *169*, 190, 193, 211, 345
Imperial College of Science, London 91
IMPERIAL CONFERENCES 11, 26, 71, 87, 92, 146, 168, *169–70*, 171
Imperial Institute, London 91
Imperial and International Communications Ltd 171
IMPERIAL PREFERENCE 71, 104, 146, *170*, 271, 305
Imperial Services College (*formerly* United Services College) 150, 198
IMPERIAL WAR CABINET AND CONFERENCE (1917) 43, 88, *170–1*, 230, 315
IMPERIAL WIRELESS AND CABLE CONFERENCE (1928) *171*, 333
IMPERIALISM *171–2*
Imphal, Battle of (1944) 56
indentured labour 167, 245
INDIA *172–3*; wars with Pakistan 29, 37, 190, 307;

384

Index

Index

Index

390

Index

Index

Index